lumes I and II of this rojected multi-

THE LETTERS OF
Henry Wadsworth Longfellow

VOLUME I

1814–1836

Longfellow, c. 1829, attributed to Thomas Badger

THE LETTERS OF
Henry Wadsworth Longfellow

EDITED BY

Andrew Hilen

———————

VOLUME I

1814-1836

The Belknap Press of Harvard University Press

Cambridge, Massachusetts

1966

Distributed in Great Britain by Oxford University Press, London

Library of Congress Catalog Card Number 66–18248

Typography by Burton Jones

Printed in the U.S.A. by Harvard University Printing Office

Acknowledgments

THE PREPARATION OF this edition of the Longfellow letters began in 1954 after the trustees of the John Simon Guggenheim Memorial Foundation had granted me a fellowship award to undertake the project. Since that time I have been given financial assistance by the University of Washington, not only with sabbatical leave periods that have enabled me to work in Eastern Seaboard and European libraries, but also with generous grants from the Graduate School Research Fund. I am very grateful for the encouragement provided by this material aid from both the Foundation and the University.

The officers of the Longfellow Trust have allowed me unhindered access to the Longfellow family papers and have granted me permission to publish the letters in these volumes. It is a pleasure to acknowledge my gratitude for their cooperation, given without condition of any kind. I am indebted, furthermore, to the following individual and institutional owners of Longfellow's manuscript letters who have allowed me to see, study, and make copies of their possessions for publication purposes: American Antiquarian Society; American Philosophical Society; Clifton Waller Barrett Collection, University of Virginia; Henry W. and Albert A. Berg Collection, New York Public Library; Berkshire Museum, Pittsfield, Mass.; Boston Athenaeum; Boston Public Library; Bowdoin College Library; Brown University Library; University of California Library, Berkeley; Paul Fenimore Cooper, Cooperstown, N. Y.; Connecticut State Library; Cornell University Library; Dartmouth College Library; Duxbury Rural and Historical Society; O. O. Fisher Collection, Detroit, Mich.; Franklin and Marshall College Library; Genealogical Society of Pennsylvania; Goddard-Roslyn Collection, Roslyn, N. Y.; Harvard University Archives; Harvard College Library; Hispanic Society of America; Henry E. Huntington Library and Art Gallery; Lehigh University Library; Lund University Library; Longfellow Trust Collection; Maine Historical Society; Massachusetts Historical Society; Mrs. Brenton Greene Meader, Providence, R. I.; Pierpont Morgan Library; National Archives, Washington, D.C.; Manuscript Division, New York Public Library; Parkman Howe, Boston, Mass.; Historical Society of Pennsylvania; Carl H. Pforzheimer Library; Princeton University Library; Rosalind Richards, Gardiner, Me.; Royal Library, Copen-

ACKNOWLEDGMENTS

hagen; Royal Library, Stockholm; Royal Society of Northern Anti-
quaries, Copenhagen; Chester M. Sawtelle, Marblehead, Massachu-
setts; E. Ross Sawtelle, Marblehead, Massachusetts; University of
Upsala Library; Victoria and Albert Museum; Wadsworth-Longfellow
House, Portland, Maine; University of Washington Library; Williams
College Library; and Yale University Library.

No editor of a body of letters as extensive as Longfellow's can
expect to bring his work to conclusion without the assistance of
hundreds of people in a variety of private and public institutions. I
am consequently indebted to many librarians, curators, government
officials, autograph dealers and collectors, literary and historical
scholars, private individuals, and friends, upon whom I have depended
as I prepared both the text and the annotation of this edition. During
his career as Curator of the Longfellow House, the late Henry Wadsworth Longfellow Dana began a catalogue of his grandfather's letters
and assembled an extensive file of subsidiary data. Professor Dana's
researches became the foundation of my own, and I have thus enjoyed
the advantage of beginning my work with materials furnished by a
predecessor in the field. Thomas H. de Valcourt, Professor Dana's
successor at the Longfellow House, has been most cooperative and
has frequently solved problems for me with his extensive knowledge
of Longfellow family matters.

Over the last several years the Longfellow trustees have transferred
many valuable papers and books from the Craigie-Longfellow House
in Cambridge to the Houghton Library of Harvard University. I have
thus had to rely heavily on the assistance of the Houghton Library
staff. The late William A. Jackson was particularly kind and cleared
a number of important paths. William Bond, Curator of Manuscripts
at Houghton during the period of preparation of these volumes,
answered many letters of inquiry and has been very helpful in a
variety of ways. During my several months of research in Cambridge,
Carolyn Jakeman kindly gave me every assistance.

Among the many libraries, societies, and government agencies (in
addition to those already listed) that responded to my requests for
information, the following were particularly cooperative: Columbia
University Library, Free Public Library of Jersey City, Genealogical
Society of Salt Lake City, Heidelberg University Library, Laval Uni-
versity Library, The Library Company of Philadelphia, Library of
Congress, Literary and Historical Society of Quebec, Medford Public
Library, New England Historic Genealogical Society, New York Gene-
alogical and Biographical Society, New-York Historical Society, New
York State Library, Old Dartmouth Historical Society and Whaling

ACKNOWLEDGMENTS

Museum, University of Oregon Library, Portland (Maine) Public Library, Redwood Library and Athenaeum, Rhode Island Historical Society, Saint Louis University Library, Staatsarchiv Koblenz, Troy Public Library, Union College Library, United States Information Agency, United States Department of the Navy, and United States Department of State.

A few librarians and curators whom I pressed into service as researchers and correspondents on many occasions deserve my special thanks: John Alden, Boston Public Library; Kenneth J. Boyer, Bowdoin College Library; Kenneth C. Elkins, Harvard University Archives; James J. Heslin, New-York Historical Society; Pauline King, New England Historic Genealogical Society; Ruth Kirk, University of Washington Library; Marian B. Rowe, Glenn B. Skilliro, and Elizabeth Ring, Maine Historical Society; Clifford K. Shipton and Marcus McCorison, American Antiquarian Society; Grace Tappan, Portland Public Library; and R. N. Williams, II, Historical Society of Pennsylvania.

In addition, many other persons helped me by running down the answers to questions, by arranging for photostats and microfilms, and by tracing Longfellow's manuscripts to their owners. Although it would be impossible to list them all, I should like especially to mention Steven Allaback, Research Assistant, University of Washington; Jean Baillou, Ministry of Foreign Affairs, Paris; Bürgermeister Baldus, Stadtverwaltung St. Goar; Professor James F. Beard, Jr., Clark University; Herbert Cahoon, Pierpont Morgan Library; Porter R. Chandler, New York City; Rear Admiral Hubert W. Chanler, Geneseo, New York; Alexander P. Clark, Princeton University Library; Helen Rose Cline, Parish Recorder, Trinity Church, New York; F. Dousset, Archives of France; Donald C. Gallup, Yale University Library; Dr. John D. Gordan, Berg Collection, New York Public Library; Louise Hubert Guyol, New Orleans; Zoltán Haraszti, Boston Public Library; Realschullehrer Th. Hardenberg, Königswinter am Rhein; Professor Fred Harrison, Portland State College; Professor William T. Hastings, Brown University; R. J. Hayes, National Library of Ireland; Dr. Hesse, Städtlisches Karl-Ernst-Osthaus-Museum, Hagen; G. Heisbourg, Luxembourg Embassy, Washington, D.C.; Ignacio Martinez de Irujo y Artazcoz, Marquis of Casa Irujo, Madrid; Professor Theodore F. Jones, New York University; William B. Jordan, Jr., Portland, Maine; the late Richard Kraft, Seattle; Dr. Robert Ladner, Austrian Embassy, Washington, D.C.; Katherine Maas, New York City; Jules Mersch, Luxembourg; Robert Monroe, University of Washington Library; Ivor Morris, Mount Allison University; Virginia M. Osborn,

ACKNOWLEDGMENTS

Town Library of Lancaster, Massachusetts; Professor Norman Holmes Pearson, Yale University; Dr. Olga Pinto, National Library, Rome; Stephen Riley, Massachusetts Historical Society; Professor Alphonse V. Roche, University of Arizona; Eleanor Hall Saunders, Washington, D.C.; Marian R. Small, Maine Historical Society; Julia Ward Stickley, Washington, D.C.; Robert E. Stocking and Anne Freudenberg, University of Virginia Library; Dr. Stollenwerk, Stadtverwaltung Boppard; Laurence Terry, Concord, Massachusetts; J. des R. Tessier, Quebec; Louise Hall Tharp, Darien, Connecticut; Professor Norman L. Torrey, Columbia University; Dr. K. G. Van Acker, University of Ghent Library; Amy Ver Nooy, Dutchess County Historical Society; Professor Edward Wagenknecht, Boston University; Dr. Weidenhaupt, Stadtarchiv, Düsseldorf; Walter Muir Whitehill, Boston Athenaeum; D. J. van Wijnen, Royal Netherlands Embassy, Washington, D.C.; and Lars Åhnebrink, University of Upsala.

I should like, finally, to acknowledge an indebtedness to my colleagues on the faculty of the University of Washington, who contributed to these volumes in many ways, and to the members of my family, who bore my frequent absences from them with understanding and restraint.

ANDREW HILEN

University of Washington
Seattle

Contents

Volume I

ILLUSTRATIONS

xi

INTRODUCTION

Introduction

LONGFELLOW AS LETTER-WRITER

1814–1843

From the time he was seven years old, in 1814, until he was thirty-six at the end of 1843, Longfellow is known to have written some 1200 letters; one may assume, in addition, that he wrote several hundred others which have disappeared, leaving no trace. Of this total, 805 have survived — most of them in manuscript but a number only in print — to form the first two volumes of this collection of his letters. No claims can be made, of course, for completeness. The publication of these volumes will doubtless bring lost manuscripts out of their hiding places in attics, minor libraries, and the files of private collectors. Yet one suspects that only a fraction of the unrecovered letters of the period will turn up in the future, for Longfellow's earlier correspondents, with less awareness of his coming fame, did not preserve his letters with the eagerness of those later correspondents who hoarded every line and every signature from the pen of the author of *Evangeline* and *Hiawatha*. Thus, one may conclude that the present volumes contain most of the surviving letters of Longfellow's childhood, youth, and early manhood.

As his correspondence grew with his literary reputation — he wrote more letters in the last twenty years of his life than in all his preceding years — Longfellow came to regard the hours devoted to it as the most tedious, the most unprofitable and uninspiring, of the day. This was not surprising, of course. After his name became a household word in America, scores of well-wishers, unpublished poets, autograph-hunters, and financially embarrassed supplicants stalked him by mail, driving him to the expression of anguished cries in his private journal. But even as a college sophomore he had disliked letter-writing, although for different reasons. On December 18, 1824, he complained to his father of the duty that drove him to his desk. "I suspect that they at home do not like to write, better than I do, and for my part, I utterly abominate it — that is letter-writing. I write so exceedingly slow, that

I

it is really a waste of time to no purpose, — for neither I nor my correspondent can be wiser for what is written. Though I am exceedingly fond of writing in general, yet I never did like to sit down patiently, and write long letters about nothing."

Stephen Longfellow, a wise man who even at that early date may have suspected that literature was to take his son from the more dependable profession of the law, hastened to remark on the value of letter-writing. "Epistolary composition," he wrote on December 26th, "is one of the most difficult kinds of style to acquire, and is at the same time a most desirable attainment; and if you mean to become iminent [sic] as a literary man you must remember that taste and scholarship are as much displayed in correspondence as in any exercise." Chastened, his son explained in a reply dated December 31st: "I still consider it rather a difficult task to write a good letter: for it seems to me, that since the style of letters is about the same as that of polite conversation, the same faculties, which give excellence in the one, give it also in the other. This inability to write good letters without great exertion is probably the reason of my dislike of letter-writing in general, for very few persons are willing to be often engaged in that pursuit, wherein they can so evidently see their own inferiority."

Longfellow's early distaste for letter-writing arose from his feeling that letters had to be composed according to rules, that the mere conveying of information was not enough, that the style of "polite conversation" had to be cultivated. This in itself reveals that he had a literary attitude toward the art of letter-writing, — no matter how often, in his eyes or in ours, he failed the art. In the letters of his early years we frequently find him attempting to inject "style" into his paragraphs by employing elegant phrases, learned allusions, poetical extracts, and what passed in his mind as humorous sallies. In his European letters of 1826-1829 he tried hardest for effect, conscious that his family wanted a narrative of his travels as well as assurances that he was warm and dry. That some of these letters, with minor modifications, found their way into his first book of sketches, *Outre-Mer,* supports the thesis that he tried to write so that his reader might be pleased with the method as well as with the matter.

He did not always, of course, attempt a formal style. He filled a good many of his early letters with questions, complaints, and gossip, in the language not of polite but of ordinary conversation; and in a number, particularly in the thirties and early forties, he dealt with business and professional matters as matter-of-factly as any Yankee merchant. He wrote none of these letters, certainly, as he later composed his poetry, with one eye on posterity; they are the spontaneous products of a mind that, in them, unwittingly revealed its own boundaries. Consequently, we can come closer to an understanding of young Longfellow from the 805 letters in these volumes than we can from any other source.

Most readers of the letters will tend to agree that they reveal Longfellow as having a keen and expansive mind, but not a particularly complex one. If he displays the nature of his training with frequent allusions to the Bible, Dante, Shakespeare, and Goethe, he also appears somewhat overimpressed by such modestly endowed writers as Mrs. Hemans, L.E.L., and the contributors to the *United States Literary Gazette* and the *Knickerbocker Magazine.* His personal philosophy, when he drops hints of it, turns out to be based on a Puritan morality, diluted by conservative Unitarianism and laced with New England shrewdness. His gossip of men and books displays few real insights into character and criticism. Even his choice of a favored correspondent, George Washington Greene — to whom he wrote some fifty letters before 1844 and hundreds afterwards — suggests a lack of intellectual discrimination. Greene, a querulous dilettante and literary failure, exercised his finest talent in playing on Longfellow's sympathy and friendship over a long lifetime. Nothing within these pages, therefore, tends to challenge the thesis underlying twentieth-century objections to his poetry: that Longfellow was a detached observer rather than a penetrating critic of manners and men.

But if Longfellow was not as deep as his critics would have him, neither was he as shallow as they sometimes imply. A precocious boy and a talented youth, he became, by the standards of his own day and of ours, a learned young man. With a more receptive than creative mind, he took to languages easily and became a versatile and skillful linguist. By the late fall of 1836 when he assumed his chair as Smith Professor of Modern Languages at Harvard, he could speak French, Spanish, Italian, and German with a considerable degree of fluency, and he had a working knowledge of Portuguese, Swedish, Danish, and Dutch. He had learned in addition Latin and Greek. Although at twenty-nine he began to neglect scholarship for the temptations and rewards of a purely literary career, he had already won a reputation as a compiler of textbooks, as the author of *Outre-Mer,* as an influential essayist for the *North American Review,* and as a graceful translator of foreign poetry. When Frances Appleton decided to marry him in 1843, he had earned international fame with *Voices of the Night, Hyperion,* and *Ballads and Other Poems.* This considerable achievement by so young a man has not always been acknowledged by those critics who have disparaged his intellectual capacities.

It should be remarked, furthermore, that the letters in these volumes fail in large part to support the conventional picture of Longfellow drawn by his brother in the standard life of the poet and cherished subsequently by an assortment of derivative biographers. Equipped with scissors and paste and a divinity-school training, Samuel Longfellow curtailed the manuscripts at his disposal — including many of these letters — and out of good intentions and family loyalty, as well as from half-truths and concealed facts, he created a portrait in soft tones of a saint without force, a man without troubles or anger or sex. Readers of his early letters will find a different Longfellow. This is not to deny that he emerges from these pages a well-mannered young man with the instincts of the genteel age; it is merely to say that he appears now with all his shortcomings and peccadilloes, all his worries and yearnings and regrets, and that the self-portrait is more interesting than the brother's idealized one.

Letters are sometimes interesting, of course, for what they do not reveal, and those of these years do little to suggest that Longfellow was to become in time the best-known poet writing in English. They contain few statements of poetical ambition and only occasional allusions to poetic theory, and his comments on the poetry of others are rarely marked by critical perception. With the knowledge that Longfellow was to become a world poet, however, one can discern in his letters the nature of his poetry; that is, the reader can discover in them those elements of his character which influenced the direction of his muse: the tendency to sentimentalize the past and present, the talent of lucid expression, a conventional morality, a lively if confined imagination, an educated taste, and strains of jocosity and melancholy. It requires no special perspicacity, therefore, to sense from his letters that Longfellow was to become a man of some literary stature; but only hindsight can discover in him, as letter-writer, the makings of a man whose name for millions was to become synonymous with the word "poet."

At least eighty of Longfellow's correspondents of the period 1814-1843 were the recipients of letters that have not been recovered for this edition. If one measures the importance of a letter by the reputation of the person who received it, little has been lost, for only a handful of the correspondents in question found their way into the biographical dictionaries. It also appears that in over half the cases only one or two letters are involved — reason enough for unconcern. It is nevertheless obvious that many of these unrecovered letters contained information that would interest both Longfellow's biographer and the critic of his poetry. Thirteen letters to George William Gray Browne might tell us much about Longfellow's literary interests during his college years; nine letters to Susan Codman might reveal details of an unsuccessful courtship, now only suspected; eleven letters to José Cortés y Sesti would illustrate Longfellow's skill in Spanish; eight letters to Cornelius Felton would supplement our knowledge of Longfellow's relationship with that Harvard colleague, now only partially documented; and twenty-two letters to Alexander H. Everett (two of which survive), eight to James G. Carter, and eight to Frederick T. Gray might give us new insights into his relationships with editors and publishers. There are in addition at least forty-three unrecovered letters to various members of the Longfellow family, twenty-three to Sam Ward, six to George Washington Greene, and thirteen to Lewis Gaylord Clark (to mention a few of his favored correspondents of the period), all of which might put our image of Longfellow into sharper focus. The same may be said for the nine lost letters to Hawthorne, four to Sumner, and six to Willis Gaylord Clark. Some of these manuscripts may still exist in various secluded corners; but until by chance they come to light, the recovered letters of this edition must provide us with the portrait of Longfellow as letter-writer, 1814-1843.

PRINCIPAL CORRESPONDENTS

1814–1843

The members of Longfellow's family preserved their records with care, in accordance with a custom not uncommon in their day and with a pride that is easily forgiven. As a result, the archives of the Longfellow Trust are rich with the letters of three generations. It is to this instinct of the family for treasuring its records that we owe the existence of three-eighths of the letters here printed. It follows naturally that Longfellow's father, mother, brothers, and sisters are leading members of the dramatis personae of the correspondence in this period. As might be expected, his principal correspondent was his father, to whom he addressed at least 200 letters, 185 of which have survived in the family files.

Stephen Longfellow (1776-1849), a fifth-generation American, was born in Gorham, Maine, and spent his adult life in Portland.

Entering Harvard at eighteen, he graduated after election to Phi Beta Kappa in the distinguished class of 1798, which included Joseph Story, Richard Sullivan, Sidney Willard, Joseph Tuckerman, and William Ellery Channing. After college he read law and gained admittance to the bar in 1801. He enjoyed a successful legal career, depending more on conscientious thoroughness than on rhetorical pyrotechnics, and took part prominently in the philanthropic and civic affairs of Portland. A Federalist in politics, he served as a delegate to the Hartford Convention of 1814, as a representative to the Massachusetts General Court in 1814 and 1815 (Maine was not admitted to the Union until 1820), as a member of the Eighteenth Congress of the United States in 1823-1825, and as a member of the Maine legislature in 1826. He was an overseer of Bowdoin College from 1811 to 1817 and a trustee from 1817 to 1836. On January 1, 1804, he married Zilpah Wadsworth, daughter of a Revolutionary general, and became the father of eight children, six of whom survived him.

A serious and cautious man, influenced by both the Puritanism of his forebears and the rationalism of the century in which he was born, Stephen Longfellow always exercised a slight restraint on the youthful enthusiasms of his son. He counseled against a purely literary career, warned of the dangers of premature publication, and discouraged the idea of a second European tour. But he advised quietly and did not command. At the same time he recognized the boy's talent early and realized the necessity of channeling it properly. Although he would have preferred Henry to follow the law, he gave encouragement and financial support to the plan that enabled him to support himself while indulging his passion for letters. One suspects that he moved discreetly behind the scenes of his son's appointment as professor at Bowdoin in 1829 and of his invitation in 1834 to join the Harvard faculty. Longfellow owed much of his success as professor and poet to the sympathy and astuteness of his father.

Although he wrote fewer letters to his mother than to his father — forty of at least forty-seven have been recovered — Longfellow inherited the most prominent features of his character from her, with the result that their relationship was marked by an intimacy in which Stephen Longfellow did not share. Zilpah Wadsworth Longfellow (1778-1851) could trace her ancestry to the Plymouth Pilgrims and owed the respectability of her social position to her father, General Peleg Wadsworth, a hero of the Revolution. In common with her husband, she enjoyed a keen intelligence and a genteel cultivation; in contrast to him, she had a deep religious faith and a sensitive appreciation of literature. Whereas Stephen Longfellow was inclined to be practical and taciturn, she was as likely to be impetuous and voluble. Her own letters, filled with the images of her lively mind, give a fine picture of the family environment in which her gifted son grew up.

During his impressionable college years Longfellow addressed his letters dealing with books and authors to his mother rather than to his father, and it seems clear that she became his confidante in such matters and perhaps the sharer of his dreams. How much she influenced Stephen Longfellow in modifying his doubts concerning their son's literary ambitions cannot be known with certainty, but they obviously discussed the problem and she as obviously represented the boy's viewpoint. In later years her role as confidante became less important. Having encouraged her son to pursue his inclinations, she watched him grow beyond the reach of her own literary understanding. But by then she could enjoy the reward of knowing she had been right in supporting him.

Of his three brothers Longfellow was closest in age to Stephen Longfellow (1805-1850), the eldest child in the family and the fifth of the name. He attended college with Stephen, defended him in his frequent hours of adolescent adversity, and sympathized with him later in the ruin of his life. No two brothers could have been more unlike. Stephen was a person of charm and ability who suffered either from a weakness of the will or from a premature conviction of the meaninglessness of conventional New England life. In any event, he too often permitted himself the luxury of drift, and his history is marked with abortive attempts and forgotten resolutions. In the end he failed as a lawyer, saw his marriage collapse, and died when, had fortune been kinder, he might have enjoyed the full rewards of his talents. Ten letters from Henry to Stephen during these early years have been recovered.

Longfellow's younger brothers contributed their share to the family life that shaped his character, but they figure insignificantly in his correspondence of this period because of disparities in age and interests. Alexander Longfellow (1814-1901) attended Bowdoin College briefly, saw something of the world with the Pacific Fleet as secretary to his uncle, Commodore Alexander Scammell Wadsworth, and at the age of twenty-three began a long career as a civil engineer. Henry is known to have written him at least ten letters at this time, six of which survive. Samuel Longfellow (1819-1892), twelve years younger than Henry, entered Harvard as these letters end, became subsequently an eminent Unitarian clergyman of Victorian tastes and temperament, and wrote the definitive biography of his brother. No letters to him exist for these years and none are known to have been written.

Two of Longfellow's sisters, Elizabeth (1808-1829) and Ellen (1818-1834), died during their young womanhood and thus disappeared from his correspondence, although not from his memory of his early life. Elizabeth was closer to him in age than any other member of the family and perhaps closer also in understanding, for at the time of her death she had received more letters from him than had any of her brothers and sisters. Six of the twelve known letters addressed to her survive. Ellen, on the other hand, like her brothers Alexander and Samuel, was too young to expect more than letters intended for the family at large, and none to her alone has been recovered. A third sister, Mary (1816-1902), to whom he wrote five letters here printed and at least one more that has been lost, survived all her brothers and sisters and through her marriage became a woman of fortune and social prominence in Cambridge. Her importance in Longfellow's correspondence belongs to a later day.

There seems to be no question that after Elizabeth's death Anne Longfellow (1810-1901) became her brother's favorite sister, and as time went on, she assumed the role of his principal family correspondent. He wrote at least fifty-two letters to her before 1844, forty-three of which are extant, and if one considers their correspondence during Longfellow's lifetime, the number reaches into the hundreds. After he returned to Brunswick in 1829, Longfellow made Anne his confidante, particularly in matters of the heart, and it was she who encouraged and helped him in his courtship of Mary Potter. Their interests and hopes were brought even closer together when on November 26, 1832, Anne married George Washington Pierce (1805-1835), Longfellow's good friend and Bowdoin classmate (the recipient of seventeen letters in this collection). Pierce died just two weeks before Mary Potter, and brother and sister seem then to have found in their mutual sense of loss an understanding of one another that lasted their lifetimes. Longfellow ultimately found a new happiness with Frances Appleton, but Anne endured widowhood for sixty-six years, supported in part by her brother's thoughtfulness and in part by the memories that surrounded her in the old family mansion on Congress Street in Portland.

One member of the household remains to be mentioned. Lucia Wadsworth (1783-1864), Zilpah's elder sister, came to help the Longfellows during the first years of their marriage and, in the tradition of maiden aunts not uncommon then, remained a fixture in the family circle. Aunt Lucia found her happiness in her sister's children, each of whom she served as nurse, disciplinarian, and consoler. Longfellow alludes to her infrequently and addresses her but once in his letters, but it seems clear that when he wrote to his parents he wrote to her as well.

Longfellow's principal correspondents outside his family during the years 1814-1843 were George Washington Greene and Samuel Ward, Jr. Greene (1811-1883), a minor historian, occasional pedagogue, and grandson of General Nathanael Greene, entered Brown University in 1825 but left before graduating to seek his health and acquire languages in Europe. There Longfellow met him in 1827, and in the Roman atmosphere of carnival, antiquity, and romance, they formed a friendship that lasted a lifetime. Greene's talents, while considerable, could not support his literary aspirations, and he leaned on his friend for encouragement, advice, and in later years for money. During the period covered in these volumes he married a young Italian girl, tried his hand at schoolmastering in Rhode Island, sought Longfellow's promotion to New York University so that he might have his place at Bowdoin, and discouraged by failure on every side, retreated to the sunnier surroundings of Italy. He subsequently served as United States Consul in Rome, as an instructor in modern languages at Brown, as a member of the Rhode Island legislature, and as the first occupant of a chair in American history at Cornell. Only his friendship with Longfellow, however, was an unqualified success. A polished but uninspired writer, he labored to establish a reputation with a definitive and adulatory biography of General Greene, which appeared in three volumes (1867-1871) and was dedicated to Longfellow, who had subsidized its publication.

What attracted Longfellow to Greene is not always easy to understand, but the evidence of forty-four extant letters written before 1844 (most of considerable length) and of hundreds later reveals an affection that survived many years and long separations. Greene can hardly have exerted an intellectual influence on his friend, for nothing in his published works or his own letters suggests any deep powers of the mind; nor could his attraction have been good humor and enthusiasm, for he was by nature a chronic complainer. His ill health — a symbol of his failure to achieve the reputation he aspired to — undoubtedly provoked sympathy in Longfellow, but sympathy alone is not enough to explain his loyalty. Perhaps the best explanation can be found in the fact that of all the friends of Longfellow's first European adventure, Greene alone remained to share his nostalgia for that halcyon period. In later years, warmed by Longfellow's wine and comforted by his cigars, he presumably displayed a charm of personality that made one forget his idiosyncracies.

During his second trip to Europe, in March, 1836, Longfellow met Samuel Ward, Jr. (1814-1884), a talented and adventurous New Yorker who became one of his most reliable correspondents, as their exchange of some 350 letters over the next forty-six years reveals. Longfellow seems to have been attracted by Ward's effervescence, earthiness, and flamboyance — qualities that his Yankee background had tended to restrain in his own personality and to which he was drawn in others. Ward was, in addition, a young man of means, which perhaps did not decrease his charm in Longfellow's eyes. Son of the prominent banker Samuel Ward and husband of the granddaughter of John Jacob Astor, Sam Ward enjoyed a social life that Longfellow could not emulate until his marriage to Frances Appleton in 1843. After that event the two conducted their correspondence sporadically because of Ward's peregrinations on three continents.

Ward's career after 1843 was as varied as Longfellow's was equable. Having gone through his inheritance, he made and lost three fortunes — in the California gold fields, in Washington as "King of the Lobby," and in Wall Street as a speculator. Everywhere he traveled — in this country, Mexico, Paraguay, Nicaragua, and Europe — he created legends about himself based on his prodigal generosity, his gustatory achievements, and his flair for the dramatic. That he was devoted to Longfellow is a fact substantiated both by his letters and by his essay entitled "Days with Longfellow," which he published in the *North American Review* two months after the poet's death (CXXXIV [May 1882], 455-466). "With me," he wrote on describing their first meeting in Germany, "it was a case of love at first sight, which has burned with the steady light of a Jewish tabernacle ever since."

During the years 1836–1843 Longfellow wrote some seventy-five letters to Ward, fifty-seven of which are included in this edition. It was a period in which Ward played an important role in Longfellow's life as a literary stimulus and agent — suggesting, criticizing, and encouraging as well as selling his friend's poems to the highest New York bidders. Greene, who might have served this function, was in Rome during most of this time; Charles Sumner, who became a more intimate confidant in the years ahead, was perhaps too occupied with his own problems and ambitions; and Longfellow's other friends were for various reasons more inclined to applaud than to help as critics and agents. Ward, however, was aggressive in his desire to be of service and was in fact the prime mover of the correspondence. A frustrated poet himself, a dramatizer, and a sharp judge of talent in others, he found in Longfellow not only a personal friend but also a writer on whom he could spend the considerable energies of his own ambition. His letters to Longfellow — frank, gossipy, and serio-comic — elicited answers in kind. With no one else was Longfellow so apt to let down the bars of his reserve.

Longfellow's letters to the various members of his family, together with those to Greene and Ward, account for slightly more than half the extant letters of 1814-1843; no other correspondents were so frequently in his mind as these. Shortly after he took up his duties as Smith Professor at Harvard, however, he began a correspondence with Charles Sumner (1811-1874), a young Boston lawyer who no one suspected would later flourish his resolute moral principles with great rhetorical skill in the United States Senate. During the period covered by these volumes Longfellow wrote only about twenty-five letters to Sumner (eighteen of which have been recovered), but in time the two became involved in an exchange of some four hundred more.

The friendship between Longfellow and Sumner was quickly established. By October, 1837, within a year after they had first met and shortly before Sumner sailed for a two-year sojourn abroad, Sumner had become, in Longfellow's phrase, "My particular friend," and after his return from Europe, where he captured other friends as effortlessly as he had captured Longfellow, he found relief from the tedium of his law practice by indulging again with Longfellow his taste for fine wines, books, and fireside conversation. Their compatability was complete. Sumner brooded with Longfellow over Frances Appleton's rejection of his suit, motivated not only by sympathy but also by his own uneasy foreknowledge that he, too, would be rejected in his pursuit of happiness through love and marriage. Although the important part of his correspondence with Sumner belongs to a later period, Longfellow's eighteen letters of 1836-1843 document the beginning of a friendship that survived the vicissitudes of time and lengthy separation.

Over the years covered in these two volumes Longfellow wrote to 220 or more correspondents, 144 of whom preserved the letters that are printed here. To some he wrote a dozen or more times, spurred by the enthusiasms of transitory friendships; to others (the German poet Ferdinand Freiligrath is a good example) he wrote irregularly but throughout the lifetime of the correspondent; and to a number of intimate friends he wrote rarely because he saw them frequently in the streets either of Portland and Brunswick or later of Boston and Cambridge. From the time of his first letter to the end of 1843 he wrote over three times as many letters to his father as to anyone else. When Stephen Longfellow died in 1849, his correspondence with his son had lasted on a fairly regular basis for thirty-five years; indeed, Longfellow's letters to his father and to Anne Longfellow Pierce (Stephen Longfellow's successor as chief family correspondent) spanned sixty-eight years, from 1814 to 1882. Similarly, although he wrote to them with less regularity, Longfellow maintained in writing his association with Greene for fifty-three years, with Ward for forty-six years, and with Sumner for thirty-seven years. These epistolary exchanges with family members and particular friends are to a large extent still available to the scholar and provide a primary source of information about Longfellow's life and the society in which he lived.

EDITORIAL PLAN

The first two volumes of this edition contain all the available letters of Longfellow, published and unpublished, written during the first thirty-six years of his life (although I have chosen not to include a few excerpts of less than fifty words from letters listed in dealers' catalogues and unrecovered in their entirety). The letters are arranged in chronological order, numbered consecutively, and placed under the full name of the recipient. When the exact date is not known, I have provided a date within brackets, justifying it when necessary in a footnote. When only the year of a letter is known, the letter is put at the end of the year; when the month and year are known, it is placed at the end of the month.

Since the object of this edition is to present authoritative texts of Longfellow's letters, I have retained as closely as possible his orthography, punctuation, paragraphing, grammar, and syntax. Longfellow wrote in a legible hand, with only an occasional lapse, and consequently bequeathed his editor few problems in interpretation. In preparing his letters for publication, however, I have felt it necessary in some instances to emend his text in the interests of clarity and readability. I have accordingly established the following editorial rules, which will apply to all volumes of the edition:

1. *Spelling* has been retained as found in the manuscripts, although a few words that appear to be the result of mere slips of the pen (*impatientient, scince, sous* for *sou, feell, vioelent, laspse, attatced*) have been silently corrected. I have preserved such spellings as *recieved, schollars, dilightful, aprehensive, phisiognomy, rappidly,*

reccollect, atlength, and *irrisistable* whenever I have established the fact that Longfellow — particularly in the letters of his youth — consistently spelled the words in that way. I have occasionally supplied a missing letter or letters within brackets, either to correct a spelling that might otherwise be considered an error in transcription (*Her[r]*, *tempe[r]ate, no[t]*) or to expand an abbreviation (see No. 5, below). Finally, I have not altered the spelling of personal names, no matter how erratic; but whenever I have made a positive identification, I have provided the proper form either within square brackets or in the note accompanying the first mention of the person.

2. *Punctuation* has not been changed except in the following instances: all sentences have been made to end with a period, which eliminates the terminal dash; dashes and other marks used to separate paragraphs have been removed; internal periods serving as commas have been changed to commas; and the double hyphen, as in *steam=ship, snow=storm,* and *rail=road,* has been converted to the conventional hyphen. In some cases I have supplied punctuation where it is clear that Longfellow inadvertently omitted it; thus, I have closed his quotations and parenthetical remarks, ended his sentences, and provided question marks when he neglected to do so and when the location of the missing points can be clearly determined. Occasionally I have silently provided punctuation, or deleted it, in order to clarify meaning. On the other hand, whenever it appeared possible that a correction, addition, or deletion in punctuation might alter the meaning that Longfellow intended, I have preferred to make no change but have sometimes in a footnote suggested clarification.

3. *Capitalization* is preserved as in the manuscripts, although for the sake of uniformity I have caused all sentences to begin with a capital letter. Whenever Longfellow's handwriting makes it difficult to determine if he used capital letters or not, I have followed modern usage.

4. *Grammar and syntax* remain the same as in the manuscripts with these exceptions: I have silently corrected Longfellow's occasional and inadvertent repetition of words and phrases (*the the; all over with tarnished all over with tarnished*); in a few instances I have deleted unnecessary words that merely obstruct meaning (*You as ask* and *all am my,* for example, become *You ask* and *all my*); and I have sometimes added a word or phrase to clarify meaning, but always within square brackets (see No. 7, below).

5. *Abbreviations and contractions* have been preserved as Longfellow used them when they occur in modern usage or when they are easily recognizable; when such is not the case (*Hard.* for *Harvard, celd.* for *celebrated, professorp.* for *professorship, Comment.* for *Com-*

mencement, mage. for *magazine*), they are expanded within square brackets and the accompanying periods or dashes deleted. The ampersand is rendered as *and* except when it is found in the names of firms and in the abbreviation *&c.* for *etc.* Superscript letters have been brought down to the line throughout and any underlying dashes or double periods replaced by a single period when the word has not been expanded within square brackets.

6. *Letters and passages in foreign languages* are reproduced exactly as in the manuscripts, regardless of spelling and grammatical irregularities, in order that the reader may judge for himself the nature of Longfellow's command of French, Spanish, Italian, and German, as well as the extent of his acquaintance with Greek, Latin, Provençal, Swedish, Danish, and Dutch. When the obscurity of his hand makes a reading problematical, I have followed correct modern usage. I have also provided translations of all passages in foreign languages (except for titles or expressions that have become a part of English usage) so that the general reader will have no difficulty in following Longfellow's meaning. Greek characters have been transliterated in italics unless their retention has some particular significance.

7. *Editorial insertions* have been held to a minimum. On occasion I have used square brackets to enclose an explanatory word or phrase omitted by Longfellow but necessary for a proper reading; to expand initials, such as *J. G. [James Greenleaf],* or names, such as *Mary [Potter Longfellow];* to include missing dates when they can be established or approximated; to provide the proper form of foreign and other words so erratically spelled as to be confusing; to supply short translations; and to insert certain italicized editorial comments, such as *[signature missing], [sentence unfinished], [in another hand],* or *[reading doubtful].* Double vertical bars enclose words, phrases, and punctuation marks lost through a defect in the manuscript and restored conjecturally. If there is no doubt about the reading of a single mutilated word, however, I have made the correction silently. Missing or illegible matter too long to be restored conjecturally has been indicated by suspension points ‖ . . . ‖ with a footnote subjoined to estimate the length of the passage.

8. *Longfellow's corrections* have been followed throughout, although I have sometimes given the original reading in a footnote if the correction seems to be of a later date or if the replaced word or words appear to have some stylistic or biographical importance.

9. *Typographical makeup* of the letters varies slightly in some instances from that of the manuscripts and printed sources. I have placed all dates and headings in run-on style at the beginning of the

letters and all postscript material (some of which appears in the originals in the margins and on the covers) at the end; I have centered the closings in run-on style and dropped Longfellow's signature below the complimentary remark; and I have indented Longfellow's paragraphs in accordance with modern usage.

10. *Basic texts* used in the preparation of the edition have been the manuscript texts whenever available. When the original letter is unrecovered, I have depended — in order of priority — on photographic reproductions, printed versions, and typed or handwritten copies. When depending on a printed version, I have reproduced the text exactly as I have found it except for obvious typographical errors or errors in transcription, which I have silently corrected.

11. Letters discovered after the manuscript went to the printer are entered in their proper chronological place and numbered like the preceding letter, with the addition of *a* or *b*; those discovered too late for inclusion will appear in an appendix to the final volume.

ANNOTATION

In preparing the annotation for this edition, I have had occasion to draw frequently from the correspondence received by Longfellow and preserved by him in a chronologically arranged series of bound volumes (now catalogued alphabetically in the Houghton Library). This correspondence, while incomplete, is a major source of information both about people and allusions in Longfellow's own letters and about the unrecovered letters indexed in the final volume of this edition. In my search for documentation I have also consulted Longfellow's unpublished journals, his study and lecture notes, scrapbook items, and literary manuscripts, as well as the family letters of Zilpah and Stephen Longfellow and their children. The list of acknowledgements will indicate some of my other sources of information.

In addition to identifications, textual clarifications, explanatory remarks, and (when I have discovered them) the sources of Longfellow's literary and other quotations, the letter endnotes contain other information of interest to a close reader of the letters: Longfellow's instructions to his correspondents ("Verte," "Turn over," etc.) as well as his own footnotes; deleted words or phrases (if they seem important for any reason); translations of lengthy passages in foreign languages; explanations of supplied dates if they are not obvious from postmarks or internal evidence; and the annotations of others appearing on the manuscripts. With a few exceptions I have identified the personae of the letters on the occasion of their first appearance; the reader who meets them subsequently may consult the index, where the identifying reference is italicized. I have in addition made use of a numbering system for letters and notes to facilitate cross reference; thus, 139.2 refers to Letter No. 139, note 2.

Unless otherwise stated, all manuscripts referred to in the introductory material and the letter endnotes are the property of the Longfellow Trust and are now on permanent deposit in the Houghton Library of Harvard University. Information concerning the location of the other manuscripts (or if the manuscript is unrecovered, the source of the text) is found at the end of each letter. In addition, when the data are available, I have included at the end of the letter the address of the recipient, legible postmarks (without, however, giving full philatelic descriptions), annotations on the address leaf, and the endorsement whenever it provides facts not already known to the reader and likely to be of interest to him (such as dates when the letter was received and/or answered). I have also provided at the end a reference to a first printing if the letter has been previously printed in its complete form; unless they are substantially complete, I have not noted the extracts and abridgements in Samuel Longfellow's *Life* and in other biographical and critical studies dealing with Longfellow.

Short titles of works cited frequently in the annotation are listed at the end of each volume. Finally, I should like to state that the textual readings, descriptive annotations, and identifications of this edition are to be considered authoritative whenever they vary from the material of my earlier publications on Longfellow.

CHRONOLOGY

1807   Birth of Henry Wadsworth Longfellow, February 27, in Portland, Maine.

1813   Enters Portland Academy, where he continues for eight years.

1821   Admitted to Bowdoin College, September, but remains at Portland Academy for freshman year.

1822   Becomes resident student at Bowdoin College, September.

1823   Stephen Longfellow begins term in U.S. House of Representatives, December, where he serves until March 1825.

1825   Graduates from Bowdoin College, September. Reads law in Stephen Longfellow's office in Portland.

1826   Publication of *Miscellaneous Poems Selected from the United States Literary Gazette* (Boston: Cummings, Hilliard and Company, and Harrison Gray), c. February. Departs for Europe, April. Resides in Paris.

1827   Resides in Madrid, March–September. Meets George Washington Greene in Marseilles, December.

1828   Resides in Italy.

1829   Studies at Göttingen, February–June. Death of Elizabeth Longfellow, May 5. Returns to America, August. Assumes duties as professor of modern languages at Bowdoin College, September.

1830   Publication of *Elements of French Grammar; French Exercises; Manuel de Proverbes Dramatiques;* and *Novelas Españolas* (Portland: Samuel Colman), c. June.

1831   Publication of "The Origin and Progress of the French Language" in the *North American Review,* April; *Le Ministre de Wakefield* and *Elements of French Grammar,* 2nd ed. (Boston: Gray & Bowen), c. June. Marries Mary Storer Potter, September 14.

1832   Publication in the *North American Review* of "The Defence of Poetry," January, "Spanish Devotional and Moral Poetry," April, and "History of the Italian Language and Dialects," October; *Syllabus de la Grammaire Italienne* and *Saggi de' Novellieri Italiani d'Ogni Secolo* (Boston: Gray & Bowen), July. Marriage of Anne Longfellow and George Washington Pierce, November 26.

1833   Publication in the *North American Review* of "Spanish Language and Literature," April, and "Old English Romances," October; *Outre-Mer, No. I* (Boston: Hilliard, Gray & Company), July; and *Coplas de Don Jorge Manrique* (Boston: Allen and Ticknor), September.

1834   Publication of *Outre-Mer, No. II* (Boston: Lilly, Wait, and Company), May. Death of Ellen Longfellow, August 12. Receives offer of Smith Professorship of Modern Languages at Harvard, December.

1835 Publication of *Outre-Mer; A Pilgrimage Beyond the Sea* (New York: Harper & Brothers), April. Departs for Europe, April 10. Visits England, Scandinavia, Holland, and Germany. Deaths of George Washington Pierce, November 15, and Mary Potter Longfellow in Rotterdam, November 29.

1836 Winters in Heidelberg. Meets Samuel Ward, Jr., March, and Frances Appleton, July 31, in Switzerland. Returns to America, October. Begins residence in Cambridge.

CHART I

Longfellow, Stephenson, Storer Genealogy

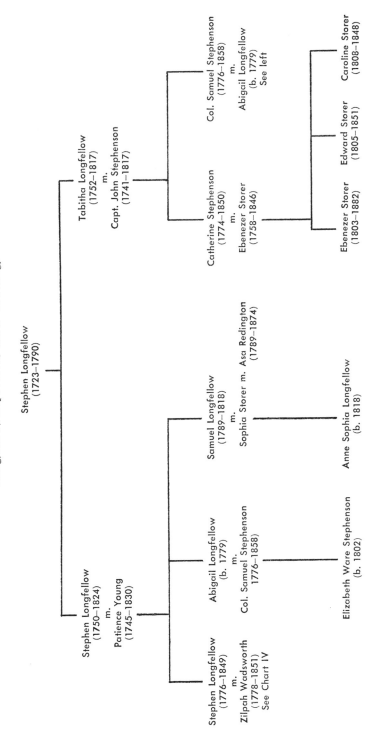

Stephen Longfellow
(1723–1790)

Stephen Longfellow
(1750–1824)
m.
Patience Young
(1745–1830)

Tabitha Longfellow
(1752–1817)
m.
Capt. John Stephenson
(1741–1817)

Stephen Longfellow
(1776–1849)
m.
Zilpah Wadsworth
(1778–1851)
See Chart IV

Abigail Longfellow
(b. 1779)
m.
Col. Samuel Stephenson
1776–1858

Samuel Longfellow
(1789–1818)
m.
Sophia Storer m. Asa Redington
(1789–1874)

Catherine Stephenson
(1774–1850)
m.
Ebenezer Storer
(1758–1846)

Col. Samuel Stephenson
(1776–1858)
m.
Abigail Longfellow
(b. 1779)
See left

Elizabeth Ware Stephenson
(b. 1802)

Anne Sophia Longfellow
(b. 1818)

Ebenezer Storer
(1803–1882)

Edward Storer
(1805–1851)

Caroline Storer
(1808–1848)

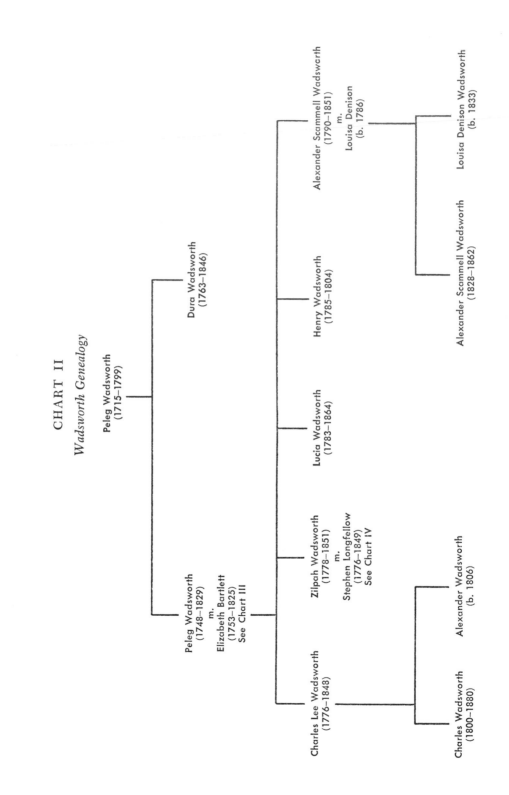

CHART II

Wadsworth Genealogy

Peleg Wadsworth
(1715–1799)

Peleg Wadsworth
(1748–1829)
m.
Elizabeth Bartlett
(1753–1825)
See Chart III

Dura Wadsworth
(1763–1846)

Charles Lee Wadsworth
(1776–1848)

Zilpah Wadsworth
(1778–1851)
m.
Stephen Longfellow
(1776–1849)
See Chart IV

Lucia Wadsworth
(1783–1864)

Henry Wadsworth
(1785–1804)

Alexander Scammell Wadsworth
(1790–1851)
m.
Louisa Denison
(b. 1786)

Charles Wadsworth
(1800–1880)

Alexander Wadsworth
(b. 1806)

Alexander Scammell Wadsworth
(1828–1862)

Louisa Denison Wadsworth
(b. 1833)

CHART III

Bartlett, Doane, Wells Genealogy

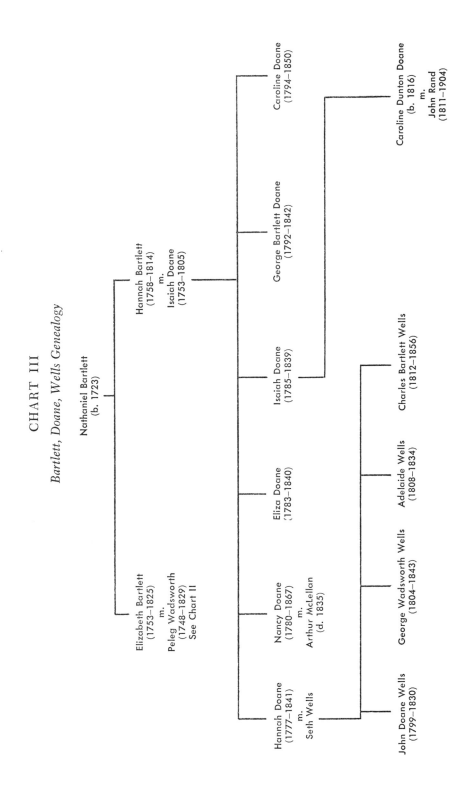

Nathaniel Bartlett
(b. 1723)

Elizabeth Bartlett
(1753–1825)
m.
Peleg Wadsworth
(1748–1829)
See Chart II

Hannah Bartlett
(1758–1814)
m.
Isaiah Doane
(1753–1805)

Hannah Doane
(1777–1841)
m.
Seth Wells

Nancy Doane
(1780–1867)
m.
Arthur McLellan
(d. 1835)

Eliza Doane
(1783–1840)

Isaiah Doane
(1785–1839)

George Bartlett Doane
(1792–1842)

Caroline Doane
(1794–1850)

John Doane Wells
(1799–1830)

George Wadsworth Wells
(1804–1843)

Adelaide Wells
(1808–1834)

Charles Bartlett Wells
(1812–1856)

Caroline Dunton Doane
(b. 1816)
m.
John Rand
(1811–1904)

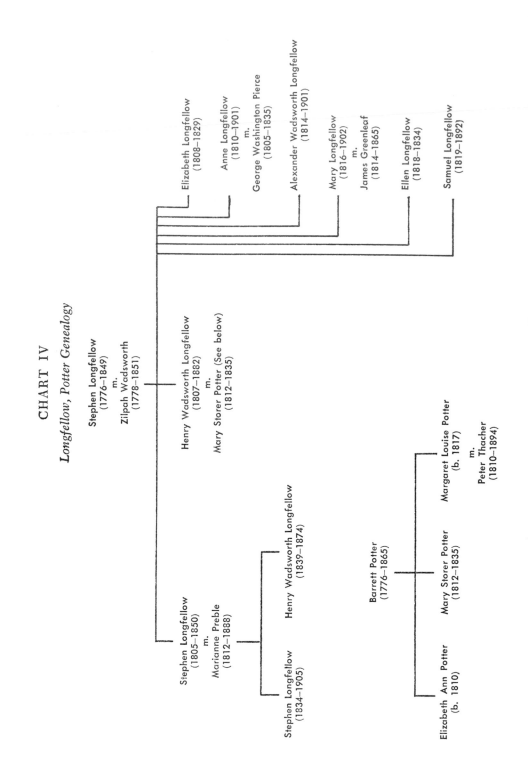

CHART IV

Longfellow, Potter Genealogy

Stephen Longfellow
(1776–1849)
m.
Zilpah Wadsworth
(1778–1851)

Elizabeth Longfellow
(1808–1829)

Anne Longfellow
(1810–1901)
m.
George Washington Pierce
(1805–1835)

Alexander Wadsworth Longfellow
(1814–1901)

Mary Longfellow
(1816–1902)
m.
James Greenleaf
(1814–1865)

Ellen Longfellow
(1818–1834)

Samuel Longfellow
(1819–1892)

Henry Wadsworth Longfellow
(1807–1882)
m.
Mary Storer Potter (See below)
(1812–1835)

Stephen Longfellow
(1805–1850)
m.
Marianne Preble
(1812–1888)

Henry Wadsworth Longfellow
(1839–1874)

Stephen Longfellow
(1834–1905)

Barrett Potter
(1776–1865)

Margaret Louise Potter
(b. 1817)
m.
Peter Thacher
(1810–1894)

Mary Storer Potter
(1812–1835)

Elizabeth Ann Potter
(b. 1810)

PART ONE

SCHOOL AND COLLEGE

1814–1826

SCHOOL AND COLLEGE

1 8 1 4 – 1 8 2 6

Eɪɢʜᴛʏ-ᴇɪɢʜᴛ ʟᴇᴛᴛᴇʀs, all but the first five and the last six written during Longfellow's four years as a Bowdoin College undergraduate, document the years of his formal education. They provide us with a record of his formal training, of his adolescent problems and adventures, and of his development into young manhood.

As a student, Longfellow depended perhaps more on a ready wit and facile memory than on disciplined concentration. He graduated fourth in a class of twenty and feigned surprise at the honor. "How I came to get so high," he wrote to his sister Anne on June 30, 1825, "is rather a mistery to me, in as much as I have never been a remarkably hard student, touching College studies." If not a "hard" student, he was nevertheless a conscientious one, who avoided the easy society of the less serious undergraduates (among them Hawthorne, who is not mentioned in the letters of this period) and who observed rather than participated in the Brunswick escapades and indiscretions. Sensitive to his obligations as son and scholar, in a way that his brother Stephen was not, he studied Latin and Greek, wrestled with mathematics and science, read history and English rhetoric, and attended with a minimum of complaint the compulsory chapels. The faculty rewarded him not only with the Fourth Oration but also with their tacit approval of the plan that was to make him their colleague. Fittingly enough, after election by his fellow students he composed and read the farewell poem to his class.

The literary allusions and quotations in his college letters establish the fact that Longfellow read both widely and indiscriminately at Bowdoin. He studied the English classics under the eye of the faculty, but his own tastes, formed in part by the contemporary British and American journals, led him to the modern poets and novelists. The list of authors mentioned or alluded to in the first group of letters is as long as it is miscellaneous: Shakespeare, Thomas Gray, Charles Brockden Brown, Isaac D'Israeli, Washington Irving, John Neal, James Fenimore Cooper, Edward Young, Thomas Campbell, James Thomson, L.E.L., Mrs. Hemans, Thomas Chatterton, William Cowper, John Milton, Lydia Maria Child, and James Gates Percival, to mention a few. The evidence of lists is not decisive, of course, but it is clear that young Longfellow found in literature the main stimulus of his intellect.

That his classmates elected him their poet suggests that they, at least, had already associated him with a literary future. He had, indeed, published both poetry and prose in Portland newspapers and in Boston and Philadelphia journals; in 1824, he had competed in Boston for the Shakespeare Jubilee prize in poetry; and as a kind of local laureate, he had celebrated in verse the arrival of Lafayette in Maine and the centennial of Lovewell's fight at Fryeburg. Having had the satisfaction of seeing his lines in print, he felt tempted in the enthusiasm of immaturity to attack the future with his pen alone. Wiser counsel prevailed, however, and he left college to acquaint himself briefly with the law before beginning the accumulation of languages. Had he been given his head by less solicitous elders, he might have become a better poet; but his own instincts for practicality urged him to embark on a less hazardous course, and he thankfully accepted the alternative of Europe and a scholarly career.

1. *To Stephen Longfellow*

Portland. [January 16, 1814][1]

Dear Papa,

Ann wants a little bible like little Betsy's. Will you please to buy her one if you can find any in Boston. I have been to school all the week and got only seven marks. I shall have a billet on monday.[2] I wish you to buy me a drum.

Henry W. Longfellow

MANUSCRIPT: Longfellow Trust Collection. ADDRESS: S. Longfellow/Boston PUBLISHED: *Life*, I, 7.

1. On January 16, 1814, Zilpah Longfellow wrote to her husband, who was in Boston attending the General Court: "Enclosed is Henry's letter, the product of some hours attentive employment. I mention this that you may appreciate it not by its appearance but by its intrinsic value." Thus the letter was written on the 16th or shortly before.

2. Henry attended at this time a private school kept by Nathaniel Hazeltine Carter (1787-1830), a Dartmouth graduate and subsequently an author of minor reputation. The seven marks were disciplinary in nature; a billet was a good-conduct letter.

2. *To Stephen Longfellow*

[Hiram] Aug. 1815.[1]

Dear Papa

I wish you would tell me in your next letter how the house comes on.[2] And I wish you would bring me a Childs Companion, for Charles

Wadsworth.[3] I do not know but I have one at home, but if you buy one I can pay you again. I believe it will cost only nine pence. I thank you for those books you sent me. I have read the riddle book through and learnt several riddles. I like the stories in the other book very well.

H. W. L.

MANUSCRIPT: Longfellow Trust Collection. ADDRESS: Stephen Longfellow Esq:/ Portland

1. On August 14 Zilpah Longfellow explained to her husband: "I wrote on Thursday [the 10th], intending to send it with Henry's by some private hand, but no opportunity offered." This narrows the date to August 9 or 10. The letter, in Zilpah's hand, bears her note at the top of the sheet: "Copy of Henry's letter." The original is missing.

2. In July, 1815, a fire damaged the Longfellow house in Portland, providing Stephen Longfellow with an opportunity to do some extensive remodeling. Henry and his mother awaited the completion of the work in Hiram with the Wadsworth grandparents.

3. Charles Wadsworth (1800-1880), son of Charles Lee Wadsworth of Hiram, was Henry's first cousin.

3. To Stephen Longfellow

Portland   September 15th 1820[1]

Dear Sir

Perhaps you are impatient to hear from us and to know how mama's health is and I now take my pen to inform you that she is better than the Doctor expected she would be at this time.[2]

This evening while I was studying my Greek, Elizabeth wrote you a letter but making some mistakes in directing it and being called for by mama, she had not time enough to finish another, and I, thinking you would wish to hear from us, took this opportunity to write you this short letter, in haste, as you will see by the writing. It is now twenty-five minutes past eight, and I am sitting in the parlour with Alexander by me almost asleep — he hangs his head upon his shoulder. Poor little boy, he wants to go to bed! A minute or two ago I called him by name—he only raised his head and without opening his eyes answered "what." Stephen is just carrying him to bed and so, if you please, I will wish you a good night.

Henry W Longfellow.

MANUSCRIPT: Longfellow Trust Collection. ADDRESS: Stephen Longfellow Jun Esqre./Augusta/State of Maine POSTMARK: PORTLAND SEP 14

1. The postmark indicates that Henry wrote this letter on the 14th or before.

2. During several weeks in the fall of 1820 while her husband attended to business and political affairs in Augusta and Wiscasset, Zilpah Longfellow suffered from a debilitating illness, the exact nature of which is not known. Dr. Samuel Weed (1774-1857) of Portland attended her.

4. *To Stephen Longfellow*

Portland, Monday, September 25 [1820]

Dear Sir

Doctor thinks mama is better to night. She set up an hour and a half to day. Instead of keepin[g] my money untill tomorrow to spend in "trifles" I thought it would be better to buy books with it and accordingly I bought two "plays." I dont much think I shall go over to the plains [1] tomorrow but stay in town and take a little bit of a ride on horse back.

Grand-papa Wadsworth [2] arrived here from Hiram this evening. You must excuse the shortness of this letter and "badness of the writing" which is owing to my not having a good pen — and not having a sha[r]p knife I am not able to make a better one.

Henry W. Longfellow [3]

MANUSCRIPT: Longfellow Trust Collection. ENDORSEMENT: H.W.L. 1820

1. That is, "Stevens Plains," then a part of the adjacent town of Westbrook and now a Portland suburb.

2. Gen. Peleg Wadsworth (1748–1829), after a distinguished career in the Revolutionary War and later in business and politics, had moved in 1807 to a 7800-acre tract of land in the Saco River valley where he founded the town of Hiram. On his subsequent visits to Portland he stayed with Stephen and Zilpah Longfellow, to whom he had left his brick mansion on Congress Street.

3. Anne Longfellow had begun a letter to her father on this sheet but had not got beyond her first sentence: "Portla[nd]/I now write you good news." Opposite this statement Henry wrote, "Anne began here but," and at the end of his own letter: "Henry finished here."

5. *To Stephen Longfellow*

Portland   October 8th 1820

Dear Sir

Mama thinks she has not amended much, for the week past, and therefore says you must not expect to find her very smart. A letter was recieved from, "your humble servant" Mr Joseph Pierce, of Boston,[1] from which I have made an extract which contains all that will be necessary for you to know, as the other part of the letter contains nothing of business nor importance.

He says that he is aprehensive that his letter of the 21st of September was not sufficiently explicit. And further that "On recurring to the copy, it appears that you might perhaps consider yourself as retained for the Twenty Associates only in the case now pending — whereas I wished it to be understood that you were retained in all cases, wherein the Twenty Associates are, or may be a party, either directly or indirectly, in any suits now commenced, or may be hereafter commenced, by them or against them. Therefore if you did not so understand it before — please consider it in that light now — and confirm it accordingly." [2]

We recieved an other letter to day (sunday) from Mr Mark L Hill Jun (Philipsburgh) [3] enclosing five dollars which Wm Davis handed him wishing him to enclose it to you, for B. Adams *who* Requested him to inform you that he will send the remainder in a few days — says that he should have sent it before but was disappointed in getting it. [4]

I like Mr Cobbs, as a preceptor, as well as any one I ever had. [5] He seems to understand the languages so well, that nothing appears to perplex him, but on the contrary, he answers all our questions with as much quickness and facility as if he had just reviewed them (the languages).

Stephen wishes to sell you, his elegant watch, which has been lately fixed and now keeps verry good time. He offers it for six dollars, which he thinks cheap enough, considering the "repairs" it has undergone which, if you buy the watch, he intends to pay for. (per order).

An address will be delivered before the Portland Benevolent Society, on Wednesday evening next, by John. P.B. Storer — Esq — [6] at which I purpose to attend.

Henry W. Longfellow.

MANUSCRIPT: Longfellow Trust Collection. ADDRESS: Stephen Longfellow Jun Esq./Wiscasset —/State of Maine.

1. One of Stephen Longfellow's clients, as the succeeding paragraph reveals.
2. Henry's footnote at this point: "this longest passage marked by double commas is the extract alluded to."
3. Phippsburg.
4. This somewhat complicated transaction was apparently in payment for legal services performed by Stephen Longfellow. All of the principals mentioned were from Phippsburg, Maine. Hill's father was Mark Langdon Hill, an overseer of Bowdoin College at this time and also a member of Congress.
5. Bezaleel Cushman was preceptor of the Portland Academy in 1820. There is no record of a Mr. Cobbs (or Cobb, a more usual Portland name) as an instructor at the Academy. Perhaps he was a temporary teacher, as the paragraph seems to imply.
6. John Parker Boyd Storer (1794-1845), member of the Bowdoin class of 1812 and a Unitarian minister.

6. To George Washington Pierce [1]

Portland   February. 16 — [1822]

Dear Friend —

As you requested me to write — and as letter-writing — in some instances — is an employment to which I am not at all averse, I shall embrace this opportunity to commence a correspondence with you. There is — with me — a little embarrassment in addressing my first letter to an acquaintance although I might consider myself quite intimate when in company with him. You must excuse me, therefore if my letter should be dull and uninteresting. You might perhaps be disposed to laugh at me were I to use the apology of some lazy correspondents who excuse themselves by saying that 'they have nothing to say' in their letters tho' I frankly confess it is particularly applicable to my situation at the present moment. There is scarcely any interesting news abroad. The common every-day occurrences would sound tediously in your ears — and besides such things are more fit for a news-paper than for the pages of a letter.

Some of my acquaintances at Brunswick seem to have forgotten me — however do not mention it to them — for if they cannot remember me without having some one to "drive it into 'em" I should choose rather to be forgotten than to be remembered.

As to my classical studies — I am still going on in *Xenophon* — and have proceeded about 17 sections in the 2nd Book of Livy — if your course of studies are different from this — or if you have proceeded farther — please to let [me] know it.

Yours respectfully
H. W Longfellow

P.S. We have proceeded — in Mathematicks as far as Tare and Trett.

MANUSCRIPT: Longfellow Trust Collection.   ADDRESS: Mr George Pierce — /Brunswick.

1. By the fall of 1821 Henry had advanced enough in his studies to be admitted to the freshman class at Bowdoin College, of which his father was a trustee. Because he was only fourteen years old, his parents decided against his residence in Brunswick during the first year of college, and he and his brother Stephen remained in Portland, following the Bowdoin curriculum under the guidance of Bezaleel Cushman. Henry had, however, visited the college grounds in May, 1821, and he was acquainted with a number of his classmates already on the campus. One of these, George Washington Pierce, became an intimate friend and the husband of his sister Anne (see Introduction).

7. *To George Washington Pierce*

Portland   June 2nd 1822

Dear Friend

I recieved yours of the 3rd — to day — and assure you that I am no less sorry than you are, that I did not recieve your former letter — which was the cause of your seeming neglect. No apology, however, was necessary — and if, indeed, it had been — I should not have considered it incumbent upon *you* to have made it. You must naturally suppose that I am desirous to know what standing Kinsman[1] holds in the Class — and whether he gets many "screwings" &c. If you have had sufficient opportunity to form an opinion upon this subject I wish you would tell me *exactly* what you think about it, and not disguise your opinion from any private motives of friendship. From what I have already heard, I have no doubt that he gets along well — but I have, as yet, had no direct information upon the subject. What do you think of Greenleaf?[2] and what is the opinion that the schollars in general entertain of him? Is he not considered as a fellow of excellent natural abilities? That is my opinion and I think that he only needs application to give him a high standing in his class. What I have heard of him since he has resided at Brunswick, rather inclines me to believe that he is not a very close applicant to his studies — and I am sorry for it, because I wish that the "Representatives from *our* Western towns" should hold high rank in the Class.

And now whilst I think of it I will ask you a question of rather a different kind. How did it happen that you passed through Portland with so much secresy that I did not even *hear* of it untill you had left town? I was expecting daily to see you but the first thing I hear'd was that you had passed through town on your way to Brunswick.

Remember me to all my friends — and tell them I am expecting letters from them and hope they will not disappoint me.

Yours &c &c
Henry W Longfellow —[3]

I shall want to know where you commence reviewing — &c — and how far the Class will probably proceed in Majora[4] — and whether we shall be examined in Algebra at Commenceme[n]t. If you will take pains to enquire — and inform me you will oblige me.

H —

MANUSCRIPT: Longfellow Trust Collection. ADDRESS: To/Mr Geo: W— Pierce./ Student at Bow: Coll:/Brunswick POSTMARK: PORTLAND ME JUNE 2

1. John Dafforne Kinsman (1806–1850) of Portland, later a lawyer in that city.
2. Patrick Henry Greenleaf (1808–1869), son of the distinguished jurist Simon Greenleaf, then residing in Portland.
3. The instruction "Verte" follows the signature.
4. Andrew Dalzel's *Collectanea Græca Majora,* the Greek text studied at Bowdoin by freshmen, sophomores, and juniors.

8. *To George Washington Pierce*

Portland — June 28 — [1822]

Dear George —

I have just recieved your letter and have already sat down to answer it. I think you will give me credit for my punctuality in writing if you cannot for anything else. For the particulars of our "Scrape" at the Academy, you must apply to Greenleaf. Preble[1] has written him particularly upon *that* subject — no doubt you will find his account very interesting. Mr Cushman was much too hasty — was governed too much by his passions — and proceeded very unadvisedly. His feelings undoubtedly were hurt — and he endeavoured to salve over the wound by the course he pursued. Had it been a small schollar, taking past occurrences into consideration, his conduct might have been justifiable: but in the present instance it is *far* from it.[2]

You must excuse the shortness of this letter. I must write to Greenleaf to day and I have very little leisure as I expect to leave town tomorrow morning. I am going up "into the bush"[3] to stay a few days and shall expect an answer to this upon my return.

Yours

H. Longfellow —

PS I wish you would be more particular in the account of your studies.

MANUSCRIPT: Longfellow Trust Collection. ADDRESS: To/Mr Geo: Pierce./Student at Bow: Coll:/Brunswick POSTMARK: PORTLAND ME JUNE 28

1. Edward Deering Preble (1806–1846), son of the naval hero Commodore Edward Preble and also a nonresident Bowdoin freshman.
2. This "scrape," the particulars of which are not known, seems to have involved one of the Bowdoin freshman under Cushman's tutelage at the Portland Academy.
3. That is, to Hiram to visit the Wadsworth grandparents.

9. *To George Washington Pierce*

Portland   Monday July 15 — [1822]

Dear Pierce

I recieved yours of the 13 to day — in which you expressed your 'hopes' that none of the country lasses had stolen my heart away. I assure you that your fears upon that point are groundless. However I was much pleased with my ride into the Country. I was at your house on Saturday the 29" — June — and since then do not feel at all disposed to laugh at Baldwin.[1] I think you have a fine view from your door, of the mountains to the south in Cornish and Limington — very fine i[n]deed — equal I think to anything of the kind I have ever seen. I drank tea with your family and was kindly pressed to pass the night there, which I extremely regret was not in my power, if it had been, I assure you I would readily have accepted the invitation.

In answer to your questions concerning chum[m]ing I answer you, that I shall probably chum with brother. We all expect to be down at Commencement and as you say "it is very uncommon for one to be turned by" — I hope we shall all enter — if we do not — "therefore recieve *'we'* the greater condemnation."[2]

I thought I had *done* troubling you with my queries about our studies — but I have something more to ask yet. I wish you would note down on paper the authors you have studied once, and those which you have reviewed, in the order in which you read them — and also to make *particular* inquiry of one of the Tutors whether we shall be examined in Algebra at commencement — and if we are to be in what particular parts of it. I wish you would make these enquiries as soon as you recieve this, and write me by the next post, as it is necess[ar]y for us to have the information as soon as *possible.* Excuse my miserable penmanship — as I am in a hurry — and believe me.

Yours with regard
H. — W Longfellow —

MANUSCRIPT: Longfellow Trust Collection. ADDRESS: Mr Geo: W— Pierce —/ Brunswick/(Me) POSTMARK: PORTLAND ME JULY 15

1. Baldwin, on the route from Portland to Hiram, was Pierce's birthplace and home.

2. Jas. 3:1. "My brethren, be not many masters, knowing that we shall receive the greater condemnation."

10. *To Zilpah and Stephen Longfellow* [1]

Brunswick   September 22nd 1822

Dear Parents,

As we have now got comfortably settled, I suppose it is about time to let you know how we go on here. I feel very well contented, and am much pleased with a College Life. Many of the students are very agreeable companions and, thus far, I have passed my time very pleasantly. The students have considerably more leisure than I expected, but as the season advances and the days grow shorter, our leisure moments must necessarily be considerably diminished. I expected, when I got here that I should have to study very hard to keep a good footing with the rest of the class; but I find I have suffi-cient time for the preperation of my lessons and for amusement, and that I am not more deficient than some of the rest of the class. I have not been "screwed" at recitation yet and shall endeavour not to be. So much for egotism!

I have very little more to write, but I will not forget to mention that by some means or other, I cannot tell what, I have either lost on my passage here, or left at home, all my cotton stockings except the one pair which I wore — and another thing is that I wish some one would get a brass ferrule put on to my cane and send it to me as soon as possible. If you have any good apples or pears I wish you would send me some — and tell the girls to send a whole parcel of Ginger-bread with them. My box of tooth powder may also be put into the bundle.

Your's affectionately,
H. W. L —

P.S. There is another thing of considerable importance which I had like to have forgotten. You do not know how much we stand in need of a good Watch. When the chapel bell rings for recitation it is only struck a few times and then is done, so that we, living so far from the College Buildings, are liable to be late — however we must do the best we can. Give my love to all and tell the Girls to write soon.

MANUSCRIPT: Longfellow Trust Collection. ADDRESS: Stephen Longfellow Jun Esq/Portland POSTMARK (*in script*): BRUNSWICK/SEPT. 23d. PUBLISHED: *Young Longfellow*, pp. 31–32.

1. Shortly before writing this letter, Henry had taken up residence in Brunswick to begin his sophomore year in college. Unable to find room in the college dormitory, he, his brother Stephen, and Ned Preble boarded with Rev. Benjamin Titcomb, a Baptist clergyman of Brunswick whose chilly house was later occupied by Harriet Beecher Stowe, who wrote *Uncle Tom's Cabin* in its inhospitable drafts.

11. *To Zilpah Longfellow*

Bowdoin College. December 7 — 1822.

My Dear Mother,

I recieved your letter of Novr 26 — as returning from church, last sunday. And now see what a scurvy trick Fortune (or rather Mis-for-tune) has played me. The reason of my silence concerning our return at Thank[s]-giving was, that I wished to take you by surprise — and therefore said nothing, but kept you in doubt. You see how it ends. We are disappointed in our mode of conveyance and forced to remain. And ther[e]in lies the rub. I do not know when I have passed a week so unpleasantly or when time has lagged so much or hung so heavily upon my hands. First, the disappointment was a serious evil: added to this the long succession of cold days and colder nights — frozen ears — cold feet and a thousand other "ills the flesh is heir to" [1] — all these make it dull living in this dreary region of the East. Heigh-ho for the vacation. We ate our Thanksgiving dinner at Professor Cleaveland's;[2] — the professor was very sociable but I had rather by half have dined at home.

I am very sorry to hear that Betsey has been indisposed and hope she has quite recovered again. I have not got well yet and what is more, do not see much prospect of "a speedy recovery." However I make two meals on "pudding and milk," that is one good thing! We have fixed our fire-place as you mentioned. I think it may be advantageous as it respects warming the room, but the chimney is more inclined to smoke and that, you know, is about as disagreeable as cold is — but to have both is rather too bad.

You say you can excuse the shortness of the letters. Be so kind as to excuse the shortness of mine! My love to all.

Your affectionate son
Henry.

ps. The letters I recieved by Mellen[3] and Preble, I shall answer soon.

MANUSCRIPT: Longfellow Trust Collection. ADDRESS: Mrs Zilpah Longfellow./ Portland/By the politeness/of Mr Story. —[4]

1. Cf. *Hamlet*, III, i, 62–63.

2. Longfellow's commemorative sonnet to Parker Cleaveland (1780–1858), written over fifty years later, eloquently reveals his admiration for Bowdoin's versatile professor of chemistry, mathematics, and mineralogy; and subsequent letters establish the fact that Cleaveland became an important influence in the young man's life.

3. Frederic Mellen (1804–1834), Longfellow's classmate and the younger brother of the poet Grenville Mellen. He and Ned Preble had brought letters from Portland, where they spent the Thanksgiving holiday.

4. Presumably Joseph Story (1779–1845), Stephen Longfellow's classmate at Harvard and at this time an associate justice of the United States Supreme Court with a circuit embracing Maine, New Hampshire, Massachusetts, and Rhode Island.

12. *To Cullen Sawtelle*[1]

Portland   Jany. 14. 1823.

My Dear Cullen,

From the various little cares which have lately obtruded themselves upon my leisure, I turn with pleasure to the calls of friendship. I do not sit down to pen you a long letter, but hoping to profit by mutual correspondence I offer you the few words that friendship dictates. It would perhaps be uninteresting to you as well as idle in me, to repeat the manner in which I have been engaged since we last shook hands at parting in B[runswic]k. Suffice it, for the present, to say, the two weeks have slipt rappidly away and agreeably too — the particulars when we meet again.

An evening or two ago I had the pleasure of seeing a sketch of your beautiful village of Norridgewock — and I assure you I was greatly delighted with it. If it is in reality as beautiful and pleasant as it seemed from that sketch to be, it is just such a village as I should like to live — die — and be buried in. I know of nothing so delightful as retiring from the smoke, noise, and dust of the town to the green fields of the country — tho' many prefer the town — noisy and dusty as it is. I feel pretty confident that life would wear smoothly away — with me — could I dwell in a neat country-house — upon the borders of some lake or river in the enjoyment of rural retirement — but this is mere talk! ! I am too continually lazy to be a farmer or any thing else, for ought I know. The sketch which I was speaking of, was taken upon the side of the Kennebeck opposite your village and either above or below the bridge, I am unable to say which. I do not recollect of having ever seen a view of any village, which has so much delighted me. I will not say that I envy you the happiness, which you must almost *necessarily* enjoy there, but I *will say* that I should like to enjoy it with you. I have heard Norridgewock spoken of as a beautiful place but I never till now formed any idea of its situation or beauty.[2]

Before I close my letter, I will give you my congratulations on the begin[n]ing of another year, and very heartily wish you a Happy New-Year. We have Carriers' and News-boys' good wishes in abundance and I suppose they are plenty with you — but the hearty good wishes of one friend are worth ten thousand of these.

And now that you may have a peep at me as I sit by the fire thinking of my old friend, yourself, — imagine to yourself a family circle drawn around the evening fire, and myself not the least amongst them. But do not, I beseech you, think that I still keep that 'sour visage' which I wore in Brunswick — for I begin to flatter myself that it is not so care-wrinkled as it was then but that it really grows a little more pleasant. So much for Egotism.

But it grows late and I perhaps, tho' unintentionally, grow tedious!! Remember me to our Class-Mate Shipley.[3] And, believe me, "forever-and-aye,"

Your affectionate friend
Hen. W. Longfellow

MANUSCRIPT: Chester M. Sawtelle, Marblehead, Massachusetts. ADDRESS: To/ Mr Cullen Sawtell[e]./Norridgewock./Me. POSTMARK: PORTLAND JAN 15 POSTAL ANNOTATION: Paid

1. Another of Longfellow's classmates, Cullen Sawtelle (1805–1887) of Norridgewock, Maine, later became a lawyer and congressman. Longfellow wrote to him from Portland during the mid-term holiday.

2. The instruction "Turn over." follows this paragraph.

3. David Shepley (1804–1881) subsequently entered the clergy and served as an overseer and trustee of Bowdoin College.

13. *To Stephen Longfellow*

Bow: Coll: *February.* 18. 1823.

My Dear Father,

We arrived here safely after a very pleasant ride of about 6 hours — dining at Codman's[1] and so on to town in the afternoon. I begin to like our boarding-house better, than I did last term, and, somehow or other, our room seems, to me, at least, ten-per-cent more pleasant. We have five new boarders at our table and more are engaged here. Two of the Medical Students are 'sojourning' in the next chamber to us — all so handy — in case of sickness — tho' by the by, they may be but new beginners. I expect that this will be a very pleasant term. If it is not I am mistaken — there seems to be more bustle and buisiness than usual and more life in this dull town than there appeared to be at the close of last term. Most of the College students are here — and I am only waiting for Spring when we shall have warmer days — and more leisure, to enjoy myself. After indulging in morning naps as I did during the vacation, I thought it might be very difficult to regain the old path again — but I find I [have] no difficulty whatever in waking at sunrise, and that this depends solely upon habit, I have no doubt. Early or late to bed, I find makes no great difference. I wake as early, when I go to bed at 12 — as when I go at 9. So *there* are 3 hours clear gain. I never retire till after 10 — never. My usual hours are 11 and 12.

As to my health I hardly know what to say — nor do. I should think it was not so good, by any means. Ever since I have been here I have been troubled — with a continual swim[m]ing and aching in my head — a fullness and heaviness — I hardly know what to call it. Sometimes a continual pain, (at times less or more violent) from morning till night. What this is owing to I can not say — probably to my sudden change of diet for I now fare upon bread and milk etc. — in stead of my pudding.

20th. I feel much better to day than usual. I have got back again to my old diet. I find it suits me better than any thing else I can take.

Stephen wants a box of herring very much. He would like to have them brought when you come on. And now for my part I wish Anne or somebody else who makes as much leisure as *she* does, should bake me an oven full of *Molasses* Gingerbread. Please to give my love to all!

Your affectionate Son
Henry.

PS. The Gingerbread is of the utmost importance.

MANUSCRIPT: Longfellow Trust Collection.   ADDRESS: Stephen Longfellow Ju[n] Esq —/Portland./By Mr Geo: Wells.[2]

    1. A tavern in Freeport.
    2. George Wadsworth Wells (1804–1843) of Boston was Longfellow's second cousin.

14. *To Zilpah Longfellow*

Bow Coll: March. 1st. 1823.

My Dear Mother.

I begin to think my health is some better than when I last wrote. As to the pills — I would take them if you will send them on to me [1] but I do not want to taste any more of Brunswick medicine; I have had quite enough of that already. Nolcini charges too much for his piano or rather, perhaps, too little allowance is made for ours.[2] His piano is a very excellent one and I wish we owned it — but it seems rather extravagant to purchase at so high a price. I rather suspect that you have the same opinion with me. Your letter was so very short that I hardly know what to say farther in answer to it. Indeed I have nothing more at present; but you shall hear again in a few days, as Stephen says he has got two letters "under weigh." I shall write to Betsey next week: please to tell her not to wait for *that* letter but write me immediately. More anon.

Good bye for the present —

Your affect. Son
Henry.

PS: March 2nd. It seems that papa passed through town to day. I was much surprised when I discovered it.

MANUSCRIPT: Longfellow Trust Collection.   ADDRESS: Mrs Zilpah Longfellow./ Portland. —/By politeness of/Mr G—— ENDORSEMENT: Henry. March 1 1823./April 6.

    1. Zilpah Longfellow, in a letter dated February 23, 1823, had suggested that he take soap and soda pills "to correct the stomach."
    2. Charles Nolcini taught music, dancing, French, and Italian in Portland during the twenties. The Longfellow children were among his pupils. See Carl L. Johnson, "Longfellow's Beginnings in Foreign Languages," *New England Quarterly*,

XX (September 1947), 318–319. In her letter of February 23, Zilpah Longfellow had written that Nolcini wanted $200 for his piano and would allow the Long-fellows $30 for theirs.

15. *To Elizabeth Longfellow*

Bow: Coll: March 12 [1823]

My Dear Sister,

Five weeks have already elapsed since I left you, and not a line, not even a word from you, have I been favoured with. But I can readily imagine the cause of your silence — I percieve that you have no idea of writing before you recieve a letter from me — therefore lest I should lose so good a correspondent as you are, I will not scruple to commence.

The Season seems to advance very tardily; thus far, since the commencement of the term, I do not think we have had more than one pleasant day, that is, pleasant throughout from morning till night. About every other day, or so, we have a snow storm, sometimes rain, and sometimes a little of both — very agreeable, you will say, without hesitation. I should like to know for the sake of curiosity how the weather has been in Portland, of late, and since we left there.

I am somewhat surprised that my papers (Gazette and Argus)[1] are not sent. I am really impatient for them and should be pleased to have them forth coming. Even "Old News" are quite agreeable here.

— Really, Betsey, I think of nothing else to say at present; and when One has nothing to say it is "contra bonos mores," a breach of good manners to say anything, at all. So good afternoon. Should I think of anything farther I will add a P.S. My Love to all friends and acquaintances.

Your affectionate brother
Henry.

MANUSCRIPT: Longfellow Trust Collection. ADDRESS: Miss. Elizabeth W. Long-fellow/Portland/By Mr McDougall. —[2]

1. The *Portland Gazette* and the *Portland Argus*. Longfellow's first published poem, "The Battle of Lovell's Pond," had appeared in the *Gazette* for November 17, 1820.

2. William McDougall (1797–1852), a Bowdoin tutor.

16. *To Stephen Longfellow*

Bow: Coll: March. 16 — 1823.

Dear Sir,

In conformity to your strict requisition I sit down to write — half asleep — half awake — and, of course, just in right trim to write a letter: but there's no alternative: so here goes. And to commence with, candidly and without prevarication, a very convenient "saying" *that* of All dull Letter-writers — "nothing to say:" — very applicable to myself, I was thinking — for seriously, all that I have said, and all that I intend to say (and I do intend to say something) shall in sum total of the matter amount to just what a person may very conscientiously call "nothing at all." Thus much for introduction! And now before proceeding farther I would mention that for the sake of brevity it is usual for me to divide my discourse into but two general heads — in themselves including a host of subdivisions — "invisible to mortal eye"[1] — as it were! but to resume the thread of my narration — as I was saying, I make use of but two general heads, the introduction and the conclusion. Having gone through with the former, undoubtedly much to your satisfaction, with much haste and right speedily I draw my *Conclusion,* in the words of the celebrated Periander

$$\text{Μελέτη τὸ πᾶν.!!!}^{[2]}$$

— Your affect. son
Henry. —

MANUSCRIPT: Longfellow Trust Collection. ADDRESS: Stephen Longfellow Jun Esq./Portland./By politeness of —/Mr McDougall.

1. Cf. John Milton, *Paradise Lost,* III, 55.
2. "Practice is everything." *Diogenes Laertius,* I, 99. Longfellow omitted the accent marks over the Greek characters.

17. *To Stephen Longfellow*

[Bowdoin College] March 29th. [1823]

Dear Sir,

I write to state my situation to you, and to let you know how affairs stand. I am afraid that my health is declining, and I have good reasons to think that my suspicions are not without foundation. I am somewhat troubled with an unpleasant feeling in my head, altho' it is not so bad as it was at the commencement of the term, and my costiveness continues as usual. My appetite is very good and I am sometimes inclined to indulge myself, altho', my food is generally light, especially at morning and evening meals. I exercise considerably, but my whole frame is so debilitated that all exercise becomes fatigue, and apparently defeats its own purpose. I know not what this may end in, but unless my health improves I shall be *very averse to continuing here.* I am sensible it would have been better for me to have gone to West Point, where they require regular exercise as well as study. Accustomed to so much relaxation from study as I took before I left

Portland, it is not surprising that I am unable to bear so much confinement as I here experience. This matter, I begin to think deserves some attention and that, too, speedily. I wish you would think upon it and let me know as soon as possible, what course is best to be pursued.[1]

Why, in the name of Goodness, does not somebody write! I have not had a letter this month — only two the whole term, whilst I have written six or more. Please to tell Betsey, she is my Debtor, and that I can by no means excuse her silence — by the way, it would not hurt Anne, to write again!

Your affectionate son
Henry —

ps. I have not recieved the Papers, yet.[2]

MANUSCRIPT: Longfellow Trust Collection. ADDRESS: Stephen Longfellow Esq./ Portland   POSTMARK (*in script*): BRUNSWICK MARCH 31

1. This complaint elicited a quick response from Stephen Longfellow, dated April 2, 1823, in which he urged Henry to guard his health as "the greatest of all temporal blessings" and proscribed a two-mile daily walk for exercise (to be increased to four when the weather improved), Zilpah's soap and soda pills, Saratoga water, and a consultation with either Dr. Wells (19.2) or Dr. Smith (38.2) of the Bowdoin Medical School.

2. The *Argus* and the *Gazette*.

18. *To Stephen Longfellow*

Bow: Coll: — April 5. 1823.

My Dear Father,

We have had a famous "scrape" here a few days past. The whole town is literally "up in arms." These are the particulars of the whole affair. Last Thursday, which was fast-day, the students were required to attend meeting. One of the Seniors was taken sick during service and vomited and was obliged to leave the house. Mr Mead[1] observed this. In the afternoon he made some remarks upon the general behaviour of students, in respect to informing against each other to the Government — touched a little upon intemperance and concluded in nearly these words "Yes, my hearers, there was an instance this forenoon, even in this house, enough to melt any heart! heart, did I say! Not a heart of flesh but a heart of stone!" Here the indignation of the students burst forth, and, as if by one impulse, they "scraped" him. At evening-prayers, the President[2] made a few observations on the conduct of the students, stating that it was decidedly wrong to behave in such a manner in the house of Worship — but *that he blamed no one,* and rather considered it as done from the impulse of the moment than from any premeditated design. Thus having the

Government (who were also displeased with some of his remarks) in our favour, we had not much to fear. On Friday, however, some of the "Good Ones" drew up a bill making concessions to Mr M — and stating that the conduct of the students was very reprehensible. About 18. signed this. The Senior Class holding a meeting, sent a delegation to Mr M — requesting him to give a little explanation of his words, which he refused to do. They then drew up a petition to the Government, requesting permission to leave Mr Mead and attend some other Preacher in his stead. The Government have not, as yet, I believe, given a decisive answer, tho' from all accounts they seem to be very favourable to it. This Petition was signed by more than 80! To the subscribers of the first mentioned paper the President observed that he did not thank them for it! So much for their officiousness! In all probability, they will now have services performed in the Chapel or permit to attend Parson Titcomb! If we attend the latter, it will afford us a fine walk of 6 miles. Some of our College Bards have been amusing themselves at his [Mead's] expence. A song is compose[d] by them, of no less than 15 stanzas. To the popular air of "Robert Kid." I have not an inclination to copy it now — one stanza will be enough to show the spirit of it. I may bring a copy with me at the end of the term.

9th. "My fame took sick and died as I preach'd, as I preach'd!
My fame took sick and died as I preach'd!
My fame took sick and died, — and my con[s]cience testified
To the downfall of my pride — as I preached!"

— And so it goes on to the conclusion, which is truly pathetic.[3]

But I must conclude my letter as I have a great many things to attend to just now, and a considerable many other correspondents to whom I am indebted.

Your affect Son,
Henry. —

MANUSCRIPT: Longfellow Trust Collection. ADDRESS: Stephen Longfellow Jun Esq./Portland./By politeness of Mr [Simon] Greenleaf —

1. Rev. Asa Mead (1792-1831), pastor of the Brunswick Congregational Church, had incurred the dislike of the students because of his rigorous orthodoxy and because attendance at his sermons was frequently compulsory.

2. William Allen (1784-1868), president of Bowdoin College during 1820-1831 and 1833-1839. Clergyman, versifier, and compiler of dictionaries, he was Longfellow's English instructor during the sophomore year.

3. For a comment on this incident see *Young Longfellow*, pp. 37-38. The intem-

perate student was George William Gray Browne (1806–1879), Longfellow's fellow townsman and good friend and a member of the class of 1823.

19. To Stephen Longfellow

[Bowdoin College, April, 1823]

My Dear Father,

All has become quiet again. Yet Mr Mead seems not to have entirely got over his tantrams. He gave the students a few back-handers the last time he preached — talking a good deal about "deeds of darkness" to be brought to light here-after and so on. A few of the students have left his meeting: and I, also, want you to permit me to attend Parson Titcomb's.[1] But I can spend no more time upon a subject so perfectly disgusting to me.

As you enquire so particularly about my health I will give you what information I am able. I can hardly tell whether I am better or about the same. I walk considerably and take a good share of exercise. The Congress Water suits very well. However, I think I am considerably better — and upon the whole, convalescent. I have no[t] consulted Dr Wells,[2] and believe I shall not at present. I did intend to, and called to see him, but he was out.

I think of nothing more to say at present. I shall write again, however, tomorrow.

Your affectionate Son
Henry.

MANUSCRIPT: Longfellow Trust Collection. ADDRESS: Stephen Longfellow Jun Esq./Portland   ENDORSEMENT: Henry April 1823.

1. In a reply dated April 12, 1823, Stephen Longfellow wrote that while Mr. Mead may have been indiscreet, the action of the students in "scraping" him was most improper. "I most sincerely hope," he wrote, "that *my sons* have had nothing to do with this unfortunate and disgraceful transaction." Although he made no reference to Henry's request to attend Parson Titcomb's church, it is clear that he did not approve it.

2. John Doane Wells (1799–1830), professor of anatomy and surgery in the recently established Bowdoin Medical School, was related through his mother to the Wadsworth family; he was Longfellow's second cousin.

20. To Zilpah Longfellow

[Bowdoin College, April, 1823]

My Dear Mother,

Your letters by Mr [Simon] Greenleaf were recieved, with great pleasure, and I now *steal* a few moments from the evening to reply to them. I say *"steal"* a few moments — and it is theft, for I ought to be about other affairs — for I have a great abundance of things to attend to just now. I have this evening been reading a few pages in Gray's Odes. I am very much pleased with them. The *Progress of Poesy* and the ode *To Eton College* are admirable. And many passages in *The Bard,* tho' I confess, quite obscure to me, seem to partake in a great degree of the sublime. Obscurity is the great objection which many urge against Gray. They do not consider that it contributes in the highest degree to sublimity. And he certainly aim'd at sublimity in these Lyrical Odes. If he did not, so much the more honour to him, for he has certainly attained it, whether sought or unsought. Tho' not in themselves entirely original, they were quite so to me — and, of course very amusing. Every one admires his Elegy and if they do not his odes, they must attribute it to their own *want of taste* — en Français *Gout.*[1]

I do not know on what grounds you can complain of want of letters. I have written *one* (at least) regularly every week. If you have not recieved them, it remains to be settled between you and the Post. You will no doubt think this short epistle as a poor return for your long one — but you can excuse me as I wish to notice Alexander's sublime Poesy.[2]

Your affectionate Son
Henry.

ps. As to health. I really do not know as I get much better. If I do not gain at the close of this term I think I would be well to spend the whole Summer term in Gorham or Hiram. Please to let me know what you and Pa think of this plan.

MANUSCRIPT: Longfellow Trust Collection. ADDRESS: Mrs Zilpah Longfellow./ Portland.—/Favoured by/S. Greenleaf Esq. ENDORSEMENT: Henry April. 1823/Ansd April 24

1. In a reply dated April 23, 1823, Zilpah Longfellow was reluctant to accept her son's correlation of obscurity with sublimity. "I am not very conversant with the poetry of Gray, dear Henry, therefore cannot tell whether I should be as much pleased with it, in general, as you are. His Elegy I have read frequently, and always with pleasure. I admire it for its truth and simplicity, and think it a charming thing. I presume you will not allow it any sublimity. Obscurity is favorable to the sublime, you think. It may be so, but I am much better pleased with those pieces that touch the feelings and improve the heart than with those that excite the imagination only and raise perhaps an indistinct admiration. That is, an admiration of we know not exactly what" (*Young Longfellow*, p. 37; *Life*, I, 30).

2. A reference to some childish poetry sent to him by his brother Alexander.

21. *To Zilpah Longfellow*

[Bowdoin College] April. 25. 1823

My Dear Mother,

The partial and uncandid manner in which Dr Johnson, criticised the poems of Gray, gives great offense to many, and is condemned by all of candid minds. The causes of his severities are generally believed to be the difference of their religious and political opinions. This is sufficient to make the opinions advanced by the great Lexicographer of little weight. Tho' he were the greatest man alive, and possessed of the greatest learning, yet this alone, without he possessed also impa[r]tiality, would not constitute him the best critick. I do not see what is so incomprehensible in the first line of the Progress of Poetry. Is it not as plain as a passage somewhat similar in the Psalms! Gray's poem commences thus:

"Awake, Aeolian Lyre, awake," . . .

and David says . . . . Awake, my glory; awake, lute and harp.[1] I know and acknowledge that I am not a competent judge, in this matter and I only advance such opinions as suggest themselves to my mind, that you may know, not embrace, them. I am in favour of letting each one think for himself, and I am very much pleased with Gray's Poems, Dr Johnson to the contrary, notwithstanding.[2]

We have just heard, to day, of Captain Porter's assassination.[3] Please to send, as soon as convenient, the papers containing the particulars! !

Your affectionate Son

Henry. —

MANUSCRIPT: Longfellow Trust Collection. ADDRESS: Mrs. Z. Longfellow/ Portland./By politeness of Mr Bodwell.[4] ENDORSEMENT: Henry April 25. 1823./May 9. PUBLISHED: *Life*, I, 31.

1. Cf. Ps. 57:8. The ellipses are Longfellow's.

2. To this, Zilpah Longfellow returned her agreement: "I do not think the Dr. possessed much sensibility for the charms of poetry, and he was sometimes most unmerciful in his criticisms" (letter of May 9, 1823, quoted in *Young Longfellow*, p. 37).

3. David Porter (1780–1843) was at this time a member of the board of navy commissioners. Within the year he would command the West Indies Squadron to suppress piracy in that area.

4. John Adams Bodwell (1797–1825), a student in the Bowdoin Medical School.

22. *To Zilpah Longfellow*

[Bowdoin College] May 11. [1823]

My Dear Mother,

The term ends in about ten days. The exhibition is to be on Thursday the 22nd and on Friday you may look for us home. Wm Codman[1] has a colloquy on the Turkish Character for his part. It is very handsomely composed, but I cannot divine with any considerable degree of accuracy what sort of a figure William will cut upon the stage. Mr Titcomb has just delivered us your letters. It seems then that Captain Porter was not assassinated — only see how a report will grow by traveling a few miles.

In my letters to Papa and Betsey, you say 'there is a promise implied to write again soon.' I reccollect something of that kind — and I then intended to have written the next day, but I do not reccollect what it was that hinder'd me. You mention something which I said about "particulars tomorrow," but it is so long ago that I wrote those letters that I am totally unable to tell what I was speaking about.

About 40 — of the students have formed themselves into a "corps du Militaire." The name of the band is the "Bowdoin Cadets." The Government of College are very much pleased with it. Saturd[a]y afternoon we paraded before Proffessor Cleavelands "by particular request" and tick[l]ed him quite.[2] I am very much employed about these times, with one little thing and another, so, I pray you, do not expect long letters nor be disappointed by recieving short ones. Anne's letter I shall answer as soon as I get leisure. For the present adieu!

Your affect. Son

Henricus.

PS I do not think it will be in my power to bring you Gray's Poems. The volume which I had was from the College Library. However I think I can get it for you in Portland. Love to all.

H. W. L.

MANUSCRIPT: Longfellow Trust Collection. ENDORSEMENT: Henry Longfellow Ap[ril]. 1823.

1. William Henry Codman (1806–1879) of Portland, a member of the class of 1824.

2. According to Thompson in *Young Longfellow*, p. 39, Longfellow soon lost interest in this drill corps and "returned to the society of his less demonstrative friends."

23. *To Stephen Longfellow*

Bow Coll: June. 22 — — 1823.

Dear Father,

If Mr Johnson will exchange that copy of Otis' Life (as no doubt he will),[1] I wish you to send me the other as soon as you can possibly find a mode of conveyance, as I have partly read it and wish to finish it.

As the Government of College did not see fit in their clemency to give us a "local habitation" in the New Building we still remain in our old room:[2] and I find it an excellent room for Summer: cool and comfortable during the heat of the day; so that it is a very good room on that account. Our board is much better here, this term than it was last.

I wish you to send me $3 to pay the initiation fee of the Peucinean Society.[3] I intend to ride up and see you on the fourth of July if you have no objections. E.D. Preble is coming up with me — in your next letter I wish you to tell me if you give your assent, (as doubtless you will).

We have had a very sudden change of weather here of late. Last Friday was a very warm and sultry day. Yesterday (Saturday) a cold rain storm came up: and to day it is clear and cold with a chilling wind from the N. East. Felt very comfortable with a fire. Please to tell the whole "posse comitatus" of the family to write and I will answer their letters. I feel very safe in making this promise for I know very well how *few* letters I shall have to answer.

Please remember me to all.

Your affect. Son
Henry.

PS. Stephen says he cannot find but two or three pair of stockings here and rather thinks that he has left them. Please to reccollect the 4th of July!!!

MANUSCRIPT: Longfellow Trust Collection. ADDRESS: To/Stephen Longfellow Jun Esq./Portland. POSTMARK (*in script*): BRUNSWICK/JUNE 24

1. Eliphalet Johnson, a Portland bookseller, had apparently sent Longfellow an imperfect copy of William Tudor's *The Life of James Otis* (Boston, 1823).

2. Longfellow and his brother Stephen moved into No. 27, New College, in October (see letter No. 27).

3. The Peucinian Society, founded in 1805, was the most prominent of the Bowdoin clubs at this time. Longfellow had been initiated on March 21.

24. *To Zilpah Longfellow*

Bow: Coll: June 29th. 1823.

My dear Mother,

I dare say you have been expecting letters from me, for some days past and have been somewhat disappointed in not hearing from me sooner, but you must reccollect also that none of you at home have written a single line. I would not have you imagine that I, by any means, wish or intend to keep an exact account of "Dr. and Cr." Nothing could be farther from my wishes and intentions. But the fact is, I do not hear from you so often as I wish. The girls ought to write more frequently than they do. I know it would be for their benefit.

It seems you are to have no Oration on the 4th of July. We are to have one here by one of the Students. The town's-people are to celebrate this great day in a very singular manner. You will recollect how very wide the principal street is here! Perhaps you will also recollect that at the foot of the hill and directly in the middle of this street is a piece of boggy, *useless* ground of which *no use* has, as yet, been made. This is to be converted into a Mall! ! All hands ahoy. This, this is to be the scene of action and the whole city is to turn out for the perfection of what I suppose is yet to be the very acme of natural and artificial excellence. The sagacious populace have formed great expectations of what is to be; whether or no they will be disappointed a few weeks or months will determine — perhaps a few days.

We had a famous Book-Auction here on Friday. I purchased Henry's Chemistry for $3.30 and Paley's Evidences for 40 cts.[1] The books sold, were the stock of the Brunswick Book Store — and one of the poorest collections of books I ever wish to meet with. I purchased nothing but these two works. The performances for Commencement are assigned, and great dissatisfaction prevails amongst the members of the Senior class, as is usually the case on similar occasions. I expect letters from home right soon, accompanied with permission to be at home on Friday &c. Till then farewell.

Your affectionate son
Henry.

MANUSCRIPT: Longfellow Trust Collection.

1. Both William Henry, *The Elements of Experimental Chemistry*, and William Paley, *Evidences of Christianity*, were used as textbooks at Bowdoin.

25. *To Stephen Longfellow*

[Bowdoin College] June 30th. 1823.

Dear Father,

I write a few lines to let you know that I recieved the bundle in safety. I am glad you was so fortunate in the exchange as to obtain a copy that is bound.[1] All I can further add at present is that you may depend upon seeing me at the end of the week, provided I can obtain leave of the President, to come. Stephen seems to have determined to remain here. The Bow: Cadets (of which he is a member) are to have a dinner on the 4th of July; at least I have so understood. Stephen says he shall stay.

Yrs. affectionately

Henry.

MANUSCRIPT: Longfellow Trust Collection. ADDRESS: Stephen Longfellow Jun Esq./Portland.

1. The reference is to Tudor's *Life of Otis* (see Letter No. 23). Stephen Longfellow wrote of his success in effecting an exchange in a letter dated June 27, 1823.

26. *To Stephen Longfellow*

Portland   Sept. 20. 1823.

Dear Sir,

I have just returned from Gorham, and supposing that you are anxious for the recovery of your father and desirous of knowing every change in his situation, sit down to write you an account of his health, as correctly as possible. I am sorry to be under the necessity of informing you that Dr Folsom [1] is of opinion that his recovery is precarious and doubtful. No other medical aid has been called as yet. Your father is averse to it and Dr F. — thinks he has already done "what man can do," and is rather despairing of a favourable change of the disorder, 'tho he advises to pursue the same course of medicine as heretofore, and not to abandon hope. He rather inclines to think also that the present is no new disease, but a change of the former disease to the stomach. The *Hiccough* continues rather violent, altho' with intervals of moderation. The continuance of this troublesome companion induces the belief that the palsy is the cause of it. Your father seems to think this is the case; — and the Cyclopaedia observes that the "hickup will sometimes continue to distress the patient, not only for several months but even for some years &c." He had quite an ill turn yesterday. In the afternoon and evening the spasms were violent and so rappid in succession and so unintermitted that he conversed with difficulty. The night was a dangerous one to him — but morning

49

found him refreshed and much better, which gave us great encouragement to hope for better things. But I fear, in my desire to give you a correct account of the state of things, I have led you to imagine worse things than actually exist. *He* was as well I think to day, as before this last severe attack. Not so well as when you were last with him — because much weaker — yet not so sick by any means as he has been during the progress of his disease. He has a strong desire for your return and mentioned to me to day — (it was just before I left him) that he wished me to request you in my letter to return *as soon as your business will possibly admit of your absence,* as he wishes to finish the remainder of a perticular business between yourself and him, which was left unfinished by you at some former period. I think of nothing else to *inform* you of, relative to your father's situation, and close my letter with *informing* you that all other friends in Gorham are well and also all at home here are in good health, and send their best respects to you.[2]

Your affect[ionat]e Son
Henry.

PS. With respect to the books (Horace) I suppose it will be best to get one at the Bookstore and purchase the other second-hand at College?

MANUSCRIPT: Longfellow Trust Collection. ADDRESS: Stephen Longfellow Jun Esqr/Wiscasset./Me. POSTMARK: PORTLAND ME SEP 21 ENDORSEMENT: Henry. Portland./to his father at Wiscasset/Sept. 1823.

1. Dr. Dudley Folsom, a general practitioner in Gorham.

2. Stephen Longfellow (1750–1824), Henry's grandfather, had lived in Gorham for almost fifty years and according to the town's historian was "one of the most distinguished and respected" of its citizens (Josiah Pierce, *A History of the Town of Gorham, Maine* [Portland, 1862], p. 185). During his lifetime he held various public offices in town and county and from 1797 to 1811 served as judge of the Court of Common Pleas. On March 13, 1824, Zilpah Longfellow wrote to her husband in Washington: "Your father has taken to drinking brandy, by the advice of his physician, but he mourns very much that he is under the necessity of changing his early and approved habit of water-drinking." Not responding to this therapy, he abandoned it and died soon after, on May 28, 1824.

27. *To Stephen Longfellow*

Bowd Coll. Oct. 3rd. [1823]

Dear Sir,

We have just got settled in our new room.[1] It is a very pleasant corner room in the third story of the North End of the new building. And I take this opportunity to send for my box of books, as it is *very necessary* to have them here before Wednesday. Our recitations commence tomorrow morning.

Please also to send the large book of music (Holyoke's Collection)[2] which I accidently left at home. You will find it in the Little Room. I have purchased two copies of Horace — one at 2$:25 cts and the other at 75 cts: both very good copies. Please to send some money to pay for them.

Your affect. Son
Henry.

I shall send you the pay for the British Poets, as soon as I can collect it.[3]

MANUSCRIPT: Longfellow Trust Collection.

1. That is, Longfellow and his brother Stephen.
2. Samuel Holyoke (1762–1820), American hymnist and teacher, was the author of several collections of music. Longfellow probably refers here to his *Harmonica Americana* (1791).
3. Sometime in July, in an unrecovered letter, Longfellow had requested his father to purchase a set of *The British Poets* for the Peucinian Society.

28. *To Elizabeth Longfellow*

Bowd. Coll. Oct. 12. 1823.

My Dear Sister,

More than a week has elapsed since I left you, but so insensibly has the time slipped away, that it seems but a day — an hour I had almost said. First the trouble and bustle of moving — next the fatigue of setting things in order again — then the difficulty of commencing new studies and the continual, uninterrupted succession of task after task have kept me so assiduously employed that the silent lapse of hours and days has been unnoticed, though of course not unknown. The return of another day of rest has given me leisure to communicate to you a few of my thoughts. The change of local situation as well as the classical advancement, which a few days have produced — the meeting of old friends and the formation of new acquaintances, you can easily suppose to be pleasant and satisfactory. The room we occupy at present, is situated in the North Eastern corner of the North College — but I forget myself! From such a description, you, who have never seen the colleges, can form no idea of its situation. And in fact I know not how to give you the location of it — this much, however, you can understand; — the bed-room window looks towards the village and Professor Cleaveland's, — the two other windows afford a delightful prospect, — no less so than the charm of an extensive woodland scenery of — pine trees, — groves, beautified by a great quantity of bushes cut during the Summer, and left, dry, withered, and sere, to bea[u]tify and vary the Autumnal landscape — a fine view of the road to Harpswell and the College Wood Yard. But within! How shall I describe it! *Yellow* floor! *Green* fire-place. Mantel and window-seats, *blueish white*, — and three great doors, *mahogany color.* But jesting apart! — the room is a very good room, although more pleasant for Summer than Winter, as it is in back, not the front of College, and on that account not so warm. You must not infer from what I have said that I dislike my room. No! far from *that!* I am very well pleased with it. I wish to be disposed to be pleased with every thing which must be mine or with which I must have dealings, that is, with every thing that cannot be bettered — to make the best of a bad bargain, — and content myself, that it is not, as it might have been, worse. This, you will say, is a sober — sentimental philosopher-like conclusion — (or more properly resolution) for so impatient a person as I am; but you know that

> Experience keeps the very best of schools —
> And keeps her rods on purpose to whip fools.[1]

I feel far better contented here — far more happy, and far less inclined to be low-spirited, than has ever been the case at any former period. This may be ascribed to *many* causes. It may be the consequence of the change of situation and the novelty necessarily accompanying this change, or perhaps it may arise from the relaxation and exercise of a pleasant vacation — more probably from both of these causes combined. You must not be supprised when I tell you, I wish not to come home. No — not yet! — not for weeks — months! You will laugh and say this is strange and novel, as coming from me, who am always complaining! But recollect my determination — my resolution and marvel not that these things are so!

Give my love to all —

Your affectionate brother
Henry

MANUSCRIPT: Bowdoin College Library. ADDRESS: Miss Elizabeth W. Longfellow/ Portland/By Mr. Cutter.[2] PUBLISHED: *Bowdoin College Bulletin*, No. 327 (December 1957), 32–33.

1. Cf. Benjamin Franklin, *Poor Richard's Almanack*: "Experience keeps a dear school, but fools will learn in no other."

2. Presumably Levi Cutter (1774–1856), a Portland merchant and an overseer of Bowdoin College.

29. *To Zilpah Longfellow*

Bowdoin College. Oct. 19th 1823.

My Dear Mother,

I recieved a very few lines from you this morning and answer them immediately, lest by procrastinating I should never answer them. I shall not however be so laconick as you were, though I have a very good plea for not being too long.

And in the first place, I shall take the liberty of anticipating a few questions, such as I presume you would have asked, if you had not been so very unseasonably interrupted at the very commencement of your letter. You wish to know what I am reading. This question I hardly know how to answer! I am reading three or four books at a time — sometimes more! A very foolish way of improving, or rather of wasting time, you will think. I know it — but when a volume grows tedious and uninteresting, I choose rather to lay it aside, than to weary my patience by poring over sleepy pages in such a manner as to derive neither advantage nor amusement. Besides I can never endure that, which is dull, when that, which is entertaining is upon my shelf — and within my reach, and requires but a change of posture to be placed open before me. But a truce with this. Thus far my reading has been mostly of the light kind. I have just closed Arthur Mervyn, a novel, — an American novel — from the elegant pen of C. B. Browne, formerly of N. York, whose writings are nearly as much read and admired in Old England, as those of Irving himself. The scene is laid in Philadelphia, at the time, when that beautiful city was desolated by the wasting breath of pestilence. The limits of a letter would by no means enable me to give a proper description either of the plot, characters, or scenes of this truly excellent novel. Besides, you have probably read the work; if so any thing I could say would of course be useless or worse than useless. The author of this book, you will recollect, as an American has never recieved from his countrymen that praise and renown, which was his due, — justly and undeniably his due, and which the stranger and the foreigner do not hesitate to bestow. And it is a silent, but eloquent rebuke to the land of his birth and his childhood, that the country already so great in literary reputation, so jealous of the beautiful wisdom of her rebellious and undutiful child, — so impatient of superiority and so suspicious of rivalship, should willingly and freely crown the brows of the off-spring of another soil with the laurel, which the unnatural mother withheld. But the reputation of Browne, as a novelist is at last breaking forth here also, and dawning upon the grave that holds his ashes.

Tired at last of caressing the children of an exotick soil and fostering the offspring of another instead of her own, our country becomes grateful too late to cheer him with hope and smiles upon him when her smiles can no longer gladden the heart that felt her frowns and her rebukes so keenly. Arthur Mervyn is the only one of his novels I have read, though I reccollect I once met with another by the same author some years ago. His writings are numerous and a writer in Blackwood's Magazine speaks highly of them. I have lately understood, that a complete edition of his work will shortly issue from one of the N. York presses. I hope this is true, for I am impatient for more.[1]

In the second place, I have read the British Spy. A series of letters purporting to have been written by an Englishman, resident for a time in this country, to his friend at home. They have been by common fame, however, decided to be the work of an American pen, and I believe it is well known that Wirt was the author. These letters were originally published in a daily journal and subsequently collected into a volume, of which the seventh edition is now before me. It is a small work and exceedingly interesting.[2] These two works constitute the principle of my reading thus far. I have commenced another work entitled "The Literary Character, illustrated by the history of Men of Genius."[3] This is a very amusing and a very instructive book and well worth reading. But my letter is already full, and yet it seems as though I had but just begun it.

I am sorry to hear Betsey is unwell again. I should think it high time for her to be more provident concerning her health, and I should also think it was not beneficial to her to walk so far to school, this damp and chilling weather. I would certainly *go no longer, on any account.* Please to tell miss Anne, that I shall write her a long letter this week, if I can find leisure, and that she must have one ready to send, as soon as she hears from me. My health is very good, though we have such a fine boarding house, that I am frequently tempted to indulge myself too much. The vacation completely recruited me, and with proper care and exercise I shall do very well as to this point. As to the room, it would be warm enough were it not for the great crack beneath the door, which admits a gale sufficient to be distinctly felt across the room. Please to send some list. The windows are very tight.

Your affectionate Son
Henry.

MANUSCRIPT: Longfellow Trust Collection. ADDRESS: To Mrs Z. Longfellow./ Portland. POSTMARK (*in script*): BRUNSWICK/OCT 23

1. The author of "On the Writings of Charles Brockden Brown and Washington Irving," *Blackwood's Edinburgh Magazine*, VI (February 1820), 554-561, seems to have helped form Longfellow's opinion of the author of *Arthur Mervyn*. Despite their unoriginality, Longfellow's remarks illustrate his early interest in the defense and promotion of American literature. *The Novels of Charles Brockden Brown* were published in Boston, 1827, in seven volumes.

2. William Wirt's *The Letters of the British Spy* — a miscellany of moral, critical, and descriptive essays, written in a luxuriant style — appeared first in the Richmond *Argus* in 1803. Published in book form in the same year, the *Letters* achieved considerable popularity and went through many editions.

3. By Isaac D'Israeli. See Letter No. 31.

30. *To Anne Longfellow*

Bowdoin College. Oct. 26 —. 1823.

My Dear Sister Anne,

In my last letter to my mother, I promised to write you a long letter, during the week, but I have delayed the fulfilment of this promise a day or two later than I intended, from causes which I shall state before the close of my letter. You ought to have written to me long ago, and not have been so ceremonious as to wait for me to write first. You must know I have no time to spare — for what little time I can steal from my college exercises, I wish to devote to reading. But with you the case is very different. You are never in a hurry, and have always time enough. You can not deny it, for I know exactly how it is with you. So I shall expect a long letter from you in answer to this — a letter, that you must take a great deal of pains with. Last Friday the appointments for the December Exhibition were given out. The part assigned me to perform, is a dialogue with JW. Bradbury.[1] Or as it was given out by the president "English Dialogue between a North American savage and an English Emigrant." We have 4 minutes a-piece: and the part is a high one, being the third in this division of the class. I think it will be a very fine subject both to write and speak upon, and although it is not the part I wished for, yet I have this consolation that it is much higher than that, which I expected, so that I have every reason to be satisfied and well pleased with this appointment.

I see by the Portland Papers that the Governour and council have appointed the twentieth of November as the day of Thanksgiving! as "Thanksgiving Day" I suppose I should have said. I think I shall come up to feast with you on the fat of the land and every good thing of Portland. I like to have such days come round. They resemble the "Merry Christmass of Old England" as the account is given of it in the Sketch Book. Although the 'Christmass Pie' is far surpassed by the "New England peculiar" baked pumpkin and pan-dowdy![2] Talking about Thanksgiving Day puts me in mind of the Pioneers and ten thousand other things, — geese, turkies, ducks, chickens, roasted pork, plumb puddings, sour apples and Molasses and pumpkin pies baked in milk-pans &c. &c. The Yankee's feast! !

Now I'll be sober again! I wish you to employ some of your leisure in making a set of card racks for me to decorate my chimney-piece with. I have asked the same favor of you before, and I believe you promised to make them for me. It was nearly a year ago, so please to begin them immediately, for unless you do, I fear I shall not get them untill they will be useless to me.

The weather has been rainy and very unpleasant to day, with a high north wind, that whistles well through the key hole and the cracks around the door. I must have some list and very soon too, or we shall all blow away up chimney. And now to conclude my letter, I shall inform you that a few good *sour* apples would be a most acceptable present from home. I prefer a mild sour to sweet — or, in fact, any kind of sour, mild or not mild. But the bell rings.

Remember me to all friends, and family,

Your affectionate Brother
Henry.

ps. Stephen says he shall write soon. And further, I wish you to make a pair of green curtains for the windows, 4 feet 7 inches in length and 3 ft 3 inch. in width, and send them down as soon as possible.

MANUSCRIPT: Longfellow Trust Collection. ADDRESS: Miss Anne Longfellow/ Portland./By the favour of/Mr RAL. Codman[3]

1. James Ware Bradbury (1805–1901), Bowdoin 1825, became a United States Senator and one of the ablest lawyers in Maine. On the occasion of Longfellow's seventy-fifth birthday Bradbury wrote a reminiscence of this college dialogue: "I recollect that at our Junior exhibition a discussion upon the respective claims of the two races of men to this continent was assigned to Longfellow and myself. He had the character of King Philip, and I of Miles Standish. He maintained that the continent was given by the Great Spirit to the Indians, and that the English were wrongful intruders. My reply, as nearly as I can recall it, was that the aborigines were claiming more than their equal share of the earth, and that the Great Spirit never intended that so few in number should hold the whole continent for hunting-grounds, and that we had a right to a share of it to improve and cultivate. Whether this occurrence had anything to do in suggesting the subject for one of his admirable poems or not, one thing is certain, that he subsequently made a great deal more of Miles Standish than I did on that occasion" (Letter to H. W. Bryant, in *Proceedings of the Maine Historical Society, February 27, 1882* [Portland, 1882], p. 128). The manuscript of the dialogue, in Longfellow's hand and dated December 10, 1823, is in the Clifton Waller Barrett Collection, University of Virginia.

2. Irving describes the traditional Christmas dish of England — the peacock pie — in the *Sketch Book* vignette entitled "The Christmas Dinner."

3. Randolph A. L. Codman (1796–1853) of Gorham had studied law under Stephen Longfellow and was currently practicing in Waterville, Maine.

31. *To Zilpah Longfellow*

Bowdoin College   Nov. 9th   1823.

To Mrs Z. Longfellow, —

My dear Mother,

I have just awoken from an afternoon nap, and find all have gone to meeting and left me alone. I dropt to sleep just before the bell rang, as I was sitting with my book by the fire, and as this slip has given me a little leisure I gladly devote it to you. And I will begin my letter by answering a few questions, that you proposed in your last of the 26th of Oct. You ask "Is not the History of men of Genius a new publication?" This question I cannot answer directly, though I am inclined to think it is. I never saw, nor heard of the book as I recollect untill a few weeks since. It was written by D'Israeli, author of 'Quarrels of Authors,' who is I believe residing in some part of England.[1] You enquire if the "British Spy" is not entirely a political book? No! It treats of matters and things in general as the spy found them in this country — American manners and customs, American oratory, — eloquence of the Bar and the pulpit; he endeavours to account for shells and other marine production being found at a distance from the sea and beneath the surface, to advocate Count De Buffon's theory of an alluvial[2] soil and supposing, as the Abbe Raynal gave as his opinion, that the whole continent of America many thousand years back was covered by water and gradually emerged to the light of the sun by the accumulation of matter produced by the action of the earth's revolution upon its own axis towards the east, and the counter current of the Ocean towards the West.[3] He discusses also a great many other topicks which it is hardly worth while to mention, for I will bring the book with me when I come home again. I did not take Foster's Essays![4] I have heard frequent mention made of Foster Coffin's "Journal"[5] and should be well pleased to read it, but at present I have not time to do this, so that Aunt [Lucia] need not trouble herself to send it to me as I had rather reserve it for winter amusement. I find my leisure time diminishing fast and since I wrote you last have not read but one volume. That is Heckewelder's 'Account of the History, Manners and Customs of the Indian Nations of Pennsylvania and the neighbouring states.'[6] This is a very interesting volume, and exhibits in a new and more agreeable light the character of this reviled and persecuted race. It appears from this account of them and of their customs, (and I see no reason why he should not be relied upon as correct, since he passed the greater part of a long life amongst the indians) that they arc a race possessing magnanimity, generousity, benevolence, and pure religion without hypocrisy. This may seem a paradox, but nevertheless I believe it true. They have been most barbarously maltreated by the whites, both in word and deed. We have heard them branded as a very scandal upon humanity, — cruel, malicious, wicked and without natural affection. Their outrages! — what ear has not heard of them a thousand times? whilst the white people, who rendered their cruelty more cruel, their barbarity more vindictive, publish abroad their crimes and thank heaven in their hypocrisy, that they are not like these persecuted heathen. I wish you could read this volume. I do not know whether it is in the Portland Library or not, though I am rather inclined to think it is. Get it as soon as you can and read it and see what a noble race have been almost entirely cut off and exterminated from the face of the earth, by the coming of the whites.

I have been thinking about taking a school this Winter Vacation, but have at length concluded, that I had rather not. I have not come ||to thi||s conclusion without some good reasons for it. One is, ||that I|| feel afraid of wasting my time, and wish to have leisure during the vacation for reading. A second is, that the confinement will be injurious to my health. I wish to ride round a little and get over the tediousness that the same things over and over again at College are apt to produce. I know I do not take sufficient exercise at present and I am confident I should not take much more whilst instructing a school.[7]

Please to tell Ann[e], that she need not buy the curtains at present, I will attend to them myself, when I come home. One of our best classmates died on Friday night or rather on Saturday morning last, after a short sickness of about 3 weeks, and all things are pretty gloomy here at present. He was one of the most mild and kindhearted students in College, bearing a character of the strictest morality. His complaints were consumptive and his loss is greatly felt amongst us. The class will attend his funeral at Freeport, tomorrow.[8] Please to remember me to all my friends.

Your affectionate Son
Henry W.

MANUSCRIPT: Longfellow Trust Collection. ADDRESS: Stephen Longfellow Jun Esqe./Portland. POSTMARK (*in script*): BRUNSWICK/NOV 10/FREE ANNOTATION (*by Longfellow*): Free

1. Isaac D'Israeli lived at this time in Bloomsbury Square. *The Literary Character, Illustrated by the History of Men of Genius* was first published in London in 1818.
2. Longfellow wrote "alluvion."

3. Wirt's geographical observations and theories may be found in Letter II of *The British Spy.*

4. Presumably *Essays in a Series of Letters to a Friend* (London, 1805) by John Foster (1770–1843).

5. Isaac Foster Coffin, *Journal of a Residence in Chile. By a young American, detained in that country, during the revolutionary scenes of 1817–18–19* (Boston, 1823). Coffin, son of Dr. Nathaniel Coffin of Portland, was acquainted with the Longfellows.

6. Published in Philadelphia in 1818. Longfellow read the book in preparation for his dialogue with Bradbury.

7. As an upperclassman, Longfellow was qualified to teach in rural schools during vacation periods. Had he done so, the Bowdoin authorities would have permitted him to leave the college two weeks in advance of the vacation and return two weeks after the next term began. He may actually have been struggling with this inducement.

8. Daniel Haraden Griffin, a member of the class of 1825, had died on November 8. He was born in 1800.

32. *To Stephen Longfellow* [1]

Bow: Coll: December 1st. 1823

My Dear Father,

I presume you will be expecting to hear from us and from home even before this letter reaches you, but not to keep you long in waiting on my account I have begun as soon as possible. Our returning ride from Portland on the Saturday we left you, was vastly disagreeable. Night overtook us long before we reached Codman's at Freeport, and we did not arrive at Brunswick until nearly nine in the evening, — heartily sick of the darkness, mud and misery. I have but little leisure at present, for the exhibition comes on next Wednesday and I wish to have my performance perfectly committed, so as to leave no opportunity for embarrassment, as far as it depends upon myself. I have too much confidence to feel any solicitude about the thing and if the contrary were true, I have too much resolution to let it be known. I wish, though, that the appointment was any thing in the catalogue but what it is at present. It is difficult in the extreme to write a good dialogue. This I find from experience. I hoped that I should have received what is here called a Single part. And I was quite disconcerted by the disappointment, though I presume I have no reason to be dissatisfied. I am rather sorry that the Exhibition falls so late in the year. The Chapel will be very cold and uncomfortable both for the performers and the spectators. I think the first part of November would be much preferable to the present time. The last of November at farthest — never during the present month; for after snow has fallen the cold is too severe to be thus detained an hour or two in a building without fire: — especially should the weather be stormy, as was the case last year!

We commenced Locke, on the Human Understanding, more than a week since. I find it thus far neither remarkably hard nor uninteresting! I began with the determination to like it at any rate and so get on very easily. How long a time did you devote to a lesson of six or seven pages? We had no recitation this afternoon. Instead thereof a discussion was proposed, to wit, "whether the Soul always thinks." This was extemporaneous, — that is, there were no written performances. Most of those that said any thing upon the subject, spoke in the affirmative, controverting Mr Locke's opinion, which was that the soul does not always think. One very original theory was advanced, bordering upon the transmigration of souls; "that we had good reason to suppose, that the souls of the inhabitants of one hemisphere whilst asleep, took up their abodes in the bodies of persons in the other," and continuing always active and in thought came and went alternately: so that the number of souls in the universe is but one half the number of inhabitants.

I wish I could be at Washington during the winter, tho' I suppose it rather vain to wish when it is almost impossible for our wishes to become realities. It would be more pleasant to get a peep at southern people and draw a breath of southern air, than to be always freezing in the north, but I have very resolutely concluded to enjoy myself heartily wherever I am. I find it most profitable to draw such conclusions and form such plans, as are least liable to failure: and I think here I am pretty safe, as it devolves mostly upon my own exertion. I think I am rather fortunate in not obtaining a school for this coming vacation, and begin already to congratulate myself upon being so free from necessary and regular employment as to have time to devote to reading.

So much for myself and now for my friends. With regard to home, I have not heard a word, nor received a line from them since I returned. I presume they are waiting to hear from me, and wondering why I do not write; but really, my leisure at present is so very limited, that [I] can scarcely find time for my necessary exercise, of which I take more than ordinary. And I find it absolutely and indispensably requisite to my health and consequently to my comfort. My chief exercise consists in walking. The small fall of snow we had here a few days since makes this rather uncomfortable, and when the snow becomes deep and drifted I hardly know what I shall do, without I take to cutting wood again, which is rather irksome. I really wish

I could do as well without exercise, for in that case I should be easier than at present.

I have learned of late to keep better hours than I used to. My ||bed|| hour is eleven, with little variation, and I rise of course pre||tty ear||ly. ||It is|| now twenty minutes past my hour for sleep, and as I am ||afraid|| of irregularity in these things, I shall close.

Your affect. Son
Henry W Longfellow.

MANUSCRIPT: Longfellow Trust Collection. ADDRESS: Hon. Stephen Longfellow Jun./Representative to Congress./Washington City. POSTMARK (*in script*): BRUNSWICK ME/DECR 3d/FREE ENDORSEMENT: H.W. Longfellow/Dec 9. 1823 [*year in a second hand*]

1. Stephen Longfellow had been elected a Federalist representative to the Eighteenth Congress, and during this and the following winter he spent considerable time in Washington, apart from his family. This and subsequent letters are addressed to him there.

33. *To Zilpah Longfellow*

Bowd. Coll: December 4th. [1823]

My dear Mother,

I received your kind letter of the 30th of Nov. to day and according to your wish write in return immediately. With regard to writing to Washington, I have already anticipated your wishes and a letter, on its way to that place from me, passed Tuesday night in the Portland Post Office. Our ride on our return from Portland after Thank[s]giving was truly uncomfortable. We did not reach this place untill about 9 o'clock in the evening. It was both dark and cold, and the road so muddy, that the horse could but just jog on at a most dignified pace and nothing was wanting but a smart rain storm and a sharp north-wester to have made it delicious.

You mention "Seventy Six" and "Randolph."[1] If you call the former of these 'over-*wrought*' I do not know what you will say of the latter. Of Randolph I have heard a good-deal said. I have also seen several long extracts from it. It seems to me, judging from these, to be a compound of reason and nonsense — drollery and absurdity — wit and nastiness. It talks about the ladies of Baltimore, — and how they "eat snuff"! And some other things ten times as bad. And still I believe there are parts of it that go far to prove it the work of Genius. I wish you would either send Seventy Six to Wm Browne or return it to the circulating Library immediately, or there will be something of a tax to be paid. I presume Mr Kelly or Mr Harding will willingly do either.[2]

This is by no means a long letter, — merely the apology for one. You must excuse me at present, for I shall write again and at greater length next week. Our Exhibition is upon Wednesday next, in the cold chapel. I pity the spectators, who must sit an hour or two in a cold room, that never knew there was such a thing as fire in existence. It will be better for the performers, for they have the liberty of going out and in when they please.

Please to remember me to all the family and tell Alexander to wait 'till next week or later for an answer to his letter, and he shall have it.

Your affectionate Son
Henry W. Longfellow.

MANUSCRIPT: Longfellow Trust Collection. ADDRESS: Stephen Longfellow Jun Esqe./Portland. POSTMARK (*in script*): BRUNSWICK/DECR 5th FREE ENDORSEMENT: Henry./Dec. 4. 1823. —

1. John Neal (1793–1876), Portland's best-known author of the day, published both these novels in 1823. *Seventy-six,* a romance of the Revolution, is perhaps his best-known work; *Randolph,* written in the form of letters, contains critical attacks on well-known Americans.

2. Stephen Longfellow left his office in Portland in the charge of Albert Livingston Kelly (1802–1885), a young law student. Charles Harding (1798–1849), a Bowdoin graduate of 1821 just turned lawyer, apparently worked with Kelly.

34. *To Stephen Longfellow*

Bowd. Coll. December 11th 1823

My Dear Father,

I presume you have received my last letter some days previous to this date, as it was put into the mail more than a week since. It is my intention to write you as often as once a week, though more than that time has now elapsed since the date of my last. The Exhibition took place last evening and I must confess I feel glad it is past. The weather was very unpleasant yesterday. There was during the day quite a violent snow-storm, and the evening was cold and uncomfortable. The audience of course was not very numerous, though the seats were better filled than I expected, considering the state of the weather. I feel a great weight is removed from my shoulders, for I could not but feel some solicitude, though I would never confess it. I shall now have a great deal more leisure, which to me is one of the sweetest things in the world. And it will really be a rarity to me, for I have seen very little of it for some weeks past. I think I now shall enjoy myself heartily.

Winter has commenced with us pretty violently. We have just weathered one tempest (if you will excuse the expression) and another seems to be threat[en]ing. I do not know that the cold has been very intense, but it takes hold of me rather harshly. The fact is we here feel every puff of wind, that blows and being so much exposed as this low-land is to the inclemencies of the weather, observe every degree of change. There is not a great quantity of snow upon the ground, but what there is, is light, which renders the walking very uncomfortable. This I should lament very much, since it deprives me of that exercise, had I not adopted another mode as a substitute, which is this. I have marked out an image upon my closet door about my own size, and when ever I feel the want of exercise I strip off my coat, and considering this image as in a posture of defense, make my motions as though in actual combat. This is a very classick amusement, and I have already become quite skillful as a pugilist. My only doubts with regard to its utility are, whether it may not be too violent. I find thus far, considerable advantage arising from it, and shall not discontinue it untill I experience some inconvenience. I rather think that my appearance is very appal[l]ing as I constantly, whilst under action, wear the leathern gauntlet or, rather more properly, mitten. I use the most exercise just before I go to bed. I know not whether this time is the most reasonable, but it is the most convenient as being less liable to interruptions. I should think exercise before each meal would be well, but the mornings and afternoons are so short at this season of the year, as to render it inconvenient and sometimes impossible at those particular times. I might get up before sun-rise and run round a little, but I am not very fond of rising in the dark.

I take the New York Statesman, edited by Mr N. H. Carter, who, the paper mentions, is now in Washington.[1] He has commenced an account of Congressional proceedings in the form of an Editorial correspondence, so that I shall have a good opportunity of seeing all that is going on at the Metropolis during the session of Congress, which from all accounts will be one of great interest. However I must confess I care but little about politicks or anything of the kind and therefore read and know but very little about them, so that the columns of my paper devoted to political speculations is to me almost as uninteresting as so many columns of the trades-man's advertisements.

The last letter I have received from home was dated the 30th and 31. of November. This cannot therefore give you anything new from that point, as you did not leave Portland untill the 31st. I cannot tell why they are so negligent about writing, for that letter was answered some days since. I presume they write to you more frequently — at least I hope they do. I suspect they feel rather lonely at home and I shall write them again very soon. The present term ends in four weeks from to day, so that I shall be with them before a great while, and enjoy the long vacation of six-weeks there.

The Students begin to drop off very fast. Most of the Senior class have left town already, and about one half of ours, so that the seats in the Chapel begin to look vacant.[2] I should like to be at Portland on the first of January and commence the new year there, but as the term ||does not|| close untill the 10th of that month, this will be inexpedient. I think of nothing more to write you at present, and as it grows rather late at night, I incline to exercise a little and crawl to bed as soon as possible. And so farewell!

Your affectionate Son
H. W. Longfellow.

PS. Stephen says he shall write you soon.

MANUSCRIPT: Longfellow Trust Collection. ADDRESS: Stephen Longfellow, Jun Esqe./Washington City. POSTMARK (*in script*): BRUNSWICK ME/DECR 13th/ FREE ENDORSEMENT: Henry W Longfellow/Dec 20/1823 [*year in a second hand*]

1. Carter had been Henry's teacher in 1814 (see 1.2). In 1819 he became editor of the *Albany Register*, later the *New York Statesman*, an organ of the DeWitt Clinton political faction.

2. President Allen's permission to upperclassmen to teach during the holiday explains this exodus.

35. *To Elizabeth Longfellow*

Bowdoin College. December. 14th. [1823]

To Miss E. W. Longfellow.

My Dear Sister,

I am at a loss how to account for your long silence, and know not what to attribute it to, unless it be indisposition or a want of inclination, for I cannot but think you have time enough. To indisposition I am unwilling to attribute it, besides had you been so much out of health as to be unable to write I should have heard of it from some other of the family. Upon your want of inclination the reason of your long silence must devolve. And here a heavy charge lies at your door, to which you must either immediately plead guilty or assert your innocence in a special manner. The only letter I find as coming from you, was written during the second week of this term and bears the date of October 8th. You see by this how negligent you are, it being more than two months since your last letter was received. For my own part I cannot imagine how you are going to excuse yourself and I shall not excuse you unless you write immediately upon the reception of this letter, or at farthest before the end of this week. It is now three weeks since I passed Thank[s]giving-Day at home with you, and not a solitary mark or token of recollection from any one of you at home excepting one letter from mother. I do not see how you can be pardoned unless you turn over a new leaf.

After a long process of time the Exhibition is at length over, and I have regained my liberty again, — that is my leisure. The performance took place on Wednesday Evening last. During the day we had a considerable snow-storm; if snow fell with you at Portland, you will know exactly what an evening it was for a publick Exhibition. However the evening came, — and the Exhibition too, — but as for the audience, — we will not say much about it. The female part was great, — say for instance two ladies, which considering the unpleasant state of the weather was in fact as many as I expected. The Chapel was however apparantly full, but whether students or town's-people I know and care not. I was glad there were but few ladies present, for my part was not such as would have pleased them, since it was so unpoetical, (as a dialogue must be,) as not to please myself. Not that ladies are always fond of poetry, but an Indian Dialogue. Oh! dear! I was very much chagrined at having such an appointment. There is no doubt but that it ranked as high as it should have ranked, but I *always* disliked any such part at an Exhibition and was very desirous of having something else instead thereof, whenever I should come upon the stage. But it is now of no great consequence, since it is all over. I presume it will be something different when I have another appointment. If it is not I shall be terribly nervous. And now I will tell you another piece of NEWS.

Your friend W. H. Codman delivered a Poem before the Athenean Society.[1] I dare say it is something new to you that he was a poet. I have known this for a year or two, but I never dreampt that the little man would mount into the pulpit to deliver a poem. I can hardly give you a description of it untill I come home. It was not at all original and yet it was quite interesting and quite as good as could have been expected, taking all things into consideration.

We had a little more snow this evening and I presume we shall have excellent sleighing for a few weeks at least. I have had one sleigh-ride already and that is begin[n]ing remarkably early for me. I rather think you folks at home, ||cann||ot amuse yourselves much in that way at present. However when I return I mean to exercise the colt, pretty often.

I have written twice to Washington, but as yet get no answers. I suppose it is hardly time to talk about them yet, though I presume you have heard from thence, before this date. And now I shall conclude my letter by strictly charging you, under the severe penalty of my royal displeasure, to write me straightway a long letter full of news, great and small, and now you may give my love to all, and I will make my best bow and retire from your presence.

Your affectionate brother
H. W. Longfellow.

PS. The term ends on the 10th of Jany.

MANUSCRIPT: Longfellow Trust Collection. ADDRESS: Miss EW./Stephen Long-fellow Jun Esqe./Portland. POSTMARK (*in script*): BRUNSWICK/DECR 16/FREE

1. The Athenæan Society was the older and more convivial rival of the Peucinean Society, to which Longfellow belonged. Among its members were Stephen Long-fellow, Franklin Pierce, and Nathaniel Hawthorne. Codman became a lawyer and, like Hawthorne, received a political appointment when Pierce was elected President.

36. *To Zilpah Longfellow*

Bowdoin College. December. 21 1823.

My dear Mother,

I cannot possibly let the opportunity of writing you by private conveyance pass without informing you, that all goes on here pretty much as usual, that I am well and want to see you again very much. The term, as I think I have mentioned in a former letter, though I will not be positive, closes on the 9th day of Jany and consequently I shall be with you again in a little more than a fortnight. I am naturally so indolent, that I anticipate a great deal of pleasure from the leisure of the vacation and the length of the winter evenings. The weather has of late been very stormy and uncomfortable. The violent rain on Wednesday has dissolved most of the snow and the whole town is literally inundated. The walking is of course exceedingly bad. In addition to this I have not a stick of wood nor anything like one, save a piece or two of bark, left to warm the room with. I had enough as I thought to last untill I should get another load, but to my great discomforture the storms came on at the begin[n]ing of the week, and I am as destitute as a man without a shirt. This is rather a curious comparison, but it conveys my meaning exactly, since I am deprived of the very "sine qua non" or in english, that which I cannot dispense with. However I have got into a good warm berth, with a good warm friend [1] and therefore do not feel the effects of my mischance, which will in all probability be made good again in a day or two. You must not expect to derive anything new or interesting from this hasty letter, for in that case you will be sadly disappointed. I write that you may see I sometimes think of home and to tell you we are both well. But as it is growing very late and I think it hardly right for me, who am but a lodger in these parts, to keep my host from his sleep, I must close my letter rather prematurely, though not without repeated solicitations for you to write immediately, for it is a very long time since I heard from you or any one of the family. I have not time to answer Alexander's letter to night, but will not put it off much longer.[2] Please to tell him so, and give my love to all.

Your affectionate Son
Henry W Longfellow.

MANUSCRIPT: Longfellow Trust Collection. ADDRESS: To Mrs Z. Longfellow/By favour of J. McKeen Esqe/Portland.[3]

1. Longfellow and his brother had separated temporarily to seek the warmth of friends' rooms.

2. This letter, if he wrote it, has not been recovered. Longfellow refers to it again in Letter No. 37.

3. The bearer of the letter could have been any one of the three sons — Joseph, John, or James — of Joseph McKeen (1757-1807), the first president of Bowdoin College. All lived in Brunswick or Topsham.

37. *To Zilpah Longfellow*

Bowdoin College. Decembr. 25. 1823.

My dear Mother,

Your letter of the 22nd is on my table before me; but it is very short and I can find nothing in it that requires a particular answer. I know not whether you will be expecting a letter from me at this time, and I write more that you may not be disappointed if you should be looking for a line, than because I have anything novel for your amusement. Indeed if you look for news to the Orient, you stand a better chance than anybody in the world, to be disappointed. We have nothing here but what is old. Like the Spaniards, we are a century behind the rest of the world. We see the newspapers after they are worn out with age, and travelling, in the mail-bag — we read a novel, after it has become obsolete everywhere else, and its author forgotten. And here the advantage in writing lies evidently upon your side. So far from telling you anything new, I am almost afraid to attempt such a thing, lest it should be like serving up a dish of minced-fish to a person on Sunday morning, when the same person dined upon a part of the fish in its original state on Saturday. I beg you to observe the delicacy of the comparison, for being very partial to the "bon vivant," this is as it were drawing a resemblance from nature. And yet, more from necessity than inclination, and I will not hesitate to acknowledge it,

I have become almost as tempe[r]ate and spare in my diet, as Daniel was, when he lived in Babylon on pulse.[1] However, all this "to the contrary notwithstanding," if I were in England now, (and I have been wishing myself there all the day long so warmly, that if my wishes could but turn to realities, I should have been there before sun-rise this morning) — I should calculate to throw off the dignity and excellence of starving one's-self to death and become a bacchanalian for a while. I do not believe any person can read the fifth number of the Sketch Book[2] without feeling at least, if not expressing a wish similar to my own. Irving, as the papers say, has already written another novel,[3] — however I have already supposed you were acquainted with this. I hope we shall have the pleasure of reading this new work of his, and also the Pilot by the author of the Spy.[4] This will afford fine winter amusement for us in the long evenings, and stormy days. I have already begun to anticipate this pleasure, and a great deal more of the same kind.

It has been a great day with us here, to-day. I do not refer to the celebration of Christmass, but you must know, if you are not aware of it, that the consociation of 'Old Sanctities,' or to speak more reverentially, of ministers, met at this place to-day. They have had exercises of a religious and publick kind both forenoon and afternoon, and I might add, morning and evening. I have been so much of a heretick and an infidel, as to be audacious enough to shut my eyes against this clear and shining light, and remain all day at home, shut up in my room; and I cannot find any-body who was present, that remembers the text of the sermon. So much for going to meeting out of mere curiosity![5] It was my intention to have written to Anne this evening, but a friend called in and interrupted, so that I have hardly time left after writing Alexander's letter, which I am apprehensive cannot be postponed any longer, with safety to myself. Besides I have not yet heard whether Anne has returned from Gorham. If she has, she must excuse my seeming negligence, which has grown to be a great word now-a-days. The Students continue to drop away one by one from College. I expect to leave about as late as any, though perhaps not.

Your affectionate Son
Henry W. Longfellow.

MANUSCRIPT: Longfellow Trust Collection. ADDRESS: Mrs Z. Longfellow/Portland./By Mr J. D. Kinsman.

1. See Dan. 1:8–16.

2. Longfellow apparently devoted part of the day to seeking holiday sentiments in the *Sketch Book*; the fifth number consisted of "Christmas," "The Stage-Coach," "Christmas Eve," and "Christmas Day."

3. Probably a reference to *Tales of a Traveller*, published in 1824.

4. Cooper's *The Pilot* had already been published. Longfellow had undoubtedly seen an advertisement of it.

5. Longfellow entertained liberal religious views from an early date, probably as a result of his parents' devotion to Rev. Ichabod Nichols, Unitarian minister of the First Church, Portland. Zilpah Longfellow underscored her son's distaste for orthodoxy in a letter to her husband on January 12, 1824, describing a family argument on religious matters: "He [Col. Samuel Stephenson, her brother-in-law] is himself highly orthodox, as usual. Though he acknowledges that Lucia [Wadsworth] and Henry are too hard for him in argument. They sat up till twelve, one night, settling points, or endeavoring to do it, but without success."

38. *To Stephen Longfellow*

Bowd. Coll. Jany 1st. 1824.

My dear Father,

I do not know how I can better employ an hour of the first evening of the year, than by devoting it to you. To commence my letter under favourable auspices, as far as the will is concerned, I wish you a very happy new year. I dare say, that both you and I have had as many of these kind wishes as if we had been at home, and perhaps more, though we have not heard them all. Stephen went off to Portland to day, and is probably now enjoying in reality, what I am enjoying in imagination; which I must confess is rather a 'scant pattern' of enjoyment, when exerted in reference to the joys of the present, though I presume not with regard to the past and future. He obtained a billet to the President for leave of absence, and has left me alone. I may well say alone, for I am the only person in the third story of this End of College. It seems pretty solitary to be sure, but I had about as lief be alone, and rather on some accounts, than have another with me. For my part, I feel no great desire to return yet. Our lessons are generally far from being difficult, the recitations short, and the evenings long. About three fourths of our class are absent, so that the time taken up in reciting is not half what it used to be. The Term closes on Friday the 9th. I do not think of leaving until very near the end. Wednesday is the day I have pitched upon as my νόστιμον ημαρ, or day of returning. We read themes this forenoon. Or more properly we did not read them, for the plan pursued by our professor is this. The themes are given to him for criticism, once a-fortnight. He returns them to us marked for correction, or not, as it may happen. We hand them to him again, and on a fixed day he reads extracts from the best written before the whole class, not mentioning the name of the writer. This course has apparently done much good, for it makes us all ambitious to excell, and the Themes are evidently written with much greater care than they were before, when we all read our own to the President. And he (Professor Newman) [1] has also made another new regulation with regard to our writing, which I should think equally beneficial with the former. This is having a strict rule of punctuality. Unless the Themes are given to him upon the day appointed, the student is fined for omission of writing, except he give a satisfactory excuse. This has had the desired effect, and where before everything seemed to lag as it were, we now go on in great order and regularity. I see by the papers, and I suppose you have seen it too, that Mr Bates of Eastport, whom Dr Smith sued for his medical fee, is dead, and buried three miles off at sea in a lead coffin &c. which is very singular indeed. [2] I think he must have been very superstitious or very whimsical, or both together. I recieved a short letter from home to-day, but no news that would be of interest to you. One student has been suspended for negligence since my last letter. This is the only suspension that has taken place during the term, so that you may see how steadily everything goes on here. But the hour is very late, so that I must close my letter with a request to be remembered to Uncle A.S.W. [3] and the repetition of my wishes for a happy NEW YEAR.

Your affectionate Son
Henry W. Longfellow.

MANUSCRIPT: Longfellow Trust Collection. ADDRESS: Stephen Longfellow Jun Esqe/City of Washington. POSTMARK (*in script*): BRUNSWICK ME/JANY 2d/FREE ENDORSEMENT: H W Longfellow/Jany 8 —/1824 [*year in a second hand*]

1. Samuel Phillips Newman (1797–1842), professor of Latin and Greek at Bowdoin, 1819–1824, and of rhetoric and oratory, 1824–1839. An excellent teacher, he apparently exerted a considerable influence on Longfellow.

2. Dr. Nathan Smith (1762–1829), a distinguished physician and professor of medicine at Yale, organized the Bowdoin Medical School and served as a professor there from 1820 to 1825. The offshore burial of his patient, Elias Bates, would not have appeared so singular to Longfellow if he had known that Bates was a former sea captain.

3. Alexander Scammell Wadsworth (1790–1851), brother of Zilpah Longfellow, entered the United States Navy as a midshipman in 1804, and by 1823 he had already had an exciting career as an officer aboard the frigate *Constitution* and other men-of-war. From 1823 to 1825 he served in the Washington navy yard. A favorite uncle, he is frequently mentioned in Longfellow's correspondence.

39. *To Stephen Longfellow*

Portland   Jan. 11. 1824.

My Dear Father,

I write to you at this time to inform you of a plan I have formed for passing a part of the present College-vacation. "Amusement reigns man's great demand" — as Dr Young says,[1] and my plan is this. To go to Boston, and spend a week there. My classmate Weld[2] is going on in the course of a week or two, and offers me a seat in his sleigh, which invitation I feel much inclination to accept. I have written to you for your approbation of this plan, which I think is a very good one. That you may the more readily think as I do, I would inform you that I was never fifty miles from Portland, in all my life, which I think is rather a sorrowful circumstance in the annals of my history. When I hear others talking, as travellers are very apt to do, about what they have seen and heard abroad, I always regret my having never been from home more than I have hitherto. So that I often wish I had not been so fond of a sedentary life. I am of an opinion, that it is better to know the world partly from observation than whol[l]y from books. You, who have seen so much of it, at least of one division of it, will know how this is, and I dare say will think so too, since most others do. This visit then may on this account be advantageous as well as agreeable. Besides I do not think it will be very expensive, since if I go in the manner before-mentioned the cost of travelling will be greatly reduced. My companion that is to be, should this plan go in to operation, has numerous relatives in Boston, and as he will take the horse to his own account, that expense will also be removed. He is going on for his sister, who is visiting there, in consequence of which, if he has my company, I shall be under the necessity of returning in the stage. I do not know as there is any kind of utility to arise from being thus minute in the statement of particulars, but I wish you to know everything 'pro and con.' I think you will be inclined to express your approbation of this measure. I wish you would write me as soon as convenient upon this subject, that I may know what answer to give Mr Weld, with regard to this. I find nothing new to write you, either by observation or by the News-papers. Colonel Stephenson returned home with Madam S. — on Saturday.[3] Since then, we have heard nothing from Gorham. I believe you have had letters from us of later date than this. We received your National Journal[4] this morning. I like this paper very well, that is what I have read, for I have not looked at the Extra Sheets yet. I find I have not power to stop Mr Carter's paper here,[5] as I was thinking I might, so that it goes on to Brunswick, much against my inclination, for I like to have as many News-papers as possible. ||If you|| subscribe to any other Washington papers I wish you would send them, after you have used them. The more Literature and the less of Politics, the better. And that is one reason why I like the Journal, because with all its Politics, there is much literary matter, and very few advertisements, which last mentioned usually take up a very good part of our Portland papers. All, of course, send their love to you.

Your affectionate Son
Henry

MANUSCRIPT: Longfellow Trust Collection. ADDRESS: Stephen Longfellow Jun Esq/City of Washington. POSTMARK: PORTLAND ME JAN 12 ENDORSE-MENT: H W Longfellow/ansd/Jan. 11. 1824 [*date in Longfellow's hand*] PUBLISHED: *Young Longfellow,* pp. 50–51.

1. In "Night II" of *Night Thoughts.*

2. Eugene Weld (1805–1849), a Bostonian, had only recently moved with his family to Brunswick. This made him an ideal traveling companion in Longfellow's eyes.

3. Col. Samuel Stephenson (1776–1858) of Gorham had married his cousin Abigail Longfellow, the sister of Stephen Longfellow. They had been visiting the Longfellow family in Portland (see 37.5).

4. A Washington newspaper, the first volume of which appeared in 1824.

5. *The New York Statesman* (see 34.1).

40. *To Cullen Sawtelle*

Portland   Jan. 20 1824

My dear friend Sawtelle,

I received and read your letter of the 14th, with great pleasure, and to save you from the death you stand in so much dread of — the death of a Cobler, I write you immediately.[1] "Old Friend Brown[e]" is again suspended to Gurnes. You will stare at this, but nevertheless it is a fact. Suspension — voluntary suspension to the land of barbarism. But then all this takes place under circumstances of a different kind from those of his former mission to the heathen.[2] The truth is he has gone to "teach the young idea"[3] — sojourning in the land, as a kind of pedagogue, — a machine like yourself maybe, though I know nothing about [the] salary of the school nor its perquisites. I have not heard from him since he left town, but I think of writing him soon, for taking all things into consideration, I like Browne very much, though he has his faults.

I suppose you are now sitting by your rousing Winter fire, with plenty of sour apples and sweet cider, cracking your jokes with the girls, or talking with the "Old bruisers" about green turnips and cabbage-leaves — improvements in Agriculture and hoe-handles, and other such like topics of a farmer's evening conversation. Now all this together with dough-nuts and molasses, and old cheese, is very pleasant. However I hold it to be very good logic and very good philosophy into the bargain, to make a vacation answer all the purposes of a vacation, that is not hurt myself by study. For my own part, if indeed you feel any inclination to know how I am passing all these hours, days, and weeks, I must acknowledge, that all I do, — no — I will not say all I do — but the principal part of my business is eating, drinking, sleeping and making poetry. Now this is very agreeable, and very economical, and all that, because it does not wear out shoes — no, — nothing but elbows and old coats. In fact I take little or no exercise, sit right down by the fire, in the morning, and hardly move a leg untill night, which is in this cold, stormy, uncomfortable weather, as well as may be. So that I am as happy as a Nabob, excepting now and then, a little sadness and melancholy. But a truce with this. If you see Eugene Weld, please to tell him from me, that he must not forget his promised visit to Portland &c. I shall write him soon — as soon as — as — as — can't say when. I have spoken to Preble about our contemplated tour to the Eastern country, during the next spring vacation. He says he is ready to join in any such scrape, so that you may calculate upon seeing us down amongst you somewhere about the second week.[4] But I can tell you about this and such things, when I come to see you again, face to face, better than I can write them now. The weather here has, since my arrival, been generally very unpleasant, which has been an unfortunate circumstance, especially if you take sleigh-rides into the consideration. But as I do not go out much I do not feel that inconvenience from it, which otherwise I might. Farewell!

Yours affectionately
Henry W. Longfellow.

MANUSCRIPT: E. Ross Sawtelle, Marblehead, Massachusetts. ADDRESS: Mr Cullen Sawtelle./Brunswick. POSTMARKS: PORTLAND MAINE JAN 21/PAID POSTAL ANNOTATION (*by Longfellow*): Paid 5.

1. Sawtelle's letter is unrecovered. The meaning of this sentence must thus remain obscure.
2. Browne had been rusticated the previous year for having been inebriated at worship, which ignited the passions of Rev. Asa Meade and caused the subsequent rebellion of the student body (see 18.3).
3. James Thomson, *The Seasons*, "Spring," l. 1153.
4. This plan probably fell through, for there is no record of Longfellow's having visited Sawtelle in Norridgewock during the spring vacation.

41. *To Stephen Longfellow*

Portland Jany. 21. 1824

My dear Father,

I have been long waiting in expectation of letters from you, in order to hear what you have to say in regard to my visit to Boston, but have waited in vain. Indeed, you write so seldom, that we are all complaining. Judge Mellen says you are "not half so good a fellow as he was, when at Washington, — for not a day passed in which he did not write to some one of his family."[1] He wants to know if you have lost the use of both your hands! I have had but one letter from you since your departure, and have written you one every week. Do write to me soon, — immediately! — that I may know what to expect with regard to this visit, — for even with your consent I am not sure of the ride. I have not yet heard from Mr Weld, who you recollect, is going with me, though I shall write him soon upon this subject. If he does not go on to Boston, I shall not be so very desirous of going myself, unless I could find some other companion as good. Weld formerly resided in Boston. R.A.L. Codman came to town on Wednesday evening, and brought our cousin E.W. Stephenson.[2] She intends to remain some days with us, and to judge of the future by the past, she will make a very merry if not a very long visit. We laughed this afternoon untill we could scarcely stand, and all this for nothing at all, — it was indeed very silly, but nevertheless we enjoyed it highly. If you had been with us, I cannot tell whether you would have laughed *with* us or *at* us, but I really think you would have laughed. Mr Codman left town this afternoon (Saturday —). He says his father intends to journey as far as Washington, in the course of the Winter. Frederick C. is at Baltimore.[3]

I presume you have already heard of the famous Caucus of the members of both branches of the Legislature, to find out their own minds upon the subject of the next President. It was farcical "in extremo" and "in toto." Mr MacDonald[4] of the Senate was in the "cheer," as he called it, and showed what a precious legislator he was. Some resolves were moved, and the motion made to have them read by the chairman — and he read them word by word and I had almost said syllable by syllable. "Re-sol-ved that" &c. When they were read he cried out with some emphasis "There, Gentlemen, I've read them!" Whilst he held the papers in his hands and before they were read from the chair, a laugh was raised at something that was said. "Well, Gentlemen, after you have done laughing I'll read them" — (another laugh). "I wish you would *be still!* &c." Now this is all very great indeed for a Senator, not to use even the proper "order" when commanding silence! He observed in the Senate to day, 'that he didn't *"keer"* whether the bill passed or not.' Wonderful! The question of the location of the seat of government has been agitated again. The inhabitants of Augusta sent to the Legislature a de‖ed for‖ thirty acres of land, requesting money for the erection of publick buildings. The consideration of this question was postponed, I think untill 1827.

But Mr Williams of the House,[5] moved for a reconsideration of the vote for postponement, and I know not what is now to be done — not much I presume! All send their best regards to you and of course wish you to write — and moreover we are all well. Stephen is now in Gorham or Hiram, we know not which.

Yours respectfully and affectionately —

Henry W. Longfellow.

MANUSCRIPT: Longfellow Trust Collection. ADDRESS: Stephen Longfellow Jun Esqe/City of Washington. POSTMARK: PORTLAND ME JAN 23 ENDORSEMENT: H W Longfellow/Jany 30/1824 [*year in a second hand*]

1. Judge Prentiss Mellen (1764–1840), chief justice of the state of Maine, had served as United States Senator from 1818 to 1820. He was the father of Grenville Mellen, the poet, and of Frederic Mellen, Longfellow's classmate at Bowdoin.

2. In January, 1825, Codman married Elizabeth Ware Stephenson, daughter of Longfellow's aunt, Abigail Longfellow Stephenson.

3. Capt. Frederick Codman was Randolph A. L. Codman's brother. They were the sons of Capt. James Codman, a shipmaster of Gorham.

4. John McDonald of York County.

5. Rufus Williams (1783–1863) of Hallowell, a prominent lawyer and politician, had been active in the promotion of Maine to an independent state. After some years of agitation Augusta was chosen as the state capital in 1827.

42. *To Stephen Longfellow*

Portland. Feby. 2nd. 1824

My dear Father,

It is several days since the reception of yours of 22nd of January,[1] and I have delayed answering it thus long not from inclination but necessity. I have been suffering from all the inconveniences of the Ophthalmia, which you mentioned you were fearful of bringing upon yourself. I do not know what was the cause of my indisposition, but it came upon me quite unawares. My eyes felt rather weak a few evenings since, and thinking it arose from using [them] too much by candle light, I took no particular notice of it, and consequently no precautions against its effects. The next morning my eyes were very much inflamed and rather painful. However the disease has been of short duration. I am nearly recovered, though I dare not read much in the evening. I hardly know what to use as a cure, for every one has a remedy, that is of course infallible, and can bring a great many examples of the efficacy of their proscription, which is offered. I concluded the remedy, which was the most *natural* was the best, and therefore used water several times a day, sometimes warm and at others cold, by way of variety and also of experiment.[2]

I have read Mr Webster's speech upon the Greek question, as

given by Mr Carter in the Statesman, and also from the Intelligencer. I was very much pleased (of course) although I did expect, that he would have appealed more to the passions of his audience, as this would seem to be the most effectual way of influencing the opinions of the majority, although not always the most just. I have not read any of the other Speeches upon the question — nor Mr W's second speech, in answer to his opponents.[3]

Edward D. Preble started for Boston this morning in the Mail-Stage. It would have been good company for me, but I have not recieved any information from Mr Weld with regard to our agreement. Mrs R. Derby is in town, and returns to Boston on Monday next. Aunt Lucia talks of accompanying her.[4]

Sam is at my elbow dictating to me what to say about himself. He is a very good boy and has eaten a frozen apple, according to his own account. The other little folks are at school. All send their best regards, and are very well. Cousin Elizabeth [Stephenson] continues to keep us in good spirits.

Yours very affectionately

H. W. Longfellow.

MANUSCRIPT: Longfellow Trust Collection. ADDRESS: Stephen Longfellow Jun Esqe/City of Washington. POSTMARK: PORTLAND ME FEB 2 ENDORSEMENT: H.W. Longfellow/Feby 8/1824. [*year in a second hand*]

1. In which Stephen Longfellow delivered a polemic on the subject of travel while granting his son permission to go to Boston. See *Young Longfellow*, pp. 51–52.

2. Longfellow had trouble with his eyes for the rest of his life, an affliction that periodically forced him in later days to seek an amanuensis. Although his ophthalmia may occasionally be attributed to hypochrondria, it was in this and many other instances the result of his habit of prolonged reading in poor light.

3. On January 19 Webster addressed the House of Representatives in support of a resolution to appoint a United States Commissioner to Greece. His remarks on "The Revolution in Greece" favored the independence of that country and made clear his hostility to the principles and methods of the Holy Alliance. Although the resolution was defeated, Webster's speech attracted international attention as the first official expression of sympathy toward the Greek revolutionists.

4. At this time Longfellow still held to the hope of traveling to Boston with his classmate Weld and consequently did not feel free to accompany Ned Preble. When the original plan fell through, he departed on February 10 with his aunt Lucia Wadsworth and Mrs. Richard C. Derby of Boston. Mrs. Derby (Martha Coffin, 1783–1832) had been visiting her father, Dr. Nathaniel Coffin of Portland.

43. *To Stephen Longfellow*

Bowdoin College. March 2nd. 1824.

My dear Father,

I have omitted writing you for so long a time, that you may well accuse me of negligence, but I know you will not condemn me without a hearing. Whilst at Boston I was too much engaged to write unless I wrote in the evening, and my eyes were so weak, that I was afraid to do that. Since my return to Brunswick I have really been too busy to write to you or to any-body else. This is my excuse for my long silence and this letter is in palliation of the offence. I will now describe to you as well and as briefly as I can my visit to Boston. As we left Portland in the Accommodating Stage, the first night was passed at Portsmouth. We arrived towards evening, and after tea I called upon my classmate Mason,[1] and we walked about the streets a little. But it was too dark to see much of the town, and too wet to be at all comfortable, so that I returned to the inn with the consoling expectation, that the storm which seemed threatening would be a storm of rain, and the morning would find no snow on the ground. Nor were these fears without foundation. When we again set off on our journey, in the morning, there was very little snow left beneath the sleigh-runners. However we drag[g]ed along untill we came to Newbury-port, where we took wheels, and arrived at the "Literary Emporium"[2] late in the evening. Aunt L. and Mrs Derby remained at Salem untill Saturday the 14th. I slept the first night, — the 11th of Feb. — at the Exchange Coffee House,[3] and could not help thinking how much my situation resembled yours, when you were first there. If this were not another building I should have imagined I occupied the same chamber, that you did in former times, for it seemed to be the very highest point of the habitable dwelling, the very apogee, so to speak. In the morning I sallied forth, in pursuit of Mrs Wells', but took the wrong direction and walked up by the mall. I however found my way back to the Coffee-House and took a guide. Neither the Dr. nor George was at home, and I did not introduce myself, but Mrs Wells soon found me out by my resemblance to Mama.[4] I had a delightful visit. We went to Charlestown, — to the Navy Yard and Breed's Hill: — to the Athaneaum, to the State House, and took a beautiful view from the dome, — To Stewart's painting room, to Dogget's Repository, — and to all places of repute excepting the Mill-dam.[5] The day we fixed upon for seeing this was so severely cold, that we relinquished the plan. I was also at Cambridge, and I must not forget the splendid ball I attended. This was a private ball given by Miss Marshall, one of the most celebrated of the City belles.[6] It was indeed a most *splendid* entertainment, more so by far than any I had ever beheld before. Here I saw and danced with Miss Eustaphieve, the daughter of the Russian Consul.[7] She is an exceedingly graceful and elegant dancer, and plays beautifully upon the Piano Forte. I furthermore was at the Theatre when the Shakespear Jubilee was represented.

This Jubilee in honour of the Bard of Avon, is nothing more than select scenes from his most celibrated Tragedies and Comedies, together with an elegant pageant, representing the Tragick Muse in a car drawn by Fiends and the Muse of Comedy, drawn by Satyrs, — severally preceeded by the standards of the tragedies and of the comedies. Mr Sprague's prize poem written for the occasion, I did not hear. And so much for the Shakespear Jubilee.[8] I saw a great number of elegant buildings in Boston, and was much pleased with the city itself, as well as with the inhabitants. I w||as|| t||here|| but eight days, and would have staid as long again had it been in my power. But this was out of the question altogether, for as it was I did not get back to College again untill after the commencement of the term. I have hardly got calmed and settled down to my studies yet, but I hope I shall be soon. I am pretty well, I may say very well, although I fear I do not take exercise enough. We attend the professor's Chemical Lectures,[9] which you know are very interesting as well as instructive. I have had no letters from home this week, but expect letters daily.

Your affectionate Son

Henry.

I will be thankful to you if you will pay Mr Carter, this years subscription for his Statesman, which amounts to $4.00.

MANUSCRIPT: Longfellow Trust Collection. ADDRESS: Stephen Longfellow Jun Esq/City of Washington. POSTMARK (*in script*): BRUNSWICK ME/MARCH 5th FREE ENDORSEMENT: H W Longfellow/March 11./1824 [*year in a second hand*]

1. Alfred Mason (1804–1828), son of Jeremiah Mason of Portsmouth, the legal rival of Daniel Webster, became a physician and died of fever during the first weeks of his internship at Bellevue Hospital, New York. He was Hawthorne's roommate during the freshman and sophomore years.

2. That is, Boston.

3. Located in Congress Square, the Exchange was the stagecoach terminal in Boston.

4. Hannah Doane Wells (1777–1841), first cousin of Zilpah Longfellow, was the Boston member of the family on whom Longfellow depended for shelter and entertainment. She was the mother of Dr. John D. Wells and George W. Wells.

5. The last three places mentioned by Longfellow are no longer in existence. The location in 1824 of the painting room of Gilbert Stuart — Longfellow's spelling is either inadvertent or misconceived — is undetermined. The repository of John Doggett & Company was located on Market Street. The Mill-dam, finished in 1821, lay across the Back Bay at what is now lower Beacon Street.

6. Emily Marshall, daughter of Josiah Marshall, a wealthy merchant of Boston, inspired Percival and Willis to poetry and other admirers to superlatives. Josiah Quincy wrote of her that "She was simply perfect in face and figure, and perfectly charming in manners" (*Figures of the Past,* ed. M. A. DeWolfe Howe [Boston, 1926], p. 281). The same age as Longfellow, she married William Foster Otis in 1831 and died at twenty-nine in 1836.

7. Alexis Eustaphieve and his daughter, a pianist of considerable reputation, were prominent in Boston musical circles. See *The Memorial History of Boston, Including Suffolk County, Massachusetts, 1630–1880.* ed. Justin Winsor (Boston, 1880–1886), IV, 416.

8. Longfellow does not mention the fact that he himself had submitted an ode to the prize competition of the Shakespeare Jubilee. This is made clear by Zilpah Longfellow in a letter to her husband dated April 4, 1824: "In Boston, at dinner, Mr Minot [presumably William Minot (1783–1873), son of George Richards Minot, the jurist and historical writer] asked Henry if he were the author of the poem written in Portland and offered for the prize at 'The Shakespeare Jubilee,' as they call it. Henry pretended not to hear, and made no answer except by blush. Very extraordinary to put such a question to a young man at such a time. There were thirty poems presented to the judges. Mr Minot was one of them, [and] in that way he knew that one was sent by 'Longfellow Portland.' The prize was adjudged to a Mr Sprague of Boston. It is fortunate I think that H. did not receive it. That would have 'turned his head.' It shews a good share of confidence in his own powers to make the attempt to win the prize. It has never been mentioned to him at home." Charles Sprague (1791–1875), a Boston banker and minor poet, took the prize with his "Ode to Shakespeare." Longfellow's contribution is identified by Lawrance Thompson in "An Inquiry into the Importance of 'Boston Prize-Poems,'" *The Colophon*, New Graphic Series, I, No. 4 (1940), 55–62.

9. Parker Cleaveland's lectures.

44. *To Zilpah Longfellow*

Bowdoin College. March 7th 1824.

My dear Mother,

I received your letters &c by Mr Abbot,[1] and as you request it I will read your letter of the 25 of Feby. again and answer each question in order. You wish to know what company I had in the stage! There were Judge Ware of Portland, Mr Shepley of Saco, Mr McLellan (a student), and one or two others, whom I did not know.[2] "Have you seen Dr Wells?" This I have already answered in the affirmative.[3] Speaking of the subject of your letters, you next ask "On what subject then shall I write?" You can yourself answer this question much better than I can. It is for you to chuse, not me. The next question is "How could we all be so thoughtless, so careless, Henry, as to let you go without the money and bills!" This needs no answer, nor comment! You then inquire whether I wish for any new shirts! that is, if I want any sent to me? I do not at present: if I should I will send for them. You then speak of crackers &c but you forgot my shoes. The crackers I do not wish for, and my reason is that I have, after one week's abstemiousness, concluded, that it is more pleasant if not more healthy, to eat dinner, as other folks do. "Had Stephen procured any wood for you!" No, he had not. He was not able to purchase any, however I found some very poor wood on monday. Now I will turn to your last letter!

Stephen did not show his letter to me, nor mention that he had received one. I have said nothing about it to him, and do not know whether he has yet received the one you refer to.[4] If you desire the whole truth I must not conceal it. His conduct seems to be pretty much as it was last term. He is absent from his room most of the time, and I do not know how much he studies, although he does not appear very well at recitation. I am now almost sorry I have told, what I have told. It is too near the beginning of the term to judge of what he will do. Excepting this apparent negligence, his conduct is perfectly regular. You see in what a very unpleasant situation you have placed me, by setting me as a spy upon him. If I do not tell you the truth of the matter, I shall not be doing my duty, and yet when I tell you the truth, I am afraid you will interpret things worse than they really are. Don't write to papa about it for I am certain he will be more apt to do so than you are. I cannot say any more.

I have not heard from Washington since I left home, that is to say, I have had no letters from thence, though I shall look for one soon. I wrote a very long letter to W. last week and dare say I shall get an answer to it, before the month is out.

I received by Mr Abbot, $77.00 — For our bill of board $45.00
                                                   This bill amounts to   44.25
$2.00 for wood.   Remains   .75 cts.
  My College bill is $14.35. You send me $14.00.
Stephen's   "   "   " $18.55. You sent but $16.00!!

I believe you forgot the bill for washing, as I cannot find it among the others; this bill you know is $4.00.

This term is a very busy one; for the studies are the most difficult of any we attend to during our whole College life. Therefore you will please to tell the girls not to write me any letters at all, but to set right down by the fire in the morning, and read novels untill midnight, for this will brighten the intellects and improve the imagination! And if Ann[e] ever thinks ||about|| card-racks again, I shall be exceedingly grieved and mortified!

Has Aunt [Lucia] done talking of Boston yet? I have not by a good many weeks yet. I have been to see Miss Weld twice. It is a very fine place to visit, I assure you. Worth all the other families in town, — mind, — I say for visiting.[5] And now it is high time, that I should begin to think of my lesson.

So, farewell.

                                    Your affectionate Son
                                         Henry.

Please to send me a quire of letter-paper! When I was in the City of Boston I sent to Philadelphia, for the "American Monthly Magazine." If you get it in Portland, I want you to send it on for me, and, as I said in my last letter, the Portland Advertiser, for all these things are exce[e]dingly pleasant. Please to send all the January numbers of the Advertiser.

MANUSCRIPT: Longfellow Trust Collection. ADDRESS: Stephen Longfellow Jun Esqe./Portland. POSTMARK (*in script*): BRUNSWICK/MARCH 8

1. John Abbot (1759–1843), treasurer of Bowdoin College and ex-officio trustee.

2. Those named by Longfellow were: Ashur Ware (1782–1873), judge of the U.S. district court of Maine; Ether Shepley (1789–1877), U.S. district attorney of Maine; and Isaac McLellan (1806–1899), a member of the Bowdoin class of 1826 and subsequently a minor author.

3. Apparently in an unrecovered letter to his mother dated March 5, 1824.

4. Stephen Longfellow, who was in Washington, had written a letter to his eldest son and namesake in which he reproved him for his poor conduct both at Bowdoin and at home and admonished him about his obligations. This letter followed young Stephen from Portland to Hiram to Brunswick before it finally caught up with him. It seems to have had only a temporary effect, for within the year the Bowdoin authorities suspended him for neglect of duties, for participating in conduct "disturbing to the quietness and dishonorable to the character of a literary institution," and for introducing spirituous liquors into the college (Bowdoin Faculty Records, December 28, 1824). Although he graduated with his class, Stephen found no satisfaction in his studies or, later, in preparation for the law. Frustrated in his ambition to follow a military career, he took refuge in irresponsibility and alcohol and consequently never achieved the success to which his talents might have led him. Henry always remained loyal to him and, as this paragraph reveals, discussed his shortcomings with reluctance.

5. Through his classmate Eugene Weld, Longfellow became acquainted with the Weld family of Brunswick, of which the Miss [Abby] Weld mentioned here was a daughter.

45. To Zilpah Longfellow

Bowdoin College   March. 11th. 1824.

My dear Mother,

I have just received your letter of the 9th and am very sorry, for many parts of your intelligence. But to proceed methodically and all in order, I would inform you that, I have not received the shoes!! To be sure, I got a bundle with the *pumps* &c. &c. And then the bill of $4.00! Are you sure I took it? If I did it is lost, for when I came to pay it, I looked for it in my memorandum-book and lo! the bird had flown! so that I took my own money to pay it and now am poor, — pennyless, — pitiful! I hope this is not quite lost, for I have not one cent of money. Do send me some soon. I was unwise enough to pay Stephen's Term bill with the money you sent, — for wood, I think it was; but this is of no great account, as we shall not probably want more wood this term.

Miss Bush[1] is very well. I was there on Sunday evening.

I dare say you are curious to know who wrote me from Philadelphia! It was the Editor of the Magazine; and he says the first 3 numbers of the work came in the same mail with the letter. Do get them immediately, and send them, as soon as you can read them. I have inclosed a letter to Dr McHenry (The Editor of the Magazine)[2] which I wish you to send to the Post Office without delay, or I shall be in a pretty dilemma. I wrote to him to put my name upon the subscription list at Philadelphia, since there was no agent in Portland. He writes back "According to your request your name is placed among the agents." Now this is not according to my request, nor any thing like it; so that I have had the trouble of writing him a second time, for fear my name should be on the cover of his work, after this fashion perhaps,

'American Monthly Magazine No. 1. —
Agent. Portland. H. W. Longfellow.'

Oh! what a blunder! Do send for those three numbers. I suspect they are in the post office or at Johnson's.[3] I would not have them lost on any account whatever. But only to think I am to be the agent. Oh dear! I am *quite* disturbed! It is *quite* amusing to be sure. I have had a good laugh about it with Deane[4] and Preble! I dare say you will all laugh too. I am afraid you will find my name upon some number already. If you should, do not scratch it out, for I should like to see it there. But do not mention this to any one out of the family, on any consideration. Stephen's health is very good and so is mine!

Your affectionate Son
Henry.

I have not heard from Washington yet.

MANUSCRIPT: Longfellow Trust Collection. ADDRESS: Stephen Longfellow Jun Esq./Portland. POSTMARK (*in script*): BRUNSWICK/MARCH 12

1. Miss Hannah Bush, a friend of the Longfellow family, was the sister of Mrs. Parker Cleaveland. She presumably lived in her brother-in-law's household at this time.

2. James McHenry (1785–1845), an Irishman, had come to the United States in 1817. In 1824 he settled in Philadelphia, where he practiced medicine, engaged in trade, and edited the *American Monthly Magazine*. He was the author of several narrative poems and historical romances.

3. The Portland bookseller (23.1).

4. Ebenezer Furbish Deane (1801–1848), Bowdoin, 1824.

46. *To Stephen Longfellow*

Bowd Coll. March. 13th. 1824.

My dear Father,

A week has now elapsed since my last letter, and again I resume my pen. The term wears away exceedingly fast, or as Horace says — "fugaces Labuntur anni; — "[1] by the way, I forgot to tell you in my last, that we were reading Horace. I admire it very much indeed: and in fact I have not met with so pleasant a study since the commencement of my college life. Moreover it is extremely easy to read, which not a little contributes to the acquisition of a thorough knowledge of every line and every Ode.

One hour each day during this Spring term, for five days in every week, is employed in attending Professor Cleaveland's Chemical Lectures. I do not recollect whether I mentioned this circumstance to you in my last letter or not, however be that as it may I think it worth repeating. Most of the lectures, which we have thus far attended have been very interesting. There were one or two upon the subject of Chemical Affinity which were not so. And yet I believe it is considered of the greatest importance, for those who would devote themselves to the study of Medical Science, to be acquainted and pretty thoroughly acquainted with the principles of this affinity. I said the Medical science, but I dare say you will tell me that an intricate connection exists between this principle and not this science only, but extends its influence to most other sciences and even to the arts.

I feel very glad that I am not to be a physician, — that there are quite enough in the world without me. And now, as somehow or other the subject has been introduced, I am curious to know what you do intend to make of me! Whether I am to study a profession or not? and if so, what profession? I hope your ideas upon this subject will agree with mine, for I have a particular and strong predilection for one course of life, to which you I fear will not agree. It will not be worth while for me to mention what this is, untill I become more acquainted with your own wishes.

My last letter from Portland was dated March 9th. Mr Hayes as you may have heard before this time, has left Portland.[2] I do not hear any news in this part of the Union, that would be interesting for you to hear. We all look to the South for news.

I wish you would be kind enough to seal, and direct the inclosed letter to "The Editor of the Christian, Care of Mr John Mortimer, the publisher, Philadelphia."[3] The letter is an acknowledgement, from the Philalethian Society[4] at College, of the reception of the first seven numbers of that paper, presented by the Editor. I dare say you have already seen this paper, devoted to "Religion, Morals, and Literature." The reason I inclose the letter to you is, that I may save the postage, being myself the Secretary of the Society, and consequently it being my duty to write.

Stephen and myself are both very well.

Yours affectionately
Henry W. Longfellow.

PS. Upon the whole I think it would be best to direct this "to the Editor of the C." and inclose it in a letter to the Publisher, together with the $3.00 I here send you, which is advanced by E.D. Preble, who wishes to take the paper.

MANUSCRIPT: Longfellow Trust Collection. ADDRESS: Stephen Longfellow Junr. Esqe./City of/Washington. POSTMARK (*in script*): BRUNSWICK ME/MARCH 15th FREE ANNOTATION (*by Stephen Longfellow*): March 20. 1824. Inclosed to Mr. John Mortimer the above letter and $3 — Bill of the Eagle Bank of New Haven No. 2914, dated Decr. 1. 1818 — Geo: Hoadly Pres[iden]t J.W.S. Ressiter Cash[ie]r. I requested him to send the Christian to Edward D. Preble, Bowdoin College, Brunswick ENDORSEMENT: Henry W Longfellow/March 21./1824 [*year in a second hand*]

1. "Our years pass away." *Odes*, II, 14.

2. Apparently David Hayes (1795–1870), a member of the Bowdoin class of 1819 and subsequently a lawyer in Westbrook, Maine. In a letter to her husband dated March 7, 1824, Zilpah Longfellow wrote: "Mr Hayes left the Office yesterday. He is so pleasant, we were sorry to have him go." Hayes either prepared for the law under Stephen Longfellow or worked in his office.

3. Mortimer, a bookseller located at 74 S. Second Street, Philadelphia, published *The Christian; a Weekly Paper, devoted to Religion, Morals, and Literature*, as well as McHenry's *American Monthly Magazine*.

4. The Unitarian Society of Bowdoin College, of which Longfellow was secretary. A fragment of the record book of the society survives, in which Longfellow on the date of this letter made the following entry: "Met according to adjournment at the Secretary's room. An assessment of 50 cts made upon each member for defraying incidental expences. The first seven numbers of 'The Christian' received, presented by the Editor, Philadelphia" (MS, Clifton Waller Barrett Collection, University of Virginia). See Letter No. 55.

47. To Stephen Longfellow

Bowd: Coll: March. 21st. 1824.

My dear Father,

Nothing that is new or that partakes of anything of interest has transpired since my last letter. The papers from Portland have very little variety in them and still less of novelty. And yet to their multitude of weekly and semi-weekly journals, they are about adding another. This is a paper entitled the "Wreath," a Literary Museum for the Ladies, the first number of which is to be issued some time next June, — if ever. I do not know who is to be the Editor, nor did I even hear of the proprietors previous to seeing their prospectus.[1] Sister E. [Elizabeth] from whom I had a letter a day or two since, says she shall not wish to read it, "if it is composed of such trash as usually fills the ladies Magazines. They pay but a poor compliment to the ladies, to think they can be pleased with such nonsense." Which I think is very well said. However we shall know in a few weeks what it is likely to be, — whether good, — bad, — or indifferent. I have lately subscribed for the American Monthly Magazine, Edited by Dr McHenry of Philadelphia. You must not think I shall call on you to pay for this, as I do for numberless other things of the kind, — e.g. the N York Statesman! No. This is to be paid for out of my spending money, and I am confident you are willing it should be appropriated in this manner.

At College all is as sober, steady and quiet as usual. The appointments for the exercises of the Spring Exhibition came out on Wednesday, and considerable dissatisfaction came out with them: which is in most cases unavoidable. It was a scene of no great interest to me, although this second assignation of parts in our class, bring[s] the appointment of my colleague and me a little higher than we before considered it. E. Weld, my particular friend, of whom I have spoken to you before, has the highest part in our class, at which, as you will naturally suppose, I am much rejoiced.

When do you think Congress will rise? I hear from home that you will return in the latter part of April, whether the Session is closed or not. We shall meet then in the Spring vacation, though I was fearful we should not. I anticipate a great deal of pleasure at meeting you again after so long an absence. Do write me again before you return!

My visit to Boston continues to afford me a great deal of pleasure in the retrospect, — even more than the anticipation of it did. It was so very pleasant, that it created a reluctance to return so soon to College. Yet here I am again, and well contented to be here, since I am to stay but little more than a year longer.

We are both well and happy.

Your affectionate Son
Henry W. Longfellow.

MANUSCRIPT: Longfellow Trust Collection. ADDRESS: Stephen Longfellow Jun. Esq./City of Washington. POSTMARK (in script): BRUNSWICK ME/MARCH 22d/FREE ENDORSEMENT: H W Longfellow/March 28/1824. [year in a second hand]

1. This journal does not seem to have survived. In his *History of the Press of Maine* (Brunswick, 1872), p. 54, Joseph Griffin writes that "The Wreath, a family paper, was commenced in 1822, by John Edwards, and afterward continued by A. W. Thayer. It lived about a year." Griffin's recollection of the date is presumably faulty.

48. *To Zilpah Longfellow*

Bowdoin College. March 22nd. 1824.

My dear Mother,

I will now acknowledge the receipt of your letter of the 13th, — the Magazines and papers by Mr Cs B.[1] and of Si[s]ter E's [Elizabeth's] letter of the 17th. The paper which you sent, was part of an outside quire, and of course, very much torn, as the outside quires always are: therefore you will be kind enough to send another half-quire and a bunch of quills. The shoes which I mentioned, I rather think you will not find about the house; they are a pair Mr Hartshorne[2] was to make and send off to the house for me. By what you said, I suspect you have not received them. No matter. I expect to take a ride up to Portland with my classmate Weld, in the course of a fortnight; I will give you information previous to our coming, if, indeed, we do come.

I had a letter today from Geo. Wells. He sends his best regards to you all. We are all well here; Dr Wells, — Miss B. [Bush] and the rest of us. This will come by [Frederic] Mellen. His eyes are so weak as to require his absence from College. The bell rings for recitation.

Yours in great haste
H. W. Longfellow.

Stephen is also in want of shoes.

MANUSCRIPT: Longfellow Trust Collection.

1. Possibly Charles Edward Barrett (1804–1894), a member of the Bowdoin class of 1822 and a law student in Portland at this time.

2. Washington Hartshorn owned the Portland Shoe Store at the corner of Cross and Middle Streets.

49. *To Stephen Longfellow*

Bowd Coll. April. 11. 1824

My dear Father,

I have been so very busy for the last month, that two or three weeks have slipped away since my last letter to you. And yet I suppose I could have found time to have written, had there been any very urgent necessity. But if I waited for this impulse, I am afraid I should wait forever as I have nothing to do with Washington, — Congress, nor Political Economy.

I have no news to tell you, — none at all! In fact I believe with Solomon, that "there is no new thing under the sun."[1] I had a letter from home yesterday, and they were all well there, but that was no news, because things that are, and are to be, are like those, that have been. You see what a reasoner I am. Shall I be a Lawyer!

But I suppose you are curious about College affairs. And with regard to *these* there is nothing *new*. Yet I will say something concerning the Lectures, — Professor Cleaveland's Lectures. The last was upon the galvanick heat produced by Prof. Hare's Deflagrator.[2] The experiments with this instrument did not, however, succeed so well as those with the battery at the two preceding lectures. I think the subject of galvanism very interesting, though the experiments with the dead dogs, in producing respiration, and 'endeavouring' to restore life, — (unsuccessful) — were more curious than pleasing. They have been trying the same upon Johnson, lately hung at New York,[3] and with as little effect. We have already had lectures upon Electricity, and Monday evening will be devoted to Oxygen Gas.

Although we in Brunswick cannot boast the mildness of your southern winters, yet we should prove ourselves very fastidious, not to be pleased with the delightful Spring mornings we have already had. Winter has abandoned us very much in a hurry, though for my own part, I heartily wish him good bye. We have had some remarkably pleasant weather, sunny and warm like summer, though sudden and great changes still continue. However there is no probability of more snow, nor of any severely cold weather, in which most of all I rejoice. I am glad to tread upon dry land again, and am now able to take more exercise than I was at the commencement of the term. Of course I feel better than I did then. I wish I had a horse here. I should in that case ride daily, when the weather permitted. This has been a very sickly term in College. A great number of students have been obliged to return home on account of ill health. However within the last week, the Government, seeing that something must be done to induce the students to exercise, recommended a game of ball now and then, which communicated such an impulse to our limbs and joints, that there is nothing now heard of, in our leisure hours, but ball — ball — ball. I cannot prophecy with any degree of accuracy concerning the continuance of this rage for play, but the effect is good, since there has been a thorough-going reformation from inactivity and torpitude.

When do you expect to turn your face Northward again? As soon as the first of May? We are all very anxious to see you again, though we know not exactly at what time to expect you. And I suppose you cannot tell yourself when Congress will rise, untill the day draws very near.

Pardon my being so cheap and common-place in my letter to night and also the dilution and dilation of a meagre subject, which I have been practising upon you. But do write me soon, lest I become apprehensive that you have forgotten me, — and so forth.

Your affectionate Son
Henry W. Longfellow.

MANUSCRIPT: Longfellow Trust Collection. ADDRESS: Stephen Longfellow. Jr. Esqr./Washington. POSTMARK (*in script*): BRUNSWICK ME/APRIL 12th FREE

1. Eccles. 1:9.

2. Robert Hare (1781–1858), professor of chemistry in the University of Pennsylvania, devised his deflagrator in 1821 for generating a high electric current.

3. John Johnson, a convicted murderer, was hanged on April 2 and his body given up to doctors for dissection and experimentation. The New York *Evening Post* contained lengthy accounts of his trial and execution.

50. *To Zilpah Longfellow*

Bowd. Coll. April. 14. 1824

My dear Mother,

I can write you but a few lines, and even these must be written in haste. I feel remarkably unwell to day, and in fact I never feel well at noon. What can be the matter! About eleven o'clock in the forenoon I begin to feel dull and exceedingly stupid, and do not have a clear Idea in my head untill supper-time. This is not only very unpleasant but it is also very inconvenient, for I cannot study to any advantage. I have had this feeling more or less, every day this term, but never so bad as at present.

Wednesday Evening. 9 o'clock

I feel much better to night, on account of going without dinner. I shall be forced to continue th[i]s fasting or else must suffer this horrible stupefaction at noon. Why does it return so regularly *then*? I am perfectly well at all other times, especially in the evening. My ey[e]s grow stronger, which is a great blessing. I have received the shoes and they fit me very well. You will, my dear Mother, excuse my short letter, when I tell you I have some other writing on hand which for the present occupies most of my leisure, and is of no little importance.[1]

Give my love to all.

Your affectionate Son
Henry W Longfellow.

ps. Mr Weld sends his regards. Please to send my Magazine[2] by Mail, if you have yet received the April Number. But I had almost forgotten to tell you in answer to your last letter, that we arrived in perfect safety, about 8 o'clock on Friday evening, after an uncomfortable ride, in a very dark evening. However we repented not of our visit.

Stephen has bought a pair of shoes of Mr Hartshorn's Agent in this town, and got them charged upon Mr H —— 's bill.

I did not intend to *charge* you this postage of so short a letter, but I do not hear of any private conveyance, so shall put into the mail. No I shalln't either. Here's captain Chase.[3]

Friday, very well to day.

MANUSCRIPT: Longfellow Trust Collection. ADDRESS: Mrs Zilpah Longfellow./ Portland./By Capt. Chase.

1. Longfellow is apparently referring to his poetical experiments. Zilpah Longfellow was his closest confidante in these matters and presumably understood the allusion.

2. The *American Monthly Magazine*.

3. Capt. Robert Chase operated a small coastal freighter that ran between Portland and Brunswick.

51. *To Stephen Longfellow*

Bowd. Coll. April 30. 1824

My dear Father,

I shall not make any apology for writing you so short a letter as this is to be, though perhaps I should apologize to myself, for writing at the expense of my eyes, which are very weak. Your letter of the 21st was particularly acceptable to me, as it was the only one I have received from you for a great many weeks, and I shall keep the cypress, from the Tomb of Washington, as a sacred relick. But in thinking to make a Lawyer of me, I fear you thought more partially than justly. I do not for my own part imagine that such a coat would suit me. I hardly think Nature designed me for the bar, or the pulpit, or the dissecting-room. I am altogether in favour of a Farmer's life. Stephen says nothing about either. Do keep the farmer's boots for me!

There has been a little disturbance here about bon-fires in the evening, which thus far has resulted in no more violent effects than heavy fines. All however is now quiet. Pray excuse my writing anything farther, for though the "spirit is willing the flesh is weak."[1]

Yours affectionately
Henry W. Longfellow.

MANUSCRIPT: Longfellow Trust Collection. ADDRESS: Stephen Longfellow. Jun. Esqr/Portland/By R.A.L. Codman Esqr. ["*Portland*" *deleted and* "*M.C./Washington*" *written in by Zilpah Longfellow, who also deleted Codman's name*] ENDORSEMENT: H. W. Longfellow/May 7./1824 [*year in a second hand*]

1. Matt. 26:41.

52. *To Zilpah Longfellow*

Bowd. Coll. May. 13th. 1824.

My dear Mother,

I sit down to acknowledge the receipt of your acceptable letter of the 2nd. inst. and also of your former letter, which came with the magazine. Your last mentioned letter was marked "Post Paid," but very unfortunately for me this mark was hidden by the envelope of the Magazine, so that the post-master in Portland did not make the usual acknowledgement of it, and I was obliged to pay, though I hesitated for fear that the government should receive double recompense. I confess with you, in regard to the A. M. Magazine, that the selections are not much to my taste. And I am sure I know not at whose door the fault lies. The Editor seems to exert himself a great deal in the cause in which he has enlisted, and is remarkably liberal in his reward to contributers and correspondents, but I hardly think he has talents either suited or adequate to the undertaking. The Copperplate Engravings are about as interesting as anything I find in those numbers, which I have already received. Have you received No. 5.? I see he still persevers in holding me up to publick view in the interesting character of his Agent, from which circumstance I am rather apprehensive, that he did not receive the letter, which contained my abdication.

With regard to the remissness of our correspondence, you have very justly rebuked me. And yet I hardly think you can complain, when you recollect that there are so many hands and heads at home and that the girls have time enough to write if they only have the will. The fact is, that it requires some time for me to write a letter, and what little leisure time remains from my College studies and bodily exercise, *must* be devoted to more general study. And then there are a thousand other things, which steal the time away, and which those who have never been at college, and know not from experience, never can know. Of such are the 3 hours spent daily in the recitation room, the time wasted in run[n]ing to and fro, and at meals, the exercises in the Chapel morning and evening, and the hour at Lecture. However I should not mention the last circumstance, as diminishing our leisure, for the Chemical Lectures, which I refer[r]ed to, are now closed. Nevertheless I have little time to devote to letters, which notwithstanding all that has been so frequently and strenuously urged in favour of Epistolary writing, and the necessity of devoting much attention to it, I must confess give more pleasure than profit, though I do not flatter myself so much as to think, that my letters give much of either. I think the best way is to have our letters, laying aside those which necessity demand[s], to have those of amusement "Like angel's visits, — few and far between."[1]

My head feels better than it did when I last wrote, a[l]though my dyspepsy, or whatever it may be, (for I am sure I do not know) is worse. This appears rather singular to me, and I dare say the business will be more fully developed in a short time.

Does the Small Pox rage with much violence in Portland? I have been vaccinated by Dr. Wells, but it did not take. I do not know the cause. He thinks, and so do I, that I have had the disease before, though no scar of any former inoculation could be found upon either arm. Did not Doct. Merrill[2] once vaccinate me at Portland? If he did, and that effectually, it ought to leave some mark to ||show|| itself. So say the Doctors, of which we have multitudes here.

My eyes are weak, — as usual, or rather more so than usual. I believe their inflam[m]ation arises from drinking cider, since I can attribute it to no other cause, half so probable as this. I believe I must leave it off, as soon as possible, and use them as seldom and as little in the evening as will answer.

Please to give my love to the whole congregation of children, old and young, and thank me for so long a letter.

Your affectionate Son
Henry W. Longfellow.

Stephen is very well.

MANUSCRIPT: Longfellow Trust Collection. ADDRESS: Mrs Zilpah Longfellow/ Portland. POSTMARK (*in script*): BRUNSWICK/MAY 8th [*sic*]

1. Thomas Campbell, *The Pleasures of Hope*, Pt. II, l. 378.
2. Dr. John Merrill (1782–1855), a member of the Harvard class of 1804, had practiced in Portland since the time of Longfellow's birth.

53. *To Zilpah Longfellow*

Bowd. Coll. June. 1824.

My dear Mother,

According to your strict injunctions I have commenced and pro-ceeded thus far toward filling half a sheet, which I shall please to call a letter. After a very pleasant ride on Thursday afternoon we arrived here soon after sunset, in all wished-for safety, though rather low in the article of spirits.[1] It looks very pleasant here, and would feel so too, were not the weather so cold. Stephen arrived yesterday fore-noon and the trunks are safe. I have no more intelligence to com-municate so that I can as conveniently stop here as — anywhere. Please to remember me to all, if "all" have not gone to Hiram.

Your affectionate Son

Henry.

If any of the girls find a broken ring of gold or brass wire lying about the house, it belongs to Mr Weld. He has lost one of this descrip-tion somewhere, and says it is very valuable to him. One thing I forgot when I left Portland, and that was a bottle of Sponge Blacking. Day-and-Martin's[2] requires too much brushing.

MANUSCRIPT: Longfellow Trust Collection.

1. After a brief holiday in Portland, Longfellow had returned to Brunswick to complete the college term.
2. An imported English shoe blacking.

54. *To Anne Longfellow*

Bowdoin College   October. 1824.

Dear Ann[e],

I suppose you are tired of waiting for an answer to your letter of the 1st of this month; but if you are not I highly commend your patience and shall act accordingly in future. The fact is, I have been very much engaged of late in writing my Latin Oration, which is to be delivered at the Exhibition, on Friday next.[1] Of course you will have no more letters from me until the close of the week. Do you know who wrote that ridiculous, lifeless, little piece of Poetry in the "Wreath" signed "H."? I am afraid folks will think I wrote it, and that I am in the habit of writing for the puny paper! Somebody has written another "Jephtha's Daughter" — do you know who it was? The signature was "Mordnant" — according to the best of my recol-lection![2] Has Nolcini finished my song yet? If he has brought it over to you, pray let me know how it sounds, and whether it's worth having, — though I presume it will be.[3]

You request a description of Miss A. Weld's wedding, and if you will wait until Thank[s]giving-day, I will tell you all I recollect about it, though I beg you to excuse me from giving the description in a letter.[4] Have you heard from C. Doane[5] since I left you? I received the bundle by W Codman, and Elizabeth's letter, which I shall answer as soon as convenient. Love to all, and excuse short letters.

Your affectionate brother
H. W. Longfellow —

There is a P.S. on the next page.

I wish you would tell Pa', that I will thank him for $3.00 — inasmuch as I have been cheated to that amount by taking a Wiscasset bill, which it seems is no better than it should be, — that is to say — good for nothing![6]

MANUSCRIPT: Longfellow Trust Collection.   ADDRESS: Miss Anne

1. According to the "Order of Exercises at Exhibition, October 29, 1824," printed in the *Eastern Argus* on November 1, Longfellow delivered a "Salutatory Oration in Latin. — Angli Poetæ" ("English Poets") as the first event of the program. Hawthorne's Latin dissertation "De Patribus Conscriptis Romanorum" ("of Roman Senators") was No. 8.

2. See 47.1. In a reply dated November 7, 1824, Anne Longfellow identified Mordnant as "The beautiful Daniel Clark" and assured her brother that nobody suspected him as the author of the poem signed "H."

3. Nolcini was apparently setting one of Longfellow's early poems to music. In her reply noted above, Anne Longfellow remarked that "your song is not finished yet."

4. Miss Abby Weld, sister of Longfellow's classmate (39.2), had recently married John Austin Stevens (1795–1874), a New York merchant, in Brunswick. The marriage was noted in the *Eastern Argus* of October 11, 1824.

5. Caroline Doane (1794–1850), Longfellow's first cousin, once removed, was the sister of Hannah Wells, with whom he had stayed on his holiday in Boston.

6. All banks at this time were permitted to issue bank notes, the value of which fluctuated in accordance with the reputed strength of the bank, the diffusion of the notes, and other factors. In a letter dated October 27, Stephen Longfellow sent his son $3.00 as well as detailed advice on how to recover the money from the bad bill.

55. *To George Wadsworth Wells*

[Bowdoin College] November — , 1824.

. . . Somehow, and yet I hardly know why, I am unwilling to study any profession. I cannot make a lawyer of any eminence, because I have not a talent for argument; I am not good enough for a minister, — and as to Physic, I utterly and absolutely detest it. . . .

I have heard nothing of your fellow-student, P — — , since he was here in August. He was resolute, though feeble enough in health, and though poor, yet he was very generous. I presume he has frequently mentioned to you our little Unitarian Society at Bowdoin. I wish something could be done for us; we are as small as a grain of mustard-seed! There are but six members, now, in college, and our library is limited to a hundred or two volumes. I wish you would exert your influence in our behalf. And I want you to purchase twenty-five or thirty copies of a little work called Objections to Unitarian Christianity Considered.[1] I want to distribute one or two of them in this section of the globe. To these you may add such other works of the Unitarian Tract Society as you think will be useful, together with Mr. Adam's State of Christianity in India, —[2] the whole amount not exceeding two or three dollars, which I will send you as soon as I receive the books.

MANUSCRIPT: unrecovered; text from *Life*, I, 52–53.

1. By William Ellery Channing, first published in 1819.
2. Rev. W. Adam, *Correspondence Relative to the Prospects of Christianity, and the Means of Promoting its Reception in India* (Cambridge, 1824).

56. *To Stephen Longfellow*

BOWD: COLL: Sunday December 5. 1824.
My dear Father,

I arrived here yesterday afternoon, after a long ride in all the mud and misery of a rainy day. It rained almost unceasingly from morning till night, — snow and hail in the evening, — and to day we have a sharp no[r]th west wind. I take this early opportunity to write to you, because I wish to know fully your inclination with regard to the profession I am to pursue, when I leave college. For my part, I have already hinted to you what would best please me. I want to spend one year at Cambridge for the purpose of reading History, and of becoming familiar with the best authors in polite literature: whilst at the same time I can be acquiring a knowledge of the Italian Language, without an acquaintance with which, I shall be shut out from one of the most beautiful departments of letters. The French I mean to understand pretty thoroughly before I leave College. After leaving Cambridge I would attach myself to some literary periodical publication, by which I could maintain myself and still enjoy the advantages of reading. Now I do not think that there is anything visionary and chimerical in my plan thus far. The fact is, — and I will not disguise it in the least, for I think I ought not, — the fact is, I most eagerly aspire after future eminence in literature, my whole soul burns most ardently for it, and every earthly thought centers in it. There may be something visionary in *this,* but I flatter myself, that I have prudence enough to keep my enthusiasm from defeating its own object by too great haste. Surely there never was a better opportunity offered for the exertion of literary talent in our own country, than is now offered. To be sure, most of our literary men, thus far, have not been professedly so, until they have studied and entered the practice of Theology, Law, or Medicine. But this is evidently lost time.

I do believe that we ought to pay more attention to the opinion of Philosophers, that "nothing but nature can qualify a man for knowledge." [1] Whether Nature has given me any capacity for knowledge or not, she has at any rate given me a very strong predilection for literary pursuits, and I am almost confident in believing, that if I can ever rise in the world, it must be by the exercise of my talents in the wide field of literature. With such a belief I must say, that I am unwilling to engage in the study of the Law. Had I an inclination to become an orator, not this inclination, nor any application to the study of oratory, could constitute me one, unless Nature had given me a genius for that pursuit. This I think will hold good in its application to all the professions of life, and of course to literary pursuits. Here, then, seems to be the starting point; and I think it best for me to float out into the world upon that tide, and in that channel, which will the soonest bring me to my destined port; — and not to struggle against both wind and tide, and by attempting what is impossible, lose everything.

I have sent three pieces of Poetry to Mr. Parsons for the U.S. Literary Gazette, and he has thought so well of them as to invite me to become a regular correspondent. [2] I intended to have shown you his letters at Thanksgiving, but forgot to take them with me when I left Brunswick. I am very much pleased with the kindness he has already shown me, and am willing to leave to his own judgement the amount of compensation, which I am justly entitled to by my contributions, and which he promises shall be satisfactory. Mr Parsons says, — I speak it without vanity because I speak it to *you,* — that he is "well satisfied that my literary talents are of no ordinary character &c" — [3] and he judges from the three short pieces I have already sent him, and speaks with so much apparent sincerity, that I should be unwilling on that account, had I no other, to think that he spoke otherwise, than as he thought. I am sorry you did not see his letters and would send them to you now, if it were not necessary for me to write an answer during the week, and if I had not already given you the most interesting parts of the information they contain.

With regard to the Philadelphia Magazine, I am fearful that I

95

must relinquish all hope of reaping the harvest of my labours. If I recieve no compensation for the numerous contributions, which they have had from me, it will argue a sad want of generosity in them ||though I|| have still the consolation of thinking, that the benefit derived from writing these communications still remains for me. I suspect this last mentioned benefit is the only one I shall ever derive from these writings. It is rather unpleasant to be treated as I apprehend I shall be, but if the publisher of the Magazine has failed in his undertaking, I must attribute my own loss to the man's misfortune, and not his ill will.[4]

But it grows late, and I close by informing you that all at home were well, when I left them.

Yours affectionately
Henry W. Longfellow.

MANUSCRIPT: Longfellow Trust Collection. ADDRESS: Stephen Longfellow Esqr./ City of Washington. POSTMARK (*in script*): BRUNSWICK ME/DECR 6th/ FREE ENDORSEMENT: Henry W. Longfellow — /Dec. 5 and 18./26 [*corrected to "1824" by a second hand*]

1. Longfellow echoes here a philosophic statement from Goldsmith's *Citizen of the World,* No. 4: "The volume of nature is the book of knowledge."

2. Theophilus Parsons (1797–1882), afterward Dane Professor of Law at Harvard, edited the *United States Literary Gazette* during 1824. Longfellow's three poems, with their dates of publication in the *Gazette,* were: "Thanksgiving," November 15, 1825; "Autumnal Nightfall," December 1, 1824; and "Italian Scenery," December 15, 1824.

3. Parsons wrote in full: "Will you permit me to add, that I am equally well satisfied, that your literary talents are of no ordinary character, and that they have not received their highest culture. I think you will not be offended by my honesty in saying, that while all the pieces which you have sent me would be creditable and useful to any journal, they are susceptible of improvement from alterations calculated not to supply deficiencies but to remove imperfections" (letter dated November 17 [1824]).

4. Three of Longfellow's contributions to the *American Monthly Magazine* can be identified: a poem entitled "To the Novice of the Convent of the Visitation" and signed "H.W.L." (I [April 1824], 365); a dramatic sketch in verse called "The Poor Student" (*ibid.,* pp. 350–360); and "Youth and Old Age," an essay signed "L." ([May 1824] pp. 453–457). His authorship of the sketch and essay is verified in *Life,* I, 41. Unfortunately he received payment from McHenry only in praise, for the magazine failed at the end of the year. See remarks in Letter No. 59.

57. *To Stephen Longfellow*

Bowdoin College. December 18. [1824]

My Dear Father,

As nothing of any importance has transpired here since I last wrote you, and as I have not yet received an answer to my last letter, I have no materials of any kind from which to manufacture another epistle. I however write to let you know that we are both well, and that everything goes on smoothly. I have not received any letters from Portland since my return to college.[1] Of course you hear oftener from home than I do; at least I should hope you do. I suspect that they at home do not like to write, better than I do, and for my part, I utterly abominate it — that is letter-writing. I write so exceedingly slow, that it is really a waste of time to no purpose, — for neither I nor my correspondent can be the wiser for what is written. Though I am exceedingly fond of writing in general, yet I never did like to sit down patiently, and write long letters about nothing. The maxim is a true one — "The least said, — the soonest amended." And yet I can hardly account for this aversion to epistolary writing. I am not very fond of conversation, and have no great talent for it: — and those who excel in conversation generally excel in letter writing; since the exertion of the same talent is called for in each. However, when I can grasp the least intelligence that I think will interest you, I shall certainly write and communicate it; but when I have in reality nothing of importance to say, I may as well say what I do say, in as few words as possible, as to be more diffuse.

Your affectionate Son
Henry.

MANUSCRIPT: Longfellow Trust Collection. ADDRESS: Stephen Longfellow Esq./ City of Washington. POSTMARK (*in script*): BRUNSWICK ME/ DECR 20th/ FREE ENDORSEMENT: December 18. 1824

1. On December 4.

58. *To George Wadsworth Wells*

[Bowdoin College] December 18, 1824.
. . . The study of divinity I always regard with the greatest reverence; and I should not wish to enter so beautiful a vineyard, — however great the harvest and few the laborers, — unless I thought that by my care the holy vine would flourish more, and its branches yield more fruit. Men, indeed, have thrown a veil of mystery over this beautiful subject, and have made it difficult for the way-faring man to walk in the light and liberty of religion; and I am confident that human systems have done much to deaden the true spirit of devotion and to render religion merely speculative. Would it not be better for mankind if we should consider it as a cheerful and social companion, given us to go through life with us from childhood to the grave, and to make us happier here as well as hereafter; and not as a stern and

chiding task-master, to whom we must cling at last through mere despair, because we have nothing else on earth to which we can cling?

I conceive that if religion is ever to benefit us, it must be incorporated with our feelings, and become in every degree identified with our happiness. And hence I love that view of Christianity which sets it in the light of a cheerful, kind-hearted friend, and which gives its thoughts a noble and a liberal turn. The doctrines of men have long been taught as the doctrines of an infinitely higher authority; and many have been led to think that faith without works is an active and saving principle. Though these are my feelings upon this subject, and I think yours will be in unison with them, yet I am not willing to pursue the profession of Divinity. I shall earnestly endeavor to reside one year in Cambridge, before I conclude upon the course of my future life. Never fear the vicinity of Boston. I have the faculty of abstraction to a wonderful degree. . . .

Have you ever seen any numbers of the Westminster Review? If you can get a number by any means, either for love or money, pray send it to me, as I have a great longing to see the work.[1]

MANUSCRIPT: unrecovered; text from *Life*, I, 54–55.

1. The *Westminster Review* had recently been founded by Jeremy Bentham and James Mill as the organ of the philosophic radicals.

59. *To Stephen Longfellow*

Bowdoin College. December. 31. [1824]

My dear Father,

When I think of my last letter to you, I must confess that I feel rather ashamed of sending it, for I suspect that you would have been equally pleased had you received none at all. And yet I still consider it rather a difficult task to write a good letter: for it seems to me, that since the style of letters is about the same as that of polite conversation, the same faculties, which give excellence in the one, give it also in the other. This inability to write good letters without great exertion is probably the reason of my dislike to letter-writing in general, for very few persons are willing to be often engaged in that pursuit, wherein they can so evidently see their own inferiority. Practice, you will say, makes perfect, and of course makes easy what was difficult; — but how many does this very difficulty discourage in the outset! I will not acknowledge that I am conquered by this alone, but I always persuade myself that I *can* employ my time to greater advantage: — whether or not I *do,* is quite another question. But my opinion upon the subject is, that to be able to maintain a correspondence with ease and elegance is no mean acquisition, — I will go so far as to say — an acquisition almost indispensable to some situations in life. And moreover I believe that I should take greater pleasure in writing to friends if they as correspondents would give me fairer opportunities.

One thing, besides affording me the greatest pleasure, will evidently result to my great advantage. I refer to my correspondence with the Editor of the Literary Gazette — Theo. Parsons. He writes me pretty regularly, and expresses himself perfectly satisfied with my communications for his paper. He seems to be a true friend, and takes great interest in my "sayings and doings," — and moreover, though it is not modesty in me to say it, he speaks in high praise of my poetical powers; — and yet his candour with regard to the faults of my writings forbids me to think he speaks otherwise than as he thinks.

From Dr McHenry I have heard nothing since the 15th of Nov. I think it high time that I received some remuneration, and shall contribute nothing farther toward the support of his Magazine until I do receive it. The amount due is about $50 — more or less according as he holds to or retreats from his contract: — but I strongly suspect, and have very good grounds for the suspicion, — that I shall be something of a loser by this business. I do not accuse Dr McHenry himself, but certainly "there's something rotten in the state of Denmark." The Editor throws the whole blame upon the publisher, and *he* is as mute as you could wish any man to be. This is ungenerous, and unless some change takes place pretty soon I shall let him know exactly what I think about the business. He may tell me at once if he pleases, that he will not pay me, and then I shall know exactly what to do about it.

I am very desirous to hear your opinion of my project of residing a year at Cambridge. Even should it be found necessary for me to study a profession, I should think a twelve-months residence at Harvard before commencing the study of that profession would be exceedingly useful. Of Divinity, Medicine, and Law, I should choose the last. And whatever I do study ought to be engaged in with all my soul — for I *will* be eminent in something. The question then is, whether or not I could engage in the Law with all that eagerness which in these times is so very necessary to success? I fear that I could not! Ought I not then to choose another path in which I can go on with better hope of success? Let me reside one year at Cambridge, — let me study Belles Lettres, — and after that time has elapsed it will not require a spirit of prophecy to predict with some degree of certainty what kind of a figure I commence to make in the literary world. If I fail here, there is still time enough left for the study of a profession:

— and whilst residing at Cambridge I shall have acquired the knowledge of some foreign languages which will be, through life, of the greatest utility.

Pray write me soon upon this subject, for I am exceedingly desirous of knowing your opinion of the matter.[1]

Your affectionate Son
Henry W. Longfellow

MANUSCRIPT: Longfellow Trust Collection. ADDRESS: Stephen Longfellow. Esq./ City of Washington. POSTMARK (*in script*): BRUNSWICK ME/JANY 1st/ FREE ENDORSEMENT: H W. Longfellow/recd. — Jany 8. 1825/Dec. 31. 1824 ["*recd. —*" *and* "*Dec. 31. 1824*" *in Longfellow's hand*]

1. Excerpts from Stephen Longfellow's answer to this letter and Letter No. 56 can be found in *Life*, I, 56–57, and in *Young Longfellow*, pp. 59–60.

60. *To Theophilus Parsons*[1]

[Bowdoin College, Dec. 1824]

In your letter of the 23rd of December, which I received a few days since, you mention a previous letter of yours containing Mr. Sparks' determination respecting my review,[2] which you think I must ere this have received: but it has never reached me. From the slight reference which you made to this subject in your last letter, I am unable to gather what the determination of the editor of [the] North American is. However I shall soon know, either from your letter which I hope is not lost, or else from the Review itself which will soon reach me. With regard to my poem before the Peucinean Society, I think it will not do for the Gazette. It is too long for such a work — amounting to about 400 lines. The subject is "The Poetry of the Dark Ages" — which perhaps you will say is a better subject for a dissertation than a poem.[3] I take great pleasure in writing for the Gazette, and shall find no difficulty in contributing regularly, if such as I can write give you satisfaction. Those who attributed "Autumnal Nightfall" to Bryant paid me the highest compliment, but an exceedingly poor one to Mr Bryant. With this gentleman and noble poet I long to be acquainted — but I fear that years must elapse first. This is an unwelcome thought. I have two copies of his poems, and I admire them exceedingly. I will thank you for the names of the writers of each No. of the Gazette, for I think it adds greatly to[4]

Woods in Winter.

When Winter winds are piercing chill,
    And through the white-thorn blows the gale,
With solemn feet I tread the hill,
    That over-brows the lonely vale.

O'er the bare upland, and away
    Through the long reach of desert woods,
The embracing sunbeams chastely play,
    And gladden their deep solitudes.

On the gray maple's crusted bark
    Its tender shoots the hoar-frost nips; —
Whilst in the frozen fountain — hark! —
    His piercing beak the bittern dips.

Where twisted round the barren oak
    The summer vine in beauty clung,
And summer winds the stillness broke, —
    The crystal icicle is hung.

Where from their frozen urns mute springs
    Pour out the river's gradual tide,
Shrilly the skater's iron rings,
    And voices fill the woodland side.

Alas! — how chang'd from the fair scene
    When birds sang out their mellow lay: [5]

P.S.S. Fairfield, a gentleman from the Southern States, now teaching the languages as a private tutor in Portland, will shortly publish there a volume of original poems. The title is "Lays of Melpomene" which is a very lugubrious title indeed: — they embrace the "Sisters of St. Clara" — the scene of which is the Portuguese convent of St. Clara. I have seen but one extract from it, and cannot, you know, from that form any opinion of its merits.[6]

MANUSCRIPT: Henry E. Huntington Library.

    1. Only two sheets of this letter survive. The second sheet contains 5½ stanzas of Longfellow's contribution entitled "Woods in Winter" (published in the *United States Literary Gazette*, I, No. 20 [February 1, 1825], 316–317) and a postscript written at right angles to the poem. Inasmuch as Longfellow's remarks have been

crossed out, leaving the poetry clear, it is apparent that Parsons used the letter as printer's copy.

2. Longfellow had written an essay review of Thomas Colley Grattan's *Highways and Byways*, First Series (London, 1823), and sent it to Parsons for the *Gazette*. Unable to use it, Parsons had forwarded it to Jared Sparks of the *North American Review*, who also refused it. For details, see *Young Longfellow*, p. 62 and note.

3. This poem is unrecovered.

4. Page end. Continuation missing.

5. Remainder of poem missing.

6. Sumner Lincoln Fairfield (1803–1844), a New Englander, had been a tutor in Georgia and South Carolina. His *Poems* (New York, 1823), *Lays of Melpomene* (Portland, 1824), and *The Sisters of St. Clara* (Portland, 1825) were devastatingly reviewed in the *United States Literary Gazette*, I, No. 21 (February 15, 1825), 326–328. He later achieved notoriety by accusing Bulwer-Lytton of having been unduly influenced by his poem *The Last Night of Pompeii* (New York, 1832).

61. *To Stephen Longfellow*

Portland. January. 16. 1825.

My dear father,

More than one week of the vacation has already elapsed but Cousin's wedding[1] and succeeding merry-makings have detained me so long in Gorham, that I have passed but few days at home. You however hear enough of home from your other correspondents in the family. If not, you could easily prophecy, — and correctly too, — that domestic concerns went on decently and in order. The Legislature commenced their session on Wednesday the 5th. and the Colonel[2] revolves pretty rapidly in his orbit, according as the attraction here or at home predominates. I have not heard any speeches yet, and indeed they have had but two discussions of any kind — one on the *election* of *door keeper*, and the other on the expediency of giving the Governor and Council power to appoint the Register of Deeds, after two unsuccessful ballotings of the people.

We have received one letter from Stephen, by which he appears to have no very strong predilections for his sojourn in the land of promise.[3] Does not Mr Little the Unitarian minister at Washington publish a Magazine there?[4] If so, I wish you would purchase one no. for me — if you can obtain single nos.

Yours affectionately
H. W. Longfellow.

MANUSCRIPT: Longfellow Trust Collection. ADDRESS: Hon. Stephen Longfellow Esqr./City of Washington. POSTMARK: PORTLAND ME JAN 17 ENDORSEMENT: Henry W Longfellow/Jany 23. 1825/28 —

1. The wedding of Elizabeth Stephenson to Randolph A. L. Codman (see 41.2).

2. Col. Samuel Stephenson.

3. Because of his misconduct in college (see 44.4), Stephen had been suspended for four months and "required to pursue the studies of his class during the period of his suspension, vacation not excepted, under the care of the Rev. Mr. Fessenden of Kennebunkport, and further to bring such testimonial of his good conduct, as is required by the laws of the College" (Bowdoin Faculty Records, December 28, 1824). Since Rev. Joseph Palmer Fessenden (1792–1861) was an ardent champion of the temperance movement, the college authorities thought him an appropriate instructor.

4. Robert Little (d. 1827), an English dissenter, was the minister of the Unitarian congregation in Washington. In 1823–1824 he edited the *Washington Quarterly Magazine of Arts, Science, and Literature* during its brief life of two issues.

62. *To Stephen Longfellow*

Portland   January 24. 1825.

My dear father

Should I pursue my accustomed course of writing you once a week alternating with a short and long letter, you would this week be entitled to the latter. But as I generally sit down to write all my letters without in the least premeditating or taking thought what I shall say, the length and substance of my letters depend upon the momentary inspiration, by which my pen moves. From the general tenor of your last letter — that is as far as my memory serves me, for I have not my files at hand — from the general tenor of your last letter, it seems to be your fixed desire, that I should choose the profession of the Law for the business of my life. I believe that I have already mentioned to you that I did not wish to enter immediately upon any profession. I am very much rejoiced to hear that you accede so readily to my proposition of studying general literature for one year at Cambridge. My grand object in doing this will be to gain as perfect a knowledge of the French and Italian languages as can be gained by study without travelling in France and Italy, though to tell the truth I intend to visit both before I die. The advantages of this step are obvious, — the means of accomplishing an end so desirable exertion must supply. I am afraid that you begin to think me rather chimerical in many of my ideas, and that I am ambitious of becoming a "rara avis in terris."[1] But you must acknowledge the propriety and usefulness of aiming high — at something which it is impossible to overshoot — perhaps to reach. The fact is, — what I have previously said to you upon the subject leads me to exhibit myself without disguise. I have a most voracious appetite for knowledge. To its acquisition I will sacrifice anything; and I now lament most bitterly the defects of my early education, that are attributable in part to myself and in part to my instructors. My advantages have been from infancy almost boundless

— and by reflecting but one moment I see how awfully I have neglected them. I knew neither the value of time nor of these advantages. I now refer to the years which I passed at the Academy. Of having misspent the portion of my College life already passed I cannot reproach myself so severely, although I have left undone a multitude of things that ought to have been done. But fortunately for me, as I grow older I grow more studious. Nothing delights me more than reading and writing: — and although this assertion, unqualified as I have made it, may savour of vanity, yet I feel the truth of it: and nothing could induce me to relinquish the pleasures of literature — little as I have as yet tasted them. But this is a wide digression. And in returning to our former subject I can only say that of all professions — I would say of the three profesions which are sometimes called the learned professions — I should prefer the Law. I am far from being a fluent speaker; — but practice must serve as a talisman, where talent is wanting. I can be a lawyer, for some lawyers are mere simpletons. This will support my *real* existence, literature an *ideal* one.

I purchased last evening a beautiful pocket edition of Sir. Wm Jones's letters[2] and have just finished reading them. Eight Languages he was critically versed in — eight more he read with a dictionary and there were still twelve more which he had studied less perfectly, but which were not wholly unknown to him; making in all twenty eight languages to which he had given his attention. ||I ha||ve somewhere seen or heard the observation, that as many languages as a person acquired, so many times was he a man. Mr Jones was equal to about sixteen men, according to that observation.

I am afraid you will accuse me of more than usual carelessness in this epistle: — but I shall plead the shortness of time in which I have written it and my desire of acquiring facility in writing. I must learn to dispatch a larger number of letters in the course of an evening, than I now do. A letter from you whenever your business will permit will be very gratifying to

Your affectionate son
H. W. Longfellow.

MANUSCRIPT: Longfellow Trust Collection.   ADDRESS: Hon. Stephen Longfellow./ City of Washington.   POSTMARK: PORTLAND ME JAN 24   ENDORSEMENT: Henry W Longfellow/Jany 30. 1825

1. "A rare bird on the earth." Juvenal, *Satires*, vi, 165.
2. Volume the First (London, 1821). This was Vol. XLV of John Sharpe's *Select Edition of the British Prose Writers*. The book, with Longfellow's autograph, is in the Longfellow House. Jones (1746–1794), a distinguished philologist and jurist, had combined a "real" and an "ideal" existence in the manner of Longfellow's ambition.

63. *To Theophilus Parsons*

Portland. January. 27. 1825.

My dear sir,

I here inclose you the first two Nos. of a series of Essays which I promised you long since. The title you are well aware is not original, for Sir R. Blackmore who plied so forcibly upon an unsinning world his Epic engine, once published a series of periodical essays under this title: still I do not think this any objection to my using it again. I have been delayed by sickness and several other circumstances from sending them sooner: and would have sent you four Nos. instead of two, had it not been for the further delay that must have been occasioned. No. 3. is "American Literature" — or rather is to be "American Literature" — for it is not yet written. No. four — is written. It is "Reminiscenses of Genius." I will send them soon. I think you may venture to publish one no. — a fortnight — that is should you be sufficiently pleased with them to publish at all.[1] Pray do not think me vain; — as you certainly will if you apply all the remarks made relative to "The Author" in No. 1. strictly to myself: — this you must recollect is my assumed character.[2] With regard to my "review" — I will thank you to inclose it in a cover, and send it to me by my classmate Mellen, who is now in Boston. If you do not meet with him, or some one else who will bring it to me, let it suffer martyrdom by fire which it richly deserves.[3] My dear sir, do be more critical with my compositions: for although criticisms are in general very unpleasant, yet in private they are both more beneficial and less painful than in public: — and I assure you that yours have been beneficial to me — at least I think they have been so.

I wish you to request Cummings, Hilliard &c[4] to procure for me the works of Thom. Chatterton. I do not inclose the money because I know not the cost of the work: — I will however send it as soon [as] I get the volumes.

Who writes "Letters from a Traveller"? Who is "Agnes"? With "G." who wrote "The Song of the Spirits" in one of your late nos. I am very intimately acquainted. Has he ceased writing for you, or has he changed his signature? I have a thousand other questions to ask you, but desist for fear of tiring you.[5] Write as soon as possible, for I am impatient to hear from you.

Yours very respectfully.

H. W. Longfellow. —

P.S. Chatterton's works I want as soon as they can be obtained, and I will be much obliged to you, if you will be kind enough to speak to

Cummings Hilliard and co. when you next see them and request them to hasten the business.

MANUSCRIPT: Boston Public Library. ADDRESS: Theophilus Parsons. Esqr./Taunton./Bristol County./Mass. POSTAL NOTE (*by Longfellow*): 2. sheets. ANNOTATION: Note — if there is anything in this for us please inform us. L. Little.[6]

1. Longfellow published five essays in the *Gazette,* using Sir Richard Blackmore's title *The Lay Monastery:* "The Author," I, No. 22 (March 1, 1825), 347–349; "Winter Months," I, No. 24 (March 15, 1825), 376–377; "The Literary Spirit of Our Country," II, No. 1 (April 1, 1825), 24–28; "Poets and Common-sense Men," II, No. 5 (June 1, 1825), 182–186; and "Valentine Writing," III, No. 1 (October 1, 1825), 25–28. "Reminiscences of Genius" appeared in the *Portland Advertiser* for May 27, 1825.

2. In his first essay Longfellow assumed the character of a solitary, melancholy, quiet man of letters, "a truant from society" who had turned from "the troubled world of realities to an ideal world" of his own.

3. See 60.2.

4. Boston publishers and booksellers.

5. The questions, of course, concern contributors to the *United States Literary Gazette.* "G" was George William Gray Browne, who was then studying law in Portland and conducting a column, "The Pedestrian," in the *Portland Advertiser.*

6. Unidentified. Presumably an associate of Parsons on the *United States Literary Gazette.*

64. *To Stephen Longfellow*

Portland. February. 7. 1825.[1]

My dear Father,

I received, some days since, your letter of January 28, and should have answered ere this the interesting propositions, which it contains, had not the arrival of my classmate Weld from Brunswick caused a short delay. Your good advice I shall hereafter follow, and have therefore sent no poetry for the next number of the Gazette, — though I have a piece written for that purpose.[2] Your opinion upon the subject of my writing coincides in a great measure with that of Mr Parsons, the editor of the United States Literary Gazette, who says that I must use more care, or rather, that it will be for my own advantage to use more care, than my communications generally exhibit. All this is very candid in him, and so far from displeasing me, is very acceptable advice. For although it may seem paradoxical, that any reference to one's defects can be pleasant to the individual, yet the difficulty vanishes, when this reference is followed by an expression of the belief, that his own exertion can remedy the defect. You need not be apprehensive that my feelings will be wounded by anything, that you deem it just to say in the way of criticism; — but, on the contrary, it will please as well as improve me, to hear what you think particularly needs improving.

You observe that you have heard nothing from me with regard to the reception of a letter from you in answer to two former ones of mine. This letter to which you refer and which you supposed has passed me and gone to Brunswick, was received by me, and answered without any particular mention of its arrival, and without any reference to the date. Perhaps the last letter which you received from me, was not the last which I have written previous to this. The date of my last was January 23rd: [3] and I believe it contained some remarks upon the plan of residing a year at Cambridge. I received a letter from George Wells, in which he observes, that the government of Harvard College are very willing to receive graduates from other colleges to reside there, with the privilege of attending all Lectures, and the use of the Library. "The only charge is $1.00 per quarter for the Library. Room Rent is from 30 to 60 dollars per year, and board from 2 to 3 dollars per week." I do not know whether I could obtain a room ready furnished or not. If I go there, I should prefer it to one, which I should be obliged to furnish myself. The expenses for one year will not be very great.

For example. Board at 2.50 would be $130.00
Room rent 50.00
Library 4.00
$184.00

This I suppose to be about a fair calculation, — neither the highest nor the lowest — but a medium between the two. However I presume that the execution of the plan depends a great deal upon circumstances and if the project fails I shall not be inconsolable.

I have written again to the Editor of the American Monthly Magazine, but without success: — I cannot get a word from him. I strongly suspect that there is some plan on foot to defraud me, and I hardly know how to act. What would you do, if you were in my situation? Cannot the publisher of the Magazine, or rather the proprietors, be compelled to fulfil their engagements with their correspondents?

With regard to Mr [Robert] Little's Magazine, as the publication is not continued, it will hardly be worth while to purchase the two numbers, which you mention are already issued.

Our state Legislature have made no donation to Bowdoin College this session. The petition was for 3000 dollars annually for 3 years: that it might be in their power to build a new chapel and establish ‖a pro‖fessorship of modern Languages: but so far from granting it, the Legislature refuse to grant us anything whatever. They think Bowdoin rich enough already: and one member of the house observed, — to use his own expression — that "they manage things there so *slick,* that the college saves annually three thousand dollars!" But it appears from facts that Bowd. College receives but $80 after the balance of receipts and expenditures — at least the remainder is very small.

It has been currently reported here, that Henry Clay has been shot in a duel. Is the report true? [4]

Yours affectionately
Henry W. Longfellow.

MANUSCRIPT: Longfellow Trust Collection. ADDRESS: Hon. Stephen Longfellow./ Washington. POSTMARK: PORTLAND ME FEB 9 ENDORSEMENT: Henry W Longfellow/Feby 15 —/1825 [*year in a second hand*]

1. Longfellow mistakenly wrote "1824."

2. Stephen Longfellow had cautioned his son against rushing into print. "You should make it a rule never to send an effusion of the moment to the press, till the ardor and feelings, with which it was written, have subsided."

3. Longfellow should have written January 24th (see Letter No. 62).

4. When Clay announced his support of the presidential candidacy of John Quincy Adams, George Kremer — a Jackson follower — leveled a "corrupt bargain" charge against him in an insulting letter in the *Columbian Observer* of Philadelphia on January 28th. Clay responded with what amounted to a challenge in the *National Intelligencer* on January 31. The duel was not fought, although the New York papers reported that it had taken place and that Clay had been killed.

65. *To Theophilus Parsons*

Bowdoin College. February 20. 1825

Dear Sir,

By the first mail after my arrival here I received your very acceptable letter of the 15th, and use all diligence to answer it, and at the same time forward you a few lines of Poetry. I have no prose on hand, and as our recitations commence tomorrow and our lectures on Tuesday, I think it extremely doubtful whether I shall find leisure to prepare any before the 28th. I have been much disappointed in not being able to send you the third and fourth numbers of the Lay Monastery, which I promised in my last letter to forward without delay: — but a visit from a classmate rendered it impossible. My wish to send them to you so soon was caused by the fear, that the first two numbers were not a sufficient guarantee for succeeding ones, and that you would desire to have more in readiness before you ventured to publish any. I was very glad to see Mr Sparks' letter, and thank you for sending it to me.[1] The tidings of your "abdication" were not so welcome to me. Will Mr Carter[2] correspond with me? I should like to make some contract with him. By the way, Cummings and Hilliard have sent me, with the last Gazette, their bill — $5.00. It would be very convenient for me, if you could pay them from what you are to allow me for my writings; and moreover it would save the trouble of sending money by mail. With regard to the want of accurate keeping in the Lay Monastery — you misapprehended me in supposing, that I meant the "care of the library" to be the bequest of a *"deceased"* uncle.[3] Perhaps I used the word "bequeath" improperly. All that I intended to express was, that he had *given* me the care of his library — he being still alive — tho' dead to such cares as this.

A Song of Savoy.[4]

As the dim twilight shrouds
    The mountain's purple crest,
And Summer's white and folded clouds
    Are glowing in the West,
Loud shouts come up the rocky dell
And voices hail the evening bell.

Faint is the goatherd's song,
    And sighing comes the breeze:
The silent river sweeps along
    Amid its bending trees, —
And the full moon shines faintly there,
And music fills the evening air.

Beneath the waving firs
    The tinkling cymbals sound;
And as the wind the foliage stirs,
    I see the dancers bound
Where the green branches, arch'd above,
Bend over this fair scene of love.

And he is there, that sought
    My young heart long ago! —
But he has left me — though I thought
    He ne'er could leave me so.
Ah! lovers' vows — how frail are they! —
And his — were made but yesterday.

Why comes he not? — I call
   In tears upon him yet! —
'Twere better ne'er to love at all,
   Than love, and then forget!
Why comes he not? — Alas! I should
Reclaim him still if weeping could.

But see — he leaves the glade,
   And bec[k]ons me away:
He comes to seek his Savoy [5] maid! —
   I cannot chide his stay. —
Glad sounds along the valley swell,
And voices hail the evening bell.

H. W. L.

Dirge over a nameless grave [6]

[1]

By yon still river, where the wave
   Is winding slow at evening's close,
The beech upon a nameless grave
   Its sadly-moving shadow throws.

[2]

O'er the fair woods the sun looks down
   Upon the many-twinkling leaves,
And twilight's mellow shades are brown,
   Where darkly the green turf upheaves.

3

The river glides in silence there,
   And hardly waves the sapling tree:
Sweet flowers are springing, and the air
   Is full of balm, — but where is she! —

4

They bade her love the son of pride,
   And leave the joys she cherish'd long:
She loved but one, — and would not hide
   A love so near allied to song. [7]

[5]

And months went sadly on, — and years: —
And she was wasting day by day:
At length she died, — and many tears
    Were shed, that she should pass away.

[6]

Then came a gray old man, and knelt
    With bitter weeping by her tomb: —
And others mourned for him, who felt
    That he had seal'd a daughter's doom.

7.

The funeral train has long past on,
    And time wip'd dry the weeper's[8] tear! —
Farewell — lost daughter![9] — there is one
    That mourns thee yet, — and he is here.

H. W. L.

I see that a Second Series of High Ways and By Ways has been published. If I can get the work in good season, however singular you may think my conduct to be after a failure, I intend to write a review of the volumes just issued and to publish the article, in connection with my former one, in the New York "Atlantic Magazine" — if the Editor will take the writings. A review of the second series would be a good pretence for bringing forward the first at so late a period. I am afraid you will think me a sort of resolute mad-man, when you come to hear this design — and I fear it will take a *very* long experience to make me sage. I wish you would write to me without *any* delay, when you receive this letter, and let me know what you think of my resolution; as I shall be governed in a great measure by your opinion upon this subject; and if I act at all, I must act immediately. Who signs "J" in the Gazette?[10]

I remain yours very respectfully
H. W. Longfellow.

MANUSCRIPT: Henry E. Huntington Library. ADDRESS: Theophilus Parsons. Esq./ Taunton./Mass. ANNOTATION (*by Parsons*): Poetry for 23 and 26 —/Col. Metcalf[11] —/Please hand this letter to Mr J.G. Carter after you have done with it./T. P — ENDORSEMENT: Brunswick Me/Feby 22

1. See *Life*, I, 60.
2. James Gordon Carter (1795-1849), an educational reformer, succeeded Parsons as editor of the *Gazette*.

3. The fictional uncle referred to appears in "The Author" (see 63.1).

4. Printed in the *United States Literary Gazette*, I, No. 24 (March 15, 1825), 379. A marginal note, in Parsons' hand, reads "For No 24."

5. Longfellow's note at this point: "Is it proper to throw the accent of the word *Sá*-voy upon the first syllable as I have here done, or should you say Sa-*voy*? If the latter be correct, it will be necessary to substitute some such word as 'mountain' in its place." Parsons made the correction to "mountain."

6. Printed in the *Gazette*, I, No. 23 (March 15, 1825), 365. Parsons' marginal note reads "For No 23."

7. Parsons corrected the stanza as follows: "They bade her wed a son of pride,/ And leave the hopes she cherish'd long:/She loved but one, — and would not hide/A love which knew no thought of wrong."

8. Corrected by Parsons to "father's."

9. Corrected by Parsons to "maiden."

10. In a letter of Feb. 25, Parsons advised sending the review to Carter. It was published in the *Gazette*, II, No. 4 (May 15, 1825), 121–129. See *Young Longfellow*, pp. 355–356. "J" is identified as "J. A. Jones, a lawyer, now in New York."

11. Eliab Wright Metcalf (1781–1835), a colonel in the state militia and head of E. W. Metcalf & Co., printers of the *Gazette*. Metcalf used this letter as printer's copy.

66. *To Stephen Longfellow*

Bowdoin College   February. 20. 1825.

My dear Father

I arrived here day before yesterday, and as our recitations do not commence immediately I have leisure enough to answer any letters from you, if indeed I had any to answer. But it so happens, as it has very frequently happened before, that you have now been long my debtor. I had a letter from Mr Parsons yesterday, in which he informs me of his intention of relinquishing his labors as Editor of the United States Lit. Gaz. on the first of April next. Mr James G. Carter is to take his place, who has lately published a work upon the Free Schools of New England.[1] Mr Parsons says he is a man of great literary merit, and he will doub[t]less do as well in the Editorial department of the Gazette as Mr Parsons has done. But the best of it is, he desired Mr P. — when he wrote to me, to request a continuance of my contributions for him. This is rather flattering to my feelings, and perhaps it would have been better for me, had he said nothing about it; though it may not be so. McHenry, the Editor of the A.M. Magazine turns out to be a scoundrel. He has all along until this time been telling me that he was not proprietor of the magazine, but merely editor, and that I must not draw upon him for my pay, but upon a certain other gentleman, who, he said, *was* the proprietor. But I saw a Mr [Sumner Lincoln] Fairfield in Portland, who was personally acquainted with him in Philadelphia, and who was also a writer in the Magazine.

He never received anything for his contributions, and furthermore says that McHenry was the proprietor of the work. Now this is very scandalous; — for it is not only cheating me but it is likewise injuring the character of the gentleman, whom he has stated to be proprietor. If you happen to see him when you return through Philadelphia, I wish you would tell him that he is "in danger of the law," — though I would by no means have you think, that I consider the affair of sufficient consequence to induce me to wish to sue the fellow. All the care I have about the business is to expose such a mean attempt to defraud.

I have written some prose Essays for the U.S.L.G. the first of which is to be published in the next number — no. 22. They are entitled "The Lay Monastery" and I am going to continue them in numbers, — writing occasionally as I have leisure. Perhaps you will say that I had better write them and not publish them; — but there is to me, in publishing, this evident advantage, apart from all others, viz. that I take greater care to finish, as far as I have power, every thing that is to go before the world, than I do my private writings. I know that there are a great many disadvantages in publishing too frequently, and I intend to be as prudent as possible.

February 23rd.

I have defer[r]ed sealing my letter until this time, that I might say a word or two about the inauguration of our Professors, which took place to day. The Boards were of course in session, and Dr Nichols, Judge Mellen and Charles Davies were here from Portland.[2] Mr Newman was made professor of Rhetorick and Oratory, and pronounced an Oration upon those subjects. Mr Packard was inaugurated as Professor of Languages. His oration was upon the erroneous methods of teaching the languages, which are now universally pursued in our schools, — for instance, the requiring the pupil to commit to memory the rules of grammar, whose application he cannot understand at the time &c. Mr Upham's Oration was upon the science of metaphysicks, of which branch he was made professor. We have our first recitation to him tomorrow noon.[3]

Do you wish me to attend Dr Wells' Lectures upon Anatomy? I thought from what you formerly said upon the subject, that such was your wish and I have consequently attended the first of the course. His second lecture is tomorrow. If you desire me to continue, it will be necessary to send me a certificate to that amount.[4]

Your affectionate Son
Henry W. Longfellow.

MANUSCRIPT: Longfellow Trust Collection. ADDRESS: Hon. Stephen Longfellow/ Washington City. POSTMARK (*in script*): BRUNSWICK ME/FEBY 24th/FREE

1. Carter's *Letters to the Hon. William Prescott, LL.D., on the Free Schools of New England, with Remarks on the Principles of Instruction* (Boston, 1824) first developed the idea of a normal school for teachers.

2. Ichabod Nichols (1784–1859), minister of the First Church, Portland, and Prentiss Mellen were trustees of Bowdoin College; Charles Stewart Daveis (1788–1865), a prominent Portland attorney, was a member of the Board of Overseers.

3. For Newman, see 38.1. In "Morituri Salutamus" Longfellow refers to Alpheus Spring Packard (1798–1884) as his last surviving teacher. Thomas Cogswell Upham (1799–1872) is praised and characterized in Letter No. 69.

4. In a letter dated February 27, 1825, Stephen Longfellow approved his son's attending these lectures.

67. *To Zilpah Longfellow*

Bowdoin College   February. 26. 1825.[1]

My dear Mother,

I presume that Mr Kelly informed you on his return of our safe arrival here on Friday evening. We have had but few recitations thus far and of course a good deal of leisure: but the number of our recitations is increased by two extra ones per week, which arrangement nobody seems to like. The inauguration of our three Professors took place on Wednesday, when each delivered an Oration upon some branch of science connected with his department of instruction. The performances were very excellent.

I have had another attack of the influenza, and have not felt well since my return to College. I am dull and stupid and everything else that is uncomfortable. However I make shift to keep along in my studies and to attend two lectures a day of an hour each, — the one on Anatomy by Dr Wells, and the other on Chemistry by Professor Cleaveland. I have received no letters from Washington since my arrival here, though I have got three numbers of the National Journal. I have had an opportunity of sending directly to Kennebunk, and have forwarded those books to Stephen, which we shall study this term, which will be a very busy term.

I sent by Mr Kelly for paper and quills and so forth; — but as I have not received them yet, I am apprehensive that he forgot to deliver his message. I sent also for Rousseau, but this I do not want. What I now wish for are a quire of letter paper, a bunch of quills and half a quire of common writing paper — together with the large french grammar that has "Henry Wadsworth's" name in it, and to be still more minute, is covered with blue paper, and gnawed a little by mice.[2] I left it in the Office; — and this is as full and correct a description as I can give of the book, since the Author's name, a very long hard name, has escaped my memory.

I send, with this, one of my shirts and the two collars to have them altered. I wish you would cut them as they are marked with the pencil-marks upon the side of the collar where the buttons are sewed on. I will thank you to finish them and return them as soon as possible as I shall be in want of them.

Mr Weld is very well, and if he were here would — I presume, send his respects to you and the rest of the family.[3] I dined with him yes-terday on Venison, which is a great rarity here, this being the first that has been brought to market in this village for a great many years.

I am now going down to the Post Office with the hope of getting a letter from Washington, and shall not therefore seal this letter until my return, that perchance I may give you a word or two from the Little City.

Your affectionate son
H. W. L.

Nothing at the Office!

March. 2nd.

I have waited long and patiently for the return of Uncle P. from his eastern excursion; but since I have neither seen nor heard of him as returning homewards, I have come to the conclusion to send my letter by mail, and the little bundle of shirts by the first private oppor-tunity. It seems to me that uncle must ere this have taken the thief, as the stage-driver told me that he had seen a person answering uncle's description of the runaway, upon the route between Hallowell and Brunswick.[4]

If you choose to read some of my prose writing, look into the U.S. Literary Gazette for March. 1. — No. 22. — under the title of "The Lay Monastery" and you will find the first number of a series of essays, which I am writing occasionally for your amusement and my own profit.

There is no wood to be had from the College Wood Yard and very little from my wood-closet, so that I will thank you to send me without delay $3.00 to buy a cord of that necessary article.

You will get the U.S. Lit. Gaz. at Hyde's book Store.[5]

Your affectionate Son
H. W. L.

MANUSCRIPT: Longfellow Trust Collection. ADDRESS: Mrs. Zilpah Longfellow/ Portland POSTMARK (*in script*): BRUNSWICK/MARCH 3/6 ENDORSEMENT: Henry. Feby. 1824. Brunswick [*date corrected to* "1825"]

1. Longfellow mistakenly wrote "1824."

2. Henry Wadsworth (1785-1804), the uncle for whom Longfellow had been named, fell in action aboard the fireship *Intrepid* during the Tripolitan War. The grammar has been identified by Carl L. Johnson ("Longfellow's Beginnings in Foreign Languages," *New England Quarterly*, XX [September 1947], 321-323) as Dr. M. Guelfi Borzacchini's *The Parisian Master; or, A New and Easy Method for Acquiring a Perfect Knowledge of the French Language in a Short Time* (Bath, England, 1789).

3. Eugene Weld (39.2) had spent his February vacation with the Longfellows in Portland. Zilpah Longfellow had written to her husband on February 7, "I know not what makes Henry so fond of him," but he seems to have been one of Longfellow's intimate friends in college.

4. Zilpah Longfellow explains this incident in a letter to her husband, dated Tuesday evening [February 22, 1825]: "Brother Peleg [Wadsworth] came in before breakfast, very much fatigued, with riding all night; he was in pursuit of a young man, one of their family, who had decamped the preceeding morning taking with him Papa's horse, and my brothers best suit of cloathes even to his boots and gloves."

5. William Hyde kept a book and stationery store at 3 Mussey's Row, Portland.

68. *To Zilpah Longfellow*

Bowdoin College   March. 13. [1825]

My dear Mother,

I enquired of Mr. Everett[1] for the bundle which according to your letter was sent me by him, but he says that he never received any from you. By the way, your letter had a threefold postage, by reason of the little strip of paper in it, — pray be more economical. But by all means send the bundle *without any delay,* for I am absolutely destitute of socks etc. — and paper — fit for a letter — as you see. You will have to send it by the Stage; — tommorrow morning if possible. I wish you would send to Hartshorn's and tell him to make me a pair of thick calf-skin boots, — no, that will not do — he has not the measure — no matter: I hardly think I shall need them. If you will make me a pair of gaiters, they will answer all purposes. I heard from S. [Stephen] a day or two since. He appears to be in very good spirits. Farewell.

Your affect. Son
Henry.

MANUSCRIPT: Longfellow Trust Collection.

1. Ebenezer Everett (1788-1869), a lawyer of Brunswick, was at this time a member of the Board of Overseers of Bowdoin College.

69. *To Zilpah Longfellow*

Bowdoin College   April 6. 1825

My dear Mother,

I take this opportunity to write you a line, in order to introduce to you our new Professor, Mr Upham, with whom you will doubtless be much pleased. No one of our government, — no — not even a student is so universally admired in college, as he is. His "sayings and doings" are altogether different from anything we have hitherto met with from our instructers and officers of college. He associates with us as if he were one of us — he visits us at our rooms and we visit him at his: — so that the formality, which has heretofore existed between the officers and students of college is fast wearing out of use, and giving place to a more agreeable, — and doubtless a profitable, — familiarity. He has politely offered to be the bearer of any letters, and I have given him this, that you may see him: — of course inviting him to call.

J. D. Kinsman will be up on Fast-day — please to send me some more letter paper. By the way, I have followed up Papa's injunctions of frequent writing so closely, that my postages of this term already amount to $1.50. All kinds of letters very thankfully received, tho' not very punctually attended to

by your affectionate son
Henry.

MANUSCRIPT: Longfellow Trust Collection. PUBLISHED: Lawrance Thompson, "Longfellow's Original Sin of Imitation," *The Colophon*, I, N.S. (1935), 104.

70. *To Stephen Longfellow*

Bowdoin College   April. 7. 1825

My dear father,

I received by to-day's mail your letter of the 5th, together with the New Monthly Magazine. The number of the European Mag. that I took from the Por[t]land Library for Preble was charged upon the books to him, as I understood it at the time: and I suspect that Mr Sewall will find it so. The number is at Mrs Preble's, and Edward will write immediately about it to her.[1]

I am sorry that you did not sooner mention to me the circumstance of my New York Statesman being paid for up to the 20th. About a week since I sent the Editors $2.00 — the last half-year's subscription, and requested them to stop the paper at the expiration of that term. It is not very interesting and I do not wish to continue it longer.

I suppose the Editors will refund the $2. ere long, at least I hope they will.

I fear that Mr Fairfield — the Editor of the "Northern Iris" of which I sent you the first number, will not be able to remain here much longer. On the night of the fire here, he was ordered into the ranks by Robert Dunlap, and in offering resistance to the RtHon: — was pushed down. He took notice in his next paper of the conduct of the firewards on the occasion, and said something about "a tall, clay-coloured, irishman-looking fellow" — in reference to Mr Dunlap. This publick notice of the affair has caused a considerable excitement in town, and added to the former prejudice existing against Mr Fairfield will go far to drive him away from this place, or at least to render his stay here very uncomfortable to him, and disagreeable to others. I wish he had never come here: — his paper is a poor weak thing — in a decline, and soon to die, — for want of patronage.[2]

I have just come from Mr Jos. McKeen's store: — whilst there, he handed me the inclosed receipt, and I paid the bill. I thought it hardly worth while to trouble him for the items of the account: — but have obtained the bills of Mr Pierce and Mr John McKeen with the items specified as you requested. I here inclose them.[3]

Your affectionate Son

Henry.

MANUSCRIPT: Longfellow Trust Collection. ADDRESS: Hon. Stephen Longfellow. Esq./Portland.

1. William Bartlett Sewall (1782-1869), a Portland attorney, had asked Stephen Longfellow to obtain the magazine from his son. Longfellow here explains its whereabouts. Edward and his widowed mother, Mary Deering Preble, lived in a mansion adjoining the Wadsworth-Longfellow house.

2. Sumner Lincoln Fairfield edited *The Northern Iris,* a Brunswick monthly, for six months in 1825. Joseph Griffin said of it, "It was edited with ability; but, depending on unsolicited patronage, it was not remunerative" (Griffin, *History of the Press of Maine,* p. 83). Fairfield, always an unpopular gentleman, hastened his journal's demise by offending such substantial citizens as Robert Pinckney Dunlap (1794-1859), a lawyer and member of the Maine Senate.

3. The receipt and bills, which concerned Stephen's college expenses, are missing. Both Joseph McKeen (1787-1865) and John McKeen (1789-1861) were Brunswick merchants (see 36.3). Pierce was apparently another storekeeper.

71. *To Zilpah Longfellow*

Bowd. Coll. April. [21][1] 1825.

My dear Mother,

Your frequent rebukes in reference to my negligence in writing have not been to me vain chidings: — I have felt them all, though you may have had reason to think otherwise.[2] With all my usual delinquency, however, I should have answered your letter of the 13th before this, had I not received on Monday "Chatterton's Works," for which I had some time since sent to Boston. It is an elegant work in three large Octavo volumes, of 536. pages each,[3] and since Monday noon I have read the greater part of two of them — besides attending two Lectures a day of an hour each and three recitations of the same length together with my study-hours for preparation. Of course I have had no time for writing letters: and this is my excuse for not writing you sooner. With Chatterton I am of course very much pleased. You will find a short account of his Life and the faults and follies of his genius, in Ree[s]'s Cyclopaedia[4] and I wish I could here spare room to copy something from his poems: as I cannot without relinquishing another plan I have in view. I shall wait another opportunity. If you will turn to "Knox's Essays" No. 144. you will find there a dolorous prose-ditty upon Chatterton, which I must confess to be rather affectedly pathetic and sentimental.[5]

In order to give a little more interest to my letters, I shall occasionally take the liberty of transcribing a tale or essay or something of the kind, which you may read or not as you fancy it. The first — of which I can send you but part at this time, — was suggested by Chatterton's Life. It is a

Reminiscence of a neglected Genius.

"This was his chamber: 'tis as when he left it."
Rogers' Italy.[6]

If ever a man died of melancholy, it was — —. But his melancholy had nothing of gloom nor of moroseness in it: it was but a shadow of intellectual light, mellowing and beautifying the features of his mind. He was an enthusiast: — but all his fine enthusiasm has gone out in death. Friendship asks "where is he?" There is a little cemetery in the hollows of his native hills, and within it a new and a nameless grave: — he is there at rest forever. It is a retired and quiet spot, and many trees spread a consecrat||ing peace|| over the place of graves. I have often strayed in the religious shades of its cool avenues, and meditated amid the mute but eloquent records of mortality. There is something in the grave of friendship, that often draws us to it. It has a voice, which speaks to the mind's ear with a thrilling emphasis, till the memory of the dead sometimes becomes more attractive than the beauty of the living. The quiet of the place steals into the heart, like the peace of holy-time: and as I stand within this sanctuary of the dead, and reflect what silent dissolution is going on around me, and how dust is gradually loosening itself from the forms into which nature had moulded it, and mingling with dust again, — I forget the world and all its cares. I feel the religion of the place — for here is set a limit to humanity — here the afflicted have found consolation and the weary rest. What a lesson is here for pride — that it must soon lay down side by side with the humblest child of clay! What a lesson for ambition — that a few feet of earth must ere long be the boundary of its possessions! What a lesson for passion, — that the grave is so cold and senseless, and that friend and foe are at rest together.

In a grave-yard I never feel alone. The green sward of the earth covers the waste and corruption of the dead, and my mournful fancy peoples anew the solitary places of the tombs. The dead are there! — but a veil is drawn over every countenance. The dead are there! — but they are revived in thought and live in memory. The multitudes that are gathered together in the voiceless chambers of the grave were once active in the theatre of life, and full of vital energies. But childhood has here forgotten the hilarity of its young days, — the vigor of maturer years has grown weak and inactive, — and age has lain down his staff and mantle at the last altar, to which the feet of man can ever come. Death is the common lot — the common level! A little handful of dust — a little measure of mouldering clay! The leaf that falls in autumn upon the grave is a memento of our mortality, and the sculptured stone which friendship erects over the grave of the departed to pe[r]petuate their memory, frail as it is, outlives the forming hand.[7]

When I write again I shall continue this, and you will then be able to see the application of the motto, which you cannot possibly do at present by any human foresight.

Yours
H. W. L.

MANUSCRIPT: Longfellow Trust Collection. ADDRESS: Hon. S. Longfellow./Portland. POSTMARK (*in script*): BRUNSWICK/APRIL 21st FREE ANNOTATION (*by Longfellow*): Free

1. The date is established by a marginal note on the manuscript, which reads: "Brunswick, April 21st."

2. Zilpah Longfellow's impatience with her son's silence had overflowed in a letter to Henry of December 26, 1824: "I should really be pleased to have a letter from you once in a term. The novelty of the thing would be quite delightful. Do you not love to write prose? Send me some theme, some speculation or essay, any thing in form of a letter will be better than this impenetrable reserve, this frigid

indifference. Seriously, not a day passes that I do not think of my absent sons, nor do I ever forget them in my daily petitions to that Being who alone can protect us. And do you not suppose it would give me great satisfaction to hear frequently that they were well and happy?"

3. Edited by Robert Southey and Amos Cottle and published by Longman and Rees, London, 1803. Samuel Longfellow described the work in *Life*, I, 62, n. 1.

4. Abraham Rees, *The New Cyclopaedia, or Universal Dictionary of Arts and Sciences . . . Biography, Geography, and History . . .* (London, 1802–1820).

5. "On the Poems Attributed to Rowley" may be found in Vicemus Knox, *Essays Moral and Literary* (1778).

6. Samuel Rogers, *Italy; a Poem*, XVII, l. 47.

7. This effusion is an incomplete draft of "Reminiscences of Genius" (63.1). See Letter No. 73.

72. *To Stephen Longfellow* [1]

Bowd. Coll. April. 1825

Dear Sir,

I write you merely to request that you will inform Stephen, as soon as possible, that the class have finished Astronomy in Enfield, and recited their first lesson in Dialing this morning.[2] I should write directly to Stephen if I had leisure to write a long letter.

I will thank you to tell Sister Elisabeth, that I have found her breastpin.

Your affect. son
Henry.

MANUSCRIPT: Longfellow Trust Collection.

1. Stephen Longfellow's term in Washington having expired, he had returned to Portland on March 16.

2. William Enfield, *Institutes of Natural Philosophy, Theoretical and Practical* (1785).

73. *To Zilpah Longfellow*

Bowdoin College. Sunday Morning. May 15. [1825]

My dear Mother

You will find the continuation of my last letter in the "Pedestrian" — Portland Advertiser. Wm. Browne writes the "Pedestrian" — and he has requested me to write a No. and I sent him what you saw the beginning of.

Our Examination is on Tuesday, but whether in the forenoon or the afternoon I cannot say. If in the forenoon I shall be with you at tea, that day — if in the afternoon, I shall come up in the evening. My great haste to get home is that I may go to Fryeburg on Wednesday — Preble is going up with me.[1] Dr Wells is very desirous to have

Aunt L. and the girls go with him to Boston when he returns. He will not go before the close of the week.

Yours in great haste
H. W. L.

Professor Upham will come up on Tuesday evening with us.

MANUSCRIPT: Longfellow Trust Collection.

1. Longfellow wished to attend the centennial celebration of the Battle of Lovewell's Pond at Fryeburg on the 19th, for which he had composed an "Ode Written for the Commemoration of Lovewell's Fight." This poem, his second on the subject, was printed in the *Eastern Argus* of May 23, 1825, in the *Portland Advertiser* of May 24, and in the *American Patriot* of May 27.

74. *To Dr. Nathaniel Low* [1]

[Bowdoin College] June 25. 1825.

Dr Sir,

Please to accept the following lines, on a very hackney'd, but a very noble subject. I intended to have given them to you when I was last in Portland. If you see Kelly before Friday, please to tell him, that I shall expect a line from him by Friday's mail, if he cannot come down for me on Saturday.

Yours, very respectfully,
H. W. L.

(communicated) [2]
Lafayette.

Here shall the Hero rest:
    True hearts are round him!
Those he has nobly bless'd,
    Nobly have crown'd him.
Many a tongue hath said
    God speed the Stranger! —
Many a heart, that bled,
    Owns its avenger. —

Ne'er shall our Eagle stoop,
    Crest-fall'n and daunted! —
Ne'er shall the banner droop
    Strong hands have planted! —
Those that in days of grief
    Conquer'd beneath it,
Now with the Olive leaf
    Hasten to wreath it.

Europe has seen from far
   Mid her thick legions,
Empire's fast-westering star
   Shine on these regions. —
Why does she wear the yoke,
   And free hearts falter? —
Why is the quench'd urn broke
   At Freedom's altar? —

Father! — we bring to thee
   Fervent devotion:
It bursts from hearts as free
   As the free Ocean! —
Here in our bosoms rest;
   True hearts are round thee!
Those thou hast nobly bless'd
   Nobly have crown'd thee! —

Pulci. — [3]

MANUSCRIPT: Longfellow Trust Collection.   ADDRESS: Dr Nathaniel Low./Portland.
POSTMARK (*in script*): BRUNSWICK/JUNE 29th

1. Low (1792–1883), of South Berwick, Maine, edited the *American Patriot*, a Portland newspaper (formerly the *Independent Statesman*), for about a year.
2. That is, an original contribution, as opposed to a reprint.
3. This poem appeared in the *American Patriot*, I, No. 7 (July 1, 1825), 2–3. Longfellow sent it to Low on the day Lafayette arrived in Portland on his famous tour of the United States. His reason for using the signature "Pulci" is enigmatic; Luigi Pulci, a fifteenth-century Italian poet, was the "sire of the half-serious rhyme" (Byron).

75. *To Longfellow Sisters*

Bowdoin College. June. 28. [1825]

My dear Sisters

I arrived here at 7 o'clock precisely — after riding 4 hours. The Students who remained here, I find, have had a mock reception of Lafayette, the particulars of which I cannot stop to write — saving that many people thought that the General had come in reality.[1]

Our appointments for commencement are not yet given out — when they are, I shall write again. The enclosed is a good description of a convent &c. written by N. H. Carter, formerly preceptor of

Portland Academy.[2] After you have read it give it to Elizabeth K —
since she has so many predilections for a nun's life.[3]

Yours in haste
H. W. L.

MANUSCRIPT: Longfellow Trust Collection.   ADDRESS: Miss Elizabeth Longfellow./
Portland

1. A note on the manuscript, in another hand, states that "*G. W. Pierce* [who
was to become Anne's husband] personated the General on this occasion." Longfellow himself had gone to Portland to see Lafayette. Stephen Longfellow, a member of the Committee on Arrangements, delivered one of the welcoming addresses.

2. Carter went to Europe in 1824 and wrote descriptive letters for the *New York
Statesman*, which were widely reproduced in other journals. Longfellow here sends
his sisters one of those letters.

3. Mary Elizabeth Knight, a friend of the Longfellows (see 76.4).

76. *To Anne Longfellow*

Bowdoin College.
Wednesday Evening. June 29. 1825

Dear Sister Ann[e],

I have been waiting very impatiently for two days to receive my
trunk from Portland, which has not yet arrived. It strikes me that
L. Bond[1] moves a little slower in this business than he ought. I wish
some one of you to jog his elbow upon the occasion. I had an exceedingly pleasant ride down,— the pleasantest I ever took from Portland
eastward.

The appointments for commencement were given out this afternoon. Little[2] has the first Oration in English — Bradbury the second
— your brother Henry the third. You must not think from this that
I am the third schollar in the class, for that would be a sad mistake.
Weld has a disquisition — Mellen a poem — and so forth and so on.

The moon is just rising over our beautiful pines, and the twilight
grows too dark for me to write without a lamp. Good night. I shall
have a word or two more for you in the morning.

Thursday Morning — June 30.

My appointment, they tell me, is considered the fourth in the class
— having only Little, Dean[3] and Bradbury above me. How I came to
get so high, is rather a mistery to me, in as much as I have never been
a remarkably hard student, touching College studies, except during
my Sophomore year, when I used to think that I was studying pretty
hard — though I might possibly have been mistaken. In five weeks we
shall be set free from college — for one month. Then comes Com-

mencement — and then — and then — I cannot say what *will be,* after that.

I have been looking again for my trunk by the stage — and have again been looking in vain. It is very strange that Bond does not send it.

Friday. July 1.

A dull, rainy, pensive, sentimental kind of a day — hardly warm enough for the first of July.

Here are some faded rose-leaves for Miss K[night]: — they must be acceptable, because they come from Mr Deering's.[4] They are dry enough, to be sure — faded — but

"All that's bright must fade!"[5]

Good bye

H. W. L.

MANUSCRIPT: Longfellow Trust Collection. ADDRESS: Miss. Ann[e] Longfellow/ Portland. POSTMARK (*in script*): BRUNSWICK/JULY 1st.

1. Leonard Bond, a Portland groceryman and butcher, apparently also served as a transfer man.

2. Josiah Stover Little (1801–1862), the first scholar in Longfellow's class, subsequently studied law, entered politics, and became president of the Atlantic and St. Lawrence Railroad. His valedictory oration was on "The Influence of Government on Literature."

3. Gorham Deane, born in 1803, died of consumption on August 11, 1825, a few weeks before Commencement. He had been assigned a "Philosophical Disquisition."

4. Miss Knight married George Deering (1796–1833), brother of Nathaniel Deering, the Portland editor and dramatist, on July 1, 1827.

5. First line and title of a poem by Thomas Moore.

77. *To Caroline Doane*

Bowd: Coll: July. 3rd. 1825.

Dear Caroline,

Positively I never knew such provoking taciturnity, as I find in you. Your last letter bears the date of April 13th: — and my last letter so full of questions, and illustrating thereby the true native spirit of New England — you cannot find an opportunity to notice.[1] Very good! I shall now turn back to your letter of March 15. Out of thine own mouth will I condemn thee.[2] You say in that letter "if you will bury in oblivion all past negligences, I will *promise* to be more punctual in future." Gentlemen of the grand jury, what say you, — is the prisoner at the bar guilty or not guilty?

Have you seen Brainard's Poems?[3] I think he has a highly poetical mind, as the piece entitled "Jerusalem" and the elegiack stanzas "on the death of Mr Woodward" sufficiently prove. But I moreover think that he has done himself great injustice as a poet, by publishing together so many trivial pieces. "Jack-frost and the Caty-did" from its simplicity is very beautiful. What think you of these lines taken from it? Jack-frost, in describing himself, says

> "A hollow hail-stone on my head,
> For a glittering helm was clasp'd:
> And a sharpened spear, like an icicle clear,
> In my cold little fingers was grasp'd." Page. 70.

The conception of this — and indeed of the whole piece is certainly very poetical, unless I am mistaken in supposing, that I know what poetical conception is; which may very probably be the case. I should extract more from these poems for your amusement, were I sure you have not already seen them. But presuming that I am telling you a "thrice-told tale," I desist.

I have an invitation to give you, and I hardly know in what way to offer it, that it may be most acceptable. The invitation is for you to come down to our commencement — the way of offering it is — but I hesitate here. I am afraid to ask you to come for the purpose of hearing our performances — lest you should say, that you felt no desire to. And should I ask your presence on a visit merely — you might answer, that you had little or no inducement to it. Well then, I know your taste and love for painting will give you a wish to examine our gallery, which I think Dr Wells will acknowledge to be very valuable and excellent: though the connoisseur — Sir Richard Derby of B.[4] would not. However — do come at Commencement — with Mrs W. — and Adelaide and all your family, who can.[5] And by the way — give my best respects to Elisabeth Chase,[6] and tell her she must come for Old Acquaintance' sake. It will be an excellent season for her long-promised visit to Portland. I have the vanity to suppose that you will wish to know, what my appointment for the occasion is; and I shall accordingly anticipate your wish, — at least the question arising from that wish, by telling you, that I have the third English oration. Now, Caroline, as you were disappointed in not seeing our *citadel here* last fall, do not disappoint your Portland friends by staying at home this. Miss Chase's invitation, you will take good care to remember and deliver.

And now I must *repeat* a question, which I asked in my last letter: —

though its second asking will savour strongly of curiosity, — perhaps too strongly for one, who has so little as I have. Who is the young lady of bad taste, that cuts up her Literary Gazettes, because I write occasionally for the same? H.W.L — says he will do anything under heaven for her — if you will but tell him who she is and what he shall do. Do have compassion for the young man, and unfold the mistery to him: — think —how many many months you have kept him with his curiosity unsatisfied. I look impatiently for the development of the affair in your next letter.[7]

How should you like to go to Niagara, with Harriet S. — ?[8] A very delightful piece of business I should call it. I suppose, however, that she will tarry a long while at the Springs, which you would not like so well as Niagara — at least, so I presume.

The Duke of Brunswick[9] continues to flourish beautifully. He stayed a day or two with [us] in Portland, when Fayette was there, and moreover he has a "disquisition" at Commencement on the "Moral Sublime" — queer enough too! Some college wags love to quiz the young man — and they have made him believe that a young lady here is in love with him, and that she spies into his windows with a glass! He takes it all for law and gospel: really I cannot help laughing at him, though he is a good-hearted fellow, and an old friend, which ought to keep me from joining in any jests at his expense. Good bye! Write soon — very soon!

Very truly yours

H. W. L.

MANUSCRIPT: Longfellow Trust Collection. ADDRESS: Miss. Caroline Doane./ Care of Dr Geo: B. Doane.[10]/Boston. POSTMARK (*in script*): BRUNSWICK ME/JULY 4th

1. This letter is unrecovered.

2. Cf. Luke 19:22.

3. John Gardiner Calkins Brainard (1796–1828), a Connecticut author, published *Occasional Pieces of Poetry* in 1825.

4. Richard C. Derby (1777–1854) of Boston was the husband of Martha Coffin (42.4) and a member of the prominent Salem merchant family.

5. Adelaide Wells (1808–1834), daughter of Mrs. Hannah Wells, was Caroline Doane's niece and Longfellow's second cousin.

6. Longfellow had met Elizabeth Chase in Boston in February, 1824. A cousin of Mary Storer Potter (whom he married in 1831), she subsequently became an acquaintance of some intimacy.

7. This letter, if it was written, is unrecovered. The identity of Longfellow's admirer, therefore, remains a mystery.

8. Longfellow had apparently met Harriot Coffin Sumner (1802–1867) during his visit to Boston in February, 1824. He was to become intimately acquainted with her in later years. Daughter of Harriot Foster Coffin and Jesse Sumner of Boston, she was the first cousin, once removed, of Longfellow's great friend Senator

Charles Sumner. As the second wife of Nathan Appleton, she was a member of Longfellow's family circle after his marriage to Frances Appleton in 1843.

9. A title apparently conferred on Eugene Weld.

10. George Bartlett Doane (1792–1842), a Boston physician, was Caroline's brother and Longfellow's first cousin, once removed.

78. *To Stephen Longfellow*

Bowd. Coll. July. 22. 1825.

My dear Sir,

I perceive you still urge the great necessity of letter writing.[1] For my part, I must confess, that I am not well satisfied that you do not attach more importance to the subject than in reality belongs to it. This proposition, which is a panacea for my conscience in all delinquenc[i]es, has certainly some good foundation in the very nature of the thing. In fact, I can prove syllogistically that there is no personal advantage whatever in letter writing.

1. Nothing can be advantageous to a person's writing, which has a tendency to injure his style, and to bring him into a superficial way of thinking.

2. Now Letter writing has these effects to an eminent degree, inasmuch as what we say must be said carelessly and familiarly, — and the topics introduced into a letter being necessarily numerous, if you would please your correspondent, — you cannot speak fully upon any one of them, and consequently there is no regular train of thought kept up in the mind, and our habits of thought become superficial.

3. A Logical Conclusion — Letter-writing is of no great benefit.

But after all syllogism is a most fallacious mode of reasoning, since of necessity it involves that egregiously poor principle — a "begging the question," — and moreover a person can prove anything under the sun by it. And although the preceding argument is strictly logical, yet I do believe that as a principle of action it may be carried too far.

With regard to our studies, we are looking over — perhaps I ought to say *overlooking* — Chemistry and Stewart's Philosophy,[2] on the review. We have about 60, 8 vo. pages at a lesson — upon which I sometimes study ten minutes — sometimes five — and at other times do not look at. Touching commencement exercises, I have written my oration long ago. The subject is "The life and Writings of Chatterton" — 7′ long.[3] I hardly know how this will answer, but am rather of the opinion that it must do. But this is not all. The class have requested me to deliver a poem on the day after Commencement, just before our final separation — which invitation I have accepted, and consequently shall be rather busy the remaining part of the term. And in fact I have been very busy thus far. To be sure I read very little, but I am continually writing. I wish I could read and write at the same time. However as the case is, I am more industrious than if I read, since I am never tired of writing, though I sometimes am of reading.

Mr. Bond ought to have paid the carriage of my trunk as he agreed to. I had to pay for it half of my whole property in the ready-money line, so that I will thank you for $1.00 any time before the close of the term, that is before a fortnight, — though I do not want it immediately.

The bell is ringing. S. and myself both well.[4]

> Your affect. son
>
> Henry.

MANUSCRIPT: Longfellow Trust Collection. ADDRESS: Stephen Longfellow. Esq./ Portland. POSTMARK (in script): BRUNSWICK/JULY 24th

1. As early as December 26, 1824, Stephen Longfellow had written to his son, "Epistolary composition is one of the most difficult kind[s] of style to acquire, and is at the same time a most desirable attainment; and if you mean to become iminent [sic] as a literary man you must remember that taste and scholarship are as much displayed in correspondence as in any exercise."

2. Dugald Stewart, Elements of the Philosophy of the Human Mind (London, 1792, 1814).

3. Longfellow subsequently abandoned this subject in favor of "Our Native Writers" (published in Every Other Saturday, I [April 12, 1884], 116). See Young Longfellow, pp. 68–70.

4. Stephen Longfellow's rustication in Kennebunkport (61.3) ended in April, 1825, but upon his return to Bowdoin he was immediately sent home to Portland for inability to produce a good conduct testimonial. He returned in June to take examinations and managed to remain in good standing until graduation in the fall (Bowdoin Faculty Records; Young Longfellow, p. 356).

79. To Caroline Doane [1]

Bowdoin College   July. 26. 1825.

Dear friend Caroline,

You have concluded not to write to me it seems! Very well! I will write to you then. Call it a breach of promise, if you please, since I promised not to write untill I heard from you, yet if you do, — remember, — it will be persecution "for conscience' sake" — since I am cavalier enough to believe, that if you do not write I am in duty, bound to; at least I will make this assertion, and it will be hard in you to think, that I would assert what I did not believe. I thought you would find enough in the ride to Hiram, which prevented me from seeing you on the 4th, — to recompense me, in description, for the loss of your company, by a sketch of your journey. I said in description, but the promised sketches in painting are to be forth-coming with all becoming speed. My Mother's letter on Saturday informs me that you "talk frequently of returning home" — but you surely will not go before I see you again. Remain only 5 weeks longer, and I will do my best to go to Boston with your ladyship, for I assure you I long — really long to go to Boston again. But though I shall use all my art of persuasion and put all my oratorical powers into requisition, yet I am afraid there will be many objections to my second visit following the first so closely. I will employ you as my advocate in this cause, — do unite your voice with mine.

You can hardly imagine how surprized I was, on returning to my room after Saturday-morning's recitation, to hear that H.C. Sumner was in town. The weather was exceeding dull and I was 3 pr. cent duller than the weather, till the Tavern Hostler knocked at the door and handed me the letter, — and then good bye Latin and Greek, — his honour did not study much more during that day, I can assure you — but in lieu thereof he passed 5 exceedin[g]ly pleasant hours, — and exceedin[g]ly short ones too — and then good bye Miss. Sumner. But I was extremely sorry the day was so wet and uncomfortable. And then she returned so quickly back again to Portland, — I grew sad again! I could indeed say

"— my winged hours of joy have been
Like angel visits, few and far between —"

Which two lines I have taken the liberty to quote from Campbell,[2] for the sake both of expressing my meaning shortly and elegantly, and also of saying something very beautiful on the occasion. If it were not for being laughed at, I could be very melancholy! I *cannot* say how Miss. Sum — enjoyed the rainy Saturday, but for my own part, — *it is useless* to say how I enjoyed it. My mother's letter observed that if it contained "ever so good advise I should not pay much attention to it," — but I can conscientiously say, that this is a very er[r]oneous opinion, for I did not, indeed, open the letter untill afternoon, but that happened to be the only part of the day, in which I stood in need of consolation and good advise. Did Mr. and Miss. S — arrive safely at Portland? Or have you not seen them since their return? They go to Boston tomorrow morning, I believe?

I have been passing a part of the evening with Professor Cleaveland, who yesterday received a letter from Dr Wells, stating that he should visit Brunswick at commencement with Mrs. W — instead of Adelaide. You will, of course, yourself remain. But alas! — what excuse have I, then, for going to Boston, if you have the Dr. for your gallant. That business is nipt in the bud I suppose! Miss Bush sends her love to all, and hopes to see you at Commencement with a whole parcel of other good folks. I, of course, join with her. And moreover as it waxes late, and I have some thoughts of getting my lesson and going to sleep, I bid you farewell, with a particular request, that you will write me immediately, — that is to say, as soon as convenient.

Yours &c.
Henry W. Longfellow.

MANUSCRIPT: Longfellow Trust Collection. ADDRESS: Miss Caroline Doane./Care of S. Longfellow Esq./Portland. POSTMARK (*in script*): BRUNSWICK/JULY 26th

1. Now in Portland visiting the Longfellow family.
2. *Pleasures of Hope*, Pt. II, ll. 377–378. Longfellow wrote "joy" for "bliss."

80. *To Jared Sparks*[1]

Portland   July. 30. 1825.

Mr. Jared Sparks,
Dr Sir,

I have never yet seen any notice of the 'life and writings of Chatterton' in any of our native Literary Journals, and as far as my observation extends, I find that little is known of him in our country, saving that such a person once existed — and, like other men, died — and some ask "Who was he?" Now it strikes me that something ought to be done to publish in our land the fame of so wonderful a genius, who as yet lives but in the memories of our literary men. In order to lead men to the inquiry of who and what Chatterton was, and when, where and how he lived and died, I have thrown together some Biographical remarks, together with a notice of the Rowley MSS. — and the controversy which originated in their pretended discovery — which I send you for the October No — of the N.A. Review. Should you discover merit enough in them to induce you to publish them, I think they may be instrumental in some measure in giving Chatterton a 'name and a place' with us. The subject is certainly one of great interest. As soon as you can run over the papers, please to drop me a line. If you should not make use of them, I will thank you to lay them by for me, as they may answer for some other journal.

Yours very respectfully
Henry. W Longfellow. —

MANUSCRIPT: Harvard College Library. ADDRESS: Rev. Jared Sparks./Boston. ENDORSEMENT: H.W. Longfellow./Aug. 5./1825

1. Sparks (1789–1866) was at this time owner and editor of the *North Ameri-*

can Review. Longfellow was later to become more closely associated with him at Harvard, where Sparks became professor of ancient and modern history in 1839 and president of the college from 1849 to 1853.

81. *To Caroline Doane*

Bowd. Coll. July. 7. 1825.
— By the way I should have said August. 7.

Dear Caroline,

This will be a dull letter, for I sit down to write it with dulness aforethought. The fact is, I ought to have written you a week ago, in answer to yours of July 8th and 14th, and to have given you absolution from the sin of long silence, on the plea of sickness — expressing at the same time my sorrow for your indisposition, and hopes for a speedy recovery. All which being done in the cold manner, — though not with the cold feelings, of a business man, — we proceed to be dull.

Nothing can induce you to visit us this fall! I am sorry that we are all so poor in gifts, — that nothing, — though we urge all things with becoming importunity — nothing can bring you away from your own "home and *fire-place*" — (excuse me from saying 'fire-*side*' this hot weather). I hope however you will change your resolution before another month elapses, and delight us with your presence at commencement — and with a visit at Portland. Adelaide will not of course wish me to be ceremonious, — she must come by all means.

The Duke,[1] (I know you will not believe me, but 'tis nevertheless a fact) — is in a high fever because he cannot get at a sprig of dried 'rue,' that a young lady in Portland cut for him merely in sport. He wanted to know why my sister did not send it on to him in my letter, and actually requested me to bring it to Brunswick at Commencement time! O fie! — moral sublime. By the way, Brother Ben is here. I never see him without thinking of Miss. C — I can imagine with what a queer kind of a look he received his dissmissal &c.[2]

Harriet S. [Sumner] is probably at Niagara. Coffin[3] was here about a fortnight ago. There is not the least alteration in him, and probably never will be. I hear slight and passing reports of the Boston beauties — of Miss Marshal's being a great Belle at Providence and so forth and so on. But I am not in proper estate to write of the ladies; for Diderot says, that "when writing on women, we should dip our pens in the rainbow, and throw over each line, instead of sand, the powder of the butterfly's wing."[4] Very fanciful. However I must say a word or two of L.E.L. When I first read her poem, I thought that she would become identified, in some measure, with her own "Improvisatrice" as Lord Byron was with his "Lara" and "Childe Harold." Miss Letitia

Elisabeth Landon (L.E.L.) has written certainly some very beautiful poetry, but she is rather too careless. She can no more compose with Mrs Hemans, then Percival can with Bryant. You are much mistaken with regard to the age of Miss Landon. You say seventeen — she is nineteen — and by no means a stranger in the literary world. In 1822 she published a poem called "The Fate of Adelaide. A Swiss romantic story." She is however a prodigy, and must be possessed of great activity of mind to write so much as she does.[5] I will copy a little piece for you, which I presume you have never yet seen, as it is just from the London. Lit. Gaz.

" — Song.

> I have a summer gift,
>   A summer gift for thee:
> See this white vase, where blooms
>   A beautiful rose tree.
> And on its crimson leaves
>   Your heart must moralize,
> For love a lesson takes
>   Of every leaf that dies.
> First you will prize the gift
>   In all its scented pride;
> — Its newness then will pass,
>   And 'twill be flung aside.
> Then Autumn rains will stain
>   Its leaves with a dark token;
> The plant will perish then,
>   And the white vase be broken.
> Will not love's tale be told
>   In the fate of the rose tree? —
> Such was at first your love
>   Then your neglect of me. — "[6]

I have read "Mr Sprague's Oration,"[7] and some short Extracts from Mad. De Genlis' Memoirs.[8] With the first I was very much pleased — of the second of course I cannot judge.

The subject of my Oration is "Native Writers."

Yours affectionately
H. W. L. —

MANUSCRIPT: Longfellow Trust Collection. ADDRESS: Miss. Caroline Doane./

Care of Dr. Geo. B. Doane./Boston. POSTMARK (*in script*): BRUNSWICK ME/AUGT 8th

1. Eugene Weld (77.9).

2. This is apparently a reference to an unsuccessful courtship of Susan Codman (1802-1877) of Portland, sister of William Henry Codman, by Frederic Benjamin Page (1798-1857), a young doctor of medicine and the brother of Dr. Jonathan Page, a Bowdoin overseer. See Letter No. 192. Longfellow himself seems to have been interested in Miss Codman; they exchanged several letters while he was in Europe, which encouraged gossip in Portland of an impending engagement (according to a letter from Anne Longfellow to Henry dated October 26, 1826). Miss Codman, admired on every side as a great beauty, apparently rejected him as a suitor in a letter dated March 8, 1830, by quoting five stanzas of a poem by Miss Sheridan beginning, "I do not love thee! no — I do not love thee!/And yet when thou art absent I am sad."

3. Possibly Harriot's brother, Nathaniel Coffin Sumner (1803-1841).

4. From Diderot's essay *Sur les femmes*. The French reads: "Quand on écrit des femmes, il faut tremper sa plume dans l'arc-en-ciel et jeter sur sa ligne la poussière des ailes du papillon."

5. Longfellow's information about Laetitia Elizabeth Landon was not entirely accurate. Born in 1802, she was twenty-three at the time of this letter. She had published *The Improvisatrice; and Other Poems* in 1824 and *The Fate of Adelaide* in 1821. Most of her early poetry appeared in the *London Literary Gazette,* and it was from this source that Longfellow formed his critical judgment of her work.

6. *The London Literary Gazette,* No. 434 (Saturday, May 14, 1825), 316. Longfellow varied the punctuation slightly and wrote "leaves" for "bloom" in l. 14.

7. Charles Sprague, *An Oration, Delivered on Monday, Fourth of July, 1825 . . .* (Boston, 1825).

8. *Memoirs of the Countess de Genlis, illustrative of the History of the Eighteenth and Nineteenth Centuries* (New York and Philadelphia, 1825).

82. *To Theophilus Parsons*

Portland. August 13. 1825.

Dear Sir

Being apprehensive that you did not receive a letter, which I wrote you from Brunswick, a few weeks since,[1] I take the liberty to write again. I shall trouble you with but few words, at this time; in as much as I have but little leisure, and you will have but little patience with me in warm weather. The letter to which I refer[r]ed above contained some suggestions upon the plausibility — or rather the possibility of my becoming connected — for one year — with the Editorial department of the Literary Gazette: — whether Mr Carter would like an assistant Editor — &c &c.

I did not write directly to Mr Carter upon the subject — for I might have been intrusive: but thinking that you could easily learn of Mr C. his inclination upon the subject, I thought it would be best to write to you touching this matter, as an affair, for the present, "inter nos."

I wish to breathe a little while a literary atmosphere, and as I shall not probably enter upon the study of my profession for a year, I wish to be connected in some way with a literary periodical work. Of course, the Literary Gazette is first in my thoughts, and I wish that it might be my lot to be associated with Mr Carter in a capacity different from that of an occasional writer for the paper.

If you will be kind enough to discover his sentiments upon the subject without mentioning my name, unless he should approve of the scheme, you will confer a great obligation upon me. It strikes me that a single Editor must be very much confined with such a work as the Lit. Gaz. and that he would be willing for the sake of more liberty and less solicitude to have a partner in the business. Pray write me as soon as possible, as it is of some importance for me to be acquainted with my prospects in this way, before Commencement.[2] By the way — I hope to see you at Bowdoin this fall, that you may be present when a parcel of us poor fellows receive the parting benediction of our young "Alma Mater." We are, to be sure, too poor in gifts to offer you any great inducements — but one I will offer you — and that is a hearty welcome.

Yours affectionately
Henry W Longfellow.

MANUSCRIPT: Boston Public Library.   ADDRESS: Theophilus Parsons Esq/Taunton/ Ms.   PUBLISHED: *Young Longfellow*, pp. 74–75.

1. This letter, dated July 10, 1825, is unrecovered.
2. Longfellow's efforts to move into the literary world after his graduation did not succeed. At commencement the trustees of Bowdoin College, including his father, voted to establish a chair of modern languages and recommended young Longfellow for it. A family decision was then made to send him to Europe to prepare for the position. But as the season was late, he delayed his departure and in the early autumn moved, impatiently, into the world of his father's law office, where with his brother Stephen and his friends George W. Pierce and Frederick Mellen he spent the next several months dutifully reading Blackstone.

83. *To Jared Sparks*

Portland   October. 9th 1825

Dear Sir

I fear you will think me obtrusive in writing to you a second time upon the subject of "Chatterton." But when I wrote that Article, I weighed in my mind — duly as I then thought — all the objections to its publication in the N. American, which you suggested in your letter of the 15th of September.[1] My conclusion was, that if you did not reject it because it was not well written, that it would be published. For I supposed that the subject was of some novelty and interest to many of your readers here, and I will confess that I continue to be of that opinion. My grounds are these.

The review of Chatterton's Works in the Edingburgh, unless my memory fails me, came out in a number of that work, which appeared about twenty years ago.[2] Now, although the Edinburgh Review is pretty widely circulated, and pretty generally read in our country, at the present day, yet from the circumstances of our political history, and state of literature amongst us at this day, I should not think it false reasoning to argue, that twenty years ago — nay even ten years, the circulation of the Edin[bur]g[h] Rev — was confined to a few subscribers. Consequently, we cannot suppose that the American public knew much of Chatterton from this source. But supposing the circulation of that Review to have been then, as great as it is now. You will, I think find, upon perusal of the article on Chatterton contained in it; that but a single quotation, and that a very short one — about twelve lines, — is given from the Old Rowley poems, upon which the author's fame chiefly rests. Besides nothing is there said of Chatterton's history, — which, you may depend upon it, is little known to most of your readers. Most of our country men have heard of Chatterton, and seen his name in the newspapers, but they know as little of the man as they do of Shirley — Ford — Heywood &c. &c. There is, it is true, a life of Chatterton — a very short sketch, in Rees' Cyclopaedia, and also in the "British Poets" by Sanford and Walsh;[3] — but you are well aware, that these are accessible to but few, and that the former is deprived of much of its interest by not being connected with any of Chatterton's writings.

A word concerning the Quarterly Review. I recollect going over most of the volumes of that work with a desire to find some notice there of Chatterton. All that I remember of finding there was in a review of a work by Chalmers, and was rather a vindication of his character against the severe remarks of Chalmers, than a notice of his life and writings.[4] From these considerations I have taken the liberty of writing you upon the subject a second time. As I said before, I fear you will think me obtrusive: — but I hope you will pardon this in a young writer, which you assuredly will do, if you will but place yourself, for a moment, in my situation. I will, sir, give you the further trouble of looking over my article again, to see, if by such alterations as should suggest themselves, you might not fit it for the January number of the North American. I feel gratified that the paper was not rejected on account of style. We cannot get new books here, till they have all been reviewed and read in other parts of the Union. How would a review of Neal's "Brother Jonathan" answer for the N.A.?

That Author deserves some severity from the American critics.[5] Very respectfully —

Your Obt. Sert. &c
Henry W. Longfellow.

MANUSCRIPT: Harvard College Library. ADDRESS: Revd. Jared Sparks./Boston. POSTMARK: ||PORTLAND|| ME ||OCT|| 9 ENDORSEMENT: Mr Longfellow/Oct. 11./1825

1. Sparks had written: "Your letter and the article on Chatterton have been received. It is now twenty two years since Chatterton's works were published, and considering they were fully handled in the Edinburgh Review, have been from time to time touched upon in the Quarterly, both of which circulate in this country, it appears to me that any formal notice at the present time will not have sufficient interest for the American public./With the first part of the article I am particularly pleased, as a specimen of chaste and agreeable writing, nor do I see any faults, unless it be the length of the quotations, and perhaps the diffuseness in the remarks, which follow. Did the subject appear to me as one of particular interest, I should gladly insert the article in the Review" (*Young Longfellow*, p. 357, n. 32).

2. *Edinburgh Review*, IV (April 1804), 214-230. The review of the Southey and Cottle edition of Chatterton (71.3) is by Sir Walter Scott.

3. Ezekiel Sanford and Robert Walsh, *The Works of the British Poets, With Lives of the Authors* (Philadelphia, 1819-1823).

4. *Quarterly Review*, XI (July 1814), 493-495. The review is of Alexander Chalmers, *The Works of the English Poets, from Chaucer to Cowper* (London, 1810).

5. While in England, John Neal wrote *Brother Jonathan*, a romantic novel dealing with colonial New England. It was published in three volumes in 1825.

84. *To Caroline Doane*

Portland   November. 1. 1825
Gentle Reader! Pray write me soon!

My dear Caroline

Perhaps you will recollect, that Mons. de Chateaubriand has in his Atala a sentiment of this kind — "if a man were restored to life a few years after his death, I doubt whether he would be welcome even to those, that shed most tears when he expired."[1] If this be true I hope it is not with our absence as with our death. And I hope, too, that this letter will come as a visible token of the resurrection of our beloved correspondence, — now dead and gone these many days. You will perhaps say to me, when you read this comparison of our correspondence to a dead man, — as Falstaff said to Prince Henry — "Thou hast the most unsavoury similes."[2] Whether it be so or not, I will speak no more in parables. But, Caroline, if it is a fair question, why have not you written me since the 8th of July, which is the date of your last letter? Like Brutus "I pause for a reply."[3]

Since I wrote you last I have been metamorphosed from a College

Student into a Student in a Lawyer's Office. But I make it my boast, that the mutabilities of life have little to do with my feelings and affections, and at these present times, — to use a worn-out similie, I am as happy as the day is long. I write very little either of prose or poetry. I believe that whatever I do write takes its colour from things around me. And being on terms of familiar friendship with one of the sweetest and most elegant girls, that I ever beheld — / Nota Bene, she's engaged/ — [4] no wonder that, should I ever write poetry, my thoughts should arrange themselves, somewhat in the following order.

> Her beauty was no mortal thing! — It was
> A glorious image of the light and beauty
> That dwell in Nature: — of the heavenly forms
> We worship in our dreams, and the soft hues
> That lie in the wild bird's wing, and flush the clouds
> When sets the golden sun. — Within her eye
> The heaven of April with its changing light,
> And when it wears the blue of May, was hung,
> And on her lip the rich red rose. Her hair
> Was like the tresses of the summer trees
> When twilight makes them brown: — and her soft cheek
> Wore all the richness of the Autumn sky
> When the warm sunset mellows it. — Her breath
> Was like the soft and gentle air of Spring,
> As from the morning's dewy flowers it comes
> Full of their fragrance, and her silver voice
> Was the rich music of a Summer bird,
> Heard in the still night, with its passionate cadence.

And so forth and so on, to the end of the chapter. Now, Caroline, though you may think me a little extravagant in this article, yet I hope you will give me the credit of having one original idea, and that is, the idea of making up an ideal beauty of my own, from the several beauties of Nature: — more of this hereafter.

You saw, then, my dearly beloved friend Miss. Mary E. Knight? She gave me and my sisters your very kind invitation to Boston, which I regret to say it will not be in our power to accept at present. Do you not think Miss. K. is very beautiful? By the way, she sends her best regards to Mrs Wells — yourself and Adelaide, in which we all devoutly join her.

Yours affectionately
H. W. L.

MANUSCRIPT: Longfellow Trust Collection. ADDRESS: Miss Caroline Doane/Care of Dr Geo: Doane/Boston.

1. Longfellow apparently quoted the sentiment from memory. The French reads: "Si un homme revenait à la lumière quelques années après sa mort, je doute qu'il fût revu avec joie par ceux-là mêmes qui ont donné le plus de larmes à sa mémoire" (*Atala, ou les amours de deux sauvages dans le desért*, section entitled *Le Drame*).

2. *King Henry IV, Part I*, I, ii, 81.

3. *Julius Caesar*, III, ii, 34.

4. Possibly Mary Elizabeth Knight (76.4).

85. *To Caroline Doane*

Portland   December 4th. 1825.

What can be the reason that I receive no letter from my dear friend Caroline? I am apprehensive that my last letter never reached her, or certainly I should ere this have received an answer, for I recollect that in a former case of delinquency, she promised to be "punctual in future."

The last time I heard from you, you said something about Mrs Hemans and L.E.L. — Miss. Landon. I will give you my opinion of their writings, for if I recollect right, you asked it. All I know of Mrs Hemans' poetry is from her publications in the London New Monthly Magazine, for her volume of poems has not reached us here in the East.[1] I think she possesses great genius, and great power over language. Her first communications in the Magazine were the best — for instance the "Songs of the Cid" — "The hour of death."[2] But lately, I must confess, though I know you are one of her admirers, that she has sadly failed in her glory. It looks as if she was writing for money not for fame, when we find her pieces long and loosely put together, as if they were thrown off in haste and sent to the press without correction. Now I happen to believe with an Ancient Writer, that "Labor is the price, that the Gods have set upon all excellence."[3] Formerly Mrs Hemans wrote but little, and her composition bore the marks of much care. She wrote most admirably then, — but of late, by her own carelessness, she has fallen short of her own excellence. Moreover, she has introduced into modern poetry a hop, skip, and jump kind of measure, which has had, in my humble opinion, a very deleterious influence in our own country. Everything nowdays must be written in the sing-song way. For instance, — I quote from Memory, —

"The wind has a language I would I could learn, —
Sometimes it is soothing — sometimes it is stern! —"[4]

Now — candidly, Caroline, does not this bear a most ludicrous resemblance to one of Old Mother Goose's Melodies,

> "There was an old woman tossed up in a blanket
> Fourteen times as high as the moon!" —

By the way, as soon as I get leisure I mean to write an Essay upon modern poetry, and introduce this quotation, for it strikes me as being a peculiarly apt one.

And now a word for L.E.L. You say she is only seventeen years old. Nineteen, — I have heard, and I suspect, that she is nearer nineteen than seventeen: — for as long ago as 1818, she published a poem called "The Fate of Adelaide, a Swiss romantic story." It is noticed in the Edingburg or Qua[r]terly Review — I forget which, for that year.[5] However, Miss Landon is a very sweet writer, with twice the tenderness and plaintiveness of Mrs H. and not half her strength and energy. But as I have filled my sheet, and as I have a very singular fact to mention in connexion with L.E.L.'s Poems, I will postpone all farther remarks until I write again, which with your leave, will be soon. In the mean time do not forget that you are indebted in the way of letters to

Your Old friend
Henry Wadsworth.

MANUSCRIPT: Longfellow Trust Collection. ADDRESS: Miss Caroline Doane/Care of Dr Geo: B. Doane/Boston. POSTMARK: PORTLAND ME DEC 5

1. Longfellow apparently refers here to *The Forest Sanctuary, and other poems* (London, 1825), published in Boston in 1827.

2. See the *New Monthly Magazine and Literary Journal* (American edition), V (January–June 1823), 307–308, 376–378, 378; and VII (January–June 1824), 60.

3. Longfellow is presumably paraphrasing a quotation from Addison's *Tatler*, No. 97: "there is nothing truly valuable which can be purchased without pains and labour. The Gods have set a price upon every real and noble pleasure." Addison, in turn, remarks that he is translating from "that noble Allegory which was written by an old Author called *Prodicus*, but recommended and embellished by *Socrates*."

4. Altered slightly from "The Wind," a poem appearing in the American edition of the *New Monthly Magazine and Literary Journal*, VIII (July–December 1824), 11, and signed "O." Longfellow's implication that Mrs. Hemans wrote the lines has no basis.

5. Miss Landon published *The Fate of Adelaide* not in 1818 but in 1821 (see 81.5). It is noticed in the "Quarterly List of New Publications," *Edinburgh Review*, XXXVI (February 1822), 571, and in "New Publications," *Quarterly Review*, XXVI (October 1821), 275.

86. *To Caroline Doane*

[Portland, Dec. 31, 1825]

"O by what words — what title or what name
Shall I entreat your pardon. —"[1]

If ever during your late long silence [I have uttered] any murmur
of reproach for your seeming neglect, ignorance of the cause of that
silence must be my excuse. At the same time, I cannot but lament
exceedingly, — my fair cousin, — that you did not write me, when
you were at Lake George, — whilst its enchanting scenery was before
your eye, and the impressions upon your mind were in all their fulness
and freshness. I hope, however, that you, in the language of L.E.L.

"on the canvass made
Those dreams of glory visible."[2]

I quote from memory, and probably have not employed the exact words
of your favorite in the modern school, but the idea is in plain English,
I hope you filled your port-folio with sketches: — one of which you
are now copying oil-colours for a Christmass and New Year's present
to your unworthy friend here — the Lawyer's clerk, who assures you
it would be the most acceptable gift you could make him. Indeed,
Caroline, a painting done [by] your hand, would be, As Cowper says

"in my heart's
Just estimation prized above all price."[3]

Again I quote from memory. Now to L.E.L. — a moment longer.
What shall I say of her? Lord Byron called the octo-syllabic verse
"fatal" when speaking of Walter Scott;[4] — I hope it will not prove so
in the case of Miss Landon, though I think she writes and publishes
with a haste that would prove fatal to most any poet. But still she is so
gentle, so passionate — so pathetic — there is so much beauty in her
ideas, and so much elegance in her language, that one cannot read
her poetry without feeling a little of her own enthusiasm. But at the
same time if she had written but half as much as she has written, it
would have been worth fifty times its present value, taking it for
granted that she bestowed the same time and labour on that half that
she has upon the whole. Her greatest fault in my opinion, is the structure of her verses. There is no art about her — she does not know

how "to *build* the lofty rhyme."[5] Moreover she imitates Tom Moore. For instance, the following passage from the Improvisatrice.

> "But quick the twilight came and fast,
> Like one of those sweet calms that last
> A moment, and no more to cheer
> The turmoil of our pathway here."[6]

Of the "Troubadour," I have seen nothing but an account of a "Combat" and a little ballad about "a faire Ladie" which were in the Newspapers.[7] By the way, talking of "Troubadours" — let me go back a little. When you gave me intelligence of a "beautiful young lady" who cut my pieces from the Gazette, you added, that I ought to write a poem for her. Thinking you to be a young lady of veracity, I supposed that there was no doubt but what I had ought so to do: — taking your jest for fact. This was before I knew of L.E.L.'s poem, and down I sat, choosing for my subject "The Troubadour!" The very next day, I saw it announced that L.E.L. had just published a poem called "The Troubadour." Of course, I threw mine aside.

Good night! Miss Knight sends her love to you. I don't know when she is to be married.[8] Good night, again; all's well at home, and we grieve with you over your domestic sorrows.[9]

> "But, howsoever,
> Let's not be *strange* — (seldom) — in [our] writing."

— as Thomas Heywood says in one of his Old Plays.[10] Write to me soon.

Yours affectionately

H. W. L.

MANUSCRIPT: Longfellow Trust Collection.   ADDRESS: Miss Caroline Doane./Care of Dr George B. Doane/Boston.   POSTMARK: PORTLAND ME DEC. 31

1. Thomas Heywood, *A Woman Killed With Kindness*, IV, v, 41–42.

2. *The Improvisatrice*, ll. 29–30. The second line should read: "My dreams of beauty visible."

3. *The Task*, II, 33–34.

4. Longfellow gives an incorrect impression here. In his dedicatory preface to *The Corsair* Byron wrote: "Scott alone, of the present generation, has hitherto completely triumphed over the fatal facility of the octo-syllabic verse."

5. John Milton, "Lycidas," l. 11.

6. *The Improvisatrice*, ll. 301–304. The first line should read: "But quick the twilight time has past."

7. L.E.L. had only recently published *The Troubadour; Catalogue of Pictures, and Historical Sketches* (London, 1825). "The Combat" and "Portrait of a Lady"

were poetic interpretations of paintings by William Etty and Sir Thomas Lawrence respectively.

8. See 76.4.

9. Presumably a reference to illnesses suffered by Mrs. Hannah Doane Wells and Caroline (see Letters No. 87 and 88).

10. *The English Traveller*, Act IV.

87. *To Caroline Doane*

Portland   Jany. 22nd 1826.

Dear Caroline,

Since my last letter to you I have seen some extracts from the "Tour in Italy," of which you speak so highly. The part to which I refer is the description of "Florence by Moonlight" which is very fine and very poetical — a critic might say too poetical for prose.[1] You see how I am situated here. I never get a new book till every body has read it — every body in Boston, I mean, for we do not pretend to read anything but novels here. To be sure, our booksellers did get the "Rebels," about a fortnight after its publication, and I read it perhaps as soon as any one. Miss Francis is certainly a fine writer, though the death of Grace Osborne reminded me very strongly of the "pride of the Village" in the "sketch book" and something is said about "looking down upon the grave of an enemy, and feeling a compunctious throb, for having warred with the poor handful of dust that lies before us" — which you will recollect having seen before in the "Rural Funerals" of Irving. N.B. — Some of Doct. Byles' jokes and puns are bad, — if I am a judge of such things.[2]

You have undoubtedly read Dr. Percival's Poem before the Yale branch of the Phi Beta Kappa.[3] As usual, I have seen some "extracts" — of course can form no opinion of the whole — though if the part I have not seen is no better than the part I have seen, — it is a miserable concern. People will find out atlength, — and you yourself, my dear friend, will ere long acknowledge that Bryant is a better poet than Percival. Bryant's poetical fame rests on a surer basis than Percival's, — because upon a more natural one. Perhaps I shall not make myself understood, in the narrow limits of a letter, but I will try. One great characteristic of Bryant is the beautiful accuracy with which he copies nature — the quick and delicate perception of little beauties, which most eyes see not — and a wonderful skill in the finishing of his poems. Consequently if his writings ever please, they must always please, since they appeal direct[l]y to those principals of our nature, which never change. And moreover the structure of his verse — his blank verse especially, — is extremely natural — very much like Cowper's, and very compact, and nicely finished withal. Now Percival places himself diametrically opposite to all this — indeed he professes to despise all sort of carefulness and art in poetry. If I were to set myself up as a judge, I should say, that the most striking characteristic of his poetry was "sensuality:" — but I would not take the usual definition of that term. What I mean is, that everything in his poems addresses itself to our passions and internal senses — to our feelings, not to the mental faculty of poetical taste. These it is true are as prevalent as our mental powers, but we soon get tired to death of sentimental sonnets, and pathetic love-stories, because it is one great law of our nature, that our passive impressions should grow weaker and weaker, as the objects which produce them, are multiplied. But I am almost sorry that I began this criticism, — since I cannot go through with it, unless I tire your patience out and out; — besides If I have not made myself intelligible you will laugh at me. Excuse me for being so very tedious!

We have all been very anxiously waiting for letters from you — longing to hear of Mrs Wells' perfect recovery, and of the health of our other friends, to whom with Mrs. W. give the best love of our family — and be assured of their kind remembrance of yourself.

Very affectionately yours ever
Henry.

MANUSCRIPT: Longfellow Trust Collection. ADDRESS: Miss. Caroline Doane./ Boston./Ford. by/Capt. S. Wadsworth [4]

1. Caroline Doane's letter mentioning this book is unrecovered. A number of such "Tours" appeared in the 1820's.

2. Lydia Maria Child, nee Francis, published *The Rebels; or, Boston Before the Revolution* in 1825. A melancholy tale, written against the backdrop of the Stamp Tax agitation, it presents Grace Osborne as a jilted heroine and Dr. Mather Byles, the celebrated clergyman, poet, and wit, as comic relief. Longfellow's quotation from "Rural Funerals" was from memory and not strictly accurate. Miss Francis paraphrased Irving's sentiment at the end of Chap. XX.

3. James Gates Percival's "The Mind" was delivered before the Connecticut Alpha of Phi Beta Kappa on September 13, 1825, and published separately in Boston in 1826.

4. Capt. Alexander Scammell Wadsworth (38.3).

88. *To Caroline Doane*

Portland   March 13th 1826

My dear Caroline,

Presuming that you are fully recovered from your Influenza, I venture to commence this letter with my most hearty congratulations. Next to these comes a general protest against one peculiarity of your letters —which is that they never contain anything about yourself.

In one of your letters you tell me you have been to Lake George — and that you began a description for me, which you never finished. And that goes for a Summer's correspondence — but not a word do you write of yourself — your own thoughts — your domestic circle — and those sweet home-feelings, which I know are always ardent and glowing in the heart of my sweet friend Caroline. I see what the difficulty is. It is not that you are so suspicious of my friendship as to suppose that I could not enter warmly into your domestic thoughts and domestic feelings. No — it would be paying you but a sorry compliment, at my own expense, to tell you such a tale: — but the difficulty is, that you modestly personate a subordinate character in your own writings, instead of coming forward as the heroine of them. Now I insist upon your making your next letter a Journal of such thoughts, feelings — domestic pastimes and occurrences, as you think it proper and befitting, that I should know. This will indeed be making me one of that domestic circle of which I think so frequently and fervently and in which I can almost imagine myself at this moment placed.

I will set you an example by telling you that I am at present looking "from the loop-holes of retreat" [1] upon a busy and bustling world with whose joys and sorrows I have very little to do. I am just as rusty as ever, by reason of my going very little into society, and joining very little in the merriment and gaieties of this town. Now and then I sally forth of an evening to chat with Miss K——[Knight] and now and then listen to the music of that excellent piece of divinity, Susan Codman. Touching literary matters, I sometimes peep into a book written in plane — unostentatious and nervous style, and sometimes a page or two of tumid swelling stuff: and the great discrepancy I find in my reading in this respect, leads me to think that it is with our thoughts as with our money, — those who have most, appear before the world in a plain dress: — but those who have little, dash out in the tawdry splendour of glaring and flaunting patches — daubed all over with tarnished lace and gilding.

With regard to Poetry, I have not stopped writing tho' I have stopped publishing for certain reasons which I cannot go into at any length in a letter, but which I will unfold when we meet again, which will [be] before the Spring is out. I take the liberty to send you a little song, founded upon a beautiful appearance in the scenery of morning, which you who are a traveller will understand, for you must have observed it.

Song.

Where from the eye of day
The dark and silent river
Pursues through tangled woods a way
O'er which the tall trees quiver —

The silver mist that breaks
From out that woodland cover
Betrays the hidden path it takes
And hangs the current over. —

So oft the thoughts that burst
From hidden springs of feeling,
Like silent streams, unseen at first
From out cold hearts are stealing: —

But soon the clouds that veil
The eye of Love, when glowing,
Betray the long unwhisper'd tale
Of thoughts in darkness flowing.[2]

— Therefore, good night! Sister Ann[e] is writing you, and will make
known to you family matters. Please to answer this letter sometime
before the Autumn sets in — if convenient.

Yrs truly
H. W. L.

MANUSCRIPT: Longfellow Trust Collection. ADDRESS: Miss Caroline Doane/Care
of Dr George B. Doane/Boston./Mr Geo: W Pierce.

1. William Cowper, The Task, IV, 88.
2. Published in the United States Literary Gazette, IV, No. 1 (April 1, 1826),
30, this poem was Longfellow's last contribution to the journal.

Stephen and Zilpah Longfellow, c. 1804, by William King

Longfellow, 1825

PLATE I

Stephen Longfellow, Jr., 1824

Stephen Longfellow, c. 1825

PLATE II

Bowdoin College, 1821

PLATE III

Letter to Stephen Longfellow, October 19, 1826 (No. 105)

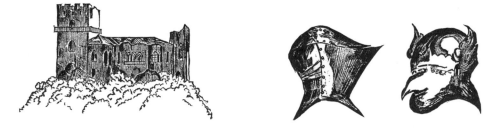

PLATE IV Sketch by Longfellow, Letter No. 144

PART TWO

EUROPE

1826–1829

EUROPE

1826–1829

LONGFELLOW LEFT PORTLAND at the end of April, 1826, stopped at Boston to collect the indispensable letters of introduction, and then proceeded over the Berkshires to Albany and down the Hudson to New York. On May 15 he sailed from America on the packet *Cadmus* for Havre de Grâce. He was nineteen years old and Bowdoin's unofficial professor-elect of the modern languages, which he had yet to learn. From the time he left home until he returned in August, 1829, he wrote over a hundred letters, sixty-six of which have been recovered for Part II of this volume. Of this group, forty-nine were written to members of the Longfellow family and represent, as far as can be determined, an almost complete file of the letters that Longfellow sent home.

Because he was at the mercy of an inefficient and expensive postal system and because of sporadic opportunities to send letters by private hand, Longfellow wrote irregularly from abroad, with the result that the details of his itinerary were not always clear to his correspondents. He left Portland with the understanding that he would spend two years in Europe, mostly in France and Spain, concentrating on the languages of those countries, and that if he accomplished his goal in good time, he could devote the remaining months to travel and study in Italy and Germany. It was a plan that lent itself to modifications. Indeed, Longfellow got no farther than Boston before George Ticknor attempted to adjust his program in favor of Germany. Eventually the two years became three, and he spent more time in Italy than anywhere else. As an exchange of letters with his father took months, he sometimes followed a travel plan before receiving authorization from home or described one that he subsequently abandoned. Readers of his letters need not share, however, the frustration of his parents, who were never quite sure where their son would be next. With the help of his journals and miscellaneous papers a fairly accurate itinerary of his travels can be plotted.

June 14–19, 1826: Arrived Havre de Grâce. En route Paris via Rouen.

June 20, 1826—February 14, 1827: Paris (c. August 3—c. September 3, Auteuil; October 3–12, excursion to Orleans, Tours, Vendôme).

February 15—March 9: En route Madrid via Orleans, Limoges, Bordeaux (c. February 20—c. March 1), Bayonne, Irun, Tolosa, Burgos.

March 10—September 1: Madrid (March or April, excursion to Segovia, St. Ildefonso, Escorial; May 24—June 7, excursion to Villaneuva del Pardillo).

September 2, 1827—January 1, 1828: En route Florence via Seville (c. September 14–23), Cadiz (September 24—c. October 1), Gibraltar (c. October 3—c. November 3), Malaga (c. November 5–20, with excursion to Granada, November 10–17), Marseilles (c. December 10–16), Toulon, Nice, Genoa (December 24–27), Pisa, Leghorn.

January 2—February 5: Florence.

February 6–11: En route Rome.

February 12—December 8: Rome (April 9–25, Naples; early July and August 1—c. September 4, L'Ariccia).

December 9, 1828—February 22, 1829: En route Göttingen via Venice (December 14–25), Trieste (December 26–c. 29), Vienna (January 1–9), Prague, Dresden (January 13—February 18), Leipzig.

February 23—June 5: Göttingen (April 15—c. May 14, excursion to England via Rhineland, Brussels, Calais-Dover, Canterbury, London [c. April 25—c. May 2], Rotterdam, Amsterdam, Utrecht, Cassel).

June 6–c. 30: En route Liverpool via Frankfurt, Mayence, Metz, Paris (June 13–22), London, Oxford, Coventry, Birmingham.

July 1—August 11: Liverpool to New York.

This extensive itinerary undoubtedly exceeded the original intentions of Stephen Longfellow, who in his own letters occasionally revealed a slight impatience with his son's apparently lighthearted wanderings over the face of Europe. He had always looked upon the experience as a practical investment, whose dividends would provide Henry with security as a college teacher if at the same time he wished to try his talents in the less stable world of literature. Yet he subsidized the journey willingly enough, with all its tours and detours, sharing vicariously his son's delight with French and Spanish countrysides, with Florence, Rome, and Göttingen. Later he prepared a careful statement of accounts in which he listed the cost of the three years abroad. The total came to $2604.24. "The above," he reminded his son, "is to be considered as an advancement in the settlement of my Estate." By 1849, when his father died, Longfellow could well afford to pay the debt.

Eventually the investment paid off more richly than Stephen Longfellow could have expected when he made out his bill of costs; but even in 1829 he must have been satisfied that he had advised wisely and well. The three years abroad had put a mark of maturity on his son. He had learned the languages, filled his mind with the images of older cultures, and enjoyed the milder indiscretions of independence. He was ready, at twenty-two, to settle into a professorship at Bowdoin College.

Nevertheless, readers of this second group of his letters can readily deduce that Longfellow did not return to America a completely trained and disciplined scholar. He had mastered most of the problems of idiom and grammar and had accumulated a sheaf of miscellaneous jottings from a variety of learned volumes. Learning the languages, however, had taken precedence over literary research. He was largely self-taught; and with the weakness of youth he had often sacrificed study to the enjoyment of the romantic scenes about him. He was therefore no Ticknor, no Bancroft or Cogswell, when he assumed his duties at Bowdoin. Rather, he was a well-educated young man with sophisticated tastes and a restless ambition. This ambition plus the demands and exigencies of instructing undergraduates first turned him toward genuine scholarship during the next years.

One final point should be made concerning this European tour. His letters reveal that Longfellow was immersed completely in the tradition of the romantic pilgrim wandering over an idealized landscape. He seems never to have outgrown this Childe Harold complex, although on later trips to the Continent other interests and problems infringed upon it. Europe in 1826–1829 existed in his mind as the "land where the golden apples grow." It was the inspiration for his first really ambitious literary work, *Outre-Mer,* and it continued to stir his imagination as long as he lived. He was quick to forget the less romantic aspects of the experience — the sicknesses, the discomforts of travel, the moral indignations, the pangs of homesickness — but he was rarely unable to conjure up images of the beleaguered city of Prague, the belfry of Bruges, the crooked streets of Nuremberg, or the cool, silent cathedrals of Italy. As the idealization of these scenes of his youth continued, he found in them a major source of poetry.

89. *To Zilpah Longfellow*

Boston   May 2nd 1826.

My good Mother,

I have been too constantly engaged since my arrival here to write you, until this last hour of my stay, when I am expecting every moment to hear the stage, which is to carry me to Northampton, drive up to the door. We were to start at 2 o'clock A.M. — but the stage is not here yet, so that I shall have at least time enough to tell you how kindly my friends have received me here, and how I have succeeded with letters &c.

I heard Dr Channing on Sunday.[1] He preached a most eloquent sermon, and preached it most eloquently. I have passed part of an evening with him since, but like Paul, I believe it is — tho' a good preacher, he is "in bodily presence weak."[2] I dined to day with Mr Ticknor.[3] He is a little Spanish-looking man, but exceedingly kind and affable. He has supplied me with letters to Washington Irving — Prof. Eichorn in Germany[4] — and Robert Southey. He strongly recommends a year's residence in Germany — and is very decidedly and strongly in favor of commencing literary studies there.

One of Dr Well's letters introduced me to Dr Lowell[5] who has given me a letter to the celebrated Mrs Grant of Laggan — author of a poem, which you will find somewhere about the house, called the "Highlanders."[6] I have several other letters which it will be useless to enumerate.

On monday I was at Cambridge and saw Pres. Kirkland.[7] He is a jolly little man — and does not pretend to put on all that dignity and high decorum, which sometimes hang — and oddly enough, too, upon the shoulders of men in office.

I am thoroughly and sadly tired every evening with running about on the hard pavements of this city all day long, and on some accounts I do not regret leaving town so soon as I shall leave it, tho' on other accounts of course I do.

I have written this miserable scrawl in the greatest haste merely to let you know a little of my "sayings and doings" here, and to inclose a receipt of $130. — from Mr Otis.[8]

Stage has come — good bye

Love to all —

Yrs
Henry[9]

MANUSCRIPT: Longfellow Trust Collection. ADDRESS: Stephen Longfellow Esq/ Portland. POSTMARK: BOSTON MS MAY 3 ANNOTATION (*by Zilpah Longfellow*): The flute arrived this morning a few hours after H's departure — we will return it to Portland the first opportunity.

1. William Ellery Channing (1780–1842), the apostle of Unitarianism, had been Stephen Longfellow's classmate at Harvard.

2. II Cor. 10:10.

3. George Ticknor (1791–1871) held the professorship of modern languages at Harvard to which Longfellow ultimately succeeded.

4. Johan Gottfried Eichhorn (1752–1827), the so-called "founder of Old Testament criticism," had been Ticknor's professor and friend at Göttingen.

5. Rev. Charles Lowell (1782–1861), pastor of the West Unitarian church in Boston, was the father of James Russell Lowell.

6. Mrs. Anne McVickar Grant of Laggan (1755–1838) had achieved a reputation in both Britain and America with her translations of Highland poetry and her *Memoirs of an American Lady* (1808), an account of her life in New York State, 1758–1768. Charles Lowell and his brother John (1769–1840) had known and admired her in Edinburgh, and the latter had donated $5000 to a fund for her

support. Longfellow did not go to Scotland and consequently did not make use of his letters of introduction.

7. John Thornton Kirkland (1770–1840), president of Harvard College, 1810–1827.

8. Presumably Harrison Gray Otis (1765–1848), Stephen Longfellow's friend and Federalist ally in the Massachusetts legislature and at the Hartford Convention in 1814.

9. Some indication of his mother's feelings and anxieties on the occasion of Longfellow's departure may be had from the following lines, which reached him before he sailed from New York on May 15: "It was very fortunate for me that your Boston stage was late, as it gave me the pleasure of receiving a letter from you, which is no small consolation in your absence. I will not say how much we miss your elastic step, your cheerful voice, your melodious flute; but will say farewell my dear son, may God be with and prosper you. May you be successful in your pursuit of knowledge, may you hold fast your integrity, and retain that purity of heart which is so interesting and endearing to friends. I feel as if you were going into a thousand perils. You must be watchful and guard against every temptation."

90. *To Stephen Longfellow*

Albany [May]¹ 5th. 1826.

My dear Father,

I have atlength reached this dirty city: — this morning from Northampton. I shall not however remain here long enough to visit any of the public buildings — not even the grand canal,² as I am to sail down river tomorrow morning in the James Kent.

With the village of Northampton I was highly delighted. The mountain and river scenery near it are certainly very beautiful, and from Round Hill — the seat of Messrs Coggswell and Bancroft's school you have an extensive view of the village and its environs.³ These gentlemen received me with the greatest kindness — and have furnished me with a number of excellent letters. They coincide with Prof. Ticknor of Cambridge in recommending a year's residence at Göttingen. Mr Ticknor says that the expenses there will not be so great as at Paris, and that it is all-important to have a knowledge of the German language. The Lectures on literary history, which he wishes me to attend there, commence in October, and he says I could before that time become sufficiently advanced [in] the language to understand them. I should take rooms there as at Paris, and should pay about one guinea for a course of Lectures. It will, he thinks, be removing me from a great deal of temptation, and moreover be laying a solid foundation for future literary acquirements.

For my own part — I must confess that this change in my original plan did not strike me very favorably at first — but the more I reflect upon it the better I like it. I wish you to write me, at New York, as soon as you receive this — and tell me what you think of the change in my plans. Mr Ticknor and Mr Bancroft have both studied at Göttingen, and of course their opinion upon the subject is of much weight.

At Northampton, I visited the Lead Mine, which lies about 8 miles from the village. They call it a Lead Mine by courtesy, because geologists say that a vein of lead ore runs somewhere in the vicinity and specimens have here and there been found. The entrance is at the side of a clay hill and the passage is roofed with timber; — and is about 3 feet in height — measuring from the surface of the water which everywhere fills the bottom of the cavern, and affords easy means of passage in and out by boat. You soon, however reach the solid granite, thro' which an excavation has been made to the distance of nine hundred feet, making the length of the whole cavern about one thousand. The height of the cave, after it reaches the granite, varies from three to ten feet: — and the whole passage is made by the traveller in a little flat bottomed boat, in which he stretches himself upon his back and is propelled forward by a kind of ragged Palinurus, who navigates the boat by pushing with his feet against the roof of the cavern, where it is low enough — and where it is not by means of a pole thrust against the rocky sides, which are on an average about 5 or 6 feet distant from each other. The whole business is very curious — and certainly the cave is a monument of human perseverance — since after more than twenty years labor no vein has been found. The Perkinses of Boston[4] are the principal proprietors, — and the man who lives in the nearest cottage has worked the mine for eleven years.

What wretched writing materials one gets on the road! This is my excuse for such wretched scribbling. My best love to all.

Your affect Son
Henry. —

I shall not go down to New York in one day — because I wish to pass the High[l]ands by day light. From the City of New York I shall write to the girls — and send Alexander's and Sam's balls, which I quite forgot at Boston.

MANUSCRIPT: Longfellow Trust Collection. ADDRESS: To/Stephen Longfellow Esq./Portland/Me. — POSTMARK (*in script*): RECD HOOK LANDING/MAY 8. 1826

1. Longfellow mistakenly wrote "April."
2. The Erie Canal, completed in 1825.
3. Joseph Green Cogswell and George Bancroft established the Round Hill School in 1823, modeling it in part after the famous Swiss schools run by Fellenberg and Pestalozzi. Both men were eager advocates of European study. For accounts of their school and their relationship with Longfellow, see Orie W. Long, *Literary Pioneers* (Cambridge, 1935) and *Young Longfellow*, pp. 83–85.

4. Thomas Handasyd Perkins (1764–1854), Boston merchant and philanthropist, and his brother James (1761–1822) had for thirty years conducted business enterprises noted for their variety and general success.

91. *To Elizabeth Longfellow*

New York   May 14th 1826.

My dear Sister,

This is the first good opportunity that I have had of informing you of the places I have visited since I left home — of the route I pursued — and of my tarrying here and there. It was a day's ride from Boston to Northampton, and I remained one day at that village, and reached Albany the next evening just as the sun was going down. The approach to that city by the Northampton road is very pleasant. As we de[s]cended into the valley of the Hudson, we had an excellent view of the city, rising on the opposite shore of the river, with its spires and roofs gilded by the setting sun — whilst behind us a double rain-bow stretched across the hills. The appearance of the city from this point is not unlike that of our own town, seen from the farthest extremity of the new bridge: — but Albany is certainly a very dirty place.

I was very desirous on leaving Albany to pass the highlands of the Hudson, and the hills of Wehawken by daylight, and consequently made arrangements to stop at Caatskill, and to ascend the mountains, my head being full of Hendrick Hudson and his crew at nine-pins — the Doolittle Inn — and Rip Van Winkle. I found it however too early in the season to put my plans into execution, in as much as travellers have not yet begun to ascend the hills and of course the means of conveyance were not at hand. I therefore stopped at Hudson, and went down by land to Red Hook, where I passed Sunday afternoon. The scenery on the North River between Albany and Hudson is very beautiful, especially where the river makes a gradual sweep round a low point of land, and you catch the last view of Albany. There is something very peculiar and singular in the style of building which one here sees in the little Dutch farm-houses — constructed partly of stone and partly of small Holland bricks — with thatch-roofed barns and out-houses. I sketched one or two of them on the back of a letter, which will give you a faint idea of them.[1]

Red Hook is a very beautiful little village — and from it you have a fine view of the blue peaks of the Caatskill Mountains "stretching up to a noble height, and lording it over the surrounding country."[2] On the afternoon of Sunday [May 7] I attended the village church. It is a small and simple building, standing upon a little eminence and surrounded by its church-yard. The villagers have a beautiful and romantic custom of placing a slender white railing around the graves of their friends, and of planting flowers within them. Some of the grave stones were over-run with moss, whilst others were covered with the wild rose, with osiers bending over them.

I left Red Hook on Monday, but did not reach this City till 4 o'clock on Tuesday morning [May 9]. I was exceedingly disappointed in not seeing The Highlands by daylight after all my delay for that purpose. I went to Philadelphia on Wednesday — remained there but one day and returned to this place on Friday — not very much delighted with my journey.

Remember me most affectionately to all the family and all my friends.

Your aff[ectionate] brother
Henry.

I have bought the Indian Rubber balls and will send them as soon as possible. I received Mama's letter this morning by P.H.G. [Patrick Henry Greenleaf] — and should have answered it to day if I could have found a moment's leisure.

MANUSCRIPT: Longfellow Trust Collection. ADDRESS: To/Miss Elisabeth W. Longfellow/Care of Stephen Longfellow. Esq./Portland. POSTMARK: NEW YORK MAY 15

1. Longfellow's sketch follows this paragraph.
2. Cf. Washington Irving, *Rip Van Winkle*.

92. *To Anne Longfellow*

New York. May 14th 1826.

My dear Ann[e],

The little note which you sent by Wm Greely [1] reached me in safety as I was walking up Broad Way, — tho' I am sorry to say that the "noble youth — of light fantastic toe" was not with me. I saw him to day for the first time. He was dressed very genteely in black — with a nice pair of Wellington boots — and a whole row of little buttons at the bottom of his pantaloons. We were of course very glad to see each other after so long an absence, and he made particular inquiries after the health of all his Portland friends. I am going to take tea with him at his sister's house this evening.[2] This, you see, is putting Uriah in "the fore-front of the battle:"[3] — but I must hasten to answer a part of your note, which was evidently written with the greatest interest of any part.

I was at Brooklyn on Wednesday — the same day on which I arrived in this city. It was about sunset, and I found both Uncle and

Aunt at home.[4] I saw them again yesterday; — dined with them, and went to the Navy Yard with them — and am every moment expecting Uncle here. I have been very much delighted with Aunt Louisa — every way delighted with her — and yet I am very well aware, that I can give you no description of her person sufficiently correct to enable you to form any idea of her appearance. She is just about your own size, but her figure is entirely different from yours; — I know not whose it resembles — nor indeed do I know who has a countenance resembling hers. Her complection is very dark — and her eyes black and brilliant — and her whole face very expressive and very intellectual. By the way — I am going over tomorrow morning to take breakfast with her, and say good bye for the last time.

I sail for Le Havre de Grace tomorrow at 10 o'clock. in the forenoon, on board the Ship Cadmus, Capt. Allen. She left the wharf yesterday noon, and the passengers are to be taken down the bay to her by the Steam Boat Nautilus. There are twenty cabin passengers, two of which are ladies — and many of the gentlemen are French, which will be of great advantage to me. The ship is a very fine one and the Capt. has the reputation of being an excellent man.[5] This will make everything as pleasant as can be; and at this season of the year I cannot but anticipate a good passage.

I was not so much pleased with Philadelphia as I expected to be. It is not half so pleasant to me as New York. Whilst there I visited Pratt's Gardens and the Water Works at Fair Mount.[6] You can get a better description of the latter at home than I can possibly give you: and of the former I can only say that I was astonished to find a man who had taste enough to expend part of his wealth in purchasing such beautiful grounds and in filling his green houses with exotics of every description from lemons and oranges down to tea and coffee — to find such a man cutting his fish-ponds into regular figures — like so many ditches.

I saw Mr and Mrs Derby and Sarah Ellen Derby[7] at Philadelphia, and went with them to a little "sociable" in the evening — where we had dancing. It is worthy of remark that in that city they dance on all occasions. Carey and Lea — the Philadelphia booksellers will publish the second volume of the Atlantic Souvenir in October next. I forgot to tell you that the pieces I wrote you[8] were entitled "The Spirit of Poetry" — "The Burial of the Minnisink" — "Song of the Birds" — and "The Dead Bird — a ballad." [9]

Love to all! Farewell!

Your affectionate Brother
Henry.

I received my flute by Patrick Greenleaf, who arrived here this morning. Had I known that William Greely would have left town before my return from Philadelphia I should have written by him to some of the family.

MANUSCRIPT: Longfellow Trust Collection. ADDRESS: To/Miss Ann[e] Longfellow/ Care of Stephen Longfellow Esq/Portland. POSTMARK: NEW YORK MAY 15

1. William E. Greeley, a commission merchant of Portland (*Portland Directory and Register for 1827*).

2. The "noble youth — of light fantastic toe" was possibly Eugene Weld, with whom Longfellow had lunch on the day of his departure (see Letter No. 117). Weld was studying medicine in New York.

3. II Sam. 11:15.

4. Capt. Alexander Scammell Wadsworth and his wife Louisa J. Denison (b. 1786), whom he had married in 1824.

5. Francis Allyn (d. 1862) was master of the Havre Line's *Cadmus* from 1824 to 1827. He was subsequently mayor of New London, Connecticut, 1838–1841.

6. Henry Pratt (1761–1838), a wealthy shipping merchant of Philadelphia, had built Lemon Hill, an estate overlooking the Schuylkill and noted for its exotic plants and decorative fishponds. Nearby the city had completed the first municipal waterworks in America in 1801. Both Lemon Hill and the waterworks are now a part of Fairmount Park.

7. Sarah Ellen Derby (b. 1805), who became the mother of John Rogers, the sculptor, was the daughter of Capt. John Derby and Eleanor Coffin Derby of Salem. Her mother, daughter of Dr. Nathaniel Coffin of Portland, was well acquainted with the Longfellows.

8. Longfellow presumably meant "for it," a correction that has been made in pencil by another hand.

9. *The Atlantic Souvenir; A Christmas and New Year's Offering, 1827* (Philadelphia, H.C. Carey & I. Lea, 1826) contains "The Song of the Birds," pp. 113–114, and "Burial of the Minnisink," pp. 200–201. "The Spirit of Poetry" appeared in the next edition of the annual. "The Dead Bird" seems never to have been published. (Luther S. Livingston, *A Bibliography of the First Editions in Book Form of the Writings of Henry Wadsworth Longfellow* [New York, 1908], pp. 4–5).

93. *To Zilpah Longfellow*

Havre de Grace. June 15th. 1826

My dear Mother,

I have atlength reached the shores of the Old World. We arrived yesterday at four o'clock P.M. and I employ the first leisure moment to send you tidings of my safety. I suppose you will wonder that I did not employ my time at sea in writing to my friends — and I almost wonder at it, too, — but there was so much confusion on board the ship — such a continual talking of French and broken English — for Frenchmen you know talk incessantly — and we had at least a dozen of them with us — that I found it utterly impossible to write a coherent epistle and threw by my first and only attempt in despair.

You will see by the date of this that our passage was thirty days. On many accounts it was a remarkably fine one. We saw none of the terrors of the sea. We had not one heavy gale, and the sea was so smooth that the whole voyage might have been safely made in a yawl boat. I forget what I used to think of a sea-voyage when on land — but I have found it a dreary blank. I had little else to do than to busy myself with my own thoughts and meditations, so few circumstances were there at sea to call me away from them. Hence I cannot describe my sensations on taking my last look of my native land and my first of a foreign one.

You perceive in what great haste I write, and must excuse me from giving any particular description of Havre, which I leave in a few minutes in the Steam Boat for Rouen. However I can give you a sketch of the city in general terms. You will get the best idea of the style of building here, which you can possibly get without seeing the place, by calling to mind the pictures in a little book which we had when children ycleped London cries.[1] The houses are all of stone or small yellow bricks — very narrow and most of them five — and many six stories high — with 'peticoat and pantaloon' dangling from the upper windows, and linen hung out to dry on little balconies. The streets are most of them paved with flat stones about six inches square, — without side-walks — and sloping down from the buildings on each side to a little gutter in the middle, something in this manner.[2]

The fortifications of the city, which are now somewhat out of repair, are very extensive. If my memory serves me they were commenced by Louis 13 — and finished by Louis 14th.[3] The eastern part of the city is defended by a double ditch forty feet in width with ramparts thirty or forty in height. Beyond these lies the most beautiful part of the city — the commercial part being very low, dingy and dirty. But east of the gates the land rises abruptly — sloping to the south east — covered with the richest verdure — with the country-houses of the citizens rising terrace above terrace to the very top. The antique buildings, with peaked roofs and tall chimneys, — peeping out from amid the trees have a very romantic and beautiful appearance — but as these gardens are private and my time here was short I did not ascend the hill.

I thought I should have written to Stephen and the girls and all of you whilst at Havre — but I did not get my trunks from the Police Office till 10 o'clock this morning — and my whole writing apparatus was contained in them, which has prevented me from putting my good designs into practice. But I know that you will be well satisfied to hear of my safe arrival, and that I am in the best possible health. Our passage was so much longer than all on board anticipated, that we have arrived barely in season to send letters by the Queen Mab, which sails this evening. Give my best love to all the family — and to all friends.

Very Affectionately Yours for aye
H. W L. —

Recollect to pay the postage of your letters as far as New York — or I shall never receive them.

MANUSCRIPT: Longfellow Trust Collection. ADDRESS: To./Stephen Longfellow Esqr./Portland/State of Maine./U.S. of America. —/By ship/Queen Mab POSTMARKS: NEW YORK JUL 31/SHIP

1. *London Cries for Children. With Twenty Elegant Wood Cuts* (Philadelphia, 1810).
2. Longfellow's sketch follows this sentence.
3. Francis I fortified Le Havre in 1516. Richelieu continued work on the fortifications during the reign of Louis XIII, and Louis XIV completed them.

94. *To Stephen Longfellow, Jr.*

Havre de Grace. June. 15th 1826

My dear brother,

Having lost my passage to Rouen by delay in obtaining a passport, I am obliged to remain another night in this city: and to complete the catastrophy, instead of journeying up the fair waters of the Seine in the Steam boat as I intended, I shall be jolted and jostled along a rough highway in a French diligence. I have been much pleased with this city, because everything about it is perfectly novel to me. What first attracted my attention, as we came slowly up the quai, was the singular construction of the houses, all of which are old and much dilapidated. No description can give you any conception of their quaint and peculiar style — though you can conceive how odd a spectacle it must be to see in a street of only one rod's width, with tall dingy houses six stories high — a grand display from every upper window of blankets and bed-cloathes — old shirts and old sheets — flapping in the wind — not to mention

> "Loose pantaloon and peticoat
> Pendant on dyer's pole afloat." — [1]

As I walked from the ship to the Hotel I was irresistably seized with divers fits of laughter. At almost every step I encountered gens-d'armes with fierce whiskers and curling beard[s] — women with wooden shoes full of feet and straw — paper hats and tight pantaloons — and the dames of Normandy with tall pyramidal caps of muslin — reaching at least two feet above the head, and adorned with long ear-lappets.

A French 'table d'hote' is well worth mentioning from its novelty to a stranger. The first dish of course is soup, — and next they will bring you a piece of meat — of what kind you choose — but no bigger than your two fingers — and then they change your plate and give you a piece of a different kind — but of the same size — and so on for ten or a dozen dishes. After the meats are removed they bring on the vegetables — then fruit — then cake. It is very amusing to see a frenchman tuck his napkin under his chin and fall to — and yesterday the very paragon of Paddy Carey[2] was at table. He was a great burly-faced dragoon — a Bold Dragoon — about seven feet high with nothing French about him but his language and his uniform and as this "proper man"[3] talked and laughed with the landlady, I could not help thinking of Widow Leary and

> "Pat so sly
> Ogle throws" — [4]

which put me in mind of Ned Preble. If Ned only knew the one hundredth part of the laughable things which I have seen during one day's residence in Havre, he would lament long and loud that he had not come to France with me.[5]

The fortifications of this city are very grand. I cannot describe them to you because I know not military terms enough to make you comprehend me: — but they seem to me to be impregnable. Beyond the gates of these, on the eastern side, are the Boulevards of the city, and beyond these a thickly wooded hill with country houses. In this direction, too, the road leads you thro' an avenue of trees to the Havre Light Houses.

But it waxes late and I start tomorrow at six. Ergo — good night. Did Pa receive a letter from me concerning going to Germany?[6] I put this in the form of a question tho' all I intend is to say that I wrote upon the subject — before I reached New York.

You will of course remember me particularly to all my particular friends without my being more particular: — and as to the family, they all know how much love I bear them, without a repetition of the old saying about poor pens and pale ink — et cetera. I shall not write again before I reach Paris — when I shall open upon Fred — and

Ned — and Pat[7] — and all who are to be my correspondents. Farewell.

Your affectionate brother
Henry —

MANUSCRIPT: Longfellow Trust Collection. ADDRESS: To/Stephen Longfellow. Jr./Portland./State of Maine./U.S. of America. — /[By the] Stephania — ANNOTATION: forwarded by R. Vassoit & Co./Le Havre 25th. June 1826 — POSTMARKS: NEW YORK AUG 4/SHIP

1. In his manuscript journal describing the Carnival in Rome, Longfellow inverts these lines and adds a third: "Pendant from Dyer's pole afloat/Loose pantaloon and peticoat —/Indignant flout the air! —" Their source has not been identified.

2. The hero of an Irish song. See the *Universal Song Book; a complete collection of the songs and ballads of Ireland* (New York, 1904), pp. 100–101.

3. *Midsummer Night's Dream*, I, ii, 84.

4. From stanza 4 of "Paddy Carey." Paddy, whose brawny shoulders and cheeks "like thumping red potatoes" made him the idol of the ladies, married the unattractive Widow Leary in order to buy a captain's commission with her money.

5. Preble had apparently considered traveling to Europe with Longfellow but chose to remain in Portland. Soon after his friend's departure, however, he made secret plans to join him in Europe (see Letter No. 105). He left America in the spring of 1828 and studied with Longfellow at Göttingen.

6. That is, Letter No. 90.

7. Frederick Mellen, Ned Preble, and Patrick Greenleaf.

95. *To Stephen Longfellow*

Paris. June. 20. 1826

My dear Father,

I arrived in this great Babylon of modern times on sunday evening — the 19th of June,[1] and am in haste to let you know exactly how I am situated before I say anything of the wonders of this city. As soon as I got out of the Diligence and my trunks had been searched to the satisfaction of the police officer, whose conscience allowed him to be satisfied with thrusting his hands down at the sides of the trunks, I jumped into a cabriolet and crossed the river for the Fauxbourg St Germain. As my first object was to find Eben. Storer[2] I went immediately to Madame Potet's — "No 49 — Rue Monsieur Le Prince Faux — St. Germ." The family were all from home, but knowing French enough to make myself understood by the servants I got my baggage taken from the cabriolet and awaited their return. They arrived about midnight, which by the way is not a very late hour here. I was received with the greatest kindness — for Cousin Eben it seems had told Madame of my coming to Paris and had procured a room for me here, where I intend to reside whilst I remain in Paris. You cannot conceive how very fortunate I am in getting into this family. Madame Potet is one of the best women in the world, and tho' I have been here but two days I feel myself perfectly at home. Madame P——— has two adopted daughters with her, the elder of which is about twelve or thirteen years old — the other about 8. The younger is engaged to a gentleman twenty one years old, which may seem strange to all of you, tho' it is the common custom in France to engage all little girls of about that age. The elder performs most elegantly on the Piano-forte, which adds much to our pleasures here; — since she plays with nearly as much ease and elegance as Nolcini himself.

I know of but one objection to my residing here whilst at Paris, and that is that there are seven of us boarders — "Sons," as Madame calls us — all Americans. Perhaps you will think there is danger of speaking too much english — and there would be indeed, if we were much together — but we seldom assemble except at meals at which all english is forbidden — and he who speaks a word of it is fined one sou. Moreover three of the boarders have resided some time in Paris and speak French well. My chamber is small but very beautifully furnished — tho' you seldom see a carpet in Paris, the floors of the houses being made of oak finely polished and waxed or of little tiles painted red. Indeed I think I could not be so well situated elsewhere, nor could I obtain a place where I should enjoy so great advantages for acquiring a knowledge of the French language. If I had my chambers at a Hotel I should have a thousand solitary hours, because I cannot speak french well enough to go into French society — but now if I wish to be alone I can shut myself up in my chamber — if I wish for society I can go at any hour into Madam's parlour — and talk my kind of French with her and her daughters, — besides the pleasure of hearing most delicious music.

I do not know whether this situation of mine will in the long run be more expensive than one at a hotel. We pay thirty six dollars a month — for our board and rooms — and our washing about 50 cents a week. But at present it is not in my power to be more particular touching expenses — after I have resided here a ||while|| longer I can give you more correct information — which I shall not fail to give from time to time. Our house is finely situated for a student — within five minutes walk of the Public Lectures on all subjects — but a few steps from the Luxembourg gardens and the Pantheon. I have reserved all description of persons — places and things in general until I have seen more of the city, and have had time to collect my thoughts a little, which are altogether in confusion from the total novelty of everything about me. I feel as happy as possible — am in the best health in the world — and delighted with Paris — where a person if he pleases can keep out of vice as well as elsewhere, tho' to be sure temptations are multiplied a thousand fold if he is willing to enter into them. Remember me very kindly and affectionately to all.

Your son
Henry. —

My address is "Chez Madame Potet, rue Monsieur Le Prince — No. 49 Fauxbourg St. Germain à Paris".

MANUSCRIPT: Longfellow Trust Collection. ADDRESS: To./Stephen Longfellow. Esq./Portland./Maine./By the Ship Cadmus POSTMARKS: NEW YORK AUG [6?]/SHIP

1. Sunday evening was June 18.
2. Ebenezer Storer (1803–1882), Longfellow's second cousin, was studying medicine in Paris. He later practiced for many years in New York City.

96. To Parker Cleaveland

Paris July. 10th. 1826.
Rue Monsieur Le Prince. 49. St. Germain. —

Dear Sir,

I take one of the earliest opportunities afforded me to inform you of my safe arrival in Paris, — but so bewildered am I in this great mart of wonders and novelties, — that I can hardly put together two coherent sentences. I am pleasantly situated in the quiet Fauxbourg of St. Germain — and within five minutes walk of the principal lecture rooms and colleges in the city — but during the few weeks I have been here I have done little else than run from one quarter of the city to another, with eyes and mouth wide open — staring into print-shops — book-stores — gardens — palaces — and prisons.

A day or two since I went to the Garden of plants — or "Jardin du Roi" — with your letters to Mr Lucas and Mr Brongniart[1] — for the latter resides during the summer at the Garden of Plants — tho' his house is in Rue St. Dominique. When I inquired for Mr Lucas, the Porter replied "Il n'y est plus" — but not knowing that this phrase was equivalent to our expression "he is no more" — I asked where he had gone. "Il est mort" — was the answer. The son died in January last[2] — and the father in April — but of what diseases I know not.

Mr Brongniart I found in the Mineralogical Cabinet, very busily engaged in making some new arrangement of shelves of minerals — or something of that kind. He is a small man — with the air of a brisk little bachelor about him — and an intelligent, good-humoured countenance, somewhat resembling Mr. Abbot's.[3] His manners, too, are exceedingly kind and affable, — but as he speaks not a word of English and I know, as yet, but precious little of speaking French, it was fortunate that I had a person with me who understood both languages. It seems he has outstripped your anticipations in the publications of his Mineralogy — for he has not only published the second edition of his work — but is now preparing the third.[4] He was so exceedingly busy when I saw him, that I presumed it would not be convenient for him to furnish me with a copy at that moment, but I will see him again before I seal my letter, and inquire more particularly about dates and the time of publication of both the second and third editions. He was kind enough to give me a ticket of admission to the "Manufacture Royale des Porcelaines" at Sèvres,[5] at which place he spends every Tuesday — Thursday — and Saturday.

I wish I had time and ability to give you the least adequate idea of the magnificent Garden of Plants — which owes so much to the labors of Buffon, and which at present employs in its various departments more than one hundred and sixty persons, and an annual expenditure of upwards of £12.000. Cuvier is still employed in the Cabinet of Comparative Anatomy: — and Public Lectures are delivered in the amphitheater on general Chemistry — pharmaceutical chemistry — the application of Chemistry to the arts and manufactures — botany — the mammalia and birds, — reptiles and fishes, — the invertebral animals — geology — iconography — and Mineralogy. And all this, too, public — perfectly public. What a noble institution!

July 11th.

I have just returned from the Garden of Plants, where I have been to make more particular inquiries of Mr. Brongniart, concerning the publication of his Mineralogy. The imperfect understanding I have of the French language when spoken, led me yesterday into a considerable error touching the different editions of Mr. Bro[n]gniart's work. I understood him to say that he had published a second edition, and was now preparing a third, but it seems he was speaking of you and your Mineralogy, — and as regards his own work, he has as yet published but one edition. It will be a long time, he says — probably a year, before the 2nd edition of his book will appear. He is, in the mean time, preparing ||another|| work on the Geology of Paris and its environs, which w||ill s||hortly be published,[6] and a copy of which he will forward to you by the earliest opportunity.

We have had a little of real American Weather here this summer. On the first of this month the thermometer was at ninety — which is the highest to which the mercury has risen. But we have none of the pleasant breezes of a summer's afternoon, which you enjoy daily at Brunswick — indeed I should hardly have known from what I have observed in Paris, that there was such a phenomenon in the natural world, as are put in motion. Remember me very affectionately to all your family — and if you please to all who care enough about me to inquire after me.

Yours very respectfully and affectionately
Henry W. Longfellow. —

MANUSCRIPT: Berg Collection, New York Public Library. ADDRESS: To/Mr. Parker Cleaveland —/Professor of Mathematics and Nat. Phil./Bowdoin College./ Brunswick. Maine. —/U.S. of America. — POSTMARKS: ‖NEW YOR‖K AUG 13/FORWARDED BY DE LAUNAY LUUYT CO HAVRE/SHIP

1. Jean André Henri Lucas (1780–1825), French mineralogist and keeper of the galleries in the Museum of Natural History, was the son of the curator of the museum. The elder Lucas was reputedly the illegitimate son of the naturalist Buffon. Alexandre Brongniart (1770–1847) had succeeded Haüy as professor of mineralogy in the museum.

2. Actually, February 6, 1825.

3. John Abbot (44.1).

4. *Introduction à la minéralogie, ou Exposé de principes de cette science* (Paris, 1824). A second edition appeared in 1825.

5. The Porcelain Manufactory, founded in 1738 at Vincennes, was transferred to Sèvres in 1756. Brongniart was its director from 1800 until his death, during which time Sèvres became the most important name in ceramic chemistry.

6. Longfellow seems still to have misunderstood. Brongniart and Cuvier originally published their *Essai sur la géographie minéralogique des environs de Paris* in 1811. At this time Brongniart was presumably at work on his *Classification et caractéres minéralogiques des rockes homogènes et hétérogènes* (Paris, 1827).

97. To Longfellow Sisters [1]

Paris. July 10th. 1826. —
Rue Mons Le Prince 49. St. Germain.

My dear Sisters,

Whenever I think how far I am from you, and how long it will be before I see you again I am half-disposed to be a little melancholy: — just as I felt when I left you like the friends of Paul — "sorrowing most of all that they should see his face no more" [2] — as William Browne says in his last letter. In truth a man has not much time to spare in melancholy thoughts when surrounded as I am by the continual gaiety of Paris, but at the same time these are thoughts, which one would not wholly banish — when they spring from the recollections of home, — and absent friends — and "auld lang syne."

I suppose you will think on reading thus far, that I am going to be exceedingly tender and sentimental throughout the whole of a long letter, but I cannot be so prodigal of my sighs and tears, — and the daffy-down-dilly style, which makes some writers so touching and pathetic. For instance, — a certain letter in verse which I treasure up as a holy relick of departed days, and in which the writer expresses himself with great ease and elegance in that fine passage —

> " — 'Tis I that regret to bid you farewell —
> 'Tis me that does wish that you would here dwell! —" [3]

— A truce with this badinage. On the next page and the last — I shall say a word or two about France in general — and then of Rouen and Paris in particular.

You can hardly imagine how delighted I was to catch a glimpse of green fields again, after a long and calm sea-voyage. And then there was such an air of novelty about everything in France — and it was so delightful to be set free from the prison of a ship's cabin, and to wander at one's "own sweet will" — like one of Wordsworth's rivers — [4] that I felt quite beside myself at my first landing. A Postillion with deer-skin breeches and ponderous jack-boots was a subject of sublime speculation to me; — and when once crowded into the capacious bowels of a French "diligence" — I thought French dust more palatable than that we have at home. But I am wandering wide from my subject. There are some remarkable features in French scenery and the lives of the peasantry, which attracted my attention at once. For instance, one seldom if ever sees a fence in France. I have never seen one. A green hedge occasionally meets the eye — or a wall covered with vines — but I saw, for the most part, in the rich and highly cultivated country thro' which I passed — large fields of ripening grain reaching to the road-side, without the least defence of hedge or railing. Every cow I saw was tied with a cord just long enough to permit it to crop the grass in the ditch at the way-side without touching the grain, which grew and ripened before its eyes day-after day — a very tantalizing situation: — and now and then, too, I saw a flock of sheep — watched by a shepherd and his dog — which of course appeared very Arcadian and very classical.

Rouen is a city of great antiquity, and at present contains about 90.000 inhabitants. One of the first places that a stranger visits there is the Cathedral, whose façade is celebrated as one of the most perfect and most splendid specimens of Gothic architecture in Europe. It is a huge pile of antique building, erected in part by William the conqueror — but finished in the taste of another century. There were formerly three towers in front — but the central and principal one was destroyed by lightning in 1822 — perhaps you recollect the mention of this circumstance in the papers of the day. Within the Cathedral are the tombs of "Richard Coeur de Lion" — his brother Henry, and "The Duke of Bedford."

Not far from the Cathedral stands the ruins of an ancient Palace built by Edward 3rd. — and once occupied as a royal dwelling, but now as public offices and halls of Justice. As you approach this from the Cathedral, you pass beneath an old and gloomy gateway, or rather arch — built in commemoration of the founder of the city — a shepherd named Rouen, if one may believe the ancient legend of the place, — who in early times fed his flocks on the very spot where the arch now stands — and thus gave origin and name to a great city. In the hollow of this arch the shepherd with his dog and flock, are represented in rude and uncouth bas-relief. Other places of interest to a stranger are the ruins of the church and convent of St. Antoine — the Gallery of Paintings — and the Public Library. In the latter is a large illuminated manuscript of the Catholic chants on festival days, with the music — in folio parchment — written by a Monk of St. Antoine *in* and *about* 1682 — for he was engaged in the work of transcribing 30 years. It is nearly four feet long, and about five inches thick — curiously and rather clumsily bound in oak and brass — with two locks. Its weight in gold — 75 lbs — has been offered for it by an Englishman. The writing and ornamental painting are done most superbly.[5]

But one place of curiosity to strangers I must not forget to mention — I mean the public square, called "La place de la Pucelle d'Orleans" — the spot where the celebrated Joan of Arc was burned. It is at the present day a kind of market for fruits and vegetables — and in the center stands a monument commemorative of the maid's death, — the lower part a fountain — the upper — a statue of Joan of Arc — and altogether a very rough and uncouth piece of architecture. Close by are the remains of the Duke of Bedford's palace, from which he beheld the execution.

I have but little room left to speak of Paris, tho' you shall hear all you wish to hear about it, either before I return or afterwards. In general terms then — Paris is a gloomy city — built all of yellow stone — streaked and defaced with smoke and dust — streets narrow and full of black mud, which comes up thro' the pavements on account of the soil on which the city is built — no sidewalks — cabriolets — fiacres and carriages of all kinds driving close to the houses — and spattering or running down whole ranks of foot passengers — and noise and stench enough to drive a man mad. But the city buys a redemption of the curse that all these inconveniences would bring upon it, by the elegance of its public gardens — its boulevards — &c — &c. &c. Here I must close — only mentioning that in the Louvre there is a painting of Venus — which is an exact portrait of Miss. Knight. I was absolutely thunderstruck, when it caught my eye — and am rejoiced to find an old friend in Paris — give my love to her — and God bless her.

Yours &c
Henry. —

MANUSCRIPT: Longfellow Trust Collection.

1. Enclosed with Letter No. 98.
2. Cf. Acts 20:38.
3. These lines are part of a crude farewell poem to Longfellow by an acquaintance named Oliver K. Barrell, a lawyer's clerk of Portland. Barrell's letter containing the verses is dated April 28, 1826. For Longfellow's attitude toward Barrell, see Letter No. 107.
4. See "Composed Upon Westminster Bridge."
5. In *Outre-Mer* Longfellow identifies this manuscript as the work of Daniel d'Aubonne (*Works*, VII, 30).

98. *To Zilpah and Stephen Longfellow*

Paris   July. 11th. 1826.
Rue Monsieur Le Prince. 49. — St. Germain. —

My dear Parents,

As usual I am in the greatest haste imaginable — not from any fault of mine, — but rather that I have had a vast multitude of letters to write, and not much leisure to devote to them. "The more haste, the worse speed" is a true maxim when applied to a man sitting down to write a letter; — and it never gives one much self-possession, when bewildered in [a] labyrinth of ideas, and not knowing where to turn, to be told that his letters for the packet must be ready at a particular moment, which is drawing on apace, for time always flies fastest, when a man, if he could, would make the sun stand still on Gibion, and the moon o'er the valley of Ajalon.[1] But I will not lengthen out this prologue.

In the first place of all, I wish you to have as exact a knowledge as possible of my affairs and finances. My board and room-rent amount to 36 dollars a month — about six francs a day. My washing costs me about 30 or 40 sous a week — and of course there are other charges for my clothing, and many little incidental expenses, which in the aggregate amount to a considerable sum, which cannot be exactly calculated at present. If I live as I do at present, at the end of my year in

France, I expect my expenses will have amounted to little if any less than $550 or $600. Perhaps you may think this too large an allowance — and as I am certainly very desirous of living as economically as I can — and at the same time live respectably and genteely, I shall endeavour to bring my expenses into a smaller compass if possible. I do not expect to remain all the summer in the very heart of the city here, but think of leaving the attractions of this most attractive of places — all behind me, and of residing till Winter in the environs — at a place called Montmorenci, the former residence of Jean Jacques Rousseau and the spot where he wrote the "Nouvelle Heloïse." I have many reasons for this which I think you cannot but approve. In the first place, I hope to live cheaper there — in the second place, I shall be more studious there, and consequently become more proficient in the French language, and consequently better able to attend the public lectures in the city during the Winter, which I now occasionally attend tho' not understanding one sentence out of fifty — tho' during my three weeks' residence in Paris I can observe a great difference in my ability to comprehend what is said. And again during the month of August it is Vacation at all schools and colleges where public Lectures are delivered, and consequently Paris loses one of its greatest attractions to a student. These, with a few others of less importance, are the reasons which influence me, and as I have not yet forgotten what I came to France for, I shall endeavour to pursue that course of conduct, which according to the best of my judgement and that of the gentlemen here, to whom I brought letters, — shall seem best adapted to the end in view.

I recollect that when I last saw Doct. Nichols, he said something about *"my friends at Cambridge"* taking an interest in my situation abroad. Not understanding what he could mean by this, I said that he meant my friends at *Brunswick*. "No" — he said — "my friends at *Cambridge"* — and from other casual expressions, which he dropped in the course of conversation, I thought he intended to hint, that he had a plain for obtaining a situation for me at Harvard — as being more to my taste than Brunswick. Has he mentioned the subject to you? And if he has not, will you take the trouble to inquire whether he has formed any plan of that kind? I have pondered again and again on the subject, and wish you to tell me when you write whether this fancy of mine has any foundation, or whether it be indeed a mere fancy. If there is a plan formed in his mind, with regard to [a] situation at Harvard, what situation can it be? Pray satisfy my curiosity as soon as possible.[2]

Doctor Wells, amongst other letters, gave me one to Mr. Storrow,[3] which has introduced me to a most delightful American family. They have resided in Paris about eight years; — and I find it very pleasant to have a visiting place, where I can almost believe myself at home again — at least in America. Mrs. Storrow is a very excellent, and withal a very handsome woman — and there are two daughters, who play — very sweetly on the piano.

But I must seal my letter for fear of missing the Packet-ship of the 15th. I meant to have written Stephen a long peculiar kind of a letter, all about Paris and nothing else — but as my time has failed me, he must take the will for the deed, and wait another week or so.

Now come the salutations and greetings: — such as love and remembrance to all the family in common and severally, and "greet Phoebe with a holy kiss"[4] — that is to say, all the little ones. Write me as soon as possible.

Your affectionate Son
Henry. —

My residence at Montmorenci will make no difference in the direction of your letters — because it is but a few miles out of the city, and Madam Potet will forward all letters to me.

MANUSCRIPT: Longfellow Trust Collection. ADDRESS: To/Stephen Longfellow Esqr./Portland. —/Maine. —/U.S. of America. — POSTMARKS: NEW YORK AUG 13/FORWARDED BY DE LAUNAY LUUYT & CO HAVRE/SHIP ENDORSE-MENT: Henry. Paris July 11. 1826/to/Parents and Sisters

1. Cf. Josh. 10:12.
2. Stephen Longfellow seems to have ignored this question, perhaps because he did not wish to encourage his son to pursue a higher ambition than the promised Bowdoin professorship.
3. Thomas Wentworth Storrow (1779-1862), a successful Boston merchant and the uncle of Thomas Wentworth Higginson, was residing temporarily in Paris for the primary purpose of educating his daughters.
4. Cf. Rom. 16:1, 16.

99. *To Harriot Sumner*

Paris   July 19th. 1826.
Rue Monsieur Le Prince. 49. —
Fauxbourg St. Germain. —

My dear friend Harriet —

I should have written you by the last New York packet — but hearing of an opportunity to send directly to Boston, I have delayed my letter a little, that you might be more sure of receiving it. This — together with a thousand wonders which I had to see in Paris — before I could write a syllable to any one — and which are forever drawing one's attention off from what is his duty and what ought to be his duty — must pass for my excuse for not writing you till midsummer, tho' I left on the first of May.

What strange adventures one meets with — and what strange characters he is jostled against, as he worries along this great thoroughfare of life — the World. How far — and how unexpectedly, too, — we are sometimes separated from all our old friends. If I had thought a year ago, that in a twelve-month's time I should have been sitting down to write you from Paris, I should have been overjoyed with the anticipation — but now that the reality has come almost unlooked for — I find that a man's old friends are all the world to him, and that without them he may be filled with a heartless kind of gaiety, but can have little of life's best enjoyment. A clown in Shakespeare says — "Now am I in the forest of Arden — the more fool I. If I were at home I should be in a better place." [1] This, I think is an excellent homily for every traveller from New England — and is one of the best commentaries in the world upon the old saying of — "Home is home — however homely." [2]

The Voyage across the sea was one of the dullest parts of my life. It was so calm — so monotonous — so lifeless — so everything that makes one's time hang heavily on his hands — as if he had a day or two more in this world than he knew what to do with. Sky — and water — and sunshine, and clouds, and rain — day after day, and week after week! And even this unvarying succession of the same monotonous scenes — would have been more tolerable, if one could have been a moment alone — and could have had a moment's silence for thought or study — but there was a crowd of ill-favoured frenchmen on board, talking — laughing — singing — playing the fiddle and playing the fool — from morning till midnight — with such an eternal volubility of tongue that everything they said became an utter abomination — a "sounding brass and tinkling cymbal," [3] to me. Hence you may be assured, — that I was glad enough to catch the first glimpse of the coast of France, and felt as light-hearted as a bird set free from its cage, — when atlength I set foot, for the first time on the shores of the Old World.

At Havre there is very little to interest a stranger but upon the opposite side of the Seine are the green highlands of Honfleur, which have become classical by being made the scene of Mr. Irving's tale of "Annette Delarbre." [4] I passed but one day at the old Norman city of Rouen — for — altho' an antiquary might revel there a year amongst the relics of old and almost forgotten days — I was contented with taking a hasty look at the grand Cathedral — the monument of "Richard Coeur de Lion" — the old Palaces of Edward ||3rd and the|| Duke of Bedford — and of the uncouth monument to commemorate the execution of Joan of Arc — ||marking the|| spot where that cruel tragedy was acted.

The truth is — I was in haste to reac||h Paris, and|| having reached it I am in no haste to leave it. ||There are|| attractions and temptations enough here, I assure ||you, to rob|| one of his time and his money and his morale ||and his|| soul in the bargain! But I shall not go in||to detail|| in a letter, because you have a good friend[5] nea||r you who|| can describe to you, much better than I can||, the scenes|| and characters, which one meets with in Paris.

Remember [me] very particularly and affectionately to your Mother and Laura[6] — and the rest of your family — and again to Mr. and Mrs. Derby, whom I left in Philadelphia — but who are probably now with you.

Yours affectionately
H — W — Longfellow —

MANUSCRIPT: Longfellow Trust Collection.   ADDRESS: To —/Miss Harriet C. Sumner/Care of Mr J. Sumner./Boston./By kindness of/Doct. McKeen[7]

1. Cf. *As You Like It*, II, iv, 15–16.
2. *Paræmiologia Anglo-Latina* (1639).
3. Cf. I Cor. 13:1.
4. In *Bracebridge Hall*.
5. Possibly Dr. James McKeen (see n. 7).
6. Elizabeth Laura Derby, daughter of Capt. John and Eleanor Coffin Derby (92.7), was Harriot Sumner's first cousin.
7. Dr. James McKeen (1797–1873), professor of obstetrics in the Bowdoin Medical School and son of the first president of the college, had just completed a tour of the hospitals of Europe.

100. *To Stephen Longfellow, Jr.*

Paris. July. 23rd. 1826. —
Rue Mons. Le Prince. 49. St. Germain

My dear brother,

After five weeks' residence in Paris I have settled down in something half-way between a Frenchman and a New Englander: — within, — all Jonathan — but outwardly a little of the Parlez-vous. That is to say, I have good home-feelings at heart — but have decorated my outward man with a long-waisted thin coat — claret-coloured — and a pair of linen pantaloons: — and on Sundays and other fête days — I appear in all the glory of a little hard French hat — glossy — and brushed — and rolled up at the sides — it makes my head ache to think of it. In this garb I jostle along amongst the crowds of the Luxembourg, which is the favorite promenade in St. Germain.

From what my own thoughts were, before I saw the Public Gardens of Paris, I imagine that you have no very correct idea of them: at least, I think that I can give you a more perfect conception of them by a short description of any one — say — for instance — the Luxembourg. This is a very extensive and beautiful garden — with long, shady gravel walks over which the tall old trees, which are all regularly planted, form perfect arches — and directly in the center, a valley or lower level of the ground in which are little plats of flowers — rows of orange trees, and a little pond with two beautiful white swans. You de[s]cend from the higher grounds to this little vale, which is an amphitheatre, open towards the palace — by flights of stone steps, which here and there interrupt the stone ballustrade around the brink. On the higher grounds, and in an oval, — parallel to this ballustrade, are placed the marble statues of the garden, each upon a high pedestal in a niche cut from the boughs of the trees. This part of the garden is the general lounge and promenade: — and is full of rush-bottomed chairs! Not to an absolute *plenum,* — but a row or two on each side of the walk, where the ladies sit to be looked at — and the gentlemen to look at them, whilst a crowd of both sexes run the gauntlet between them. Here the people gather every evening at about six o'clock and laugh and talk 'till the gates are closed — at 10. It is very pleasant, I assure you to take a high seat in the synagogue here, and review the multitude passing and repassing, in all the ridiculous peculiarity of French dress, and with all the ridiculous variety of French countenance. This must answer for the Luxembourg.

But after all the Boulevards are the most attractive places of resort of a warm summer's evening. These — you know consist of a wide fine street passing round the city like a girdle, — with excellent sidewalks, and a double row of trees on each side. The Italian Boulevards — that division of the whole, which lies to the north — are the oldest and the most frequented. The trees there have gained a noble height and overhang the pathway with their mingled branches, forming a delightful shade at noon-day and a high gloomy arch at night. At the Italian Boulevards are the most splendid Cafès in Paris. There the people of quality crowd in their coaches to taste ice-creams, &c. &c — and persons of every character and description throng the footpath — a living mass — wedged together and moving together, like the crowd in the aisle of a church on the 4th of July! [Mem[o] — who delivered the Oration at Portland this summer?].[1] You cannot concieve what "carryings on" there are there at all hours of the day and evening!

Musicians singing and playing the harp — jugglers — fiddlers, — jewish cymbals and cat-calls — blind beggars and lame beggars, — and beggars without any qualifying term, except importunity, — men with monkeys — raree shows — venders of tooth-pick||s and|| cheap wares — Turks in the oriental costume — Frenchmen with curling whiskers, and round-plated straw-hats — long skirted coats and tight wrinkled trowsers — real nankeen-ers — coblers — book-sellers with their stalls — little *boutiques* where no article is sold for more than 15 sous — &c — &c — &c.

At this Boulevard there are several minor theatres where parodies and farces are performed. But a few months ago a most splendid opera was brought forward, called "Mars and Venus," and a little while ago I attended the parody of it at the Theatre of Varieties: — and saw Apollo in a red hat and striped pantaloons — Vulcan was dressed up in a flame coloured coat, and a monstrous heavy man played the part of Zephyr — with a little sugar-loaf hat — blue-coat, tight white pantaloons and the belly of an alderman![2] They are very fond of taking off John Bull at all the little theatres in Paris, and I have seen his lordship represented by a clumsy fellow of a Frenchman — in a flat hat and deer-skin breechess — singing "Auld Lang Syn" — with most ludicrous trills and quavers.

I mentioned in one of my letters something about going to reside at Montmorenci, near Paris. I have given up the idea — for one can live no cheaper there than at Paris. Besides I am unwilling to leave Madame Potet — it is such an excellent situation for one to learn the language — and Madame takes such unwearied pains to instruct me. I am coming on famously I assure you. Tell all my friends to write me soon, and with my most affectionate remembrances to all the family — yourself remember

Harry. —

There is a book at home — Belknap's "Foresters" — which I bor-rowed of Mr Cushman: with my respects to him — return it if you please.[3]

MANUSCRIPT: Longfellow Trust Collection. ADDRESS: To —/Mr. Stephen Long-fellow. Jr/Portland/Maine. — POSTMARK: BOSTON MS SEP 7

1. Longfellow's brackets.

2. *Mars et Vénus ou les Filets de Vulcain*, a ballet by Blache and Schneitzhoeffer, was first performed in Paris on May 29, 1826.

3. In *The Foresters, an American Tale* (Boston, 1792), Jeremy Belknap de-scribed the development of the British colonies in a humorous and allegorical style. Longfellow had borrowed the book from Bezaleel Cushman, his old schoolmaster.

101. *To Stephen Longfellow*

The Village of Auteuil. August. 12th. 1826.

My dear Father,

One would think that nothing could be easier to a stranger in France, than to find every facility for making himself acquainted with the language: — hence you can hardly imagine the perplexities I have been surrounded with in searching out a situation, which should offer any advantage, at all peculiar and remarkable, to a foreigner wishing to acquire the French language purely and correctly. I mentioned in one of my former letters, that I thought of residing a month or two at Montmorency. I went then to see if I could obtain an agreeable situation — but not being successful, I returned to Paris, after visiting the Hermitage of Rous[s]eau, and sitting upon the rock upon which he composed the "Nouvelle Heloise." What was to be done then! At Madam Potet's there were other Americans — we spoke our own language too much — I could not, and did not attempt to persuade myself to the contrary.

I found atlength a young French gentleman who was my fellow-passenger from America — who recommended me to the house in which I am at present residing. It is what in the language of the country is called a "Maison de Santè" or "house of health" — where, retired from the noise and dust of the city, valetudinarians can breath the country air and become healed of their infirmities. Attached to the house is an extensive garden full of fruit-trees — and bowers, and alcoves, where the boarders ramble and talk from morning till night. This makes the situation an excellent one for me, for I can at anytime hear french conversation —for the French are always talking. Besides the conversation is the purest of French — inasmuch as persons from the highest circles in Paris are residing here. Amongst others — an old gentleman who was of the household of Louis Sixteenth in the days of the revolution — [1] and a Madam de Sailly — daughter to a celebrated advocate named Bèrier, who was the defender of Marshal Ney in his impeachment of treason.[2] There is also a young student at Law — here,[3] who is my almost constant companion — and who corrects all my mistakes in speaking and writing the French. As he is not much older than I am, I do not feel so much embarrassment in speaking to him, as I do in speaking to others. This will undoubtedly advance me a great deal in the language: — and besides — after we return to Paris I shall have the advantage of his acquaintance, and also of that of Mad. de Sailly, who has invited me to visit her at Paris. These are some of the advantages which I enjoy here, and you can easily imagine others, which a country residence offers over that of a city — during the vacation of the literary institutions at Paris — and the cessation of their lectures.

And now comes one great disadvantage. One of the ladies here is learning the English language — and as she [is] far advanced in speaking it — she thinks it amazingly uncivil if I do not converse with her — and dictate to her from english books some part of every day. And this is the disadvantage attending almost every situation in polished society here — some member of the family has studied our own language, and they take care to let you know this by murdering it in your presence. Besides there are so many thousand Englishmen in Paris, that they fill up every chink and cranny, in those families which would otherwise be eligible situations for a student of the French tongue. I am in hopes of finding a family all French before my month at Auteuil is finished — and the Public Lectures at Paris commence.

I forwarded the letters to Dodge & Oxnard at Marseilles all in good time. They have made Mr Welles my banker. His address is "Messrs Welles &c Rue Taitbout — 24." All my letters in future had best be sent to his care; — so that in whatever part of Paris I may here after reside I shall be sure of receiving them.[4]

My health continues to be excellent, and trusting that you and all the family are in as good health and spirits as I am

I remain Your affect. Son

Henry.

Before sealing my letter I wish to inform you that I have atlength found a situation at Paris in a family which takes boarders and where there are no English. Particulars here-after when I have inquired more particularly about the place, and have concluded whether to go there or not.

MANUSCRIPT: Longfellow Trust Collection. ADDRESS: To/Stephen Longfellow Esq./Portland/Maine/U.S. of America. POSTMARKS: NEW YORK OCT 11/ SHIP ENDORSEMENT: Henry to his father and mother/Auteuil Augt of 1826/ [Rec] Oct 14/[Ans] Nov 26.

1. Possibly M. d'Argentuille, the sexagenarian described in *Outre-Mer* (*Works*, VII, 64-69).

2. Pierre-Nicolas Berryer (1757-1841) could not save Ney, who was executed on December 7, 1815.

3. Louis Camus, who according to Longfellow's journal entry for Sept. 14, 1836, later practiced law at Rue de Porte foin No. 14, Paris.

4. Stephen Longfellow had provided his son with a letter of credit on Dodge & Oxnard, to be used "only in case of necessity," as he wrote on November 26, 1826. This firm was presumably chosen because one of the partners, Thomas Oxnard (1775-1840), was a native of Portland. Samuel Welles (1778-1841), Longfellow's banker and general agent during his sojourn in Europe, was a trans-

planted American, whose connections with the first banking houses of Europe and the United States brought him considerable wealth and prestige.

102. *To Zilpah Longfellow* [1]

Auteuil. August 17. 1826. —

My dear Mother,

I have been residing for the last fortnight at this pleasant village of Auteuil. It is situated about three miles northward from Paris — and watered on one side by the Seine, — whilst the Wood of Bologne shades the other, and affords a delightful promenade, morning and evening. As to the village itself — there is nothing remarkable about [it] — at least nothing further, than that it was formerly the residence of Ben Franklin [2] and the famous tragic poet Racine. This may have sanctified the place, by making it classic ground, but after all a French village in its best estate can be little to the taste of Brother Jonathan. There is so little about it — except, indeed, its quiet and tranquility, — to remind one that he is out of town — no corn-fields garnished with yellow pumpkins — no green trees, and orchards by the road side — no slab-fences — no well-poles — no painted cottages, with huge barns and outhouses, — ornamented in front with monstrous piles of wood for winter-firing: — nothing in fine to bring to the mind of an American a remembrance of the beautiful villages of his native land. In every respect — as far as regards its construction — it resembles the city. You have the same paved streets — the same dark, narrow alleys without sidewalks — the same dingy stone houses — each peeping into its neighbour's windows — the same eternal stone walls, shutting in from the eye of the stranger all the beauty of the place, — and opposing an inhospitable barrier to the lover of natural scenery. Indeed — a French Village looks like a deserted town — deserted, because your ears are not disturbed with the continual uproar of the streets — and in the village there is not that selfish business air about every-body and everything that we always find in the city. But you know how fresh and cheerful and breezy, a New England village is — how marked its features — so different from the town — so peculiar — so delightful! And I think you would hardly wish to find yourself more than once in a village of Normandy or Seine. I hope that in the Vine Country and the south of France, I shall find some more distinguishing and characteristic features in the village and the city.

Unless my memory fails me, I have committed one great fault in my former letters in not describing to you particularly the style of building in France. If an English man or an American had a house lot, he would erect his mansion upon it in such a manner as to leave a grass-plot in front or something like a garden in the rear — but a Frenchman would build a great castle of an edifice close upon the street — in the form of a hollow square — sky-high — with a paved court in the interior, — into which the staircases of the house would open — and the entrance of which from the street would be through a huge arched gate-way much resembling the large doors of a barn — and which a porter should open [and] shut whenever one wished to enter or go out. This is the style of building at Paris. The lower apartments upon the street are generally occupied by tradesmen and have no connexion with the rest of the house. What we call the second story is called the "Entre-sol," and after this is passed, they begin to number, calling *that* story the *first,* which we call the *third,* and run[n]ing up to a fourth, fifth and sixth, — making in all seven or eight, as the case may be. A French house, then, is something like a pile of one-story houses, placed one above another, for each story is occupied by a different family, and is composed of a suite of rooms — a dozen or twenty, opening into each-other. When you have rung at the outer door, and obtained admittance into the court you have by no means got into the house, but are under the necessity of getting further information relative to the family you are in search of — whether they are in the first — second — or fiftieth story. You then ascend — and ring again, — and after waiting upon a staircase which is a throughfare for five or six families, you are atlength ushered into the house.

The apartments of French families are generally very elegant — always much more so than the dirty entrance would lead one to anticipate: — for there is generally a pile of filth and decaying vegetables garnishing the outer-door, and an odour of anything but sanctity upon the stair-case.

But I will cut short this dull and detailed account by inquiring about family affairs with you. I suppose that Captain Wadsworth and his wife, and cousin Caroline Storer[3] are already with you, as I heard from cousin Ebenezer — that they would visit you together this summer. I wish I could step in amongst you some evening; — and although it is impossible to be bodily present with you, I assure you I am often so in thought. This is almost the only consolation which I have in my absence from you, — and this at best is a very melancholy one. Hence you can easily imagine with what impatience I am waiting for the arrival of your letters, which I know must before this time be somewhere near the coast of France. The style of direction should be as follows —

"A Monsieur —
Monsieur H. W. Longfellow
Aux soins de Messrs. Welles & co.
Rue Taitbout. No. 24. — à Paris. —"

They always give a double title here — two monsieurs. Be kind enough to remember me to all my friends in Portland and the country — kiss the little ones for me — and for yourself receive my kindest love.

> Your most affectionate son
> Henry. —

MANUSCRIPT: Longfellow Trust Collection.

1. Enclosed with Letter No. 101.
2. Franklin lived at nearby Passy during his term as commissioner to France.
3. Sister of Ebenezer (95.2) and Longfellow's second cousin.

103. *To George Bancroft*

> The Village of Auteuil. — Wood of Bologne.
> August. 20th. — 1826.

Dear Sir,

The wonders which distract the thoughts of a stranger on his first arrival at Paris, have hitherto prevented me from fulfilling very punctiliously all my duties as a correspondent with the friends I have left behind me. You, who have been a traveller, can easily imagine how the novelties of this Old World would unfit a mind so little subject to severe discipline as mine is, for anything like sober thought. I was so bewildered in the crowds and noise of Paris, — what I saw wore an air so foreign from what I had imagined — and everything around me was so unique and so peculiar — that it was a long time before I collected my thoughts sufficiently to write a line. I had not imagined so vast a change.

> Urbem quam dicunt Paris, Melibae, putavi
> Stultus ego, huic nostrae similem. — [1]

And when I found that I had a new World to study, I had little disposition to attend to other affairs.

You will see by the date of this letter that I am at present residing at Auteuil. You without doubt know this little village, which was once the residence of Racine, Boileau, and Franklin: — and, I assure you, I am passing a very delightful month in these classic shades, reading Virgil — and Madame de Sévigné — and Henri de St. Pierre,[2] though so far from being inspired by the genius of [the] place, I grow daily more certain of the fact, — that when I left my native land I left with it whatever little poetical inspiration Heaven had blessed me with. The fact is there is no Literary Gazette here; — but there is something of the same origin, which is infinitely worse, I mean the Collection of Poems — which haunts me like a pestilence.[3]

I can write you little concerning Paris which would in the least interest you, since at this season of year all the literary men are out of the city. Hence all my letters with one exception remain upon my hands. The only subject which fills the mouths of men is Talma's sickness, who has for some weeks been hanging like Mahomet's coffin between heaven and earth — that is to say has been at the point of death:[4] — and the singing of Madam Pasta and Mademoiselle Sontag — stars at the Opera![5] From your side of the water, we hear of the death of Adams and Jefferson — but not much in detail.[6] All the Americans at Paris are in mourning on the occasion — a black crape upon the left arm, to show the French, who have so little respect for their Kings — that so far from looking upon our rulers as opp[r]essors who keep us, in a disgraceful vassallage, they are held by us to be indeed the fathers of their people: — or else it is a Yankee notion — I do not know which.

Mr. Cooper reached Paris more than a month since.[7] He took lodgings at first at the Hotel Montmorenci, and on leaving, behaved very disgracefully, — declaring that his bill was too unreasonable, and commanding the Landlady to leave his room. At present he is in the Fauxbourg St. Germain; — his wife and one of his daughters are sick with the scarlet fever. So much for *our* Scot[t]. I understand that the last No: of the North American has been unusually severe with him.[8] This is a capricious world, but for my own part, I confess myself happy in being near a writer who has gained so much reputation at home and abroad.

I am sorry to trouble you with such a letter as this is, — but I assure you I am quite out of the reach of the news; but if you will so far pardon me, as to write me a line in return, I promise better things in future.

Very respectfully Your Obt. Servt.

Henry W. Longfellow.

Be kind enough to address to the care of Messrs Well[e]s &co. Rue Taitbout. No 24. I have written to Mr Cogswell by the same ship that brings you this.[9] Paris Sept. 7th.

MANUSCRIPT: Massachusetts Historical Society. ADDRESS: À Monsieur/Monsieur George Bancroft./Northampton./Mass. —/United States of America. POST-

MARK: NEW-YORK NOV 7   ANNOTATION: Recd Forward New York Nov 8. 1826./by Ys. Re[spectfull]y Edwd Storer [10]   ENDORSEMENT: Henry W. Long-fellow/August 20 1826/Rec. Nov. 1826

1. "The city they call Paris, Meliboeus, I foolishly imagined to be similar to ours." Vergil, *Eclogues*, I, 19–20. Longfellow substitutes "Paris" for "Rome."

2. Jacques Henri Bernardin de Saint-Pierre (1737–1814), friend of Rousseau and the author of *Paul et Virginie* (1789).

3. Longfellow presumably refers to *Miscellaneous Poems Selected from the United States Literary Gazette* (Boston, 1826), in which he was represented by fourteen poems.

4. François Joseph Talma (1763–1826), the celebrated tragedian, died on October 19. See Letter No. 107.

5. Giuditta Pasta (1798–1865), Italian soprano, was famous for her dramatic impersonations; Henrietta Gertrude Walpurgis Sontag (1806–1854), German soprano, had only recently made her Paris debut.

6. John Adams and Jefferson both died on July 4, 1826, the fiftieth anniversary of the Declaration of Independence.

7. Cooper and his family actually arrived in Paris on July 22, 1826 (James Franklin Beard, ed., *The Letters and Journals of James Fenimore Cooper* [Cambridge, 1960], I, 145).

8. A critical review of *The Last of the Mohicans* and *The Pioneers* appeared in the *North American Review*, XXIII (July 1826), 150–197.

9. This letter has not survived.

10. Edward Storer (1805–1851), Eben's brother, was a purser in the U.S. Navy.

104. *To Stephen Longfellow*

Paris   October 2nd   1826.

My dear Father,

I was overjoyed a day or two ago in receiving your letter of August 11th, the first which I have received from home since my arrival in France. Indeed you cannot conceive the joy it gave me, for I had been many weeks in all the despondency of "hope deferred" [1] — knowing that you had written me but receiving no letters. What a pity that your letter on the subject of going to Germany should have been lost! It is a subject in which of course I feel very deeply interested, and I really hope that it may be in my power to attend the lectures at Goettingen before my return.

I am convinced that what you say of Spain, will be impossible. [2] You either over-rate my abilities and my advantages, if you think that I am already master of the French: or I have sadly misimproved them both, which I do not wish to allow. But I will confess, that I had no idea of the difficulties attending my situation — no idea, that it was indeed so difficult to learn a language. If I had known before leaving home how hard a task I was undertaking, I should have shrunk. My friends at home, and especially my young friends, imagine that I am enjoying a most delightful existence, without care and without labor, surrounded by all the allurements of a splendid metropolis, and living in continual delight. But nothing can be further from the truth. There are allurements enough around me, it is true, but I do not feel myself at liberty to indulge in them: — and there is splendor enough, but it is a splendor in which I have no share. No! The truth is, that the heavy responsibility which I have taken upon myself — the disappointments I have met with, in not finding my advantages so great as I had fancied them — and in finding my progress comparatively slow: — together with the continual solicitude about the final result of my studies, and the fear that you will be displeased with my expenses — are hanging with a terrible weight upon me. I never imagined the business I have taken in hand a very light affair, but I thought there would be fewer perplexities attending it.

I am convinced that if I remain here but two years, I had better relinquish the Spanish language for the German — since I cannot acquire a thorough knowledge of four languages in so short a time. This was the advice, which Mr Bancroft and Mr Cogswell gave me, who of course are well qualified to judge upon the subject. If you are of the same opinion, — the plan which strikes me as being most plausable is to pursue the French most vigorously for a few months — then commence Italian — learn its principles thoroughly — spend the Spring in Italy to speak the language, and then spend the Summer and succeeding Winter in Germany. This to be sure is changing our plans, from the very foundation, since the year which I intended to pass in Paris, will be essentially shortened. I think, however, that this change will be a good one, inasmuch as the German language is infinitely more important than the Spanish, being infinitely more rich in literary resources.

Unfortunately there is no one at Paris to whom I can apply for advice, most of the persons to whom I have letters being still at their country residences. In this particular my arrival at the commencement of the summer, was rather disadvantageous: — indeed I have delivered but one introductory letter to Frenchmen. This has made my advantages at Paris much inferior to what I still hope to find them during the Winter; — and has strengthened me in one resolution which I have taken, and will explain to you.

I mentioned in a former letter my month's residence at Auteuil, a delightful little village in the environs of Paris: — and, indeed, I wrote you from that place. The time I passed there was very agreably and very profitably spent: — but the expenses were equally great with my expenses at Paris. Thus one end I had in view in leaving Paris was defeated, and it is now a month since I have returned to the city. Still I am not satisfied with the rate of my living: — and the lectures which I expected would commence the first of September do not in reality commence before the first of November. I have therefore resolved to leave Paris a second time, and to go to Tours, where good french is spoken — living is cheaper — and the country delightful. One great reason — for this step is that I must break up at once the society of Americans which seems to be increasing around me every day; — it is hard to avoid our own countrymen in this manner — especially in a land of strangers — but I must do it — I must do something at once which will be decisive — and I know no better course to follow. When the Winter has really set in I shall wish to return to Paris again, in order to get what good I can hope to derive from my letters of introduction, and also to cultivate the excellent French society into which I have had the good fortune to be introduced.

But you caution me against going too much into society. I can assure you, however, that the practise of conversing with good company is the only way to acquire readily a good pronunciation, and a habit of easy conversation, the want of which is the greatest impediment which lies in my way.

But to return a moment to my departure for Tours. I cannot — you will readily conceive, — explain in this place the many little circumstances which influence me to this step, but I dare say they will readily suggest themselves to you. The principle inducements, I have already referred to — namely — a diminution of expenses — and an absence from English society. I hope you will think this course beneficial — at least profitable, since my expenses exceed your expectation. I assure you that upon that point I was astonished. It gave me — and still gives me a great deal of uneasiness. But I am resolved to live as cheap as possible, and set my heart at ease upon the subject, since it is vain to indulge in unavailing regrets.

I met General Lafayette in the street not long ago: — he was alone — on foot — and nobody seemed to notice him particularly! What a difference from what it was in America! He gives a great dinner to all the Americans in Paris on the Anniversary of his return to France. I have not yet been at Lagrange.[3] It is said that there are never less than thirty or forty at his table daily. So many visiters must be a great burden to him — this restrains me from going at present. He sends his regards to you.

My love to all — and farewell! I expected letters from Stephen and the girls long before this. My health was never better. I hope you will be able to read all this letter; but it blots so much that I doubt it. It is the wretched French paper and ink. They make all their letter paper very thin, because postages go by weight here. One might almost as well write on blotting-paper — with water. Once more farewell! Remember me most affectionately to all concerned. I have ten thousand things to write, but not the time.

Your son
Henry.

I am acquainted with a young gentleman, who has just arrived at Paris, via Spain. He has travelled through the country, and says it is very unpleasant[4] — and very dangerous, on account of the dissentions which distract the country and the frequent assassinations which take place there.

Upon more mature reflexion I have renounced the idea of residing at Tours. I fear that too many changes in my situation will not be advantageous. I shall endeavour to diminish my expenses by changing the qua[r]ter of the city, in which I live — and going to a part very distant from the center. I shall write again very soon in continuation, because half is not said.

MANUSCRIPT: Longfellow Trust Collection. ADDRESS: To./Stephen Longfellow Esq./Portland. Maine./U.S. of America. POSTMARKS: NEW YORK DEC 9/ FORWARDED BY DELAUNEY LUUYT & CO HAVRE/SHIP ENDORSEMENT: Henry to his father/Oct 2 1826/Decr. 13/A[ns]. Oct and Jan

1. Prov. 13:12.
2. In his letter Stephen Longfellow had suggested that Henry remain in Paris until he had mastered the language and that he then visit Spain "early the next winter or in the autumn," after which he could spend a few months in Italy and the remaining summer and winter in Göttingen.
3. Lafayette's residence. For Lafayette's letter to Longfellow from there on June 29, 1826, see *Life*, I, 89.
4. The direction "next page" follows.

105. *To Stephen Longfellow*

Paris. October 19th 1826.

My dear Father,

I have read your last letter — the first which I have received from you — dated August 11th. — a thousand times over; and sit down to write you a second answer to it — for if I kept an exact count of De—— and Cr—— with my correspondents at home they would hear very little of me. The more I think of your propositions concerning Spain and Italy — the more they astonish me. At the same time I most heartily wish that I could conform to them to the very letter. But I fear — and have good reason to think, that it will be impossible,

and the oftener I reflect upon the course I am to follow on leaving
Paris, the more I wish to change our original plan: though there is
one part of it which I would not change.

Our first intention, you will recollect, was that I should remain
one year in Paris. You can readily imagine that I was somewhat surprised to hear you speak of going into Spain early in the Winter or in
Autumn. Tomorrow night finishes four months that I have lived in
Paris — or perhaps I should speak more correctly were I to say that
yesterday morning finished four months that I have been in France.
When I first stept foot on shore I could not ask the simplest question —
nor understand the simplest answer. Now I can converse tolerably
well — though I will not flatter myself by saying anything more.
What I knew of the French language, when I arrived, was not much.
My pronunciation of it was far from correct. D'Eon was a very poor
instructor [1] — his pronunciation very bad. It is impossible that he
should have been a Parisien. He was a German — no doubt one of
the German Swiss guards — there are thousands of them here with
a phisiognomy strikingly resembling his — and their pronunciation
is to the Parisian what the sound of the Scotch dialect is to pure English. This was exceedingly unfortunate for me — inasmuch as I have
had to unlearn as well as to learn, and it is not the easiest thing in the
world to divest one'self of habitual errors. And this has been not only
unfortunate but absolutely discouraging: — to find myself speaking
French with a German as well as an English accent. But I have been
wearing off these accents — very slowly to be sure — but I hope ef-
fectually — and look forward for a pronunciation as perfect as a foreigner can acquire. Indeed if I teach the language — this will of
course be necessary — but it can only be acquired with time.

Why then do you speak of leaving France in the first of Winter?
I[f] it be found necessary to shorten my residence in Paris — why
shorten it so much? And in the Winter, too, — which offers more
advantages to a student in Paris than all the other seasons of the year.
Besides, my dear Sir, — I have not yet received any advantage from
my letters of introduction and it does not seem advantageous to retire
from this city at [the] very moment when my prospects of improvement were greatest, and when I had just got to enjoy French society
from the excellent part which I have had the good fortune to know: —
having reason to say that "my lot has fallen unto me in pleasant
places." [2] I do not say it boastingly — for I do not find in it a subject
of boasting — but I say it rejoicingly, that I have become acquainted
in some of the first families — where the French is most purely and
most beautifully spoken. This is an advantage which ought not to be

underrated — and it would be an incalculable advantage if I could reside in such families instead of visiting them occasionally. But [this] is impossible — utterly impossible. You see that I take your example as a good one and write across the page.[3] French letter paper will not allow of this generally speaking — but I have a sheet thicker than ordinary — and as it has become quite an object to save postage, since I write so much — I find this method an excellent one.

But let us return to our subject. I expressed a wish to remain as long as possible at Paris in order to reap all the advantages which my situation affords me. Yes — I had rather give up the Spanish and the Italian for the present, than leave the French half-acquired and miss a glorious opportunity of acquiring it. I think indeed that I must give up the Spanish; at all events I must give up the idea of visiting Spain. That country is filled with all the horrors of a civil war. It is as much as one's life is worth to visit it. We get most terrible accounts from every quarter — and as I never desired to come to my end by the dagger of an assassin or the pistol of a robber, I think it at least prudent to leave Spain like the "man who fell among thieves" and "pass by on t'other side."[4] Indeed I have given up all hope of visiting it: — and think that we may well set ourselves at rest upon that subject. The question then will be which is the most important for me as a scholar: the German language or the Italian? All those who have spoken to me upon the subject in America have told me by all means to become a German scholar — that the language was rich in literary resources — and that no student ever regretted a years residence at Goettingen. Mr Ticknor said "give up the Italian for the German" — and moreover urged me very strenuously to go first to Germany — tho' for my own part I am well satisfied with the learning the French first. Mr Bancroft and Mr Cogswell — both said that the German was all important and advised me to lengthen my residence in Europe rather than return without a knowledge of it. So much for our counsellors. For my own part I do [not] imagine that I could learn to speak the German with correctness and fluency in the space of a year — but if I go there in the Spring instead of going into Italy, I shall learn the language perfectly enough to read it, and to understand the Literary lectures which commence in November or the last of Octob. I must confess that this is the course which I wish to adopt. I had rather be master of the German and French than to know them superficially together with the Italian and Spanish, and I make the proposition to you as the one which of all others I should choose — though in my last letter I proposed going into Italy in the Spring. But let us take all possible suppositions and propositions into view and then decide. Spain — I must give up — which then to choose — the German or Italian? If I can have but one it should be German: if both the Italian last. Hence I am for remaining here in my comfortable Winter quarters until March or April and then for passing into Germany to remain a year. And now I will tell you a secret which every one who reads this letter must keep as a profound secret since it was imparted to me in confidence. Edward Preble writes me that he will come out in the Spring and attend lectures with me at Gottingen, but he would not have it known for fear of disappointment and the imputation of "wild scheme" and "roving turn." Please to talk to him upon the subject and advise him to the step, if you conclude to let me go. I wish we could all three have an intervue upon this important subject — we could do more in five minutes than by scribbling over quires of paper. But I await your final decision. Any of the gentlemen of whom I have spoken above as advising me to go to Gottingen will of course be very ready to give you any information upon the subject — and upon the advantages of the German literature and language — and I think will persuade you if any persuasion be necessary, — to send me to the University of Gottingen.

This will be a very interesting letter to you and Mama — but the girls will think it rather dry — except in the abstract, by which I mean — the decision which it will lead you to form. Farewell.

Affectionately Your Son
H. —

I always take it for granted that you had rather have these business letters, than any other kind — and since somebody must have them it seems proper that they should come to you who are most interested in the concern. But when we get the troublesome affairs well settled, we will turn to other things. I have set my heart at rest upon the subject of funds — inasmuch as I now live as economically as possible — and at a rate much less than formerly. I find it cheaper to take my own advise than any other person's — and as I am now acquainted with the manners and customs I shall jog on more economically and therefore more pleasantly.

MANUSCRIPT: Longfellow Trust Collection. ADDRESS: To/Stephen Longfellow Esqr/Portland. Maine/U.S. of America. POSTMARKS: NEW YORK NOV 26/ FORWARDED BY DE LAUNAY LUUYT & CO HAVRE/SHIP   ENDORSEMENT: Henry to his Parents/Paris Oct 19 1826/Nov. 30./Dec. 3. 1826.

1. F. D'Eon gave private lessons in German, French, and sword-handling in Portland in 1825. His advertisement, offering thirty-six lessons for six dollars, appeared first in the *Eastern Argus* for February 10, 1825. Longfellow presumably studied French with him after his graduation from Bowdoin.

2. Cf. Ps. 16:6.

3. In this and other letters from abroad Longfellow wrote both horizontally and vertically on the page to save postage. See Plate IV.

4. Cf. Luke 10:30, 31.

106. *To Zilpah Longfellow* [1]

Paris   October 19th 1826.
Rue de Racine No 5.

My dear Mother, —

I write this from "Winter Quarters:" — Rue de Racine Fauxbourg St. Germain. If ever man deserved a comfortable dwelling-place, I do — for no man ever toiled harder to fine one. But atlength I believe I am suited. I have found a little nook in this quiet part of the city, where I shall stay the Autumn out, and from which I hope to give you in due season a few sketches of "Winter in Paris." I am within a few steps of the house where I resided when I first came to the city — and as my movements since I left that house for the Village of Auteuil may be a little obscure to your eyes, I will relate them all to you in "short metre."

I left my first boarding house because there were a great number of Americans there, and as I could not speak French I was continually speaking English: though were I to return back again to the same place, this objection would be in a great measure removed, because I could speak French if I choosed. I went to Auteuil in the beginning of August: — after I had spent six weeks in Paris and as I have already written you an account of my residence there, I shall not trouble you with further particulars at present. It was very singular however that I should have got into [a] "Maison de Santé." It was by accident — a very lucky accident for me. A young friend of mine — a Frenchman — told me he knew of a good situation for a stranger in a French family at Auteuil, where I should see good society and be comfortably situated, and offered to go with me to see the house. We went: and being pleased with the society and the beautiful garden, I engaged a room for one month. As we came out of the gate I observed to him "How pale and sick they all look!" "There is a good reason for it" — said he, "they are all just recovering from sickness and have come out here to take the country air!" This astonished me — but it was too late to retract — so I became an inhabitant of the house, and thereby made many valuable acquaintances — and very pleasant ones too. I should never have gone to such a place, if I had known what it was — but I was afterwards very glad of my mistake, and enjoyed myself very much during the warm month of August, rambling in the garden and in the woods with the convalescent.

When I returned from Auteuil I again found a situation in a French family: — but it has given me a disgust to that way of living in Paris, and I am now keeping Bachelor's Hall — that is to say, I am living in college style — a chamber to myself. The truth is I cannot endure the manner of living in such families as I and other strangers can have access to. There are to be sure some fine families in Paris who take boarders, but you must pay fifty dollars a month — and that I cannot well afford. Those which are cheaper in price are cheaper every way — despicable — mean — avaricious. All they want is your money — and when they are sure of that they take no kind of pains to make your residence agreable. I have become heartily disgusted with their deceptions and hollow-heartedness. Should I live a century in France I would never go into a French boarding-house again, unless I could find one expensive enough to be decent — and I had money enough to defray the expenses. This has determined me to hire my chamber separately, and to dine at a Restarateur's or at a "Table d'hote" — that is to say at a table where a certain number meet daily, and pay so much each. This is very convenient, I can assure you, for in whatever part of this great city you may happen to be, you are sure of not losing your din[n]er. You have only to step into a "restaurant-[eur]'s" — and immediately a bill of fare is handed you, with the price of each dish marked: so that your din[n]er costs what you please or rather what your appetite pleases. But the price of the "Table d'hote" is fixed, and all sit at one table — whereas at a Restarateur's the rooms are fitted with small tables of two, — four, — or six plates each.

The general breakfast hour is ten o'clock; and all the French take at this hour their "Déj[e]une[r] à la fourchette" — a breakfast eaten with a fork — very much like one of our dinners — hot cutlets — beefstakes — poultry — and vegetables. The Dinner hour is 5: — and I am sure you would wonder at a French dinner: — such an endless variety — nobody but a Frenchman can "endure unto the end." [2] For my own part I generally hold out more than half way through — but never quite through the affair — dessert and all. And now that I am free from the dangerous temptation of eating too much at a family table,[3] I shall seldom visit a "table d'hote," but dine cheaply and simply at a Restarateur's. It strikes a person very singular at first — and he can hardly bring himself to sit down at a little table by himself, and eat before ten thousand strangers — but it is the custom of the place — and though before coming to France I thought I should never be able to eat in such a multitude — yet at present I find no difficulty — and can cry "garçon" to the servant as loud and bold as anybody.

No Frenchman is overstocked with modesty — and what would pass for a praiseworthy portion of it in our country in Paris would be downright sheepishness.

But I have made a wide digression from my subject and am getting entangled in all the labayrinths of a subject worthy of the pen of Briggs and a place in the "Cookery." [4] Let us go back a little. I said that [I] had become disgusted with life in a French family — always excepting Madame Potet's, which is indeed a home to the American in Paris. With that exception — let the stranger who is unacquainted with the language and customs of France avoid a French family. He can live much cheaper and much more agreably as I am now living — and as I have described to you full-length. I told you of my return from Auteuil into a family at Paris. I remained there but one month. I was discontented, unhappy — and of course could not improve my time to the best advantage. Moreover I despaired of finding a place to suit me — and in fine I determined to leave Paris altogether and go to Tours — but upon reflection found it would be very foolish to leave at present — at least for any length of time. But I was melancholy — down-hearted — dispirited — almost disconsolate — and I therefore resolved to take a short vacation, and leave my cares behind me. So I shouldered my knapsack and made an excursion on foot upon the beautiful banks of the Loire — from the city of Orleans as far as Tours — and back to Paris by the way of Vendome. I was absent ten days — during which time I spoke not a word of English but advanced rapidly in the French. Part of the rout was most delightful — as you may readily suppose — and though I wandered Goldsmith like — alone with my k[n]apsack upon my back — I was in good spirits all the way and constantly pleased with the novel and rural life around me. I was induced thus to run away from my studies — perhaps from my duties — by the consideration that perhaps I should never have an opportunity of seeing that part of France — certainly never in the season of the Vintage. At the same time I found the excursion of the greatest advantage to me every way. It nursed my funds a little — for I travelled very cheaply — being most of the way on foot — and moreover exercised me in speaking the language and gave me confidence in my own powers, which a man who is learning to speak a language can never have too much of. It would be very bad policy to begin a description of my ramble at the end of such an intricate, interwoven letter as this is. I shall therefore devote my first leisure moments to describe to you at large my route and the wonders and beauties of that land of song, which Goldsmith painted more poetically than truly. [5] I wished first of all to make my apology for taking such a journey without leave — though I have no reason to think that you will call the step an unwise one — when I enumerate its advantages and tell you that I spoke not an English word the whole route — and that it is impossible to pass ten days in Paris without conversing as many times in one's native tongue. So that in fact I was a gainer rather than a loser: — and I assure you that I shall remember that foot excursion with delight to the latest day of my life — even were I to live a century.

But it is indeed time to "sheath the pen — and spare mankind." I am growing very garrulous in my correspondence — and whenever I take up my pen to write you never know when to lay it down again. My constant hope has been to receive a letter from you, but each packet arrives in turn with succession of disappointments. Four months in France and only one letter — very extraordinary and very true! Only one letter from home — and so many hands to write — whilst I have written almost a thousand long-winded epistles — and crowded them upon you by nearly every packet: not to mention about twenty other correspondents, which I can count out of the house — who are also kind enough to let me do all the writing. But good night! I hope you will be able to find the commencement — and perhaps I ought also to pray that you may have strength to reach the end of it. I said something in the begin[n]ing about "short metre." I would correct the expression. It should be "six-hundred line long metre." Give my best love to all — and recollect that I am always blessed with good health.

Most affectionately your absent Son
Henri. —

MANUSCRIPT: Longfellow Trust Collection.

1. Presumably enclosed with Letter No. 105.
2. Matt. 24:13.
3. The instruction "first page" follows at this point.
4. Richard Briggs, *The English Art of Cookery* (London, 1788) and *The New Art of Cookery* (Philadelphia, 1792).
5. In *The Traveller*.

107. *To Patrick Greenleaf*

Paris   October 23rd 1826.
Rue de Racine No 5

— I am glad — my dear Pat — that in sitting down to write this letter, I am able to do it in the consc[i]ousness that I am writing to an old friend, whom I can address with all the familiarity of old acquaintance "in regular standing." This removes me at once from a thousand embar[r]assments and from the necessity of as many apologies, which one is apt to think is his duty to make, when he sits down to write to a stranger without any previous reflexion. It is this freedom which gives the great charm to a friendly correspondence — and makes it like a fire-side conversation — a kind of "Q in the corner"[1] affair, where a fellow can kick his boots off — thrust his feet into his slippers, — and feels himself at home. I know that your taste in this matter agrees perfectly with my own, because your letter of the "glorious and evanescent" twenty seventh was an excellent specimen of the order "night-gown and slippers." Indeed a stiff letter galls one like a stiff shirt collar — whilst a sheet garnished here and there with a careless blot — and here and there a dash — but in the main full of excellent matter, is like a clever fellow in a dirty shirt whom we value for the good humour he brings with him and not for the garb he wears.

And now for Parisian news. The mouths of men and the columns of the journals are full of the death of Talma — the celebrated French tragedian, who finished his part in life's great drama about three days since. I have never seen him — neither upon the stage nor elsewhere — but you know what a reputation he enjoyed, and can easily imagine what a sensation his final exit has produced. The journals are full of elegies and eulogies — all speak of his wonderful power — his force — his *character* — as an actor, — and of his benevolence, — his generosity — and his noble feelings as a man and a private citizen. But the green curtain has come down — or rather what may be called the "drop-scene" of life. Like Voltaire he was a free-thinker — and like Voltaire tormented by the importunities of Priests when on his death-bed. The Arch Bishop of Paris was urgent to be admitted to see him. "Tell the Arch Bishop — " said he — "that I will call upon him when I get better" — which was as much as saying like Voltaire "Let me die in peace."

— But one thing is well known concerning Talma in private life — and that is that he was a gambler — and that he several times expended his whole fortune in that way. He was much patronised by Napoleon — who more than once payed his gambling debts. These things are not much thought of here — but you will oftener hear this passion of gambling spoken of than his good and generous qualities — proving that

> The evil that men do lives after them —
> The good is oft interred with their bones. —[2]

Speaking of Talma, who was the greatest French tragedian — it will be a-propos to speak also of Mademoiselle Mars — who is probably the

finest actress in genteel comedy who is now living.[3] She is certainly
a most wonderful woman — not only in her performances but also
in her personal appearance. She is now upwards of fifty — and if you
should see her on the stage, you would take her for a young lady of
twenty six: — and then such extraordinary talents for the drama! —
'tis strange, 'tis passing strange [4] — you would be enchanted in some
of those characters in which I have seen [her] — everything is so
delicate — so simple — so innocent — so touching; and yet in private
life she has more intrigues than any woman in Paris. Indeed this part
of a mistress — she played long ago — in Napoleon's time — for the
Emperor kept her formerly — and now she keeps a half-dozen of
lovers — perhaps more — for I do not like to speak with certainty on
so delicate a subject. What a devil of an old woman.[5]

But after all Mlle. Mars must not be judged more strictly than other
French women — for all French women are naughty women: — as a
general rule. To be sure there are exceptions — for the Dutchess
D'Angoulême [6] not only prays for the remission of her own sins but
also for those of the Dutchess of Berry [7] — who takes pleasure where
she can find it and not content with keeping the Arch Bishop of
Paris, she puts all the "Garde du corps" under severe contribution.
But I suppose that I should not tell tales out of school — and you may
think it no compliment to your taste to fill a letter with such matters —
as if they would relish well — but you must recollect that I am speaking in all the freedom of conversation and if you judge me too severely
— I shall be "screwed up" as Fred says. And by the way — why does
not Fred write me — why does not Pitt Fessend[en] write me — and
Geordie Pierce — and Doctor Page and Bill Browne? [8] I wrote to one
and all of them long and long ago — and you will confer a favour on
your absent friend if you will hint to them the propriety of answers
as soon as possible: — because if my letters are worth anything they
are worth an answer and if they are not worth anything I shall not
write any more. This is rather too bad is it not — to write — and then
write again to beg for an answer. And this puts me in mind to answer
your letter of the 27th, whose reception I have hardly acknowledged.
It gave me great pleasure I can assure you — for it was the first or
rather with the first which I received from Portland. The packet
brought me one from my father — one from you; — one from Ned
[Preble] — and another from — but guess who — why from Oliver
Barrel[l] — this last affair — this letter of Oliver quite overwhelmed
me — because I was not anticipating such a favour. He means well
enough and seems to be in reality full of good feeling towards me —
therefore I wished to have been spared the unpleasant alternative

of cutting him short with no answer, or of involving myself in a correspondence with him. However, I prefer the former. He will probably think the letter miscarried if I make no answer — and if he does not just tell him that I am so much engaged that I cannot answer immediately — and that the last are always best as woman was the "Heaven's last best gift." [9] You know what a fond and silly heart he has towards the fair sex — any pill goes down with him that is administered by the hand or gilded with the name of woman. You have been to the White Mountains, then, this summer. You must have been there just before the dreadful affair of the Avalanch[e]. What a terrible catastrophe — another Goldeau. I have been reading long and minute accounts of it. [10] I assure [you] it struck me most forcibly — because I have loitered amongst those beautiful and sublime scenes — and rested in the very cottage whose inmates have found what John Neal in describing a similar event calls a "mountain pall." [11] Tell Fred [Mellen] to write a piece upon the subject and to send it to me over the sea: the subject is enough to inspire apathy itself with the noble sentiments of genius. When you mentioned passing an evening with Miss Codman and Miss Derby [12] I actually envied you the pleasure you had enjoyed — and perhaps that covetousness was justifiable in me, who am thus cut off from all that innocent and purifying intercourse with the young and beautiful that you are surrounded with and in whose society I have found better lessons of virtue than in all the sermons I ever heard. Indeed there is no book in which I read with so much interest as the face of a woman. This is a very gallant confession — but you know my old habits — and when I find myself so shut out of the world of my old friends — the thoughts of former intimacy now finished and in some instances finished forever come over me like a cloud. "It is a melancholy of my own, in which very often contemplation wraps me in a most humorous sadness" [13] — and sometimes in a most bitter sadness. If you ever come to Europe do not come alone. I have sometimes found [in] Paris the ||greatest s||olitude in the world — because I am all alone.

And now Pat a little business for you. I wish you to rummage about amongst all the old American papers that you can lay your hands on, and when you come across a file of those published when Fayette was in America I wish you to cut out all the ridiculous pieces of poetry touching him — all accounts of country celebrations — all toasts &c &c &c. All, in fine, which is the least peculiar. Make them up into a package and direct it to me — then put a second invellope over it directed to "D. C. Porter. Paris" — then a third — directed to his agents "De Launay Luuyt & Co. Havre." This method is the safest, and I shall have very little postage to pay — but if you send this directly to me I shall have letter postage to pay — which if the bundle were any way considerable in bulk would be a heavy duty on old Newspapers. The use to which I am going to put these musty old documents, I cannot now explain to you. I will explain all hereafter.[14] But do not forget the commission. Send them before March, as I expect to [go to] Germany in March. The reason that Ned will not travel must be very peculiar. Tell him that I say his only reason is that he means to be married soon. Push him, and make him confess it. It would be a fine affair — would not it. Equals to Nol's elopement.[15]

You see how I fill up the corners of my letters. I have so much to say that I can not find room to say it in. Be of good cheer — and write often. My best regards to your sister and all at your house.

Most affectionately yours.

H. W. L.

MANUSCRIPT: Bowdoin College Library. ADDRESS: To/Mr Patrick H. Greenleaf/ Portland Maine/U.S. of America POSTMARKS: NEW YORK NOV 26/FORWARDED BY DE LAUNAY LUUYT & CO HAVRE/SHIP ENDORSEMENT: H. W. Longfellow —/Dated Paris Oct 23. 1826/Recd Nov 29. 1826.

1. An expression, now obsolete, which is apparently the equivalent of "Puss in the corner." It appears in Fanny Burney, *Cecilia*, I, 41.

2. *Julius Caesar*, III, ii, 76–77.

3. Mlle. Mars [Anne Françoise Hyppolyte Boutet] (1779–1847) was the leading comedienne of the Comédie Française.

4. Cf. *Othello*, I, iii, 160.

5. The instruction "Turn to the first page" follows this sentence.

6. Marie-Thérèse Charlotte (1778–1851), daughter of Louis XVI and Marie Antoinette, married her cousin Louis-Antoine de Bourbon, duke of Angoulême, in 1799. He was the last dauphin of France and she, according to Napoleon, "the only man of her family."

7. Caroline Ferdinande Louise (1798–1870), eldest daughter of King Francis I of Naples, was the widow of Charles Ferdinand, duke of Berry. More accomplished as a social than as a political intriguer, she was exiled from France in 1833.

8. Longfellow refers to his classmates Frederic Mellen and George Pierce, and to his friends George William Gray Browne and William Pitt Fessenden (1806–1869). Fessenden, who later enjoyed a distinguished political career in the U.S. Senate, was at this time studying law in Portland and courting Longfellow's sister Elizabeth. Dr. Page is either Dr. Frederic Benjamin Page or his brother Dr. Jonathan Page (see 81.2).

9. Milton, *Paradise Lost*, V, 19.

10. A description of the famous Willey Slide in Crawford Notch, August 26, 1826, is contained in Stephen Longfellow's letter to his son, September 24, 1826: "If you see our newspapers you are apprised of the melancholy disaster which happened at the White Mountains. A long continuation of violent rains has so loosened the soil rocks and trees on the sides of the mountains that it produced a great number [of] avalanches in different places, the most destructive of which buried the notch house where Mr. Wylie lived, in ruins, and with it the whole family,

consisting [of] nine persons. The road is filled with rocks, earth and trees for several miles, so that the bed of the river is changed, and it is apprehended by many that the road can never be repaired." Hawthorne based "The Ambitious Guest" (1835) on the Willey family tragedy.

11. "O, I have lost ye all!/Parents — and home — and friends:/Ye sleep beneath a mountain pall" (in *Goldau; or, the Maniac Harper*).

12. Presumably Sarah Ellen Derby and Susan Codman.

13. Cf. *As You Like It*, IV, i, 16.

14. Although no explanation is forthcoming in any of the extant letters, it is apparent that Longfellow used this material in preparing a sketch called "The Bald Eagle Tavern." See Letter No. 145.

15. Nolcini had eloped with a Miss Murray of Portland (Susan Codman to Longfellow, August 19, 1826).

108. *To Stephen Longfellow, Jr.*

Paris   October 26. 1826.

My dear brother S —

I am going to describe to you as well as I can in the compass of a single letter a foot-expedition which I made a few weeks ago, and which I mentioned in the letters I sent by yesterday's packet; and which, in fine, makes a fine epoch in my life. It was a journey of a few days along the romantic borders of the Loire and Cher — of a few days, stolen from the melancholy of a city life — and filled with all the joy and light-heartedness which a foot traveller feels, when leaving his cares behind him — he shoulders his knapsack — to wander away to the ends of the earth! But first a word of Orleans — celebrated, you know, for its siege, and as the birth-place of Joan of Arc. This was the first city I had seen whose ancient walls remained — and the sensations which it excited were of a powerful and thrilling kind — for though what is now left of the fortifications of the place has been changed to a public promenade — looking upon a rich cultivated landscape and shaded with fine old trees — still all the thoughts and associations which pass through a stranger's mind, on first seeing the ruins of an ancient wall — are of other days. Orleans is very delightfully situated upon the northern banks of the Loire — and its environs are really enchanting — a wide fertile plain in all the beauty of the richest cultivation. All that will attract a stranger, who visits the place without introductory letters — all that will attract him within the walls of the city will be the façade of the cathedral begun as long ago as Henri Quatre's time — and not yet entirely finished — and a most exquisite bronze statue of Jeanne d'Arc which stands in the market place — and by the force of contrast reminds one of the clumsy monument erected to her memory in Rouen, the place of her execution.

From Orleans I started on foot for Tours. Oct. 5th. October is my favorite month of the twelve: — and when I reflected that if I remained at Paris I should lose the only opportunity I might ever enjoy of seeing the centre of France in all the glory of its vintage, and all the glory of its Autumn I "shut the book-lid" — and took wing — with a little knapsack on my back, and a blue cap, not exactly like Quentin Durward's — but perhaps a little. More anon of him. I went as far as Orleans in the diligence, because the rout is through a dull uninteresting country. And after passing one day in that city, I was on my way on foot and alone. I began the pedestrian part of my journey on one of those dull melancholy days, which you will find uttering a mournful voice in Sewal's almanack — "expect — much — rain — about — this — time! — very miscellaneous weather — for sundry purposes"[1] — but not for a journey on foot, thought I. But I had a merry heart, and it went all day, till about sundown, when I found myself about seven leagues on my way — and one beyond Beaugency — a village which is put down in the maps — you will easily find it. I found the rout one continued vineyard: — on each side of the road as far as the eye could reach — there was nothing but vines save here and there a glimpse of the Loire and the turrets of an old chateaux or of a village church. Fortunately the clouds had passed away with the morning — and I had made a fine day's journey of it: — turning aside from the main road — cutting across the country, traversing vineyards — and living in all the luxury of thought which the occasion inspired. I recollect at sunset — I had entered a path which wound amongst a wide vineyard — where the villagers were still at the labour of the vintage — and I was loitering along — talking with the peasantry — and searching for an Auberge to pass the night in. I was presently overtaken by a band of the villagers — returning from their labours — and as I made it a rule to speak to every one I encountered, I of course wished them a good evening — and finding that the girls of the party were going to village at a short distance I joined myself to the band. The great secret of the matter was — I wanted to get into one of the cottages if possible — in order, you know — to study character.[2]

— And another great secret was — that I had a flute in my knapsack — and I thought it would be very pretty to touch up at a cottage-door — Goldsmith like: — though I would not have done it for the world without an invitation. Well — before long I determined to get an invitation if possible: so I addressed myself to the girl who was walking beside me — told her I had a flute in my sack, and asked her if she should like to dance. Now laugh long and loud! What do you suppose the answer was. She said she liked to dance but she did not know what a flute was! Lord! — what havoc that made among my romantic ideas! However my quietus was made. I said no more about a flute the whole journey through: — but I thought that nothing but starvation would drive me to strike up at the entrance of a village as Goldsmith did. The company I was in, conducted me to the village of Tivher — the most beautiful and romantic little village — I was ever in — I make no exception. I found the village inn — and fell asleep at night with the thought that perhaps a part of the "Traveller" was written in that very village. When I awoke the next morning — a clear bright autumn sun was shining upon the romantic valley of Tivher — the villagers were already at their work — the ducks were gabbling in a sunny pool — the wine-press laboured in the shade — a grist-mill was a-going and so was I! I continued the same rout upon the northern bank of the Loire as far as Mer — where I crossed the river, and without meeting with any adventure worthy of record — arrived at nightfall at the very celebrated old chateau of Chambord. The chateau of Chambord is celebrated as being the most splendid of the old gothic chateaux in France, but at present it is in a very desolate state — unoccupied and falling into decay. I can by no means give you a perfect idea of it: — if you can call to mind any engraving of a French chateau — you will have a more perfect picture before you than I can paint in a letter. Ned Preble used to make excellent ones on the covers of old writing-books at school — with battlements and peaked roofs — stuck all round with little spires and curious uncouth ornaments. Within are magnificent halls — splendid staircases — long corridors — ceilings in stucco work — but the only piece of furniture is a massive oak table of the Mareschal de Saxe to whom Louis XV. gave the chateau after the battle of Fontenoy[3] — which puts me in mind of a paraphrase of Robinson Crusoe which I attempted once — and of which two lines have always closely adhered to my memory — viz —

> "His eldest boy
> Was killed at Fontenoy." —[4]

Travellers have covered the walls and battlements of the old edifice entirely over with their names — thousands and thousands, but for my own part I was content to commemorate my visit by breaking off the head of a little stone dragon which I found amongst other ornaments upon the principal staircase — which I shall bring home as a trophy of my journey. The next day I reached Blois. At this place is a most immense castelated chateau — at present the garrison of the gendarmerie, but formerly the scene of the assassination of the Guises.[5]

There is [a] chamber in which is shown one of Louis eleventh's infernal machines for secret murders — a kind of well — set round with sythes and sharp edged instruments — into which the victim was dropped — bound hand and foot. What a fatality there is about human greatness! The chamber of Catherine de Medicis in the same chateau is now occupied by a fourrier — the officer whose care is the lodgement of the soldiery!

I was now half way on my rout to Tours which was to be the boundary of my journey. The next day carried me to Amboise on the south side of the Loire. On the rout I saw many houses of the pe[a]santry cut into the solid rock of the hillside, and overhung from the vineyards on top with the thick foliage of the vine. They have a very singular appearance — but rather bespeak poverty than choice. I peeped into one of them — it was dark and damp like a dungeon — and they seemed at best good for nothing but wine cellars.

— I said that I should say something of Quentin Durward and the road I took of course suggested his name — but I have not time to finish my history — therefore we will adjourn. I shall however take the earliest opportunity to finish what I have begun in this letter — and fill up what little remains blank in this sheet by telling you that I am living in college style here — and as the weather is now quite cold enough for a fire, — I keep mostly within doors and begin to study very hard. I come on well in French tho' I say it who should not say it: — and shall begin German soon. Why do not you write me. I should think you had no quill-drivers amongst you. I have as yet received but one letter and that I received nearly a month ago. It was from Papa — and I have answered it long ago. I find I get very long winded in all my letters — but I cannot help it. It is the same as if I were talking with you at home there. But do not forget nor neglect to write — for you know I am almost alone in this Old World — no old friends around me as you have — and the reception of a letter is quite an era of good feelings with me. None of my correspondents seem to care about answering my letters. There was Mellen — and Pierce and Fessenden — and Browne — and Doctor Page and a host of worthies there! Tell all hands to write. Write, no matter what — only write. Because only one letter for four months — five months is rather short allowance. God bless you good bye. Amor ad omnes. Haud immemor mali — succerere disco [6] — which means I write you two for one.

Yours

Henry.

MANUSCRIPT: Longfellow Trust Collection. ADDRESS: To/Stephen Longfellow

Jr/Portland Me./U.S. of America POSTMARKS: NEW YORK DEC 9/FOR-
WARDED BY DE LAUNAY LUUYT & CO HAVRE/SHIP   ENDORSEMENT: Henry
to Stephen/Octr 26 1826/Decr. 13

1. Longfellow apparently refers to *The Farmer's Almanac*, edited in 1822–1824
by William B. Sewall (70.1). There were a number of Sewalls, however, who
compiled New England almanacs.

2. The instruction "First page —" follows this sentence.

3. The Battle of Fontenoy took place in 1745. Maurice de Saxe's victory over the
English and their allies earned him the chateau in 1748 and the title "Marshal
General of the King's Camps and Armies."

4. Robinson Crusoe's eldest brother "was killed at the battle near Dunkirk against
the Spaniards." Longfellow's attempted paraphrase does not survive. See *Young
Longfellow*, p. 345.

5. Henri de Lorraine, 3rd duc de Guise, and his brother Louis de Lorraine,
cardinal de Guise, were murdered by order of Henri III in December, 1588 — the
one in the king's chamber and the other in the dungeon of the chateau.

6. "Love to all. Not unmindful of evil — I am learning how to help." Longfellow's
Latin suggests that he remembered the words of Dido to Aeneas: "Non ignara mali
miseris succurrere disco" ("Not being unacquainted with evil, I am learning how
to help those in trouble"). *Aeneid*, I, 630.

109. *To Stephen Longfellow, Jr.*

Paris   November 19th 1826.

I believe I left you, my dear brother, in my description of the center
of France, somewhere in the environs of Blois. I mentioned an ancient
chateau at that place, tho' I think I did not mention that in one of the
chambers are still to be seen some of the cruel machines for execu-
tions, contrived by Louis Eleventh: such as round holes or wells in the
floor down which the condemned was cast in a standing position bound
hand and foot: — at a certain depth he was received between two
wheels armed with sword blades and sharp points which tore the
body in pieces, and from which it dropped into a pit of lime. The road
from Blois to Tours upon the northern bank of the Loire is exceedingly uninteresting to a foot traveller — the country being very flat
and on one side of your path the river — on the other an unbroken
line of poplar trees. I found it very monotonous and tedious, and by
taking it in preference to the South bank, lost the view of the Chateau
of Chaumont, in which Madame de Staël was permitted to reside
during her *banishment from France*.[1] All I saw of it was the slated
roof and tapering spires rising from a clump of thick leafy trees. I
found the route so uninteresting, that I took the first opportunity of
crossing the river, which was at a little village called Moines. I then
found myself in a very delicious country and trudged on merrily to the

town of Amboise. On the road I met an old fellow, who said he was a sailor at the siege of Rochelle. I asked him if he knew Lord Nelson — and afterwards he managed to turn this to his account by pretending that he thought me Lord Nelson's son, and upon the strength of that begging a few sous to drink "the commodore's health."

I had no reason to like the town of Amboise — for apart from its being a dirty place, my Landlady charged me most enormously for my lodging and breakfast. There is however in the place an old chateau built by Charles Seventh, which I did not take the trouble to enter.[2] From Amboise I crossed the country to the banks of the Cher. Here I saw the beautiful chateau of Chenonçeau, which was built by François first — for Diane de Poitiers, his mistress.[3] It is a most magnificent Chateau, erected upon arches over the Cher, under which pass all the boats and barges of the river. It is the only ancient chateau in France which contains the furniture of the times of Old. In the principal entry you see the armour of François 1st — shields — helms — and lances, rusting on the wall — not to mention an old gun already rusty — something like twelve feet long — a real old bruiser. From this a door opens into a long corridor hung round with faded pictures, and reaching quite across the cheateau — from the windows of which on each side you get fine views up and down the river. Above you are shown the bed and bed-chamber of Diane de Poitiers et those also of the cruel Catherine de Medici — an arm chair and a litter of Henri Quatre — and in an old lab[o]ratory amongst broken crucibles, neck-less retorts, old drums and trumpets — skins of wild beasts — and other lumber of the kind, are wisely kept for show the bed-posts of François first. Everything about this building is enchanting — its park in which Rousseau resided — its noble fortifications — and the beau-ties of the river scenery on each side. I lingered near it as long as my time would permit and turned back at every two steps to take another last look. A bend in the Cher hid the old edifice from my view, and I jogged on towards Tours and that night arrived within four miles of it. The next day was heavy — dull — rainy — melancholy — so I jumped into a cabriolet and so reached Tours. This is a fine city tho' I saw it under very unfavorable circumstances: — for on awaking the morning after my arrival I found the sky black with clouds. There is not much, however, to interest a stranger in the place — so I found my promenade very dull — the Cathedral being no great affair, and the old Abbaye of St. Martin being turned into a shot-tower. At least half of the in-habitants are English — attracted thither I suppose by the beautiful situation of the town and the great air of the city. I met several Eng-lish Ladies in my walk. After returning from the survey of the city —

I found it dull enough — and like other idlers went to scribbling on my walls.[4]

From Tours I went south, as far as Savon[n]ieres — a little village on the banks of the Cher, celebrated for its "caves gout[t]ieres." There is a fine description of this in the guide books; and I thought I should afterwards repent if I neglected seeing any of the curiosities of the country. So down I went in spite of mud and mire in search of the wonderful caverns and also of Plessis-les-Tours — which lies some-where upon the same rout, and was once very celebrated you know.[5] I persuaded myself that there was once such a personage as Quentin Durward and when I came to [a] ford in the river, felt pretty sure that it was the same at which he crossed. But Plessis-les-Tours I could not find — no body knew anything about [it] — and those who pre-tended to direct me directed me wrong — inasmuch as there are a thousand Plessis in the environs of Tours. It was more to say that I had been there that prompted me to inquire about it — for I knew from a traveller who had seen all that remains there, that there is nothing to be seen but the old cellars. So away I went for the "Caves Gouttieres" — which my guide book painted in such glowing colours. I expected to find large elegant chambers under ground, with columns of white stalactites — and all glowing — and bright — and beautiful. Instead of which I had to slide down a bank of clay — rendered very proper for that purpose by the rain over night, — and after searching round with a farthing candle for the splendid apartments with alabas-ter pillars — scrambling through dirty holes, and stumbling over heaps of clay, found nothing to reward my pains but a few miserable fossil shells. N.B. I tore a hole in the back of my coat, which added much to the young man's general appearance, and induced him to start off forthwith on his return to Paris. I of course did not pursue the same route back that I had taken in coming — but took a more direct route by Vendome and Chartres. At Vendome I saw the ruins of a fine old castle, built by Jeanne D'Albret — mother of Henry fourth, and in which he received his early education, and spent his youthful days. It is situated upon the top of a high and steep hill — and absolutely overhangs the town. When in its strength it must have been impregnable, but the Vandalism of the French Revolution finished the ravages that time had begun, and nothing is now left but here and there a solitary tower slowly dropping to decay. The only way to enter them is by climbing in at the windows, which of course I did without ceremony, as they are uninhabited. In one of them is the tomb of Jeanne d'Albret — the inscription nearly effaced, tho' enough remained to inform the curi-ous, that there reposed the mother of the "bon Henri" — to which was added the request of respect for the repose of the dead — a request which has not been in the least regarded. From Vendôme I took the route to Chartres and thence on to Paris without a single event worthy of record.

I am now fixed for the rest of my sojourn in Paris in very comfortable quarters, and very near Eben Storer, tho' not in the same house. My chamber is a very handsome and a very ||spacious|| one, and I feel much at my ease and very happy. I associate very little with English Society. I feel however a little solicitude about the future, and do not like the idea of going alone either into Germany or Italy. Pray urge Ned to come out before I leave Paris. I can assure him that he will not be happy here without one of his old friends. Tell him that I will stay as long in Paris as my circumstances will possibly permit, and as long as I can get permission to stay. French comes on famously. I have now got to enjoy the society around me and of course begin to enjoy "Life in Paris" — but it was dull enough at first, as it must necessarily be to one who cannot speak French and does not wish to speak English. The last Packet brought me no letters. I was very much disappointed — indeed I could hardly believe that there were none for me. I have been here five months and have received but two letters — one of the 11th of August — the other the sixth of September. None as yet from you — none from our sisters. Truly "there is something rotten in the state of Denmark." Write me a letter from the office — all of you together — and ask Pitt [Fessenden], and Browne if they have ever received my letters. Good night! I think of no more last words, excepting that Mr. Carter [6] is here — and lives but a few doors from me. He has just returned from Italy, and will pass the Winter in Paris. Of course you will have descriptions enough of "what's done i' the capital." When I saw him last he desired his remembrance to the family when I should write. You are a very negligent correspondent, as well as some others that I could mention but forbear to for Charity's sake. Farewell. Say a good word for me to all who make enquiries.

Affectionately your brother
Henry.

I intended to have inclosed a letter for the girls, but find I cannot spare time — so I postponed it for the next packet. My letters I fear do not all reach you. Be kind enough to keep an exact account of all the dates, of my letters. I shall do of all yours and let me, if you please, know from these notes from time to time — *pretty often* what you have already received from over the sea. Why for charity's sake do not the girls take time to write? They certainly might fill very easily page after page with all their little household sayings and affairs which would of course interest me much. Two letters for 5 months is rather short allowance for one away from all his friends. Eben Storer and a friend of his are all the Americans, I associate with; they both leave for England the first of January. It was nothing but a joke — my queer figure in French clothes: what clothes I have had made was all after the English model.[7]

MANUSCRIPT: Longfellow Trust Collection. ADDRESS: To/Mr. Stephen Longfellow. Jr./Portland. Maine/U.S. of America. POSTMARKS: NEW YORK JAN 11/FORWARDED BY DE LAUNAY LUUYT & CO HAVRE/SHIP ENDORSEMENT: Henry to Stephen/Paris Novr. 19. 1826/Re[c]d. Jany 15 —

1. In 1803 Napoleon directed Mme. de Staël not to reside within forty leagues of Paris. During this exile she spent a few days at Chaumont in 1809.

2. Longfellow thus missed seeing the tomb of Leonardo da Vinci, who lies buried in the castle.

3. The story that Diane de Poitiers was the mistress of Francis I is without serious foundation. As the mistress of Henry II, however, she occupied the chateau of Chenonceaux until his death in 1559, when Catherine de' Medici acquired it.

4. The instruction "First page." follows this sentence.

5. Sir Walter Scott had reconstructed the chateau in *Quentin Durward* (1823).

6. N. H. Carter had arrived in Europe the previous year and was writing descriptive letters about his travels, which were being widely published in American newspapers, including the *Eastern Argus* of Portland.

7. Longfellow's description of his appearance in Letter No. 100 had brought forth a mild reprimand from his father in a letter dated September 24, 1826: "It seems that you have changed your costume to that of a Parisian. You will allow me to doubt the expediency of conforming your dress to the fashion of the country in which you may reside for a short time. You will find it expensive to you, as your french dress would be useless to you in Spain or any other country, for an American in Spain, Italy, or Germany decked out in the dress of a frenchman will exhibit a very singular appearance. You should remember that you are an American, and as you are a visitor for a short time only in a place, you should retain your own National Costume. You will find it much more convenient and less expensive."

110. *To Zilpah Longfellow*

Paris   Decemb. 23rd. 1826

My dear Mother,

I need not tell you that I was overjoyed in receiving your letter of October 18th. If I tell you it was the first I had received wholly from you, you can imagine the rest. But how time flies. When I look at the date of your letter, I say to myself — two months ago — this was in my mother's hand. She was then thinking of me — of me who have left you all and wandered away to the ends of the earth, like a leaf that has fallen from its parent tree, and been wafted away by the winds. I never think how swiftly time passes, except when something occurs to call up within me old recollections and familiar associations. Day after day — and week after week — and then I feel that they are passed — not that they are passing. But when I receive a letter from home it makes me sensible of the silent and ceaseless lapse of days and months. It makes me sensible, too, that time as well as distance separates us — that it is not the natural sea alone but the sea of time, which cuts us off one from another. In this way I moralize upon the past, and then I look forward to the distant — distant day of our meeting, until my heart swells into my throat and tears into my eyes — for I cannot help thinking it a very pardonable weakness, to let a tear fall now and then upon unavailing regrets and thus blot them out forever!

I do not know how I came to fall into this "meditation-among-the-tombs" kind of style, but I think it must be owing to the weather, which is dull and rainy and of course melancholy. Every day for six weeks, we have had rain, or a damp heavy atmosphere. This is the legitimate Parisian Winter. It is not cold — not the clear cold of our New England winter, which braces a man into good health in spite of himself — and whilst it pinches ones nose off, puts him into a cheerful and b[u]oyant humour — but a gloomy — chill — damp air — that gives one the rheumatism and makes him sad. I no sooner set my foot upon wet cold pavements of the street than I begin to think of a grave-yard — and whole hosts of pale ghostlike beings, with overshoes shaped like coffins — by reason that all French people wear square-toed shoes — are apt to put me into a doleful way of thinking. Indeed I think I should have passed altogether a melancholy life of it even amid the gaieties of Paris, if Cousin Eben Storer had not been here. He leaves in a week or two for London — and I shall not stay here long after his departure. All that keeps me now is the Carnival, which commences in a few days, and the strong desire I have of profiting by the kindness of some new French acquaintances which I have lately had the good fortune to make. Cousin Eben and myself became accidental[l]y acquainted with a French gentleman by the Name of Guillet (pron. Ge-yea). He was an ancient acquaintance of La Fayette in the time of the Revolution and afterwards Secretary — or rather Interpreting Secretary of Foreign Affairs under Napoleon. He is a very learned and a very singular man. He speaks six or seven different languages — English, French — German — Italian — Spanish — Latin — Modern Greek —and I do not know but some others: —but tho' so wise he is always in a frolick — and exhibits what I should call a good specimen of the green old age of a French-man of the "Ancien Regime."[1] He has been exceedingly kind to us — and

moreover exceedingly useful. He has introduced us to his family —
to the soirées or evening parties of a celebrated traveller — where we
go once a week if we choose — and where we always find high literary
society.[2] For example — we meet there Sir Sidney Smith[3] — Mr
Cooper — our novelist — Mr Carter &c &c. Here he made us
acquainted with Mr Julian, Editor of the French E[n]cyclopedic
Review,[4] who has the correspondence of all the literary and scientific
men, both in Europe and America, and who offers us letters to any
quarter of the continent — and to England — which we both think
very kind in him. Mr Warden, also, former consul from the United
States,[5] has treated us very politely and being himself a member of the
Institute, has introduced us to some private meetings — where we
had our curiosity gratified by a peep at the wise heads of Cuvier the
great Naturalist — La Place — Legendre — Gay Lussac et cetera.[6]
But to return to our friend Mr Guillet. He intends visiting America
the next Spring — and you will see him of course — as he intends
visiting every State in the Union, and will take letters to you. He will
tell you all about Paris and our manner of life here and I have no
doubt that you will be very much pleased — at all events very much
amused with such a specimen of France — and such a "walking
Dictionary" as he calls himself. He will be as good as a description of
Paris — or a guide-book through France, for the efforts he has made
in learning so many languages, have made talking a habit with him
so that he can pass for a fair specimen of "Narrative Old Age."[7]

You seem no way pleased with my idea of visiting Germany, and
your first reason is my own personal safety, which you think would be
in danger. Now for my own part, I have not the least apprehension
on this score for I never had any particular fondness for a duel. Your
second reason for my not visiting the country is much more plausible
— its lengthening my stay in Europe. It would be useless to go into
Germany unless I could remain at least a year — and I suppose you
would object to this on more than one account. When I wrote my last
letter upon the subject, speaking of my going to Gottingen as a matter
almost certain, I thought I could learn the language and get some
insight into the literature in a shorter time than a twelve month, but
those who are best acquainted with the subject tell me no. The
language is so exceedingly difficult that it will not be worth while to
attempt to speak it unless I have much time to devote to it. I must
come back again to my original destination: France — Spain and
Italy. But Italy before Spain on many accounts. The dangerous state
of the country — the suspicion naturally attached to an Englishman
if the War[8] continues long — would not detain me though I once

thought they would. But then I should wish to make sure of Italy and its language first — for fear that if I went first into Spain I should lose Italy by some untoward circumstances — such as being under the necessity of returning before the time anticipated. &c. Thus we see how much the events of life depend upon momentary circumstances — and how much the apprehension of some mischance will change ones plans and resolutions. I have been talking considerably with Mr Carter upon the subject, who advises me most decidedly to go to Italy in the first instance — and then to Spain. You will hear from me soon, then, in Italy. What a delightful prospect for me! With how much delight I shall leave the populous and noisy streets of Paris for the sunny regions of the south, and the eternal summer of the Italian valleys! Then indeed the distance between us will become more perceptable, because our intercourse by letters will be more interrupted and more uncertain. I shall, instead of regular letters, keep a journal for you — a thing that I have not done in France on many accounts — and chiefly on account of the little interest I attach to anything in Paris, and a thorough disgust for French manners and customs.

The day of my departure is not yet fixed — but I shall probably leave Paris in twenty days — more or less depending somewhat upon the information I shall receive from those who have been in Italy relative to the Carnival and Holy Week at Rome — and partly upon your letters, — which I expect every day. I told Edward Preble that I would go with him to Germany in March, but I know very well that he will not be here before Summer, when he will find me in Italy or Spain. Farewell! It is but half after 3 o'clock — but so dark that I can hardly see to finish my letter. This is the French gloomy climate — darkness visible at noon-day. Good night. Mr Carter desires to be remembered in all my letters to you — so hereafter you will take for granted. Best love to all, not excepting — Mary — and Ellen and Samuel.

Most affectionately Your Son
Henry W. L.

P.S. — I would acknowledge the reception of Anne's letter of October 26th, which came with yours. I should have answered it by the packet which brings you this, — but a small accident has prevented me. She will receive a letter next week — that is to say a week after you receive this. The dates of letters received from home are August 11th — September 6th — and two of October 26 making four.

MANUSCRIPT: Longfellow Trust Collection.   ADDRESS: To/Stephen Longfellow Esq./Portland./Maine./U.S. of America./pr Bayard [*in another hand*] POST-

MARKS: FORWARDED BY YR. OBT. SERVT. WELLES & CO./SHIP ENDORSE-
MENT: Henry to his Parents/Paris Decr 23d 1826/Re[c]d Feby 19 1827/
A[ns.] Feby 27 —

1. Records in the archives of the Ministry of Foreign Affairs, Paris, reveal that
Isadore Guillet (b. 1772) had been employed in 1794 and 1795 as a translator
for the Secretary of the Commission on Foreign Relations (Commission des Relations extérieures).

2. The instruction "first page" follows this sentence.

3. Admiral Sir William Sidney Smith (1764-1840) had retired to Paris after
a distinguished career in the Royal Navy, during which he won fame for the defence of Acre in 1799.

4. Marc Antoine Jullien de Paris (1775-1848), publicist and founder of the
Revue Encyclopédique in 1818.

5. David Bailie Warden (1778-1845), born in Ireland and educated in the
United States, was consul in Paris for some forty years, distinguishing himself
there for his scientific attainments and general learning.

6. Georges Cuvier (1769-1832), Pierre Simon Laplace (1749-1827), Adrien
Marie Legendre (1752-1834), and Joseph Louis Gay-Lussac (1778-1850) were
all members of the Institut de France.

7. Cf. Pope, *The Iliad*, III, 200. Guillet apparently did not visit the United States
until several years later (see 524.2).

8. That is, the campaign of coercion by Ferdinand VII to reduce opposition to
his autocratic regime.

111. *To Longfellow Sisters* [1]

[Paris]   January 1st 1827.

— "A happy New Year!" — my dear Sisters: — a salutation that
you have heard from a thousand tongues today, but which will not
on that account reach your ears with a less welcome accent from this
side of the water. I was not awakened at sun-rise, as I dare say you
were, — by the footsteps of the children in the entry — the door
cautiously unlatched or a shout of young voices at your bedside, —
eager to give the first greetings of the New Year: — but I awoke to the
sad con[s]ciousness of being shut out from your family circle; — for
a holiday in this distant land always brings with it a peculiar melancholy, arising from associations of the past and the uncertainties of
the future.

New Year's day in France is always a day of great gaiety and
rejoicing — a holiday for all classes of people. The streets are filled
with people — and every passage — lane — and blind alley pours
forth its turbulent tide of men — women and children. It is a day of
glory for pastry-cooks and confectioners. Their windows are decorated with all that is sublime in pie and sugar plumb: and the wistful
eye and watery mouth of many a sweep and pennyless urchin bears
witness to the complete victory of matter over mind.

Frivolity and lightheartedness are proverbial characteristics of the French. The holiday customs of the New Year's Day afford an excellent proof and illustration of their peculiar levity. Here, as in some parts of our own country, those who are in society, expect a visit from each of their friends. Of course a gallant man — who would sin against a point of etiquette, and thereby bring death into the little world of his pretensions — if he omitted a duty of such regular standing as are the morning calls of this day — has little to do but run round with his visiting cards from morning till night. This may be well enough for ought I know — but the French make light of the business by expecting in addition to the visit a pocket full of sugar-plumbs. This custom of giving pep[p]er-mints — and lozenges —

"Lol[l]ipops and bull's-eyes
With sugar-plums of full size — "[2]

prevails through all classes — and a lady in the first circles would think herself not a little slighted if a gentleman should call on New Year's morning without the customary offering of a paper of "Bonbons." Thus fashion rules us — and gives to frivolity the name and sanction of a wise and venerable custom.

There were village customs at Auteuil which pleased me more than this. First was the marriage festival. It was an amusing sight, to see the procession moving to the church — for in the little French Villages the marriage vows are consummated there: — and as "friends and relations are requested to attend" — as at our funerals — there is always something of a stir and a procession in the streets. The bridegroom smirking and glorying in the rich estate of a large blue coat and spacious white waistcoat, with a bunch of flowers stuck in the bosom. The bride walking in silk attire — with rose-wreaths in her hair — ribbons and garlands — kid gloves and satin slippers — and "timid down-cast eye"! Then follow the rejoicing relatives — and village idlers. Foremost the town musicians lead the way — a jolly little fiddler in the van — and then an octave flute — and a man labouring hard at an asthmatic clarionet.

"Sound the sweet, melodious flute
To hail the nuptial morning!"

as Little Jones used to sing at the Theatre.[3] And so onward to the Village church — to the lively music of an old familiar air: — whilst for the moment all labor ceases in the little world of the village —

the chamber-maid thrusts her head from the garret window — the curious gather at the corner of the street — the cobler leaves his little all [awl]. Of course the black-smith's bellows heave a long expiring sigh — and so of course the bride!

There are, too, the burial customs of the village, which are interesting from being peculiar to Catholic countries. But there is an air of mock-solemnity about them, which takes away all that deep moral feeling, that the burial service is, in itself, so calculated to inspire. Still, the first impression upon hearing the dirge, breaking through the silence of a summer evening, is strong and affecting. There is something peculiarly thrilling in the catholic chant — hear it where you will — but when thus connected with death — and its melancholy associations — when it mingles with the sound of the funeral bell — and you hear it unexpectedly in the tranquility of evening — it is most solemn and touching. But as the funeral procession approaches, the solemnity of the scene diminishes. An aged priest comes first — directing the chant with an instrument called a serpent — a kind of crooked horn — of black wood, with sound much resembling that of a bassoon. Next comes a boy — bearing the consecrated wafer — the symbol of the faith of the departed — then two other priests in white robes — with the banners of the church, representing some misteries of their religion — then the corpse — born upon a bier — the pall-bearers — again the religious banners — and lastly the hired mourners — with a crowd of followers — sauntering carelessly along — laughing and disputing — and at the same time most piously performing those last impressive duties to the dead — which as being the last, call for a decent observance! My love to all.

Most affecty. yours
H. W. L.

MANUSCRIPT: Longfellow Trust Collection.

1. Possibly enclosed with Letter No. 110.
2. From a parody on Leigh Hunt entitled "A Nursery Ode" by William Gifford in *Warreniana* (Boston, 1824), p. 35. Longfellow inverts the lines.
3. J. Jones, of Boston, was a performer of comic songs and dances.

112. *To Stephen Longfellow*

Paris   February 13th 1827.

My dear Father,

I mentioned in the postscript of my last letter the reception of yours of the 26th of November [1] — and as I have already virtually answered it — by sending a particular account of the situation of my money matters — I shall pass at once to your letter of 3rd Decr. which reached me after a week's interval. You mention the circumstance of your being two months without letters. This would have astonished me — had I not known from a sad experience how very easily letters miscarry — and I hardly need assure you — that this was no fault of mine. Indeed I make it something of a boast, that I am one of the most regular and attentive correspondents in the world: and with one solitary exception have never let a fortnight pass — without writing to some one of the family. I have a distinct recollection of writing a large double letter from Auteuil — a second double letter just before I left Paris for the Loire about the first of October — two long letters upon my return, giving a description of my jaunt as well as I could in so short a space [2] — and since then at the regular intervals of fifteen days without fail. You can judge from this how sorry I was to hear that you had been two months without letters. This uncertainty attending the reception of letters always discourages me when I sit down to write. Perhaps you will participate in this discouragement, when I assure you, that having applied repeatedly at the Post Office, — I have come atlength to the conclusion that your first letters are irrecoverably lost. But I am too much in haste to discuss this grief of ours at greater length.

I am very glad I can answer your wishes and expectations with regard to an instructer. I have always such a crowd of thoughts pressing upon me when I sit down to write you, that I have always omitted mentioning the circumstance of my taking an instructer. And indeed I always presumed that it was taken for granted. At Auteuil — one month — I was without one — because there were none there — but immediately after my return I commenced anew my lessons — and continued them as long as I thought it necessary. It is now exactly eight months since my arrival in Paris — and setting all boasting aside — I must say that I am well satisfied with the knowledge I have acquired of the french language. My friends all tell me that I have a good pronunciation — and altho' I do not pretend to anything like perfection — yet in comparison with what others have done — I am confident that I have done well. I cannot imagine who told you that six months was enough for the French — he would have been more correct if he had said six years — that is — speaking of perfection in the language.

— I shall leave Paris for Spain on Wednesday — day after tomorrow. I shall write again before leaving the city,[3] with all the particulars of my plan and route &c but at present I am in too great haste — for I must close my letter to be in season for the packet of the fifteenth.

You can hardly imagine how much I regret, that Edward P. —
[Preble] is not here — tho' I do not know whether he would visit
Spain. I fear we shall not meet for a long time to come. I regret it
exceedingly.

— My letters will be directed as heretofore — to the care of Messrs
Welles &co — who will forward them to me. But we cannot hope for
so regular a correspondence as heretofore — because all our letters
must traverse France from frontier to frontier — which necessarily
doubles the chances of loss.

— My health continues excellent — with the exception of the little
circumstance mentioned in my last — which is in a favorable way at
present.[4] My family physician Cousin Eben Storer — leaves for London on Friday. I have sent a few books by the packet of the 15th to
the care of Edward Storer — New York. A few dictionaries, grammars &c. I shall send a few engravings by Eben Storer. I am expecting
letters from Stephen every day but none reach me.

— My best love to all.

Most affectionately yrs
H. W. L. —

MANUSCRIPT: Longfellow Trust Collection. ADDRESS: Stephen Longfellow Esqr./
Portland. Maine/U.S. of America POSTMARKS: NEW YORK MAR 22/FOR-
WARDED BY ED QUESNEL L'AINÉ HAVRE/SHIP ENDORSEMENT: Henry to his
Father — /Paris Feby 13. 1827./R[ec]. and Ans: March 26.—

1. The letter containing this acknowledgment is missing.
2. The specific references are to Letters No. 101, 102, 104, 105, and 106. Letter
No. 104 is not a double letter, however; if Longfellow also wrote to his mother at
this time, the manuscript is lost.
3. This letter, if written, is unrecovered.
4. In a letter to his son on March 25, 1827, Stephen Longfellow wrote: "We
were very sorry to hear by your letter of Jany 1. that so unpleasant a cause would
be likely to detain you some time longer in Paris." Since the letter referred to is
missing, the "little circumstance" cannot be more accurately described.

113. *To Stephen Longfellow*

Bordeaux. Feby. 26. 1827.

My dear father,

There were a thousand things at Paris, whose descriptions might
well have filled my letters — but which were omitted — as printers
say — for want of room — and now that I have left that city probably
for ever — come thronging into my recollection. Such were for example — the church of St. Denis — in the environs — the burial place
of the Kings of France — the palace and gardens of Versailles — particularly that called the Little Trianon — visit to the prison of Marie

Antoinette — and the celebrated cemetery of Père La Chaise. I regret this much — for a short description of places so noted — would no doubt have amused you: and that I may no longer sin in the same way, I will improve a few moments of the last day of my nineteenth year in describing to you how I have been engaged since leaving Paris.

The route I pursued in coming to this city, was that of Orleans — Châteauroux — Limoges — Perigueux — &c. I wished to penetrate into the very heart of the kingdom — and by so doing I had the toil of five days and four nights through a mountainous country — more resembling ours than any part of France, which I have visited. Particuarly — the high-lands about Perigueux — resemble much the fine mountain scenery in the vicinity of Lebanon Springs. But the towns I passed thro', are all unworthy of description. The place I wished most to see — to my great sorrow, we passed during the night — for we rode day and night. This was the little town of Chalus — remarkable for the ruins of its chateau, and an old tower at the base of which Richard Coeur de Lion was killed. In sober sadness — I had a most cold and uncomfortable ride of it: — and I assure you I felt my heart leap within me, when I heard the horses' hoofs clatter upon the stone bridge of Bordeaux.

This is the most beautiful city I have seen in France. The climate, I think must be delicious — for to day, when you [are] shivering over the brands of a huge wood fire — around me the breath of Spring is breathing with a freshness to renovate the departed strength of Old Age. But the Spring — they say — is a tardy one — and not a tree has yet put forth its leaf. The city is situated on the left bank of the Garonne, which sweeps away to the northward in a long regular curve: — and the houses upon the quai form the arc of a circle — concave towards the city. From the bridge — one of the finest in France, it is said; you get a fine front view of the place; and on either side of you the eye rests upon a thick forest of masts — the best kind of forest that a commercial town can be surrounded with. The public walks of the city are numerous and beautiful; — and the commerce of all kinds carried on here gives the place an air of life and activity delightful to a traveller. The population is 91,000.

— Thus you see me on my way to Spain: and I cannot say that I leave France with much regret. It may be, that my curiosity leaves no room for feelings of this kind, by painting the land to which I am going as fairer than that I am leaving — or it may be a secret disappointment lurking in my heart, — at having found more perplexities to escape — and more difficulties to encounter than I had anticipated: — but true it is that I look forward to a happier life in Spain, than

I have led in France. The impression, however, which I carry away with me is, that the French are a hospitable kind-hearted people — and much more enthusiastic than we are. They have not that unbounded levity and light-heartedness which is generally ascribed to them; and when the writers of Salmagundi said that a Frenchman passed one third of his time between heaven and earth[1] — they meant a Frenchman of the Old Regime — not one of the present century. Indeed — the young people here seem quite as sedate as we are — and I have been frequently told by some of the "ancient landmarks" of politeness that in this particular feature of the national character, the Revolution has produced as great a change as it did in politicks — and a much more durable one. Strange as it may appear — after the awful and bloody experience of that Revolution — and the most appal[l]ing warning it thunders continually in the ears of rulers — the French ministry is laboring hard to shackle the spirit of the nation — and with the most bold shame-facedness endeavouring to retrench their liberty of thought by retrenching that of the Press. It is the dark and dangerous policy of the priesthood that is doing this. The Jesuits rule the mind of a weak good-hearted king — and you know it is a point with them, to keep the people in utter darkness — lest the coming of an intellectual day should show to the astonis[h]ed proselytes of a misterious creed, the rottenness of the system they upheld. Think — with what strides a nation is going back to the dark ages — when a printer is publickly prosecuted for publishing the moral precepts of the Evangelists without the miracles! — which took place at Paris last Summer. The "Law Projects" — as it is called — concerning the Liberty of the Press — now in full discussion in the two branches of the national government — the Chamber of Peers, and that of Deputies, — excites everywhere a most lively interest: — and I have seen many a frenchman in speaking of it shake his head profoundly — shrug his shoulders — and with a sigh exclaim "Ah! Mon Dieu! Another Revolution!"[2]

But I suppose I am giving you all this second handed — as you have probably seen the substance of it in the papers. I shall leave this city for Madrid — day after tomorrow, and shall probably be about five days on the road. I hope you received my last letters from Paris — written a day or two before I left — and full of little particulars. I received no letters by the packet of the fifth nor of the first of this month — the fifteenth has not yet arrived.

— My kind remembrance to all friends.

Affectionately Yours
Henry W. Longfellow

I am afraid that you will find my writing almost illegible upon such thin paper — but [it] is the thickest, — best, — and most economical, that my port-folio affords.

MANUSCRIPT: Longfellow Trust Collection. ADDRESS: To/Stephen Longfellow Esq./Portland. Maine/Aux États Unis. —/via Philadelphia. POSTMARKS: PHIL 4[?] MAY/SHIP ENDORSEMENT: Henry to his father/Bordeaux Feby 26. 1827./Recd. May 15. 1827/A[ns.] May 27 —

1. Cf. *Salmagundi*, No. I, Saturday, January 24, 1807.

2. Longfellow's analysis of the French political scene, with due allowance for his Unitarian bias, seems accurate enough. After the accession of Charles X in 1824 the pro-Jesuit ultraroyalists dominated the court. In 1826 a measure was introduced in the Chamber of Deputies to modify a restrictive law of 1822 that had reduced the liberal press almost to silence. After considerable debate the measure failed.

114. *To Stephen Longfellow*

                              No. 1.   Madrid   March. 20th   1827
My dear father,

If the letter I wrote you from Bordeaux by the way of Philadelphia has reached you — you will not be surprised at hearing from me from this place — and the great No. [1.] which I have planted in the corner of this sheet, as suggested in your letter of the 14th of January — will show you, that that letter has reached me here. Notwithstanding the accounts of the troubled and dangerous state of Spain which filled my ears at Paris — and the tales of all that is wild and wonderful in bloody murder and highway robbery — which my friends recited to me there, to turn me away from the Spanish border — I have reached the very heart of the empire — without falling among thieves — or becoming such a melancholy illustration of Spanish blood-guiltiness, as some of my friends anticipated. All is at present tranquil — as quiet and peaceful as France itself. True — there are "rumors of wars" [1] — we hear almost daily that the King will immediately march off his troops to Portugal: — then a royal guard marches up the street and then marches down again — and so the matter ends. In this city I feel as quiet and secure as you could wish. The traveller alone has cause for apprehension — for in sober sadness the country is infested nook and corner with hordes of Banditti. These are not organised bands — but "gentlemen of respectability" who assemble from neighbouring villages — commit robbery on the highway — murder if necessary — and then disperse to the bosom of their families and wash their crimes away in a little Holy Water. They are very bold and fearless in these little excursions: and a band of these volunteers, who have taken their stand as sentinels on a frequented road — will remain from morning till night at their station and in broad glare of day soberly and righteously rob every traveller that comes that way — and tie them one by one beneath a tree at the roadside — that no information may reach the neighbouring towns.

But I am wandering away into themes which will come in more properly hereafter. It will not of course be necessary to explain very fully my motives in coming to Madrid in preference to any other city in Spain — with a view of making the language my study: — because I know that the same reasons which actuated me will suggest themselves forcibly to your own mind. The metropolis of a country is always the great literary mart: — then — literary advantages are always greater — books always more numerous and more accessible: — and in this country, where the art of printing itself has nearly fallen into disuse from the rigorous censorship of the press — and consequently all the editions of works whose spirit is at all liberal and elevated, — are old editions — it is important that a student should resort to the Capital; for there only will he find literary fountains unsealed and flowing. There are the provincial accents, too, which cannot be too assiduously avoided — and my expenses are much less here than at Paris. I dare say I shall not regret my coming. From the little experience I have in these things — I should hardly attempt to learn a language to speak, out of its own country. Indeed — I would as readily learn Spanish at home as in Paris.

With Madrid I am very much delighted. I have not seen a city in Europe which has pleased my fancy so much, as a place of residence. I anticipate no inconvenience whatever from the excessive heat of the Summer months — because the sunshine is easily avoided — and in the shade the excess of heat is not much felt, they tell me — on account of the great purity of the atmosphere. The situation of the city, too, is very favorable to health — for its site is an extensive plain — in the neighbourhood of high mountains — and standing eighteen hundred feet above the level of the sea. But this vicinity of snowy mountains — which tempers the warmth of Summer — has proved a dangerous one in Winter. The months of January and February have been severely cold the past season. The piercing winds from the Guadarama mountains which lie to the West of the city — came like a pestilence upon the inhabitants. In the space of Six weeks, there were upwards of four thousand deaths: — a great proportion of them pulmonary complaints that swept off the sick person very suddenly — after a sickness of two or three days. This militates a little against what I at first said of the healthy situation of the city — but it was an unusual occurrence, — and I spoke of the place as a Summer residence.

— I forgot to mention the day of my arrival: — it was the 9th of this month. I soon found a situation in a family — which would be vacant in a fortnight from that time. As I always dislike to be lingering about a Hotel — after looking around the city a day or two — and delivering my letters of introduction — I made a short tour into the environs to fill up the short interval which would elapse before I could enter the family I spoke of. I took this occasion to visit Segovia — St. Ildefonso — and the Escuriel — all of which a Stranger should make it a point to visit. You will find descriptions of this tour — and of my journey from Bordeaux to Madrid inclosed. As it will be impossible to write very fully and frequently from such a distance — I shall endeavour to supply the deficiencies of my correspondence by a kind of Journal. Farewell.

Affectionately yours —
Henry W. Longfellow

The price which I pay for my board and chamber is one dollar per day. Of my mode of living etc I shall give some account in future letters.

[*Enclosure to Letter* No. 114.]

Bordeaux. I left this pleasant city — just as the melancholy days of Lent were closing like a curtain over the noise and gaiety of the last scene of the Carnival. The streets and public walks were thronged with merry groups in masks — at every corner crowds were listening to the discordant tones of the wandering ballad-singers — and grotesque figures mounted on stilts and dressed in the garb of the shepherds of the Landes of Gascony — were stalking up and down — like merry and noisy cranes: — indeed, all was so full of mirth, that even beggary seemed to have forgotten that it was wretched, and gloried in the ragged masquerade of one poor holiday. There were multitudes of musicians, too, — pipers, — and fiddlers, and organ grinders — groups of young and old that amused themselves with the tricks and grimaces of little monkeys disguised like little men — bowing to the ladies and figuring away in red coats and ruffles: — and here and there a band of little chimney-sweeps from Savoy were staring in stupid wonder at the miracles of a Showman's box.

— But these scenes of gaiety I soon left behind me, when I had seated myself in a French Diligence, and enveloped in a cloud of dust the ponderous vehicle thundered away to the sandy deserts of the

Landes. I can give you no better idea of that province of France called the Landes of Gascony, than by telling you that it resembles precisely the pine plains which surround the village of Brunswick; which makes me wonder that the French do not place a college there — it would keep the students out of temptation! From Bordeaux to Bayonne, the road winds through immense forests of Pine — with here and there a miserable looking hut — and a little patch of cultivated land blooming in the desert. The distance between these two places is sixty six leagues: and as like Stern[e] "I hate the man that can travel from Dan to Beersheba, — and say 'tis all barren"[2] — I must tell you that the way is occasionally diversified by towns and straggling villages, and one evening I was quite delighted to find the romantic little village of Roquefort — built upon the sides of the green valley of the river Douze — that has scooped out a hollow for it, in the midst of an immense sandy plain. Thus — I should characterise the Landes as a long level of sand spotted here and there with towns — and when too barren for the habitation of man — tufted with clumps of pine.

Bayonne is a dirty little city — worthy of no description, but such as you will find in guide books and gazetteers. I was forced to drag out one dull day there, and on the morrow was on my way for the Spanish Frontier, through the Basques. The Basque girls are very beautiful — they are litterally "nut-brown maids." They appear to be very industrious, and several of them earn a livelihood, by conducting travellers on horseback from Bayonne to Irun. This is a very singular and very agreable mode of travelling. At the gate of Bayonne you find these girls stationed with their horses. The saddle is constructed with a large frame-work extending two feet on each side of the horse, and covered with a cushion — so that the traveller and the guide sit balancing each other, with their feet hanging down in front, by the horse's neck. We saw a great many persons travelling in this way — and I wished myself out of the Diligence a thousand times. I said that the Basque girls were handsome. They have most beautiful dark eyes — fine teeth — a sun-burnt complexion — and glossy black hair — parted over the forehead —gathered behind the ears — and falling down to the knees in a large beautiful braid. The finest I saw were those travelling in the way described; one in particular — whose image haunts me still — a most cheerful looking girl — in the dress of the peasantry — her hair braided — and a large gipsey straw hat thrown over her shoulder. And then that comfortable way of jogging on together![3] As I am not expert in drawing horses' legs — you will please to imagine, in the above sketch, that they are hidden by a hill, — or that the horse has none — or what you will. With regard to the gentleman's — if they are too long or too short — imagine his knees bent at such an angle as will bring them right. With regard to the lady's — I decline interfering.

South from Bayonne the scene suddenly changes from the waste sands to a broken and mountainous country. On this road I caught glimpses of the sea, as it came tumbling in among the rocks. It was the first time I had seen it for nearly a twelve-month. I was glad to hear its old familiar voice: and you can hardly imagine what feelings it awakened within me. I thought I was quite near you again. It seemed but a step — a little step — from one shore to the other — and with my mind's eye I saw White Head looming thro' the mists that gathered in the horizon: — White Head — Bangs' Island — Pooduck — and the Light House — and — old Freeman — all as usual.[4]

The little river Bidassoa is the boundary between France and Spain, and you cross it at Irun — on the Spanish side. We passed it at night and when the morning broke we were high up amongst the mountains of St. Salvador — the continuation of the chain of the Pyrenees. In the little of Pyrenean scenery, which I saw in thus passing — there was nothing remarkably bold and striking. The mountain sides were neither rugged nor precipitous — and the trace of the ploughshare was occasionally seen quite to their summits. Besides there was no forest-scenery to cheer the eye — and as the season of vegetation had not commenced — the huge outline of the mountains lay black, and barren, and uninviting. What gave romance to the scene was the dashing of a little mountain brook — that we followed for miles thro' the valley — now breaking into a cascade — now foaming under a rural bridge.

— One of the first things which attracts the attention of the traveller on entering the northern provinces of Spain, is the poverty-stricken appearance of everything around him. The country seems deserted. There are no herds in the fields — no flocks by the way-side. The villages are half-depopulated — the cottages ruinous and falling away piecemeal — whilst the people have nothing left them but rags and religion. Of these — such as they are — they have enough. Among the bleak and barren mountains — the traveller will frequently find a little chapel with a cluster of not more than six cottages around it — where as soon as the bell sounds for noon-day all within hearing fall to prayer: and whenever you stop on the road the village children come about the doors of the carriage with little crucifixes, curiously ornamented and set off with many-colored ribbons. As you pass through the towns, too, you see an idle and ragged population — lounging about at the corners and, wrapped in tattered brown cloaks, sunning themselves on the south sides of the houses and walls.

Everybody in Spain wears a cloak — rich or poor — high or low — old or young. To be sure this with the poorer classes sometimes dwindles down to a blanket — but it is always gracefully worn — and you see the muleteers sitting on their saddles — with their cloaks wrapped round them and the corner thrown over the left shoulder — and riding along with all the dignity of dons and noblemen. But throughout Biscay and the northern provinces — such as Old and New Castille — the poor classes are clad with brown rags.

— The route I pursued on leaving Irun lay through Tolosa — Victoria [Vitoria] and Burgos — thence directly south through Aranda to Madrid. Part of the distance an armed guard accompanies the diligence. This sounds very formidable — but happening to be alone in the carriage the first night of my journey — this guard consisted of a mere scare-crow of a soldier with a flannel jacket and a gun, who slept as soundly as was becoming to a good sentinel, and so we kept guard over each other. But to be guarded in this way was rather irritating — for it only kept me sensible of the danger I was in when I most wished to forget it. In broad daylight, too, one who travels in this country has always something to remind him of the perilous ways he is treading in. The cold, inhospitable — uncultivated look of the country itself — the dark fiendish countenances which peep at him from the folds of the Spanish cloak in every town and village, but more than all the little black crosses which one comes upon at almost every step — standing by the roadside in commemoration of a murder or other violent death which has taken place upon the spot — these keep his fancy busy.

— Besides these general remarks — I have little to say of my journey to Madrid. I was hurrying on night and day with all possible speed — and regretted only that I could not tarry a little at Burgos, the capital of Old Castille, to see the tomb of the Cid — the Campeador — so celebrated in the Moorish wars. Thus my journey was by no means fruitful in adventures — being neither robbed and pillaged, nor having the honor of a little black cross by the roadside.

— I have already so overrun all bounds in this letter of mine that I must postpone to another occasion the description of my ride to Segovia and the Escuriel. Behold me then in Madrid most happily situated — and with most brilliant prospects before me. I must not forget to mention that I have immediately taken a Spanish Instructer — and feel enough enthousiasm about the language to make good progress in it.

The society of the Americans is very limited here. Mr Everett and family — Mr. Smith his secretary — Mr. Rich the consul — Washington Irving and his brother, — Lieut. Slidell of the Navy — and myself, compose the whole.[5] Mrs Everett is a very pleasant lady — and we pass very pleasant ev[en]ings at her house. She has not all the 'pomp and circumstance' which Ambassadors' wives sometimes put on — and receives one in a friendly — not an official way. Mr. Rich's family circle is also a very agreable one — and Washington Irving — who resides in the same house — always makes one there in the evening. This is altogether delightful — for he is one of those men who put you at ease with them in a moment. He makes no ceremony whatever with one — and of course is a very fine man in society — all mirth and good humor. He has a most beautiful countenance — and at the same time a very intellectual one — but he has some halting and hesitating in his conversation — and says very pleasant, agreable things in a husky — weak — peculiar voice. He has a dark complexion — dark hair: — whiskers already a little grey. This is a very off-hand portrait of so illustrious a man: but after writing through three sheets of paper at a sitting, I do not feel much in the spirit of minute descriptions of any kind.[6]

The family with whom I reside, is a very kind and attentive one. It consists of an elderly gentleman and lady, with their daughter — a young lady about eighteen — who has already become quite a sister to me.[7] Under her attentions I hope to find the acquisition of the Spanish a delightful task.

I regret almost daily that Edward Preble did not reach Paris before I left it: — so that he might have come with me. Singular fellow! — he never writes me — so like the rest of the world. I am in the dark as to his movements and intentions. He had better come to Europe — and if he should conclude to make the voyage — advise him by all means not to return without seeing Spain.

— Indeed it is like going back two centuries in this old world, — this visit to Spain. There is so little change in the Spanish character, that you find everything as it is said to have been two hundred years ago. You see the same dresses and the same equipages, that are represented in the old plates of Gil Blas and Don Quixotte — the same leather doublets — trunk hose — and odd-looking little carriages. But I am becoming garrulous on my old theme — so let me bring things to a close.

I have been looking long and wistfully for a letter from Stephen — but somehow or other they all miscarry — for I have not received a line from him. And you, my dear Sisters — write me often and fully.

Good night. My best love to all — quite down to Ellen and Sammy — and tell Alexander and Mary to write in some of your letters. I want to see how they come on in writing. Letters to be addressed as usual "aux soins de Messrs. Welles &co."

MANUSCRIPT: Longfellow Trust Collection. ADDRESS: To/Stephen Longfellow Esq./Portland Maine. —/U.S. of America. ENDORSEMENT: Henry to his father/Madrid March 20. 1827./Recd — May 24./[Ansd] May 27 —

1. Matt. 24:6.

2. *A Sentimental Journey*: "In the Street. Calais."

3. Longfellow's sketch of a traveler and his Basque guide follows this sentence. See Plate V.

4. White Head, the northeastern end of Peak's Island, and Bang's Island, now Cushing Island, are prominent landmarks in Portland Harbor; Pooduck (Purpooduck) is an old name for a part of Cape Elizabeth where in 1791 the Portland Head Light was constructed; old Freeman refers possibly to Samuel Freeman (1743–1831), a familiar Portland patriot and jurist.

5. Alexander Hill Everett (1792–1847) was United States minister to Spain, 1825–1829. Later, as editor of the *North American Review,* he encouraged Longfellow in his literary career. John Adams Smith was secretary of legation at Madrid, Washington Irving was attaché, and Obadiah Rich (1777–1850), the bibliophile, was consul. Peter Irving (1771–1838) had resided in Europe since 1809. Alexander Slidell [Mackenzie] (1803–1848), on leave from the Navy at this time, later achieved notoriety as the leading character in the "Somers Mutiny" (see 794.2).

6. Longfellow carried letters to Irving from T. W. Storrow and, presumably, a letter of introduction from Pierre Irving (158.7), whom he had known in Paris.

7. Longfellow lived in Madrid with Señor Don Valentín González, his wife, and his daughter Florencia at the foot of the Calle de la Montera. He described his quarters in *Outre-Mer* (*Works,* VII, 144).

115. *To Zilpah Longfellow* [1]

No. 2. Madrid. May 13. 1827.

My dear Mother,

If my first letters from this city have safely arrived, you will not yet have forgotten the promise they contained of a description of my excursion to Segovia. You will have had time, too, to recover from your surprise at finding me in Spain instead of Italy: — for by the letter I received about three weeks ago from my father and sister Ann[e] — dated Feby. 28. — I find that you suppose me travelling on in that great thoroughfare of all European "voyageurs" Italy. To be sure, it was my own fault: as I wrote you from Paris, that I should go there first. But after forming twenty different plans — comparing them together as many different times — considering and reconsidering — reading old letters from home, and consulting your wishes — and the best method of attaining the end for which I crossed the sea — I concluded that it would be more advantageous to visit Spain first, and trust to future circumstances for a poetic pilgrimage through

Italy. Thus I have penetrated into the territories of the proud Castil-
lian, though with fear and trembling: — for in sober sadness, the
moment a traveller crosses the frontier he may look upon all he has
as publick property, and cheer himself with the idea that he will soon
"come upon the parish": — for every gorge in the hills is filled with
robbers — and Spain may be strictly compared to the man who "fell
among thieves" — all travellers pass by on the other side, and it is a
rare occurrence that a good Samaritan like myself stops to pour oil
into its wounds and give "two-pence to the host." [2]

The Tour to Segovia. In a huge covered waggon, drawn by six
mules — and in its ponderous construction resembling one of the
travelling equipages of the Backwoodsmen of our own country, when
sick of the quiet of the fruitful valleys of New England he bundles
his wife and children, together with pots and kettles and household
gods into a lumbering wain, and shouldering his axe trudges off to
Ohio, — on a fine sunny morning in April, we thundered out of the
northern gate of the city. Our driver, who was also proprietor of the
vehicle, was a stout healthy young fellow in blue velvet jacket, and
brown homespun small-clothes — with a red sash around his waist
and a little round hat, like a porringer, perched on one side of his
head. He sat in front of the vehicle, smoking a little paper cigar —
now and then urging his mules into trot, and occasionally breaking
forth into a stave of some old national song. Beside him sat his companion — co-partner of his cares and his waggon — asleep in the
folds of a tattered cloak, with his head resting upon a jolly little goat-
skin filled with wine, and hanging by a peg from the side of the cart.
For fellow passengers, I had only the friend, who was making the
tour with me, Lieut Slidell of the Navy: — who has since left Madrid
for Gibralter.

You can hardly imagine how little there is in the provinces of Old
and New Castille to interest the traveller. The country lies waste and
open to the sun — you see the traces of former tillage — and here and
there a ruined village deserted by its inhabitants, presents the melancholy picture of falling roofs and mouldering walls. The country
looks stripped and barren — and you can everywhere trace the steps
of desolation passing over the vestiges of former prosperity. I was
glad when the shades of evening hid these sad momentos from my
sight; — and as we rattled into a little village in the hollow of the
mountains all mournful reflexions were put to flight by the glare of
a cheerful fire from the open door of the village inn. Without ceremony we entered the inn-kitchen. At the further extremity blazed a
huge wood-fire against the wall, sending up volumes of pitchy smoke

through a kind of tunnel in the roof, and lighting the whole appart-
ment with its blaze. Beside it was a seat covered with mats of straw,
upon which was seated "mine host" — a "little, round, fat, oily"[3] pot-
bellied man, in black breeches — and a little narrow-brim[m]ed oil-
cloth hat surmounted with a red cockade, showing the wearer to be
a faithful subject of the king and a Volunteer in the royal cause.
Here and there upon the benches sat a weary muleteer, patiently
waiting his supper from the hand of the busy cook-maid who was
scouring about the kitchen with all the busy importance of her station. Apart from the rest I observed a hungry peasant plying heartily
away at his flagon and trencher, and only relaxing his mighty exer-
tions, to catch a glance of the figures that entered. He was seated at a
little table in the middle of the floor — lighted by a little lamp in the
shape of a pot-hook suspended from the ceiling — such as you find
in the plates of Don Quixotte. As a new-comer entered the room, he
would pause with the spoon raised to his mouth and lift up his voice —
"Does it please your grace to eat with me?" Which invitation the
Spanish peasants always give on sitting down to table. I mention it as
a peculiarity. I suppose it has been a custom with them time out
of mind.

In the morning we were on our way before day break. As the day
opened we found ourselves among the winding mountain paths.
Beneath stretched a wide sweeping valley — half hidden by mists —
and all around us were barren hills

> "Bounded afar by peak aspiring bold,
> Like giant capt with helm of burnished gold."[4]

But I have no time for scenery — and shall step over the second day's
journey as being but a rep[et]ition of the first — which step will
introduce you at once into a little chamber about twelve feet square
— with a little balcony looking out upon the public square of the
ancient city of Segovia. There we arrived in the afternoon of the
second day — and after dinner sallied forth to visit the city and its
curiosities. Segovia is one of the most ancient cities of Spain, and
posses[s]es some antiquities well worth a weary journey to see. There
is [the] grand Roman aqueduct stretching across the valley of the city,
dating its origin from Vespasian's time: a most noble structure, built
of huge stones — without the least cement or mortar — solid — endur-
ing for centuries — and yet apparently so light, that it would seem
that the least rude blast might topple it down. Even at this day it is
in almost entire preservation — nothing but some of the lighter work

at the top having crumbled beneath the hand of time. Its structure is remarkably simple: — a double row of arches — one range above another — without the least ornament — and at the greatest depth of the valley about 90 feet in height. At one extremity a rude stair-caise winds up the hill side, and leads you to the second range of arcades — where you hear the water tinkling along and seeming to rejoice in the pride and ignorance of old Rome that has built so noble a structure to carry it forth to the nooks and corners of the city — instead of condemning it to wander and grope its way along in the dark highway of a leaden pipe or hollow log.

One part of the city of Segovia is situated in a valley — another part extends upon a high rocky promontory, terminating in a rugged precipice of a hundred and fifty or two hundred feet. On the very brow of this precipice stands the Alcazar, a fine monument of ancient architecture, — once a royal palace — then a prison — and at present a military school. It was built by the Moors: [5] — and you will find mention of it in Gil Blas, — who was imprisoned in its tower — if you have faith to believe it. The most antique part of the building is an immense square turret, with battlements. It has a very imposing appearance, and perhaps is nearly the only part which owes its orrigin to the Moors, as many of the other buildings around it bear evident marks of more modern birth. In the different appartements of this tower the ceilings are most curiously ornamented with moorish sculpture — and in a large hall there is a singular painting of a battle between the Moors and Spaniards — showing the warlike costumes of the olden times, and evidently the workmanship of hands that have mouldered into dust centuries ago. From the highest windows of the turret you have a fine view of the surrounding country. Directly beneath you the eye glances down upon the rugged front of the precipice — with here and there a withered tree clinging to the crevices of the rock — a solitary bird taking wing from its mossy nest — and a green vine clambering up the rocky way, and wreathing its tendrils around the barren foundations of the old tower. Farther down lies the green valley of the Eresma: — a little river winding away like a silver riband, with gardens and patches of cultivated land sloping along its banks and whitewashed cottages sprinkled at intervals beside it. A range of snowy mountains shuts in the scene.

The cathedral of Segovia is considered among the curiosities of the place: — but after seeing the fine cathedrals of France, I confess it little struck me. It is gothic: — so that with this, — the Moorish Alcazar and the Roman aqueduct you have three orders of ancient architecture under your eye at once. The last made the strongest and most lasting impression upon me. We left Segovia the next morning in a gig — a square-topt antiquity! — which carried us safely to La Granja. Adieu.

Most affectionately yours
H. W. Longfellow

MANUSCRIPT: Longfellow Trust Collection.

1. This letter was presumably enclosed in a letter to Stephen Longfellow, May 20, 1827, now lost.
2. Cf. Luke 10:30, 35.
3. James Thomson, *Castle of Indolence*, Canto I, lxix, 3.
4. Longfellow quotes the same lines in *Outre-Mer* (*Works*, VII, 130), without naming the source.
5. Actually built by Alfonso VI of Castile in the eleventh century.

116. *To Anne Longfellow*

[Madrid, May 13? 1827][1]

My dear sister Anne,

Your long and excellent letter of Feby. 27th gave me, I dare say, much more pleasure than you anticipated in writing it. I like such peeps into the little world of friends around you — and when a letter reaches me full of family doings and pictures of every-day life, I feel as if you were offering me a chair by your fireside. Changes it seems are already going on in your neighborhood. I do not mean that Mr. Lincoln is elected governor: [2] — nor that — Bill Gorham[3] has failed: — nor that, to use the words of one of my elegant correspondents "the block built by Mr. Morton has rendered the situation of your father's house rather unpleasant."[4] But that the Ethiopian should have changed his skin — that a certain neighbour of yours from a bold batchelor should have become a delicate wooer,

> "Sighing like a furnace — with a woful ballad
> Made to his mistress' eye-brow."[5]

This was bad news for me. I had been expecting him in Europe — but I must bid farewell to that hope, unless cruel absence has already snuffed out the farthing rushlight of poor Damon's love, and the short and chivalrous romance "closed with a crash and ushered in Hard Times." You must excuse the propensity I often exhibit to make my introduction longer than my letter. We grow garrulous as we grow old — you know; — and as you seem to think yourself already on the downhill of life, I shall claim the privilege of calling myself an old man — and my garrulity the garrulity of Old Age.

San Ildefonse. At the close of the letter, in which this is enclosed, you will find me doubled up in a little nut-shell of a chaise, jogging patiently along the road from Segovia to La Granja or San Ildefonse. As the ride was a very cold and unpleasant one, I shall not request you to accompany me over the ground — but rather beg of you to imagine me alighting at the door of a country inn, in the village of La Granja. In entering a Spanish tavern you have in general to pass through the stable, or rather through a dirty shed opening into the stable, and filled with rubbish, from which you are ushered into your chamber on the second floor. You are always regaled on these occasions with the sight of a crowd of loaded mules huddling together in a corner — groups of lazy muleteers lying idly about among baggage of different kinds — together with an abundant odor of wet straw. A Spanish inn-kitchen, too, is really a curiosity for a New England man. I have seen one — nothing but chimney: — a regular smoke-house — a hearth in the center with benches all round it, and about six feet from the ground the walls sloping up in the form of a four-sided pyramid with an aperture at the vertex for the passage of the smoke. There were no windows — and the light came down from the opening at the top, and displayed to the eyes of the hungry traveller a goodly array of pots and kettles, and a long range of hard-looking hams, hanging in the smoke and soot of the tapering roof. But as this was not at La Granja, I know not why it should intrude itself here. Let us get back to our subject again.

The village of La Granja — the summer residence of the Spanish court, is shut in by an amphitheatre of high mountains, and the neighbourhood of their snows renders it a cool and delicious retreat from the heat of the summer sun. The palace and its gardens are the principal if not the only attraction, which the place holds out to travellers. This palace was built by Philip the Fifth in imitation of Versailles. It is a large pile of brick and stone building, — irregular in its construction and very ordinary in its appearance. Behind it are its gardens — stretching up the south side of the mountains and terminating upon the borders of an artificial lake, shaded by a screen of green underwood and forest trees. This lake is the grand reservoir of the waters of the gardens — and feeds the thousand fountains which spout from every bower and shade. To describe these fountains would take a volume. Versailles enjoys the reputation of possessing water-works which are the wonder of the world and beyond all competition: — but those of La Granja are infinitely superior and infinitely more numerous. The statues which adorn the fountains are of the most exquisite workmanship: — most of them are of lead, — and are often in groups representing some fable of the Heathen mythology. The principal group represents fauns mounted upon Pegasus — with various other figures: — twenty feet is the height of the fountain, with the artificial rock, upon which the statues are placed, and the water is thrown in an immense column to the elevation of a hundred feet, and may be seen at the distance of many leagues. Unfortunately I did not see the fountains play — but I could easily imagine what a splendid sight they must exhibit. But enough of palaces and fountains. It is time to leave La Granja.

The Muleteers. When we returned to the inn we found a group around the door. A band of muleteers had just arrived, and were unloading their mules at the tavern door. The singularity of their dress attracted at once my attention. A description of one will serve you as a fair sample of all. He was an old weather-beaten fellow — with a free careless gait — and the air of a hardy rugged mountaineer. His brown and sunburnt visage was shaded by a shock of black curly hair, that peeped out from beneath the wide brim of a round slouched hat, such as is universal[l]y worn by the peasants of Spain, and has no mean representative in the goodly helmet of an uncle of ours from the Old Colony — meaning the "identical Hat" you speak so feelingly of in your last.[6] Around his body he wore a leather jerkin — fitted close to the neck — whole in front, like a breast plate — buttoned at the sides — and reaching to the hips, where it was gathered and fasten'd by a belt of the same material, and spread out below in something like a ruffle. From the belt hung on oneside a little leather wallet, resembling a small ca[r]tridge box, and on the other a little wooden bottle, full of wine so generous, that the inconvenient appendage called a stopper, was dispensed with. A pair of brown breeches reaching a little below the knees and met by a stout pair of black leather gaiters, strapped and buckled around the calf of the leg, — finished the rude costume of the muleteer.

The guide. It was about noon when we left La Granja for the Escurial. Our route lay across the Guardarama mountains: and we had chosen to perform the journey on mules, because it was uncertain whether we should find the passes of the mountains open. Above I have given you a description of a muleteer of the best class. I cannot deny myself the pleasure of recalling trait for trait the portrait of our guide and of giving you a second description of a muleteer of the lowest order. Figure to yourself a tall, wind-dried anatomy, with a woe-begone visage — and a dress of such odds and ends as equip the gallant scare-crow of a New England corn-field, and you have this poor pilgarlic to the life. Our host, who by the way, was a little tipsy, had ushered him into the chamber with great display — recommending him as a very honest and trust worthy man; — and as the poor muleteer doffed his fox-tail cap to make his salutations, forth came a little bullet head — the hair cut as close as shears could cut it, leaving only a little border around the forehead — parted in the middle and hanging down on each side in meager cork-screw curls. Downward he was arrayed in the glory of dirty shirt and ragged brown jacket — with two huge hands "that dangled a mile out of the sleeves."[7] His breeches were of the same material with his jacket, — quite as ragged — and at the knee sadly indicating how "loop and button both gave way."[8] Below the knee, instead of gaiters, he wore a piece of white cloth tied close about the leg and reaching to the ankle. His feet were bound up in skins — impenetrable to the mountain snows he had to traverse — and in the place of shoes he wore a pair of sandals, laced over the instep, and leaving the motion of the foot perfectly free.

To the guidance of this ourang-outang we trusted our lives and knapsacks. The road led us through the finest scenery I have seen in Spain, winding along the brow of a hill — then de[s]cending into a deep valley and loosing itself among fine forest trees. Laying our baggage upon our mules, we trudged merrily along on foot, with all that lightness and buoyancy of spirit, which springs from a pure air — and fine health. In a few hours we reached the last house upon the mountains. It was a little cottage, situated in the shelter of the hills, beside a deep ravine, along which came a mountain brook, dashing and foaming under the arch of a high stone bridge, and mingling its roar with the sound of the winds and woods. At the door sat two hunters, who had just come down from the pass we were to cross. They gave us the unwelcome tidings — that it was impassable for mules: — so there we will rest awhile. Farewell.

Your affectionate brother

Henry.

MANUSCRIPT: Longfellow Trust Collection.

1. Since this letter was enclosed with Letter No. 115, it was written on or shortly after May 13.

2. Enoch Lincoln (1788–1829), governor of Maine, 1827–1829.

3. The *Portland Directory and Register for 1827* lists William Gorham, Lottery Office, Middle Street.

4. A statement contained in a letter from Oliver K. Barrell, August 27, 1826.

5. *As You Like It*, II, vii, 148–149. Longfellow applies the quotation to his friend Preble.

6. Anne Longfellow had written on February 27, 1827, "Uncle *Dura* with his wife arrived this afternoon — and oh dear Henry! that very identical *HAT* — the very recollection of it makes you smile methinks." Dura Wadsworth (1763–1846) was Longfellow's great uncle.

7. From Irving's description of Ichabod Crane in "The Legend of Sleepy Hollow."
8. Cf. William Cowper, "The Diverting History of John Gilpin," stanza 26.

117. *To Elizabeth Longfellow* [1]

Madrid   May 15th 1827.

My dear Sister Elizabeth,

It is just a year to-day since I said "My Native Land — good night!" [2] and I need hardly assure you that every circumstance of the departure is still fresh in my memory. Indeed, it seems to me but yesterday and the taste of the luncheon of ham and porter which I took on board ship with Greenleaf and Weld, is still lingering in my mouth — or else I fancy it so. How soon the year has stolen away from me! I should really be disposed to quarrel with Old Time, for shifting so rapidly the scenes of Life's little drama, were it not, that he promises me, that each succeeding one shall be brighter than the last, and I have the comfortable assurance that as soon as he gets through with this slack-wire performance in Europe, he will light up the theatre anew for a happy little scene on your side of the water: in which will be introduced the much admired demi-chorus of

"Captain Clapp's a-coming home,
I shall die!" [3]

In the mean time, as Ann[e]'s letter left me in an uncomfortable situation, half-way up the Guadarama mountains, — I shall beg leave to continue my journey.

Foot-travelling. In spite of the bad news of the mountain being impassable, which we received at the inn, we resolved to continue our jaunt, and left the house in excellent good-humor with our guide for having led us into such a perplexity. We were soon among the snows: — and then our mules began to show their laudable spirit of patience and long-suffering, by quietly lying down in the road, — to kicks and cuffs "burn-proof." A great part of the way we found a path already cut: and fortunately encountering a troup[e] of rough mountaineers, who were continuing to clear away a foot-path in the snows, we left our mules in charge with them, to be taken back to the inn — and piling our luggage upon the shoulders of our guide, together with a multitude of blessings for his sagacity — we pushed on. It was getting late — and the sun was lingering on the snowy peaks of the mountains, when we emerged upon their southern declivity, into the smile of the sun and the [warm] breath of the wind. Here we had a long weary de[s]cent to make, and it was already twilight before we arrived at a little cluster of cottages at the foot of the mountains. We had still several leagues to walk — because, I will confess, we were rather startled at the idea of sleeping in a lonely Spanish inn among the hills. Here a new calamity befel[l] us. The spirit of our guide began to flag: — his knees smote together — it was just in front of the tavern door: — and he, like his mules — refused to go. But as we had not paid him, he found upon reflexion that this resolution was rather premature: and having spirited up his courage with a bottle of generous wine, he began again to drag his slow length along. The people at the door of the inn shook their heads at us as we passed, and we soon discovered the real cause of our guide's reluctance to proceed farther, which was not so much fatigue as the fear of robbers, with which he said the road was haunted. As we de[s]cended into a wooded hollow, the last ray of day-light forsook us, and with it the last ray of hope vanished from the soul of our Palinurus. He told us in a low cautious voice that the valley we were entering was the scene of many a mid-night robbery and the burial-place of many a belated traveller: and for about three miles we followed our path through an open uncultivated country, passing all cross-roads and open gates with the speed and lightness, with which a school-boy would pass a grave-yard after dark, — startled at the least noise — holding our breath even at the whisper of the night-wind in the trees — and looking with fearful expectation that from behind every bush would peer the head of [a] "bold highwayman" — or the terrible apparition of Raw-head and Bloody-bones. Atlength this suspense was alleviated by the twinkle of a cheerful light at a distance, and soon after the friendly bark of a dog informed us that we were near the habitation of man. I never heard sweeter music: and seldom have seen a more agreable sight than the dusky and indistinct towers of a village church, that caught our eye — rising from the top of a hillock and rearing themselves against the evening sky. I[t] was the village at which we had stopped the first night after leaving Madrid: — and "faint and wearily the way-worn traveller"[4] entered the inn-kitchen of which I have before given a description. After a foot-journey of twenty miles need I say how joyfully I took "mine ease in mine own inn"?[5]

The Escorial. As you have probably [had] enough of way-faring by this time, I shall not detail the continuation of our route the next morning which brought us to the Escorial. It will be enough to say that it was also on foot — and from the sad condition of my boots, was something like making a penitential pilgrimage with peas in one's shoes. But notwithstanding these inconveniences, the day was not much advanced when we reached our resting place.

The Escorial is at once a Palace, a Convent — and a Sepulchre. It was built by Philip 2nd, in fulfilment of a vow he had made in the battle of St. Quentin, that if he were victorious he would build and dedicate to the saint on whose day that battle was fought — a convent that should out-rival the richest of the world. The vow has been gloriously accomplished, and the colossal edifice seen at seven leagues distance in the bosom of the hills, seems as imperishable as the works of nature around it. There is very very little ornament about the building — all is simple — grand and massive — of a solidity to rival that of the Egyptian Pyramids. I have never seen anything that gave me such a vast idea of human power — as this melancholy and imposing edifice. It is constructed of a dark sombre granite, and the church is magnificently grand. I could not help lingering among its gloomy arches, and indulging in that pleasant kind of melancholy which such scenes are apt to inspire. I heard mass said in the twilight of its long-drawn aisles — and as the chaunt of the priests reached my ear at intervals, with the peal of the organ echoing amid the arches and dying away in indistinct murmurs along the roof and vaults — the effect was most powerful.

From the church you de[s]cend by a magnificent marble staircase in the Pantheon — or Tomb of the kings of Spain. It is a circular vault of forty or fifty feet in diameter, lighted by a sepulchral lamp which hangs from the ceiling in the centre. It is finished in black marble — and the coffins of the kings are ranged round the walls one above the other — all in the same gloomy livery of death — the black marble of the chamber. From the church, too, you pass into the sacristy of the Convent: where you are shown a fine painting of Raphael's, one of the most celebrated and valuable in the world — called the "Pearl" — from its great value. It represents the Holy Family. Other appartments of the convent are full of fine paintings, but as I am an amateur in things of the kind I shall not attempt any description — for which I dare say you will thank me.

With this very meagre account of the Escurial, I leave you to form the best idea you can of its grandeur. However, to assist your fancy, it may not be out of place to say that it is built to represent a gridiron upside down — the towers representing the legs, and different ranges of chambers the bars, — an idea worthy of the Dark Ages, — and which took birth in the artist's imagination from the circumstance, that St. Lorenzo, — to whom the monastery is dedicated, suffered martyrdom upon a gridiron.

The Return — and Chapter the last. This chapter I shall dispatch in a very few words, being somewhat "a-weary of the world."[6] We were only one day at the Escurial: which we left for Madrid our abiding city, mounted on mules. I was rejoiced beyond measure when I saw the spires of the city rising at a distance, but rather weary and woe-begone with my thirty miles ride. Since then times have changed; — and for six weeks we have had nothing but wind and rain, which have laid me up with a glorious fit of rheumatism. I am now just emerging from the gloom of a sick chamber, and thanks to a change in the weather and to the "warm good feeling" of an old pair of flannel drawers, am fast getting rid of my troublesome companion. I cannot conceive how I should be subject to the rheumatism: — unless it be an inheritance from Old Dick Richards, which has come down to me together with the cottage "under the hill." [7]

I know that it will give you joy to know that I am pleasantly situated here. Indeed, I am in one of the kindest families possible. The whole house is goodness — from the mistress down to the domestic: — and the daughter, a young lady of "sweet sixteen" with the romantic name of Florence, supplies the place of a sister much better than I had anticipated could be possible.[8] I find much more frank and sincere feeling of kindness towards me as a stranger here in Spain — than I ever found in France. In France I found a good deal of the whited sepulchre: — here all is generous sincerity. The out-side of the Spanish character is proud, and on that account at first a little forbid[d]ing — but there is a warm current of noble sentiment flowing round the heart. The Spaniards are, at the same time, perhaps the most courteous people in the world. You cannot imagine how very punctilious they are. In saluting a lady — the common phrase is "Señora, I throw my-self at your grace's feet!" The Lady replies — "I kiss your grace's hand, Señor!" How would that do in Portland? You must say a thousand good things from me to all my fair friends around you, in general and particular: — and also to all the children of the family, of whom I think very often. Write me soon and very particularly.

Most affectionately your brother
Henry.

MANUSCRIPT: Longfellow Trust Collection.

1. This letter was enclosed with Letter No. 115.

2. *Childe Harold*, Canto I, xiii, 1.

3. The reference is presumably to Capt. Asa Clapp (1762–1848), a prominent Portland merchant. In 1793 he became something of a *cause célèbre* when, while commanding a ship traveling between the United States and England, he was captured by Sir Sidney Smith (110.3), detained in England for six months, and permitted to return home with full indemnity for his cargo.

4. These words are unidentified but are reminiscent of James Montgomery's "The Wanderer of Switzerland."

5. *Henry IV, Part I,* III, iii, 91.

6. Cf. *Merchant of Venice,* I, ii, 1–2.

7. Samuel Longfellow identifies Dick Richards as a Negro servant who had carried Longfellow, "when a little boy, to school, and who had always promised to bequeath to him his cottage on Munjoy's Hill" (*Life,* I, 116).

8. See 114.7.

118. *To Stephen Longfellow*

No 3. Madrid   July 16th 1827.

My dear father,

A day or two ago I had the pleasure of receiving your letter of the 27 of May, and in acknowledging the reception of it I would also mention — that since I last wrote you I have received yours of the 25 March and Mama's of the 6th of May. The news of a further remittance were very acceptable to me, for although I live with all decent economy, yet I must confess that European economy would be extravagance in New England, and in residing at Madrid my expenses have been greater than they would have been in a Provincial town. But unfortunately it is only in New and Old Castille, that the language is spoken with purity, and if I had gone to Barcelona or Valencia I should have learnt a jargon fit for the tower of Babel, and not the language of Cervantes.

In looking over a few notes which I have taken at intervals since my residence in Spain, I find short notices of many things which to be well described should have been described, whilst the impression was fresh in my mind. I have still a lively recollection of many scenes, which I think will please you in the recital, as you cannot have the reality before you. There are others, too, whose frequent recurrence keeps them vivid in my memory. Such are the religious ceremonies of the Catholic Church, which in Spain are still celebrated with all the pomp and circumstance of darker ages. The Spaniards in their faith are the most obedient people in the world: they will believe everything a priest tells them to, without asking why or wherefore: but at the same time, as you may readily infer from this, they have as little pure religion as can be found upon the face of the earth. In fact their religion may very justly be compared to one of those little grocery stores in the purlieus of Green street, which has its whole stock of sugar hats and gingerbread images stuck up at the windows.

The ceremony most frequently witnessed is the passage of the Host, or the "consecrated wafer" — or in other words and as the Spaniard firmly believes it to be, God himself, to the death bed of some poor child of mortality. Whatever remorse he feels in his last hour — however sinful his life has been — the moment the priest places the consecrated wafer upon his dying lips, his sins and his sufferings are washed away — and he feels as sure of entering the gate of heaven as those should feel, who have led holy lives. The "wafer" is carried upon the end of a silver staff by some reverend bare-headed friar — preceeded by the banners of the church and a short procession of priests with wax candles, and the tinkling of a little bell. As the procession passes through the street the people take off their hats and throw themselves upon their knees — the noise and bustle of the city ceases — and you see nothing but the multitude prostrated upon the pavement and hear nothing but the tinkling of the bell. But these are the common every day processions; others on the occasion of some church festival are much more imposing. The most remarkable which I have seen, was that of the "Corpus Christi." It passed through the principal streets of the city, — which were shaded from the mid-day sun by curtains stretched across them from the roofs of the houses and the pavement covered with sand. The balconies on both sides of the street were decorated with tapestry and yellow and crimson hangings, and filled with ladies in their gala dresses: and beneath, the procession passed slowly and solemnly along through a double file of soldiery. First came the children of the charity hospitals — then a band of music — friars from all the different religious orders and convents with the banners of their parishes — the Host with its music — and last of all a guard of soldiers. On such occasions the streets of Madrid have the appearance of a crowded and brilliant theatre. But the other night I witnessed a scene much more imposing. I was at the Opera, and in the midst of the scene — the tap of the drum at the door and the sound of the friar's bell announced the approach of the Host. In an instant the music ceased — a hush ran through the house — the actors and actrices on the stage with their brilliant dresses kneeled and bowed their heads — and the whole audience turned towards the street and threw themselves upon their knees. It was a most singular spectacle: — the sudden silence — the immense crowd of the theatre — the group upon the stage — and the decorations of the scene produced most peculiar sensations in my mind.

A few months ago, I saw two remarkable ceromonies at the Palace, which are worthy of being mentioned. The first was a dinner given to twelve poor women, at which the Queen served as a domestick. A long table was placed on an elevated platform in a large hall of the palace, and on one side sat the twelve poor women decently dressed in black. The rest of the hall was occupied by the spectators, which crowd in throngs to the celebration of this pious annual festival. The King and royal family were in a kind of balcony at one extremity of the hall. The Queen entered very simply dressed in white — with short sleeves, and her arms bare, — and ascended the platform. Mass was then said, and afterwards her majesty washed the hands of the poor women in a bason of water held by one of the maids of honor. She then put a towel around her waist, and began to serve at table. Each of the poor had twenty different dishes allot[t]ed her, and they were placed successively before her by the queen, who received them one after another from the hands of her Maids, and placing them for an instant upon the table to receive the refusal of the poor women, who sat like so many female Tantali, passed them into the hands of a priest, and thus they were stowed away under the table in twelve great baskets. After this dinner, when nothing was eaten, a table cloth and towels were given to each of the poor — the Queen joined the rest of the royal family — and the old women trudged off, each with her table cloth under her arm, and followed by two servants with her great untasted dinner packed away — fish, flesh and fowl — dishes and dessert — all together in the bowels of a great basket. I would just observe, by the way, that all the Maids of Honor are remarkably old and ugly: — and moreover that the Queen is eaten up by the ||effects|| of a most gloomy and melancholy religious frenzy, — and writes poetry.

About a month afterwards the King fed an equal number of poor men. But there was no difference in the festival, except that he washed their feet instead of their hands.[1]

I suppose you almost wonder at my being so long in Madrid without mentioning the Prado, nor saying a word of the bullfights. I shall take another opportunity of describing both to you before I leave the country, which will be very soon. You will also receive a few Spanish books, which I shall send to Boston by the way of Bilboa. Have you received the books I sent from Paris? You do not know how much I regret that they are so few. Books are so very cheap in Paris — that it seems a pity not to buy a decent library. But at Brunswick they have an excellent French library. Do you know whether they have also any Spanish books? As nobody can work without tools, it might not be amiss to enquire. I am still in my former intention of going to Germany by the way of Marseilles, unless some objection should offer itself, previous to my departure from the south of Europe. Pray do not think me too change[a]ble in my designs — many of them are rather suggestions than mature plans — but rest assured that I shall do what will result most to my advantage, so far as I am capable of judging. Do not believe too much of what people tell you of learning the French language in six months and the Spanish in three. Were I guided by such counsellors I should return a sheer charlatan: and though I might deceive others as to the amount of my knowledge, I cannot deceive myself so easily: for whatever vanity I may possess with regard to my natural abilities, I have very little with regard to my acquisitions. We did not celebrate the "glorious fourth" here — though it so happened that the day "was ushered in" — as the newspapers say — by the firing of cannon, and the ringing of convent bells, which ring every day and all day. I dare say you had the usual allowance of orations and poetry: — and I hope for your sakes they were better than usual. Kind remembrances to all friends and love to all the family.

Most affectionately yours.

H. W. L.

MANUSCRIPT: Longfellow Trust Collection.   ADDRESS: Stephen Longfellow Esqr./ Portland./Maine./U.S. of America.   ENDORSEMENT: Henry to his Parents/ Madrid July 16 — 1827/Recd Octr 10 —/A[ns] Nov. 26 —

1. The date of this event can be established by a notice in the *Gentleman's Magazine*, XCVII (April 1827), 357: "From Madrid we have an account of one of those disgusting scenes of religious foolery which King Ferdinand has so frequently exhibited. On 24th March, his Majesty washed the feet of some poor people, and afterwards waited upon them at their repast, in the presence of a number of Grandees."

119. *To Zilpah Longfellow*[1]

Madrid. [July] 16th 1827.

My dear Mother,

Since I last wrote you I have spent a week or two in the country, to enjoy a little Rural Life in Spain, and see if the shepherds, which inhabit the green valleys of Castille, are the same with those that sigh through whole pages of pastoral romance. In the villages of the North of Spain, there is little to tempt one away from the city. You see nothing but a cluster of one-story huts of a dirty yellowish stone, roofed with thatch or red tiles, and thrown disorderly together in some nook among the hills. There is seldom a tree to be seen for miles, and those who are lovers of "the babble of green fields"[2] — in the place of soft velvet meadows and waving woods must content themselves with the matter-of-fact beauty of beans and barley. At the same time I had the good fortune to find a village, which enjoyed the shadow of a few trees. It is called [Villanueva del] Pardillo, and is situated on the southern slope of the Guardarama mountains about four leagues from this city.

It is the most pictoresque village I have yet seen in Spain, and the view of the surrounding country — sprinkled here and there with clumps of forest trees — and cultivated uplands — and shut in by a curve of bare and stormy mountains, was very delightful. The beauty of this valley, and the occasional gathering of a storm about the peaks of the mountains afforded many a fine evening scene.

It was the morning of a village holiday when we arrived — and as we entered the street we encountered groups of the peasantry in their best dresses, adorned with flowers and ribands, moving along to church. The church was an irregular little building, built of the same rude materials as the cottages, with the tombstone of some hoary village patriarch, placed as a step at the door, and a large shady tree in front. I recollect lingering about the humble edifice the day of our arrival — and listening to the voice of the priest within and the mournful voice of a poor little organ, that was groaning most sadly beneath the heavy hands of the grey-headed sacristan. After mass the villagers hurried away to their sports: for in catholic countries, all saints' days and sundays are consecrated to merriment, after the religious duties have been performed. In the evening we had a rustic dance in front of the house, in which we were residing. There is something very amusing in these village dances. One almost thinks he has got back into old pastoral times, and the peculiar dress of the Spanish peasantry adds much to this romantic self-deception. They wear a short jacket of brown or black cloth — with breeches of the same material and white stockings or black leather gaiters. Their vest is generally of some bright colour, and below it around the waistband of the breeches passes a red sash, which serves in lieu of suspenders. The back of the head is covered with the folds of a coloured handkerchief, and the round Spanish hat with velvet band and tassels cocked a little on one side. In the dress of the peasant girls there is nothing at all peculiar. The music of these rural festivities consists of two or three guitars of different tones, accompanied by a voice — the tap of a tambour and castagnets, which are nothing but two circular pieces of wood — a little hollowed in the centre, and attached to the thumb with a silken cord. The dance of which I saw most, was called Manchegas — a dance of the province of La Mancha of chivalrous memory. There seems to be no regular step, but every one swings his legs about like a pendulum, and balances his arms in all directions. For my own part, I used occasionally to join in with the rest; and I very distinctly recollect, that the first motion of my arms in the air was so violent and well directed as to deprive the manager of his hat, and the first swing of my leg brought my dirty boots into a col[l]ision with a pair of nice white sunday stockings: — manoeuvres which excited universal approbation and unbounded applause.

Near the Village of [Villanueva del] Pardillo stand the ruins of the castle of Villa Franca — an ancient strong-hold of the Moors of the fifteenth century. It is very finely situated upon the brow of a hill of easy ascent on one side, and precipitous and inaccessible on the other. It consists of a large square tower, — and spacious court-yard with ruined battlements around it. At the corners are round towers of solid stone work with turrets, and here and there apart from the principal building stand several circular basements, whose towers have fallen and mouldered away. From the top of the principal turrett you have [a] fine wide view of cultivated and woodland scenery, and beneath in the depth of the valley lies a beautiful grove alive with the song of nightingales. Only the second story of the building is now occupied — the rest is ruinous. The wind whistles through the broken casement and "the long grass waves on the wall."[3] On its summit the cross has taken the place of the crescent banner. Seen from a distance, it has a very beautiful effect — and adds much to the charm of the landscape. It is not frequently the case that one meets these old ruins in the north of Spain: but they are more numerous in Andalousia.

By the kindness of Mr. Irving, who introduced me to the Marchioness of Casa-Yrugo, I have had an opportunity of a peep or two into good Spanish Society. The Marchioness is a Philadelphia lady; — she married one of the Spanish ministers, and since her husband's death has become the heiress of a large property.[4] She is now somewhat advanced in life — but still gives large parties, and goes much into the fashionable world. I have been several times to some of her evening jams — but as it was during Lent, there was no dancing. Some childish sport took the place of it: and I have seen a whole roomful of the "highborn Spanish noblemen" — and daughters of Dons and Cavaliers engaged in such games as in our country only belong to children. For my own part, I went as a mere spectator. I was pleased to see the grand world, though they say there is nothing so baleful to a little man, as the shade of a great one. It is not the fashion, either in France nor here to introduce a gentleman to any of the ladies, as in our country, — you merely make your bow to the lady of the house — and trust to providence for a good opportunity to enter into conversation with the ladies.

But the society which I have at home pleases me most. The daughter of the old lady with whom I am residing is one of the sweetest-tempered little girls that I have ever met with: — and added to this, the grace of the Spanish women and the beauty of their language makes her conversation quite fa[s]cinating. I could not receive greater kindness than I receive at the hands of this good family, who on all occasions exhibit the greatest, and most disinterested affection for me. I shall feel the most sincere regret in bidding them farewell for ever. There is also another family in the house with which I am acquainted. It is a Malaga lady with her daughter, — a very handsome young lady of about seventeen — a very white skin — light blue eyes — and fine auburn hair. She frequently reminds me of sister Ann[e], and by the way, has the same name.[5] As the two young ladies are very intimate together, I have a great deal of good society. Whilst I write, I see them in the balcony below me, busy with their needles and their tongues — little dreaming that I am thus sending tidings of them across the sea. I confess that I feel very little desire to leave Madrid, as you may imagine; — but as you claim me for your own, and as I have just thrown my purse out of the window, because it was full of holes and told no flattering tale — I shall not be able to linger much longer in this land of the Sun. Indeed, I shall take my departure as soon as the immoderate heat of the weather abates a little, so as to permit one to travel, if not comfortably, at least without perishing. The Summer was very late here, but is now very hot. The greatest heat is about five o'clock in the afternoon. At that hour the thermometer in an elevated and exposed situation just out of the city gives every day from 90° upwards — and in the streets at the same hour — with the reflection of the pavements and the walls of the houses we have at least 120. I seldom go out, excepting very early in the morning to bathe in the river, or at nine o'clock at night to take a walk in the Prado.

This celebrated public walk — the Prado, may be described to you in a very few words. It is situated just within the eastern gate of the city, in a little hollow or valley made by a gentle slope of the grounds on either side. The principal street of the city passes across it at one extremity, and the other leads to one of the south gates, and to the convent of the Atocha. The saloon of the Prado — so called I suppose, because the most crow[d]ed walk — is a wide open area — with stone benches at short intervals from each other at each side — skirted on the right hand by a double avenue of trees, and on the left by a carriage-road in which the young bucks of the city show their dexterity in driving tandem and those who are of too high estate to go on foot jog along in their curricles and take the dust which the crowd on foot raises in great abundance for them. Beyond this road runs another double avenue of trees. At each extremity of the Saloon stands a large fountain — with statues in stone — one of them represents neptune drawn by seahorses — the other, if my recollection serves me, Ceres. In the middle of the Saloon, beneath the shade of the trees on one side, is another beautiful fountain — with a group representing the four seasons. These are the principal fountains — there are others of inferior note. On Sundays the Saloon of the Prado is so crowded just after sunset that one can hardly elbow his way along, nor see through the cloud of dust which envelopes him. This the Spaniards seem to enjoy highly — God bless them in such enjoyments! Farewell. Affectionate remembrances to all.

Your son
Henry.

MANUSCRIPT: Longfellow Trust Collection.

1. Included with Letter No. 118.
2. Cf. *King Henry V*, II, iii, 17.
3. Cf. Oliver Goldsmith, "The Deserted Village," l. 48.
4. Sarah Armitage McKean (1780–1841), daughter of Thomas McKean (American patriot, signer of the Declaration of Independence, and governor of Pennsylvania) married Don Carlos Maria Martinez, Spanish minister to the United States, in 1798. Martinez received the title Marquis of Casa Irujo in 1802 as a reward for distinguished diplomatic service. He died in 1824.
5. The Malaga lady was a Señora Beltrand; her daughter's name was Anita. See Letter No. 129.

120. *To Washington Irving*

Cadiz.　September 24. 1827.

My dear Sir,

It was my intention to have written you from Seville, but I was there so short a time, and that short time was so fully occupied, that I found it impossible to fulfil that intention. I can assure you, that that day which saw me safely entering the gates of Seville was a jubilee for me. I have been fortunate enough thus far to have escaped robbery and "bloody murder": — and no wooden cross by the way side designates my burial place, nor melancholy pile of stones cries aloud of Spanish blood-guiltiness. I hope you will be as fortunate as I have been.

But if I have been fortunate in this respect, I have been unfortunate in every other: — for let one be as happy as you will, he always has some secret sorrow lurking about his heart, which makes him imagine himself the most miserable wretch alive. I came very near giving up the ghost on board the Galera: — I was parched by the sun; choked by the dust: — torn to atoms by the motion of the vehicle: — and finally reached Seville with a fever, that lingered about me all the time I was there. These however are but slight inconveniences, when one suffers them in good company: — but in bad company it puts life itself in danger.

Let me be more particular. You, of course have seen a Galera — the manner of travelling in them is this. After stowing in the baggage, which nearly fills the whole vehicle, they place a number of straw beds upon it, and the passengers lay extended cross-wise, the feet of one dancing about the ears of another. You can easily imagine how very inconvenient this posture is — laying stretched upon your back all day long — with your head thumping against the edge of a cart and a pair of feet directly under your nostrils — in Summer! We were ten — packed away in this uncerimonious way: — twelve days — twelve days of long suffering! And then you find yourself in such wretched low society, that human nature cannot endure it more than a fortnight. Upon my conscience — I cannot, my dear Sir — advise you to come in a Galera.

At the same time I will not advise you to take the diligence. I shall merely state what I have seen, and you will form your own conclusions; for were you in consequence of any direct advice of mine, to start in the diligence and be robbed, I should feel as badly as if I had taken a part in the robbery. You are already aware that the Diligence is guarded by robbers. This is not a mere supposition — it is certain. In the village of Manzanares — about half way between Madrid and Andujar we stopp'd to dine at the same hotel and at the same time with the diligence. In conversation with the guard — one of them confessed to the Mayoral of our galera that not a month before he had been engaged in robbing the diligence, that he was then guarding! In the diligence you will be but four days and a half on the road — in every other conveyance at least twelve days — and as the conversation always turns upon the dangers of the road, you may be said to live a fortnight in continual ap[p]rehension. So you must choose — "Slavery or death"!

At Seville you will find very good accom[m]odations in the "Fonda de los Americanos — Calle de la Sierpe" — the No. I have forgotten — but you will easily find it. You may live there for 12 reals a day — and very well, too, — including chamber &c &c — everything very well arranged. This is the lowest price — if you wish for better dinners and suppers of course you pay more. You will find the prices put up on one of the posts at the entrance of the patio.

From Seville you will take the Steam boat to this city. You will find the price at the hotels exorbitant. As soon as I landed I went up into the principle street and enquired for a "Casa de Pupilos" — in plain english, Boarding House — and was fortunate enough to find one which suits me exactly. I have the most delightful chambers, that you can imagine. A neat bed chamber, and a sitting room — that looks out upon the principal square of the city — with a fine sea-breeze coming past window during the heat of the day. I think I will be ||delighted|| with the situation. The family appears to be a ||very k||ind one — but as I have been here but two days and have not yet dined at home I cannot say what style they live in, as regards the table. You can have your meals alone, should you like the house. I pay but 15 reals a day — a hotel would cost me two dollars. The house is situated "Plaza de San Antonio No 4. Piso alto" — kept by "la Señora Lopez." If you are not fond of upper stories I find that in the lower stories of the same house there are also chambers to let.

Thus I have written you a few notes without head or tail, according to your wish and the inclination of a lazy man, who hates to take pen in hand. Farewell. Should you find leisure to write me, you know how delighted I should be to hear from you. A letter will reach me in Gibralter — care of the Consul. I do not know when I shall leave Cadiz. If I had the means of honest decent subsistance I would stay here a year — it's heaven on earth!

My best respects to Mr Rich and his family — and the Secretary — and very kind remembrances to your brother.

Respectfully and Affectionately Your friend and Servt.
Henry W. Longfellow.

MANUSCRIPT: Berg Collection, New York Public Library. ADDRESS: Al Sr. Dr. Washington Irving./Al Cuidado de S.E. el Em-/baxador de los Estados Unidos/ en/Madrid   POSTMARK: CADIZ

121. *To George Guelph Barrell*[1]

Marseilles. December — 13th 1827.

My dear sir,

I take the earliest opportunity to inform you of my safe arrival at Marseilles. We were detained two days in Adra; and about seven days after getting our cargo in were in the Gulf of Lyons. I was delighted with the shortness of the passage, and flattered myself with the idea that in a day or two at furthest I should be quietly seated by my fireside in Marseilles. But the wind bloweth where it listeth: and a north-western gale gave us leave of absence for a week, which we employed in a circuitous route by Toulon. After creeping along the coast a day or two we atlength reached the very entrance of the harbour [and] had taken that all important personage the pilot on board, when to my utter dismay a terrible gale from the north sent us back to Toulon again. This last gale, however, was of shorter duration — and two days afterwards we were safe within this port.

Very fortunately there was no Quarentaine — so that there was no further delay than that of the wind and waves. The letters I have received from home bring me good tidings. I am to pass the winter in Italy, and have permission to remain another year in Europe, a part of which I shall devote to the study of the german language in one of the Universities of that country. I know not how the solitary gloom of a German university will suit me, after lingering among the green valleys of Tuscany and beneath the glorious sky of Naples: — and I sometimes sigh to think that all this rambling and roving about the world must so soon pass away like a dream. But no matter: — "whilst the lamp holds out to burn"[2] — I will enjoy its light — and when at last that light is fled, I will live on recollection. This is a kind of philosophy which necessity teaches us.

The U.S. schooner Porpoise is here. Several of the Officers are going on to Genoa — Pisa and Leghorn by land. We shall probably go in company. If so the journey will be very pleasant. I must confess, however, that I do not enter Italy with all the enthusiastic feelings I experienced on entering Spain. So much the better: — there is less danger of being disappointed. I think I shall remain in Florence till Spring. Thence I shall go south — and on my return pass through the Tyrrol and down the Rhine.

My most affectionate remembrance to Mr Emmerson.[3] Every body inquires particularly after him. I hope he goes on better and better daily — and that you — my dear Sir, enjoy as good health as when I was with you in Malaga.

Most truly and affectionately Yours

Henry W. Longfellow

MANUSCRIPT: Pierpont Morgan Library.

1. Longfellow wrote of Barrell (1788-1838): "The consul at Malaga Mr. Geo: G. Barrel[l] — was formerly a midshipman in the Service of the U.S. on board the same vessel and at the same time with Henry Wadsworth . . . He is one of the most generous — free — noble hearted men I ever met with" (Journal, 1827; cf. *Life*, I, 130). He was the uncle of Longfellow's classmate George B. Cheever, who had possibly provided a letter of introduction.

2. Isaac Watts, *Hymns and Spiritual Songs*, Bk. I, No. 88.

3. There is nothing in the Barrell correspondence, now at the American Antiquarian Society, Worcester, to identify this man; nor do the Malaga consulate papers in the National Archives throw light on his identity. Longfellow spells the name "Emerson" in Letter No. 128 and may be referring to William Samuel Emerson (1801-1837), Harvard, 1823, and Bowdoin Medical School, 1827, whose

mother was a Barrell — although efforts to place him in Malaga at this time have not succeeded.

122. *To Stephen Longfellow*

Marseilles. December 14th 1827.

My dear father,

About the commencement of the last month, I wrote you from Gibraltar,[1] and with the letter forwarded a few notes upon my journey through La Mancha and Andalusia. I hope these papers reached you in safety; which they doubtless did — for when a letter miscarries there is always room for suspicion that I am negligent in writing you. From Gibraltar I also sent you a box of raisins and a jar of grapes: — I hope they turned out to be good, for I bought them as the best.

In Gibraltar I was detained a month, waiting for a passage to this place. Being at length tired of throwing away my precious time, I embarked for Malaga, where I found a Swedish ship bound here, on board of which I took passage. Before sailing, however, I took occasion to visit Granada. It is the most interesting spot I have seen in Europe. It is not a fine city: but its ancient moorish relics are such and so many, that to see Granada alone is worth a journey across the Atlantic.

On my return to Malaga I remained there but two days — making in all eight. It is rather a dirty, insignificant city — looked upon as a city: — though by no means insignificant as a commercial place. It has a fine cathedral — rather modern than otherwise — and a public walk with a fountain. But of all these things I shall write you very particularly as soon as I reach winter quarters and get one quiet moment to do it in. I shall have a great deal to say to you about Granada, and that part of the country: but as this must necessarily be a kind of business letter, I must be laconic, and shall introduce no descriptions here for fear of mutilating them too much.

We sailed from Malaga on the 22nd of November, and after taking in a cargo of lead at Adra — a small village some leagues east of Malaga — we proceeded onward. At the end of a week we reached the entrance of the gulf of Lyons — where we met with a very cold reception from a blustering north-wester, which continued four days and blew us off towards Corsica. We atlength got up near Toulon — and creeping cautiously along the coast, took our pilot on board and were just steering into the harbour of Marseilles, when a second gale more tremendous than the first, again sent us forth seafaring. Fortunately it was of very short duration: and two days afterwards we were comfortably sitting by our firesides in this city.

I have now been here six days: — and am very much pleased with

Marseilles. It is a very fine city — doubtless one of the finest in Europe. I speak of what is called the new city: the old being very dirty, and very ancient, and very ugly. More of this hereafter. On arriving I went forthwith to Mr Oxnard's [2] — whom I found confined to his bed by a violent fit of the gout. I am glad to add that he is since somewhat relieved. As I had received no letters since the month of July — having early in August requested Mr. Welles to forward such as might come to hand to Marseilles, I naturally expected to find a budget of them in waiting for me. In this, however, I was disappointed as I found only one from Mrs. Derby, inclosing two letters of introduction from Joseph Bonaparte: [3] — one from another correspondent of Portland — and yours of the 25th August and 10th of September. What a pity that those letters did not reach me before I left Spain! If they had, I could have arranged a journey of a much finer route, by embarking for Naples instead of Marseilles. But at present, I must do the best in my power, which is to go to Florence, where I hope to master the Italian in a very short time: — since from its resemblance to the Spanish I find I can read it without much difficulty. At the close of the winter, I think of making a tour to Rome and Naples — if I receive no counter orders from you — and returning by the way of Venice — pass through the Tyrol and down the Rhine to Gottingen — or from Venice to Milan and through Switzerland. The latter route perhaps will be the best. Mr. Carter, I see has published his letters. [4] What a large work it is! I regret it is not in a more portable form — as I could derive the greatest advantage from it.

In the letters I wrote from Gibraltar I sent you an exact account of my expenditures: so that you know precisely their amount in case those letters have not been lost. You may be assured that I shall exercise all my prudence as an economist during my residence in Italy — and if in continuation I reside a year at Gottingen I think that in such a place there can be no doubt of living ||very|| cheap.

We start for Toulon day after tomorrow — the 16th instant. I go in company with Lieutenants [John A.] Carr and [John L.] Saunders — and Mr — [Gwinn] Harris — purser of the U.S. Schooner Porpoise [5] — which is now at this place. Another young gentleman by the name of Greene [6] — a grandson of the old General — goes with us. I am very happy to have such excellent company to travel with. I shall leave them all at Pisa — and proceed on to Florence where I shall put myself into a family without loss of time.

Letters to be addressed as usual to the care of Welles & co — (by the way it's "aux soins" with an "x" and an "s.") — and whatever remittances you may deem it necessary to make had better go into the same hands.

Tell mama and all the family, not forgetting my good Aunt Lucia
— that before I left them I did not know how much I loved them.

> Very affectionately Yrs.
>
> H. W. Longfellow

MANUSCRIPT: Longfellow Trust Collection. ADDRESS: Stephen Longfellow Esq./
Portland — State of Maine/United States of/America. POSTMARKS: NEW
YORK MAR 8/SHIP ANNOTATION (*in Longfellow's hand*): Marseilles Dec 14.
1827 ENDORSEMENT: Henry to his father/Marseilles Decr. 14. 1827./R[ec]d.
March 12. 1828./An[s]d March 25. 1828.

1. This letter is unrecovered.
2. Of the firm of Dodge & Oxnard, bankers, of Marseilles (see 101.4).
3. He was living at this time in the United States (see 124.5).
4. Nathaniel Hazeltine Carter, *Letters from Europe; comprising the journal of
a tour through Ireland, England, Scotland, France, Italy, and Switzerland in the
years 1825, '26, and '27* (New York, 1827).
5. The *Porpoise* had recently fought an engagement with Greek pirates in which
Lieutenant Carr had distinguished himself by singling out and killing the pirate
chieftain.
6. This is the first mention of George Washington Greene, one of Longfellow's
most intimate friends henceforth (see Introduction).

123. *To Stephen Longfellow*

> Florence   January 13. 1828.

My dear Father,

Yesterday I had the pleasure of receiving yours of the 17th of July
last, inclosing letters from Mama — Alexander — and Mary. A very
long interval has elapsed between the writing and reception of those
letters, but I need not say that they were not the less acceptable on
that account. I would also acknowledge the receipt of yrs. of Nov. 25th
which reached me about a week since, together with one from Messrs.
Welles &co. informing of the arrival of the Bill of 2000 francs on
J. Winslow. Havre.

In Gibraltar I wrote you an account of my expenditures up to the
date of that letter.[1] But that there may be no mistake — nor misunderstanding from the miscarriage of letters, I will here copy from my
book the amount of my expenditures, and the Bankers upon whom I
have drawn by order of Messrs. Welles &co.

Paris — Rec. from Messrs. Welles. &co.		frcs	2300	
At Bayonne	Messrs. Garcia &co	"	200	
" Madrid	from Messrs Adoin Garcia &co			$400
" Seville	" Peter Garcia			" 50
" Gibraltar	" Messrs Lagrave & Lapoutide			"200
" Marseilles	" Messrs. Fitch Brothers &co	frcs	500	
		Frcs 3000. and $650.		

This gives you an exact view of my expenses up to the first of January 1828. I should think it best to make all remittances to Messrs. Welles &co. Their correspondence is so very extensive, and the firm on so safe a footing — that it is not only the most convenient but the surest mode of placing funds in my hands: — so in a word, whether I be in Italy or Germany — be kind enough to forward all letters and bills to those gentlemen. I have only to add, that tho' I find travelling and residing in foreign countries very expensive, I make it my object to live as cheap as I can.

With regard to the purchase of Spanish Books for the College Library — I regret that I had not been authorised to purchase such as were wanted at Madrid. I could have purchased thousands of them very cheap — and under the direction of Mr. Rich our consul — who is very deeply read in Spanish Literature, could have made a very valuable selection. But at present I know of no one at Madrid who could attend to the purchase of books — and unless some one attends to it personally, the business will be badly done. Mr. Rich has left Madrid and established himself in London: but I presume he has his agents in Madrid. As he is very extensively engaged in the sale of Spanish books, he would be the best person to apply to upon this subject. I know not the comparative value of Spanish books in Paris — but I should always prefer Spanish editions on account of the greater correctness of the text. I will take pains to inform myself upon the subject: — and should any order be sent me, will attend to it with the greatest pleasure — as there is nothing I am so fond of in the way of business as buying books.

I have now been in Florence about a for[t]night: — I arrived on New Year's Day. I propose remaining a month or six weeks longer: and then going to Rome. On my return I shall pass up through Switzerland — and down [the] Rhine to Gottingen. This is giving you in three words a sketch of my plan of operations: but I cannot yet say how long it will be necessary to remain in Italy in order to acquire its language and see its wonders. I shall, however, divide the time principally between this place and Rome. The language is more grammatically spoken here than elsewhere, but the accent is very harsh: whereas at Rome, with a little less correctness they have a great deal more music in their manner of speaking. I find the language very easy to read, and not very difficult to understand when spoken: — at the same time, when I attempt to speak it myself I find some difficulty in keeping clear of Spanish words. There is a great deal of similarity between the two languages — but perhaps there are not a dozen words precisely the same in both — always some slight shade of difference

— a letter added — or a letter taken away — which perplexes me very much.

I should think that time had at least four pair of wings here in Florence. A fortnight already gone — and as yet I am hardly ready to begin. The carnival is now about commencing. There are seven theatres open — some of them as low as *five cents* entrance. For *eleven cents* you attend one of the most charming theatres I ever entered — and see a performance of tragedy or comedy by some of the best actors I have ever seen. Theatres are at half price during the carnival, and all so crowded that it is difficult to get a seat. The masquerade balls are also commencing: I have not attended any yet.

In our consul here I find not only an excellent kind man, but also an old acquaintance of yours. It is Mr. Ambrosi who was in Portland in 1802.[2] He desires his particular remembrance to you — and speaks very often of your kindness to him when sick with the yellow fever at Mr. Cutter's tavern in Portland. He takes great pleasure in repaying them to me, and has been exceedingly kind in introducing [me] into the very first society of Florence, of which I shall send you a few *very* hasty sketches — I should say *hasty notes,* as my time will not allow me to make them anything else.

When I look upon my table and see about twenty unanswered letters, and then reflect how exorbitant some of my correspondents are — and what kind of letters are generally expected from a man travelling in Italy — I am almost desperate. If I take the time necessary to write a correct long letter, with phrases — flourishes and rounded periods — I should never find a moment to devote to my French — Italian — and Spanish studies, all of which I have to carry on together: — and for the same reason I keep no journal: — nothing more than a few loose notes of passing events. So much English writing tears my time all to tatters. It is to the family only that I write with out care or solicitude: — for it matters not to you whether my pen is good or bad — my ink pale or black — provided you can read the letter.

Have you received a few French books which I sent from Paris to the care of Edward Storer, New York — and also a small box of Spanish books which I forwarded from Madrid to Boston via Bilboa, to the care of Dr. Wells? If not, please make some inquiry after them — if convenient. I should not wish to lose them. With the most affectionate remembrance to all the family

Yours &c &c —

H. W. Longfellow.

P.S. I intend to leave Florence about the 5th of next month, so as to pass the last week of the carnival at Rome. I should wish to pass the Spring in Italy were it not for going to Germany. Do you hear anything said about the University at Bonn on the banks of the Rhine? Mr. Everett spoke to me about it and gave me letters to some of the professors.

[*Enclosure to Letter* No. 123.][3]

Demidoff's! ! !

A few evenings ago I was at "Demidoff's"! It was peeping into [a] world where little men like myself seldom venture! "God help the peeper! — who has thus been peeping at great men through the little end of a telescope!" — Vide John Neal.[4]

When I reached Florence — the first thing I heard and the only thing I heard was Demidoff — Demidoff — Demidoff. If I asked who such a lady was — oh! she's so and so — saw her t'other night at Demidoff's! Do you go to the Opera to night? Opera ho! you're joking — quite facetious to day — no — I'm going to Demidoff's! Well, I am going to the play. Pray tell me is there a French theatre here in Florence? Oh yes certainly there is! And where is it? Where! At Demidoff's! ! !

I at length grew desperate. Who the deuce is Demidoff — said I. Ah, don't know him, eh! — haven't been presented — sorry for you — indeed I am! Well who is he! Why my dear fellow he's —

Demidoff.

— I atlength got at the truth of the matter. Demidoff — is a Russian Count of immense wealth — living on an income of a million dollars a year — about *two a minute!* He is now on the down hill of life — but fond of the pleasures of Society — he gives splendid balls and parties three times a week — which, after being once presented, you attend when you please, without any further invitation.

A few evenings since I was presented there by the Consul, in company with one or two other American gentlemen. Passing through the antichambers, we found the company assembled in the Theatre: — for the Count has a private company of French Comedians attached to his suite, to lend a hand in clearing away the rubbish of his million a-year. The room used for these theatrical exhibitions was very neatly carpeted and furnished, and contained chairs enough to accommodate about one hundred spectators. Near the door sat the old Count, in an elbow chair, with two large wheels, attached to it in order to trundle the poor remnant of mortality from one room to another — his infirmities being such that he cannot walk. There were not a great many persons present — most of them were English.

The play was what the French call a Vaudeville — a genteel kind of farce interspersed with Songs. The acting was very indifferent — but as it cost nothing to the audience, they could not in conscience be out of humour — and so the play went off very well, and was more or less applauded by all present, lest it should be thought they did not understand the language.

When the play was over the Count was rolled off in his triumphal car to his fireside in the saloon — and the company being too small to entertain itself — after chatting awhile about the weather and the play — dispersed.

Two days after this there was a ball and supper at the Count's — but the night was so rainy and dark that I thought I should be more comfortable at my own fireside — and consequently did not go.

— I must confess, that I hardly understand the old Count's philosophy! I should not think he could be happy with so much revelry and dissipation around him! His countenance bespeaks a great deal of benevolence — and you hear of him as being very generous in his charities to the poor. He likes to see the world happy around him: and I dare say has more than one passing regret that he cannot break that two wheel chair of his, and figure away in a rigadoon with the best of them.

— Have I anything more to say of Demidoff? No.

MANUSCRIPT: Longfellow Trust Collection. ADDRESS: To/Stephen Longfellow Esq./Portland — Maine./U.S. of America. ENDORSEMENT: Henry to his parents —/Florence Jany 13. 18. 23. 1828./Recd. May 7th./[Ans.] Augt. 8. 1828.

1. This letter is unrecovered.

2. James Ombrosi, a native of Tuscany, represented the United States in Florence as consul or commercial agent from 1823 until his death in 1852 (State Department Records).

3. This sketch is placed here on the authority of Samuel Longfellow, *Life*, I, 138–139, and is presumably one of the *"hasty notes"* referred to above, although written some days later. Nikolai Nikitich Demidoff (1773–1828), whom Longfellow met on January 12, was a philanthropist of wide repute. The description of his soirees does not seem to be exaggerated. Cf. N. H. Carter, *Letters from Europe*, II, 404–407.

4. Longfellow approximates the words of John Neal in a review of Harriet Vaughn Cheney, *A Peep at the Pilgrims* (*Blackwood's Magazine*, XVIII [September 1825], 319).

124. *To Zilpah Longfellow*[1]

Florence   January 18. 1828.

My dear Mother,

Your letter of July 17th 1827 — after travelling through about as much of Spain, as I myself did, has atlength reached me here in Florence: — and though the date was rather ancient and — but filial love sees no difference in dates.

I suppose the very names of Florence — the Arno — and Vallombrosa are full of romance and poetry for you who have not seen them: — and that you imagine me sitting at night in the shadow of some olive grove — watching the rising moon — and listening to the song of the Italian boatman, or the chime of a convent bell! Alas! — distance and poetry have so much magic about them! Can you believe that the Arno — "that glassy river — "

"Rolling his crystal tide through classic vales — "[2]

is a stream of yellow, muddy water almost entirely dry in Summer! — and that Italian go[n]doliers — and convent bells — and white-robed nuns — and all the rigmarole of midnight song and soft serenade, are not altogether so deligh[t]ful in reality as we sometimes fancy them to be! But I must not tell tales! I may spoil the market for some beautiful effussion, that at the very moment when I write, is making its appearance in the delicate folds of Oliver's "State Banner!"[3]

There is a very excellent society in Florence — tho' it is chiefly composed of French and English. By the kindness of Mrs. Derby, I have been enabled to visit in the former — and been received with great kindness. When at Marseilles I received a letter from her inclosing an introduction to Princess Charlotte, the daughter of Joseph Bonaparte, at present residing at Florence. I assure you I feel very grateful to Mrs. Derby for the kind favour which has been of infinite utility to me. I had no sooner deliv[er]ed the letter — (I should say left it with my card — for the Princess was not at home when I called) — than I received an invitation to pass the evening with her ladyship. I of course accepted. There was very little company there — most of some connexion of the family. The princess is a small delicate figure about your own size. She is married to Prince Napoleon — son of Louis, former king of Holland. The old gentleman[4] is quite decrepit — he has the rheumatism so badly that he can hardly walk. The Countess of Survilliers — wife of Joseph Bonaparte was also present — a fine sensible old lady — with a countenance marking a great deal of firmness and character.[5] Several other female members of the family were there — and also the Duchess of Istria [6] — a *beautiful French beauty*: — nor must I forget to mention that I made the acquaintance of the son of Marshal Soult.[7]

The evening slipped away very pleasantly. It was then I saw for the first time an Improvisator. I was talking with a gentleman in a corner of the room, when from the opposite I heard the sound of a piano, and a moment afterwards a voice neither singing nor declaiming — but something between them both. I turned round to listen — and was told that was an Improvisator. He was reciting the Invasion of Italy by Hannibal — with a good deal of action: — whilst another person accompanied the intonations of his voice by a voluntary upon the piano. The next subject given him was the Battle of Navarin[o]. He paused a few moments — and commenced in the same recitative tone as before — with a suitable accompaniment: — and without any hesitation carried his subject through. After this a list of rhymes was written down upon a sheet of paper — and nine different subjects given him: — each of which he was obliged to adapt to those rhymes — composing extemporaneously nine different pieces of poetry with the same rhymes. I did not understand Italian well enough to judge of his performance — but the occasional applause bestowed upon him by those who did understand, led me to conclude that some parts were beautiful if not brilliant.

The next day I dined with the Countess of Survilliers.[8] She gave a very plain good dinner, without any kind of cerimony. There was at table an Italian lady — de[s]cendant of Michel Angelo, with her daughter, who sung in the evening most divinely. After dinner the same society I had seen the day preceeding dropped in — and I felt quite at home. But there was no Improvisator — in place of one — the Princess Charlotte played Yankee Doodle for me! Of course I was "ravi" — "charmé — et infiniment obligé."

You can hardly imagine how many English travellers there are in Italy. Last night I met one who was really an original. He has just returned from the south. He travels with a double barreled gun and two pair of pistols — but never shoots — and to wind up — a violin without a bow! He has been at Naples without seeing Mount Vesuvius — and would not visit Pompeii and Herculaneum — because they told him "it was hardly worth seeing — nothing but a parcel of dark streets and old walls!" But what is worst of all he went to Rome and did not see the Vatican! — almost incredible.

I believe somebody has been putting oil in my ink, for I can hardly form a letter — and if you make out to read what I have written, —

it is all I can wish! I suppose you wonder, that in writing you from Florence, I say nothing about the Venus de Medicis. It is rather strange, but the fact is, that I can give you no idea of it by describing it — so I prefer an "expressive silence." [9] Thanks to Alex. and Mary for their letters. I was very much pleased with them: and was very glad to see them so well written. Good Bye. Love to all —

Most affectionately yours
H. W. L.

Jany. 23. — I have left my letter unsealed for a few days — in hopes of having the pleasure of acknowledging the receipt of news from you or some other of my Portland correspondents: but the fear of losing the opportunity of forwarding these letters induced me to close them at once, and send them off to Leghorn, in order not to keep you waiting.

I shall stay but a few days longer in Florence. I feel anxious to get into Germany — at least as much so as I do to see Rome and Naples. I must confess it! It is rather singular — but I must confess it. I am travelling through Italy without any enthousiasm — and just curiosity enough to keep me awake! I feel no excitement — no — nothing of that romantic feeling which everybody else has — or pretends to have. The fact is I am homesick for Spain. I want to go back there again. The recollections of it completely ruin Italy for me: and next to going home — let me go to Spain.

I forgot to mention a splendid ball at the English Embassador's a few nights ago, at which we were present. I never saw anything so splendid. He gives a masked ball on Monday next — to which we are also invited. I intend to go from motives of curiosity — tho' I do not expect to perform a very brilliant part in the comedy.

I regret very much that I am so much engaged at present with my studies, that I cannot give you a short description of my visit to Granada — my passage to Marseilles and my subsequent journey to Nice — Genoa — Pisa — Leghorn — and so to this place. But I have taken a few notes to refresh my memory — so that we can talk the matter over amongst the family when we meet again. Until then farewell. It will probably be some time before you hear from me again — the opportunities of sending letters from Italy are so few — and I shall now be constantly on the move until I anchor at a German University.

H. W. L.

p.s. You see that after all I could not resist the temptation of sending you a few short notes upon Granada. That they will amuse you as much in reading as they have me in writing is more than I can hope for.[10] My health is always so very good that I never think to tell you of it: so that when I say nothing to the contrary you must always take it for granted that I am well.

MANUSCRIPT: Longfellow Trust Collection.

1. Enclosed with Letter No. 123.
2. John Pierpont, "Power of Music," ll. 20 and 3.
3. Oliver K. Barrell had "issued a prospectus for a new paper to be called the State Banner. So you see strange things are occurring" (Stephen Longfellow to Longfellow, November 25, 1827).
4. Louis (1778–1846), brother of Napoleon. His son was Napoleon Louis Bonaparte (1804–1831).
5. Joseph Bonaparte had fled to the United States in 1815 under the assumed name of the Count of Survilliers. His wife, sister of Désirée, the crown princess of Sweden, had remained in Europe.
6. The Duchess, the former Marie-Jeanne Lapeyrière (1782–1840) married Jean-Baptiste Bessières (1768–1813) in 1801. Bessières, a marshal of France, received the title duke of Istria from Napoleon in 1809.
7. Napoleon Hector Soult (1801–1857), son of Nicolas Jean de Dieu Soult (1769–1851), duke of Dalmatia and marshal of France.
8. That is, on January 16. The date is established by the Countess's invitation (MS, University of Washington Library), sent to Longfellow at his lodgings at "Place Ste. Marie Novella No. 4600."
9. James Thomson, *A Hymn on the Seasons*, l. 118. The Medici Venus is in the Uffizi Palace.
10. These notes are arranged in the Longfellow papers with the Journal. See *Life*, I, 131–134.

125. *To Zilpah Longfellow*

Rome   March. 26. 1828.

My dear Mother,

An interval of nearly three months has elapsed since receiving any letters from the family — or from any of my correspondents — on your side of the world. Indeed I get so few letters now-a-days, that I find my own epistolary zeal growing cool within me: and were it the same with my recollections of home — I fear that the wheels of our correspondence would ere long cease moving. This, Heaven avert.

You can only imagine how great my desire and anxiety to hear from you sometimes become — by refer[r]ing to your own sensations: — where after a long silence — you begin to wonder why I do not write — and see the post coming in every night with letters from all the world, but me. Upon my word, I'm quite as ignorant of your sayings and doings for nearly a year — as if I had been travelling in the Moon: — thus far you are great debtors to my curiosity: — and with regard to the anxiety we reciprocally feel — as I am only *one* and you at home are ten — mine is to yours in the inverse ratio of those numbers — that is ten per cent greatest. Excuse my arithmetic.

I have been in Rome six weeks: — but I have as yet hardly commenced seeing Rome. I have been pursuing my studies with some little care — and the busy days of Carnival hardly left room to visit curiosities. But I am rather anticipating myself. I should have told you that I remained in Florence but a month. The fact was — I disliked very much the sound of the Tuscan pronunciation. I got quite out of humor with the language and concluded that I would not give further attention to speaking — but would make my way through Italy with the little I had acquired — and be contented with reading, — without making much pretension to speaking it. I accordingly left Florence — and arrived here with the intention of seeing the city in a few weeks and after taking a peep at Naples — go north — visit Venice — and Milan, and pass through Switzerland into Germany.

On arriving at Rome I found a friend of mine — Mr. Greene — of Greenwitch, Rhode Island, — with whom I [had] travelled from Marseilles to Leghorn — and went into the same family where he was residing. And such a delightful family! I could write you a volume upon my good fortune in getting so pleasant a situation. The family was once very rich, — political changes have reduced it somewhat — reduced I mean in a pecuniary way — and I feel that I am now in it by peculiar privilege. There are three young ladies — who have all been excellently educated — and speak besides their native tongue — both English and French. They are great musicians, also: — and one plays the harp with great perfection — the other the piano with the skill of a professor — and both sing — the youngest of the three is not so highly gifted in these particulars. But the family is so very kind — so very genteel — we see so much good society [in] the evening — and I have so good an opportunity for practicing French — Spanish and Italian, that I shall make my residence in Italy something longer than I had intended on leaving Florence.[1] Next week is the "Holy Week" so known and noted in the Catholic world, and so splendid in its ceremonies at Rome. At present we are surrounded with all the gloom of "passion Week:" — and our ears are filled with the doleful sound of church and convent bells.

A few days ago we received the news from Naples, that there was an eruption of Vesuvius. Most all the English travellers at Rome set off post for Naples — and you hardly see the face of a foreigner in the streets at present — so powerful was the curiosity excited. For my own part I felt it and still feel it — but the uncertainty of reaching Naples before all should be finished — and the fear of not getting back for Holy Week at Rome — determined me to remain quiet: — always hoping that the final eruption will not take place for some weeks to come. Perhaps however that even now whilst I write, the splendid phenomenon is taking place. A month or two ago the shock of an earthquake was experienced at Naples — and a small island in the vicinity greatly injured — a village upon it being nearly destroyed and a great many people killed. From this and other prognostics of the eruption it was thought, that it would be violent. I regret exceedingly that I am not at Naples to witness it. Since the first report, we have received no further accounts, excepting confirmation of the fact.

As soon as "holy Week" is passed I shall go to Naples — and if all is over must content myself with looking at the lava — and the cinders and ashes. I hope that Pompeii and Herculaneum will not be buried again. On my return I intend to pass a week or two more at Rome — because Rome cannot be seen in a day. Afterwards I set out again in my wanderings Northward — to Venice and Milan — and into Germany.

My two years are nearly finished; — it seems impossible. Time, unlike all other things, feels not the decrepitude of age — but as he grows older — quickens his pace. I look back upon two years as one short dream. Nothing but again meeting you — and seeing ‖all the‖ changes, that have taken place during my long absence — can make me really feel that it is long. I very frequently sit down to think upon you all — and enjoy the pleasure of meeting, in pleasant dreams and anticipation: — but at the same time I do not feel quite satisfied with what I have seen and done in Europe yet.

Within I enclose you a few more Notes.[2] Have mercy upon me — and be lenient in your criticism — for really I have not time to devote to journalising. Mr. Carter's great book upon Europe will give you ample occupation for a century. Pray tell the girls to write me — not to forget they have a brother in Europe. So many heads, and hearts, and hands, as you have amongst you all — ought not to keep me in fasting and prayer. My best love and best wishes to all — and kind remembrances to all friends in town and country.

Most affectionately yours
Henry W. Longfellow.

There is one subject upon which I have for a long time wished and intended to write you — that is, to set the girls to studying French — or one of the languages of greatest utility. If you could get instruction for the Spanish in Portland — begin with that language. It is much simpler in its principles and easier in its pronunciation than either of the other living languages — but do let them learn some one language. Let the youngest learn it also — it is never too young — and the more I study myself the more I am interested. The fact is, I am completely engrossed with the subject. With this study of the languages I am completely enchanted. Indeed I am very passionately fond of it. So much so that I wish my brothers and sisters to go hand in hand with me — and when I return, it will be so delightful to pursue our studies together! The first language is always difficult — afterwards the difficulty vanishes rapidly.

I have just heard that the eruption at N‖aples‖ was very slight — so that those who reached Naples in time to see it — will hardly be paid the troub‖le and‖ those who are late — will have the pleasure of returning.

MANUSCRIPT: Longfellow Trust Collection. ADDRESS: To/Stephen Longfellow Esq./Portland./Maine./Aux Etats Unis. ENDORSEMENT: Henry to his mother/Rome March 26. 1828./Recd July 26. 1828/An[s]d. Augt 9. 1828

1. The Persiani family, with whom Longfellow lived while he was in Rome during the next ten months, occupied the second floor of the Palazzo Crispoldi, Piazza Navona No. 21, a focal point for foreign students and artists. Innocenzo Persiani, the head of the household, was a druggist, fifty-five years old in 1828; his wife, Marianna Marzili, was seven years his senior. The three daughters were Giulia (b. 1804), Virginia (b. 1808), and Luisa (b. 1813). Giulia, in whom Longfellow became romantically interested (see Letters No. 495 and 516), was the widow of Antonio de Cesaris, whom she had married at thirteen. There was also an eighteen-year-old son, Fabio Persiani. (Information from the parish register of San Luigi dei Francesi).

2. Unidentified, but presumably among the notes arranged in the Longfellow papers with the Journal.

126. *To Stephen Longfellow, Jr.*[1]

Naples. 22nd April. 1828.

My dear brother,

It is just a fortnight to-day that I have been sojourning in this delightful land, in whose description poetry can mingle little of soft and beautiful imagery, which has not here "a local habitation and a name."[2] Indeed — you see nature here as it glows in painting and blooms in song: — not that nature is not always more lovely in herself — than in the Poet's album and the Painter's sketch book: — but you find in the scenery of Naples those rich combinations — which, were they found every where, would make the world we live in, too much of a Paradise.

My windows overlook the bay of Naples — and directly in front of me on the other side of the water rises the broken cone of Vesuvius

— with a thin light cloud of smoke wreathing itself about its summit — and fading away into the blue of the atmosphere. The long curve of the sea shore is lined with white villages — beyond, the blue promontory of Sor[r]entum juts into the sea — and farther out lies the island of Caprea, so famous as the scene of the retirement of Augustus and the follies of Tiberius.

It is not however my intention to go into minute descriptions because they are tedious as well as useless. I shall merely notice hastily some of the greatest curiosities in the environs of Naples; and promise you before hand not to weary you with long details.

On the sea-shore, and directly at the base of Vesuvius stand the Villages of Portici and Resino [Resina] — built upon the lava which covers Herculaneum. This ancient city, you know, was buried at the same time with Pompeii by the stones and ashes thrown from the Volcano in the eruption of '79: — later eruptions have covered it with successive layers of lava. Several excavations have been made and filled up again, because it would be dangerous to undermine the towns of Portici and Resino. The only thing worthy of the traveller's notice at Herculaneum is the excavated Theatre. Even in this, the excavation is very imperfect.

[*Rome, later*] I find this commencement of a letter amongst my papers and am half disposed to destroy it: — but I think upon the whole it would be better to fill up the sheet and send it to you. By the date you will find when I was in Naples, and that will save me the trouble of telling you that I have been there. I was there about three weeks — and as far as beauty of scenery and poetical association are concerned it is one of the most interesting spots I have visited.

One of the most interesting jaunts I made whilst at Naples, was to Baiae and the Elysian fields. On my way I visited lake Acheron — though the scene is now changed. The thick black forests, which the Poets describe as surrounding it, no longer exist: and instead of Charron's boat, that wherried the disembodied spirit across those waters, — a little flat-bottomed scow took me accross to an oysterhouse for two cents! The only truth in Virgil's description is the "Facilis de[s]census Averno est"[3] — for the lake is situated in a hollow among the hills, with steep banks inclosing it. There is a ruin of the temple of Apollo upon its brink. The Tomb of Virgil at Pausilippo [Posilippo] is also a spot full of interest: — and at sunset it is lovely beyond description. In a word, I could give you the names of a thousand delightful rides about Naples — the names and very little more.

I did not find the inhabitants of the country between Rome and

Naples so poverty-stricken as books describe them. There are however beggars enough. Their manner of asking charity is sometimes very singular — it is always in the name of some Saint or of the Madonna: — and there is occasionally such a strange mixture of holy and unholy in their language, that it amuses one. I recollect an old woman in one of the Villages on the road — who cried to me "Ah! Signor[e]! — per carità! — qualche piccola cosa! — Vi diró la buona Ventura! — C'è una bella Signorina — che Vi ama molto! — Per il Sacro Sacramento! — per la Madonna! —" [Ah! Sir — a trifle for charity! — I will tell your fortune for you. There is a beautiful lady that loves you well! — for the sake of the Holy Sacrament! — for the Madonna! —][4] — Others of the kind I could mention but one is sufficient.

Were I not well aware of the antipathy you have to pen, ink and paper — I should be very much disposed to quarrel with you, for letting two years pass without writing: — but I promise an entire amnisty — and peace, if you will write me a line or two soon. You mustn't think, that, because I never complain, I do not feel your neglect. Sometimes it makes me a little melancholy. I have some other very negligent correspondents, who must think me very idle, or very much in love with them, if they expect any more letters from me. Though you at home must not keep me long in want of letters from you. Every little circumstance which takes place in Portland is interesting to me: — from the Brazen Nose of Temple Bar (which I understand has been again snoring its inspiration among the Boe[o]tians of Fish Street) — down to David Ross going round Trull's corner in a windy day.[5] By the way I wish you of Temple Bar would keep me a kind of journal or day book — recording interesting facts, and send it to me once or [twice a] month. Amongst so many of you it would cost you nothing to make a few loose notes and illustrations.

I feel particularly desirous to know if the books I sent from Paris — comprising amongst others a large German Dictionary — and also those I forwarded from Madrid to the care of Dr. [John Doane] Welles, Boston, — have reached you. I hope so — for to me they were particularly valuable. Also inform me if you have received a package of letters and descriptions from Gibraltar — and another from Rome. You proposed numbering your letters — and forgot the proposition at No 1. I forgot to follow the rule, but as it is never too late to begin, I will recommence. I have also to tell you — what I should have told you long ago — to seal your letters with wafers. Sealing wax weighs too much: — and I suppose that sending these letters to Paris will cost me nearly two dollars. Postage goes by weight in France. Hence the use of such thin paper — as some of my letters are written on. When you receive a letter from me written on thick paper, you may be sure I send it by private conveyance.

A few months ago I received a long letter from Pitt Fessenden, which I intend to answer soon. I am also in debt to my most punctual correspondent — Greenleaf: — for which I reproach myself very much, for I really feel *grateful* to him for his kind letters. Please tell him that the package he mentions having sent me has never reached [me] — tho' I suppose it is in Paris. And so farewell! I most heartily wish that one of you Templars would come out and spend with me the rest of my sojourn in Europe. You must make Ned Preble "Chargé d'affaires et Envoyé Extraordinaire" — to my Court at Göttingen whose venerable walls I hope yet to see, though all depends upon the letters which I am waiting for from home. I shall write upon this subject and upon the amount of my expenses — (as I have already from Florence) — by the next packet. Until then Adieu. A thousand kind remembrances to all friends — in town and country: — with my warmest love to every member of the family. Mama and the girls will have letters from me soon. Write soon.

Most affectionately yours

H. W. L —

MANUSCRIPT: Longfellow Trust Collection.

  1. Enclosed with Letter No. 134.
  2. *A Midsummer Night's Dream*, V, i, 17.
  3. "Easy is the descent to Avernus." *Aeneid*, VI, 126.
  4. Longfellow's brackets. Cf. *Outre-Mer* (*Works*, I, 247–248).
  5. Before Longfellow left for Europe he and other law students in his father's office had organized the "Knights of the Temple Bar," a brotherhood dedicated to the advancement of nonsense in the *Portland Advertiser* through a series of essays from "Brazen Nose College." See *Young Longfellow*, pp. 80–81. David Ross may have been employed at Trull's grocery on Main Street.

127. *To George W. Greene*

Rome. Sabato mattina. — [April 26, 1828]

Caro amico mio,

Sono arrivato quì jeri, a le due dopo mezzo giorno, un poco stanco del viaggio, ma benissimo di salute. Ho trovato qui en casa due lettere per voi, che adesso vi mando, ma veramente non ho il tempo di scrivere una lettera, perche Madama sta aspettanda la carrozza, è andiamo tutti a — San Pietro in Montorio! ! ! Questo vi fa rabia! — ma come si fa? — non posso meno che accompagnarle. Addio! Vi scriverò per la posta di Lunedì.

Vostro Amico

Enrico W Longfellow.

Questo poi è grazioso assai. In tanto che stava sc[r]ivendo queste poche parole, Madama e tutta la famiglia sono andate via nella carrozza senza dirme niente, e me hanno lasciato finire la mia lettera en pace. Dunque torno a cominciare: — e comincio per dirvi, che la prima giornata del mio viaggio è stata una di piccole disgrazie. Dopo di partire da Santa Luccia No. 28 mi hanno fatto aspettare due hore en carozza: — e poi nella strada hanno suc[c]esse tante piccole cose. Il postiglione è caduto e mancava poco di amazzarse; e una volta tre cavalli sono cascati ensieme e la carrozza se ha rotta — di sorte, che non siamo arrivati en Roma prima di le due dopo mezzo giorno — come gia hò detto sopra.

Le 5 della sera: —
Era veramente un gran piacere di rivedere la famiglia e le nostre stanze un' altra volta. Anche ho avuto molto piacere in rivedere il caro viso della Signora Cook, che sta bene, e vuole molto a vederca. Il Signore Cook non ho veduto ancora: — perche sta tutto il giorno a San Pietro, occupato con quella copia de la chiesa, che ha cominciato un pezzo fa.[1] Ma anch' egli sta bene — e vi ha scritto a Sicilia, come voi avete detto prima nelle vostre lettere, di mandare lì ciò che scrivesse.

Quasi tutti gli Americani sono partiti da Roma. Ma sta qui la signora La Roche col suo marito, chi abbiamo veduti dal signore Hodge in Marsiglia — vi ricordate? Vanno a Napoli subito, di maniera che voi avrete il piacere di riverderle. Ma badate à voi — perche gia è arrivata in Napoli la signora Eichenshoult ò some si chiama — la Svedese!!! Notizie veramente importanti!

Sono stato da Bowman — ma non l'ho trovato. E andato a Frascati — torna a Roma domani sera. Il signore *Gentnér* — no sò come si scrive il suo nome — è partito per Livorno; — e adesso restano soltanto Bowman e Woodbridge.[2]

Questo sono le piccole notizie che ho sentito nel poco tempo che stò in Roma. Il peggiore è, che non trovo nessuna lettera dalla mia famiglia. Adesso propria vado dal console per vedere si ne ha ricevuto.

Ho molte cose che dire, ma non c'e tempo. Sono tanto inquieto in non ricevere lettere che veramente non posso scriverne. Addio. Vi scriverò presto — in tanto non vi dimenticate di me — e scrivetemi

Vostro Amico
H. W. L. —

MANUSCRIPT: Longfellow Trust Collection. ADDRESS: Monsieur/Monsieur Geo. W. Greene./Santa Luccia 28./Terzo Piano./Napoli. POSTMARKS: NAP 1828 28 APR/ROMA ANNOTATION (*by Longfellow on address cover*): — Dont be frightened at these black and ominous seals. There are no bad news inside.

EUROPE

TRANSLATION:

Rome. Saturday morning.

My dear friend,

I arrived here yesterday at two in the afternoon, rather tired by the journey but very well in health. I found here at home two letters for you, which I now send you, but really I haven't time to write a letter because Madame is waiting for the carriage, and we are all going to — San Pietro in Montorio! ! ! This will make you angry! But what can one do? I can't do less than accompany them. Adieu! I will write to you by Monday's post.

Your Friend
Henry W Longfellow.

Now this is very charming. While I was writing these few words, Madame and the whole family have gone off in the carriage without saying a thing to me and have left me to finish my letter in peace. So I come back to begin: and I begin by telling you that the first day of my journey was one of minor misfortunes. After leaving Santa Luccia No. 28, they made me wait two hours in the carriage; and then on the way many small things occurred. The postilion fell off and only narrowly escaped killing himself; and once three of the horses fell down together and the carriage broke down — so that we did not arrive in Rome before two in the afternoon — as I have said above.

5 in the evening:

It was indeed a great pleasure to see the family and our rooms again. I was also very pleased to see again the dear face of Mrs. Cook, who is well and much desires to see us. Mr. Cook I have not yet seen because he spends the whole day at San Pietro, busy with that drawing of the church which he began some time ago.[1] But he too is well — and has written to you in Sicily, since you had previously told him in your letters to send there anything he might write.

Almost all the Americans have left Rome. But Mrs. La Roche and her husband are here, whom we met at Mr. Hodge's in Marseilles — do you remember? They are going to Naples immediately, so you will have the pleasure of seeing them again. But be careful, because Mrs. Eichenshoult or whatever her name is — the Swedish woman — has already arrived in Naples! ! !

I called on Bowman — but didn't see him. He has gone to Frascati. He returns to Rome tomorrow evening. Mr. *Gentnér* — I don't know how to spell his name — has gone to Leghorn; and now only Bowman and Woodbridge remain.[2]

These are the small [scraps of] news I have heard in the short time I have been in Rome. The worst thing is that I have no letters from my family. I am, in fact, now going to the Consul's to see if he has received any.

I have many things to say, but there isn't time. I am so worried at not receiving letters that I really cannot write any. Adieu. I will write to you soon — meanwhile don't forget me — and write to me

Your friend
H.W.L. —

1. Longfellow describes George Cooke (1793–1849) in *Outre-Mer* (*Works*, VII, 256) as "an artist, an enthusiast, and a man of 'infinite jest.' " A Marylander, he studied in France and Italy in 1826–1831 and subsequently established himself as a portrait, historical, and landscape painter in New York and Washington. He had married Maria Heath in 1816.

2. Of the people mentioned in these paragraphs, only one is certainly identified. Margareta Charlotta Heijkenskjöld (1781–1834), a wealthy Swedish woman, at-

tracted considerable attention during the next years by traveling about Europe alone. She was a friend and patroness of the Swedish poet Nicander (133.1). Longfellow may also refer here to William Channing Woodbridge (1794-1845), the educator, who was in Europe from 1824 to 1829. Hodge is presumably Joshua Dodge, the American consul in Marseilles, appointed from Massachusetts (State Department Records).

128. *To George Guelph Barrell*

[Rome, May 6, 1828][1]

My dear Sir

This will be presented you by my friend Mr. Geo: W. Greene, grandson of General Greene, whose name is so conspicuously written in the annals of our revolutionary history. Mr. Greene intends passing a few months with you in Malaga — and I take great pleasure in introducing him to your acquaintance, knowing with what friendly and kind hospitality you welcome the stranger from our side of the sea.

I met with Mr. Greene at Marseilles soon after leaving you, and since [then] we have been almost constantly together. I doubt not — my dear Sir, — that he will leave Malaga with the same sentiments of love towards you, and regret at leaving you, that I experienced on a similar occasion, and that have since made me home-sick for Spain.

I wrote you a few lines from Marseilles — which I fear have never reached you;[2] — though I really hope they may have come to hand, for I would not willingly fall under the imputation of forgetfulness, in a point upon which I am rather sensitive.

I suppose Mr. Emerson has already left you, and I hope in perfect health. If not, Mr. Greene will take great delight in joining him in those amusements which we Yankees always find by the sea-shore. You can hardly imagine how much, amongst a thousand other things, I regret those morning baths at sun-rise. To tell the truth I have not seen the sun rise since.

With my kindest regards — and best wishes to Mr. Emerson if he be still with you, and sentiments of the warmest friendship towards yourself — I have the honor to be

Most respectfully Your Obt. Servt.

Henry W. Longfellow.

MANUSCRIPT: Longfellow Trust Collection. ADDRESS: To/Geo: G. Barrell. Esq./ Consul of the United States/Malaga./Presenting Mr. Greene

1. Since one can assume that Longfellow wrote this and the following four letters of introduction for Greene on the same day, the date is established by Letter No. 129. Greene seems not to have delivered any of the letters.

2. See Letter No. 121.

129. *To Señora Beltrand*[1]

Roma — el 6. de Mayo. 1828

Muy Señora mia,

Me aprovecho de la ocasion que me so ofrece ahora por la primera vez, de enviar à Vms. noticias mias, si ya Vms. no se han olvidados de mi. El dador de esta — el Señor Don Jorge Greene de los Estados Unidos — un joven de muy buenas prendas y muy amigo mio, pasando a Malaga con intencion de quedarse algunos meses en èsa, yo hè tomado la libertad de presentarle a Vms. estando seguro que Vms. tendrian mucho gusto en conocerle: y èl otro tanto en el conocimiento de Vm. y su muy apreciable familia.

Déspues que sali de esa, hè pasado algunos malos ratos y algunos buenos, — he tenido gustos y disgustos — gozando tal qual los bienes que tengo y esperando mayores: — como hacen generalmente todos los que viagen. Dentre de pocos dias salgo de esta, para irme en Alemania — donde pienso de restar un año entero.

En tanto, espero que Vms. — lo pasen bien: y en lo tocante a su apreciable salud de Vm. y la de su familia — que le gozen todos muy buena.

Muchisimas memorias a la Anita, y digale Vm. que siempre tengo mucho gusto en acordarme de esos tiempos pasados, quando he gozado tanto de su conocimiento, y amabile sociedad.

Expresiones a su marido di Vm. — y crèeme Vm.

Su amigo y Servidor, Q. S. M. B.

Don Enrique.

MANUSCRIPT: Longfellow Trust Collection. ADDRESS: La Señora Beltrand./ Malaga./España./Presentando el Sñr./Don Jorge Greene. PUBLISHED: *Longfellow and Spain*, pp. 87–88.

TRANSLATION:

Rome, the 6th of May, 1828

Dear Madame,

I take advantage of the opportunity that is presented to me now for the first time to send you some information about me, if you have not already forgotten me. Since the bearer of this letter — Mr. George Greene of the United States — a young man of very fine qualities and a very close friend of mine, is going to Malaga for the purpose of staying a few months in that city, I have taken the liberty of presenting him to you, feeling certain that you would be glad to meet him, and he to meet you and your fine family.

Since I left that city, I have had a few bad times and some good ones. I have had pleasures and annoyances — enjoying as they come the good things that I have and hoping for greater ones — as all those who travel generally do. In a few days I am leaving this city in order to go to Germany — where I intend to stay a whole year.

Meanwhile, I hope that you get along well; and insofar as your health and that of your family is concerned, may all of you enjoy good [health].

Best regards to Anita, and tell her that I always have great pleasure in remembering those bygone days, when I enjoyed so much her acquaintance and her pleasant companionship.

Regards to your husband and believe me

Your friend and servant, Who kisses your hand

Henry

1. See Letter No. 119 and n. 5.

130. *To Louis Camus* [1]

[Rome, May 6, 1828]

Mon cher Monsieur,

Je saisis avec empressement l'occasion qui m'est offerte à present de vous presenter un de mes amis, qui peut vous donner de mes nouvelles. Mr. G. W. Greene voyage en France pour ètudier la langue Française, et s'informer des usages du pais: et se proposant de fai[r]e un sejour de quelques mois dans votre ville, je ne saurais mieux lui temoigner mon amitiè, qu'en faisant pour lui une connaissance, qui m'a toujours ètè chère, et dont, je suis bien persuadé, il fera beaucoup de cas. Vous aussi, — qui aimez tant les Americains et notre chère patrie, — vous serez bien content de connaitre Mr. Greene; — cependant je ne vous donne pas d'avance son caractère; parceque je ne veux pas vous priver du pl[a]isir qu'il doit vous donner de le savoir en lui parlant.

J'èspère que votre santé est meilleure, que quand je vous ai vu la dernière fois. Je vous prie de presenter mes respects à Monsieur votre frère et sa famille. Je ne sais pas quand j'aurai encore le plaisir de vous voir, mais espère qu'il serait bientôt. Adieu.

Votre ami et Serviteur

Henry W. Longfellow.

Monsieur Louis Camus.

MANUSCRIPT: Longfellow Trust Collection. ADDRESS: A Monsieur/Monsieur Louis Camus. —/Rue de Porte-foins/Paris./Monsieur Greene.

TRANSLATION:

My dear Sir,

With eagerness I take the opportunity now offered me to introduce to you one of my friends who will be able to give you news of me. Mr. G. W. Greene is traveling to France to study the French language and to acquaint himself with the customs of the country; and as he proposes to make a visit of some months in your city, I know no better way of showing him my friendship than to provide him with an acquaintance that has always been dear to me and which, I am very sure, he will value highly. You also — who very much like Americans and our dear country — you will be very happy to know Mr. Greene; nevertheless, I do not comment on his character beforehand because I do not wish to deprive you of the pleasure that you will surely derive as you get to know it from talking to him.

I hope that your health is better than it was when I saw you the last time. I beg you to present my regards to your brother and his family. I do not know when I shall again have the pleasure of seeing you but hope that it may be soon. Adieu.

Your friend and servant
Henry W. Longfellow.

1. Longfellow had met Louis Camus, a "young student at Law," at Auteuil. See Letter No. 101 and n.3.

131. *To José Cortés*[1]

[Rome, May 6, 1828]

Querido Pepè,

El dador de esta el Señor Don Jorge W. Greene, tu veciberàs con mucha amistad y afecto: pues es muy guapo sujeto y un amigo que aprecio mucho, y en el cual tu encontraras principios y costumbres que te daran gusto. En viajando en España tiene el mismo objeto, que tenia yo: — eso es decir, ver el paes — aprender la lengua — y aprovecharse de todos esas ventajas que suelen ofrecerse a los que corren cortes. Tu harás cuanto puedes para hacerle gustar "la heroica Villa" de Madrid — y para facilitarle en ver todas las cosas que se encuentran dignas de verse en la corte. Por el cual, tu recibiràs muchas gracias adelantadas y otras tantas cuando te dè un abrazo: — que siempre espero sea presto.

A dios — amigo mio. Acuerdate de mi — y no te olvidas que te tengo como uno de los mejores amigos que Dios me ha concedido. Cuidate mucho — y cuidado con las muchachas, — que las hay y muy lindas en España.

Tu amigo — que desea mucho verte —

Enrique.

MANUSCRIPT: Longfellow Trust Collection. ADDRESS: Al Señor Don Josè Cortès y Sesti./De la guardia real./Madrid./El Señor Don/Jorge W. Greene. PUBLISHED: *Longfellow and Spain*, p. 89.

TRANSLATION:

Dear Pepè,

The bearer of this letter, Mr. George W. Greene, you will receive with much friendship and pleasure, for he is a very lively person and a friend whom I esteem greatly, and in whom you will find principles and habits that will please you. While traveling in Spain, he has the same purpose that I had: that is to say, to see the country, to learn the language, and to take profit from all those advantages that generally offer themselves to those who visit capitals. You will do all you can to make him enjoy "the heroic Town" of Madrid and to help him see all the things that are found worthy of being seen in the capital. For which you will receive many thanks in advance and as many others when I embrace you — which I always hope will be soon.

Good bye, my friend. Remember me, and don't forget that I consider you to be one of the best friends that God has granted me. Take good care of yourself — and be careful about the young girls, for there are some very pretty ones in Spain.

Your friend — who is very anxious to see you —

Henry.

1. José Cortés y Sesti (b. 1810), whom Longfellow met in Madrid, became his most important Spanish correspondent. He later came to America to seek his fortune, taught Spanish in Portland and Boston, and frequently visited the Longfellows in Brunswick.

132. *To Don Valentín González*

[Rome, May 6, 1828]

Mi Querido Patron,

Esta serà entregada a Vm. por un paysano mio, el señor Don Jorge W. Greene, que viage en España para estudiar las costumbres y la literatura del pais. Sè muy bien, que el saber que es amigo mio bastarà para que sea bien recibido en su casa: y como es muy hombre de bien y de un trato muy amabile, — Vms. tendran mucho gusto en hacer su conocimiento — tambien que èl en hacer suyo y el de su familia.

Vm. me harà un favor muy grande, si, algun dia quando no tiene ocupacion, — Vm. irà con èl al [Villanueva del] Pardillo, para enseñarle esos sitios que me han gustados tanto, y donde hemos pasados unos dias de quietud y felicidad con la buena gente de ese lugar.

Memorias las mas finas a Brigida, y la Florencita, y digar las que no se olviden de mi, y que se mantengan buenas y se cuiden mucho.

B. S. M. de Vm. Su Servidor y fiel amigo
Enrique W. Longfellow.

MANUSCRIPT: Longfellow Trust Collection.   ADDRESS: Al Señor Don Valentin Gonsalez./Calle de la Montera./No. 16 y 17. Cuarto Secundo/Madrid./El Señor Don/Jorge W. Greene.   PUBLISHED: *Longfellow and Spain*, p. 88.

TRANSLATION:

My Dear Landlord,

This letter will be handed to you by a fellow countryman of mine, Mr. George W. Greene, who is traveling in Spain in order to study the customs and the literature of the country. I know very well that knowing he is a friend of mine will be sufficient for him to be well received in your house; and since he is a very honorable man and of very pleasant comportment, you will be very glad to meet him — just as he [will be glad] to make your acquaintance and that of your family.

You will do me a great favor if someday, when you are not busy, you will go with him to the [Villanueva del] Pardillo to show him those places that pleased me so much, and where we spent a few days of quiet and joy with the good people of the place.

My best regards to Brigida and Florencita, and tell them not to forget me, and to keep in good health and to take good care of themselves.

I kiss your hand, Your servant and faithful friend

Henry W. Longfellow.

133. *To Karl August Nicander*[1]

Rome. June 10. 1828.

My dear friend,

I received with the greatest pleasure yours of the 6[2] — inclosing a letter of introduction to a friend of yours in Bonn, for which I beg you to receive my warmest thanks. I am very well pleased to hear, that you are diverting yourself at Naples, and hope that you will be as much delighted with Baïe and Puzz[u]ol[i] — Vesuvius — and the Tomb of Virgil, as I was. Indeed I hardly know a spot of more interest to the poet, than Naples and its environs. It is a scene that the Poets of other days loved to consecrate by filling it with the beings of their own imagination: — and *One* of them — perhaps the sweetest of all — sleeps amid the scenes he loved in life, and hallows in death.

In return for the good news you send us of yourself and your doings, I am very happy to inform you, that Madam Julia [Persiani] has almost entirely recovered from the wound in her foot, and walks about as merrily as ever. This is the most important information, that I can send you from Rome — and I think with all your friendship for Julia, you could not desire better news than this.

I assure you — my dear friend — that the "voce secreta" which whispers you that we should meet again, told you no false tale. If you return from Naples as soon as you intended, when you left us — we shall meet once more in the "Eternal City": — because I have concluded to remain here until the second week in July.

Good bye. Amuse yourself well, and return soon. Julia — Madama Persiani — and all the family send their best regards to you, and wish you all the amusement, which can possibly be drawn from the scenes around you. For my own part, I send you my best wishes, and a warm return for the friendly sentiments you expressed for me in your letter. In the hope of hearing from you again — of soon seeing you in Rome — I am

affectionately and respectfully yours
Henry W. Longfellow.

MANUSCRIPT: Royal Library, Stockholm. ADDRESS: A Monsieur/Monsieur Charles

A. Nicander/Naples./Poste Restante. POSTMARK: NAP 1828 [*remainder illegible*] PUBLISHED: "Some Unpublished Longfellow Letters," pp. 177-178.

1. Longfellow had met Nicander, the Swedish poet (1799-1839), as early as March 2, 1828, for the latter mentions him in his journal entry for that date (*Longfellow and Scandinavia*, p. 3).
2. Nicander's letter is printed in *Longfellow and Scandinavia*, p. 162.

134. *To Stephen Longfellow, Jr.*

No 1. New Series.!!!   Rome   June 28. 1828.

My dear Brother,

It is now about six months that I have not received letters from home. The last I received whilst at Florence — the first week in January. However I attribute this to accident and not to any negligence of the family: because I doubt not that letters have been written — and can only lament that they have not reached me. Of course I am utterly in the dark with regard to Portland news: — though a few weeks since I saw, in carelessly running over an old newspaper, that Doctor Nichols had been appointed President of Harvard University.[1] I feel very desirous to know if he has accepted the appointment.

For my own part — I have so many things to say, that I hardly know how to choose amongst them. As you see by the date, I am still in Rome: where I only wait letters from home. As soon as they reach me I shall take my leave: — and if they do not come soon — I shall leave without them. Did you receive my letters from Florence — and those I have written since my arrival here? I have been so much delighted with Rome, that I have extended my residence in Italy much beyond my original intention. There is so much in this city to delay the stranger — the villages in the environs are so beautiful — and there is such a quiet and stillness about everything, that were it in my power I should be induced to remain the whole year round. You can imagine nothing equal to the ruins of Rome. The Foro Romano and the Colos[s]eum are beyond all I had ever fancied them: — and the ruined temples — the mausoleums — and the old mouldering acqueducts which are scattered in every direction over the immense plain which surrounds the city — give you an idea of the ancient grandeur of the Romans, and produce in your mind ideas, which cannot be easily defined, nor communicated.

But how different from Ancient Rome is Modern. Perhaps it is hard to criticise manners and customs — but I wish to mention one or two facts which have fallen under my observation, and which in our country would not be considered altogether orthodox. I speak of the dissoluteness of manners — but I shall make no comments. I know a certain Duchess — now verging towards half a century, who has two fine daughters — to whom she sets a brilliant example of Roman virtue, by keeping a young English lover, and introducing him into the highest circles of society.[2] There seems to be no kind of shame attached to it — for her daughters visit our house frequently — and tell all the little amorous quarrels — and in a word all the manoevres of the camp. I have heard a Neapolitan gentleman — talk of his mistresses in society here — as people do with us of their wives. I have even seen him show the different rings and jewels he had received from different persons — and rather make a boast than a secret of his amours! I will add one more. Whenever I please to go to the principle street of the city at the hour for walking I see a lady of the highest ton — who has a rich young banker for her "cicisbeo" — riding in her carriage with her daughter — her husband and her lover! — and even with such corruption there are many instances of the purest morality — and families of manners and morals as uncorrupted as ours. Though in morality as in geography — a great deal depends upon difference of longitude: — and in Europe playing cards — and dancing — and going to the Theatre Sunday night — is thought a very innocent amusement. Nobody here has the least suspicion of its being immoral, any more than we have of the immorality of eating dinner on Sunday. The only idea they have of hallowing the seventh day is that of going to Mass in the morning: and all other festivals of the Church are kept just as holy as the Sabbath.

At Rome there is a great deal of religious superstition. You find a picture of the Virgin Mary, with lamps burning before her at almost every corner of the streets: — and at the "Ave Maria" — that is to say an hour after sunset — vespers are sung to the most "fashionable" virgin: — for you must know, that sometimes one virgin is in vogue and sometimes another.

There are also an immense number of processions and festivals in honor of Patron-saints. Tomorrow is Saint Peter's: — and the grand Church of St. Peters — which is certainly one of the wonders of the world — will be illuminated: — and also there is to be a grand display of fireworks. I have already seen this illumination and the fireworks twice, on other occasions of public rejoicing: — they are splendid in the extreme, and the vast cupola of St — Peters — seen from a distance — glowing with ten thousand lamps, looks like a golden palace — such as we read of in Fairy Tales. About a week since was the festival of St. Louis. I w‖rite of‖ it because there is one circumstance attending the celebration which will be interesting to you. St. Louis is a favorite saint with the Romans. They write letters to him — and send him petitions &c &c. I saw a great quantity of these letters — which are thrown at the foot of the altar — and probably read by — — the priests! The day after the festival I went into the church — and ventured inside the rail of the altar so as to read the direction of these letters. One of them was as follows. "All' Angelico Giovane S. Luigi Gonzaga — Paradiso" — (To the Angelic youth St. Louis Gonzaga — Paradise). But as this letter was not marked paid, I suppose it will not go. I asked one of the soldiers who guarded the letter-box, when the stage went out — and if the post-office was closed![3] But I have been so long in Catholic countries that the abuses of this religion have little effect upon me. Its principles are as pure and holy as could be wished.

P.S. You must not be astonished at what I have written you with regard to the corruption of manners at Rome. It is a problem easily solved. The great folly of mingling together religion and politics explains the matter at once. All offices of any note are held by the Reverend clergy: — and the Pope[4] signs death-warrants. The carreer which is open to a young man — and the only one, is that of the church. This implies celibacy — hence a young man who can have no wife of his own — is not scrupulous with his neighbours. Marriage in Rome shuts the door to all advancement. Indeed the Pope is so violently opposed to it, that he has lately discharged his barber, because the poor fellow wished to get married. When the Pope was young — he was one of the gayest young men of the day: — and now that the evil days are come, in which he has no pleasures — he has such a pious regard for the peace of families, that he seems to think that a man's wife should belong to the parish.

MANUSCRIPT: Longfellow Trust Collection. ADDRESS: Stephen Longfellow Jr./ Portland./Maine [*in another hand*]/Aux Etats Unis d'Amerique./Aux Soins de Messrs. Welles & Co/Rue Taitbout 24./Paris./Pr Montano — POST-MARKS: JUILLET 14 1828/NEW YORK SEPT 2/FORWARDED BY YR OB SERVT WELLES & CO. PARIS/SHIP ENDORSEMENT: Henry to Stephen/Naples April 22 and Rome June 28./Recd. Sept. 1828.

1. Either Longfellow or the newspaper was in error, although Ichabod Nichols seems to have been considered for the position. In a letter to her son dated April 12, 1828, Zilpah Longfellow wrote, "We were fearing we should lose Dr Nichols, supposing he would be invited to accept the Presidency of Harvard on the resignation of Dr Kirkland, an event we have sometime anticipated. It is now three weeks since it occurred — we hear of no appointment to supply the vacancy and we begin to take comfort."

2. The Duchess Margarita, second wife of Duke Vincenzo Lante della Rovere, whom Longfellow mentions specifically in a letter to G. W. Greene, January 2, 1840 (Letter No. 516). The Duchess, famed in middle age for her beauty and amorous propensities, was the mother of four daughters.

3. Cf. *Outre-Mer* (*Works*, VII, 246).

4. Leo XII.

135. *To Zilpah Longfellow*

No. 2. New Series   Rome   July 11. 1828.

My dear Mother,

It is now more than six months, since I received your last letters: and being for so long a period entirely in the dark with regard to your family history, I feel quite shut out of the pale of the church. To what I ought to attribute this famine in our correspondence, I know not: but certain it is — that since the first week in January I have not received a single word either from you, nor any of my American correspondents. Nor do I get any answers to the repeated letters I write to my bankers in Paris. Of course I am in doubt which way to move: — whether homeward — or to Paris, or to Germany. Hence I shall remain where I am until I get letters.

I find your last letter bears the date of May 6. — 1827. Something more than a year ago! Since which time you have occasionally written a line or two in other letters. I see by this letter that you do not wish me to go to Germany: — for my own part I feel desirous of going there, but I find my funds almost exhausted: and without letters from home, I know not what to do. But my principal anxiety is to know if you are all well. For my own part [I] have always enjoyed good health — with a few slight exceptions, and hope that you are not deprived of this blessing, which above all others gives one a light heart.

Since writing to Stephen No. 1. of this new series — I have been to pass a few days in the country, at the village of Arriccia — about fifteen miles from the city. It is a very delightful spot — situated on a gentle hill, and surrounded for miles with beautiful forest scenery. The roads, and mountain paths leading from the village are arched and shaded with fine large trees: — and the interchange of hill and vale — of woodland and cultivated fields, reminds me more of New England than anything I have seen on the continent. Every day I made some excursion to the neighbouring villages and convents. Not far distant is the Lake of Nemi — called by the ancients the "mirror of Diana" — on account of the purity of its waters. Lord Byron has a description of it in the fourth Canto of his Child Harrold, where he says

"Lo Nemi! — navell'd in the woody hills —" [1]

which description and particularly the epithet "navelled" — conveys you a perfect picture of the scene. It continues

"And, near, Albano's scarce divided waves
Shine from a sister valley —" &c [2]

All which is very correct and topographical: — the lake of Albano being near that of Nemi, and like it buried in the hollow of wooded hills. There is a convent of Capuchin monks upon its borders. At no great distance is the convent of Monte Cavi[cavo] — upon a very high eminence — from which your eye runs over an immense extent of scenery. Rome — with its antiquities lies hardly distinguished, almost beneath your feet. You see the Mediterranean — and even the island of Corsica — and you have the scene of the last half of the Æniad of Virgil spread like a map before you. I cannot at present speak more particularly of these scenes. But, I intend returning to Arricia — and will write more particularly from the spot itself.

You can judge from my long residence in Italy, that I am much pleased with it. Its language is very beautiful; — but more difficult than the Spanish. I have been paying a little attention to the German, but find it very difficult; though I must confess, that the little progress I have made does not enable me to form any opinion of the difficulties of that language. I hope you have a good french instructor in Portland for the girls: — and that if they have not commenced that language they will lose no time in so ||doing.|| At the same time do not let them learn of a foreigner — of a Frenchman or not at all. They can learn to read the language without an instructor.

I can only repeat, before closing my letter, that my love for you all, and consequently my desire to see you, increases daily. But the day of our meeting — I know not why — seems long to me. I am often with you in my dreams — and in my wishes always. I feel no alienation from distance — nor change from time: and hope that in my heart I am as thoroughly *homespun* as ever.

> "Whatever lands — whatever climes I see,
> My heart untravelled still returns to thee! —"[3]

I have not written very often from Italy — because I have had not many occasions direct: — and the expense attending the forwarding of letters by way of Paris is very considerable. I have, however, on two occasions sent considerable packages — besides several single letters. It seems that my American correspondants are doing all they can by their long silence to ruin the post-office revenue. I have abandoned all hope of seeing any of my old friends in Europe. Those who can come, will not come, and those who will, cannot. Farewell. A great deal of love to all the family, and kind remembrances to all friends in town and country.

Your affectionate son
Henry.

MANUSCRIPT: Longfellow Trust Collection. ADDRESS: Hon. Stephen Longfellow. Esq./Portland./Maine./Etats Unis./*Per* John Hale — [*in another hand*] POSTMARKS: BOSTON SEP 20 [?]/FORWARDED BY YR OBT SERVT WELLES & CO PARIS/SHIP ENDORSEMENT: Henry to his mother/ Rome July 11.1828./Recd. Septr. 21. 1828./A[ns]. Sept. 27. 1828.

1. CLXXIII, 1.
2. CLXXIV, 1-2.
3. Cf. Oliver Goldsmith, *The Traveller*, ll. 7-8.

136. *To Stephen Longfellow*

No. 3. New Series   L'Ariccia. August. 4. 1828.

My dear Father,

You will doubtless be not a little surprised, to find by the date of my letter that I am still in the environs of Rome; it being probably your intention, as well as my own, that long ere this I should have been established and pursuing my studies at the University of Goetingen. But circumstances out of my power either to foresee or to prevent have broken in upon these plans. Since the first week in January, I have not received any letters from America, nor any from Mr. Welles in Paris. To Mr. Welles I have written repeatedly: — and one of my letters at least must have reached him, for it was favoured by private conveyance: however I do not get a word in reply. Mr. Welles has always been so very pu[n]ctual and obliging in his letters, that I cannot for a moment accuse him of the slightest negligence. My only fear is, that my letters, which he may have forwarded regularly have all miscarried.

As I have no letters of credit for Germany, and of course look to Mr. Welles for them, this long and unaccountable silence has been very unpleasant to me. Consequently when I was ready to leave Rome, and felt myself well enough advanced in the Italian Language to set out for another foreign country, I was greatly incommoded by this want of letters: — from you, to know your decisions upon the course I was to take, after knowing my expenses thus far, an exact account of which I forwarded you in my last letter to you: [1] — and also from Mr. Welles, forwarding me letters of credit for Germany. I was thus delayed by "hope deferred, that maketh the heart sick." [2] Thus week after week slipped away — whilst I waited patiently in daily expectation of the arrival of letters. The season advanced, and warm weather came on. The summer, you know, in Rome is very unhealthy for foreigners: and so it proved to me: — and I who have hardly know[n] until this what sickness is — am now an invalid seeking my health in a little village among the hills in the vicinity of Rome. I am however happy to tell you that I am no longer in danger: and find myself gradually gaining strength and activity.

In the beginning of July I took a violent cold, which of course gave me no alarm, as I am seldom free from some affection of the kind. Feeling, however, a little feverish at night, on going to bed I took the usual remedy of something to throw open the pores, and in a day or two felt well enough to venture out. But I had anticipated my time. For a few days afterwards I felt poorly — and took the advice of a phisician, who was himself taken sick immediately after his first visit. For my own part I grew worse, and was atlength obliged to take to my bed with a raging fever. Of course another phisician was instantly called — but there was no checking the fever — we were obliged to let it have its course and come to a crisis. It proved to be an inflamatory rheumatic fever — and grew very high and dangerous. It was one of those fevers, however, which are violent and rapid in their course, and throw the die of life and death in a very short space of time. My medical aid was of the highest order — and the crisis passed favorably for me. Medical aid, migh[t] however have been of no avail, had I not very fortunately been situated in a very kind family, whose attentions were most zealous and unremitting. Indeed, next to [the] hand of Providence, it is to the care of this most excellent and kind hearted family, that I owe my life.[3] I have been in the house ever since my arrival in Rome, and have always experienced from them the greatest kindness. Had I been a son of the family nothing more could have been done for me, during my sickness, than what has been done. The extent of my gratitude, it would be difficult to concieve: and more so perhaps, when I mention as an instance of the attention I received, that during the seven days I was languishing upon a sick-bed, every moment, some one of the family was by me, both day and night. I am, however, most indebted to the ever-watchful care of Mrs. Julia, the oldest daughter, who having the freedom of a married woman, which the other daughters had not, was of course my nurse: — and a better one I think could not be found. It is to her, I may say, I owe my life, for having administered to me a gentle dose of medicine, as I lay almost gasping for breath, from violent oppression of the chest, and having prevented the surgeon from bleeding me a fourth time; — and this too without orders from the doctor, who on coming in and finding me so much better and the dangerous crisis thus past — was loud in his praises.

It is now four days since I left Rome, and am residing at this village, where the air is pure and delightfully cool — even in the heat of August. My strength is slowly returning: but I shall not take a step upon my travels northward, until I find myself entirely restored. This is quite a new sphere of existence to me, who have never before been a valetudinarian. It is delightful to feel one'sself getting well. When I reached this village I was completely shattered and wrecked. But the country air is working out its effect. My best love to Mama and all the family. Should you write to Mr. Welles, pray say nothing upon the subject of my letters — at least not as implying negligence in him.

Your affectionate son
Henry.

I wrote No 2. to Mama, about three weeks ago. Please to number your letters likewise.

I shall write again soon to my sisters, but they must not wait my letter in order to write an answer — the[y] can anticipate a little.

MANUSCRIPT: Longfellow Trust Collection. ADDRESS: Hon. Stephen Longfellow./ Portland. Maine. —/U.S. of America./Aux Soins de Messrs. Welles & Com-[pagni]e/Rue de Taitbout 24/à Paris/pr. France [*in another hand*]   POST-MARKS: Août 18 1828/NEW YORK OCT 6/FORWARDED BY YR OBT SERVT WELLES & CO. PARIS/SHIP   ENDORSEMENT: Henry to his Mother [*sic*]/ Rome Augt 4. 1828/Recd Oct 7 and ans. Nov. 2/1828

1. See Letter No. 123.
2. Prov. 13:12.
3. That is, the Persiani family (125.1).

137. *To Longfellow Sisters*

No. 4. L'Ariccia. 1 September. 1828.

My dear Sisters,

You will see by the date of this that I am still at l'Ariccia — the village from which my last letters were dated. The month, which was to be the limit of my sojourn here — is nearly finished: — and I shall return to Rome in a few days, with my health perfectly restored — and of course in very good spirits. I think, however, that my heart would be much lighter — and an occasional moment of gloom and sadness would be spared me — were I to receive now and then a letter from home; — a blessing denied me for many months past. Can you believe, that the last letter I have received from your side of the water, was dated a year ago! And it was but three weeks ago, that I even heard *of* you. A letter from Edward Preble at Göttingen — informed me that you were all well in April last.

In such a long interval, you may easily suppose that my feelings have not been without some agitation: — for except the letter, which Edward Preble says he has for me, I do not hear of more than one letter's having been written, — which letter was lost somewhere between Paris and Rome. I know not how it is: — my American friends at Rome receive their letters regularly — some of them dated but a month or six weeks before — whilst I — with so many brothers and sisters hardly hear from [them] once a year.

I dare say you have wondered not a little that in none of my letters I have spoken of Rome in the rapturous language of a modern tourist. But with me — all deep impressions are silent ones. I like to live on, and enjoy them, without telling those around me that I do enjoy them. Besides when I attempt a description — I find the effect it produces in reading, so infinitely inferior to the effect I think it should produce — and all I have seen described in painting and poetry, so very inadequate to convey an idea of what Rome is — that when I sit down to my task, I find it a very cold and ungrateful one. From this motive, I have sent you nothing from Rome, but a short description of the buffooneries of Carnival — and I do not know whether this ever reached you.[1]

But I assure you, there is something in the ruins of Old Rome, which is grand and beautiful beyond conception; and the effect it produces on you is almost delirious. I do not believe there is a finer view in the world, than that from the eastern gate of the city — embracing the "Campagna" of Rome — with its ruined acqueducts diverging in long broken arcades — and terminated by the sweep of the Albanian hills, — sprinkled with their white villages — and celebrated in song and story! But the great charm of the scene springs from association: — and though everything in Italy is really picturesque — yet strip the country of its historic recollections — think merely of what it is — and not of what it has been — and you will find the dream to be fading away.

You would be shocked at the misery of the people — especially in the Pope's dominions: — but their element seems to be in rags and misery — and with the mummery of their religion and the holidays of the church — which average nearly three a week, they are poor — and lazy, and happy — I mean happy in their way: — for the negro slaves within the precincts of the Southern States are their equals in liberty, and infinitely their superiors in every comfort: — so you may judge what *happiness* is among the poorer classes of Italians.

This, however, is a subject which can hardly be of much interest to you. Indeed, when I write to you — my dear sisters, — I feel very little disposition to write upon any other subject than yourselves. I think two years may have changed you: — and as far as regards your persons outwardly — I suppose that when I return I shall find myself amongst strangers: — tho' heaven forbid, that any absence however long, should alienate one particle of that brotherly love — which I feel so strong towards you — and which I know to be kindly reciprocal within your own bosoms.

You know not what a longing desire I have to get some of your Portland news. There must be a great budget of them for me somewhere — but where to look for them, — and whence — and when I may expect them, I know not. When you next write, tell me every little particular you can lay your hands on.

Are you studying French or Spanish now-a-days? If not, you should lose no time in commencing: for I have become so very devoted to the study of languages, — that I think a person is inexcusable who is deterred by those difficulties, which always impede the first steps we take in every science. Do not let my admonitions be vain: — for I assure you — that by every language you learn, a new world is opened before you. It is like being born again: — and new ideas break upon the mind with all the freshness and delight — with which we may suppose the first dawn of intellect to be accompanied.

In the mean time, farewell. Remember me kindly to all my Portland friends — particularly those of the feminine gender: — and above all do not forget to write me soon, and to let me have all your news, good bad and indifferent. Nor must you forget my respectful remembrance to our relations out of town — but whenever you see them, call me to mind, — and tell them I often think of them. Once more, my dear girls, farewell.

Most affectionately your brother

Henry. —

MANUSCRIPT: Longfellow Trust Collection.

1. This description is included in the Longfellow papers with the Journal.

138. *To Karl August Nicander*

Piazza Madama — den 29. Oct. 1828.

Lieber Freünd,

Der Brief, der sie hatten die Güte dieser morgen mir zü schreiben, kann ich nicht verstehen. Ci vorrá una settimana per leg[g]erla. Ho capito peró, "Aüch heüte kann ich nicht kommen" — e quando ho letto tutto vi risponderó.

Per non far aspettare, quello che m'ha portato il vostro bigl[i]etto, corto cammino, e mi rassegno,

Il vostro amico et servitore —

Enrico W. Longfellow.

MANUSCRIPT: Royal Library, Stockholm. ADDRESS: Al P[ad]rone Ill[ustrissi]mo/Il

Signor Auguste Nicander/Villa Malta./Roma. PUBLISHED: "Some Unpublished Longfellow Letters," p. 192.

TRANSLATION:

Piazza Madama — 29 Oct. 1828.

Dear Friend,

I cannot understand the letter that you have had the goodness to write to me this morning. It will take a week to read it. I did, however, understand, "Also I cannot come today" — and when I have read the whole, I will reply to you.

So as not to delay the man who brought me your letter, I cut this short, and give up,

Your friend and servant —
Henry W. Longfellow

139. *To Zilpah Longfellow*

[Rome, November 27, 1828]

My dear Mother,

I reproach myself a little for not having sooner answered your kind and long letter of April 12. which, as I have already mentioned in the letter in which this is inclosed, reached me not long ago by way of Germany. But I am happy that in answering it now, I can also acknowledge the receipt of another, dated Aug. 9th. For me, a line from my Mother is more efficacious than all the homilies preached in Lent: and I find more incitives to virtue in merely looking at your hand writing, than in a whole volume of ethics and moral discourses. Indeed there is no book in which I read with so much interest and profit, as one of your letters. I can only regret, that I have not this pleasure more frequently.

I think that to-day must be Thanksgiving Day with you.[1] To a wanderer like myself, there is no season which so vividly recals the endearments of home, and so fully awakens the recollection of its blessings, as the return of those annual holidays, which signalise the close of the year. They are jubilees, that gather friends and relatives together, and call in from the thoroughfares of the world, those that have been thrown out of the family circle, and jostled apart in the crowd. At such times, the heart clings to home, as the dying man clings to life. As I have no friends around me, my heart fills up the blank with tender recollections: and I imagine myself seated in the midst of you — recalling earlier days, and renewing the broken links that absence has made in the social chain!

Here, too, the Winter festivals are just commencing: and the toy-shops are full of dolls and gew-gaws for the Bifana, who acts here the same comedy for children, that Santiclaus does in America. The Piferari, or Pipers, begin to come in from the neighbouring villages, to play before the images of the[2] Virgin, and hail the approach of merry Christmass. This little sketch represents two of them, playing before one of the thousand images of the Madonna, that are stuck up at every corner of the city. One of them plays upon a kind of bagpipe and the other upon a flageolet. There is something very wild and pleasing in the airs they play, — and produces an effect upon one's feelings, that much more elaborate music often fails to do. Excuse me for taking up so large a space with this rude sketch: if it does not amuse you — there are some around you whom it will amuse.

The month of October is also a merry month in Rome. It is the Vintage time, and there are a thousand little social parties in the different vineyards near the city. This year there was a great concourse of all classes twice a week at the garden of the Villa Borgese: — when the lower clas[s]es decked out in their Sunday finery danced beneath the trees to the music of tamborines. These dancing groups scattered here and there among the groves and over the lawns of the park — with the splendid equipages moving along the stately avenues — produced a very pleasing picture. All this merry-making finished with the month of October: and November ushered in the melancholy festival of the Dead — and for eight days you could hear nothing but the mournful knell of funeral bells. It was a great tribulation to me, for I live between two churches: — it was "a smoke in my nose."[3] —

Rome is now becoming quite gay. The crowd of English, who have come to winter here, is immense. Walter Scott and Mr. Cooper are both expected here. There are also great crowds from other qua[r]ters of the world: — and amongst other notable personages a Russian Princess, who is travelling with a suite of forty, and who pays at the hotel at which she resides here, eight thousand dollars a month! This is on a large scale. I know an English lady here, the Baroness of Bourkard,[4] an acquaintance of Mrs. Derby — that is to say she was, fifteen years ago. She says Mrs. D. is the handsomest woman she ever saw — which is saying a great deal, when one has travelled all over Europe. However I think for beauty, our American ladies bear away the palm. I do not think so highly of European beauty as many do: — but perhaps I am biassed in my judgement by national prejudices. I will not assert the contrary for fear of being in something similar to the Englishman, who said that if he knew himself, he had no national prejudices: — but he did hate a Frenchman!

I am sorry to hear of Sister Elisabeth's illness, but hope that ere this it is favourably terminated. With regard to her engagement with Mr.

F. — I am highly gratified with it: I most cordially congratulate her. Mr. F — —'s cousin, Lieut. Fessenden of the Army is now in Rome.[5] I shall communicate the news, when I next see him.

All my correspondents congratulate me upon my happy meeting with Preble. I can only say, I wish I were as happy as they desire me to be: — I have still this pleasure in anticipation, and probably shall have until the Spring: — when I suppose we shall meet, only to say farewell. He is just beginning a traveller's life, and I am just closing it. Like all other people, the traveller has his cares and sorrows: — sometimes he is gay — at others sad: — sometimes he feels like a bird encaged: — and then again he seems to "drag at each remove a lengthened chain."[6] But my sheet is full — my pen worn to a stump: and my exhausted lamp just expiring. I can only see to trace the letters — and those hardly legibly. It is after midnight. At so lonely an hour, my thoughts return homeward with double force, to center in the happy circle, which is now gathered around your fireside. So wishing one and all a merry Thanksgiving — a merry Christmass — a happy New Year — and a good night — I am

your affectionate Son
Henry.

MANUSCRIPT: Longfellow Trust Collection.

1. This remark apparently establishes the date of the letter as the 27th of November. It was probably included with the letter written on November 24 and now missing.

2. Longfellow's sketch of the pipers interrupts the sentence here. See Plate V.

3. Isa. 65:5.

4. This unidentified baroness does not seem to have been a member of the English peerage. She may possibly have married into the prominent Swiss-German family of Bourcart (Burhardt, Burkard).

5. Elizabeth Longfellow's marriage to William Pitt Fessenden was frustrated by her death (of scrofula) on May 5, 1829. John Milton Fessenden (1802–1883) resigned his commission in 1831 and became a prominent railroad engineer.

6. Cf. Oliver Goldsmith, *The Traveller*, l. 10.

140. *To George Washington Greene*

Venise. December 17. 1828.

Dear Green[e],

It is rather a singular circumstance, that the day when we first met, and last parted, should so nearly coincide. It was a year ago — about the middle of December — that chance threw us together — and without further ceremony made us friends. All the incidents of our early acquaintance, as well as those of our first travels together must still be fresh and vivid in your recollection. In mine, they are almost too much so: for you will call to mind those expressive words of Dante in the melancholy little story of Francesca di Rimini

> "—: nessun maggior dolore
> Che ricordarsi del tempo felice
> Nella miseria: —"[1]

It was at this season of the year, too, that we were together in Genoa. I remember it, as if it were but yesterday. The view from our windows — and the terrace overlooking the bay. When I turn back to my notes, I recal many little circumstances, that time had almost effaced from my memory. You cannot have forgotten Christmass Eve. I remember we sat together until midnight. Perhaps I can recal to your mind still more forcibly the scene if I copy you two or three lines from my Note-Book — "It is Christmass Eve. The moon is shining sweetly upon the sea, and here and there a boatman's lantern glimmers upon its surface. It is near midnight: and the bells are ringing out their glad jubilee at the approach of the Nativity." When I call to mind all this — and reflect that it was but a year ago: the lapse of time seems a dream. Still how fruitful of events has that little space of time been to both of us. Chance that threw us together then, has now jostled us apart again. For my own part, I fear that the past year, has only made me older: — for I should hardly dare assert that I am either much wiser or much better than I was a year ago: — though I am very happy in believing that you are both.

You see by my date, that I am in Venise. Indeed my present situation recalls to my mind very vividly ours [of] a year ago. My windows look out upon the bay of Venise: it is a winter night: — the moon is shining quietly upon the water: — and occasionally a little gondola, with its lighted lamp, flits by, and disappears in some dark alley. As I write, too, the sound of the Austrian drum, and the distant ringing of bells reaches my ear. Nothing is wanting to complete my illusion, and to make the shadow go back one year on the dial plate of time, but to see you enter the door.

I dislike to be alone at Christmass time. I feel as if I were an outcast from the world. The return of these annual holidays is the signal for bringing friends together, and uniting around the family fireside. Even the Italians — little as they have of true home-feeling about them — seem to feel this: and I find more than one wanderer turning his footsteps homeward to pass Christmass with his friends. They have a proverb, too,

"Natale coi tuoi, —
Pasqua — dove puoi!"[2]

It is capital, is it not?

Decr. 18.

I[n] reading over what I have written, I feel very much disposed to tear up the sheet. I find I have fallen unawares into a long train of melancholy reflexion. Excuse me: — but I feel so sad and down-hearted, that let my thoughts be scattered as they may, the[y] finally concentrate in the same point. You will understand me. I have purposely avoided the subject in my letter: it is too painful for me to dwell upon: though I assure you it haunts me continually.[3]

Venise is the most wonderful city I ever beheld. You will be delighted with it. The Italian language in the mouth of a Venitian woman is perfect music: you cannot conceive how soft it is. Indeed I have not yet heard a harsh sound — even among the common people. I am very sorry I left Childe Harold in Rome. Mr. Hooper[4] has it: you must get it from him: it will serve you, when you come on here. The Europa is the best hotel here, and is very reasonable. I pay two francs a day for my room. I am very much occupied, as I think of leaving next monday. Write me immediately — and address to the care of Messrs. H. M. Bassinge & ce. *Dresde[n]*. On my arrival at that city, you shall hear from me again. Be very particular in your letters to let me know all that passes, with regard to — hai capito? Oggi scriverò pure al Signor Cooke. Addio. Salutami tanto tutti in casa Persiani: et talora non ti scorda[r] di me.

Tuo affet[tuosissi] mo amico
Enrico W. Longfellow

Si tu hai fatto la conoscenza della Signora Baronessa Bourkard tu mi farai il piacere di salutarla da parte ||mia|| e pure Madama Hooper.[5]

MANUSCRIPT: Longfellow Trust Collection. ADDRESS: À Monsieur/Monsieur George W. Greene./à Rome. POSTMARK: VENEZIA 25 DEC 1828

1. "There is no greater sorrow/Than to be mindful of the happy time/In misery." Longfellow's translation of the *Inferno*, V, 121–123.

2. Samuel Longfellow translates this proverb in *Life*, I, 154: "Christmas with your clan;/Easter — where you can!"

3. Possibly an allusion to Longfellow's interest in Giulia Persiani (see 125.1).

4. Nothing is known of this man except that Longfellow knew him and his wife in Rome. On April 6, 1830, George W. Greene wrote from Paris: "I saw Mr. Hooper also. He was as well and good-humored as ever — his lady as usual was sick."

5. " — you understand? I will also write today to Mr. Cooke. Adieu. Give my very

best wishes to everyone at the Persiani's, and remember me from time to time./ Your very affectionate friend/Henry W. Longfellow/If you have had the chance to meet the Signora Baroness Bourkard, be kind enough to give her my regards, and also Mrs. Hooper."

141. *To Stephen Longfellow* [1]

Venice. December. 19. 1828.

My dear father,

On receiving yours of the 15th Septemb. I left Rome immediately. I unsealed your letter with the usual delightful feelings of hearing from home: but I assure you the perusal of it caused me great pain. The tidings that the anticipated appointment at Bowdoin has been refused me, were very unexpected and very jarring to my feelings. And more so, because it was a situation, which neither yourself, nor I, had solicitated, but which had been gratuitously offered me upon certain conditions — the which I have scrupulously fulfilled.[2]

I assure you — my dear father — I am very indignant at this. They say I am too young! Were they not aware of this three years ago? If I am not capable of performing the duties of the office, they may be very sure of my not accepting it. I know not in what light they may look upon it, but for my own part I do not in the least regard it as a favor conferred upon me. It is no sinecure: and if my services are an equivalent to my salary, — there is no favor done me: — if they be not, I do not desire the situation. If they think I would accept the place they offer me, — as I presume they do, — they are much mistaken in my character. No Sir — I am not yet reduced to this. I am not a dog to eat the crumbs, that fall from such a table. Excuse my warmth, but I feel rather hurt and indignant. It is a pitiful policy, — that, whilst other institutions send abroad their professors to qualify themselves for their stations and pay their expenses, — they should offer me an uncertain and precarious office — for it is a probationary one, if I understand them, — in which the labours of six years would hardly reimburse the sum I have expended in three. I do not think so meanly of myself as to accept such an appointment. It was not necessary to come to Europe for such an office as they offer me: it could have been had at a much cheaper rate — and at an earlier hour.

I am led to employ such language as this, because I feel no kind of anxiety for my future prospects. Thanks to your goodness, I have received a good education. I am ashamed to touch upon this point again: I though[t] that what I said in my last letter, would be the last I should ever have occasion to say in my own justification. But now I feel it a duty I owe to myself to speak even more fully. I know you cannot be dissatisfied with the progress I have made in my studies. I do not speak this from any feeling of self-complacency, nor do I wish that parental partialities should bias your judgement. I speak honestly — not boastingly. With the French and Spanish languages I am familiarly conversant — so as to speak them correctly — and write them with as much ease and fluency as I do the English. The Portugese I read without difficulty: — and with regard to my proficiency in the Italian, I have only to say, that when I came to this city, all at the Hotel, where I lodge took me for an Italian, until I gave them my passport, and told them I was an American. Do you, then, advise to accept of such a situation as is proffered me? No, I think you cannot. For myself, I have the greatest abhorrence to such a step. I beg of you not to think that this springs from any undue degree of arrogance: I arrogate nothing: but I must assert a freedom of thought and of speech.

I intend leaving Venice in a few days for Dresden, where I think of remaining until the opening of Spring. I do not wish to return without a competent knowledge of German — and all that I can do to acquire it shall be done. The time is short — but short as it is I hope to turn it to good advantage.

In the mean time please to give my kindest remembrances and most cordial thanks to those friends who have taken so much interest in my behalf: particularly to Judge Preble,[3] and Prof. Cleaveland. I should be sorry that my refusal of what has been so kindly solicited by them should cause them any pain: — but more so should it cause you any. In continuation, I have only to assure you that whatever suspicions my long stay in Italy may have occasioned you, they are wholly without foundation, as you will be satisfied of, in reading my last letters.

Trieste. December. 27.

I can hardly reconcile myself to the idea of relinquishing my studies at a German University. I become daily more and more impressed with the importance of it. My familiarity with the modern languages will unlock to me all those springs of litterature, which formerly would have been as sealed books to me. I have often had to lament, that I was obliged to leave the different countries I have visited, at the critical moment when the knowledge I had attained of their several languages rendered a longer residence peculiarly desirable. You see how it is with Washington Irving. He has remained in Spain upwards of three years — and you see what profit he reaps from it. Whoever first makes a Sketch Book of Spain will necessarily make a very interesting book.

I see by the papers that Mr. Irving has collected from old MSS. in the archives of the Library of the Arch Bishop of Seville a series of Moorish Tales.⁴ I have no doubts they will be delightfully interesting. He is a fortunate man: and deserves to be so, for he is a good man.

MANUSCRIPT: Longfellow Trust Collection. ADDRESS: To/Stephen Longfellow Esq./Portland. Maine. Etats Unis./Aux soins du Messrs Welles & c[i]e./Rue Taitbout. No. 24. Paris. ANNOTATION (*by Longfellow, on address cover*): Venice Dec 19. 1828.

1. Enclosed in Letter No. 143.

2. Stephen Longfellow's letter of September 15 is lost, but it concerned the refusal of the Bowdoin overseers to support the action of the trustees in appointing Longfellow a professor. This is made clear by Stephen Longfellow's explanatory letter of April 9, 1828, quoted in *Young Longfellow*, p. 374.

3. William Pitt Preble (1783–1857) was at this time an associate justice of the Supreme Court of Maine and a trustee of Bowdoin College.

4. Irving published these tales as *A Chronicle of the Conquest of Granada* in 1829.

142. *To Zilpah Longfellow*¹

Venice. December. 20. 1828.

My dear Mother,

I have been in this city about five days. My journey from Rome was a very uncomfortable one. Rainy days — sleepless nights — wind and cold — and "stumbling among dark mountains"² compose not one half the melancholy catalogue of my woes. But I will spare you the detail. Your imagination can readily picture the miseries of a traveller at this season of the year. Italy's eternal summer blo[o]ms only in song.

I shall never forget the delightful feelings awakened within me on approaching Venice, and entering its principal canal. It was a bright moonlight night: and a thousand lamps glimmered in the distance along the water's edge. Above rose the palaces, and domes and spires of the city, emerging from the sea. Occasionally a gondola, with its little lamp, darted like a shooting star along the water, and disappeared in some dark alley. The only sound that reached me was the distant chime, measuring the march of time — the dashing of an oar, or the voice of a gondolier. There was something so like enchantment in the scene, that I almost expected to see it sink into the sea, and disappear like an optical delusion, or some magic city in the clouds. Indeed all is so visionary and fairy-like here, that one is almost afraid of setting foot upon the ground, lest he should sink the city.

Since my arrival I have been pretty busily occupied in examining those objects, which most excite the stranger's attention, and are most worthy of remark. The object that has most interested me is the old Palace of the Doges. It is an immense pile of building — principally Arabic in its architecture, — dating from the middle of the fourteenth century — the days of Marino Faliero. I stood upon the spot where he was crowned, and where he was beheaded. It is at the top of the grand marble staircase, leading from the courtyard to the palace. His portrait is not among those of the other Doges, which adorn the grand hall now occupied as the library. In the place of it is painted a black curtain, with this inscription upon it in latin. "This is the place of Marino Faliero — beheaded for his crimes." The sight of this record of eternal ignominy, produces a strong impression upon the beholder.[3] Not less powerful are those he experiences on passing through the silent halls of the ancient Senate — of the Council of Ten — and of the Inquisitory. Beneath are the dungeons in which so many noble hearts have broken. The spot is shown you, where it is supposed that those upon whom the sentence of death was passed were strangled secretly. A little door, now walled up, led out from this dungeon to the canal. The old dungeons are also shown you. Most of them are entirely dark: into others a feeble ray of daylight struggles. From the walls of one of them I copied the following inscription — traced in rude characters by some hard instrument. "Confide in no one — think and be silent, if thou wishest to escape the snares and treachery of spies. Sorrow and repentance avail not here." The Bridge of Sighs leads from the halls of the criminal tribunal to the prison. It is a small covered bridge, thrown over a canal, high in air. Across it the prisoners were dragged to the judgement seat, and back to their dungeons. I cannot say with Lord Byron,

"I stood in Venice on the bridge of Sighs —"[4]

for the Tribunals being closed at this season, I know of no method of gaining admittance. To draw your thoughts from so melancholy a theme, I will mention a little incident that befel me upon the spot. As I was busily engaged in sketching the Bridge of Sighs, a wench of a chambermaid emptied a pitcher of water from a chamber window of the palace directly onto my head: and to show how little I cared for cold water even at this cold season of the year, I came very near slipping into the canal.

Yesterday I took a boat upon the grand canal, and floated from one extremity to the other. On the borders of this canal stand some of the most magnificent palaces I ever beheld. Still you trace in many of them the melancholy marks of decay and desolation. Nearly all of them look sombre and desolate. In some the windows are closed up:

— in others the casements without glass! My gondoleer pointed out to me as we passed the habitation of Lord Byron. He had formerly served him as gondoleer — and recited to me a sonnet he had composed to his lordship. It is very curious. He told me also several anecdotes of his manner of life at Venice. He said he was a "piccol' uomo, pallido, ma pien' di spirito e di talento:" — (a little pale man, but full of vivacity and talent.) In fact every body at Venice knows Lord Byron, and I have heard a good deal of his private life, — which I do not wish to write you, but which will serve for conversation at some future day. My gondoleer was quite a poet: and sung me two or three stanzas from Tasso. This morning he called and brought me a copy of his sonnet to Lord Byron. I told him to write one for me — which he did. It is too long to be copied here, but you will see it one of these days. It is a very singular composition.[5]

[December] 21.

I left my letter last night to go to a conversazione at Madame Benzon's[6] — at half past eleven o'clock! It is the house where Lord Byron visited constantly. She is an elderly lady, and receives company every evening from ten or eleven o'clock until three in the morning. These are fas[h]ionable hours at Venice — because they go after the theatre to finish the evening, or rather the night, in society. The Venitian ladies are not handsome, but they have a great deal of vivacity. They are also very profligate. Indeed Venice is noted even in Italy for its intrigues and infidelities.

I intend leaving tomorrow evening for Verona, on my way to Dresden. I do not anticipate a very delightful journey. The weather is very cold and uncomfortable even here, and I cannot hope for a diminution of its severity on advancing further north. You must not think however, that because I am cold, that I am deprived of all your New England comforts. On the contrary: my good landlady has promised me baked-pumpkin and hasty-pudding for dinner to day! I suppose you will think these exotics here in Venice — but they are sold in great quantities here in the street.

Farewell. I hope that ere this sister E. [Elizabeth] is entirely well. My best love to her, and to all the rest of the family — and also to my Grandparents and friends in the country.

Most affectionately your son
Henry.

MANUSCRIPT: Longfellow Trust Collection.

1. Enclosed in Letter No. 143.
2. Cf. Jer. 13:16.

3. Faliero (1274–1355) became doge of Venice in 1354. He was executed for conspiring to establish himself as dictator. Longfellow had presumably read Byron's poetic drama *Marino Faliero, Doge of Venice*, which helps explain his interest in this scene.

4. *Childe Harold*, Canto IV, i, 1.

5. Longfellow printed a short notice of Toni Toscan, the gondolier, as well as the sonnets to Byron and to himself, in his article on "The History of the Italian Language and Dialects," *North American Review*, XXXV (October 1832), 323–325.

6. Contessa Marina Querini Benzon (1757–1839), the celebrated heroine of Antonio Lamberti's "La Biondina in Gondoleta," maintained for years one of the best-known salons of Venice. She had introduced Byron to Teresa Guiccioli, his mistress.

143. *To Stephen Longfellow*

Trieste. Decemb. 27. 1828.

My dear Father,

I reached this city yesterday on my way to Dresden, and shall leave it tomorrow to pursue my journey. Inclosed are letters from Venice.[1] In reading over what I have written you — I feel much disposed to destroy the letter: but not having time to write another — nor indeed wishing to write again upon so painful a theme — I think it best to send you what I have written. If my language is too violent, excuse me: — it was not written in passion — but I feel too sensitive upon the subject. Such were and still are my sentiments: but they are alway[s] subject to your own wishes. I will do as you desire.

I mentioned in my letter from Venice — that I intended to remain at Dresden until Spring. This however depends altogether upon circumstances. I shall not unless I find it very cheap living there. Indeed I am not decided. I feel so very melancholy and down-hearted — that I am more disposed to go as soon as possible to find Mr. Preble at Göttingen — and seek the consolations of friendship in his society. This step would doubtless be the best, on some accounts, that I could take: but it would impede my progress in German. On reaching Dresden I shall be better able to judge of the plausibility of remaining there or going to Göttingen. Immediately on reaching Dresden I shall have letters from you — at least I hope to have them. Of course they will guide me.

We have had very dull melancholy weather of late: — continual fogs and rain: so that the sun has hardly shown his face for a fortnight. This makes everything look gloomy. I visit these charming countries under very unfavourable circumstances. The road from Venice to this city lies over an immense plain, beautified by harvest fields and the richness of the vine in their season — but now solitary with the frosts and bar[r]enness of Winter. You drive through long avenues — or rather through one long avenue of trees — and the level road stretches in an unbroken perspective before and behind you. The country seems to be prosperous — even under the yoke of Austrian dominion. Trieste is a busy commercial city — with wide streets intersecting each-other at right-angles: and its active population and houses of modern construction give it an aspect widely different from the old and ruinous cities I have lately visited — such as Bologna — Ferrara — Padua — &c. There is however very little in the city to interest any but a commercial man. Still I am much amused in seeing all the nations of the world brought into contact with each other, as they are here. The different costumes — and the different languages — and the different national phisiognomies around you — please the eye and the ear. Greek — Turck — Italian — German —French and English, you hear at every corner and in every coffee-house: and the various costumes and countenances afford an amusing and instructive study for the traveller, who is pleased with novelties — and is willing to be pleased.

I took this road to Dresden in order to pass through Vienna — and see one of the finest capitals in the World. Perhaps the road by Verona — and thence through the Tyrol to Munich — and so on to Dresden would have been more direct — but I felt rather reluctant to make so long a journey at this inclement season among the dangerous passes of those mountains. I should have gained little in point of time — and should have lost much in point of interest and conveniance. To Dresden I have a great many introductory letters from Washington Irving[2] — to whom I am indebted for many kindnesses. This makes me desirous of remaining there in preference to any other place — should I find my expenses moderate, and my advantages for study good. But these long journeys eat up great quantities of money: and a city-residence must necessarily be more expensive than a country-one.

I write you this from a coffee-house — where I am surrounded by noisy groups of all nations — some dosing over the columns of the gazettes — others talking the daily gossip — and others smoking over their coffee. I am afraid my letter will exhale the fumes of pipes and beer — and not of midnight oil.

Farewell. I shall write again soon. My kindest regards to all friends — particularly to Dr. Nichols. In the mean time, I hope something may be done more favourable in regard to my prospects touching the Professorship at Bowdoin.

Your most affectionate Son
Henry W. Longfellow.

MANUSCRIPT: Longfellow Trust Collection. ADDRESS: To/Stephen Longfellow. Esqr. —/Portland. Maine./United States of/America/*Per* Circupian [*in another hand*] POSTAL ANNOTATION: forw[arde]d by Y.O.etc.!/Geo Moore/ Trieste POSTMARKS: NEW YORK MAR 30/SHIP ENDORSEMENT: Henry to his Parents/Venice and Trieste —/Dec. 20. and 27. 1828./Recd. Apr. 3 — 1829./Ans. April 9. —

1. Letters No. 141 and 142.
2. Including letters to Karl August Böttiger, the archaeologist; Baron Woldemar von Löwenstern; and Comte de Rumigny, the French minister to Saxony (S. T. Williams, *The Life of Washington Irving* [New York, 1935], I, 477).

144. *To Stephen Longfellow, Jr.*

Vienna, January 3, 1829.

I write you this from the banks of the Danube. To the usual congratulations of the season I would add the kindest good wishes of brotherly affection, and repeat that, though far from you in reality, I am not so in imagination. I am continually coming upon some object which vividly presents your image to my mind and makes me regret that you are not with me. Such was the case this morning, in visiting a large collection of antique armor. Such helmets as these would have been chronicles to you.[1] They are of burnished steel, more than a quarter of an inch in thickness. The corresponding parts for the body are equally curious.

Yesterday I took a carriage and drove to Greifenstein, to see the ruins of an ancient castle, celebrated as having been the prison of Richard of the Lion-heart. It is about sixteen miles from Vienna, upon the summit of a steep hill "bosomed high in tufted trees."[2] Beneath it winds the lordly Danube, spreading its dark waters over the lowland. The little village of Greifenstein stands at the foot of the hill, from which a winding pathway leads to the old castle. Upon the angle of the rock on which the castle stands, is the impression of a human hand. This, according to tradition, gave rise to the name. *Greifen* answers to our *grip;* and *stein* is *stone.* Every knight, when he entered and gave his right hand to his host, laid his left hand on the stone [as a guard against a treacherous blow].[3] So, in process of time, the stone was worn away, and the impression of a hand remains. The chamber of Richard's confinement is in the large square tower.[4]

I have before me a copy of a song made by Richard during his confinement, which I picked up in France among some old troubadour poetry of the twelfth century. It is in the dialect of Provence. He begins by lamenting his sad fate, and says that his friends should blush to leave him "nearly two years in chains."

Let them know, my noble barons,
English, Normans, and Gascons,
That never so poor a yeoman had I
That I would not have bought his liberty.
I may not reproach their noble line,
But chains and a dungeon still are mine!

He then calls upon his fellow-troubadours, — for Richard himself
was a troubadour, — and tells them to name him in their songs.

Troubadours and friends of mine,
Generous Chail and Pensavin, —
Ye whom I love and have loved so long, —
Repeat to the foeman in your song
That little glory will be to him
In quenching a flame already dim;
That never yet did Richard show
A heart that was false to friend or foe;
And that he more shame than glory gains
Who wars with an enemy in chains.

It is throughout very simple and beautiful, — the most so of any
troubadour poetry I have read. I would translate the whole for you;
but what I have already written is so lame and inexpressive that
I desist.[5]

Prague, 11th.

I left Vienna on the 9th, and reached this city to-day at noon. I
travelled in company with a Hungarian noble and his *"homme
d'affaires."* The route was not very interesting. The Bohemian pine-
forests reminded me of Brunswick; and Bohemian small beer, of old
Uncle Trench's.[6] Prague is a pretty city, and very ancient; situated on
the banks of the Moldau, which divides it into the old and new city.
A beautiful stone bridge connects them.

I shall leave to-morrow for Dresden. Good-night!

MANUSCRIPT: unrecovered; text from *Life*, I, 160–161.

   1. Longfellow's sketch of two helmets follows here. See Plate IV.
   2. Milton, *L'Allegro,* l. 78.
   3. Samuel Longfellow's interpolation within brackets.
   4. A sketch of the castle follows. See Plate IV.
   5. Longfellow subsequently revised his translation and printed it in *Poets and
Poetry of Europe,* p. 437.
   6. A purveyor of gingerbread and root beer to Bowdoin students.

145. *To Carey & Lea, Publishers*

Dresden   15 Jany. 1829.[1]

Messrs Carey & Lea:
Dear Sirs,

Permit me to renew an acquaintance which has been long inter-rupted by time and absence, with the usual congratulations of the season, and the friendly good wishes, that always signalise the advent of a New Year. I recur with pleasure to the circumstances of my first acquaintance with you, and often recall the kindnesses I received at your hands, during the few days I passed in Philadelphia.[2]

My object in visiting Europe has been a literary one. Sin[c]e my residence on the continent, the difference between the Old World and the New has struck me very forcibly: and I have thought that a series of papers upon the scenes and customs of my Native Land might not be an unacceptable offering to the literary world. Accordingly I have commenced a Sketch Book of New England, in the stile of Irving's Sketch Book of Old England and from the variety of topics which naturally present themselves to the mind of an American, when in a foreign land, he recalls the blessings and endearments of home, I hope to give sufficient interest to the work to secure its success. Of course everything will depend upon the stile of the work, and the manner in which its subjects are treated. Upon my own stile it does not become me to speak, and with regard to the subjects of my papers, they are such as recollection furnishes me with. Thus far, I have written but two Nos. The contents I here subjoin. Each no. I suppose, if printed in a fair type, and an ornamental manner, will make, with the usual "remplissage" of index — title pages &c. about a hundred pages 8°. Perhaps I over-rate: you can judge when you see the manuscript.

No. 1.
"The Author" — his account of himself.
"Home Feelings" — recollections of my Native Land.
"Rural Scenery." — peculiarities of New England.
"The Bald Eagle Tavern" — humorous description of the prepara-tions made by the inhabitants of an inland New England Village for the reception of General Lafayette, when on his tour in America.[3]
"The Indian Summer"   a Tale.[4]

No. 2.
"Scenes of Childhood." — return to them after long absence.
"The Village Graveyard."

"Blind Tom" — a Tale.
"Harvest Home in New England."
"Dixy Bull, the Pirate" — a Tale.

Thus you have an inventory of my literary wares: a kind of "Programme du Spectacle." Instead thereof I would send you the MS. did I know of any mode of conveyance. You shall have it as soon as possible: with the title, mottos — &c &c all in order.

With regard to the terms of publication, I leave that to you: only I should wish to retain the copy-right in my own hands — as the publication is an experiment. With regard to the rest, I will enter into what arrangements you may propose: Allowing you whatever share of the profits you may deem just, on condition that you share with me the risk of failure.

The Nos. are not to appear at any fixed periods — but as the work may accumulate on my hands. Be kind enough to write me upon the subject, directing to the care of Messrs. Welles & c[i]e. 24 Rue Taitbout, à Paris.

With sentiments of esteem and respect, I am

Your Obt. Servt —
Henry W. Longfellow.

P.S. In thus making known to you my secret, Gentlemen, I have confidence in you, that you will not betray me: for in case of failure, it might injure my after-prospects as a literary man, were my name known, for the same reason I publish in nos. since in putting out a pamphlet, one has not much at stake — and at all events the loss cannot be great in any point of view. Farther — the two nos. I have written, I have written with the utmost care, and attention to the stile. I intend to do the same with the others: and in so doing, I assure you I do not anticipate a failure. Only let me again pray you not to let my name be known. I have a good many materials on hand and in part worked up for future nos. I wish always to keep one no. in advance.[5]

MANUSCRIPT: Longfellow Trust Collection. ADDRESS: To/Messrs. Carey & Lea./ Philadelphia./Über Hamburg./Messrs. Welles & Cie. 24 Taitbout./à Paris. POSTMARKS: DRESDEN 12 JAN 29/NEW YORK MAY 11/NAPOSTTYD/FRANCO/ SHIP ENDORSEMENT: An[s]d. May 13 — PUBLISHED: Lawrance R. Thompson, "Longfellow's Projected Sketch Book of New England," *The Colophon*, Pt. 15 (1933).

1. This date is apparently incorrect. See postmark.
2. See Letter No. 92.
3. Published in *The Token and Atlantic Souvenir*, ed. S. G. Goodrich (Boston, 1833), pp. 74–89.
4. Published in *The Token*, ed. S. G. Goodrich (Boston, 1832), pp. 24–35.

5. Lawrance Thompson discusses this abortive project in "Longfellow's Projected Sketch Book of New England," *The Colophon*, Pt. 15 (1933), and in *Young Longfellow*, pp. 132–135, 375.

146. *To Stephen Longfellow*

No. 10. Göttingen. Feby. 27. 1829.

My dear father,

In my last letters written at Dresden,[1] I told you it was my intention to remain in that city until the opening of Spring. Such *was* my intention when I wrote: but finding several inconveniences for a studious life, which counterbalanced the conveniencies of a residence there: and added to this, feeling a strong desire to see my old friend Preble, — I came to the resolution of leaving Dresden for this city. I arrived here on the twenty second inst. — and found Preble in good health and very comfortably situated. He will, however, leave me at the commencing of the vacation, — in about ten days — on a visit to some of the principal cities of Germany: but returns to pass the Summer here.

For my own part, I shall remain here this vacation: and should like to, the next term, unless circumstances should render my return this summer absolutely necessary. With regard to Bowdoin College, the more I think of it, the more I am dissatisfied. So much so, indeed, that I am averse to going there at all, if any other situation can be procured me. I dislike the manner in which things are conducted there. Their illiberality in point of religion — and their narrow-minded views upon many other points, need no comment. Had I the means of a bare subsistance, I would *now* refuse a Professorship there. I say *now*: I mean since they have offered me a lower office. I am inclined to think that the opposition came from the younger professors. I suppose they did not like the idea of seeing so young a man step at once into the chair of prof. without serving the usual apprenticeship. I have but one question to ask. Do the Professors of Bowdoin College speak the languages they teach? No — not one of them. I have another plan to suggest to your consideration which to me holds out better inducements than the first.

Finding Göttingen everything I had imagined it, my desire to pass a year here springs up anew. Allow me, at least, then, to pass the Summer here: and in the meantime my friends can probably think of some other situation equally good for me as a professorship at Brunswick. If they cannot, upon my return I might be permitted to deliver a course of lectures on modern literature at the Portland Atheneum, and in the mean time, I could look out for myself. As I have already told you, upon this point I feel not the slightest anxiety or mistrust. But I will not anticipate — at present let us speak of the present. I find living at Göttingen very cheap. As I have just arrived I cannot give you any just idea of what my expenses will be monthly: but as soon as I have been here a little longer I will send you a continuation of what my last letters contained. The Library here is the largest in Germany and is full of choise rare works: and the advantages for a student of my particular pursuits are certainly not overrated in the universal fame of the University of Göttingen.

Whilst at Dresden, I felt no other desire than that of returning home once more to the bosom of the family. I had got discouraged and a little down-hearted. But meeting with an old and good friend, has given new elasticity to my spirits: — they have again taken their wonted tone, and I am contented and happy. In this disposition, I am a little unwilling to give up what is now in my reach: and as I shall never again be in Europe, I should think it were better to lengthen a little my absence from home at present, than by not so doing to have subject for future regret. I brought letters to several of the Professors here, from Bancroft, and Ticknor:[2] and have been well received. Göttingen is a small city — and there are no amusements here whatever: so there is no alternitive but study. With regard to duelling, for which all the German Universities are more or less notorious, you will find a description of them in the North American for July 1828. — page 87.[3] They are considered by the students as sport: and it is not uncommon to hear of six being fought in one afternoon and on the same spot. There is however no possibility either of Preble or myself being engaged in these affairs, as we do not know the broad-sword exercise, and are of course *hors de combat.* There are about 14 or 15 hundred students here: as in all Universities some *scholars* — and others high wild fellows. He who wishes to be distinguished among the latter, must fight his way into distinction: but he who wishes to pursue his studies quietly, is no more molested here than at one of our colleges.

I find Preble improved every way. He is everything I could wish a friend to be. His associates are entirely from the studious class: — and if his mother could see every action of his during the twenty four hours of the day, she could not wish one of them changed. This is saying a great deal, but it is so.

Please write me immediately upon the subject of this, and t‖ell me‖ if you think my suggestions practicable. In the mean time, I have other literary projects in view, which shall be duly set in order and made known to you, when the time arrives in which I can put them into ‖execution.‖ Pray set your mind perfectly at rest upon all points, that may have occasioned you any uneasiness.

Kindest remembrances to all friends in town and country. To day I send a few engravings to Stephen by way of Hamburg illustrating the Burschen or high-life of the Students of Göttingen. From Dresden I sent him a letter dated at Vienna.[4] I shall expect an answer. What Preble tells me of the improvements going on in Portland delights me. It might be made one of the most beautiful cities in the world. I have never seen a finer situation in all the countries I have visited. Besides, he tells me the "march of mind" goes forward with giant strides. I see Mr. Neal attributes it to his "preface to Niagara!"[5] Mr. de Beaufort — who by the way refused the situation of Instructor at Bow: Coll: — has probably done something in this way.[6]

Most Affectionately your Son
Henry W. Longfellow.

MANUSCRIPT: Longfellow Trust Collection. ADDRESS: Stephen Longfellow — Esq —/Portland. Maine. —/Aux soins de Messrs. Welles & cie./Rue Taitbout 24. —/à Paris./Per Montano — [in another hand] ANNOTATION: Göttingen. — March. 2nd. Will Messrs Welles & co have the goodness to forward my letters to Göttingen — Bey Leo — Rothe Strasse — H.W.L. — POSTMARKS: GÖTTINGEN 4 MAR/MA[R] 9 1829/NEW YORK APR[?]/FORWARDED BY YR. OBT. SER[V]T. WELLES & CO. PARIS/PP. ENDORSEMENT: Henry to his father/Göttingen Feby 27. 1829 —/An[s]d May 7 —

1. These letters are unrecovered.
2. See Letter No. 89.
3. *North American Review*, XXVII.
4. Letter No. 144.
5. In a rambling preface to the second edition of *The Battle of Niagara* (Baltimore, 1819) John Neal castigates a New York editor (who had not reviewed the first edition of the poem) for preferring British to American literature and makes a plea for native writers: "If you would see the literature of your country take a stand worthy of her reputation — *you must watch it — encourage it — pray for it*" (p. xxxix).
6. The *General Catalogue of Bowdoin College, 1794–1912* lists a Charles de Beaufort as "Instructor, French, 1828–29."

147. *To Stephen Longfellow*

Göttingen   March 10. 1829.

My dear father,

I have of late been reading a little and thinking much on the subject of Education. The public mind on both sides of the Atlantic seems at the present day to be directing its attention particularly to the point: — I may say too its energies. The prevalent opinion is that in England and America the subject calls loudly for reform: but more so in America than elsewhere. And ours is an age and a country, in which the clearsighted and practical views of the community see nothing venerable even in antiquity itself, when errors and abuses take shelter beneath its gray hairs. There is something so operative and thorough-going in freedom of thought and of the press — I may add too, in the matter-of-fact way of thinking prevalent in our country — that to my mind the conclusion seems irrisistable, that public opinion, which is directing its currents from all quarters of the land towards the abuses of education, as it exists with us, will ere long undermine the foundation of our present erroneous systems, and sweep them from the face of the earth.

Germany and France may well boast of their schools and Universities. Good Heavens! what advantages have they not in these countries! Here indeed the gates of wisdom may be emphatically said to be swung wide open. There is a voice of free grace crying to all, that the fountains of their salvation are open. May it soon be heard in our own happy land, swelling above the voice of worldly gain, and the war of political strife.

What has heretofore been the idea of an University with us? The answer is a simple one. Two or three large brick buildings with a chapel, and a President to pray in it. I say University, because with us University and College, have till now been almost synonomous terms. Mr. Jefferson it is true made a bold attempt — but it failed — if not totally — at least in part — it failed — and why? Because, with all due respect, he does not seem to have begun right. He began where everybody else in *our* country would have begun, — by building college halls and then trying to stock them with Students.[1] But that is not the way to found an University. European Universities were never founded in this manner. Indeed, as far as regards University buildings — one might live in Göttingen from one year's end to the other without having the slightest idea of its being the seat of a University. No — it was by collecting together professors in whom "the spirit moved"[2] — who were well enough known to attract students to themselves — and after they had assembled them capable of teaching them something they did not know before. It was so with the Italian — Spanish — German and French Universities — and when there is an American University, it must and will be so with that. Then, instead of seeing a new College ushered into existence every winter by a petition to the Legislature for funds to put up a parcel of Woolen-Factory buildings for students — we should see capital better employed in enriching the libraries of the country and making them *public*! —

and instead of seeing the youth of our country chained together like galley slaves and "scourged to their dungeons"[3] — as it were — our eyes would be cheered by the grateful spectacle of mind throwing its fetters off — and education freed from its chains and shackles.

Next to our own free government I think the University of Paris the sublimest of all human institutions! When I say the University of Paris — I mean to include in the expression the Public Libraries, because tho' not in reality connected with the University, as they are open every day, one may derive the same advantages from them, as if they were. At the Garden of Plants are lectures on Botany — Nat. Hist — Mineralogy &c with illustrations from museums, and a garden containing almost every, if not every plant and animal in the world. At the Sorbonne are daily lectures on Geog. — Static[s] — History — ancient and modern literature — the dead and living languages — Philosophy — &c &c &c making the course more complete than even at Göttingen. At the Law Schools are law lectures — and at the Medical college — lectures on surgery and medicine — with the privilege of accompanying the instructor, through the Hospital under his care — assisting at his dissections — and even of having bodies for private dissection. This is a hasty and imperfect sketch of some of the advantages for a literary and scientific education at Paris: and all these advantages are perfectly and entirely — *gratis*. The meanest boor, that trundles a barrow through the street, has free access to all these — and students do not pay a sou for their education. We think in America, that there is nothing but frivolity in France — would God we had a little *such* frivolity in our country. Is not such an institution noble — sublime! It outstrips all rivalship — no other nation can boast so much.

Take this, and the German universities for models. Let two or three Professors — begin the work — let them deliver lectures in some *town* — (Portland seems to me better adapted for it than any other place in our part of the country) — not in a village — not in the woods if their lectures be worth anything — they will have hearers and disciples enough — and a *nucleus* will thus be formed around which is to grow an University. In the outset, lectures could not be *gratis* — no, the profits arising therefrom should be the Professor's support. Every one should rely upon his own talents for support — and his pay would in consequence be in proportion to his ability.

I am now coming to the application of my remarks. I told you in my last, that I wished to have nothing to do with Bowdoin Co||ll.|| The system is too limited and superficial. Instead of going there I wish if possible to sow the seeds of an University after the models of those quoted above, in our own State and our own town. Portland is just the spot for an *University* — (not a College) — it is neither too large nor too small. Yes, let Portland set an example to the whole U. States. Let us begin forth-with. As soon as I return — if the matter seems at all plausible — I mean to proffer my humble endeavours to the execution of such a plan — and put my shoulder to the wheel. The present is just the moment: we must now take the tide there is in the affairs of men.[4] Even before I left home, you had seriously thought of reading Law Lectures — and of gradually giving up the practice of law. This is just what is wanted: and should it meet with good success, as it doubtless would, you would benefit your health thereby — and remove a weight of care and anxiety from your mind. When I return I will also read those lectures I had proposed reading elsewhere. Let not a word be said about an University but let lectures upon different subjects be read — and students will collect. Thus we may steal silently upon the world with these innovations — and without Legislative grants, or College buildings, our State will see an University springing into existence in its very bosom — without its having even an intimation of its origin.

[March] 15. The third of my discourse was broken short: — my sheet is full — but I have a thousand things to say on the subject of early education &c &c which can better be said *viva voce,* than written.

I like Göttingen more and more daily — my health and spirits are good. I have made the acquaintance of Prof. Heeren, whose writings must be already known to you: also of the cel[ibrate]d Naturalist Blumingbuch: — and of Dr. Bode, who was at Northampton at the Round Hill school — and with whom I am much pleased.[5]

P.S. The remittance from Bow. Coll. for books mentioned in your last has not yet reached [me]. Speaking of this subject — pray speak to Dr. Nichols and some of those good men who take an interest in the Portland library, and see if a remittance from them — from the Portland Library association cannot also be sent out for the purchase of books in the living foreign languages. Perhaps the *Town* would do something towards enriching the Library — at least they should be requested so to do — importuned I may say — and to repay them — if they are willing to contribute something — let the Library be made *public.* I will here give you what I think a good model or plan.

Let a librarian be appointed by the *town,* with a moderate salary. Let his duty be to attend the library rooms daily — morning and afternoon. Let the Library rooms be furnished with tables and chairs — and writing materials: — then throw open its doors — and let it be as public as the town pump. The only privilege that the regular *Sub-*

scribers, who *pay* are to have over the rest of the world who read, is, that they can take books to their houses as they now do — whilst those who are not Subscribers and do not pay — will be obliged to read in the Library rooms — not having the privilege of taking books home.

Now this would be setting things on a liberal footing. Without diminishing our own advantages, as Subscribers, we should give the means of a mental livelihood to many a starving wretch — who now sees the fruit hanging just beyond his reach, and the water retiring from his lips. How many are there who would gladly subscribe to a Library — and would do all they could in its support — if they had the means of doing it! Remove the stumbling block out of the way of such men. Quench not the spirit! The Library too should be furnished with books in foreign languages as well as in the vernacular. As much attention has of late been given to modern languages in Portland — the means of pursuing those studies — and of investigating more or less the literature of different nations, is of great and vital importance. In order to preserve a knowledge of any language, one must have constant exercise in it. This exercise of course consi[s]ts in conversation and in reading. Now in Portland opportunities for conversation in French, Italian — Spanish and German are comparatively rare — hence in order to preserve a familiarity with a language in whose acquisition we have passed months if not years — and of course would not willingly forget — tho' nothing is easier than to forget a language — we have no other resource than books: at all events upon books we must place our principal reliance. If these books be not within our reach — there is no remedy — we must forget what we have learned by laborious study. Indeed — one month — when our thoughts are turned into other channels, will do more towards forgetting a language than the labor of six towards its acquisition. The importance of furnishing our library with standard authors becomes at once evident. I mean authors in *all* the four principal foreign languages. This can be done at Paris — at a very moderate expense. I should be exceedingly happy to execute any commissions. German books must be bought in Germany — the peculiarity of the German printing letters rendering *errata* in foreign editions more abundant than in French, Spanish or Italian books. Besides booksellers in Germany furnish their merchandise on the most liberal terms. They will deliver any quantity ready for embarcation at Hambourg or any other German sea-port, at a discount of 20 pr-cent.

Preble tells me that this will not do — that they are opposed to having foreign books in the Library. I think a few might oppose it — *but at all events you ought* to have some foreign books.

— My love to all the family — and kind remembrances to all friends,

Very affectionately your Son
Henry W. Longfellow.

MANUSCRIPT: Longfellow Trust Collection. ADDRESS: To/Stephen Longfellow. Esq./Portland./Maine./Aux soins de Messieurs Welles & cie —/Rue Taitbout 24. à/Paris./Per Chs. Carroll — [*in another hand*] POSTMARKS: GÖTTINGEN 16 MAR/MARS 21 1829/NEW YORK MAY 13/ALLEMAGNE PAR FORBACH/FORWARDED BY YR. OB. SERV. WELLES & CO. PARIS/SHIP ENDORSEMENT: Henry to his father/Gottingen March 10. & 15. 1829/Rec. May 15. —/ Ans. May 25 —

1. Longfellow refers to the University of Virginia.
2. Cf. Gen. 1:2.
3. Cf. Bryant, "Thanatopsis," l. 78.
4. Cf. *Julius Caesar*, IV, iii, 216.
5. Arnold Hermann Ludwig Heeren (1760–1842) pioneered the movement for the economic interpretation of history; Johann Friedrich Blumenbach (1752–1840) founded the science of anthropology; Georg Heinrich Bode (1802–1846) had begun a promising career in classical scholarship.

148. *To Elizabeth Longfellow, Lucia Wadsworth, and Anne Longfellow*

Göttingen. 28 March: 1829.[1]

My dear Sister Elisabeth,

After spending an idle hour in a vain attempt to put into English verse, a lovely little Portuguese song, which I got from the Library to day, I have thrown the book aside for some other and perhaps more fortunate moment, and will devote the little remnant of daylight which remains, to kindly recollections of an absent Sister. My failure in the translation, I attribute solely to a cold in the head, which does not allow the requisite circulation in the *bump*: — and to show you how very badly I have succeeded, I will here transcribe you one verse of the song just as it lies before me on my paper — as exactly as I can imitate the hand writing — the corrections, additions &c &c. — premising that the subject is the Poet's farewell to his Lyre:

> How oft — alas! when lonely
>   Awakening from my slumbers,
>   Thou lyre of gentle numbers,
> My hand hath tun'd thy strings! —
>   Thou, said I, and thou only
>   Canst soothe my soul! I borrow
>   From thee my joy in sorrow —
> From thee —"   — — ings!!![2]

You must get Sammy to fill up the hiatus. Now, after reading this, I think you can easily imagine me sitting alone in my chamber, at the close of a chill melancholy day in March, — with a leaden sky overhead, and twilight stealing slowly in at the window. It is a disheartening, gloomy day " — and then its hue, — Who ever saw so fine a *blue?*" One of those days, which makes us just sad enough to translate a sad ballad — and just poor enough in spirit to make a poor translation.

I dare say, now, you will think me pedantic: and tell me I had much better have filled up the space with assurances of brotherly love than with a "woful ballad."[3] Indeed it is but too true: — but then there is room for all this too. Besides I think you have too much confidence in your brother, to need constant assurances of his affection. Is it not so![4]

I have lighted my lamp, and am going forthwith to write you a letter about myself. I am all alone. Preble has gone to Berlin — and will not be back again for some weeks: so that at the moment I write I am the only American here. It is now vacation — and every body but myself is travelling. For my own part I remain — entrenched behind a rampart of books — and with intellectual provision enough to hold out a siege quite through the Vacation. With Göttingen I am much delighted: though I do not go at all into society. I have no other society than my books. My studies — you already know what they are — modern languages and modern literature. My poetic career is finished. Since I left America, I have hardly put two lines together. I may indeed say, that my muse has been sent to the House of Correction — and her last offspring were laid at the door of one of those Foundling Hospitals for poor poetry — a New Year's "Souvenir."[5] So you see the Dark Ages have come upon me: — and no soft poetic ray has irradiated my heart — since the Goths and Vandals swept over the Rubicon of the "front entry" and turned the Sanctum Sanctorum of the "Little Room" into a China Closet.[6]

"If you have tears — prepare to shed them now."[7] I mean tears of joy: — for other tears would be misplaced amid the congratulations of friends upon a certain subject that you "wot of."[8] The muse being in the Penitentiary, I can write you no epithalamium: but I can write you a volume of good-wishes, which, with all due deference, I think much better. I wish you, then, all happiness — all rest — all confidence — and withal a love that passeth all understanding; — for as Jeremy Taylor says in his Marriage Ring "She that is loved, is safe: and he that loves is joyful!"[9] May you be safe — and he joyful —

And when with envy, Time transported,
Shall think to rob you of your joys,
You in your girls again be courted,
And he go wooing in his boys —[10]

— as an Old Poet singeth. As I was tumbling over some old papers in one of my drawers this morning, I found a billet sent me, according to the custom of the country, by a Spanish lady — a few days after her marriage. It runs thus. "Don Gonzale de Heredia and Dona Clementina de Onis give your grace a share in their marriage — and offer you their house." I had rather have had a share in the wedding-cake — for all that was meant by this flourish of trumpets was, that "his grace" was at liberty to make a morning call upon the bride and bridegroom, — when he pleased.

Good bye. My love to all the family — and kind remembrance to Mr. P.[11] Ask Anne, if I have answered her last letter. If not — kiss her for me — and tell her I shall write soon. Do the same to all the children who wrote their brother Henry last Spring. Most affectionately your Brother Henry. — who takes the liberty of writing a few lines to his Aunt in your letter.

My dear Aunt Lucia.

Your kind an[d] excellent letter of April 25. 1828 — took me so completely unawares — that my philosophy lost its balance and my heart trembled with delight, like a demisemiquaver on the end of Deacon Freeman's [12] nose at the conclusion of a long-metre doxology. I make it a point not to be surprised at anything: but you had so long mused my praise in "expressive silence" [13] — at least I presume you had, — and I knew so well your reluctance to writing, that your letter did indeed surprise me tho' very agreeably I assure you. The more welcome was it because unexpected: and I hope you will surprise me in the same way often before my return.

You must pardon me, my dear Aunt, for not having answered your letter sooner. I have no apology — but in the multitude of my occupations. The great quantity of letters, too, I am forced to write, — sometimes no less than fifteen in the course of a fortnight — as was the case not long ago — makes me start back from a sheet of blank paper as I should from a sheeted Spectre.

There are some of my correspondents who keep an exact account of Dr. and Cr. with me. You must know that this makes me a martyr, for I am scarcely ever Dr. Indeed I have no paragon except Mr. O. K.

Barrel[l]: who writes on, with an ardour and perseverance worthy a better cause, bearing the whole burden of our correspondence upon his own shoulders, and setting at nought all the safeguards and barriers, which human prudence has devised in similar cases of peril. Now setting aside the family — and Oliver, with his Paul and Barnabas epistles on morality, and "Who-killed-Cock-Robin" poetry — not a friend, except George Pierce — wrote me by Preble. 'Tis true Greenleaf slipped a postscript into Stephen's letter — but it was merely to tell me that Preble was to act as deputy pay-master for all epistolary debts. This was highly flattering every way: and I can hardly find terms to express my gratitude for such favours. But I do not know why I should scold you about it. Instead thereof let me reciprocate your kind remembrances and good wishes — and assure you that wherever I may be, I shall always bear in mind your goodness and your love.

Very affectionately yours
Henry W.

My dear Sister Anne —

The place you occupy in my heart is much larger than the place assigned you in this letter. There is however some analogy, — for you are at the bottom of both. The account you gave me in your last of the manner in which you had *Furbish'd* up your mind,[14] was very interesting to me: — and I hope you will soon *demonstrate* to me your affection, in a long letter — that is, in *"straight lines produced to infinity"* — and not in an epistle cut up like this into "vulgar fractions."

Affectionately your Brother,
Henry. —

MANUSCRIPT: Longfellow Trust Collection. ADDRESS: To/Stephen Longfellow Esq./Portland. Maine./Aux soins de Messrs. Welles & Cie/Rue Taitbout 24./ à Paris. — ANNOTATION: Will Messrs. Welles & co. have the goodness to for-/ward this to its address?/Yours &c H. W. Longfellow./Göttingen. 27 March. POSTMARKS: GÖTTINGEN 27 MAR/APRIL 2 1829/ALLEMAGNE PAR FORBACH ENDORSEMENT: Henry to Eliz[abet]h, Lucia and Anne/Gottingen March 28. 1829./Recd. May 24. 1829 —

1. Longfellow's annotation and the postmark reveal that this letter was actually written on March 27 or before. Elizabeth Longfellow died almost three weeks before the letter arrived.

2. This appears to be the third and fourth stanzas of Claudio Manoel da Costa's "The Lyre," Thomas Roscoe's version of which Longfellow subsequently included in *Poets and Poetry of Europe*, p. 758. He began abortively with "How oft — alas how oft — " and first wrote "I've" for "hath" in l. 4.

3. *As You Like It*, II, vii, 148.

4. Longfellow used this paragraph to fill in the space on each side of his translation.

5. Longfellow presumably refers to "The Song of the Birds" and "Burial of the Minnisink," published in *The Atlantic Souvenir; a Christmas and New Year's Offering* (Philadelphia, 1827), and to "The Spirit of Poetry," published in *The Souvenir* for the following year.

6. The meaning is vague but applies apparently to Longfellow's study room in Portland, which was converted to other uses.

7. *Julius Caesar*, III, ii, 169.

8. That is, Elizabeth's engagement to William Pitt Fessenden.

9. Sermon XVIII, Pt. II, Sec. 2.

10. Cf. the last stanza of "Winifreda" in Thomas Percy, *Reliques of Ancient English Poetry*.

11. The identity of "Mr. P" is not clear, but it may be a reference to Pitt Fessenden.

12. Presumably Samuel Freeman (114.4), a deacon of the First Parish Church, Portland.

13. Cf. James Thomson, *A Hymn on the Seasons*, l. 118.

14. The subject of this play on words was James Furbish (1796–1878), instructor in the Portland Academy. He later became head of the Female High School of Portland, one of whose trustees was Stephen Longfellow. He was remembered by his pupils for having "waved his great silk handkerchief to and fro, while seemingly half to himself and half to his pupils, he elucidated Greek or Latin" (Edward Elwell, *The Schools of Portland* [Portland, 1888], p. 34).

149. *To Margaret L. Potter*[1] *and Ellen Longfellow*

[Göttingen, March, 1829][2]

My dear little *Marge*
I will not enlarge
   On the famous beggars' petition:
The *Law* gives protection: —
I see no objection
Why the House of Correction
   Should not bring you all to contrition.

Pray let me alone
With your "Eau de Cologne" —
   I here send you half, of a box
Of "Marina Farina:"
You will not decline a
Bottle — none finer —
   I send it to you — Mrs – F ——[3]

Tell Miss Ellen Long-
fellow — she is all wrong,
To go thus a begging for water:
You can't say *"Eau"* dear,
For it's very cheap here, —
So don't interfere —
But give the Professor some quarter.

One thing more — only one —
And then I have done —
But *this* I beg you remember,
If Caroline Doane
Wants some Eau de Cologne,
She must let it be known
Before the 1st of December.

MANUSCRIPT: Longfellow Trust Collection. ADDRESS: To/Miss Margaret L. Pot-
ter:and/Ellen Longfellow —/Beggars./Portland.

1. Margaret Louisa Potter (b. 1817) was the younger sister of Mary Storer
Potter, whom Longfellow married in 1831.
2. The place and date are questionable. It is likely, however, that Longfellow
composed this verse-letter in Germany and possible that he enclosed it in Letter
No. 148. Although he left Germany in June, his admonition to Caroline Doane in
the last line to write "Before the 1st of December" need not invalidate this theory,
for Longfellow thought as late as May that he would finish out the year at Göttingen.
3. Obviously a reference to a Mrs. Fox — possibly to Mrs. Eunice Fox (d. 1837),
a friend of Zilpah Longfellow.

150. *To Stephen Longfellow*

Göttingen   May 15 1829.

My dear Father,

I have employed [a part of] [1] the College vacation to make a journey
through the Country of the Rhine — and visit London. I thought it
best to do this at a time when there were no lectures here — in order
to enable me to pursue them to the end of the course this summer,
which I could not have done, had I postponed visiting England. I
hoped, too, to find Judge Preble in London — and to learn from him
something with regard to my prospects on my return. In this I was
however disappointed. I am now very much occupied with my studies
— but unfortunately there are no lectures on modern literary history.
The courses I attend are Wen[d]t [2] on "Natural Law." Heeren on
"Ancient History" — and a third on "Modern History" by the same.
This occupies three hours of the day. The remainder is occupied in

study of the language — under the guidance of an able professor: and in pursuing other branches of mod. literature. I am also writing a book — a kind of Sketch Book of sce‖nes in‖ France, Spain, and Italy — one volume of which I hope to get finished this Summer. This is what I spoke of [in my]¹ last letter;³ I hope by it to prove that I *have not* wasted my time: though I have no longer a very high opinion of my own prudence or my own talents. The farther I advance the more I see to be done — and the less time to do it in. The more, too, am I persuaded of the charlatanism of literary men. For the rest — my fervent wish is — and long has been, to return home. I would not remain a moment, were it not from the persuasion of its necessity: — but the German language is beyond measure difficult — not to read — no — that is not so hard: — but to write it — and one must write, and write correctly, too, in order to teach. I can only promise you to do my best. I can most assuredly lay a good foundation — and much more I cannot expect to do. If I can have the Professorship at Bow. Coll. — I should like it — but I must have it on fair grounds: — with the same privileges as the other professors. No state of probation — and no calling me a boy — and retrenching my salary. That was a very unlucky attempt at Economy. In my last letter, I wrote you with regard to the Books for B.C. Have you received it?⁴

With my most affectionate remembrances to all my friends — I remain most affectionately

your Son

Henry W. Longfellow

Preble is very well — and very studious. We keep house together — breakfast and dine together — and attend the same lectures.

MANUSCRIPT: Longfellow Trust Collection. ADDRESS: Stephen Longfellow Esq.—/ Portland. U.S. of/America./Aux Soins de Messrs Welles &c[i]e./Rue Taitbout 24 à Paris/Per Sully. — [*in another hand*] POSTMARKS: NEW YORK JUL 14/ FORWARDED BY YR. OB. SERVT. WELLES & CO. PARIS/SHIP SIGNATURE (*on cover and on flap*): Henry W. Longfellow ENDORSEMENT: Henry to his Parents —/Gottingen. May 15. 1829 — /Re[c]d. July 17. — An[s]d. July 18. and 25

1. The words in brackets were added later in pencil.
2. Amadeus Wendt (1783–1836), philosopher and art critic.
3. There is no mention of this project in the preceding letter to Stephen Longfellow, written March 10, 1829 (No. 147). He may have referred to it in one of the letters from Dresden, now lost. This is the first notice in any of the surviving letters of his plans for *Outre-Mer*.
4. Letter No. 147.

151. *To Zilpah Longfellow* [1]

— Göttingen. May 15. 1829.

My dear Mother,

It is to day three years since I left America. In running my eye over this lapse of time, it seems to me more like an interlude in the drama of life, than a part of the play. My own part in this world's comedy is so connected with the parts my friends at home have to act on the same stage, that without their presence I am not sure of my own identity: — and hence I look upon this visit to Europe as a song sung between the acts: and I am sorry that some of the variations lately introduced have not gained me much applause. [2]

I have just returned to Göttingen from a journey through Flanders to London and back by the way of Holland. With a map you may easily trace my course. From Göttingen I went to Cassel — thence to Frankfort — and to Mayence. At Mayence I took the steamboat on the Rhine and descended the river as far as Cologne. You have heard of the beauties of the Rhine: for they are told in tales and sung in ballads. It is a noble river: but not so fine as the Hudson. The ruins of old castles and monasteries which look down upon it from every eminence along its banks, give it a most picturesque appearance. The most beautiful and sublime scene is at the Bingerloch — the "Highlands" of the Rhine. It is there the river makes its great bend. The Nahe empties into it at the same spot, — and at their junction stands the beautiful village of Bingen. The river rushes in shallow rapids round the bend, and below spreads out into a long silver sheet — over which looks the most beautiful ruin of the Rhine. It is the old castle of Vautsberg — and stands upon the edge of a rugged precipice several hundred feet high, overhanging the river. I never saw a more picturesque object: and seldom a more lovely view.

The Village of Bingen — at Bingerloch — from b[e]low the bend. [3]

From this little sketch you may get an outline of the scene. Farther down and directly opposite Coblentz stands the celebrated fortress of Ehrenbreitstein. From Coblenz to Cologne the river grows less and less interesting. Bonn is the "ultima Thule" of its beauties — and afterwards it loses itself in the sands and canals of Holland.

From Coblenz I went to Aix-la-Chapelle — renowned in ancient days as the Court of Charlemagne — in modern for its mineral waters and hot springs. From Aix to Brussels. Visited the field of Waterloo: and past a day in walking over the battle ground. But a description of all this must be postponed until we meet. I went through Lille to Calais — and took the Steamboat to Dover. The white cliffs of Dover were invelloped in fog, and it rained. I thought of poor King Lear, and the samphire gatherer who looked "no bigger than his head."[4] Rode to Canterbury the same evening. Canterbury is a very interesting old place. Its Cathedral is one of the finest in England. The Shrine of Thomas-à-Becket is there — so renowned for the pilgrimages of olden time. Chaucer you recollect sings them in his Canterbury tales.

What shall I say of London — of my own pilgrimages to Temple Bar — Eastcheap and Little Brittain! Indeed, I know not what to say. We will talk of these things hereafter.

If I hurry you along with too much speed — bear in mind, that I was also hurried along through scenes in which I would fain have lingered. I remained but a week in London, and then embarked for Rotterdam. From Rotterdam I made a tour through Holland — visiting Delft — the Hague — Leyden — Haarlem — Amsterdam and Utrecht: — and retur[n]ed to this place by way of Nimwegen, Düsseldorf, and Elberfeld. With Holland I was much delighted. There is something pleasingly novel in its canals, with rural bridges thrown over them — the quaint old-fas[h]ioned houses of small bricks — with gable ends, sloping roofs — and looking-glasses at the window — so placed that one may look up and down street, without moving from his chair: — whilst the tall tapering stone windmills, which flap their long wings high above the roofs and chimneys of every town and village, give a busy and stirring look to the landscape. I was pleased, too, with the happy look of the people. The Dutch women are not handsome: but they possess that beauty which springs from health and quiet peaceful life: — and I read an assurance of ease and plenty in the fair rotundity and bright buttons of the contented tradesman, whose golden face, like the round and ruddy phisiognomy of the sun on the sign of a village tavern, seemed to say "Good Entertainment here!"

Harlem I think the prettiest of the Dutch cities. It is celebrated for its Organ, which I had the good fortune to hear: and for its tulips — some of whose bulbs have been sold for 50 dollars — and in former days, if records be true, one single root was sold for 5000 dolls. This may be exaggerated: but it is a matter of history, that a rage for flowers was once so strong here, as to prove destructive to many a respectable family. The Organ has 8000 pipes — some of them 32 feet long.[5]

In the vicinity of Amsterdam stands the little village of Broek — peculiar as the strong hold of Dutch neatness. No carriages are permitted to enter: — and to prevent this, the streets are in most parts of the village too narrow to allow of it. They are rather paved pathways — run[n]ing along the banks of the canals — bordered on one side by trees — and on the other by cottages, constructed of wood, and sometimes grotesq[ue]ly painted. Little canals intersect them, crossed by wooden bridges. Each cottage has its little garden in front, fantastically arranged, with a paved or gravel walk around it, and a flower-pot in the center. It is a universal custom with the inhabitants to keep the front doors and front appartments of their cottages closed from one year's end to another. They go in at the back door — and occupy the back part of the house. The front door is never oppened except on great occasions — such as a baptism — or the melancholy event of death — or marriage.

I went into one of the finest houses — I mean into the kitchen, no farther. It was neat in extreme — the floor of marble — the cooking utensils as bright, as if never used — and even a brass stop-cock for water, covered with a piece of wood — to keep it from tarnishing when turned by the hand. The proprietor of this establishment is an Old Bachelor. I also visited the cow-house — and the dairy-woman's cottage. The family were all in their stocking feet — and their wooden shoes at the door! She showed me the "awful realm" of the front room. It was full of neat, quaint old furniture — a piramid of painted milk-pails and cheese tubs in the center — and a cheese-press, fantastically painted and gilded. The impregnable front door was barricaded with a round oaken table.

I have not time to give you a more particular account of this very interesting town. I was exactly a month absent: and now that lectures have begun again — I am so very busy — that I have hardly a moment for writing letters. But not having written for a month, I must not be longer silent.

With love to all — and hoping of my Sister's entire recovery,[6] I am most affectionately

your Son
Henry.

MANUSCRIPT: Longfellow Trust Collection.

1. Enclosed in Letter No. 150.

2. Longfellow refers to the fact that some of his decisions — in particular his long sojourn in Italy — had not been approved by his father. See *Young Longfellow*, p. 142.

3. Longfellow's sketch follows, with locations marked for the "Castle of Ehrenfells," the "Castle of Vautsberg," the "Road to Coblenz," and the "Rapids of Bingerloch." See Plate V.

4. *King Lear*, IV, vi, 17.

5. Longfellow exaggerates when describing the famous Groote Kerk organ. Constructed in 1735–1738 by Christopher Müller, it has 3 keyboards, 60 stops, and 5000 pipes.

6. Elizabeth Longfellow had died ten days before this letter was written (see 139.5).

152. *To George Washington Greene*

Paris   June 18. 1829

Dear Greene,

I write you two lines — no more — merely to say good bye. I was obliged to leave Göttingen, on account of letters from home requiring my return. My parents think I have been long enough absent, and in addition to this by my last news, I learn that one of my sisters is dangerously sick. I was at London in May — and soon after my return to Göttingen, I received this unpleasant intelligence. Attribute to no other reasons than these my long silence. I had intended to write you very minutely respecting the University of Göttingen — but I have now no time — being hurried to death. I can only say — do not on any account omit studying there — if your health will permit. I never saw so great advantages for a student, — and living is moderate.

Day before yesterday evening I was at General Lafayette's soirèe. All the family spoke very affectionately of you — and wished to know why you did not come to France again.

I shall write to Mr. Cook[e] by the same post that brings you this — presuming you are both in Florence, as I have been told you are.

And so — good bye: — do not study *too* hard: and let me hear from you as soon as possible in Portland. Wishing you all success in studies — and good health — and *good spirits* — and good friends — I say farewell. I shall expect a visit from you as soon as you return to the United States: dont forget it. Good bye.

Very affectionately Yours
Henry W. Longfellow.

MANUSCRIPT: Longfellow Trust Collection. ADDRESS: À Monsieur/Monsieur George W. Greene./Poste Restante/à Florence. POSTMARKS: 18 JUN 1829/ 29 GIUGNO 1829/C.F.4.R/PONT BEAUVOISIN

153. *To Stephen Longfellow*

New York   11 of August   1829

My dear Father,

I have the pleasure of informing you of my safe return to my native land: which I reached this afternoon about 5 o'clock. I found the Constellation about to sail: — and met Uncle Alexander — who told me that he should set sail tomorrow. I breakfast with him on board.[1] Aunt Louisa is at Portsmouth. So much for news — if it be news to you.

I shall be with you as soon as possible — in about seven or eight days — I think. Of course the melancholy news contained in your last letter,[2] which reached me at Paris — makes me still more anxious to reach home.

My health is very robust. I shall write again from Boston.

Most affectionately yrs
Henry.

MANUSCRIPT: Longfellow Trust Collection.   ADDRESS: Hon. Stephen Longfellow./ Portland.   POSTMARK: NEW YORK AUG 12

1. Capt. Wadsworth had recently been made commanding officer of the *Constellation,* assigned to the Mediterranean squadron.

2. Informing Longfellow of the death of his sister Elizabeth.

154. *To Stephen Longfellow*

[Boston] August 17. 1829.

My dear Father,

I am now in Boston — am well — and shall be in Portland on Thursday. All friends here are well. They insist upon it that I am Professor at Bowdoin. I hear a great deal of news from all quarters — particularly of our own family. I was at Mrs. Derby's last night. Mr. D. says you are all well — and with this assurance I bid you farewell until Thursday. Very affectionately

Your Son
Henry.

MANUSCRIPT: Longfellow Trust Collection.

PART THREE

PROFESSOR AT BOWDOIN COLLEGE

1829–1835

PROFESSOR AT BOWDOIN COLLEGE

1 8 2 9 – 1 8 3 5

Upon his return to America, Longfellow entered upon his duties as professor of modern languages at Bowdoin College, a position that he held for the next six years. During this time he did his first serious work as a scholar, published his first poetic translations as well as his first extensive work in prose, became the husband of the fragile Mary Storer Potter, and began to seek wider horizons for his talents than the isolated college could afford. He also wrote some 268 known letters, of which 149 have been recovered for this collection.

It is clear from this third group of letters that Longfellow now devoted himself to scholarship with a new purposefulness, aware of the necessity of displaying his superiority before students who in some instances were nearly as old as he. The preparation of textbooks for his classes sharpened his French, Spanish, and Italian; and his essays for the *North American Review* on the "Origin and Progress of the French Language," the "History of the Italian Language and Dialects," and the "Spanish Language and Literature" carried his name beyond Brunswick and impressed his contemporaries with the scope of his researches. Longfellow soon discovered that a scholarly reputation would be the best means of taking him toward the brighter worlds of Boston and New York. Pushed by the desire to act in a larger limelight, he bought and borrowed books, read late into the night, and developed from a promising to a reputable scholar. Later critics, with more training and less knowledge, have not always been kind to this accomplishment. Although it may be admitted that Longfellow never became a formidable scholar by modern standards, he was certainly a distinguished one when judged by the standards of his own day. To George Ticknor, indeed, his knowledge of the Romance languages and literatures seemed "extraordinary."

In the meantime, Longfellow indulged his interest in imaginative literature by occasional experiments in poetry and prose. Most of these efforts were modest — a poem for the Harvard Phi Beta Kappa Society and a handful of contributions to parlor magazines and gift books. With *Coplas de Manrique,* however, a thin volume of skillfully turned poems from the Spanish, he displayed for the first time between covers his rare gifts as a translator. Although the book now has more bibliographical than literary

319

value, in it he developed the techniques that he later employed to achieve some of the most sensitive translations in the language. With *Outre-Mer,* on the other hand, he revealed no more than a derivative talent. This unabashed offspring of the *Sketchbook* clearly exhibits those tendencies of his mind — sentimentality, antiquarianism, gentle humor, romantic melancholy, and reverence for European culture — that remained always a part of his creative nature. His predilection during this period for translating and for Irvingesque romancing is not difficult to explain. His sensitive mind had not yet received the compelling stimulus of deep personal emotion; until it did, he remained an imitative author who practiced primarily with verbal skills and borrowed passions.

Unfortunately, the role of Mary Storer Potter (1812-1835) in Longfellow's emotional life is only vaguely suggested by the letters of this period. Longfellow describes her virtues in a formal letter to her father on the occasion of his engagement, but refers to her infrequently during the four years of their life in Brunswick. Although known for her gentle manners and translucent beauty, Mary Potter was by no means as remarkable a woman as Longfellow's second wife, Fanny Appleton; and one suspects that his playful epithet for her, "Little Mary," was inspired more by a sentimental affection than by a rich, deep-seated love. In any event, he deprived us of the details of his courtship and his first years with his young wife by burning her journals after her death, together with any love letters that they may have exchanged.

The years in Brunswick seemed long to Longfellow, despite the pleasures of marriage and the excitement of seeing his first books through the press. To one who had thrived in the capitals of Europe, the little town with its uncomplicated social life and its bitter winters seemed provincial and dull. Shortly after establishing his bride in a boarding house, he began to plot an escape to a larger stage, convinced that Bowdoin College could not contain his talents nor his ambition. The Brunswick letters show how, in desperate succession, he considered the notion of founding a girls' school in New York, coveted the position of secretary of legation in Madrid, bargained for the Round Hill School in Northampton, inquired after a position at the University of Virginia, and in a final reckless gesture formally applied for a professorship without salary at New York University. In the meantime, while he dreamed and schemed, his reputation as a scholar found its way to President Josiah Quincy of Harvard College.

On December 1, 1834, President Quincy offered to nominate Longfellow for the office of Smith Professor of Modern Languages, to succeed George Ticknor, and suggested at the same time that he might wish to spend a year or eighteen months abroad, at his own expense, "for the purpose of a more perfect attainment of the German." Although he permitted himself the small luxury of negotiation, Longfellow decided at once to accept the providential opportunity to escape Brunswick and, as an added fillip, to return to the wells of knowledge in Europe. During his last hurried months at Bowdoin he parried the arguments of those who would dissuade him from traveling, sold his furniture and some of his books to increase his ready money, and agreed to chaperone through Europe his wife's good friends Mary Caroline Goddard and Clara Crowninshield. On April 10, 1835, the little party of four sailed from New York for England, and Longfellow's first experience with deep, personal tragedy began.

155. *To William Allen*

Portland   August 27. 1829.

Dear Sir

Your letter to my father, dated Sept. 26, 1828, and enclosing a copy of the vote of the Trustees and Overseers of Bowdoin College, by which they have elected me Instructer of the Modern Languages in that institution, has been duly handed me.

I am sorry, that under existing circumstances, I cannot accept the appointment. The Professorship of Modern Languages, with a salary equal to that of the other Professors, would certainly not have been refused. But having at great expense, devoted four years to the acquisition of the French, Spanish, Italian, and German, languages, I cannot accept a subordinate station with a salary so disproportionate to the duties required.

I have the honor to be, Sir,

Very respectfully Your Obt. Ser[v]t.

Henry W. Longfellow.

Revd. Wm. Allen D. D.
President of Bowd. Coll.

MANUSCRIPT: Bowdoin College Library. ADDRESS: Revd Wm Allen, D.D./President of Bowd. Coll./Brunswick POSTMARK: PORTLAND ME AUG 27 PUBLISHED: *Young Longfellow*, pp. 147–148.

156. *To Ebenezer Everett*

Brunswick, Sept. 2, 1829.

Eben[eze]r Everett, Esq.
Dear Sir,

In answer to your communication this morning, announcing to me the vote of the Trustees and Overseers of Bowdoin College, by which I have been elected Professor of Modern Languages in that institution,

I have the honor of informing you — that I willingly accept the appointment — with the understanding that my salary shall at some future day be made equal to that of the other professors.

> Respectfully Your Obt. Servt.
> Henry W. Longfellow.[1]

MANUSCRIPT: Bowdoin College Library. ADDRESS: Ebenezer Everett, Esq./Secretary of the Trustees/of Bowdoin College/Brunswick

1. For facts and commentary concerning Longfellow's appointment to the Bowdoin faculty, see *Life*, I, 178–179, and *Young Longfellow*, pp. 147–148 and 377–378.

157. *To Mary Longfellow*

> Bowdoin College. Sunday. Oct 8th [1829]

My dear Sister Mary,

In answer to your billet, ||I must|| say, that you had better pursue french at presen||t, as I|| *have the books necessary.* I should however pref||er Mr.|| Giradot as an instructor — to any other person, ||as he is|| a Frenchman.[1] With regard to Mr. Furbish's pronunciation, I know nothing — never having heard ||him speak.|| Do not buy a new grammar. I will send ||you one|| soon — which you will find much simpler than those generally in use. I advise you to study French. You will no doubt be much pleased with it: and will make great progress in it.

My love to all. I shall write sister Anne very soon — but to-day I have not time.

> Very affectionately yours
> Henry W. Longfellow.

MANUSCRIPT: Longfellow Trust Collection. ADDRESS: To/Miss. Mary Longfellow./Portland.

1. F. Girardot taught French in both Boston and Portland. Nothing more is known of him.

158. *To Alexander Slidell [Mackenzie]*

> Bowdoin College   Oct. 15. 1829.

Dear Slidell,

I trust to your friendship to pardon my long silence, after having promised you, as I held your hand at parting, to write you immediately.[1] You will find my apology in what I am now about to say of myself. Having concluded to accept my appointment as Prof. at this College, I was sometime busy in making the necessary arrangements for taking up my abode here: which arrangements, together with visiting of friends in town and country — completely consumed the vacation: and since the commencement of the term I have been very much occupied — as the business of instruction is new to me, and I have also the charge of the Library, which occupies one hour every day. You know very well how the little ever[y]day occurrences of life are linked into each other, so as to form one long continued chain; — and though every[2] one of them separately is insignificant, yet all together make up no small portion of our existance. Besides after having corrected upwards of forty exercises from Levisac's grammar[3] — which I have to do daily — I hate the sight of pen ink and paper.

I am also very busy in translating an elementary grammar from the French — intended for my own use as instructer here — and for the use of Schools. It is already in a state of forwardness — and I shall put it to press without delay. I will send you a copy as soon as it is out.

Your book on Spain is very much admired here.[4] It makes me, however, very melancholy when I read it, for open where I will, I find something unknown to me before. I was as long in Spain as you were — enjoyed the same advantages whilst there — and now having before my eye a record of what you did, and the information you collected there, I feel rather sad, that I should have effected so little, where you have effected so much: for instead of a treasure of useful and valuable information, such as you have brought away from Spain, I have only dreamy sensations, and vague recollections of a sunny land. I quarrel with myself everyday for not having seen more Bullfights — and sometimes fret myself into a fever for not having been hard-hearted enough to see the tragedies of the Plaza de Cebada.[5] Nothing, which I omitted seeing, but now rises up in judgement against me: and I shall erelong be driven back to Spain in despair.

How unstable and precarious an acquisition is that of the languages! I refer to the facility of speaking them. My foothold is slip[p]ing from under me daily: and it is a subject on which I feel pretty sensitive *now*: having placed myself in a situation peculiarly liable to animadversion. The only consolation I have is that at some future day I shall be forced to go back to Europe again for nobody in this part of the world pretends to speak anything but English — and some might dispute them even that prerogative.

I am a little in the "pensoroso" to night||, so|| farewel[l]. I must turn from the indulgence of friendly recollections to wallowing in the mire of Levisac: — or rather I should say to the contemplation of such sublime truths as "L'âme de l'homme, sans culture, est comme un diamant brut!"[6] — and so to the end of the chapter.

Write soon — and let me know what you are doing and what you mean to do this winter — and whether I may indulge the hope of seeing you at the North.

Very affectionately your friend

Henry W. Longfellow. —

Remember me if you please to Irving and Berdan.[7] They will hear from me before long.

MANUSCRIPT: Longfellow Trust Collection. ADDRESS: Lieut. Alexander Slidell/ United States' Navy/New York. POSTMARK: BRUNSWICK MAINE. OCT. 19 PUBLISHED: *Young Longfellow*, pp. 150–151.

1. Longfellow had presumably seen Slidell in New York in August.

2. The word "every," in pencil, is substituted for "each" (deleted).

3. Lecoutz de Lévizac, *A Theoretical and Practical Grammar of the French Tongue* (London, 1799). There were subsequently many editions, both English and American.

4. *A Year in Spain*. By a Young American (Boston, 1829).

5. A reference to the execution of criminals in the Plazuela de la Cebada in Madrid. For a detailed description, see *A Year in Spain*, I, 268–281.

6. "The soul of man, without cultivation, is like a diamond in the rough." Lévizac's *Grammar*, Chap. II.

7. In 1826 in Paris, Longfellow had met Pierre Irving (1803–1876), the nephew of Washington Irving, and his friend James Berdan, now practicing law in New York.

---

159. *To Stephen Longfellow*

Bowdoin College

Saturday Night. Oct. 15.[1] 1829.

My dear father,

I sent a letter to Alexander on Wednesday by Doctor Parsons,[2] who was good enough to offer his services, if I had any commands for Portland. In that letter, I stated all that seemed necessary with regard to Alexander's coming to Brunswick:[3] and hope he will answer it soon.

All goes on very well except my great lamp, which leads me into a great deal of temptation and oil. The little entry lamp answers my purpose so well that I wish you woul||d sen||d me two more of the kind, for my room: — a little handso||mer if|| you should see any, though the same kind will do very well. They will give more light, and be less troublesome than the present unwieldy thing. I should like also a small fender, for my fire-place: — our wood here is all dry, and snaps in the fire; so that without something of the kind I shall lose my carpet.

I shall publish my grammar soon.[4] An edition of 500 Copies will cost about $72.00 — including paper.

$$
\begin{array}{lll}
\text{The type-work will cost} - \$45.00 \\
\text{press-work} \quad " \quad " \quad " \quad 7.00 \\
\text{Paper (5 reams)} \quad " \quad \quad "20.00 \\
\hline
\quad \quad \quad \quad \quad \quad \quad \quad \$72.
\end{array}
$$

With great love to all, I am

very affectionately yours
Henry W. Longfellow

Be kind enough to send me the address of Wm. Browne.

MANUSCRIPT: Longfellow Trust Collection. ADDRESS: Stephen Longfellow Esq/ Portland. POSTMARK: BRUNSWICK MAINE. OCT. 19

1. Saturday was October 17.
2. Presumably Edwin Parsons, a surgeon-dentist of Portland. The letter referred to is unrecovered.
3. Alexander spent two years at Bowdoin, 1830–1832. In the April, 1833, catalogue he is listed as a student in the Medical School, but he abandoned this career to become his uncle's private secretary. See 240.2. In 1889 Bowdoin gave him an honorary A.M.
4. *Elements of French Grammar; By M. Lhomond, Professeur-Erémite in the University of Paris. Translated from the French, with Notes, and such Illustrations as were thought necessary for the American Pupil. For the Use of Schools.* By an Instructor (Samuel Colman, Portland; Griffin's Press, Brunswick; 1830).

160. *To Stephen Longfellow*

Bowdoin College.
Saturday Evening   October 24. 1829.

My dear father,

I had the pleasure of duly receiving yours of the 21st inst. I have spoken with Mrs. Barnes on the subject of Alexander's board.[1] She says she will take him at $1.75 per week, not including washing which will amount to 12½ more per week: making in all $1.87½. I should object to his boarding at Common's Hall: because the students generally discuss College Affairs and College Officers pretty freely there, and they would not probably wish to have the brother of a College Officer among them. On the same account the situation would be disagreable to Alexander. I am however very desirous to have him here. I want him to instruct me in gymnastics, of which exercise I stand much in need: and to which I can devote a half-hour every morning as well as not, when the Students are at recitation: their Apparatus being now put under cover.

With regard to my book, I do not think your view of the subject correct. In the first place, it is not a work of my own compiling; but a grammar, which has long been in universal use throughout France as a schoolbook — and which has been recommended by Mr. Gallatin [2] as the best grammar in use. So that in regard to reputation, I risk nothing, for the work is a translation — and what notes I myself shall add will be only some principles taken from other grammars, to supply what is wanting in mine in order to adapt it to the understanding of the American pupil.

You say there is no immediate urgency for such a work. I think there is. The study of french is now going extensively into the course of studies pursued in all our Schools and Academies: even in our country schools — as for example *here,* and in the town of China. An elementary book is wanted: — for all existing grammars are too large — excepting Mr. Fowle's of Boston, which is too small.[3] Upon this point M. L'Hommond, my author says: "We have already good *French Grammars*: but I doubt whether the same can be said of the abridgements which have been made for beginners." He further says: "Engaged in the duties of public instruction for twenty years, I have been so placed as to make children my study, to measure their strength, and to feel what is adapted to their capacities. It is this knowledge, which only experience can give, that has determined me to compose this elementary work."

You perceive I do not translate the work with particular reference to College Students: though I shall probably introduce it at some future day. Nor is its being adapted to the capacities of children an objection: for let a man be as old and as learned in other things as you please — yet when he begins a language — of which he knows nothing, he is a child. We often over-reach ourselves by reaching too far.

The expense, on calculation, I find will not be so much as you anticipate. The books would be bound in boards with cambric backs. I have spoken with our book binder, who offers to do them at 6 cents a piece. I think Mr. Colman [4] will be able to get them done for five cents a piece. So that the whole expense may be reckoned at $115.00. For the paper, and probably for the binding, I can have 6 months credit: for the rest, I should choose to pay forthwith.

The book is now ready for the press: and after taking into consideration what I have stated above, I think you will not object to proceeding with it.

With regard to the fender, I will try to do without it for the present: my old tin one must answer. The book[s] arrived safely: and Uncle

Tony [5] is paid, for them and furniture. The cost of Mr. Packard's Books will be about $17.00.

With kind remembrances to Mama, Marianne [6] etc etc etc

Most Affectionately Yrs.
Henry W. Longfellow.

MANUSCRIPT: Longfellow Trust Collection.   ADDRESS: Stephen Longfellow Esq./ Portland.

1. Mrs. Barnes was Longfellow's landlady in Brunswick.

2. Albert Gallatin (1761–1849), the statesman and linguist.

3. William B. Fowle, *The French Accidence, or Elements of French Grammar* (Boston, 1828).

4. Samuel Colman, a Portland bookseller and publisher, brought out Longfellow's early grammars and readers. He later removed to New York, where in 1839 he published *Hyperion*. He was the father of Samuel Colman (1832–1920) the landscape painter.

5. Presumably an expressman.

6. Marianne Preble (1812–1888), daughter of Judge Preble, later married Longfellow's brother Stephen.

161. *To Stephen Longfellow*

Bowdoin College. Decemb. 20. 1829

Dear Sir,

Our examinations are atlength over, and the College closed. I now occupy Dr. Welles's room at Mrs. Barnes's, near Prof. Cleaveland's — where I intend to pass a greater part of the vacation. The reasons which induce me to do this, in stead of passing the winter with you, as my intention was when I last saw you, are very simple ones, but such as I did not anticipate three weeks since.

The Executive government have thought it advisable to introduce some considerable changes into the proposed plan of studies for the year, upon which plan we have acted thus far. The new arrang[e]-ment puts a hard-laboring oar into my hands, and will give me three [1] recitations per day, besides the hour occupied in the Library.

The Junior Class will as usual recite French every afternoon. The Seniors will have three recitations a week in French — and three in Spanish — at noon. The Sophomore class will recite French every morning. This, you perceive, gives me three recitations per diem. through the week, saturday afternoons excepted. Besides this, I am to have a private lesson in German: and the prospect before me seems thick-sown with occupations, promising me little leisure for my private studies, which on account of my busy life the last term, already begin to assume a retrograde march. Before closing this catalogue, I must add, that I have also an Inaugural Address to write for next term, and a Poem before the Phi Beta at Commencement.[2]

What detains me in Brunswick at the present moment is my Grammar, which is not yet from under the press. The notes and additions have rendered it larger than I anticipated, and the trouble of correcting Griffin's[3] proofs, is not to be expressed in words. This, however, does not discourage me from engaging further in the same occupation. Among the French books in the Library, I have just found a few volumes, which have pleased me so much and are so much what is wanted for a text-book, that I have concluded to make a selection from them, for the use of my pupils, and such other scholars as may want.[4] The Book is intended for those who are already a little advanced in the language, and who wish for a manual of polite conversation on familiar topics. The work from which I make the selection is a collection of Dramatic Proverbs, or small plays, such as are performed in Paris by ladies and gentlemen in private society. The book is so exactly what we stand in need of, that I am only surprised that something of the kind has not appeared before. I need not tell you, how delighted I am with the idea of having found this treasure. The more I see of the life of an instructer the more I wonder at the course generally pursued by teachers. They seem to forget, that the youthful mind is to be *interested* in order to be instructed: or at least they overlook the means, by which they may best lead on the mental faculties, at an age when amusement is a more powerful incitement than improvement. In proof of this, look at the text books generally in use. What are they? Extracts from the best and most polished writers of the nation; food for maturer minds: but a fruit that hangs beyond[5] the reach of children, and those whom[6] ignorance of a foreign language puts on the same footing with children. But the little collection of dramas, which I now propose to publish, unites all the simplicity, and ease of conversation, with the interest of a short comedy, whose point turns upon some humorous situation in com[m]on life, and whose plot illustrates some familiar proverb, which stands at its head by way of motto.

I think you cannot but approve my plan, which can better be discussed face to face than in a letter. For my own part, I am so much engrossed with the idea, that for the present I should be ill at ease anywhere but just where I am. I shall, however, pay you a visit as soon as I get my grammar finished, if the roads should then be in a good state for travelling.

I wrote Dr. Nichols a few days since, and sent him the outline of a Prospectus for the new Female High School, which I drew up at his request. I hope they do not mean to let the subject die. If you should see Mr. Furbish, pray assure him from me, that I have the matter as much at heart as ever.[7]

If my creditors are clamorous, I will send you money per. post: if not, I will bring it with me when I come. When does Mr. Daveis leave for Europe: I shall wish to send a few letters, if agreable to him.[8]

Your affectionate Son
Henry W. Longfellow.

MANUSCRIPT: Longfellow Trust Collection. ADDRESS: Stephen Longfellow Esq./ Portland. POSTMARK: BRUNSWICK MAINE. DEC 21

1. The word "three," in pencil, is substituted for "four" (deleted).

2. For unknown reasons, Longfellow did not deliver this poem. He called his inaugural address the "Origin and Growth of the Languages of Southern Europe and of their Literature." It was delivered on September 2, 1830, and published at Brunswick in 1907.

3. Joseph Griffin (1798–1874), Brunswick bookseller and printer.

4. This selection became his *Manuel de Proverbes Dramatiques* (Samuel Colman, Portland; Griffin's Press, Brunswick; 1830).

5. The word "beyond," in pencil, is substitued for "without" (deleted).

6. The word "whom," in pencil, is substitued for "that" (deleted).

7. The Female High School of Portland became a reality some months later, with James Furbish as preceptor and Ichabod Nichols and Stephen Longfellow, among others, as trustees. See the *Portland Directory and Register for 1832.*

8. Charles S. Daveis left New York on January 11, 1830, as a special agent to present evidence to the king of the Netherlands, the arbitrator in the Maine boundary dispute between the United States and Great Britain. Nothing is known of the letters Longfellow sent by him.

162. *To Stephen Longfellow, Jr.*[1]

Bowd: Coll: Decemb 23rd. 1829.

My dear Brother,

You see by the date of this, that I am still in the shades of Pejepscot. Contrary to my inclinations and my intentions, I am obliged to pass the winter vacation here; the reasons, which induce me so to do, you will find in the sequel of this letter.

A few moments since I received a letter from home informing me that Mr. Daveis would leave Portland day-after-tomorrow-evening. You see there is no time for parlay: and though driven to the top of my speed by proof-sheets of my grammar, and watched over by the eye of the guardian *Griffin* of the East, I must steal a few moments to prepare my part of the *budget,* and to wish you and Marianne a happy-new Year.[2]

My daily avocations are too well known to you to need a recapitulation, though true, the vacation has stepped in, and taken the weight of recitations from my shoulders. Still I am chained to the oar. You know that I am literally "un homme á Projets" [a schemer] — and that for the moment I ride my hobby pretty hard. I am now engaged in two grand designs, which with their subordinate branches and ramifications keep my imagination active and serve as a catholicon for ennui, etc. The first is in aiding and abetting the establishment of a grand High School for Young Ladies, at Portland: in which Furbish is to teach the usual English studies: Geradot, the French: Señor Correa,[3] (a Spaniard, friend of Geradot) the Spanish: and Nolcini, Italian and Music. Such is a rough outline of the plan, which I leave it to your own imagination to fill up, premising only, that you must do it so as to promote the public weal in the best and cheapest manner.

But what I am most particularly engaged in at present is the publication of a collection of French Plays, for the use of Colleges and Schools. It is merely a compilation, from some books in the College Library, and my only labor will be to select, and afterwards to correct the press and the orthography, which is a little antiquated. They are all Comedies, and very short, and to me amusing: — full of easy flowing conversation: — and abounding, of course, in colloquial phrases and familiar turns of expression. The best of the joke is, that I have fully persuaded myself, that the book is a "desideratum," and that by publishing it, I am going to benefit the world at large. This may be an illusion: but at all events, I shall benefit myself and my pupils; for every artist works best with his own tools. As soon as the book works its way through the press, I shall improve the first opportunity to send you a copy; and you will then be able to judge for yourself.[4]

News. So short a period has elapsed since you left us, that I shall not be able to communicate anything very new, or worthy of note. Whatever little matters there may be, I shall note down without order. Imprimis: Wyatt, the bookseller, shot himself through the heart with a pistol-ball. Cooly and deliberately done: after taking off his coat and seating himself upon the bed.[5] Item: Peter O'Slender (Alden) has written an angry letter to the President, published in the Androscoggin free Press: because in inviting the communicants on Sunday, instead of the customary phraseology of "all members of other Churches, *in regular Standing:*" he said "all members of other churches, *in fellowship with* this." O'Slender is becoming quite a notorious scribbler: and he always dips his pen in gall. With one dash he has almost annihilated Deacon Perry: saying that he mixed New England rum with W.I. and sold it for Santa Cruz.[6]

Item. Will Howard is engaged to Miss. Page of Hallowell: [7] so the story goes. And I believe that is all. No: they have voted *not* to form a City Government in Portland: and that closes my short Catalogue. The rest of my letter I shall fill up with congratulations on your (supposed) safe arrival: for no tidings good or bad have yet reached us. Whatever Ideas you may have formed of Europe in general, and of Holland in particular, the reality will if anything outstrip them. You may sometimes sigh after New England, and I know Marianne will, but the advantages within your reach are certainly cheaply purchased at the price of a little home-sickness and a few misgivings of the heart. I dare say *she* wished herself back, fifty times over, before she was half across the sea: but I presume you are made of sterner stuff. I shall be very impatient to hear from you, and to know how you are pleased with the Hague and the Opera: whether they suit your humour or whether "Galleo cared for none of these things." [8]

The enclosed letters you will be kind enough to send to the post: and pray dont forget to ask if anything must be paid on them. You may have some letters from Spain directed to your care for me. If you see Ned [Preble], greet him cordially from me, and tell him a letter from him would be looked upon in this latitude as a very particular favour.

Of family affairs you will have abundant intelligence from other sources. For my own part I am as ignorant of them as you are. Amongst all the gaieties and magnificence around you, dont forget, that there are those on this side of the water, whose good wishes are constantly with you, and who will always be happy in receiving the kind assurances of your friendship and remembrance, as often as leisure and inclination may prompt you to inform them of your outgoings and incomings. With my best regards to his Excellency — to Mrs. Preble: and in a word to one and all, I am your affectionate brother

Henry.

MANUSCRIPT: Longfellow Trust Collection. ADDRESS: Stephen Longfellow Jr. Esq./at the Hague./Holland.

1. After studying law with his father, Stephen took a position as private secretary to Judge William Pitt Preble, who had just been appointed ambassador extraordinary to the Hague. He left Portland early in December, 1829, and returned a year later.

2. Stephen was apparently engaged to Marianne Preble, whom he married in August, 1831.

3. According to an advertisement in the *Eastern Argus*, January 29, 1830, Correa Bottino offered instruction in Spanish and the use of the small sword at his academy on Church Street, Portland.

4. See 161.4.

5. Samuel D. Wyatt (1803–1829), a native of Portsmouth, operated a book

and stationery shop in partnership with John T. Robinson at 8 Mussey's Row, Middle Street, Portland. He committed suicide on December 15, 1829.

6. Peter O. Alden (1772–1843), a large and bulky Brunswick lawyer, had a reputation for irritability. The victim of his choler here was John Perry (1772–1846), a Brunswick businessman and deacon of the Congregational Church.

7. Records in the Maine Historical Society reveal that Capt. William A. Howard and Adelaide W. Page were married in Hallowell on May 24, 1832. Howard was a friend of the Longfellow family.

8. Acts 18:17.

163. To Zilpah Longfellow

Bowdoin College. January. 3rd. 1830

My dear Mother,

If you will turn to the last page of this letter you will find it there bears another date.[1] I was interrupted just as I was going to say, that I very seldom saw the day when I felt perfectly at leisure: and that consequently you ought not to be surprised if my letters were few, and my correspondence very irregular.

We have nothing very new here — excepting the year: — which I wish may be a happy one to you and the family. The weather has been very delightfully warm and Spring-like: but this afternoon we have all the usual prognostications of a snow-storm. I expect to be in Portland next Saturday: and if it snows before that day, perhaps the Misses Cleaveland[2] will come with me.

Very affectionately Your Son
Henry W. Longfellow.

MANUSCRIPT: Longfellow Trust Collection.   ENDORSEMENT: From HWL Brunswick/Jan and Feby 1830

1. This part of the letter is missing.
2. The daughters of Prof. Parker Cleaveland — Martha Ann (1812–1881), Elizabeth Abigail (1814–c.1880), and Mary Ackley (1816–1876).

164. To James Berdan

Portland   Jany. 4. 1830.

Dear Berdan,

This will be handed you by my friend Mr. J. Furbish of Portland, who will pass a few days in your city, on his way to Philadelphia. I shall be very much beholden to you, if you will devote a part of the leisure your professional avocations may leave you, to rendering Mr. F —— 's stay in New York pleasant to him.

Very sincerely your friend
Henry W. Longfellow.

MANUSCRIPT: Clifton Waller Barrett Collection, University of Virginia. ADDRESS: To/James Berdan Esq./New York./Presenting Mr. Furbish. ANNOTATION (*in another hand*): Please excuse Mr F. for not presenting this note in person. He is now at the Washington Hotel, and will call on Mr Berdan if possible, before leaving the city — F WORD UNDER ADDRESS: Present

165. *To Alexander Slidell [Mackenzie]*

Bowdoin College. Jany 7. 1830.

Dear Slidel[l],

I write merely to wish you a "happy New Year," and to tell you that thus far our New England winter rivals that of Italy. The buds are shooting from the trees: snow-storms have given place, it would seem, to "a babble of green fields": [1] — the air is soft and spring-like, and everyone exclaims, "Who ever saw such weather in January?" Mere animal life seems to be a luxury under such bright skies: — one feels happy even in existing. Under such genial influences, how can anyone help most cordially and sincerely wishing a happy new year to his absent friends. To be sure, in giving and receiving the congratulations of this season, there is nothing like the cheerful sound of friendly voices; they give them animation and a meaning: something seems to evaporate, when we come to put them down on paper; though a letter from a friend is very much like a good hearty shake of the hand, and what a man writes to an absent friend, is generally just what he would say to him were he present. Receive then, my good friend, this letter — a shake of the hand — and my very best wishes towards you in every way.

Have you seen the last North American? The review of your book was written by a Mr Phillips.[2] À-propos, your work has great celebrity in these parts, and my copy — which by the way, is the only one in town, is in great demand. People are very curious about the author: they want to know who you are — what you are — and where you are: and I assure you it is very gratifying to me to be able to say, in answer to their enquiries, "he's a friend of mine." What else I say is not for you to know. Let me ask you why more copies have not been sent this way?

For my own part, I am as when I last wrote you, pursuing the "even tenor of my way."[3] My Grammar is printed, and will soon be published. In the mean time, I am engaged in the publication of another book, which I intend to make one of my text-books in teaching french. It is a collection of small comedies in french, such as are performed in the Soirées of Paris. I hardly know what name I shall give it: perhaps "Manuel de Proverbes Dramatiques"; as "proverbes dramatiques" is the title of the whole collection from which I make the choise. What think you? I shall send you the "première livraison" with the grammar: for from necessity I shall be obliged to publish the work in parts, wanting it for immediate use in one of my classes. You cannot think what a book-making race we are here. All hands seem to have turned Compositors and pressmen. You know [4]

MANUSCRIPT: Massachusetts Historical Society.

1. Cf. *King Henry V*, II, iii, 17.
2. Willard Phillips (1784–1873) reviewed Slidell's *A Year in Spain* in the *North American Review*, XXX (January 1830), 237–259.
3. Cf. Gray, "*Elegy in a Country Churchyard*," stanza 19.
4. The manuscript is fragmentary. Some notion of the missing part may be had from Slidell's answer, dated February 20, 1830: "Your notices of Cortes, of Don Valentin, and Don Diego were all delightful to me . . . You say that you could tell me some stories of Don Valentin which would make me split with laughter."

166. *To George Barrell Cheever* [1]

Bowdoin College. March 13. 1830

Dear Sir,

A few days since I had the pleasure of receiving your pamphlet on the Indian Question.[2] This mark of your recollection was very grateful to me. I have perused the book with great pleasure: and am delighted to see you enter with so lively a zeal into the defence of a people upon whose rights we have already too often trampled. Permit me to take this occasion as an old friend to add my voice to the many that have already complimented you on your success as a writer: and to thank you for favouring me with a seat among worthier names in your "Readings in Poetry."[3] Be assured of my sincere friendship: and when you pass eastward again do not go through Brunswick without passing a day or two with me.

Very truly yours
Henry W. Longfellow.

MANUSCRIPT: American Antiquarian Society. ADDRESS: Mr. Geo. B. Cheever/ Theological Institution/Andover. POSTMARK: BRUNSWICK MAINE. MAR [13? 15?]

1. Cheever (1807–1890), who had been a member of Longfellow's class at Bowdoin, was at this time preparing himself for the ministry at the Andover Theological Seminary. He subsequently enjoyed a distinguished career as author, editor, and clergyman.
2. *The Removal of the Indians — an Article from the* American Monthly Magazine: *an Examination of an Article in the* North American Review, *and an Exhibition of the Advancement of the Southern Tribes in Civilization and Christianity* (Boston, 1830).

3. *Studies in Poetry* (Boston, 1830). Cheever included Longfellow's poems "The Indian Hunter" and "Woods in Winter" (see pp. 427–429).

167. *To Anne Longfellow*

Bowd. Coll. April 5. 1830.

My dear Sister Anne,

I avail myself of a moment's leisure before breakfast, to tell you that I am in the most flourishing state of health imaginable. I attribute it to my early rising and to drinking milk. Let me prescribe to you a remedy for lassitude far better than your dumb-bells — its a universal panacea — a true catholicon.

☞ You must rise with the sun — or to be uniform, at six o'clock: and as soon as you are out of bed take a tumbler of milk with an egg in it — which you must swallow whole. After this go and take a short walk, as much in the *shade* as possible. ☜

If you will have faith in me, and I speak from experience — you will find this exceedingly beneficial. Why, the person who rises early enjoys ten per cent more of life at this season, than he who drags himself down to breakfast at ten.

We have delightful weather here at present, and our streets are already quite dusty. How chearing the opening of Spring is — how many new rills of comfort begin to flow into one's heart! Love to all.

Very affectionately yours,
Henry.

P.S. Please send that cotton for the Grammars *by stage.*[1]

MANUSCRIPT: Longfellow Trust Collection. ADDRESS: Miss. Anne Longfellow./ Portland.

1. The words "or packet" have been deleted.

168. *To Mary Longfellow*

Bowdoin College. April 10. 1830.

My dear Sister Mary,

I have been intending to write you a few lines in answer to your last, ever since I received it, but have never been able to find leisure. I will not however let the present opportunity slip.

I am very sorry it is not in my power to go to Portland this afternoon with Mrs. McLellan,[1] but it would not be in my power to do it without neglecting my duties here, which you know will not answer. Next Saturday, however, I intend to make you a visit, if the roads improve. You must tell Alexander to come down for me on Friday afternoon — and we will go together on Saturday. I think I can make arrangements to stay with you until Monday morning — which will be much better than travelling Sunday afternoon.

The Exercises to my Grammar will soon be published — and so will the Book of Comedies. I shall send you and Ellen — a copy of each, as soon as they are finished.

I am waiting for the purple cotton to bind the Grammars in. Pray get it for me soon. It must be two thirds of a yard wide — otherwise it will cut very much to waste.

Dr. Wells is much better, and will doubtless soon be quite well.[2]

Give my love to all the pretty girls in Portland. Write me a long letter soon: and let me know how you go on in French. Ellen must do the same: for I wish very much to know if you find the Grammar an easy one — or if you like the other better.

Adelaide Wells[3] is expecting a letter from Samuel — which he must not fail to write soon.

What kind of cloth will make good curtains for my windows? How much do you think it will cost for three windows? And will you and Ellen make the curtains?

Very affectionately Your Brother
Henry.

You see, how I scribble — you must not imitate me.

MANUSCRIPT: Longfellow Trust Collection. ADDRESS: Miss. Mary Longfellow/ Portland./Kindness of Mrs McLellan

1. Mrs. Nancy Doane McLellan (1780–1867), Zilpah Longfellow's first cousin and the wife of Arthur McLellan, president of the Bank of Portland.

2. Longfellow was overly optimistic; Wells died of a rapid consumption on July 25.

3. The sister of Dr. John Doane Wells, Adelaide presumably nursed her brother during his last illness.

169. To George Washington Greene

Bowdoin College: Brunswick. April 13. 1830.

Dear Greene,

I received but a moment since yours of the 6th, which has just found its way from Portland: and to show you how much I value your early remembrance of me, I am determined that the post shall not leave town without bearing you my felicitations on your marriage and on your safe return home.[1] Of the latter of these events your letter gives me the first intelligence: of the former I was already aware, having seen it announced in the newspapers. Corpo di Bacco [what the deuce]?

It seems almost incredible that you should thus have got the start of me. I wish you all joy on the occasion: and am happy in believing that you are tenfold happier in your present condition than you could possibly be in any other.

> "The treasures of the deep are not so precious
> As are the concealed comforts of a man
> Lock'd up in woman's love." — [2]

For my own part, I am still a Bachelor: *where,* the date of this will inform you. I reached home in August last: and immediately entered upon my duties as Professor of Modern Languages in this College, where I drive a pretty extensive team, and where, my dear friend, I hope to have the pleasure of seeing you in the course of the summer, if leisure and inclination should lead you to think of travelling. You can hardly imagine how I long to talk over old times with you, and to converse of scenes we visited together, and of events concerning which we once said "hic [haec] olim meminisse juvabit." [3] I have also the greatest possible curiosity to see your better half, and to hear once more the gentle accents of a Roman tongue. Permit me to kiss the fair hand of your lady, and to express the wish that her life in New England may be as bright and cloudless as the skies of her own enchanting Italy.

I am exceedingly disposed to quarrel with you for writing me so short a letter, and for not saying a word about what you are at present engaged in. You have also most provokingly left me to imagine when you returned from Europe: otherwise I should not have been guilty of the "sproposito" [indiscretion] of asking you what you are now engaged in; for a moment's reflection would show me that, supposing you had just arrived, you were busy in receiving the eager congratulations of your friends.

Pray write me a deal about yourself soon — all the little minutia — if you a[re] fatter or thinner than formerly — what kind of a coat you wear — in a word, anything that can give the image of you as you are now, a local habitation in my imagination, and convince me of your personal identity with him, who used to tremble at the "mistral" in Marseilles, and grow pale at the Roman Sirocco.

You will not find me changed a hair's breadth. I do not find that the professorial chair has added a particle of dignity to my person, or magnified me a whit in my own eyes: [I may add in parenthesis — nor in those of any one else.] [4] Do you remain still in the intention of pursuing a profession similar to mine? It has a thousand charms: —

you would be delighted with it. When does Mr. Cooke return? Excellent man. I long to meet him once more. Dont forget to write something about him in your next, which I pray may not be long in coming. In the mean time believe me very sincerely your friend

Henry W. Longfellow.

P.S. You see it will be impossible for me to accept your kind invitation to visit you: but I must insist upon seeing you this way.

When I write you again I shall go more into particulars — and give you some more definite idea of my present situation and prospects.

MANUSCRIPT: Longfellow Trust Collection. ADDRESS: Mr. Geo: W. Greene./ East Greenwich/R. Island. POSTMARK: BRUNSWICK MAINE. APR 14

1. Greene had married Carlotta Sforzosi, a young Roman girl, in Paris on January 3, 1830 (*Vital Records of Rhode Island 1636-1850*, XVII [1908], 333-334), and had returned temporarily to his home in East Greenwich, Rhode Island.

2. Thomas Middleton, *Women Beware Women*, III, i, 84-86.

3. "It will be a pleasure to remember these things some day." *Aeneid*, I, 203.

4. Longfellow's brackets.

170. *To James Berdan*

Bowdoin College   April. 14. 1830.

My dear Friend,

I should have answered your very welcome Post[s]cript last week, as intimated in my letter to Pierre [Irving],[1] had I not been for the last four days half crazy with a tendency of blood to the head, to which I am occasionally subject. Our Spring developes itself so much by fits and starts — we have such sudden changes of weather — a climate so very capricious, that it is impossible for a nervous gentleman to keep his equilibrium: — and as my spirits vary with the barometer, I cannot promise myself in sitting down to write a letter, that I shall finish it in the same mood in which I begin it.

How very singular, that I should not have heard a word about Pierre's marriage?[2] I was ashamed to tell him so: but as he neglected to send me a newspaper, announcing the same, I cannot conceive that it was my fault. I hope you will never place me in a similar dilemma: at all events I will not place you in one. I say this because you manifest some anxiety upon the subject of my matrimonial speculations. Upon that subject you may set your heart at rest: for I am not a whit nearer "that Bourn etc"[3] — than when I last saw you. I must confess however, that the lively colours in which Pierre describes his happy lot — make me very discontented with my present inglorious estate, and I take this occasion to publish my manifesto, declaring my intention to

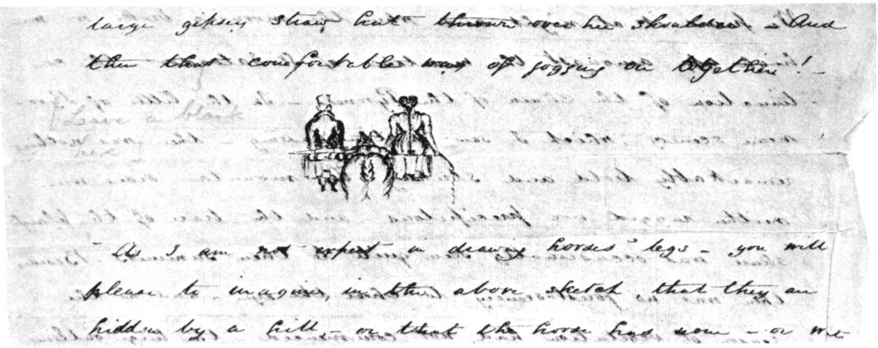

large gipsey straw hat thrown over her shoulders — And then that comfortable way of jogging on together! —

As I am not expert in drawing horses' legs — you will please to imagine, in the above sketch, that they are hidden by a hill — or that the horse has none — or

Sketch by Longfellow, Letter No. 114

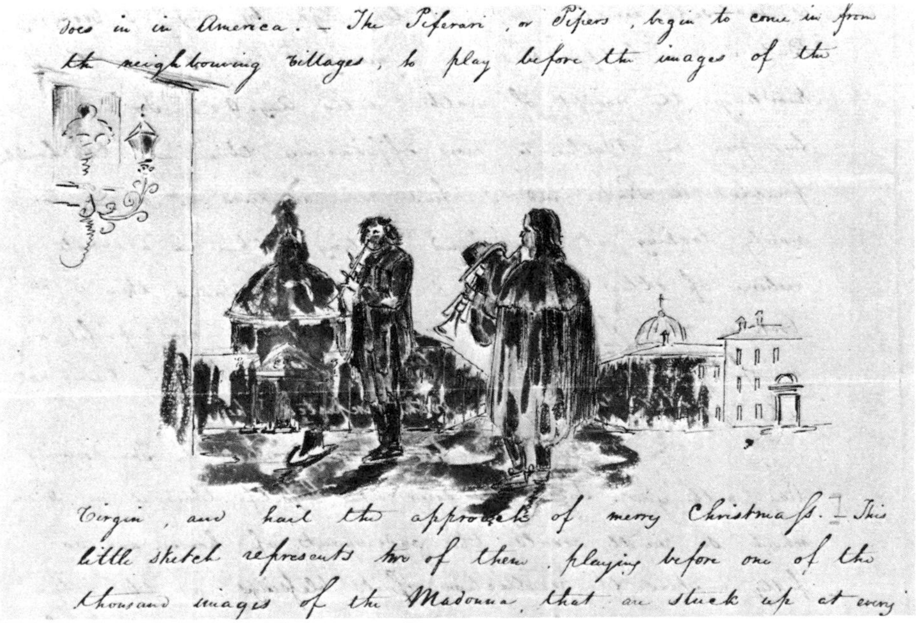

does in America. — The Piferari, or Pipers, begin to come in from the neighbouring villages, to play before the images of the

Virgin, and hail the approach of merry Christmass. — This little sketch represents two of them, playing before one of the thousand images of the Madonna, that are stuck up at every

Sketch by Longfellow, Letter No. 139

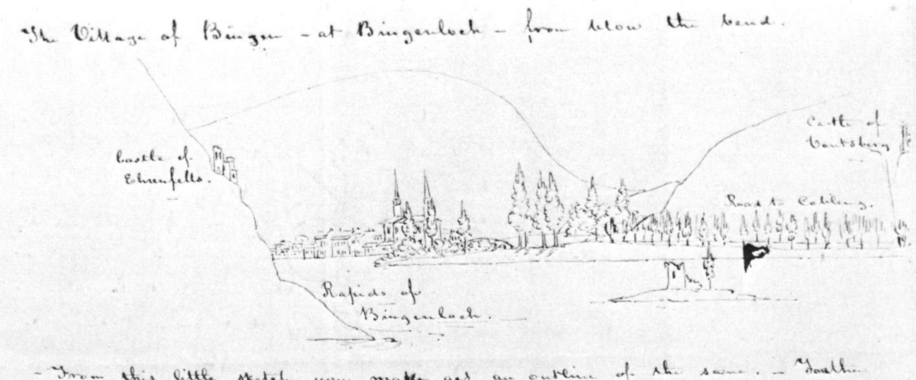

The Village of Bingen — at Bingenloch — from below the bend.

— From this little sketch you may get an outline of the same. — Farther down, and directly opposite Coblentz stands the celebrated fortress of Ehrenbreitstein.

Sketch by Longfellow, Letter No. 151

PLATE V

Mary Storer Potter Longfellow, c. 1830

PLATE VI

Longfellow, 1835, by Maria Christina Röhl

PLATE VII

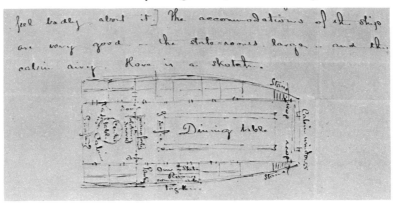

Caricature by Longfellow, Letter No. 232

Sketch by Longfellow, Letter No. 306

Heidelberg, 1836, Letter No. 348

PLATE VIII

enter into the holy alliance, as soon as circumstances shall permit me to commence negociations with the other party concerned. But I promise you at the same time, that this shall not interfere in the least with your visit in the summer, — upon which I count with certainty. As I am not yet engaged, there is no danger of my being married then.

Have you and Pierre got through with your Lawbook?[4] I fancy we shall appear as brother book-makers at about the same time: for I shall soon send you on a Grammar and Exercises — together with a volume of French plays, which are forthcoming from the prolific press of our Village Printer. They are books which I use in the study of French in my College Classes: though I hope to get the grammar introduced into schools: if I do not — woe is me! I shall never save the expense of printing.

When you write, let me know what you are engaged in — so that knowing your pursuits, I may enter more into your feelings. For my own part, buried in the dust and cobwebs of this country college, moth and rust begin to consume me. I am *with* them but not *of* them, may I truly say of those around me. I devote myself almost exclusively to the duties of my profession: and in pursuance thereof I am going to write a spanish grammar, according to my own ideas.[5] You see what an affection I have for grammars. The fact is, I do it for my own improvement — that being the best way to study a language thoroughly, and systematically.

My best respects to the Doctor's whiskers à-la-*Cordwainer*. Long may they flourish in immortal youth. I am sincerely glad to hear that his practice is increasing, as well as his family. Nor will you forget, when you next see my cousins, to say something agreeable from me, for I have a great deal of esteem for them all.[6]

What have you new in the literary world? In this quarter we have nothing but what is furnished from the West and South — and when our stock is exhausted we are content to read Congress Speeches, which are inexhaustible.

Do you still continue bathing? I have been obliged to ||leave|| it, for we have no bathing-house in Brunswick. My ||only exercise|| consists in capering about on a white horse with one eye: which exercise gives me a voracious appetite and strengthens the muscles of my arms most amazingly. This exercise I take all alone, for I lead the life of an anchorite; — to be sure I have many *acquaintances*, — mais elles ne sont pas du bois dont on fait les amis [but they are not the stuff of which friends are made].

My most particular regards to Pierre and madame: and to Cleaveland;[7] and whenever you may have a moment's leisure be assured I shall be very happy to hear from you, and to give you a prompt and loving reply.

Very sincerely your friend

Henry W. Longfellow.

MANUSCRIPT: Longfellow Trust Collection. ADDRESS: James Berdan Esq./Maiden Lane./New York. POSTMARK: BRUNSWICK MAINE. APR 14 ENDORSEMENT: Recd May 3d. 1830

1. This letter is unrecovered.

2. Irving had recently married a Miss Berdan, possibly the sister of Longfellow's correspondent.

3. Cf. *Hamlet*, III, i, 79–80.

4. There is no evidence that Irving and Berdan ever published a lawbook.

5. Longfellow did not pursue this project.

6. Longfellow's second cousins, the Storers of New York City. Dr. Ebenezer Storer, whom he had last seen in Paris, had recently begun a medical practice.

7. Possibly John Cleaveland (1804–1863), a member of the Bowdoin class of 1826, who was studying law in New York at this time.

171. *To Anne Longfellow*

Bowdoin College. June 8. 1830.

My dear Sister,

I have just left a most delightful tête-à-tête [1] with Miss. Margaret P. in order to write you this, which will be delivered you by her fair hand. Pray write me: — or dictate to George,[2] and let him write. I am very anxious to hear from you — and to know exactly the state of your health.[3]

It grieves me much to hear that the indisposition of the poney has thrown an obstacle in the way of Mary's ride into the country. I have consulted all the most celebrated farriers of the town — and they say it is nothing but the effect of a little too great exertion — the poney having led rather a *sedentary* life. I shall come up next Saturday — if I cannot get a safe opportunity of having him driven up by some one who wants to *work his passage* to Portland. Excuse haste and agitation. I am afraid I shall keep Miss P. waiting. My best to all.

Affectionately, your brother

Henry.

MANUSCRIPT: Longfellow Trust Collection. ADDRESS: Miss Anne Longfellow/ Portland./By the kindness/of Miss. M. Potter.

1. "Dont quiz me — 'please don't.' ¡Happy man!" was Longfellow's footnote here. The subject of this tête-à-tête was Mary Potter, to whom he later became engaged.

2. George Pierce, Longfellow's classmate and Anne's fiancé.

3. In this and subsequent letters to his sister, Longfellow reveals his concern for her health. For well over a year in 1830–1831 Anne suffered from a debility that

worried her family and caused her to seek country air and other remedies. Thompson (*Young Longfellow*, p. 383) concludes that she had a nervous breakdown after the death of her sister Elizabeth in 1829. She survived her trials, of course, and lived until 1901.

172. *To Benjamin Peirce* [1]

Bowdoin College   June 26. 1830.

Dear Sir,

I take the liberty of sending you two small volumes, which I have lately published for the use of students of this institution — and of Academies and schools in general.

I am, Sir, very respectfully Yours etc
Henry W. Longfellow.

Mr. Pierce
Librarian of Harvard.

MANUSCRIPT: Harvard College Library. ADDRESS: Mr Pierce — Librarian of/ Harvard University./Cambridge

1. The librarian of Harvard College, Peirce (1778–1831) was father of the celebrated mathematician of the same name.

173. *To George Washington Greene*

Bowdoin College   June 27. 1830.

Dear Greene,

Yours of the 16th April was just what I wanted — that is, it was a letter which gave me so graphic a picture of yourself and your situation that I almost imagined I saw the whole before me. I could see you at your study window, enjoying in Narraghansett and Mount Hope a delightful reminiscence of the Bay of Naples and Vesuvius. It is then your Tasso and Ariosto sound sweetest to your ear — that the "dolce far niente" of a summer evening is most heavenly — and that you take most delight in reading your own happiness

"dentro de pozzette
Che forma un dolce riso in bella guancia." [1]

For my own part — my window looks out upon a balm-of-Gillead tree and the college Chapel — and by way of back-ground, I have a fine view of the president's barn and the great road to Portland. I rise at six in the morning and hear a french recitation [Sophs.] [2] immediately. At seven I breakfast and am then master of my time till eleven — when I hear a Spanish lesson [Senior Class]. [2] After recitation I take a lunch — and at 12 o'clock go into the Library where I remain till one. I am then at leisure for the afternoon till five when I have another french recitation [Juniors][2] — at six I take coffee — walk and visit friends till nine — study till twelve, and then sleep till six — when I begin the same round again. Such is the outline of my life. The intervals of college duty, I fill up with my own studies. Last term I was publishing books for the use of my pupils, in whom I take a very deep interest. This term I am writing a course of lectures on Modern Literature — or rather on French, Spanish, and Italian Literature — which I am to deliver in Portland next winter. It will also be my college course, and I shall commence lecturing in a few days to the two up[p]er classes. So much for myself — or, as "Il Signor *Powelluccio*"[3] used to say, *my*-self. You see I lead a very sober, jog-trot kind of a life. My circle of acquaintances in town is very limited, and I have taken great pains that it should be so — I am on very intimate terms in three families, and that is quite enough. I dont care for general society. I like *intimate footings.*

I sent you my grammar and exercises, and a volume of french comedies, about three weeks since, by *a certain* Mr. Fuller of Providence.[4] Has he delivered them to you? Touching the matter of the Italian Grammar, I wish there was a good elementary grammar in existence — and I should delight to have one from your hand: but if your object is to gain money let me advise you not to publish it on your *own account.* Agree before hand with some bookseller to take the first edition: otherwise your expenditure will be great in the first instance — and what returns there may be from the sales of the work will come in piecemeal ||and|| at long intervals. This I know from sad experience: for although my grammar etc are used here by my pupils — and have been introduced into the schools in Portland, Boston, and some other places — the expenses of printing are not yet half-paid. It is very hard work to get a school book into general use. Almost everybody is supplied with grammars and such books — and the Italian, you know, is comparatively little studied in our country. Unless you can make the arrangement I mentioned above, let me rather suggest to you to prepare a course of lectures on the Italian language and literature, and deliver them in Providence the coming winter. You will have ample time for this before January next — and you will find most deligh[t]ful occupation in it: — you will have an opportunity to distinguish yourself, and I can assure you it will be more profitable than the grammar. I am very glad that you persevere in your intentions of becoming a professor. Did you make any propositions to the President of your Alma Mater[5] — or is the chair already occupied? If I were you I would not trouble myself about Greek for the present: believe me, my dear fellow, the mod. lang. are more in demand.

I am delighted daily more and more with the profession I have embraced — and I hope ere long to see you in a situation similar to my own. I very warmly reciprocate your desire that we should be in the same institution but that seems impracticable for the present. One expedient, however, suggests itself to me, which if successful would bring us a little nearer together if not exactly in contact. About sixty miles from this place, on the banks of the Kennebeck (turn to your maps if you please) there is a village called Waterville — which contains a college.[6] Now what the state of this college is, and what are its endowments I am altogether ignorant — but I will immediately set such enquiries on foot, as will decide me with regard to its being a fit and becoming place for you — and whether all the professorial chairs are fitted. Its charter was granted about 10 years since if I recollect right — and though it might not hold out to you inducements as a permanent situation — it might as a temporary one. I have friends residing at Waterville — and will write immediately to enquire whether a place is open for a professor.[7]

I am proud to have your favourable opinion of those little poetic attempts, which date so many years back. I had long ceased to attach any kind of value to them, and indeed to think of them — and I concluded it was so with others. Since my return I have written a piece and a half, but have not published a line. You need not be alarmed on that score. I am all prudence, now, since I can form a more accurate judgement of the merit of poetry. If I ever publish a volume it will be many years first. Indeed I find such an engrossing interest in the studies of my profession, that I write very seldom, except in connection with those studies. And what say you in regard to your own muse? Do you write often? and do you ever publish in any periodicals?

My best regards to your signora sposa [lady wife] — and to all your family — whom I desire much to see.

Very sincerely yours
Henry W. Longfellow.

MANUSCRIPT: Chapin Library, Williams College. ADDRESS: Mr. Geo: W. Greene/ East Greenwich/R. Island   POSTMARK: BRUNSWICK MAINE. JUNE 28

1. Samuel Longfellow translates these lines in *Life*, I, 187, as follows: "within the little pits/Which a sweet smile forms in a lovely cheek."

2. Longfellow's brackets.

3. Powell was presumably an acquaintance in Rome and, as the Italian suffix and the dialectical "*my*-self" suggest, an object of ridicule.

4. Longfellow may be referring to Rev. Samuel Fuller, Jr., pastor of Grace Church, Providence. The identification must, however, remain tentative, since

the *Providence Directory* for 1830 lists several Fullers and the letter from Fuller to Longfellow mentioned in Letter No. 174 does not survive.

5. Greene attended Brown University before his trip to Europe but did not graduate.

6. Waterville College, now Colby College.

7. No such letters are recovered.

174. *To Anne Longfellow*

Bowdoin College   July 11. 1830.

My dear Anne,

I was very much disappointed when Eugene [Weld] and Bowdoin [1] returned without bringing me letters from you. They did not enter Portland on their return: for as it was late in the afternoon when they reached Stevens's Plains, they were obliged to take the shortest road to Brunswick. But why have you not written by mail? Only think — I have not heard a word from you since a fortnight ago: and you know very well that I feel very desirous to know the effect of your remedies. Dont fail to write soon.

I yesterday took a ride towards Bath — by the old road — as it is called: — the scenery is charming: — you must come down, and see it in the course of the Summer. By the way, I have been trying to persuade Mrs. Cleaveland [2] to let Martha Anne go to Portland and make you a visit. A line from you would, I think, bring the thing about, for Martha Anne wishes very much to visit you — and her parents must be persuaded. She has a vacation this week — so that if you wish it, I doubt not she would come, and when once there, you know, you might persuade her mother to let her stay.

The other day, when I went to dinner I found a large fig-drum, or as I supposed drum of figs, directed to me. I could not conceive what good friend should have favoured me with such a present. I thought of every lady of my acquaintance, and with no little self complacency began to remove the paper envellope. Out fell a letter, and who should be the donor, but Mr — Fuller!! I proceeded to open the box — when to my utter astonishment I found — not *figs* but — you shall hear. The drum was full of a substance which appeared to be half tar, half saw-dust, from the midst of which I drew forth two little papers of ground-nuts directed to a Topsham Lady — half a pound of dates, half a pound of prunes, — a rotten pine-apple, — four coccoa-nut cakes — the jar of preserved peaches, which I send you: — and then the rest of the drum was filled with a promiscuous mass of cherries and tar. The jar of peaches was the only object worth having — so I send it to you — in a nest of cedar, which I cut yesterday with my own hands expressly for you. Present one sprig to Mrs. Deering,[3] and another to Miss Margaret [Potter], with her veil, which she left at Moorehead's — and which Mrs Moorehead gave me to day.[4] The slippers must be sent back to Hay and Norton's:[5] they will not do for me: — the other package to its direction, if you please. If you want any more cedar you have only to say the word — and you shall have it sent forthwith.

Tell Mrs. Preble that I have had a letter from Edward, dated at the university of Bonn on the banks of the Rhine. He talks of returning in the Fall.

I had a letter from George [Pierce] about a fortnight since, and shall answer it soon: — but I have a busy fit just now — and cannot very conveniently attend to anything transitory and perishable.

How does Mary find herself at Fryburg? Happy and well? or homesick and weary with pine groves?

News to night from Dr. Wells — stating that he is better — walks about the house — visits the kitchen — eats well — and talks of travelling.

There, my dear Anne, there is a letter written within and without, though not like Jeremiah's with lamentation and woe. Love to all.

Yrs.

Henry.

P.S. Had a letter yesterday from Mrs. Derby: she and Susan C.[6] have gone to the Springs.

MANUSCRIPT: Longfellow Trust Collection.

1. James Bowdoin Cleaveland (1809–1854), the second son of Parker Cleaveland, who was studying law with Stephen Longfellow in Portland.

2. Martha Bush Cleaveland (1787–1854), wife of Prof. Cleaveland.

3. Almira Ilsley Deering (1766–1855), wife of James Deering, the "Merchant Prince of Portland."

4. Mrs. Moorehead was presumably the wife of Alexander Moorehead, the proprietor of Moorehead's Tavern, a public stage house located in the northwest corner of the college yard.

5. A Portland shoe store operated by Joseph Hay and Thomas Norton.

6. Susan Codman was the niece of Mrs. Derby.

175. To Anne Longfellow

[Bowdoin College]

Sunday morning. 10 o.clock. [June–July, 1830][1]

Dear Anne,

This half-sheet lies so invitingly open before me, that I cannot help making a few dots and lines upon it. I think I should have written you this passed week had I not been very busy: for I wanted to say to George that the report of the Committee on the "American Author" has been received and meets with the most decided and unequivocal approbation.[2] All necessary alterations have been made: and a new communication will be forthwith submitted to their consideration. Beside this there is nothing new in the East.

¿ How are Mrs Welles — Adelaide — and the Doctor? and when do they return? ¿ Do you go to Paris tomorrow? If so — a pleasant journey to you.

I shall return on Saturday next — or if possible on Friday — and the Examinations will be on Wednesday and Thursday.

Very affectionately yours

Henry.

MANUSCRIPT: Longfellow Trust Collection. ADDRESS: Miss Anne Longfellow/ Portland.

1. The date of this latter is questionable. Inasmuch as Longfellow refers to Dr. Wells, who died on July 25, it seems likely that he wrote the letter in June or early July.

2. Among the papers in the Longfellow Trust Collection is a "Report of the Committee upon the *American Author*," n.d., signed by George W. Pierce and William P. Fessenden. It was apparently returned with a manuscript by Longfellow, unidentified, which his friends had read and criticized.

176. *To Anne Longfellow*

Bowdoin College   July 13. 1830.

Dear Anne,

Here I am again — so — how do you do. I am not a-going to intrude. I only call to leave a letter for the Captain, who has had the goodness to send me a ticket for the Ball tomorrow evening — for which I am very much obliged. This however you will keep secret from everyone, even George [Pierce] himself. For I fancy that if the Judge finds out that I have written a letter to his daughter, he will stand on the defensive.[1] So please hand it to her ladyship when no one is nigh — and she may do as she pleases about making it public.

Did you get the basket of cedar I sent yesterday? All well here. E. Orr.[2] sends her love.

I am &c.

H. W. L.

MANUSCRIPT: Longfellow Trust Collection. ADDRESS: To/Miss Anne Longfellow./ Portland. POSTMARK: BRUNSWICK MAINE. JUL. 14

1. Barrett Potter (1776–1865), judge of probate, Cumberland County, was noted for the strictness with which he guarded his three motherless daughters. Longfellow

here asks Anne to smuggle a letter to Mary Potter, whom he refers to facetiously as "the Captain." The letter is unrecovered.

2. Elizabeth Orr, a friend of Anne, was the daughter of Benjamin Orr, a trustee of Bowdoin College until his death in 1828.

177. *To Anne Longfellow*

Bowdoin College   July 28. 1830

My dear Sister,

I am very glad to know that you are taking the shower-bath. You are quite at the top of the ton in these *showery* days. What a dreadful nervous change in the weather! Upon my word — its *horrible*! If you are getting better under such unfavorable auspices, I shall not despair of seeing you in Brunswick ere long — as strait as a may-pole and as prim as the *ancient stomacher and stays,* can make you.

Brunswick affords not one particle of interesting gossip wherewith to enliven three dull pages of an epistle. Miss Orr is well — and the Misses Cleaveland are well — and all are well.[1]

MANUSCRIPT: Longfellow Trust Collection. ADDRESS: Miss Anne Longfellow./ Portland.

1. The letter is unsigned.

178. *To Anne Longfellow*

Bowdoin College —
Tuesday morning   August. 1830.

My dear Sister,

I cannot let Colonel Kinsman go without writing you a line or two. What a pity I should have hurried off so on Sunday last: I might have staid till monday noon, as well as not: for on reaching Freeport on Sunday night, it became so dark that I could not see the horse's head, and I was obliged to pass the night there.

The great object of my writing today is business. I was invited to a party last night, and on hunting up my pantaloons I could find only one pair of black — which were so short, as with difficulty to reach the tops of my socks. I believe you will find a pair belonging to me in one of the drawers of my bureau. Please look for them, and send them next week. If they are not to be found please send word to Stewart[1] to make a pair of black *cassimer.* My best regards in Free Street.[2]

Very affectionately yours
Henry.

MANUSCRIPT: Longfellow Trust Collection. ADDRESS: To/Miss Anne Longfellow./ Portland./Fav[ore]d by J. D. Kinsman Esq.

1. James G. Stewart, a tailor of Portland.
2. That is, to the Potters, who lived on Free Street.

179. *To Barrett Potter*

Bowdoin College, Sept. 26, 1830

Dear Sir, —

I regretted that I had not the opportunity of conversing with you before leaving town on Wednesday morning, but the hurry of departure rendered it impossible. I wished to express the grateful acknowledgment I owe you, for the confidence you have reposed in me in placing in my hands the happiness of a daughter, and in part your own. I most ardently hope, my dear sir, that you may never have the slightest occasion to think that your confidence has been misplaced. I certainly believe you never will have: and this belief is founded upon the attachment I feel for Mary, in whom I find the inestimable virtues of a pure heart and guileless disposition — qualities which not only excite an ardent affection, but which tend to make it as durable as it is ardent.

I think I have formed a just estimate of the excellence of Mary's character. I can say to your ear, what I would not often say to hers — that I have never seen a woman in whom every look, and word, and action seemed to proceed from so gentle and innocent a spirit. Indeed, how much she possesses of all we most admire in the female character!

On this account I esteem myself highly privileged beyond the common lot in having engaged her affection and secured your approval. I hope to merit both by attention and tenderness to her, and promise myself a life of happiness in the social intercourse of your fireside and the domestic quiet of my own.

I am, dear sir, most respectfully and affectionately yours,

Henry W. Longfellow.

MANUSCRIPT: unrecovered; text from "New Longfellow Letters," p. 779.

180. *To Anne Longfellow*

Bowdoin College. October. 4th 1830

Dear Anne,

You know where Free Street is — and you can read *joining-hand*.[1]

I go to Augusta tomorrow at *my own expense*, to be carped at and criticised by everybody that pleases.[2] It is like paying for being put in the pil[l]ory. On Friday I shall go to Portland at my own expense. Please be ready to receive me between five and six o'clock.

Very truly your affectionate brother
Henry.

MANUSCRIPT: Longfellow Trust Collection. ADDRESS: Miss Anne Longfellow./ Portland./Fav[ore]d by Dr. Barrett.[3]

1. The remark refers to Longfellow's engagement to Mary Potter.
2. He delivered a lecture on "female education" (see *Young Longfellow*, p. 381).
3. John Barrett (1802–1842), a physician of Portland.

181. *To Anne Longfellow*

Bowdoin College   Oct. 12. 1830

Dear Anne,

Should it be a pleasant day on Friday next, as I hope it will be, I intend to leave Brunswick at about 1 o'clock, and *walk towards* Portland. I want you to request your father to let Bowdoin take our horse and ||gig|| and, leaving town at about 2 o'clock P.M. come to meet me on the way. I want the exercise of walking: and whenever I begin to grow fatigued I will stop and wait for Bowdoin.

Your affectionate brother
Henry. —

MANUSCRIPT: Longfellow Trust Collection. ADDRESS: Miss Anne Longfellow/ Portland./Fav[ore]d by Mr. Cleaveland.

182. *To George Washington Greene*

Bowdoin College   Oct. 20. 1830.

Dear Greene,

Yours of the 12th inst. from Pawtuck has just come to hand: absence from town prevented me from having the pleasure of unsealing it at an earlier date. I am quite surprised at your intention of revisiting Europe so soon; but of this I am thoroughly persuaded, that in no part of the world, could you pass two years more profitably ||than|| in Germany. I of course shall not take it upon myself to advise you at which of the Universities you ought to reside. I presume you intend to try more than one. I will send you letters to my friends and instructers in Göttingen,[1] and will procure you others to Schlegel,[2] the celebrated philologist in *Bonn* — on the Rhine, which place I hope you will not fail to visit. I wish you would spend time to give me a little more definite idea of your intended plan of operations; and recollect, that if I can in any possible way be of use to you, you have only to speak the word.

With regard to Spanish. The language of Don Quixotte is obsolete: that of Gil Blas is not: but pray be careful how you make use of expressions out of either for conversation — unless you wish to *talk like a book*, which by the way, I presume you do not. Gil Blas is a good text-book: so is Gonzalo de Cordoba.[3] The one I commence with here, is a little thing I have published for my own use; entitled "Novelas Españolas." It consists of two stories paraphrased from Washington Irving, and published with other tales at Madrid about two years ago.[4] I will send it to you.

Please let me know how I shall send the book and letters — or to what place rather, and how soon you must have them: I will endeavour to find some conveyance.

The reason your last letter was not answered is that from my numerous occupations it has been out of my power. You will, however, excuse this shabby treatment of your epistle: I know you will, when I tell you that I have been obliged to prepare since its reception, and deliver in public three discourses on different subjects. Add to this my college duties at the commencement of the year, and you have I think apology enough.

My best regards to Madame, and believe me always very sincerely your friend

Henry W. Longfellow.

P.S. Have you done anything farther in regard to the Ital. Gram?

MANUSCRIPT: Longfellow Trust Collection. ADDRESS: Mr. Geo: W. Greene/East Greenwich/R.I. POSTMARK: BRUNSWICK MAINE. OCT 21 [*date questionable*]

1. These letters are unrecovered.

2. Longfellow himself did not meet August Wilhelm von Schlegel (1767–1845) until his second trip to Europe in 1835. See 336.2.

3. That is, *Crónica del Gran Capitán* by Gonzalo Fernández de Córdoba (1453–1515), the celebrated Spanish general known as "the Great Captain."

4. Longfellow refers to George Washington Montgomery's *Tareas de un Soliterio, ó nueva colección de novelas* (Madrid, 1829). He had selected two of Montgomery's tales, contributed a preface, and published them as *Novelas Españolas* (Brunswick, 1830). See S. T. Williams, "The First Version of the Writings of Washington Irving in Spanish," *Modern Philology*, XXVIII (November 1930), 186–187.

183. *To Anne Longfellow*

Bowdoin College. Wednesday morning. 1830.[1]

Dear Anne,

I drop you a line because I have an opportunity of sending it, and I am always ready and desirous to wish you a good morning. I am in the greatest hurry in the world; else I should *devote* a letter to you and another to Mary [Potter]. Give my love to her; and tell her I shall come up as soon ||as I find it pra||cticable.

MANUSCRIPT: Longfellow Trust Collection. ADDRESS: Miss Annie Longfellow.

1. The date of this fragment may perhaps be restricted to the autumn of 1830 following Longfellow's engagement to Mary Potter in September.

184. *To Anne Longfellow*

[Bowdoin College] Friday Afternoon. [1830][1]

My dear Anne,

I send you this antepast of a letter to encourage you to write again soon, and to inform you that I stand in great need of my *nightcap*, of which you can probably give some very satisfactory account.

The lamp excites universal admiration, particular[l]y the gauze and tin — by Cross &co.

I hereby forward a letter to Mrs McLellan in answer to her very polite invitation to tea on Thursday last. I hope she did not wait tea on my account. Please seal and deliver the letter yourself — because there will be a great many excuses necessary for not having answered it sooner — my reputation is of course at stake — and I do not know that I could consign it into better hands than yrs.[2]

Love to all — adieu.

Your brother Henry, who intends writing you a *letter* ere long.

MANUSCRIPT: Longfellow Trust Collection. ADDRESS: Miss Anne Longfellow/ Portland.

1. The year is questionable.
2. This letter is unrecovered.

185. *To James Berdan*

Portland   Jany. 4. 1831.

Dear Berdan,

After a silence of so many months common courtesy seems to demand, that this letter should commence with an apology. I received your last in the busy preparation of an Inaugural discourse.[1] A fortnight after I had delivered that, I pronounced a dis[c]ourse of a different kind before a society in this town — and within the course of two months afterward — two more public addresses, one here and another in Hallowell. In all these instances, circumstances were such, that I could not refuse, though I wished to, and endeavoured to. Add to this my college duties — and it would be an idle question to ask whether I was sick of the sight of pen, ink and paper. I have, too, been very busily employed, in every interval, in writing my Lectures on modern literature. The few letters, which I have written during this period, are limited to those which bore the superscription of a young lady of Portland, to whom I have sworn fealty. You saw the same lady in New York, last Summer — Miss Mary S. Potter. Please communicate the news — if news it be — to all Mr. Storer's family. Surely that is quite as succinct and categorical a statement of the case, as could well be made out.

There you have my reasons for the long silence I have guarded. I hope you will find them of weight. The few lines I wrote you in September[2] I fear did not reach you in season to determine you to take a northward journey. If that was the cause of your not coming, I sincerely regret it. Giving you the information you desired, too late for you to avail yourself of it, is what Pierre would call *shabby treatment.* But I imagine that other circumstances prevented you from visiting Maine: besides were it not so, my negligence has surely been sufficiently punished by my being deprived of the pleasure of seeing you.

I have given Mr. Furbish, a Portlander, a letter of introduction to you.[3] He is an odd kind of a man: but I think you will be pleased with some of his ideas on matters and things in general. He will probably be in New York in the course of a week or ten days — perhaps *not at all.* To him I refer you for all that can possibly interest you in this land of Barbarians — this miserable Down East. I feel as if I were living in exile here: and it will be a deed of charity in you to come and make a long visit as soon as you can find leisure.

Give my best regards to all my cousins,[4] and friends one and all. Pray write me soon, for though a miserable correspondent I am very fond of hearing of my friends, and receiving letters from them. Is Slidell in New York? I have long owed him a letter — six months at least. I wish he would waive ceremony.

Most sincerely your friend
H. W. Longfellow.

MANUSCRIPT: Clifton Waller Barrett Collection, University of Virginia.　ADDRESS: To/James Berdan Esq./New York.　ENDORSEMENT: Recd Jany 7th 1831

1. See 161.2.
2. This letter is unrecovered.
3. See Letter No. 164.
4. The Storers.

186. *To La Comtesse de Sailly* [1]

Portland. February 3. 1831.

My dear Madam,

Permit me so far to avail myself of your ancient, and I fondly hope still continued friendship, as to introduce to your kind attentions my friends Mr. and Mrs Greene, of East Greenwich.

I take great pleasure in thus renewing our own acquaintance, and in making my friends acquainted with one, whose name is associated with my most dilightful recollections of France. I feel anxious to secure to them the same source of pleasant souvenirs, which I enjoy and in presenting them, I feel confident I shall be doing you a pleasure, whilst I secure to them a benefit.

With sentiments of great esteem I have the honor to be, Madam,

your friend and Obt. Servt.

Henry W. Longfellow.

MANUSCRIPT: Longfellow Trust Collection.

1. See Letter No. 101. This and Letter No. 187 were written on the same sheet of paper, folded once. It is unlikely that Greene delivered them to the Comtesse.

187. *To La Comtesse de Sailly*

[Portland] Feby. 3. 1831.

My dear Madam de Sailly,

How shall I atone for my long protracted silence? How shall I answer for broken promises, and neglect of my repeated assurances to write you on my return to my native land? Indeed I can offer neither atonement nor palliation for my offence: and my conscience often upbraids me with neglect towards a friend, who has always taken so much interest in my welfare as you have done.

All I can say then is, that I will soon write you a long letter, and communicate all that has transpired since I last saw you. [1] In the mean time my friend Mr. Greene, will tell you *where* and *how* I am now situated.

I remain, with sincerest wishes for your health and happiness, very truly yours,

H. W. Longfellow.

P.S. Be kind enough to proffer my best regards to all my old friends, who esteem me enough to speak of me.

MANUSCRIPT: Longfellow Trust Collection. ADDRESS: À Madame/Madame La Comtesse de Sailly./À Paris.

1. There is no record that Longfellow wrote this letter.

188. *To Jared Sparks*

Portland   Feb. 8. 1831.

Dear Sir,

I am going to avail myself of the friendly assistance you had the goodness to offer me, when we last met, in regard to the publication of books etc. The first Edition of my translation of Lhommond's grammar is nearly sold, and a Portland Bookseller makes me certain offers for the copyright of a second edition, which, though they do not at present seem very favorable to me, I shall be obliged to accept, unless I can do better with a Boston publisher. The first edition, consisting of 500 copies, was published about a year ago. The sale, you perceive, has not been *very* rapid: but considering the circumstances of the case, that the work was a *grammar,* that it had to fight its way into schools, where other grammers had been long in use — that it was badly printed, and on poor paper, and above all that it was published Down East, I confess the sale has been quite as rapid as could have been expected. My present object is to bring the book forward under more favorable auspices. I wish to sell the copy-right to some publisher in Boston, who will have a good edition printed at the Cambridge University Press, as you suggested last Summer. I take the liberty of asking your advice upon this subject. To what publisher had I best apply? [1]

You see, my dear Sir, that I take you at your word on this occasion. I do so, because I know you intended I should. I do not however wish that you should put yourself to any inconvenience upon the subject. When you have a few moments leisure, I hope to hear from you. A letter will find me at Brunswick.

I had the pleasure of seeing Mr. and Mrs. Ticknor at Brunswick last Autumn. It was after your return to Boston from [your] Canadian Tour. They told me of your journey through the wilderness etc. etc. I presume you found as much pleasure in the journey as you anticipated. I hoped to have seen you this winter: but I have been prevented from visiting Boston by indisposition.

Do you recollect my asking you whether I should direct to you as the Revd. or as Esq? I shall to-day give you the latter title: — hereafter as you please.

Can I be of any service to you in this part of the world? If I can — pray use me as convenience requires.

Very sincerely and respect[full]y.
Your friend and Ob. Ser[v]t.
Henry W. Longfellow.

MANUSCRIPT: Harvard College Library.   ADDRESS: To/Jared Sparks Esq./Boston.

[Boston *deleted and* Philadelphia Pa. *added.* Philadelphia Pa. *deleted and* New York City *added*] POSTMARKS: PORTLAND ME FEB 7/BOSTON MS FEB 9/PAID POSTAL ANNOTATION: Forw[arde]d ANNOTATION (*by Longfellow*): Paid ENDORSEMENT: From H. W. Longfellow/Feb. 25. 1831

1. In his response from New York dated March 19, 1831, Sparks stated that he was unable to recommend a publisher. A second edition of the French grammar (together with a second edition of *French Exercises*) was published by Gray & Bowen in Boston later in 1831. This was the first book to have Longfellow's name on the title page.

189. *To Stephen Longfellow*

Bowdoin College. March. 24. 1831.

My dear Sir,

I have received proposals from Messrs Gray & Bowen of Boston for publishing a second edition of my French Grammar, much more favorable, than those offered me by another Bookseller through Mr. Colman, and which I mentioned to you at the time. They make me two offers. The first is to print the work handsomely, advertise, and do all they can to get it into general circulation, and to give me 100 copies and 12 1/2 cents pr. copy (on the number of copies printed), which will be 1000. This sum to be paid on a fair credit, as may be hereafter agreed upon. The second proposal is to publish, and give me 15 cents pr. copy (on the number of copies *sold*) payable every six months.

Now I do not think there can be much doubt in regard to these offers: but as you may possibly see some things in this negociation which escape my eye, I wish to know your opinion. My own, is decidedly in favor of the first proposal of 12 1/2 cents for each copy printed, which on an edition of 1000, will give me $125: — and the 100 copies in sheets will be worth to me $50 more. Prof. Cleaveland is also of this opinion. If I accept this proposal, I shall try to make the following arrangement in regard to payments: to receive a small portion on the day of publication: and the remainder in installments of 3 and 6 months credit: or, if this is not agreeable to the gentlemen, to receive the pay[men]t in installments of 3, 6, and 9 months credit. I begin to think that the publication will turn out pretty well after all: and if by publishing a handsome edition, I can get the work into large schools, and pretty general circulation, it will be a profitable business in the long run. I shall also try to do something with the French Comedies.

I see by the Courier that the College Question is at length decided. We were all prepared for it, and therefore it has created no very unpleasant sensation. The President, however, has just had his eyes opened to his true situation. Mr. Ellenwood of Bath was friend enough to do this unpleasant deed;[1] and told him exactly how he stood in the public estimation, what was thought and said of him, and, in fine, that he stood on the edge of a precipice. What the effect ||will be|| I cannot foresee: though no one here is of opinion that he will think of resigning his office.[2]

If you are of a different opinion from me in regard to the proposals for the Grammar, please write me by return of mail: if not, at your leisure. I am very sorry to hear of the death of Capt. Stevenson:[3] it is indeed a heavy calamity to his family.

Very sincerely and affectionately yours
Henry W. Longfellow.

I wrote to Anne on monday last.[4]

MANUSCRIPT: Longfellow Trust Collection. ADDRESS: To/Stephen Longfellow Esq./Portland. ENDORSEMENT: Henry W Longfellow/Gray & Bowens proposals

1. John W. Ellingwood (1782–1860), a clergyman of Bath, was a member of the Board of Overseers of Bowdoin.

2. Longfellow refers here to the unpopularity of President Allen and to a measure taken to remove him from office. A few days later, on March 31, the Maine Legislature passed an act making the presidency annually elective. In September the trustees of the college forced Allen from his position, but he took his case to court and in 1833 won reinstatement. He retired in 1839.

3. Capt. Stephen Stephenson of Gorham, brother of Col. Samuel Stephenson, had died on March 19, age fifty-three.

4. This letter is unrecovered.

190. *To Stephen Longfellow*

Bowdoin College   April 20. 1831.

My dear Sir,

The present will be handed you by Dr. Mussey,[1] whom you already know so well by reputation, that I need only mention his name. He will remain in Portland until monday next: and I feel very anxious, that he should visit Anne during his stay in town.

Very truly and affectionately yours
Henry W. Longfellow.

S. Longfellow. Esq.

MANUSCRIPT: Longfellow Trust Collection. ADDRESS: To/Stephen Longfellow. Esq./Portland./Dr. Mussey.

1. Dr. Reuben Dimond Mussey (1780–1866), a professor of medicine at Dartmouth, lectured at the Bowdoin Medical School, 1831–1835.

191. *To Anne Longfellow*

Bowdoin College   July 10. 1831

My dear Anne,

I am very sorry, that I have not been able to write to you before; but I have had such a constant pressure of affairs of one kind and another, that it has been quite out of my power. Never, in all my life, have I been so hurried, and beset with cares as at the present moment. I never have a moment which I can call my own. That is all I have to complain of at the present time. In other respects, I feel very comfortably. My health — need I mention it? I wish yours was as good.

Brunswick affords no news but bad news. Poor Elisabeth Orr has just met with another affliction in the death of her brother Benjamin. She was expecting his return almost daily, when the intelligence came. I have not seen her since: but I understand that she seems to feel the loss more than even that of her parents. The blow was entirely unexpected. He died at sea, after a sickness of four days only.

I have concluded to remain at least one term more with Mrs. Fales.[1] I should prefer house-keeping were it possible, but I cannot procure a tenement. I do not think that Mary will like to board out: but I do not tell her so, since there is no remedy. The marriage ceremony will take place in the second week in September. You are very respectfully invited to attend. It is the week after Commencement.

The Brunswick Ladies are going to have a Fair for the benefit of the Infant School. I wish them all success: but I confess I have my doubts in regard to its success. Time will prove all things.

I of course visited Portland on the 4th. The weather, however, was so excessively hot that I did not attend either of the Orations. Mr. Daveis's is well spoken of. He appeared in the Professorial gown. I was very much disappointed in not seeing mother but as she is with you, I cannot regret it so much.

How flourish the evergreen pines of Fryeburg? Does it not seem to you that there is some resemblance between Fryeburg and Brunswick? The same soil — the same growth of woodland. The air, I think, is different. You are much higher from the level of the sea. But you have morning and evening fogs — from the river: we have them from the sea. After you have tried Fryeburg long enough, I shall insist upon your trying Brunswick. I shall have a chamber expressly devoted to your comfort: and we should like your company vastly. When do you mean to return? Pray let me hea||r from|| you soon; if it is only a line or two, merely to say how you are. I cannot in conscience ask you to write me a long letter: for it is hard work to write from such a village as Fryeburg: I know this by comparison.

Give my love to mother: and my best regards to Dr. Griswold and his family, and to Miss Barrows, and in fine to all friends.[2]

Very affectionately yours
H. W. Longfellow.

MANUSCRIPT: Longfellow Trust Collection. ADDRESS: To/Miss. Anne Longfellow./ Care of Dr. Griswold/Fryeburg./Maine[3] POSTMARKS: PORTLAND ME JUL 11/PAID POSTAL ANNOTATION: Paid/S. L.

1. Mrs. Mary Ann Fales, his landlady. See *Young Longfellow*, p. 383.
2. Dr. Oliver Griswold (1777–1833) had practiced medicine in Fryeburg since 1798. Anne had put herself in his care and was living in the Griswold home on River Street. Miss Barrows may have been the daughter of Dr. Reuel Barrows, another Fryeburg physician. In a letter to his mother dated March 10, 1831 (MS, Longfellow House), Alexander Longfellow refers to her as Mary Barrows.
3. "Care of Dr. Griswold" and "Maine" in Stephen Longfellow's hand.

192. *To Anne Longfellow*

Bowdoin College   July 17. 1831.

My dear Sister,

I have an opportunity of sending so directly to you, that I cannot help stealing a few moments from college time, to send my love to you. I hope also to be first to communicate the welcome intelligence of the arrival of Judge Preble and "sa chère famille."[1] I suppose Steve is on tip-toe, or more probably on the way to New York: in which case we shall probably see Marianne before he does; for there seems always a fatality attending this going out to meet friends.

Of course you have heard of Pitt's engagement: I could not make up my mouth to congratulate him; so I only wished him much joy and happiness, which I certainly do wish him.[2]

Susan Codman is to be married on the first of August. I suppose Dr. Page will hang himself: for you know he still cherished the tender flame, though it cannot be said that he lets "concealment, like a worm i' th' bud, prey on his damask cheek."[3] Another precious item of intelligence is that *Master* Burke, turns out to be a *woman*: a capital *hoax* for the Bostonians! Good![4]

I have not seen "little Mary" for more than a fortnight. I have grown quite *abstemious*: and now that you are not at home, I do not visit Portland but once in three weeks.

I wish you could see the bearer of this letter, Mr Hill: — the Revd Mr. Hill of Worcester Mass. His Wife, who is with him is a charming little woman. They pass through Fryeburg on their way to the White Hills. But they will not probably stay long in Fryeburg.[5]

Nothing farther. Very affectionate remembrance to mother, regards to friends, and *brotherly* love to yourself.

most truly yours

H. W. Longfellow.

P.S. I hereby send you a Magazine for your amusement. I wrote "The Schoolmaster," and the translation from Luis de Gongora. Read "the late Joseph Natterstrom." It is good.[6]

MANUSCRIPT: Longfellow Trust Collection. ADDRESS: To/Miss. Anne Longfellow./At Dr. Griswold's/Fryeburg./By the kindness/of the Revd. Mr. Hill.

1. From Europe, where the Judge had served as ambassador to the Hague (see 162.1).

2. William Pitt Fessenden, who had been engaged to Elizabeth Longfellow before her death in 1829, married Ellen Maria Deering (1809–1857) in April 1832.

3. Cf. *Twelfth Night*, II, iv, 111–112. Susan Codman married Benjamin Welles (1781–1860), of the Harvard class of 1800, after apparently rejecting the earlier suit of Dr. Frederic Benjamin Page.

4. Longfellow's information is incorrect. Master Joseph Burke, the "Irish Roscius," was a child prodigy of the day who specialized in conducting orchestras and playing Richard III, Shylock, and other popular roles. He was thirteen at this time.

5. Rev. Alonzo Hill (1800–1871) was the pastor of the Second Parish (First Unitarian) Church of Worcester. About six months before Longfellow met him he had married Frances Mary Clark of Boston.

6. The magazine was the *New-England Magazine*, edited by Joseph T. Buckingham. The translation from the Spanish of Luis de Gongora, signed "L," appears in I (July 1, 1831), 59. William Austin (1778–1841) wrote the fanciful tale called "The Late Joseph Natterstrom" (pp. 11–19). For Longfellow's various "Schoolmaster" essays, see *Young Longfellow*, pp. 382–383.

193. *To Joseph Tinker Buckingham and Edwin Buckingham*[1]

Bowdoin College   July 18. 1831

Gentlemen,

I received your favor of the 30[th of] June with the 1st No of the Magazine, by due course of mail. I have delayed answering you, in the hope of finding some private opportunity of sending you a communication for No 2: but as none offers, and it grows late in the month I hereby send you a paper by mail.[2] I am very much pleased with the appearance of the Magazine and every one seems to be gratified with it. I should, however, read it with more pleasure, did I know the writers. Would it be agreeable to you to send me the names of the contributors to each No: or is it your wish that they should not be known? I shall be very glad to correct the proofs as you suggest. With thanks for the Mag[azin]e, I am, Gentlemen, very respectfully yours

Henry W. Longfellow.

359

P.S. I am desirous that what I here send, should go into the next No. if it be possible.

MANUSCRIPT: Parkman Howe, Boston. ADDRESS: To/Messrs. J. T. and E. Buckingham/Boston POSTMARKS: BRUNSWICK MAINE. JUL 19/PAID.

1. See 192.6. Edwin Buckingham assisted his father on the *New-England Magazine*.

2. A copy of his poem "To a Mountain Brook." See 195.2.

194. *David Humphreys Storer* [1]

Bowdoin College: August. 11. 1831.

My dear Sir,

About a fortnight since I had the pleasure of receiving from you a tract on "Entomology," which I have read with great interest: the more so, as you were kind enough to send it in token of remembrance.[2] It is a subject to which I have never given any attention, though so far from being one of those to whom it is repugnant, I think I should derive great delight from its study, had I time to pursue it properly. But the butterflies I chase are ideal, and not real ones.

I regretted very much that it was not in my power to see you again before leaving Boston in June last. I promised to call and take letters from your wife; but during the morning of the day I left, I was detained at the Hotel by visitors, and at noon the heat became so very oppressive, that it was with difficulty I got even so far as Mrs. Goddard's.[3]

I was very glad to see Mr. and Mrs. Goddard in the East: and I assure you it would afford great pleasure both to myself and Mary S. P. if you and your lady would visit us. I fear, however, that you have no vacation in your profession; and that if you had, we could hardly offer you sufficient inducements to persuade you to set your faces eastward. At all events we should be very glad to see you, and more particularly so after we get established in Brunswick, which will be in the course of next month.

With my best regards to your wife, and to Mrs. Goddard and family,

I am very truly yours
Henry W. Longfellow.

MANUSCRIPT: Massachusetts Historical Society.

1. Dr. Storer (1804–1891), a prominent Boston obstetrician and naturalist, was Mary Storer Potter's half-uncle. In 1829 he married Abby Jane Brewer of Boston, sister of the ornithologist Thomas Mayo Brewer.

2. A "List of Published Writings of David Humphreys Storer" (*Bowdoin College Library Bibliographical Contributions*, No. 2, August 1892) reveals that Storer was not the author of this tract.

3. Mrs. Goddard, wife of William Goddard (1781–1835), a Boston merchant,

was the mother of Mary Caroline Goddard, who accompanied the Longfellows on their ill-fated trip to Europe in 1835.

195. *To Anne Longfellow*

Bowdoin College   Aug. 21. 1831

My dear Annie,

Yours of Thursday last gave me great and unexpected pleasure. I thought the understanding between us was, that I should do all the writing in our *correspondence* and you all the reading: and knowing how difficult it is for you to write, I did not expect, and in fact, I hardly wished you to send me any answer to my letters. My silence of late has been owing to other reasons, then, than that of not hearing from you. The truth is, I have been to Portland very frequently, and that always crowds business a little on my return. My last visit was accompanied by a disappointment, as I perceive you are already aware.[1] The disappointment was not, however, a tenth part so great to me as to some others. Marianne was very solemnly romantic on the occasion: and when I told her in the evening that I had come to console her in her widowhood, she told me that it was no subject for jesting — that she had met with so many misfortunes in the course of her life, etc, etc. — you know what a doleful event she will make it appear. I really wished that all the sentimental novels she had read, had never been written. I wish she would lay aside romance and sentimentality. Accidents will happen — disappointments we must suffer: and that education is greatly defective, which does not prepare us for them. Ahem! — new and profound.

But what most interests me just at the present moment is the good news your letter contains, touching your own health. I thought it would be so, when you breathed the invigorating air of the mountains, and got your spirits raised a little. I came within an ace of paying you a visit last Sunday: nothing but the excessive heat of the weather prevented me. I hope to see you before long, and shall if possible before Commencement: but not in Portland: for I think the country air is *everything* for you now, and you must not come home till you have derived all possible benefit from your present situation. We *would* postpone our wedding, dear Anne, on your account, if circumstances would permit: but the vacation is but 3 weeks, — and we have now fixed the wedding-day in the second: — so that we shall have barely time to get comfortably settled in Brunswick, before I shall be forced to commence grinding in the knowledge mill again. You call it a dog's life: it is indeed — my dear Anne: I do not believe that I was born for such a lot. I have aimed higher than this: and I cannot believe that all my aspirations are to terminate in the drudgery of a situation, which gives me no opportunity to distinguish myself, and in point of worldly gain, does not even pay me for my labor. Besides, one loses ||ground|| so fast in these out of the way places: the mind has no stimulus to exertion — grows sluggish in its movements and narrow in its sphere — and there's the end of a man. We will see.

I have just received a letter from Portland informing me of Stephen's wedding, which took place on Wednesday evening last.

I herewith send you No. 2. of the Magazine. You will find a piece of poetry signed L. which was written by me.[2] I wrote nothing more in No. 2.

We have had a slight rumpus in College the past week. A student, who went to see Master Burke, after permission had been denied him, was suspended, and his friends feeling aggrieved, made a bit of a row: but all is now quiet.

Elisabeth Orr has been absent for some time past: she ret. from Minot last week. I called to see her, but she was out. I understand that she is well. Your message to Little Mary shall be delivered, and you shall have all the desired information touching the Wedding. We were published to day.[3] Regards to Mrs. and Miss P.[4]

> Most truly and affectionately your brother
> Henry.

MANUSCRIPT: Longfellow Trust Collection. ADDRESS: To/Miss Anne Longfellow./ At Mrs. Pierce's/Baldwin.

1. Marianne Preble and Longfellow's brother Stephen were to have been married on August 14, but the wedding had to be postponed when Stephen became ill. They were married on August 17, as a later paragraph reveals.

2. "To a Mountain Brook," *New-England Magazine*, I (August 1831), 164.

3. That is, a public announcement was made of the wedding, to be held on September 14 in the First Parish Church (Unitarian) of Portland.

4. Mrs. Josiah (Hannah) Pierce, the mother of Anne's fiancé, and her daughter. Anne was staying with the Pierce family in Baldwin.

196. *To Mary Longfellow*

Bowdoin College. Sept. 11. 1831.

My dear Mary,

I write to inform you, that I have invited two young ladies to pass the present week with you, and to be of the wedding party. They are Martha Anne Cleaveland and Mary Fales.[1] The latter has accepted the invitation, and the former will come if her health is good enough, which I very much doubt, as *she is now taking medicine*. We shall be in Portland on Tuesday next, in the Accommod. Stage: and I hope you will be in readiness to receive us and very glad to see us.

Very affectionately your brother

Henry.

MANUSCRIPT: Longfellow Trust Collection. ADDRESS: To Miss Mary Longfellow./ Portland.

1. Mary Turrell Fales, the daughter of Longfellow's landlady in Brunswick (see 191.1).

197. *To Mary Longfellow*

[Bowdoin College, December, 1831][1]

Dear Mary,

I have concluded to pass a great part, if not all the vacation in Brunswick. I shall however come to pass a few days with you in Portland. The reason of all this is, that next term I shall have ||four|| recitations per day: and must improve this winter for my own private studies. Yesterday and to-day are examination days: and of course I am very busy. I shall write to Papa the first moment of leisure I can get. Love to all. Very affectionately

Your brother

Henry

MANUSCRIPT: Longfellow Trust Collection. ADDRESS (*by Alexander Longfellow*): To/Miss Mary Longfellow:/Care of Hon Stephen Longfellow/Portland/ Maine ENDORSEMENT: Brunswick Dec. 1831.

1. Longfellow appended this brief note to a letter from Alexander Longfellow to Mary, dated "Brunswick December." The endorsement, apparently by Zilpah Longfellow, provides the year.

198. *To Charles Folsom*[1]

Portland   Feb. 12. 1832.

My dear Sir,

I am once more "entre mes [dieux] Lares" [among my household gods]. We left Boston on Tuesday evening, as was my intention when I last saw you, and after passing a cold and doleful night in the stage-coach, were finally ushered into Portland by the sound of the 11 o'clock bell.

I take an early opportunity to send you a list of errata. To my great surprise, on looking over my papers yesterday, I found but 4 signatures of the Grammar among them.[2] These I have reperused and here send you the result. For the rest, I shall rely upon you, as I presume the other signatures, which I took with me from Cambridge were left among my books, in Boston, and consequently will not reach me in season to be of any service. I feel quite confident, that our Table of Errata will not be very long. There are some trifling errors which of course we should not think of noticing: as for example on p. 3 near the bottom LA in *small caps.* instead of *La* in italics. The following are all I have found worthy of note.

Errata.

Page   2; *ligne* 15; *pour* EXAMPLES, *lisez* EXEMPLES.
  ”   4;   ”   24;   ”   Maurs,   ”   Maures.
  ”   5;   ”   2;   ”   liason,   ”   liaison
  ”   15;   ”   20;   ”   oblig,   ”   obligé
Pages 26, 35 *et* 40; *pour* 2me *lisez* 2nde.

In the sheets I have I can find nothing else worth notice. Quere, would it not be better to leave this whole table without punctuation thus

Page 2 *ligne* 15 *pour* EXAMPLES *lisez* EXEMPLES.

This is just as you please — just as the prevailing custom demands. Either way will suit me.

Be kind enough to remember me to the Colonel,[3] and tell him not to forget to strike off the 12 extra copies of the first sheet, and to send them with all speed to Gray & Bowen.

In the 'Saggi de' Novellieri'[4] don't forget the Belfagor of Macchiavelli. I will send you the notice of his life in due season.

Mrs. L. joins me in kind regards to yourself and lady, and in the hope that your family are now all restored to health.

Very truly yours
H. W. Longfellow.

P.S. My regards to Profs. Willard and Felton when you meet them.[5]

MANUSCRIPT: Boston Public Library. ADDRESS: To/Charles Folsom Esq./Cambridge POSTMARKS: PORTLAND [*date illegible*]/PAID POSTAL ANNOTATION: Paid/S — L.

1. After his marriage to Mary Potter, Longfellow neglected his correspondence for some months while pursuing, among other things, his interest in textbooks. In January he took his bride to Cambridge, where he met Charles Folsom (1794-1872), a classical scholar, subsequently librarian of the Boston Athenaeum and at that time an editor for the University Press. Over the next year and a half he wrote some twenty-five letters to Folsom, dealing for the most part with the publication of his grammars and readers.

2. A reference to *Syllabus de la Grammaire Italienne* (Boston, 1832).

3. E. W. Metcalf (65.11), printer of the Italian grammar.

4. *Saggi de' Novellieri Italiani d'Ogni* (Boston, 1832). Gray & Bowen published both this book and the Italian grammar.

5. Sidney Willard (1780–1856), Hancock Professor of Hebrew and Oriental Languages; and Cornelius Conway Felton (1807–1862), professor of Greek at Harvard. Felton, later president of Harvard, became one of Longfellow's intimate friends.

199. *To Charles Folsom*

[Bowdoin College] Monday noon. [Feb. 19, 1832]

My dear Sir,

I here send you the Biog. Notice of Machiavelli, which is to stand at the head of his Belfagor in the Saggi. As I have arranged the Authors alphabetically, the *date* of Machiavelli will indicate his place in the collection.

I have just received a letter from Mr. Gray.[1] He says "Mr Metcalf makes a heavy charge for correction of proofs of Grammar. Was not the copy good?" I shall refer him to you for an answer. I made very few *alterations*: hardly anything, save cancelling two pages, as you will recollect. I can think of nothing else which could authorise the Col. to make extra charges.

My best regards to Mrs. F. In these my lady would join me were she here. I left her in Portland.

Very truly yours

H. W. Longfellow.

MANUSCRIPT: Boston Public Library. ADDRESS: To/Charles Folsom Esq./Cambridge/Mass. POSTMARKS: BRUNSWICK MAINE. FEB 20/PAID POSTAL ANNOTATION (*by Longfellow*): Paid. H.W.L.

1. Frederick T. Gray (1804–1855), a partner in Gray & Bowen.

200. *To Charles Folsom*

Bowdoin College   March 3rd 1832.

My dear Sir,

I am going to trouble you with a word or two concerning the "Saggi de' Novellieri." The sheets sent reached me safely, and I have been using them for a week. Of course, as I go over them with new-beginners, it is difficult for an error to escape our scrutiny. I have accordingly picked up one or two little stragglers, and send them back to you by to-day's mail with a mark upon their foreheads.

I think it will be necessary to *reprint* the first *two pages*. The reason is that in the first line of the Biog. Notice of Soave I have used the article before the word *autore*, which is incorrect, inasmuch as the article should not be employed before a noun, which expresses the quality of a preceding noun. I think it best therefore to strike out the words *"l'autore di questa Novella* [the author of this tale]" — as you will see by the sheet I send you by this evening's mail. It is possible that the sentence as it now stands may be justified by usage; but I think it cannot be, and am therefore very desirous to have the page reprinted. This is such a carping world, and I have thrown myself open to criticism so much by writing the Notices in Italian, that I must be upon my guard to parry every home thrust. I presume that Gray and Bowen will not object to this as I shall bear all the expense of the reprint. I shall write to them this evening upon the subject. Please send me a proof if reprinted.

Be kind enough to send me also a proof of the Title-page and Introduction. By the way — perhaps you can so contrive it so as to make the *reprint* come on to the last pages of the title-page signature. No doubt you can; and if so — so much the better.

I intend to prepare a Vocabulary of the antiquated words in the Older Writers, which must go in on the last signature. In order to prepare this, I must have the sheets of the work before me. Will you be good enough to send them to me as soon as you can by mail. You may send those already struck off *now*, if you please; and so continue them as they come out of press.

The little *Grammaire* looks finely in her *red coat*. I am quite pleased with the little *shaver*. The table of *Errata* was not printed. Why? I can now increase it a little with the following, the first and second of which are real[l]y *strange — prodigious*: —

Page	2nd. line 10	for (di *el*) read (di *il*)
"	" " 11	["] (a *el*) " (a *il*)
"	19 one line from bott. masculi*n* " masculi*ns*.
Page.	34. 4th line of the French — add — "et ton maître le sait."
"	131. 1[st] line from bottom for *le* read *les*.

Present my best regards and those of Mrs. L. to your lady, and consider me very truly yours

Henry W. Longfellow.

MANUSCRIPT: Boston Public Library. ADDRESS: To/Charles Folsom Esq./Cambridge./(Mass.) POSTMARKS: BRUNSWICK MAINE. MAY 4/PAID POSTAL ANNOTATION (*by Longfellow*): Paid. H. W. L.

201. *To Charles Folsom*

Bowdoin College   March 12. 1832.

My dear Sir,

Your favor of the 6th has just reached me. The sheets of the Novellieri came last night, by which I infer that your letter was delayed a day upon its journey as you mention sending all by the same mail. This will account for my not writing you by yesterday's mail, as you doubtless expected me to do.

I had a line a few days ago from Gray & Bowen, respecting a new edition of the Proverbes Dramatiques.[1] I did not know, that they wished to have a new-edition put to press so soon, or I should have taken the books to Cambridge with me in the Winter in order to have consulted with you upon the subject. Since receiving their letter, I have given all my leisure time to the subject, and have made farther selections so as to increase the quantity of matter contained in the work, and the value of it. I have also some changes to make in the arrangement of the pieces, which I shall presently mention. I am sorry Gray & Bowen talk of having it printed in the style you mention. The names of the speakers, we both of us thought, should go *before* the text, and not *above* as now: but it never entered my head to have them in *Italic*. They ought to be in *Small Caps*. I will tell you how I wish to have it done: — just like the dramatic extracts from Goldoni *etc* in Bacchi's *Prose*.[2] And then again the *paper* — I know you will agree with me there — the paper must not be like that of the *Vicar!*[3] As I have just remarked, the quantity of matter will be increased: — quite a number of what I think *capital* pieces will be added; — I intend to write, by way of introduction, a sketch of the origin and progress of the French drama — and to put my name on the title-page, and, as a matter of course, I want the book to be a handsome one. The truth is I think VERY HIGHLY of these Proverbes: I think they are finely written; and that there never was a school-book more liked by pupils. Had I not liked the work *exceedingly* I never should have *expended the money upon it, which the first edition cost me, but which I do not regret.* I will send you *corrected* copy by mail: and the *Original work*, from which the pieces are extracted, by first opportunity: — though a worse specimen of printing I think you never yet beheld. Touching the changes I wish to make in the order, they are these: 1st to intersperse the *additional plays* among the others, and not put them at the end: and 2nd to place all the pieces containing *bad french*, (whose number will be increased) at the end of the whole by themselves. Would it not be well to divide the book into parts: Part. 1. to contain the Proverbes in pure French: Part. 2nd. — those in *im*pure french, and Part 3rd. — (if it should not swell the volume too much) the "Bourgeois Gentilhomme"? What think you of this? The *Poulet* will lead the *van* as before: The names may be thus contracted, I should think. D'ORV. — FRÉM. — COMT. — LA BRIE needs no curtailing. For the other plays I will send the contractions with the copy. You ask if there are no *errors*? If you have read the first signature you can answer your own question. *Quand vous aurez* FINI LE POULET, *vous saurez y répondre vous-même* [When you have finished "le Poulet," you will be able to answer it yourself]. Yes indeed — a great many — but nothing quite equal to "*la Traité.*" By the way that leaf ought to be reprinted: I will pay for it, rather than have it go forth as it is. I have not the copy nor have I seen it since I left you: — my impression was that it remained at the Printing Office. I think however the mistake must have been the compositor's — though after such a dialect as *di el,* I will not be positive. I have not yet had time to go over the whole Grammaire with a critic's eye. Parts of it I have — the *most important* parts, I may say: but if the table of *errata* is not yet printed — and you can wait a few days longer I will do so — and let you know the result.

The *third* page of your letter quite *alarms* me, lest I should have said something amiss, touching the Colonel's *charge*. I did not exactly understand Gray & Bowen when they wrote, but as their words were those I quoted in my letter on the subject — "*no inconsiderable item of the whole expense*" — I took the liberty of adverting to the subject. The expression was evidently a *Gray-and-Bowen-ism*. Why, certainly they ought not to complain. The charge seems to me light — now that I understand it. But how happens it that your reading the proofs is not taken into the account? There must be something there, which I do not understand; for I always regarded you as the *principal* reader — and myself as accessary. I thought I was helping *you*, and not you helping *me!* — and of course presumed that you were to present your account, the same as if I had been a thousand miles off. If the case be not so, you must have thought me exceedingly uncourteous not even to have thanked you for your attention and corrections. This however we will discuss at full length when we meet again — for as you see I have not room enough left to make a handsome bow: and if I had, I should make it to Mrs. Folsom, to whom please present my lady's kind regards, and mine.

Very truly, and with much regard, yours
H. W. Longfellow

March. 13.

I have an opportunity to send the *Original* volumes of the *Proverbes*, and avail myself of it: — though I have not had time to mark all the *errors* in the pieces I intend to add. I will drop a line to you in a day or two by mail in regard to the *order* of the pieces. For the 2nd you may take if you please, "L'Âne dans le Potager" as it is rather short — and on that account had better precede the longer pieces. The contraction in the names may run — GOURCH. — ADEL. BROUTE. (No contraction in monosyllables) ST. AND. — GERM. It seems hardly worth while to prefix the M. — MLLE. &c.

P.S. I am very glad you made those corrections in Bandello. If not too late please make one in Boccaccio. Leave out in the description of *Nuta* the *fante di cucina* [scullery wench] this line (*e con un paio di poppe che parevan due ceston da letame* [and with a pair of dugs that looked like two manure-baskets]. But how very small the volume will be! I wish I could make additions to it, — a few tales more from Boccaccio. Would not Gray & Bowen like this, think you?

MANUSCRIPT: Boston Public Library. ADDRESS: To/Charles Folsom Esq./Cambridge./Mass. POSTAL ANNOTATION (*by Longfellow*): Paid. H.W.L.

1. A second and revised edition of *Manuel de Proverbes Dramatiques* was published in Boston by Gray & Bowen during 1832.

2. Pietro Bachi, *Scelta di prose italiane, tratte da' più celebri scrittori antichi e moderni* (Cambridge, 1828). Bachi (1787–1853) taught Italian and Spanish at Harvard, 1826–1846.

3. Longfellow's first book for Gray & Bowen was *Le Ministre de Wakefield* (Boston, 1831), an edition of a French translation of Goldsmith's novel.

202. *To Charles Folsom*

Bowdoin College   March 19. 1832.

My dear Sir,

Yours of the 17th reached me last evening, and though I am in as great haste as you could have been when you wrote, I will not delay an answer which may be of importance. I presume Gray & Bowen would have no objection to the addition of a few pages more to the Novellieri; I will however write to them upon the subject, though if you could drop them a single line asking the question, it would answer all purposes. If they say *yes,* please go on by adding one more tale from Boccaccio (leaving out oaths etc). The one I have selected is *Novella* 3; Giornata 8; describing the adventures of Calandrino in pursuit of the Stone to render him invisible. In the mean time I will have something else in readiness.

Please strike from the Glossary I sent the following words:

Gli *in vece di* [instead of] li BOCC —
Li ”   ”   ”   i ”

I thought these might embarrass the scholar — but upon reflection I think not. They are both grammatical forms — and sufficiently clear.

Please reprint *la Traité*. I think it best, taking all things into consideration. A critic could not have a better handle. I will willingly bear the expense.

With regard to the *Proverbes,* I am trying to negociate with Gray & Bowen: — have requested better paper, etc. Touching the idea of putting the *bad* French in Italic — it pleases me: the only difficulty would be with the bad, in correct *idioms*. The incorrect orthography could be easily marked by the italic type — but if you marked the incorrect and inelegant *idioms* in the same way, you would get nearly the whole into italic. I will see what plan can be devised.

More fully upon this point in my next.

Very truly yours,
H. W. Longfellow.

MANUSCRIPT: Boston Public Library. ADDRESS: To/Charles Folsom Esq/Cambridge POSTMARK: BRUNSWICK MAINE. MAR 19

203. *To Gray & Bowen*

Messrs Gray & Bowen

Bowdoin College   March. 29. 1832.
Gentlemen,

Yours of the 26th inst. has just reached me. You can hardly imagine the *consternation* it caused me.[1] Why — a fortnight ago I sent Mr. Folsom additional matter to continue the Italian Reading-book with — and have been waiting to hear from him again — in order to supply more which I have prepared. My letter must have been lost.[2] I regret this more than you can — because I hoped that in the course of a week or ten days I should have the books to go on with my classes. I have now a class of 8 or 10 — who have finished what was sent in sheets — and in about ten days shall commence with another class of about 30! What is to be done? Would it not be well to do up 40 or 50 copies in paper — and then when the remainder is finished all can be bound up together? Please write me on this point.

Under the circumstances you mention you must of course go on with the Proverbes Dramatiques. I will do the best I can with those

I have on hand. By to day's mail I send *copy No 1.* just as I wish to have it. Please make some inquiries about the ill-fated letter I wrote to Mr. Folsom, as I made some remarks therein upon this point. I should like to see the *first* proof; and would request also to have the sheets sent me as fast as printed, that I may judge what additions to make. I do not think you will find them any too numerous.

To recur to the Italian Book again: — you need feel no allarm concerning the size, for I have matter on hand to increase it *to any number of pages you wish.* I here subjoin references for farther copy, which Mr. Folsom will understand.

Boccaccio. Giornata 2. Novella. 4. Title "Landolfo Ruffolo, il Corsale di Ravello."

Giornata 5. Novella 3. Title "Il Castello di Campo di Fiore."

Giornata 6. Novella 4. Title "La Gru con un piè."

————— 8 ————— 3 ——— "I tre Pittori di Firenze."

Mr Folsom
Please omit all obscene oaths and thing[s] of the kind.

H. W. L.

More copy whenever you wish.

MANUSCRIPT: Boston Public Library.

1. Gray & Bowen had written, "The Italian Reading Book [*Saggi de' Novellieri Italiani d'Ogni Secolo*] is still unfinished — we keep it in status quo in hopes that you will make some additions. When we first commenced the Grammar, you told us that the Grammar would make about 60 or 70 pages and the Reading Book 140 or 150. As we were desirous of some uniformity in appearance and price if possible, we bought a very *thick* paper for the Grammar and a *thin* one for the Reader. The result has overset our scheme and nonplus'd us altogether, — the Grammar is 104 pages and the Reader 90!! The smallest book has the thinnest paper. This circumstance makes us very desirous to enlarge the Reader if possible. Please inform us by return mail whether you can do this."

2. See the preceding letter.

204. *To Jared Sparks*

Bowdoin College   April 21. 1832.

My dear Sir,

I hear nothing farther said concerning the sale of Mr. Elliot's library, upon which subject I had a short conversation with you the last time I saw you. I am very desirous of purchasing the 'Classici Italiani,' and wish to inquire of you whether the work can be purchased in case the entire Library should not be sold.[1] Would you have the goodness, when you can do it without inconvenience, to ask some one, who would be likely to know, if the work can be purchased, and at what price.

Very truly yours
H. W. Longfellow.

P.S. It was not in my power to call upon you in order to visit Mr. E.'s library, as was agreed upon. Please pardon me for breaking the appointment.

When you meet Charley Amory[2] in company, if you have not anything in particular to say, you may remember me to him, by way of exordium.

MANUSCRIPT: Harvard College Library.   ADDRESS: To/Jared Sparks. Esq./Boston./ To be left at/Gray & Bowens.   ENDORSEMENT: From H. W. Longfellow/ Apl. 28th. 1832

1. Longfellow apparently refers to William Havard Eliot, a member of the Harvard class of 1815 and builder of the Tremont House, the most imposing hotel in the country for several years. Eliot had died in 1831, age thirty-five. The work that Longfellow wished to purchase was *Classici Italiani* (Milano, 1802–1818), 250 vols.

2. Longfellow had met Charles Amory (1808–1898), a Harvard medical student, in Göttingen.

205. *To Charles Folsom*

[Bowdoin College, April, 1832]

Mr. Folsom,
Dear Sir,

Have you been able to find the meaning of two words I sent you some time since,[1] one in the Neapolitan, the other in the Roman dialect? They were

Neapolitan — *Saraca*; "Amor me ha *bruscoliato* come una *saraca*."[2]
Roman —   *Sciutè*: "Un certo sciutè
                   Me dette fino a tre
                   Botti nella testa."[3]
Quere? is *Sciutè* vulg. for *ciotto*?[4]

MANUSCRIPT: Boston Public Library.

1. This letter is unrecovered. Longfellow needed the definitions for his essay on the "History of the Italian Language and Dialects," *North American Review,* XXXV (October 1832), 283–342. For his use of the two terms and their source, see the essay, pp. 315 and 317.

2. "Love has roasted me like a herring."

3. "A certain ragamuffin/gave me as many as three/Blows upon the head."

4. In his reply of April 24, 1832, Folsom sent Longfellow a definition of *Saraca* from Giuseppi Boerio, *Dizionario del dialetto Veneziano* (Venezia, 1829) but confessed, "I am obliged to give up 'sciutè,' as hopeless."

206. *To Charles Folsom*

Bowdoin College   May 18. 1832.

My dear Sir,

I had the pleasure of receiving last night the *Vocab. Mantov.* you were kind enough to send. It helps to throw some light upon Galeotti's *Canzonetta*, though I am not yet sure that I have made out the whole of it with unerring precision.[1]

I shall be in Boston next week, and shall of course have the pleasure of seeing you in Cambridge. I shall bring with me the remainder of the *Vocab. delle Voci Antiche* etc etc for the *Sagg. Novel.* as what I sent was very imperfect.[2]

Very truly yours

H. W. Longfellow.

MANUSCRIPT: Boston Public Library. ADDRESS: To/Charles Folsom Esq/Cambridge/Gray & Bowen

1. Longfellow refers to Francesco Cherubini's *Vocabolario Mantovano-Italiano* (Milano, 1827). Giovanni Maria Galeotti had written his songs in the dialect of Mantua.

2. A reference to the "Indice" of the *Saggi de' Novellieri Italiani d' Ogni Secolo.*

207. *To George Washington Greene*

Brunswick   June 2nd 1832.

My dear Geordie,

Yours of the 29th April has just reached me, on my arrival from Boston. What a misfortune has befallen me! To be so near seeing you, and yet not to see you! To be within a half-day's journey of you, and yet not visit you! Why, if you had put your letter into the mail one day — *one single day* earlier, I should have received it a fortnight ago, and should have posted on to welcome your return to New England,[1] in my own bodily presence, instead of sending you this sheet, blotted with pale ink and scrawled with a barbarous pen, from a chamber in the "Tontine Hotel" of this village. Our vacation has *just closed;* — the Summer term commenced to-day; and I returned to town this afternoon. Half the vacation I have passed in Boston, and as my time was wholly at my disposal, had I known of your return, I should have been in East Greenwich before the set of sun. Your letter is dated "April 29th" and bears the post-mark "*May* 18th": — it must have reached this place the same evening, that I left it for Portland. But adieu regrets! — let the past hold its peace and be still, whilst the voice of friendship welcomes you home again, and the future promises a happy meeting. I long to see you and your fair young wife. Greet her most cordially from me, and tell her in your purest Tuscan, with the softest Roman accent, that my lady very warmly reciprocates her friendly salutation.

I mingle my tears with yours at the loss of your books.[2] What a loss! Truly you are a philosopher; and you deserve to have a situation, where a noble library shall console you for your present calamity and deprivation. Still I can offer you little consolation, for after all, the acquisition of new books can never supply the loss of old ones, any more than the acquisition of new friends can make good the place of the old and true.

Your suggestions concerning the chair of Mod. Lang. in the University of New York please me very much.[3] I would gladly make the exchange; and yet I know not why I say so, for I know nothing of the proposed endowments in the N. York University, nor of the salary, or tuition, or perquisites of the Professors. Will you be good enough to write me upon this point; and tell me what will probably be the duties, and what the income of the Prof. of modern languages? It would be wrong, you know, to solicit a situation of this kind, without having first resolved to accept the appointment, in case I should prove successful in my application: — and, of course, I cannot decide upon this point, without first knowing all the circumstances of the case. *If faut s'informer des tenans et des aboutissans* [One must inform oneself about the particulars]. You see how cooly I weigh matters. I hope you will give me the credit of talking like an *old one*. And beside, how do you know that Bowdoin would please you? You may not like the town — you may not like the College — in a word, there are a thousand things, which may not exactly suit you. Jump right into the Boston stage-coach; — take the steam-boat to Portland; and in four hours after your arrival in Portland you will be with me in Brunswick; — for the distance between the two latter places is but 25 miles. This would give us an opportunity of conversing fully upon the subject, and you could judge, from personal observation, how Brunswick would suit you. In case you cannot do this, our only way is to communicate freely by letters. Taking for granted, then, that the Professorship of Mod. Lang. in the N. York University will be placed upon a good footing in regard to income — (for you know a married man is obliged to consider such matters) I doubt not that I should be highly delighted with the situation. On first commencing my Professorial duties, I was actuated by the same feelings, which seem now to influence you. I sought retirement; and I am confident I did wisely. Next September completes 3 years, that I have been laboring on in this little solitude; and I now feel a strong desire to tread a stage on which I can take longer strides, and *spout* to a larger audience. In short, I coincide with you in the opinions you express upon this subject, leaving it to others to judge, whether I am capable of filling the chair with credit to the institution and to myself. And now in regard to yourself — I think you would like the seclusion of this village — coming to it as you would with a very strong zest for quiet, uninterrupted study. Nor do I think there would be much, if any difficulty in securing the place to you, in case I should leave. The boards of Trustees and Overseers of the College meet in September, and should a vacancy occur in the professorship of Mod. Lang. I think there is no doubt, that it would be filled immediately, such is the fever at present in this part of the country for the study of French, Spanish, etc. The regular salary of the Profs. is $1000, per annum: but for the first year or two they give but 800. To this you may add the Office of Librarian, as I have done, which yields 100 more. Living is very cheap here, so that the salary is a good one, compared with those given elsewhere. You will not be *required* to lecture, though this, I think, you would do from choice. During the first year of my residence here I gave instruction in French and Spanish: — last year and this present year, I have instructed in German, French, Spanish, and Italian. *French* is the only study *required* by law: the others are optional; you can manage about as you please with them; as your opinion and wishes will be a kind of law upon the subject. But you must come on and see us this summer. I am sorry I have not a house to invite you to; but thus far I have been obliged to take chambers in a boarding-house, not having been able to procure a house exactly suited to my mind. I hope, however, to find one before long. You can have a chamber in the house where I am, whenever you will do me the favor to occupy it; for I keep one to spare for my friends, and though I may be obliged to play the host on a small scale, you shall not be the less welcome on that account. I am not, however, quite ready for you yet, for I have to paint and paper — this week; and then another week will be necessary for drying. This is a plague — *ma che volete? — in un villaggio non si può stare con tutti i suoi commodi* [but what can one do? — in a village one can't have all the conveniences].

In conclusion I must thank you for the lively interest you still take in what relates to me, and assure you that the interest I have always taken in your advancement remains undiminished. I am glad you have undertaken the translation of Guizot.[4] You will thereby introduce into our literature a valuable work, and I doubt not do yourself great credit. You ask what I have been doing of late. I have no very satisfactory answer to give. Last Winter I published a little "Syllabus de la Grammaire Italienne" — a small Italian Grammar written in French for the use of my classes here, and a reading-book is just issuing from the press, under the title of "Saggi de' Novellieri Italiani d' Ogni Secolo etc." I will send you copies by the first opportunity. I trust this little grammar will not interfere in the least with the plan you once proposed; and I confess, one reason I had for writing it in French was to avoid the possibility of interfering with your proposed work.[5] My design is to make such a *Syllabus* of the Grammar of each language I teach. Besides these books I have on hand a "Cours de Langue Française," of which I will speak with you hereafter.[6] In addition to these things, which, as you see, are in the way of my profession, I have occasionally sent an article to the N. A. Review. In the last No. I wrote a paper on the "Moral and Devotional Poetry of Spain," and in the No. for January 1832. a paper on "The Defence of Poetry," which you must read, and give me your opinion of.[7]

Most truly yours

H. W. L.

P.S. I presume you will gladly excuse me for not having given you a long description of my lady. It would be useless, when I hope to see you so soon. Once more my kind regards to all your family — and to that of *"il Signor Cooke"* when you see them or write to them.

P.S. The wrath exhibited on your first page is quite amusing. I offer no apology for my long neglect of my old friend. All I can say is, that it was very *shabby* in me to suffer your letter to remain unanswered for so long a time. I trust the confession of my error will obtain grace therefor, and absolution.

Write me again without delay, and tell me what kind of certificate or credentials are wanting, and how soon they must be sent on to you. I hope it is not already too late. Unless I have been misinfor[m]ed, the salaries at N. York will be small, and the Profs. have the Tuition beside their salaries. Is it so?

MANUSCRIPT: Longfellow Trust Collection. ADDRESS: To/Mr. Geo: W. Greene./East Greenwich/R. Island. POSTMARK: BRUNSWICK MAINE. JUN. 3

1. Greene had returned to America in March after about a year abroad.

2. In his letter of April 29 Greene had described how the books he sent from Europe were severely damaged when the ship carrying them went aground off Long Island.

3. Greene had proposed that Longfellow try for the professorship at New York University and, if successful, arrange for Greene's appointment at Bowdoin.

4. Greene had written, "I am at present engaged in translating Guizot's history

of European civilization." He seems to have finished the manuscript, although he never published it. See Letter No. 372.

5. Greene eventually published an Italian grammar entitled *Primary Lessons in Italian* (New York, 1865).

6. Under the general title "Cours de Langue Française" Longfellow intended to issue a series of four books. For details, described in a prospectus bound in the 1831 edition of the *Elements of French Grammar,* see Luther S. Livingston, *A Bibliography of the First Editions in Book Form of the Writings of Henry Wadsworth Longfellow* (New York, 1908), p. 11.

7. For these essays see the *North American Review,* XXXIV (April 1832), 277–315, and (January 1832), 56–78.

208. *To Charles Folsom*

Bowdoin College   June — 1832.[1]

My dear Sir,

These in great haste, in order to furnish you with more copy for the Proverbes Dram. After what was last sent take the following:

L'Histoire   in Tome 2.
Le Persifleur   ”   ”   8.
Le Comédien Bourgeois; corrected copy sent with this.
L'Uniforme de Campagne. Tome 8
L'Amateur du Tragique: cor. copy sent with this.

By the way, there is one piece, the name of which I forgot to note down, and have forgotten; — but which I am desirous of introducing. It will come in with those containing *bad French,* as it affords some delectable specimens. There is a Swiss corporal in the play, whose superior officer is sick. The Physician orders him to procure a *garde-malade* [male nurse] and he not exactly understanding the order — sends for a guard of ten soldiers. The piece is full of blunders of the kind. I think the title is "Le Suisse Malade."

With regard to the Proverbes, which are printed from the Original and not from my book, you must not rely upon my marks, as I sent you the books before I had finished marking them. Among other things you will find the pu[n]ctuation very bad.

Very truly yours
H. W. Longfellow[2]

I must again request your particular care in regard to the orthography and *grammatical correctness* even of the *old books* from which you reprint. Otherwise errors will slip in to the new edition. Thus I find on p. 40. about the middle *ces généreux jeunes gens* [these fine young people], instead of *"généreuses jeunes gens"* — *gens* is feminine when the adjective precedes it. P. 84. — just above the middle, the expression "DU *depuis*" for *depuis*. P. 96 — middle, *"ne biovent, ni* NE *mangent"* [neither drink nor eat]; — NE is *un de trop* [one too many]. I am sorry to give you this additional trouble; but thinking you wanted the books immediately, I sent them without revising my own corrections, or even completing them.

Sunday afternoon.
Miss C. Danforth, daughter of the late celebrated Dr. Danforth, died here yesterday morning, of a disease in the heart and liver.[3]
Mrs L. joins me in kind regards to your lady and yourself.
I sent the College Library books a fortnight ago by Mr. Gray. I presume you received them.
Please send me more *sheets*. I have on hand 11 signatures. — pp. 132.

MANUSCRIPT: Boston Public Library.

1. Longfellow possibly wrote this letter on June 22 or 23. Caroline Danforth, mentioned in the "Sunday afternoon" postscript, made out her will at the house of Mrs. Mary Ann Fales on June 18. The "Sunday afternoon" is presumably June 24.
2. The direction "(over)" follows the signature.
3. Dr. Samuel Danforth (1740–1827), a prominent Tory during the Revolution, had enjoyed one of the most respected medical practices in Boston. His daughter Caroline, a single woman of Boston, died in the Fales House while Longfellow and his wife were boarders there.

209. *To Charles Folsom*

Bowdoin College   July 2nd 1832.
My dear Sir,
I have just recd. signatures 12 to 17 inclusive of the Proverbes Dramatiques. I am in great dismay at beholding the "Sot Ami" and "La Recommendation" — as I did not intend to have these printed.[1] Please write me a line by return of mail, and tell me what plays you have recd for printing; as I sadly fear some one of my letters has not reached you.
In great haste, very truly yours
H. W. Longfellow.

MANUSCRIPT: Boston Public Library.   ADDRESS: To/Charles Folsom Esq./Cambridge

1. These stories were printed, however, in all editions of the *Proverbes Dramatiques*.

210. *To George Washington Greene*

Bowdoin College   July 6. 1832.

My dear Greene,

I wrote you a long letter about a month since[1] in answer to your last, and in reference to the Professorship in the New York University, and as I have heard nothing from you, I fear the letter may not have reached you. I want to get some more particular information respecting the new university; and moreover I am very desirous to have you visit me this summer, in order to converse more fully upon the matter, and that you may see our college and our Executive, and see how the appearance of things pleases you at the north. Besides I want to see you, independently of all these things, — and above all I want to see your wife. So please present to her the affectionate regards of my Lady and myself, and assure her that we should both be very much delighted to see her in Brunswick as soon as possible.

How far advanced are you in your translation of Guizot? Who is to be your publisher? I hope you have already made arrangements in regard to the publication of the work. If you have not I shall take the liberty of advising you, as in the case of your proposed Italian Grammar, not to publish *on your own account*, as the phrase of common parlance runs. You *must* have some well-known publisher engaged in the work; otherwise, whatever may be its merits, there is no hope of a good sale. Therefore, I beg of you, attend to this most prosaic and *material* part of the business without delay. I know you will translate the work well — for you will do it *con amore*; — but that is not enough to insure success. You must have a good publisher interested in the matter, otherwise after spending much precious time in the completion of your translation, the result — in sorrow be it said and heaven forfend — may be both mortifying and disheartening. Now don't set me down as a *sinister corvex*, — an old croaker, nor an envious rival, because I most sincerely and ardently wish you all success — and in order that you may be more sure of it, advise you not to omit the necessary preliminary steps. This, however, may be entirely useless, as you may have already pursued the very course I am now advising you to take. Mais, Monsieur, que ne vous faites-vous auteur? Pourquoi vous borner à de simples traductions? Que n'écrivez-vous pour les *Revues*? Il vaudrait mieux, selon mon avis, débuter par là; en même temps, vous mettrez en train *le grand ouvrage*, avec tout l'attirail nécessaire pour emporter les applaudissemens du public par un coup de main. Tâchez, donc, de nous donner quelque chose dans votre genre; — un Essai sur l'état actuel de la Langue et de la Litterature

379

Italiennes, — par exemple; — ou un Aperçu de la Poésie Italienne du dixneuvièmc Siècle. Qu'en pensez-vous?

Quant à moi, je ne saurais vous dire rien de nouveau. Mon petit livre, "Saggi de' Novellieri Italiani" paraîtra incessamment, et la seconde édition des "Proverbes Dramatiques" est actuellement sous presse. Je vous enverrai des exemplaires de tous les deux, aussitôt publiés, ainsi que de ma "Grammaire Italienne."

J'attends de jour en jour l'arrivée d'un de mes amis de Madrid. C'est un Garde-du-corps du Roi Ferdinand; — un beau jeune homme de beaucoup d'esprit, et à-peu-près de votre âge. Je l'ai prié très-souvent de venir en Amérique, et en fin il a cédé à mes instances pressantes, et va s'embarquer à Gibraltar pour se rendra chez moi. J'espère qu'il s'est déjà mis en route, puisqu'il m'a mandé qu'il ne tarderait guère. Je voudrais bien que vous fussiez ici au moment de son arriv‖ée,‖ cela serait un agrément de plus, car je ne doute pas que vous eussiez bien du plaisir à faire sa connaissance; — au moins la vôtre, serait-elle un grand advantage pour lui.

Ecrivez-moi bientôt. Mes complimens chez vous, et croyez-moi toujours votre très affectionné ami [2]

H. W. Longfellow.

MANUSCRIPT: Harvard College Library. ADDRESS: To/Mr. Geo. W. Greene/ East Greenwich/Rhode Island POSTMARK: BRUNSWICK MAINE. JUL 7.

1. Letter No. 207.
2. "But Monsieur, why do you not turn author? Why do you limit yourself to simple translations? Why do you not write for the *Reviews*? It would be better, according to my judgment, to begin in this way; at the same time, you can get the *great work* underway, with all the paraphernalia necessary to earn the public's applause with a surprise attack. Try, therefore, to give us something in your style; — an essay on the present state of the Italian language and literature, — for example; — or a sketch of the Italian poetry of the nineteenth century. What do you think?/As for me, I know nothing new to tell you. My little book 'Saggi de' Novellieri Italiani,' is appearing soon, and the second edition of 'Proverbes Dramatiques' is actually now in press. I will send you copies of both, as soon as they are published, as also my 'Grammaire Italienne.'/I expect daily the arrival of one of my friends from Madrid [José Cortés y Sesti]. He is a guardsman of King Ferdinand; — a handsome young fellow with a lot of wit, and nearly your age. I have very often begged him to come to America, and finally he has yielded to my urgent entreaties, and is embarking at Gibraltar to come visit me. I hope that he is already on his way, since he sent word to me that he would not be much delayed. I hope very much that you will be here at the time of his arrival — that will be an additional pleasure — for I do not doubt that you will be much pleased to make his acquaintance; — at least making your acquaintance would be of great advantage to him./ Write me soon. My compliments to all of you, and believe me always your very affectionate friend"

211. *To Charles Folsom*

Bowdoin College Library   July 13. 1832.

My dear Sir,

Your letter reached me this morning, and as I have a good opportunity of sending you a speedy reply by Mr. Gray, who leaves town at 1 o'clock this afternoon, I take the largest piece of letter paper the Library affords and send greeting[s]. I recollect marking the several plays you mention so that it was no fault of yours that they were printed. On re-perusing them, however, I changed my mind; and the only difficulty was, that I did not notify you of the change until too late. It is of no great consequence.

From the account you give me, I think you and your family must present a *moving* spectacle. So far from being an inconvenience to be living as you are between your old and new house, I think you must find it a great advantage as it is *nearer the printing office*.[1]

Excuse these vile attempts to be witty. I will shortly write you in full. If you want copy — that is if you have got through the "Comédien Bourgeois" including all the pieces in the former edition excepting the "Bossu" and "Les Deux Auteurs" you may go on with the Plays containing bad French.

Mrs L. joins me in kind regards to your Lady and yourself.

In great haste and harrassed with many doubts as to the legibility of this note, I am very truly yours

H. W. Longfellow

MANUSCRIPT: Boston Public Library.   ADDRESS: To/Charles Folsom Esq./Cambridge/By Mr. Gray.

1. On July 10, 1832, Folsom had written that he was moving to the house lately occupied by Professor Willard. "I say, could you see me in my *transition* state with a house no where — you would pity and perhaps pardon the sad writer of this wretched scrawl."

212. *To Elizabeth Chase Howard*[1]

Bowdoin College   July 14. 1832.

My dear Elizabeth,

You do not know how ashamed I am of this long delay in writing you. It is both ungallant and unfriendly; and the emphatic phrase of "horrid old men!" keeps ringing in my ears. No cause, however, is so bad, but what something may be said in its favor, and no pecadillo so far beyond redemption, that nothing can be brought in extenuation. So it is in my case. I have certain reasons, which stifle "the still small voice"[2] within; and at times render me rather *hard of hearing*, as to any friendly reproaches from without. The truth is I am much occupied; and even when I have a moment's leisure, there is always some temptation near at hand which claims its appropriation. The leisure of a student, you know, is not like the leisure of any other man whatever. The man of business often fills up his hours of recreation with books and writing; but the student never. He, whose profession is to read and write, seldom thinks of looking to either for amusement. All this goes to show why, in the hum-drum life of this Eastern solitude, I had rather take *one* ride than write *fifty* letters. There — there's a whole page of apology; and I dare say you had rather pardon my negligence without more ado, than to have me fill two more pages, with the same kind of logic.

And what are you all doing in West-Street? Eliza [Potter] [3] I presume is still with you. I am very happy to hear, that she is enjoying herself so much in Boston. I know exactly how much of her enjoyment she owes to you and the Doctor, because I have *data* to judge from. I understand that *all Boston* is moving out of town, to enjoy the sea-breeze and the country air. I suppose you remain content with what comes over the Common and steals through *that orthodox blind.* Shall you leave Boston, when the Cholera arrives there? I hope you will: — and that you will take that opportunity to visit us in Brunswick. Mary wants to see you sadly, and so do I. This village of ours is so secluded, that the visit of a friend is doubly delightful: for we have it all to ourselves. And then the streets are so wide and airy, that we hope to escape the pestilence.

By the way, I must not forget to acknowledge the favor of your little pencil note of June 13th reminding me of my *promise.* [4] I am very glad the Rock-of-Gibraltar breast-pin pleases you, and shall be proud — (laying my hand upon my heart) — to have it worn by you in remembrance of your absent friend.

Mr. Cunningham called upon us on his way from Bangor to Boston. I was very sorry not to see him, but being at college at the time, I was deprived of the pleasure. Some one told me a few days ago that there had been a *jar* between him and his lady. Think — how gossip flies on the wings of the wind. I contradicted the gentleman's report — and said it was another Mr. Cunningham. But all this, of course, is *under the rose*; for I would not be thought to give credence or currency to any such vague and unpleasant rumors. [5]

I have very little news to send you about Mary or myself. We do not have even lovers' quarrels to relieve the *monotony of married life.* The only point upon which we disagree is *smoking.* This sometimes gives rise to animated discussions — and ends in a promise never to smoke again in her parlor: — which promise, like all promises *extorted by violence*, I consider as by no means obligatory, and of course it ends *in smoke*, and thus gives me the pleasure of making another.

We hear that your cousin Sally Sullivan is soon to reside at "41 Great Marlborough Street."[6] There is something of discrepancy in the ages — but saving that, I should think it an excellent match. They both have genius — and taste; — and as they are fond of music they can sing an eternal *duet* through life. *His* last song seems to be "Come o'er the sea — maiden, with me": — which he sings to some purpose. Write me about this, will you, dear, — and congratulate the bridegroom.

Farewell. My kindest regards to the Doctor, and to all Mrs. Howard's family including Mrs. Cunningham. "Little Mary" joins me in this, and in much love to yourself and Eliza. Do me the favor to write soon, and I will be for once in my life a circumspect and punctual correspondent.

If I write three lines more, I shall miss the post; — so once more farewell.

Very truly and affectionately yours
Henry W. Longfellow.

MANUSCRIPT: unrecovered; text from photostat, Longfellow Trust Collection. ADDRESS: To/Mrs. J. C. Howard./Care of Dr. Howard/West Street./Boston POSTMARK: BRUNSWICK MAINE. JUL 14

1. Elizabeth Chase (77.5) married John Clark Howard (1805-1844), a Boston physician, in 1829.

2. I Kings 19:12.

3. Elizabeth Ann Potter (b. 1810), Mary Potter Longfellow's elder sister.

4. Since the note does not survive, Longfellow's promise is unknown.

5. James Cunningham, a Boston merchant, was the husband of Catherine Hays Howard, sister-in-law of Longfellow's correspondent.

6. Sarah Williams Sullivan (1810-1892), daughter of William Sullivan, a well-known Boston lawyer and author, married Gilbert Stuart Newton (1797-1835) on August 22, 1832. Newton, the celebrated artist and friend of Washington Irving, took his bride to live in London in October.

213. *To Charles Folsom*

[Bowdoin College, July 26, 1832]

My dear Sir,

The foregoing, together with an instance or two of the word *déjà* without any accent on the final *a*, are all the errors I have been able to find in the sheets.[1] You will perceive I have noted down the most minute as well as those of greater importance. All marked √ I should think it necessary to print: the rest had better be omitted. For many of them might pass, and would pass, and *do* pass every day in conversation as current as any classic idiom, and perhaps more so. Take for example "Qu'est-ce que ce Monsieur Tibia?" — instead of "Qui est-ce que" etc. However in this matter ‖"je‖ m'en rapporte à vous [I leave it to you]," as usual: you may eith‖er increase‖ or diminish the list of the condemned.

In the greatest haste most truly yours,

H. W. Longfellow.

In regard to the *Preface,* I have hardly decided what to do. Please give me your advice. Would you strike out the *Avis* [foreword] in French, and put in its place a short English Advertisement? Or would you let the *Avis* remain, and add to it an English Advertisement? I incline to the *former,* and will send you in a few days all the introductory matter necessary.

MANUSCRIPT: Boston Public Library. ADDRESS: To/Charles Folsom Esq./Cambridge/Mass. POSTMARK: BRUNSWICK MAINE. JUL. 26 POSTAL ANNOTATION (*by Longfellow*): Paid. H.W.L./No. 2

1. The list of errors is missing. The book referred to is *Manuel de Proverbes Dramatiques.*

214. *To Charles Folsom* [1]

[Bowdoin College, c. August 1, 1832]

ADVERTISEMENT.

This collection of dramatic pieces has been prepared as a Second Class-book in the study of the French language, and is intended to serve as an introduction to the higher and more classic Drama. It consists of short and amusing comedies, in which, as the title denotes, some popular proverb is illustrated. The original work, from which the selection has been made, was published at Paris between the years 1768 and 1782, in eight volumes 8vo, under the title of Proverbes Dramatiques. The name of the author is unknown.

The present edition contains several pieces not inserted in the first; and those containing incorrect French are placed together at the close of the volume. They may be used with great advantage in a course of instruction, by causing the pupil to correct and explain the errors contained in them.

H. W. L. [2]

[...] place. I believe I have said all that is necessary. People *some-times* take the trouble to read *short* advertisements, but *long* ones seldom or *never*. Have the goodness to send me a *proof* of the title page and advertisement. It shall be returned, *if I find anything to alter*, by return of mail: — *otherwise* you may strike it off.

Would you have the kindness to lend me from the College Library the "Coplas de Don Jorge Manrique." I wish to translate the whole of that fine Ode. I wrote Mr. Felton, a few days since, requesting him to copy for me the stanzas which I have not.[3] I was sorry afterwards; for I hear that his eyes [are not] better, which is probably the reason I have not heard from him directly. If you can *conveniently* send me the book during the course of the present month, you might mention it to Mr. Felton, and save him the trouble of copying. I am slowly preparing some Spanish Translations for the press, so that you and the *Colonel* need not forget me.

Very truly yours
H. W. Longfellow.

MANUSCRIPT: Boston Public Library. ADDRESS: To/Charles Folsom Esq./Cambridge./By Mr Gray.[4]

1. The following fragment begins with the Advertisement prepared by Longfellow for the second edition of *Manuel de Proverbes Dramatiques* and concludes with the ending of the covering letter.

2. A note by Folsom appears beside this Advertisement: "Col. M. [Metcalf] Please to have this set up as the Preface to the book of French Plays."

3. This letter is unrecovered.

4. The address appears on a separate sheet, roughly the same size as the letter and filed with it. The penciled date "c. August. 1832" appears on this sheet. Mr. Gray was presumably Frederick T. Gray (199.1).

215. *To George Washington Pierce, Monsieur Rigaud,[1]
and Anne Longfellow*

Bowdoin College   August. 5. 1832

My dear George,

I am disappointed in not being able to visit you this week; and also in not seeing Anne in Brunswick. We hope she will come soon; for commencement is near at hand, and now our Summer fruits are in perfection — *blue-berries* and *raspberries* in abundance.

Has Mr. Rigaud left town? If not, will you have the goodness to hand him the following.

Very truly yours
H. W. Longfellow

Monsieur Rigaud,

    voulez-vous avoir la complaisance de me traduire *littéralement* en Français le fable suivante, écrite en Langue Provençale, et de me dire s'il y a beaucoup de différence entre cette langue et le Languedocien du département Tarn et Garonne. Et veuillez bien en recevoir mes remercimens d'avance.

J'ai l'honneur d'être
Votre très humble serviteur,
H. W. Longfellow.

L'Esquiroou et la Castaigno.

    Un Esquiroou troubet à jun
    Uno castaigno doou gros grun,
Lizo, fresco, couroüe. Bon, dis din soun lengagi,
    Eissoto va ben! — boüen couragi;
    Veici tout just ce que mi foou,
Per countenta ma fam et rampli me bedeno.
    Esquiroous, coumo cadun soou
    Eme pau cauvo fan calleno.
Tout jouïous s'en sesis, s'asseto encountinen;
Requanquillo sa coüe, puis din sei pato viro,
    Reviro, sente, admiro
Esto castaigno, et puis li calo un coou de dent,
    Mai reneguet ben leou sa vido
    Quand la troubet touto pourrido,
    Vermenoüe, nue noun valie ren.
    Aquel esquiroou nous apren
A pas jugea dei gens, coumo eou de la castaigno,
    N'en vian souven
Qu'an lou defuero beou, de dintre es la magaigno.[2]

My dear little Annie,

    We are quite out of pat[i]ence with you for delaying your visit so long: but we take it for granted that you have some good reason for so doing, or we should have had the pleasure of seeing you before this time. But you must make haste. This is the pleasant season in Brunswick, and erelong the Autumn fogs will be upon us, and then the air is harsh and unhealthy.

    I have been relying upon visiting you this week: but I fear the ride would prove too fatiguing for "little Mary" and therefore it is given up.[3] I do not expect to be in Portland till about Commencement — perhaps not till after commencement is over.

My love to all. Tell Sammy that his young friend "Negus" is well, and talks a good-deal about him. He cuts a famous figure, with the *gymnic* jacket and a pair of tights striped with blue and white.[4]

Very affectionately your brother

Henry.

MANUSCRIPT: Longfellow Trust Collection. ADDRESS: To/Geo. W. Pierce Esq./ Portland.   POSTMARK: BRUNSWICK MAINE. AUG 4 [*sic*]/PAID   POSTAL ANNOTATION (*by Longfellow*): Paid H.W.L./No 4.   ENDORSEMENT: H. W. Longfellow/Aug 11

TRANSLATION:

Monsieur Rigaud,

Would you have the kindness to translate *literally* into French the following fable, written in the Provençal language, and to tell me if there is a great difference between this language and the Languedocian [language] of the Departments of Tarn and Garonne. And will you please accept my thanks in advance.

I have the honor to be
Your very humble servant,
H. W. Longfellow.

The Squirrel and the Chestnut.

A hungry squirrel found
A chestnut of great size,
Smooth and fresh. "Fine," he said in his own language,
"This is going well! — Courage, now;
This is just what I needed
To satisfy my hunger and fill my belly."
Squirrels, as everyone knows,
Can have a feast with very little.
He sat down very happily, he seated himself at once,
Shook his tail, then turned the chestnut over and over
In his paws, sniffed it, admired it, and finally took a bite.
But he quickly cursed his luck
When he found it quite rotten,
Worm-eaten and worthless.
That squirrel teaches us
Not to judge people, like the chestnut,
Who often seem
Beautiful on the outside, but inside are rogues.[2]

1. Unidentified.

2. Inasmuch as no answer from Rigaud is to be found among the Longfellow papers, it is unlikely that this request was ever delivered.

3. Mary Longfellow was probably pregnant at this time, since on October 7 (Letter No. 219) Longfellow informed Greene that she had suffered a miscarriage.

4. This is possibly a reference to the "Mr. Banister" mentioned in Letter No. 234.

216. *To Charles Folsom*

Bowdoin College   August 16. 1832.

My dear Sir,

"Don Jorge Manrique" reached Brunswick in safety about a week ago, and I hardly need say that he met with a most gracious reception. The plays and the proof of the title page arrived this morning. I like your suggestion respecting the addition to the "Advertisement." The second clause may read as follows.

"The present edition contains several pieces not inserted in the first; and two of those contained in the first are here omitted. The pieces added are the following:

> Dame Jeanne;
> L'Enragé;
> Le Sourd;
> La Rose Rouge;
> L'Histoire;
> Le Persifleur;
> L'Uniforme de Compagne;
> Le [Suisse Malade][1] (insert the name of the
> piece containing the Swiss Corporal.)"

These titles may be thus printed, or run along in the text, as you please. I believe I have omitted none; if I have, please supply the deficiency.

The pieces omitted are Le Bossu and Les deux Auteurs. Those containing *"etc"* as before; — saving in the last line where for *"express"* read *"explain."* Of course the "Étranger" goes in, though I believe I did not mark it.

Will you have the goodness to make out the Index, (I should say *Table*) as follows.

"LE POULET. LES BATTUS PAIENT L'AMENDE [The losers are always in the wrong]; *page* 3." etc, etc putting the *mot du proverbe* [meaning of the proverb] in the same type in which it now stands at the head of each play, and the *title* a size larger.

I see no change to be made in the title-page you sent, excepting the addition of "Seconde Edition" and the *frenchification* of "Gray *and* Bowen" into "Gray *et* Bowen." But I must have another title page besides this, instead of a *fly* title. It might run as follows:

388

COURS

DE

LANGUE FRANÇAISE.

———————— (rule)

COURSE OF STUDY

IN THE

FRENCH LANGUAGE

———————— (rule)

BY HENRY W. LONGFELLOW

PROFESSOR OF MODERN LANGUAGES IN BOWDOIN COLLEGE.

———————— (rule)

VOLUME II.

PROVERBES DRAMATIQUES.

———————— (rule)

BOSTON;

GRAY AND BOWEN

1832

I think that this volume had better be called Vol 2nd the advertisement in the N. American to the contrary notwithstanding — and let the Grammar go *on its own hook*. The new collection of Tales now in preparation will make Vol 1. and the Poetry Vol 3. What think you?

This title-page need not go into all the copies, but I think it essential that it should go into some. To the table of Errata add *"Page* 308 *ligne* 19; *pour* il toujours *lisez* il y va toujours."

Please send me *proofs* of the title-pages and Advertisement before they are struck off.

The Article on the Italian Language, which I showed you in the Spring is *being printed* in the *next* North American.[2] I read the proofs myself, with great care, and hope — yet hardly dare to hope, that I shall have everything correct. But, unfortunately, in some of the dialects I shall have to trust to my poor memory, having no copy before me. I suppose you know what this is a prelude to: — another book from the College Library — Adelung's Mithridates[3] — the volume I had before. That will assist me much, if it can be spared by the Librarian from his shelves, at this time.

As soon as our Commencement is over, I shall give myself up for a month or two to the Spanish Muse with the utmost devotion. I shall speed along with the translation ye wot of, and shall prepare an Article on the Spanish and Portuguese languages for some future No. of the N.A.R.[4] Any sweet morsel of Spanish Moral or devotional Poetry you may chance to have running in your mind, or anything curious concerning the Span. and Portuguese languages you may chance to meet with in your multifarious reading, please communicate: for you must recollect that *here* I am single-handed. Can I have the following books from the Coll. Library?

Aldrete. Del Origen y Principio de la Lang. Castellana.
Latassa. Bib. Ant. de Aragon.
—— Bib. Mod. de Aragon.
Goldman. De Ling. Vasconum, etc, etc,
Murray. Hist. Europ. Lang.
Perrin. Essai sur l'Orig. et Antiq. des Langues.
Mayans y Siscar. Orig. de la Lang. Española.
Ramis y Ramis. Princip. de la Lecture Menorquiana.
—— (Antonio) Antiq. Milicia de Menorca.
Perez. Glosa Famosa sobre las Coplas de Manrique.[5]

If I can have all these books, I will undergo all necessary *bonds* for their security: and our friend Mr Gray will do me the favor to see them safely forwarded to me.

There is also one work, which, being a ponderous folio or two, and of course to[o] large to be *transplanted* to Brunswick, I will thank you to consult for me. It is "Ximeno: Escritores de Valencia";[6] — I suppose it must contain Specimens of the *Valenciano* dialect. But do this at your leisure; there is no haste; and should it contain anything of importance to the history of the language, please inform me.

Is there anything in the library on the history of the Portuguese Language? I apprehend that books upon that subject are scarce.

My lady joins me in kind regards to Mrs. Folsom.

Very truly yours,
Henry W. Longfellow.

MANUSCRIPT: Boston Public Library. ADDRESS: To/Charles Folsom Esq/Cambridge/Mass. POSTMARKS: BRUNSWICK MAINE. AUG 18/PAID POSTAL ANNOTATION (*by Longfellow*): Paid. H.W.L./No 7.

1. Supplied by Folsom.
2. See 205.1.
3. Johann Christoph Adelung, *Mithridates, oder allgemeine Sprachenkunde* (Berlin, 1806–1817), 4 vols.
4. Longfellow refers to his translation of *Coplas de Don Jorge Manrique* (Boston, 1833) and to "Spanish Language and Literature," *North American Review*, XXXVI (April 1833), 316–344.
5. Bernardo José Aldrete, *Del origen y principio de la lengua Castellana ò Romáce que oi se usa en España* (Roma, 1606); Félix da Latassa y Ortin, *Bibliotheca antigua de los Escritores Aragoneses, que florecieron desde la venida de Christo hasta el año 1500* (Zaragoza, 1796); Latassa, *Bibliotheca nueva de les Escritores Aragones*

que florecieron desde el año de 1500 hasta 1599 (Pamplona, 1798–1802); G. A. F. Goldmann, *De Linguis Vasconum, Belgarum, et Celtarum* (Gottingæ, 1807); Alexander Murray, *History of the European Languages* (Edinburgh, 1823); Jean-Baptiste Perrin, *Essai sur l'origine et l'antiquité des langues* (Londres, 1767); Gregorio Mayans y Siscar, *Origenes de la Lengua Española* (Madrid, 1737); Juan Ramis y Ramis, *Principis de la lectura menorquina* (Mahò, 1804); Antonio Ramis y Ramis, "Antigua Milicia de Menorca," *Diario de Menorca*, Núm. 194, 195 (1820), pp. 809–813; Luis Perez, *Glosa famosa sobre las coplas de Don J. Manrique* (1564). Folsom has annotated this list for the guidance of the College librarian and inserted the note: "27 Oct. 1832. For Prof. Longfellow (ten vols.) C. Folsom."

6. Vicente Ximeno, *Escritores del Reyno de Valencia, chronologicamente ordenados desde el año MCCXXXVIII . . . hasta el de MDCCXLVIII* (Valencia, 1747–1749).

217. *To Charles Folsom*

Bowdoin College   Aug. 28. 1832.

My dear Mr. Folsom,

In the greatest haste these [lines], returning the Volume you were kind enough to send, containing Manrique. Mithridates and the Spanish-Italian Grammar came duly to hand. Who can I get to publish my Spanish Translation, should Gray & Bowen decline? I intend to begin soon.

Very truly yours

H. W. Longfellow.

MANUSCRIPT: Boston Public Library.   ADDRESS: To/Charles Folsom Esq./Cambridge

218. *To Charles Folsom*

Brunswick   October 1. 1832.

My dear Sir,

Absence from town must be my excuse for not returning the last proof-sheets more speedily, and the fact of my being now in what you are pleased to call a *transition state* (moving)[1] must atone for my not having written you since my return. Even now I write you from the borders of the Land of Nod, into whose dominions I am most rapidly posting.

Nod No 1. I am much obliged to you for the trouble you have taken to procure me Portugueze books from Mr. Pickering.[2] I shall go about the Art. immediately on receiving the documents from you, so as not to detain the books too long; — and yet I begin to fear, that so much about the Mod. Lang. and Dialects, though interesting to all such good fellows as you and I are, — may prove rather a *drug* to those for whom Mr. Everett caters.

Nod. No 2. The principle I went upon in reducing the table of Errata was this. I first struck out those, which were merely an accent omitted or inverted, as being, upon the whole, the least important. I next struck off such expressions as *"du depuis"* which coming properly under the head of vulgarisms, are hardly fair subjects for a table of errata. I have forgotten how I got over the rest; — and though you may think me rather indiscriminate in my pardon of the proscribed, yet I went upon a plan satisfactory to my own mind.

Nod No 3. You and Mr Felton have almost frightened me out of the idea of publishing the Spanish Translation. I am fearful they may not meet your expectations very fully. It is not at present my intention to extend them beyond the "Moral and Devotional." I have not looked at them for a month or two, and I begin to doubt whether they will stand the ordeal of my own partial criticism.

Nod No 4. My miserable *vinegar* ink is worse than your *radiographic* pen; — and therefore

Nod No 5, and last. Good night. Sleep folds itself around me "like a blanket." Tomorrow morning at 6 o'clock I hear a recitation in *"Folsom's Livy"*; [3] — so that I shall think of you tomorrow earlier than you will think of me.

Mrs. Longfellow joins me in kind regards to your Lady and yourself.

Most truly yours

Henry W. Longfellow.

October 2nd. — Rain — rain — rain! It has been raining four days in succession and without intermission; and that too just as I had "pulled up stakes" — thereby leaving me no opportunity to stick them down again, which operation I hope to effect in the course of the present week. After which time I shall be very happy to have an opportunity of reciprocating the many civilities I have received at your hands.

You ask "why not visit us this Vacation." I am always glad enough to follow the "star of empire" — and 'take my way westward'; [4] — but our autumn vacation is a short one; and I have been obliged to collect matters and things in general for "my own hired house." I am now going to live in a kind of *glory*; — for I shall have a French gentleman with me as a pupil, and am daily expecting the arrival of a Spanish friend, from Madrid, who will remain with me an *indefinitely long period of time*; — viz. until he gets tired of Brunswick.[5] I shall make the Mod. Langs. flourish in the *granite State*.

Have you read the Rev. of Mrs Trollope in the Edinburgh? [6] If not read it: — it is good. And talking of Reviews, I hope you will have the patience to wade through the Art. on the *Ital. Lang.* in the October No. of the N.A.R. Tell me its weak points — and find as many as you can: — I shall take it all kindly from you.

I like Mr. Bachi's books very much.[7] There are however some errors in [the] *Spanish* half of the last one which need correction; — something worse than my *'de il,'* etc. They are however slips of the pen. More of this anon.

Of my *Italian* books, I see but one notice: — in the N. York American (Newspaper).[8] Have you seen it?

MANUSCRIPT: Boston Public Library. ADDRESS: To/Charles Folsom Esq/Cambridge/Mass. POSTMARK: BRUNSWICK MAINE. OCT 2

1. He moved from Mrs. Fales's boarding house to the Robert Dunlap House on Federal Street. See *Young Longfellow*, p. 384.

2. John Pickering (1777-1846), Boston lawyer, politician, and linguist, was one of the chief founders of American comparative philology.

3. *Additional Selections from Livy* (Cambridge, 1829).

4. A paraphrase of Bishop George Berkeley's famous line, "Westward the course of empire takes its way" (*On the Prospect of Planting Arts and Learning in America*).

5. Who the French gentleman was is not known; the Spanish friend was Señor Cortés (131.1).

6. "The Americans and their Detractors," a review of *Domestic Manners of the Americans* (London, 1832). See the *Edinburgh Review*, LV (July 1832), 479-526.

7. Bachi had sent copies of the following books to Longfellow: his *Scelta di prose italiane* (201.2), *Gl' Inni Giovenili della Signora Anna Letizia Barbauld, tradotti in Italiano* (Boston, 1832), and *A Comparative View of the Spanish and Portuguese Languages* (Cambridge, 1831). Longfellow here comments on the latter work.

8. The *New York American* for Saturday evening, August 4, 1832, concluded a brief notice of the *Grammaire Italienne* and the *Novellieri Italiani* with the statement, "It is not a common occurrence, — tho', in a Professor of modern languages, certainly it should not be deemed extraordinary, — to see an American writing thus well two modern languages."

219. *To George Washington Greene*

Bowdoin College   October 7. 1832

My dear Greene,

Absence from town must be my excuse for delay and apparent negligence in sending the grammars and class-books, you requested in your last dated Sept. 18. The first thing I did on my return was to put up the books, and send them, as you directed, to Marshall and Brown, Providence. The package contained

12 French Grammar
12 Ministre de Wakefield
12 Novelas Españolas

In the same bundle was a small package directed to you, containing a copy of each of the above-mentioned works, and also copies of the "Grammaire Italienne" and the "Saggi de' Novellieri." About three months ago I sent you copies of the last mentioned, but as you have not acknowledged the receipt of them, I presume they never reached you. I therefore sent other copies, which I hope are already in your hands.

I am not sorry to hear that you are at Kingston instead of New York.[1] To tell you the truth, I have always felt rather suspicious of the New York University, and my suspicions are not removed by running over the list of Professors. Why is not *Anthon*,[2] whose name is so well known among the *Romans,* admitted to take part in the great design? Before three years are gone, I fear the University will be flat on its back — *patas arriba* [heels over head]!

Write me as soon as you can, about your Academy. Who is Mr. Comstock?[3] The name sounds familiar, and yet strange. I hope he is a good fellow, and I wish you all the succes[s] in your undertaking which you merit, which is a good wish, and a good deal.

You are right in what you say of elementary class books, and as soon as I undertake anything new I will inform you. You will of course do the same towards me, and we shall not clash in our movements. All I have in view at present is a collection of French Tales to take the place of the "Ministre de Wakefield" — and a selection of French Poetry to complete the course.

I am very sorry to say, that I am not the happy owner either of "Schlegel" or of "Müller." Of Schlegel's Lectures we have a *poor* translation in the College Library,[4] which is at your service, though I presume you can get it nearer home.

If you can find time to read a long article on the Italian Language and its dialects, have the goodness to look into the last No. of the North American Review (October No). You will there find a paper upon the subject, which I took considerable pains to write, and to have *correctly* printed. As I corrected the proofs myself I am answerable for all inaccuracies. Please read, and criticise. You will see that of two or three Dialects I had no specimens. Can you supply the *lacune?* — and have you any specimens of those dialects in which I had nothing but the Lord's Prayer? If so please communicate them to me. I am going on to complete the series of papers for Mr. Everett of the N.A.R. taking up next the Spanish and Portuguese Languages and afterwards the German and English. The French was treated of before. If you have any *specimens* of these languages which are rare or curious, you will do me a great favor by informing me thereof.

When will your translation of Guizot appear? I am very anxious to see it — to see you fairly launched into the career of authorship. I wish also, very much to make you a visit in your cool retreat on Kingston Hill. I mean that the next journey I make out of the state shall reach as far as Rhode Island. I think it quite too bad, that we should not see each other again after so long a separation.

Mrs L. joins with me in fair greetings to your fair lady. Ma pauvre femme est malade: elle a fait une fausse couche [My poor wife is ill: she has suffered a miscarriage].

Very truly yours as ever
Henry W. Longfellow.

MANUSCRIPT: Longfellow Trust Collection. ADDRESS: To/Geo. W. Greene Esq/ Kingston./R. I. POSTMARK: BRUNSWICK MAINE. OCT 7.

1. Greene had accepted a position as "Instructor in the Classical Department" of the Kingston Academy, Kingston, R. I.

2. Charles Anthon (1797–1867), professor of Greek and Latin at Columbia College.

3. Christopher Comstock was the "Instructor in the English Department" of the Kingston Academy.

4. Frederick Schlegel, *Lectures on the History of Literature, Ancient and Modern,* trans. from the German by J. G. Lockhart (Philadelphia, 1818). Longfellow later became the owner of Wilhelm Müller's *Bibliothek Deutscher Dichter des siebzehnten Jahrhunderts* (Leipzig, 1822), 14 vols., and his *Vermischte Schriften* (Leipzig, 1830), 5 vols.

220. *To Charles Folsom*

Bowdoin College   October 11. 1832

My dear Sir,

Your very acceptable letter, with the accompanying No. of the "Bulletin des Sciences" reached me three days ago, having been more than a week on the road. I should have returned an immediate answer; but from that day to this I have been quite indisposed — my wife is still confined to her chamber — we are just *half-moved* — so that I stand Colossus like astride, — one foot in my own house and one in a boarding-house. I know that these circumstances will sufficiently exculpate me from the charge of unnecessary delay, particularly in the eyes of one who has lately been, as I am now, — "quaerentem sedes domumque [seeking house and home]."

I had seen your advertisement in the North American before receiving your letter. I like your plan very much, and I think you may feel confident of complete success. I feel, too, very highly gratified with your friendly recollection of me in connexion with your work. I will readily undertake the translation of Paris' *Lettre,* and will do

it moreover with great care and fidelity, and as well as in me lies.
Nor have I any objection to my name's being given. I will set about
the work immediately; — and I wish you to inform me, in your next
letter, when you wish to have it on hand. I shall probably find it
necessary to avail myself of the privilege you give me of adding a
few notes.[1]

I hardly need assure you, that I shall take a lively interest in the
success of the Journal, and that I shall most cheerfully coöperate in
the advancement of so good a cause.

I think of commencing soon the publication of the Spanish Translations. As there is some risk in regard to the success of the undertaking I shall at first make but a small volume, confined to the Devotional and Moral poetry. If the work succeeds to my wishes I shall add
another volume, and so increase the work. This plan came into my
head this morning, and has determined me to begin, as soon as I can
make the necessary arrangements with Gray & Bowen, to whom I
shall write by this evening's mail.[2] I wish to have the work done at
the University Press, so that the sheets may pass under your eye first,
and then be sent to me, as some alterations in the translation may
suggest themselves on the passage of the work through the press. The
original text is to be given *en regard* [opposite]; and I hope to have
a book *without one* typographical error, which you will pronounce at
once to be impossible.

I see that Mr. Willard has favored me with a short notice; — very
decent and circumspect, — and far better than a *puff direct*. When
you see him, please present him my thanks for the same. Who
wrote it?[3]

I hope Dr. Bachi will not be offended at my delay in acknowledging
the receipt of his books. I shall write him the first leisure.

The last proof-sheet of the Proverbes Dramatiques was sent by the
mail of the 1st inst; and I presume it went safely to its destination.

Please present my best respects to Mr. Norton; and remind Mrs.
Folsom of *our* constant regard and remembrance.

Very truly yours
Henry W. Longfellow.

MANUSCRIPT: Boston Public Library. ADDRESS: To/Charles Folsom Esq/Cam-
bridge/Mass. POSTMARK: BRUNSWICK MAINE. OCT 11

1. Longfellow refers to the *Select Journal of Foreign Periodical Literature,* about
to be launched by Folsom and Andrews Norton (see 226.1). For the fourth article of
the first number he prepared a translation entitled "A Letter to M. de Monmerqué
upon the Romances of the Twelve Peers of France; by M. Paulin Paris" (I [January
1833], 125–152). The letter had originally appeared in France in the *Bulletin Uni-*

versel des Sciences Historiques, Antiquités, Philologie, XIX (Octobre 1831), 92–117. For the same article, see "Ancient French Romances," *Works,* VII, 279–315.

2. The letter is unrecovered. The book referred to is *Coplas de Don Jorge Manrique.* Longfellow tried unsuccessfully to obtain Gray & Bowen, Hilliard, Gray & Company, and Carter & Hendee as publishers of the translation before finally persuading Allen & Ticknor to undertake it.

3. A review of Longfellow's two Italian textbooks appeared in the *American Monthly Review,* II (October 1832), 332–333. Sidney Willard, the editor of the journal, may have written the notice.

221. *To Hilliard, Gray & Company*

Bowdoin College   October 17. 1832.

Gentlemen,

As I propose publishing in the course of the autumn a collection of translations from the "Moral and Devotional poetry of Spain" with an introductory Essay, I should be very happy to have you undertake the work. The Essay will be the Article upon that subject which appeared in the January No. of the North American Review; 1832. The book will be small — about 150 or 200 pages 12mo. I offer it to you on the following terms;

1. That the book be printed on as good paper, and in the same form and style as the "Syllabus de la Grammaire Italienne" published by Gray and Bowen last Spring.

2. That the work be done at the University Press, Cambridge.

3. That the proofs be sent me for correction after they have been read by Mr. Folsom. And

4. That I shall have 25 copies of the work for distribution, and half the profits arising from the sales, after the expenses have been paid.

My wish is to make rather an elegant book than a large one; and as the number of pages is rather small it will be a matter of some importance to have the paper thick. The Spanish original will be on one side of the page and the translation opposite. I am now ready to commence.

Hoping, Gentlemen, that you may be induced to undertake the work,

I remain very truly yours
Henry W. Longfellow.

MANUSCRIPT: Clifton Waller Barrett Collection, University of Virginia. ADDRESS: To/Hilliard, Gray & Co/Boston. POSTMARKS: BRUNSWICK MAINE. OCT 18/ 12 1/2 PAID PUBLISHED: Luther S. Livingston, *A Bibliography of the First Editions in Book Form of the Writings of Henry Wadsworth Longfellow* (New York, 1908), pp. 17–18.

222. *To Dr. John Clark Howard*

Bowdoin College   October 29. 1832.

My dear Sir,

Permit me to present to your friendly civilities my friend Mr. Cortés, a Spanish gentleman, whose acquaintance I made several years ago in Madrid. He is a Don of noble family, and one of the King's body guard; and is on his way to visit me at Brunswick. His stay in Boston will be short — not more than a day or two; — and any attention it may be in your power to offer him will be very grateful to him, as a stranger, and to me as a friend.

Very truly yours
Henry W. Longfellow

Mr. Cortés is an entire stranger in this country, having arrived at your port but a day or two since from Cadiz or Gibraltar, I am not certain which. Perhaps the worst *matters* for a stranger to manage are his money *matters*. If my friend should be in any embar[r]assment on this head — from ignorance of exchange, or any oversight or inadvertance of his, — be kind enough to furnish him with what he may stand in need of, and I will see the same transmitted to you on his arrival here.

We are all well here. Eliza [Potter] is with us and both she and Mary send much love to your lady, in which I most cordially join.

H. W. L.

MANUSCRIPT: unrecovered; text from photostat, Longfellow Trust Collection. ADDRESS: Dr. John C. Howard/West Street/Boston.

223. *To Charles Folsom*

Bowdoin College   October 31. 1832.

My dear Sir,

I read your last of the 24th with the greatest pleasure. I feel much flattered by the polite invitation of the Committee of the Phi Beta Kappa to be their next poet, and am happy, moreover, to think, that I am indebted to *you* for this honorable distinction.

"Quod bonum, faustum, felixque sit mihi vobisque."[1] I accept the appointment with much pleasure, and of course shall endeavor so to demean myself as to give you no cause to regret your friendly intervention in my behalf.

You make me quite curious to know why the *next* commencement is the best time. You say that hereafter the reasons therefor will be apparent. You see I follow your advice implicitly, and pronounce the reasons good, before knowing them, — on your authority. I hope soon to be enlightened thereupon; and I trust you will not keep me *languishing* longer than is necessary.[2]

I am sorry to have been so long in translating the paper for the Review. Had my situation been other than it was, you should have had it sooner. It is, however, at length finished, except a part of one of the poetic extracts, which I shall complete to night, if I have time. I shall not add a great many notes, nor any very long ones, because the Article, as it now stands, is quite long enough. If you are in haste, you can have it without any notes; — though by the way, the notes will be written before I hear from you again. How shall the *book* (the original) and the ms. be sent?

I shall have to abandon for the present the publication of the Spanish translations. Gray and Bowen refuse: — so do Hilliard, Gray &co to whom I next applied, in order that the work might be done at the University press. I do not like to go any farther. It is not, however, a great disappointment. It is only deferring the thing to a more convenient season, when a larger amount of materials shall have accumulated. Meanwhile, *"Manrique"* has gone to pay his respects to Buckingham. Perhaps he may decline — as the ode is one of the longest. If not, you shall read and *criticise* it in the next No. of the New England Magazine.[3] In the No for November 1. (tomorrow) is a Sonnet (The two harvests) from Francisco de Medrano, to the translation of which I plead guilty.[4]

It is hardly necessary to say that I shall be a subscriber to your Review. Please have my Nos. sent in an envelope to Colman &co Portland, — if convenient.

I have at length got seated in my new house. It is one of the pleasantest in town, and one of the most convenient. It suits me *exactly*. The only thing that annoys me is the style of the paper-hangings, which cry aloud against the taste of my landlord and predecessor. *Stripes* of the most odious colors in *all* the parlors and chambers — and in the front entry *green parrots dancing on the slack wire*. Vrai, comme je suis ici [As true as I am here]! If you doubt it, come and see; — a consummation devoutly to be wished; for nothing could please us more, than to have a visit from you and your lady; to whom, our most cordial remembrance.

I see the Token rather meets with the *rubbers*. It will make the Editor more careful in future; though I do not know how far the Newspaper critics can be relied on, not having seen the volume.[5]

Are the Spanish books to be expected soon?

Do you wish a more *official answer* in regard to the Phi Beta performance?

With much regard, very truly yours
Henry W. Longfellow.

MANUSCRIPT: Boston Public Library. ADDRESS: To/Charles Folsom Esq/Cambridge/Mass. POSTMARK: BRUNSWICK MAINE. NOV 1

1. "May it be good, favorable, and fortunate for me and for you." Cf. Cicero, *De Divinatione*, I, 45, 102.

2. When sending Longfellow the official invitation to be Phi Beta Kappa poet at Harvard, Folsom had included a personal letter, dated October 24, 1832, in which he wrote: "This appointment I would privately, as a friend, urge on you to accept, unless there be insuperable objections. Hereafter the reasons of my urgency for your accepting the appointment for the *next* anniversary will be apparent. I go on the supposition that you are, at *some* time, to be our Poet. Now is the *best* time, from various circumstances, which you will hereafter know . . . Again I repeat it, as a friend, I think you ought to accept *this present* appointment, for reasons, which you will hereafter pronounce good, and weightier than any reason for *deferring* which I am acquainted with." On November 27 he partially explained the mystery by writing: "My reason for wishing you to perform next year was the character of the Orator, whom I am not authorized to make known to you officially or otherwise, except in friendly confidence at my peril. Please then to confine it to your own bosom. Your colleague is no other than the author of the 'Conquest of Ireland.'" Folsom's plan to bring Longfellow and John Quincy Adams together on the same platform, however, did not materialize; the orator on that occasion was Edward Everett.

3. Buckingham printed the poem, unsigned, in the *New-England Magazine,* III (December 1832), 454–457.

4. *Ibid.,* p. 414.

5. A reference to critical rebukes of *The Token and Atlantic Souvenir. A Christmas and New Year's Present,* ed. S. G. Goodrich (Boston: Gray & Bowen, 1833). Longfellow published two pieces in the volume: "The Bald Eagle," pp. 74–89, and "An Evening in Autumn," pp. 150–152.

224. *To Anne Longfellow*

[Bowdoin College] Wednesday Morning. [1832][1]

Dear Sister Anne,

I send hereby a pair of pantaloons — so that in case I walk up on Friday I shall not be destitute.

Yrs.
H. W. L.

MANUSCRIPT: Longfellow Trust Collection. ADDRESS: Miss Anne Longfellow./ Portland. ANNOTATION (*below signature, in another hand*): Dr John De Lamater[2]

1. The date of this letter, supplied by H. W. L. Dana, is questionable. The address indicates that Longfellow wrote it before November 26, 1832, when Anne Longfellow became Mrs. Pierce.

2. John Delamater (1787–1867), professor of medicine at Bowdoin, may have been the bearer of the pantaloons.

225. *To Charles Folsom*

Bowdoin College   November 11. 1832.

My dear Sir,

I avail myself at the earliest opportunity which has offered itself to send you the long-delayed translation,[1] together with its original. I hope it may meet your wishes in *all particulars,* though as this can hardly be expected, I would remark here, that you must never let any *friendly delicacy* prevent you from making without reserve all such alterations, as you may deem expedient, either in this or any future communications. I hold that an Editor should be as arbitrary as the Autocrat of the Russias.

One of the translations in poetry you will find to be *monorhyme* like the original; — the other which is *monorhyme* in the original, I did not think it necessary to make so in the translation.[2]

There is one Note (Note 9) which I wished to write but found no materials therefor in my books. If you have time to supply it please do so: if not erase the reference.

Very truly yours, in haste
Henry W. Longfellow.

MANUSCRIPT: Boston Public Library.   ADDRESS: To/Charles Folsom Esq/Cambridge

1. See 220.1.
2. Longfellow refers to the poems on pp. 138 and 144–145 of the translated article.

226. *To Charles Folsom*

Bowdoin College   Novemr. 12. 1832

My dear Mr. Folsom,

Permit me *sans cérémonie* to present to your acquaintance — (by this *draught* payable at sight) — my friend Mr. Geo: W. Greene, of East Greenwich Rhode Island. Mr. Greene is a thorough-going scholar — and *literally* wedded to the *Italian tongue* — having married a wife in Italy. If you would have the goodness to make him acquainted with Dr. Harris and the Library, I shall feel much obliged to you; and if you could present him to Mr. Norton, it would be a great favor.[1]

Very truly yours
H. W. Longfellow.

MANUSCRIPT: Boston Public Library.

1. Thaddeus William Harris (1795–1856), entomologist, was the librarian of Harvard College; Andrews Norton (1786–1852) had retired in 1830 from a professorship in the Harvard Divinity School and was coeditor with Folsom of the *Select Journal of Foreign Periodical Literature* (220.1).

227. *To Charles Folsom*

Bowdoin College
Wednesday evening. Novr. [14] 1832.

My dear Sir,

I presume that the translation of the Letter upon the old French poetic romances is already in your hands: if not, it is now on its way, and will not be long in reaching its destination. I gave it to a gentleman (not knowing what else to do with it, as I received no directions from you) who went from this place to Portland on Monday last, and who said that he would endeavor to send it to Boston by the Steamboat of that evening. In case he could find no safe opportunity, he was to keep it in his possession till Thursday (tomorrow) when he intended to take the boat for Boston, and was to leave it with Hilliard, Gray &co. to whose care the package was directed. So that if it has not already reached you it will not be delayed much longer.

You will find all the Notes, which I thought it expedient to add, at the end of the ms. This was done for my own convenience; and not with the intention of having them so printed; for I should prefer, and I presume you would, to have them introduced in their proper places at the bottom of each page.

I hope the manuscript will not ar[r]ive too late for your first No. for I feel so lively an interest in the projected Review, that I am desirous of appearing in the first No. which issues; — not that the Review would gain thereby, but from the vague wish — which I cannot define to my own satisfaction, — of being present in the *first encounter.*

Thursday morning [November 15].

I thought the mail of last evening might possibly bring me a letter from you — and have kept the present unsealed for that emergency. But in vain: no letter came.

What think you of the Ex-president's Narrative poem? I have been reading it this morning; and have finished the first Canto. If the others are not better, I shall wish he had not published it.[1]

Heigho! I am out of humor with matters and things in general. This teaching boys their a, b, c, is growing somewhat irksome. Morning, noon, night — *toujours perdrix!*[2] I mean to turn author and write a book — not a *grammar.*[3]

Farewell. Write me soon; and with much regard to your lady, in which Mrs. L. joins, believe me

most sincerely yours
Henry W. Longfellow.

MANUSCRIPT: Boston Public Library. ADDRESS: To/Charles Folsom Esq/Cambridge. POSTMARK: BRUNSWICK MAINE. NOV 15

1. See John Quincy Adams, *Dermot MacMorrogh, or the Conquest of Ireland, an Historical Tale of the 12th Century. In 4 Cantos* (Boston, 1832).

2. "Always partridge." Henri IV is said to have ordered only partridge for a confessor who had rebuked him for his liaisons.

3. This seems to be a hint of *Outre-Mer*.

228. *To George Washington Pierce* [1]

[Bowdoin College, November 25, 1832]

My dear George,

Your letter was duly received and duly weighed and considered. It would be very pleasant to pass the winter in Portland, as you have kindly planned; — but having *guests* at home, it will [be] quite impossible. I hope, however, that you will join your entreaties to ours, and persuade Anne to come and sojourn with us in Brunswick, during your stay in Augusta.[2]

I heartily regret Jackson's reëlection: it is one of the bitter fruits of *democracy;* — the arraying one class of society against another. However, Jackson has now an opportunity to retrieve his *blasted* character, and I hope he will do it, in spite of whiskered Martin[3] and *id genus omne* [all that sort].

Yours etc
H. W. L.

MANUSCRIPT: Wadsworth-Longfellow House, Portland. ADDRESS (*in Mary Potter Longfellow's hand*): For/Miss Anne Longfellow/Hon. Stephen Longfellow./Portland. POSTMARK: BRUNSWICK MAINE. NOV 25 ENDORSEMENT: Mary P. L./Novr. 25th. 1832.

1. A postscript to a letter from Mary Potter Longfellow to Anne Longfellow, November 25, 1832. At the end of his wife's letter is the note: "The above receives my approbation. H. W. Longfellow."

2. Pierce's letter to Longfellow is unrecovered, but according to Mary Potter Longfellow he had invited them to pass "the winter in Portland" (that is, the winter vacation). For the guests who prevented acceptance of this invitation, see Letter No. 234. Anne Pierce spent a month in Brunswick while her husband attended a session of the legislature in Augusta as a member of the House of Representatives.

3. Martin Van Buren, Jackson's Vice-President.

229. *To Anne Longfellow*

[Bowdoin College, November, 1832][1]

Little Anne,

Certainly she shall — she shall have a book "because she's his sister." You should have had one without so much apology and preface, as your note contained. I would send you one for yourself, also, had I another copy to spare; but I have not; so that you must be content for the present to read one that is not yours.

We have no news in B. as Eliza and Margaret [Potter] will duly inform you. Give my love to George, — and cut the *puffs* out of the Argus for me. Good night.

Yours ever affectionately
Henry.

MANUSCRIPT: Longfellow Trust Collection. ADDRESS: Mrs Georgiana Pierce./ Portland.

1. The date, supplied by H. W. L. Dana, is questionable. The address indicates that the letter was written after November 26, 1832, when Anne Longfellow married George Pierce. If the book mentioned within the text is *Coplas de Don Jorge Manrique*, the letter must have been written some months later. On the other hand, Longfellow may have been referring to the Gray & Bowen edition of *Manuel de Proverbes Dramatiques*.

230. *To George Washington Greene*

Bowdoin College   December 23. 1832.[1]

My dear Greene,

I have not yet answered that part of your *penultimate* which related to the edition of Cicero which you talked of publishing for the use of schools and Academies. I am almost provoked with you for undertaking so many things, in which it will be impossible for me to assist you. I have told you already how matters stood here with regard to procuring you any scholars for your school;[2] and I am sorry to say that my assistance will be of as little use to you in the affair of the new publication. The reason is this. We have already in use in our schools an edition of Cicero, published in Cambridge by Mr. Folsom,[3] an excellent scholar, and a friend, to whom I am under many obligations. You see at once, then, that it would be an ungenerous thing in me to attempt to supplant his books, to make place *even* for *yours,* though I feel perfectly confident that your edition will be extremely well executed in all respects.

Now to your *ultimate,* — which put me out of humor and made me *cross at breakfast* — an unheard of thing before. I am really very sorry that you did not reach Brunswick — we should have been so glad to see you. The more so as I do not expect to visit Boston this winter. I shall enjoy the leisure of a long vacation in my study, before a good fire; for I still preserve a most *tingling* recollection of my ride to Boston last winter, and have resolved never to go there again at that season of the year. The fact is, that in such a climate as ours, the only way for a decent man is to stay at home in the Winter. In the month of *August* next, however, I shall be in Boston — in as much as I am to deliver the Phi Beta Kappa poem in Cambridge — and then, if no untoward event forbids, I shall make you a short visit in Greenwich.

Do not fail, when you write to give me a full account of all your literary doings, and prospects, and plans. Let me know [if] your school succeeds, and what you are writing and have written. By the way — concerning the Italian Dialects; — if by chance you have seen the last No. of the N. A. Review, and have had the patience to look through my long Article on the Italian Language,[4] you will see exactly what I am deficient in. Any dialect not there exemplified by an extract, would be acceptable to me, and any *specimen, book* or *books containing specimens, that you could procure from Italy without too much trouble,* would be extremely useful.

You did not mention in your last, whether the letters I sent you when in Boston, ever reached you.[5] I hope they did, and that they were of service to you during your visit.

Mrs L. joins me in kindest regards to your ‖lady.‖ Let me have a letter from you soon, and believe me

Very truly yours
Henry W. Longfellow.

MANUSCRIPT: Longfellow Trust Collection. ADDRESS: George W. Greene Esq/ East Greenwich/Rhode Island. POSTMARK: BRUNSWICK MAINE. DEC 22

1. This date is not consistent with the postmark, which is December 22.
2. Green was planning to open a private academy in East Greenwich. See 244.2. Longfellow's letter about procuring scholars for the academy is unrecovered.
3. *M. T. Ciceronis Orationes quaedam selectae, notis illustratae* (Bostoniae, 1828).
4. See 205.1.
5. Only one of these letters survives: No. 226.

231. *To Charles Folsom*

Bowdoin College   Jany 8th 1833

My dear Sir,

The books you were kind enough to send me from the Library, and which you mention in your letter of the 27th Novemb. reached me in perfect safety. They shall be returned to you in the course of a few days. They have been of the greatest service to me.[1]

The 'Select Journal' has just come to hand. Need I say that I am delighted with its appearance? Its whole external is extremely *avenant* [pleasing], and its contents (excuse my blushes) very interesting. I have read most of the papers it contains, and with great pleasure. Perhaps the compliment you have vouchsafed to me in the 'Prefatory note' has put me into good humor. Be this as it may, I am certainly highly delighted with the appearance of the work — even down to the very cover. I prophecy signal success in the undertaking.[2]

I suppose you are now busier than ever, for I conclude that the burden of superintending the publication of the Journal falls mainly upon your shoulders. I wish I could witness your labors — your trudgings to and fro — those toils and troubles, and *cassemens de tête* [head-splitting anxieties], in which you take so much delight. But this the unpropitious gods deny. In all probability I shall not visit the borders of the *Cam* before August next. And that reminds me of my poem. Perhaps you know that the most difficult part of the business is to select a subject, which will suit the occasion. I think the sermon should be short — and perhaps rather serio-comico; though I doubt concerning this last. And, now, from the store-house of your memory, or the fields of imagination, can you furnish me with a topic of discourse, which has not been used on similar occasions more than twenty times? If you can, please to say *aye,* and send it, as soon as convenient, as I wish to turn my mind to the subject without delay, and not have the business sitting like a nightmare upon me all the year round.

I have the article on [the] Spanish language nearly completed. It will probably be in the next No. of the N. A. unless Mr. Everett finds it too stupid.[3] The Italian article in the October No. was found to be *"dull and* LEARNED*"* — so I understand. Such disquisitions do not seem to suit the taste of periodical readers. I shall try another key soon.

Is there in the Cambridge Library a Dictionary of the old Langue d'Oc in which the Troubadours wrote? I want to study their poetry more thoroughly — and have great quantities of it before me — but I have no dictionary, and, moreover, no faculty of guessing out meanings. If you can find me such a book you will do me much service.

Mr. F. T. Gray is here, and on his return to Boston, which will be in a week or ten days, I shall send back all the books I have from Cambridge Library, together with those from yours, which I have kept so long. Mr. Felton does not write me — which I suppose you will say is none of *your* business. But you can tell him how patient I am. Mr. Gray tells me that his eyes are again bad.

Mrs L. joins in kind regards to you and yours.

Most sincerely yours
H. W. Longfellow

MANUSCRIPT: Boston Public Library. ADDRESS: To/Charles Folsom Esq/Cambridge/Mass. POSTMARK: BRUNSWICK ME. JAN 9

1. According to Folsom's letter, he had sent the books requested in Letter No. 216 with the exception of Perrin, Ximeno, and Ramis y Ramis, "Antigua Milicia de Menorca." He had also sent eight copies of *Proverbes Dramatiques,* Romualdo Zotti's revision of Giovanni Veneroni's *Grammaire Française et Italienne* (Londres, 1800), some volumes of Boccaccio, and six volumes of *Memorias Literarias* by the Portuguese Academy.

2. Longfellow's optimism for the *Select Journal of Foreign Periodical Literature* was premature. It ceased publication in 1834.

3. "Spanish Language and Literature," *North American Review,* XXXVI (April 1833), 316–344.

232. *To George Washington Pierce*

[Bowdoin College, January 22, 1833]

Mr Speaker,

I agrees with the *gentleman last up.* Them are's my sentiments. I'm all hollow for encouraging the *fisheries,* and the march of intellect, — and the progress of Society.[1]

MANUSCRIPT: Longfellow Trust Collection. ADDRESS: Geo: W. Pierce Esq/Augusta/Me. POSTMARK: BRUNSWICK ME. JAN 22 ENDORSEMENT: Henry W. Longfellow/Jany 23. 1833

1. The allusions here are puzzling, but they undoubtedly refer to President Allen and his troubles with the college and the legislature (see 189.2). The letter accompanies an illustration of a sitting eagle, altered with pen and ink and entitled "Mr. Allen." Along the side of the caricature Longfellow wrote: "The gentleman what jest sat down." See Plate VIII.

233. *To George Washington Greene*

Bowdoin College　March 9. 1833

My dear Greene,

Out of a pile of twelve unanswered letters I take yours first; — not because it has the oldest date, for it has none at all, — but because I have been thinking of you this evening, and feel more disposed to write to you than to any one else.

Till I read your last letter I thought I was a great babbler about myself, and my concerns. And now that you tell me I am not, I certainly shall be. So prepare yourself to hear me *prose,* for I am determined you shall know all I have published since my return from Europe. And so,

1. Jany. 1. 1831. Art. on French. Lang. in the N. A. Review. [XXXII, 227-317]

2. Jany. 1. 1832. Art. on the Defense of Poetry in the same. [XXXIV, 56-78]

3. April. 1. 1832. Art. on the Moral and Devotional Poetry of Spain: same. [XXXIV, 277-315]

4. October 1. 1832. Art. on Italian Lang. and Dialects: — same. [XXXV, 283-342]

5. July. 1. 1832. Art. (short notice) of an Italian Reading book by Mr. Bachi of Boston: in the Cambridge "Monthly Review."[1]

6. Sundry papers of prose and verse at different times and upon different subjects in Buckingham's "Monthly Magazine."[2]

7. In the Token for 1832: Story called "The Indian Summer."

8. In the same for 1833. Story called "The Bald Eagle."[3]

To these add, — delivered in *public* but not *published* — 1 Poem, (by courtesy so called) — Item, 1 Inaugural Address — Item, 1 Address before Literary Society of Portland, — Item, 1 Address before Benevolent Society of Portland; Item, 1 Address on Female Education; — and sundry Lectures in the way of my profession.

There, I believe that is all, excepting the Translation of a paper on the Old French Romances, published in January last in a new periodical issued at Cambridge, and entitled "Select Journal of Foreign Periodical Literature." And now, surely, you have not half so good reason to complain as I have, for you have never told me half your own doings, though I hope you will follow my example, and do in this as I have just done. And in future I will send you an exact account of all my *penmanship.*

And shall I tell you what I am engaged in now? Well, I am writing a book — a kind of Sketch Book of France, Spain, Germany, and Italy; — composed of descriptions — sketches of character — tales, illustrating manners and customs, and tales illustrating nothing in particular. Whether the book will ever see the light is yet uncertain. If I finally conclude to publish it, I think I shall put it out in Nos. or parts: — and shall of course send you a copy as soon as it *peeps.* However, it is very possible that the book will remain for aye in manuscript.[4] I find that it requires but little courage to publish grammars and school-books — but in the department of *fine-writing,* or attempts at fine writing, — it requires vastly more courage.

Two whole pages about myself — by our Lady! Now — a word or

two about *you* and your affairs. You never told me, that you studied with Jacotot,[5] nor when and where you studied German. By the way, as Jacotot's method of teaching is very little known in our country, why cannot you write a paper or general *exposé* of his plan, and publish it in the N. A. Review? I think it would be very acceptable to a great many readers.

I wish you all success in your school. The paper you sent me, I transmitted to my father in Portland, and I shall endeavor to procure you some pupils, if possible; though, as I wrote you in my last, it is very doubtful whether I can prevail upon any one to send their children so far. I really wish I could get you a scholar or two from this part of the country, for the privilege of being in your family and of speaking the Italian and French with you, is an advantage offered by no other school in the country. Be assured, that if it is possible for me to do anything to advance your interests in this or other matters, I shall be right glad to do it.

You dont know how much I want to see your lady. Please tell her so — and that I hope the long-deferred pleasure will at length be mine.

Have you heard lately from Mr. Cook[e]? Where is he? With kind regards to Mrs. Greene, in which Mrs. L. joins,

I am most truly yours
Henry W. Longfellow.

I forgot to thank you for noticing my French Grammar in the Annals of Education. I have not yet seen the notice, but shall endeavor to procure a copy of the No. containing it as soon as possible.[6]

MANUSCRIPT: Longfellow Trust Collection. ADDRESS: George W. Greene Esq/ East Greenwich/Rhode Island. POSTMARK: BRUNSWICK ME. MAR 10

1. In a commendatory review of Bachi's *Gl' Inni Giovenili della Signora Anna Letizia Barbauld* (218.7), Longfellow approved "the study of languages in childhood." See the *American Monthly Review*, II (July 1832), 80–81.

2. That is, the *New-England Magazine*. For Longfellow's contributions to it, see Edward Wagenknecht, *Longfellow: A Full-Length Portrait* (New York, London, Toronto, 1955), p. 330.

3. As well as the poem entitled "An Evening in Autumn."

4. *Outre-Mer; A Pilgrimage Beyond the Sea.* No. I (Boston: Hilliard, Gray & Company, 1833) was followed by No. II (Boston: Lilly, Wait & Company, 1834) and the complete, two-volume edition (New York: Harper & Brothers, 1835).

5. Joseph Jacotot (1770–1840), French educationist, devised the theory of learning a language from the nucleus of a single paragraph.

6. Greene's notice, unsigned, appeared in *American Annals of Education and Instruction, for the year 1832*, ed. William C. Woodbridge (Boston, 1832), II, 603. He concluded his few remarks on the book by stating, ". . . we can cordially recommend it as one of the best elementary grammars we have ever seen."

234. *To Elizabeth Chase Howard*

Bowdoin College   March 10. 1833

My dear Elizabeth,

You dont know how *very* glad I was to receive your letter; for to tell the truth I began to think in good earnest, that you were never going to write; so that the letter, when it *did* come, was a very agreeable disappointment. You are not, however, to think, that I ever reproached your silence; for I begin to find that the cares of a family are more serious matters, than most people imagine, before they try them; and I well recollect how very little time you, who are *doomed* to live in a large city, can fairly call your own.

Mr. Banister is still here. I have procured a chamber for him, very *near* me, and very *far* from college: — so that he will be able to pursue his studies with little or no interruption from students. I am afraid, that both you and the Dr. drew a wrong inference from what I said about Mr. B. in my last letter.[1] I have never seen any disposition on his part to seek for dissipated society. Far from it; he is always in his room, and I believe very studious. What I feared was from the bad influence others might exert upon him. By changing his qua[r]ters, I think there will be nothing to fear. I hardly know what to make of him yet. He certainly has some talent; but he is *very green*.[2]

Winter at length is over; or as people say in these parts, "its back is broken." To-day the sun shines warm, — and the snow is sinking fast, — and I can say for one, that my heart leaps for joy. I can endure almost anything but a cold, cheerless, winter! Give me Summer's heat and dust — give me Autumn rains — give me mud and mire in Spring — but Oh! spare me from the frozen fingers and blue cheeks of Winter!

Brunswick furnishes me no theme whereon to enlarge with any hope — any *reasonable* hope of interesting you. Our family is now quite numerous. We have Miss. Crowninshield[3] and my sister Mary with us, and Mr. Cortés and a younger brother of mine.[4] So that my poor lady has nought but care. To-day, however, she has a headache besides; and is lying on the sofa at my elbow. She intends, notwithstanding, to summon strength enough to add a postscript to this. Therefore I make my bow, and retire. Commend me to the Dr. and give *our* best regards to his mother's family.

Most sincerely yours
Henry W. Longfellow.[5]

MANUSCRIPT: Yale University Library.   ADDRESS: To/Mrs. E. W. Howard/care of Dr. J. C. Howard/Boston.   POSTMARK: BRUNSWICK ME. MAR 10

1. This letter is unrecovered.

2. There is no record of a student named Banister (or Bannister) attending Bowdoin College at this time. In a postscript to this letter, Mary Potter Longfellow writes of him: "Poor Bannister affords us a good deal of amusement; he sees with his *olfactory nerves* — talks of the *soliloquy* between Romeo and Juliet and the *tragedy of Paul Pry*; and what we call 'Bannister's last' is this, he said that pers-ons who went to bed at 9 in the evening and slept till 9 the next morning, he thought were very remarkable instances of *somnambulism*. He does not appear to understand the true meaning of words at all and really makes such blunders continually."

3. Clara Crowninshield (1811–1907), the natural daughter of the renowned merchant and yachtsman of Salem, George Crowninshield, Jr., had attended Miss Cushing's School in Hingham with the Potter sisters. She accompanied the Longfellows to Europe in 1835. For her relationship with them, see the *Diary of Clara Crowninshield*.

4. Alexander Longfellow.

5. A letter by Mary Potter Longfellow follows the signature.

235. *To Jared Sparks*

Bowdoin College   March 22nd 1833.

Dear Sir,

I have incidentally heard, that you are engaged in preparing an edition of Franklin's Letters; and having accidentally met with the following characteristic epistle of the philosopher, I take the liberty of sending it to you. I found it in an old No. of "The Universal Asylum and Columbian Magazine" published in Philadelphia in 1790. It is *very probable* that a copy of the letter is already in your hands; but as there is a *possibility* of its having escaped you, I cannot resist the wish to send it to you.[1]

Very truly yours etc
Henry W. Longfellow.

A Letter from Dr. Franklin, on the death of his brother, Mr. John Franklin; to Miss Hubbard.[2]

Philadelphia, February 22nd 1756.

I condole with you, we have lost a most dear and valuable relation, but it is the will of God and Nature, that these mortal bodies be laid aside, when the soul is to enter into real life; 'tis rather an embrio state, a preparation for living; a man is not completely born until he be dead: why then should we grieve that a new child is born among the immortals? A new member added to their happy society? We are spirits. That bodies should be lent us, while they can afford us pleasure, assist us in acquiring knowledge, or doing good to our fellow creatures, is a kind and benevolent act of God — when they become

unfit for these purposes, and afford us pain instead of pleasure —
instead of an aid, become an incumbrance, and answer none of the
intentions for which they were given, it is equally kind and benevolent
that a way is provided by which we may get rid of them. Death is
that way. We ourselves prudently choose a partial death. In some
cases a mangled painful limb, which cannot be restored, we willingly
cut off. He who plucks out a tooth parts with it freely, since the pain
goes with it; and he that quits the whole body, parts at once with all
pains, and possibilities of pains and diseases it was liable to, or capable
of making him suffer.

Our friend and we are invited abroad on a party of pleasure —
that is to last forever. His chair was first ready, and he is gone before
us — we could not all conveniently start together, and why should
you and I be grieved at this, since we are soon to follow, and we know
where to find him.

Adieu,

B. F.

MANUSCRIPT: Harvard College Library. ADDRESS: To/Jared Sparks Esq/Boston.
POSTMARKS: BRUNSWICK Me. MAR 22/PAID POSTAL ANNOTATION (*by
Longfellow*): Paid. H. W. L. ENDORSEMENT: From/H. W. Longfellow/
March 25th. 1833

1. Sparks printed the letter in his edition of the *Works of Benjamin Franklin*
(Boston, 1836–1840), VII, 113–114; but since the text differs from Longfellow's
copy in a number of insignificant ways, it is likely that he had it from another
source.

2. Longfellow's note at this point: "It is worthy of remark that this letter was
published, in the Federal Gazette, on the evening of the Doctor's death." Miss
Hubbard was the daughter of John Franklin's second wife by a former marriage.

236. *To Stephen Longfellow, Jr. and George Washington Pierce*

Brunswick. March 29. 1833.

My dear Brother,

Cortés, for the want of something better to do, has an idea of
teaching Spanish in Portland, should a sufficient number of pupils
offer themselves. I think it will be a pleasant way for him to pass the
Summer, whilst looking out for occupation more permanent and
profitable. No very definite arrangements have as yet been made: but
I think his best way will be to take a chamber in the central part of
the town, and hear his classes there.

Anything which you can do to facilitate his arrangements, should
he conclude to commence, will be very grateful to him. You will find

his terms on the next leaf,[1] which please hand to Pitt [Fessenden], when you have read it.

Remember us kindly to Marianne.

Truly yours
H. W. Longfellow.

The next page to George.

March 29. 1833.

My dear George,

You will see by the preceeding page, that my friend Cortés has an idea of teaching the "noble Spanish tongue" to the Portlanders, if they see fit to offer him sufficient encouragement.

I want you to do whatever suggests itself to you as most favorable to the undertaking.

Remember us to Anne;

Yours etc.
Henry W. Longfellow.

MANUSCRIPT: Longfellow Trust Collection.

1. In a printed form, dated from Portland, May 4, 1833, Cortés offered to "teach the Spanish Language to Ladies and Gentlemen, in classes, at his rooms in the office lately occupied by C. S. Daveis, Esq. in Court Street, where he may be found during the forenoon of every day."

237. *To Charles Folsom*

Bowdoin College. April 7. 1833.

My dear Sir,

Your last letter dates from before the flood: that is to say, it is as old as Novr. 27. 1832. It came as a fore-runner of the books, you were so good as to send me, and which I have been so *very* negligent in returning. When I last wrote you it was my intention to send them by Mr. Gray: but he slipped through my fingers in a single sleigh, and as he had a trunk with him, it would have been very inconvenient for him to have taken a box of books in addition. Since then I have had no *good* opportunity of sending them until yesterday; when I *slooped* them on board the fast-sailing *sloop* Hope, Captain Woodward; directed to the care of Charles Bowen;[1] and to-day a letter goes to him, by the same mail that brings you this, requesting him to take charge of the box and forward it to Cambridge. If the wind blows fair, then, the books will reach you almost as soon as this letter. In the same box you will find

1. The Books belonging to the College Library.

2. The volumes of Italian Dialects etc belonging to you.

3. A volume, which Mr. Felton lent Mr Packard, and which is done up in a separate paper. All the others are together, so that you will have the trouble of separating them.

For the use of these books, receive my warmest thanks. You will find them uninjured; for I have taken good care of them here, and they are carefully packed; so that, saving untoward accident upon the way, they will reach your hands in as good condition as they left them.

Pray what is going on in your quarter of the world? I have not heard a whisper for the whole winter through. For my own part I have been busy in writing down some of my reminiscences of Europe, and if you should see a thin volume of sketches in a brown cover, and lettered —— —— [Outre-Mer] No. 1. — quietly reposing some morning of May in your pigeon-hole at the Post-Office, — you must not be surprised; for stranger things have happened. Mr Gray is trying to find me [a] publisher; but I fancy he finds it rather hard work, since I hear nothing from him upon the subject. I have not, however, ful||ly con||cluded upon the publication; though I have ||decided|| upon the subject, unless my father, who i||s reading|| my ms. throws too much cold water upon the project, and thereby *dishes* it.

How prospers the *Journal*? I hope you answer *"famously"* — for so it *should* be, an||d will be|| eventually, if not already.

Mrs Longfellow joins me in cordial remembrance to your lady; and begging you to write me as soon as you can "steal away from study and care" and the *press* of business, — I am

Very truly your friend
Henry W. Longfellow.

MANUSCRIPT: Boston Public Library. ADDRESS: To/Charles Folsom Esq/Cambridge/Mass. POSTMARK: BRUNSWICK ME. APR 7

1. Bowen (1807–1845) was a partner in Gray & Bowen, Longfellow's publishers. A man of promise, he drowned tragically with his wife and one child in the Mississippi River.

238. *To Allen & Ticknor*

Bowdoin College   May 5. 1833.

Gentlemen,

A month or two ago I wrote to Messrs. Carter and Hendee concerning the publication of a small volume of translations from the "Moral and Devotional Poetry of Spain."[1] In declining the publication they said, that it was not improbable, that you might be willing to undertake it; and in consequence of this opinion, I take the liberty of writing you a line upon the subject.

What I have in readiness for the press will make a 12mo of about 100– or perhaps 150 pages. The Spanish will be printed on one page — and on the opposite page the translation. There will be an introductory essay.

Perhaps such a work would not meet with a very rapid sale; but I think it would rather more than pay the expenses. I offer it to you on these terms: — that if after paying all expenses any thing remains, it shall be equally divided between author and publisher.

If you desire it — I will take whatever might be my profit in books from your stock.

If you will have the goodness to think of this and send me an answer *during the week* I shall be much obliged to you.

Very respectfully yours
Henry W. Longfellow.

MANUSCRIPT: Clifton Waller Barrett Collection, University of Virginia. ADDRESS: To/Messrs Allen & Ticknor/Boston POSTMARKS: BRUNSWICK ME. MAY 7/ PAID POSTAL ANNOTATION (*by Longfellow*): Paid. H. W. L.

1. This letter is unrecovered.

239. *To Allen & Ticknor*

Portland. May 25. 1833.

Gentlemen,

I send you by to-day's mail the "Introductory Essay" of the Specimens of Spanish Poetry.[1] I wish you to send me the proof-sheets, as I shall feel great anxiety to have everything perfectly correct; and as the copy may not in all instances be perfectly intelligible, many errors might on that account slip into the work.

If it can be done, without interfering with previous engagements, I feel very desirous of having the book printed at the University press in Cambridge. Mr. Folsom is, as you well know, a thorough scholar; and as part of the work is to be in a foreign language, it would be a great advantage to have it appear under his supervision. Besides, having a Library at hand, he would be able to furnish all the Spanish part of the work therefrom, and would thus save me the trouble of much copying.

One thing more; — in addition to my share of any profits, which may arise from the work, I shall expect you will allow me a few copies — say eight or ten — for distribution among my friends; as it is absolutely necessary to send round a present of the kind to those, who have done me the same favor with their own publications.

If you get out a proof before the middle of next week — that is before the 1st of June, please send it to me *here*. Otherwise send it to Brunswick.

In great haste, very respectfully yours
H. W. Longfellow.

MANUSCRIPT: Parkman Howe, Boston. ADDRESS: To/Messrs Allen & Ticknor/ Boston POSTMARK: PORTLAND ME MAY 26

1. "Introductory Essay on the Moral and Devotional Poetry of Spain," *Coplas de Don Jorge Manrique*, pp. 1–27.

240. *To Alexander Scammell Wadsworth* [1]

[Portland, May 28, 1833]

My dear Sir,

Alexander has left me room for a few lines, and I write to bid you farewell, and to enquire, whether you have any situation on board ship, in which the services of a young Spanish gentleman would be acceptable. A Spanish friend of mine, a gentleman whom I first knew as one of the King's body guard in Madrid — has been passing the Winter with me at Brunswick, studying the English language — and if he could obtain a situation on board your vessel in any honest capacity he would like well to visit the scenes you will probably visit. I know not whether an instructor in Spanish might be of service to some of the officers — as I understand you will be long in the neighborhood of Chile etc. Mr. Cortés speaks English tolerably well.

Please consider this as a *question* — and not in the light of a *solicitation*; and with much regard to yourself and lady, believe me

Very truly yours
Henry W. Longfellow.

P.S. I shall not trouble you with a separate answer to this letter: but if you write Alex. again, it will be sufficient to say *yes* or *no*.[2]

MANUSCRIPT: Longfellow Trust Collection. ADDRESS (*by Alexander Longfellow*): Capt Alexander S. Wadsworth/U. S. Navy/Washington/D. C. POSTMARKS: PORTLAND ME MAY 30/SHIP POSTAL ANNOTATION: Paid/S. L. ENDORSEMENT: Alex W Longfellow/May 28. 1833

1. This letter is included as part of Alexander W. Longfellow's letter to Capt. Wadsworth, May 28, 1833.
2. Whatever the answer was, Cortés did not sail with Capt. Wadsworth, who had recently been assigned to duty as commodore of the Pacific Squadron. Alexander Longfellow accompanied his uncle on this cruise as a private secretary.

241. *To Hilliard, Gray & Company*

Brunswick   June 30. 1833

MM. Hilliard, Gray &co
Gentlemen,

Mr. Griffin reached town to-day, and has just handed me your proposition in regard to the purchase and publication of my little book of sketches.[1] The offer you make me is better than I expected; and all that prevents me from accepting it at once is the obligation in respect to any future Nos. of the work.

Whether any future Nos. are to see the light must depend upon circumstances beyond my control; — after September next, the place of my residence is uncertain; I may be so far from this part of the country, that even if the work should be completed it would be impossible or inconvenient to comply with that part of the contract which relates to the printing. These circumstances lead me to refuse an offer, which under other circumstances, I should be glad to accept.[2]

I wish, however, that you would have the goodness to act as Agent for the work. I put the *nominal retail* price at .62 1/2 per No. upon which I make you a discount of 35 per cent.

500 copies have been printed. 425 I shall send you; 25 of which are for gratuitous distribution; 25 more, I shall myself distribute; and 50 copies will remain in Mr. Griffin's hands for the market here and in Portland.

The books shall be sent as soon as they can be done up.

I wish you to take out a copy-right in your name, for I do not wish to appear as the author of the work. I am well aware, that this would be no *remedy* against any one who should chose to pilfer, but it would be a strong *preventative*.

Allen & Ticknor, who are now publishing for me a work of a different kind,[3] have offered to act as agents in this. For certain reasons, however, which it would be unnecessary to mention, I have given you the preference. As this might create hard feelings on their part, were it known, I wish that the arrangement between us may be kept secret.

Thanking you for your generous offer, and for any interest you may take in the success of my little work, I am

very respectfully yours
Henry W. Longfellow.

P.S. In regard to time of payt., I shall be satisfied with whatever is customary. Upon this point and others, which may arise, I will converse with you in August next, when I shall have the pleasure of seeing you in Boston.

MANUSCRIPT: Berg Collection, New York Public Library. ADDRESS: Hilliard, Gray &co./Boston. POSTMARKS: BRUNSWICK ME. JUL 1/PAID POSTAL ANNOTATION (*by Longfellow*): Paid. H. W. L. ENDORSEMENT: H. W. Longfellow/June 30. 1833 PUBLISHED: *Young Longfellow,* pp. 187–188.

1. *Outre-Mer,* No. I.
2. During this period Longfellow conceived various projects to escape his restlessness in Brunswick. Here he refers apparently to an abortive plan to revisit Europe. See *Young Longfellow,* pp. 188–189.
3. *Coplas de Don Jorge Manrique.*

242. *To Charles Folsom*

Bowdoin College   July 7. 1833.

My dear Sir,

I herewith send you No 1. of the sketches of Europe, concerning which I wrote you some time since. The publication has been delayed from day to day, beyond all patience, by a thousand "lets and stops" [1] quite beyond my control. But the work is at length completed, and will *appear incessantly; — il paraîtra incessamment.*

The Phi Beta Poem is upon the anvil, and nearly completed. It will be ready in season, and something to-boot.

Did you know, that you were a *sad, old rogue* for not writing me since December? Well; if you will not write *to* me, I shall make you write *for* me. You must know, that my prolific brain has conceived the mad project of leaving this College, and establishing a Female School in the city of New York, where I understand great things may be done in that way. I am anxious, however, to have more definite information upon this point; and as I understand that your friend W. C. Bryant takes a good deal of interest in the subject of female education, you would do me a great favor, if you would write him two or three lines requesting information in this matter. [2]

Kind regards to your lady.

In great haste very truly yours
H. W. Longfellow

MANUSCRIPT: Boston Public Library. ADDRESS: Charles Folsom Esq/Cambridge

1. From Roger Ascham, *The Schoolmaster,* "A Preface to the Reader."
2. Folsom's letter to Bryant is printed in part in *Young Longfellow,* pp. 191–192. Nothing came of the project. Writing to Parke Godwin on October 26, 1880, Longfellow asks that Folsom's letter not be published: "It relates to a matter of no importance, and which never took the shape of a fixed plan, but was only a question asked, and nothing more" (MS, New York Public Library).

243. *To Alexander Hill Everett*

Bowdoin College   July 16. 1833

My dear Sir,

Yours of June 18 was duly received; and since that date the North American has come to hand. I have not had time to read all the Arts. but from what I have read it appears to me to be an excellent No. I feel highly flattered, that you should miss me; though I think in the next No. to spare myself that gratification. I have been intending for some time past to send you a paper on the Old English Prose romances; a subject which has considerable attractions, when set forth in the proper light. I have not, however, as yet found the right moment for writing the Art. but shall commence it as soon as I have leisure. I hope to bring it with me, when I next visit Boston, which will be in August next.[1]

A few days ago I sent you Outre Mer No 1. being the first number of the European Sketches, we were speaking of. I fear they may strike you as rather too trival in their character. My object is to give variety, and in the next No. which will appear in the Fall, I shall endeavor to give something of a different shade and hue. I presume the package reached you in safety; it was directed to the care of Hilliard, Gray & co.

You will see by the papers that Pres. Allen was received with some glee by the students; I suspect it was only for *the fun of it*. I was not present at his *entrée*, being then on a visit at Portland. Things have taken their old course; and matters move on smoothly. We are all very glad to be beyond the reach of further Legislative interference, though some of us would not be sorry to have Dr Allen resign.[2]

Cortés is now in Portland. He is quite desirous, I find, to engage in commercial pursuits. If you should hear of any situation, which would be suitable for him, you will oblige me much by informing me of the same. I see in the papers the death of the Spanish Consul for the port of Boston. Why could he not obtain that post?

Please present my warmest regards to your lady. In these my wife joins me.

Very sincerely and respectfully
Henry W. Longfellow.

July 17th.

P.S. I have taken my letter from the office to say, that I have seen by this morning's papers the death of Mr Walsh, Secretary of Legation at Madrid.[3] I am very desirous of making application for the place,

thus left vacant; and as you have much experience in such matters —
I wish you to advise me how I am to proceed. I hope you will not refuse
me your influence in this thing. I wish you would be kind enough to
write immediately to the Secretary of State at Washington, or to him
who has the disposal of such places. Your being a leading man in the
Opposition, will not I think diminish your influence at the present
time. It is a kind of era of good feelings now; and doubtless the
President entertains very friendly feelings towards you all in Boston,
after the splendid reception you gave him. I shall certainly be under
very great obligations to you if you will write to Washington upon this
subject without delay. Will it be necessary for me to make a personal
application? If so to whom? — and how?

You will excuse me for importuning you so much; but here I am
in a corner, beyond the reach of almost every body, and with only
one or two friends, to whom I must apply in every emergency.

The present seems to be an opportunity of realizing some of my
fondest wishes, which I ought not to let slip without an effort.

Will you have the goodness to write me a line upon this subject
by return of mail? [4]

MANUSCRIPT: Longfellow Trust Collection.   ADDRESS: Hon. A. H. Everett./Boston.
    POSTMARK: BRUNSWICK ME. JUL 18

1. Longfellow's essay "Old English Romances" appeared in the *North American
Review*, XXXVII (October 1833), 374–419.

2. See 189.2.

3. Charles S. Walsh of Pennsylvania had been appointed secretary of legation
to Madrid in 1828. He died on May 13, 1833 (State Department Records).

4. In his reply of July 20, 1833, Everett sent the discouraging news that Walsh's
successor had already been appointed and that in any event it would be difficult
for Longfellow to obtain political preferment during Jackson's administration.

244. *To George Washington Greene*

Bowdoin College   July 16. 1833.

My dear Greene,

With what fatal haste Time strides over the pages of an unanswered
letter! When I received your last, my determination was to write you
by return of mail, for the melancholy tone of your letter showed me,
that you were much depressed in spirits. Something, however, prevented me, and the moment slipped by unimproved; and since then
sundry matters and things have chained the wheels of our correspondence. But I now hope, that your sadness has passed away, and that
your bodily indisposition is also over. Do be careful of that hateful
pain in your breast; and above all things avoid *late hours*. I have
abjured them as very treacherous friends; and if I go on as I have

begun, I bid fair to become one of the Seven Sleepers. You recollect I could always beat *you* at that game.

Last week I sent you by mail, the first No. of "Outre-Mer." I do not yet know how the book will succeed with the public, as it is just published, and I have not heard from my booksellers. No 2. will be put forth sometime in Autumn.[1]

I have, also, another little book in the press, a translation of the "Coplas de Don Jorge Manrique á la Muerte de su Padre;" — the original to be printed with the translation — *le texte en regard*, as we say in France. There is also an Introductory Essay, and a few additional Specimens of the Moral and Devotional Poetry of Spain. I know not when it will be finished — for at the rate the printer creeps along I should think it would take him two years. It is printing in Boston.

Well — and what do you suppose the profits of this writing, and printing to be? A mere nothing: I do maintain, that the publishers of our country are as niggardly a set as ever snapped fingers at a poor devil author. If the whole edition of Outre-Mer No 1. sells, I shall make *fifty dollars!* Of the other book, I am to have half the *profits* if there are any — in books from the publishers store! Prodigiously encouraging!

I hope you continue to like your situation in Providence; though I regret that the people around you treated you so *shabbily* in regard to the other institution. It is truly astonishing how little a good education is esteemed by parents in general. They seem to go upon the principle, that the *cheaper* a school is, the *better* it is. They send their children to school — and they think their duty done.[2]

I hope, however, that ere long you will have a situation offered you more analogous to your wishes, and your deserts. You never told me how those negociations with Brown Univy. terminated. I feel pretty sure that something will turn up before long, to place you where you ought to be.

When you next write to Italy, do not forget my commission in regard to the *dialects*, about which I wrote you sometime ago. Anything upon that subject will be most acceptable to me.

Mrs L. joins me in kind regards to your lady. We anticipate the greatest pleasure in meeting you in Boston, at the latter end of August.[3]

Do write me soon, and keep a stout heart in the *drudgery* of your profession, which cannot be greater than that, which I endure daily with the most exemplary patience.

Most sincerely your affectionate friend
H. W. L.

MANUSCRIPT: Berg Collection, New York Public Library. ADDRESS: To/Geo:e W. Greene Esq./Providence./R. I. POSTMARK: BRUNSWICK ME. JUL 17

1. Longfellow was overly optimistic, for the second number did not appear until the spring of 1834.

2. A neighboring institution with lower rates had forced Greene to abandon his plan to open a private academy.

3. At which time Longfellow would deliver his Phi Beta Kappa poem at Harvard.

245. *To George Washington Pierce*

Bowdoin College — Thursday aft. July —
date unknown [July 18, 1833]

My dear George,

You must help me now or never. I see by the Boston papers of to-day, that Mr. Walsh, Secretary of Legation at Madrid, is dead; and I mean to apply for the situation. In this you can be of the greatest service to me. You are personally acquainted with Secretary Woodbury, and very intimate with Mr. Olney; who, if he were willing, could doubtless do much in gaining me the good-will of Mr. Woodbury.[1] If I can obtain his interest at *Court*, it will be a great point gained; for it is generally believed, and I suppose upon good grounds, that he has much influence with the President.

I wish that you would communicate this plan of mine to Judge Ware, in strict confidence, and ask him if he is willing to use his influence in my behalf. If so, I wish that he also would write to Washington upon this subject. By seasonable application, and proper effort I have strong hopes of success. I am well aware, that I have no claims to urge; and I do not put the application upon that ground. But I have some qualifications for such a situation, in my knowledge of the Spanish and French languages, which might be some recommendation. At all events, I am resolved to make the trial, and I hope I may rely upon your hearty assistance in advancing my designs. Whatever is done, must be done *now*; without a moment's delay; and I want you to write me a line by return of mail, informing me what you and Judge Ware think of this, and how far I can promise myself your assistance.

And now, not a whisper of this to any one but Judge Ware, — and enjoin secrecy on him. I shall not ask the opinion nor the influence of Judge Preble; he is so *savage* just now, that I think he would rather thwart my plans, than advance them, if he had the power of doing either.[2]

My love to Anne, and all our family, and do not fail to write me tomorrow.

Very sincerely yours

H. W. L.

P.S. Be sparing of your *cold water.*

MANUSCRIPT: Longfellow Trust Collection. ADDRESS: George W. Pierce Esq/Portland. POSTMARK: BRUNSWICK ME. JUL 18 ENDORSEMENT: H. W. Longfellow/July 19. 1833

1. Levi Woodbury (1789–1851), Secretary of the Navy under Jackson, later became a justice of the Supreme Court. Mr. Olney was presumably a local Democratic politician with whom Pierce, also a Democrat, had become acquainted at party functions.

2. The cause of Judge Preble's savagery at this time is unknown, but he had a reputation for choler. "He was of strong logical powers, clear and discriminating; well informed in his profession; of imperious will; of warm temperament, easily aroused, — unfortunately for himself, and uncomfortably for those who experienced it." Nehemiah Cleaveland and Alpheus Spring Packard, *History of Bowdoin College* (Boston, 1882), p. 55.

246. *To James G. Stewart*

Brunswick, Aug. 10, 1833.

Dear Sir,

The vest you sent me fits exactly, but I cannot say so much for the coat. Somehow or other you have made a miss of it. I am very sorry for it, because it is too late to remedy the matter, as I shall not be able to stop in Portland till after my return from the West. I am therefore under the necessity of returning you the coat.

Respectfully yours,

H. W. Longfellow

MANUSCRIPT: Bowdoin College Library. ADDRESS: To/Mr. James G. Stewart/Portland.

247. *To George Washington Greene*

Bowdoin College. October 27. 1833

My dear Greene,

I have just received yours of the 22nd and am glad to see you write in such buoyant spirits; — but confound you, I wish you would ever acknowledge the receipt of a letter, and not leave it to be inferred, as you always do! Do, for pity's sake, say "Yours of so and so, came duly to hand" — or "came by due course of mail" or "is now lying before me," or some short, pithy and business-like equivalent, so that

423

I may have the satisfaction of knowing, whether my letters reach you or not. The fact is, I wrote you a long epistle about a week ago;[1] and as your letter, though dated 22nd. was put into the post-office on the 25th, according to the tell-tale post-mark on the outside, I begin to think, that the foresaid epistle has loitered on the way. All I should regret its loss for, would be, that it contains a very pretty piece of music for your wife.

I fear it will not be in my power to deliver a poem before the "United Brothers,"[2] even should they desire it. Your Commencement happens at a time, when my presence is required here. To be sure, I was absent last August; but on that very account I cannot be next August. I was excused this year by special favor, and at no small inconvenience to all concerned. Besides, I have now on hand too many engagements to think of writing a poem. I must, therefore, refuse to accept an invitation; which refusal you will of course express to any person or persons interested therein, much more politely, than I have thought it necessary to *pen* it here. Your *cotton* manufacturers, (excuse me — do —) will all become *worsted*.

I am right glad to hear that your school flourishes so well. To be sure, it is no more than you deserve; but there is always some satisfaction in seeing our efforts crowned with success, apart from the consideration that — that — that — you know what I mean to say, — though I do not. That sentence fairly broke down under me. No matter; it is not the first time.

I received the "Literary Journal," and read the same with much pleasure; — of course — being therein puffed high. Did you write both articles; or am I to thank some one beside you, for these favorable notices of *my feeble endeavors?* — (modesty).[3]

When you criticised the trees *what* ogled themselves you forgot, that they were *French* trees. Please bow, and acknowledge the propriety of their conduct.[4]

My love to your lady, *"if it is not too familiar"* as Mr. Cooke said, when he sent his *respects* to mine; — and farewell.

Very sincerely thine,
Longfellow.

MANUSCRIPT: Longfellow Trust Collection. ADDRESS: George W. Greene Esq./ Providence/R. I. POSTMARK: BRUNSWICK ME. OCT 27

1. This letter is unrecovered.
2. A literary society of Brown University, of which Longfellow had been made an honorary member earlier in the month.
3. A review of *Outre-Mer* and a notice of *Coplas de Manrique,* which appeared in the *Providence Literary Journal* for October 20, 1833.

4. The reference is to a description in *Outre-Mer* in the chapter entitled "The Village of Auteuil."

248. *To the Editor of the* New York Atlas and Constellation [1]

[Bowdoin College, 1833]

Dear Sir, —

I am much obliged to you for your kindness in sending me the last No. of your paper, in which a question is started concerning the source from which I drew the incident of the tale of "Martin Franc and the Monk of St. Anthony." In the remarks preceding this tale in OUTRE-MER, it is stated to have been taken from "an ancient manuscript of the Middle Ages." Indeed, during the thirteenth century this story seems to have been a very popular one; and several versions of it, each differing from the other in the details of the narrative, are in existence. The following references will show you where they may be found: —

1. *Du Segretain Moine*, vide *Fabliaux et Contes des Poetes François des XI. XII. XIII. XIV. et XV. Siecles.* Par [Étienne] Barbazan. [Paris, 1808] Tome 1. p. 242. It is from this old poem that I took the plot of Martin Franc.

2. *Du Prestre c'on porte, ou la Longue Nuit.* Barbazan. T. iv. p. 20. This is an imitation of the preceding varied in some of its details.

3. *D'Estourmi.* Barbazan. T. iv. p. 432 [452]. Another imitation of the same.

4. *Dane Hew, the Monk of Leicestre.* Vide *Ancient Metrical Tales.* Edited by the Rev. C. H. Hartshorne. [London, 1829] p. 316. This also is in imitation of the *Segretain Moine*: the old English poets borrowed much from the Norman Trouveres. From this version of the story I took one of my mottos.

5. The same tale is cited, and its principal incidents given, in a *Memoire sur les Fabliaux*; par M. le Comte de Caylus. Vide *Mem-[oires de Littérature, tirés des registres] de l'Acad[émie Royale des Inscriptiones et Belles-Lettres* (Paris, 1753)] T. xx. p. 364.

This may seem to be tracing up the matter far enough; but I must go one step farther. The leading idea of the story was not original with the old author of the *Segretain Moine.* He probably borrowed it from the East: for it is a fact pretty well established in Literary History, that during the times of the Crusades, the early French Poets brought from the East many of the tales that make the ground-work of their poems. The *Segretain Moine* was doubtless drawn from "The Story of the Little Hunchback," a tale of the Arabian Nights Entertainments.

Thus the story has passed through as many hands as did the body of the Friar Gui. Mr. Colman evidently drew the incidents of "The Knight and the Friar" from the same source whence I drew those of Martin Franc.[2] Had I known of the existence of the former before the publication of the latter, I certainly should have left Mr. Colman undisputed possession of the field. Unfortunately I was not aware, till after the publication of OUTRE-MER No. 1. that any modern writer had availed himself of this old fiction.

In conclusion I would say, that I have never had any desire to conceal the origin of this tale. In this quarter it is quite an old story, inasmuch as the Professor you speak of has always cited it in his College Lectures as a specimen of the fictions of the early poets of France.

Give my best respects to John. His idea, that Colman borrowed the story from me, is ingenious. I can certainly say with truth, that he is as much indebted to me for it, as I am to him. When I next visit your city, I shall expect from John an invitation to the Club-room.

Meanwhile I remain, Sir, very respectfully yours,

THE AUTHOR OF OUTRE-MER.

MANUSCRIPT: unrecovered; text from the *New York Atlas and Constellation*, undated clipping in the Longfellow Trust Collection.

1. The circumstances that called forth this letter are explained by the editor of the *New York Atlas and Constellation* in an editorial note as follows: "PROF. LONGFELLOW, GEO. COLMAN, AND 'OURSELF.'/Those of our readers who are fond of perusing the Tales that we from week to week spread upon our sheet, will recollect the very amusing and high wrought story of 'Martin Franc,' which we copied from 'Outre Mer' by Professor Longfellow, of Bowdoin College. Our readers may also remember that in the succeeding number of our paper, we inserted a communication over the signature of 'John,' charging the Author of 'Outre Mer' with downright plagiarism from Geo. Colman, who had told the same story in verse. On examination we found the assertion of our correspondent entirely corroborated so far as this, that Colman's *'Knight and the Friar'* and Prof. L.'s *'Martin Franc'* were one and the same story in every essential particular. Thus confirmed in the matter of fact, we were puzzled to conjecture how this most extraordinary *coincidence* could have occurred but in the manner suggested by 'John.' Still the high literary standing and virtuous-mindedness of so approved a scholar as Prof. L. forbids the conviction that it could be an attempted plagiarism from that popular humourist Geo. Colman, and thus doubting and fearing and hoping and believing that the 'Bowring of America,' as Prof. L. has sometimes been called, could best solve the riddle, we sent him a copy of our paper containing the charge of 'John' and our own cogitations on the same. It *now* affords us great satisfaction and pleasure to acknowledge the kindness and urbanity of Prof. L. in sending us the subjoined letter from his own hand, in which he most conclusively vindicates himself, and at the same time enables us to do him the justice of repairing an unintentional injury, however trivial or unheeded./In no way can we do this so well as by allowing the amiable and ingenious Professor to plead his justification in his own candid and happy manner. We therefore give his letter entire — believing he will forgive the freedom of substituting his private communication for any crude remarks of

our own." The issues of the *New York Atlas and Constellation* that contain the excerpt from *Outre-Mer*, the communication from "John," and Longfellow's reply have apparently not survived. The letter, preserved by Longfellow as a scrapbook clipping, was written sometime between July, when *Outre-Mer No. I* was published, and November, 1833, when the newspaper in which it appeared ceased publication. William T. Porter (1809–1858), whose name is associated primarily with sporting journals, was the editor to whom Longfellow addressed his remarks.

2. "The Knight and the Friar," a humorous poem in two parts, was originally published by George Colman (the younger) in his *Broad Grins* (London, 1802). It differs from "Martin Franc and the Monk of Saint Anthony" in enough details to substantiate Longfellow's argument.

249. *To Edward Everett*

Bowdoin College   Decr. 13   1833

Dear Sir,

I had the pleasure of receiving a day or two since the copy of your Phi Beta Kappa Address, which you were kind enough to send me, and for which I beg you to receive my best acknowledgments.

If a voice from the *far East* can add anything to the general applause which has elsewhere greeted its appearance, be assured that we have read it here with feelings of delight and admiration.[1]

I have the honor to be very respectfully

Your Obt. Ser[v]t.
Henry W. Longfellow.

Hon. E. Everett.

MANUSCRIPT: Massachusetts Historical Society.

1. Everett's address had followed Longfellow's Phi Beta Kappa poem, "The Past and the Present," at Cambridge in August. See *Life*, I, 195.

250. *To George Ticknor*

Bowdoin College   Decr 15   1833.

Dear Sir,

I was very much gratified at the reception of your friendly letter of the 6th, and I wish I could persuade myself, that my translations from the Spanish were worthy of the very flattering estimation in which you hold them.

The delay in the publication of Outre Mer No. 2 is rather annoying. It has been solely owing to the negligence of my publishers Lilly & Wait, who have kept back the paper for nearly three months, for what reason I know not. What I shall finally make out [of] this book I hardly know; as it is not yet fully written out. If I can complete my plan satisfactorily, I hope the work will not be without its merits; or to speak with the *modesty*, and in the language of a Troubadour,

E s'ieu podi' acabar
So que m'a fait comensar
Mos *sobresforcius* talens,
Alexandres fon niens
Contra qu'ieu seria.[1]

Speaking of the Troubadours — if you can lend me a Dictionary of the Langue d'Oc, you will do me a great favor. I cannot procure one. I have sent repeatedly to France, but from some reason unknown to me, I get no returns therefrom. If you have one, which you can conveniently send me, please leave it with Lilly, Wait & Co, who will see it safely sent.

The Phi Beta poem will not be published at present; it is too incomplete — a fragment merely.

Your letter reminds me of my want of courtesy towards you; inasmuch as I have never yet thanked you for the copy of your Lecture on the best method of teaching the Modn. Langs. which you were kind enough to send me, and which I read with much pleasure and advantage.[2]

Present, if you please, my best respects to your lady, and believe me, very sincerely

Your friend and Obt. Ser[v]t.

Henry W. Longfellow.

MANUSCRIPT: Dartmouth College Library. ADDRESS: To/George Ticknor Esq/ Boston. POSTMARKS: BRUNSWICK ME. DEC 16/PAID POSTAL ANNOTATION (*by Longfellow*): Paid. H. W. L. ENDORSEMENT: Bowdoin College/17 Decr 1833/Henry W Longfellow

1. "And if I could finish what my excessive desire has made me begin, Alexander would be nothing compared to what I would be." Stanza ii, lines 11-15, of a poem by Peire Vidal (fl. 1175-1215) beginning "Si m laissava de chantar."

2. *Lecture on the Best Methods of Teaching the Living Languages.* Delivered before the American Institute, August 24, 1832 (Boston, 1833). Reprinted by Henry Grattan Doyle in the *Modern Language Journal*, XXII (October 1937), 19-37.

251. *To George Washington Pierce*

[Bowdoin College]

Thursday eve[nin]g. [February 12, 1834]

My dear George

This will be handed you by a Polish Officer — Vincent Nivengosky, who has been sick for a long time at Quebec. He is on his way to Boston and if you will get the stage agent to let him go on at half-price you will do a good deal. Inclosed is a letter from my friend Nault of Quebec which will explain more particularly the circumstances of the case.[1]

Truly yours
H. W. Longfellow

MANUSCRIPT: Longfellow Trust Collection. ADDRESS: George W. Pierce Esq/ Exchange Street/Portland ENDORSEMENT: Henry W./Longfellow./Feb. 12.

1. Dr. Jean Zéphirin Nault (1810–1864) subsequently became secretary of the Bureau du Conseil de Médicine de Québec, 1835–1837, and in 1853 a professor at Laval University. Longfellow may have met him in 1826 in France (see Letter No. 300). It is likely that the Polish officer, a victim of the Asiatic cholera then prevalent in Quebec, had been one of Dr. Nault's patients. Nault's letter to Longfellow is unrecovered.

252. *To George Washington Greene*

Bowdoin College   Feby. 14. 1834.

My dear Geordie,

I suppose you think I am dead. But it is not so; I am only *buried* — in Brunswick again, after a most fatiguing and almost useless journey *westward*-ho! which I am about to lay before you in detail.

About the time I received your first letter, and the books — whose arrival I should have made known to you at the time, had not my brain been too full of thick-coming fancies, to allow me to write even a letter — I heard that Mr. Cogswell of Northampton was about to relinquish the Round Hill School at that place — a school, whose renown must have reached your ears.[1] It seemed to me a glorious opening; and I determined *instanter* to go and see for myself, what were the situation, capabilities, and prospects of this school. So off I started on the coldest day, this *mild* winter has vouchsafed to the children of the North. I stopped a day or two in Boston, to attend to some business of a friend and to get disappointed in a way, which you shall hear of anon. I reached Northampton safe and sound — and remained there two days, devoted to the business of investigating the school. The spot is lovely indeed — lovely even beneath its mantle of snow. I have seen it in Summer — and I believe it one of the most beautiful places in New England. But I will not pause to describe it now.

Mr. Cogswell's propositions were these; Rent of the buildings from next June to January *1836*, including taxes etc $1,400. For use of furniture during same time $350; in addition to which he required an advance of $1600. These terms — though they seem high — are not unreasonable when everything is taken into consideration. The school however is *run down*; and as nothing could warrant such an outlay, but certainty of success — I found it would be necessary to pause and consider. On my return to Boston I consulted with those whose opinions I most valued — and they said the scheme was a bad one — that the school was out of favor with the public — and that it would be very difficult to get it upon its feet again — in short, that I ought not to think of such an undertaking. My friends in Portland are of the same opinion — so that I consider the whole business as blown into thin air — and I awake as from a dream — vanished the pleasant visions of our wandering together through those romantic groves — and of the *golden age* we were to lead in that still retirement.

And now for my disappointment in Boston — and the reason I had for not paying you a flying visit in Prov[idenc]e which, by the way, you must have thought deuced strange. When I left Portland I took only money enough to pay my way to Boston, expecting there to receive money from my books *etc.* Silly swain that I was! One of my publishers said up and down, that he could not pay me a farthing — and what was most mortifying of all — Allen & Ticknor — to whom I repaired in full-blown confidence — told me with the greatest sang-froid, that not enough copies of the Coplas de Manrique had been sold to defray the expenses of publication! So, not a farthing from them. In fine I was obliged to borrow money to defray my expenses to Northampton. Under these circumstances I could not think of going even to Providence; and this will explain to you the whole mystery of my being in Boston without going to see you.

And now for the School in Boston. I find the most influential men there are opposed to Jacotot; and the whole way in which schools are managed there disgusted me. It is a mere matter of whim and caprice. Every new *notion* takes — is a seven-day's wonder — and then no more is heard of it. A school is full to-day, and empty tomorrow. Rents are high — living expensive — and the profits would be nothing. The sum and substance of the whole is, that I have had a most unlucky, disastrous journey. I was cold and sick — *and had to borrow money* — and I have atlength got back again with this lesson — that we had better look before we leap. I think we ought to remain where we are — until we can have the *assurance* — no‖t the‖ mere *hope*, of gaining by an exchange.[2]

Your business with Sparks I did not neglect. He ‖says‖ that the plan of his work is not adapted to such a life of your Grandfather as should be written. He says it should be a large and complete history by itself — from which such a short sketch as would suit the character of his work, might afterwards be compiled. The life of Genl. Greene is not a matter to be done up in fifty pages; and when you see his work, you will find that each volume is to contain several lives.[3]

As to the school you speak of in your last. I know of no one in this region, who could take it now — not before September next — when, if the place is not filled, I can send a person, who will fill it well.[4]

I reached Brunswick last night. My wife comes tomorrow; I precede her to get the house in readiness, and the rooms warm, like a dutiful and affectionate husband, as I am.

Addio. I shall write you again soon, for I have not had room to say half what I wished to.

Very truly yours

H. W. L.

Due parole per la Signora Maria Carlotta.

Carissima Signora Maria — tornando a Brunswick iersera ho trovato col maggior piacere la vostra lettera. Mille grazie per questa bella e lunga lettera; — ma come potrò dirvi la pena che m'ha cagionata! Sento moltissimo, che abbiate fatto un viaggio in questa stagione, e che io sia stato la cagione di sconcertar le vostre speranze, nel minimo grado, benchè fosse senza colpa mia. Ma di questo si parlerà un'altra volta. Domani tornerà la mia moglie, e vi scriveremo una lettera bella e lunga, e presto. Addio. Vostro sincero amico.

Enrico[5]

MANUSCRIPT: Longfellow Trust Collection. ADDRESS: To/George W. Greene Esq/Providence/R. Island. POSTMARK: BRUNSWICK ME. FEB 15

1. See 90.3.

2. Longfellow and Greene may have once discussed starting a school together in Boston to offer the Jacotot method of language instruction.

3. Greene's original plan prevailed, however. He wrote a one-volume life of Nathanael Greene for Sparks's *Library of American Biography* (1846) and a definitive work in three volumes that he published with Longfellow's financial assistance in 1867–1871.

4. In a letter from Providence postmarked January 22 [1834], Greene had asked Longfellow to recommend a preceptor for the "Academy at E. Greenwich."

5. "Two words for Signora Maria Carlotta./Dearest Signora Maria — on my return to Brunswick last night I had the greatest pleasure in finding your letter. A thousand thanks for this beautiful long letter; — but how can I tell you the pain it caused me! I am extremely distressed that you should have made a journey at this time of year, and that I should, even in the slightest degree, have disappointed your hopes, even though it was not my fault. But of this we will speak some other time. Tomorrow my wife returns, and we will write you a beautiful long letter, immediately. Adieu. Your sincere friend./Henry"

253. *To Anne Longfellow Pierce* [1]

[Bowdoin College, February 16, 1834]

My dear little An-aconda,

I have not a word to say to you — excepting that we want you here very much. Aunt Lucia is sitting by the fire thinking of you, and will not be perfectly happy until you come. She and Mary *arriv* last night, squired by Sweet-Sir William [2] — as Mary has probably told you already in the foregoing epistle. I will write George as soon as I collect witticisms enough to fill a letter. Meanwhile — you can tell him that the Northampton bubble has burst.

Very affectionately yours

Harry-come-parry.

MANUSCRIPT: unrecovered; text from photostat, Longfellow Trust Collection. ADDRESS: To/George W. Pierce Esq/For Mrs. Pierce./Augusta POSTMARK: BRUNSWICK ME. FEB 17 ENDORSEMENT: Mary P. L. — /Feby. 16th. 1834.

1. A postscript to Mary Potter Longfellow's letter to Anne Longfellow Pierce of February 16, 1834.
2. William Sweetser (1797–1875), a lecturer in the Bowdoin Medical School.

254. *To Edward Everett*

Bowdoin College   Feby. 23rd 1834.

Hon Edward Everett.

Dear Sir,

In troubling you with the present letter, I rely for an apology upon your kindness, and the wish I have to serve a friend of mine. I see by the newspapers, that four American artists are to be employed to fill four vacant pannels in the Rotunda of the Capitol with paintings upon historic subjects. Mr. George Cooke, a gentleman with whom I passed nearly a year in Italy, is very desirous of being employed in a work like this, as it is a golden opportunity to gain himself a name. He is a man of genius, and of an highly cultivated taste; — and has lately passed four or five years in Europe — among the beautiful models of his art. There was a copy of the "Transfiguration," painted by him, at Harding's room [1] in Boston last summer, which perhaps you saw. I think there were also several other pieces by his hand, some copies and others original, exhibited there. If you did not see them, I can say of *them*, and of Mr. Cooke's paintings in general, that they are very beautiful, both in drawing and coloring. If, however, you saw the pieces at Harding's room, I feel confident you would most willingly use your influence in behalf of Mr. Cooke.

Our representative Mr. Jarvis [2] is a member of the Committee to whom this subject is refer[r]ed; and if it should be convenient for you to say to him, what I have written, you will confer a favor upon an artist, who is ambitious to distinguish himself by some great work.[3]

Pardon, Sir, the liberty I have taken in writing thus unceremoniously; and be assured, that I should be most happy to render any service to a friend of yours, who might need my poor assistance.

Very respectfully
Your Obt. Ser[v]t.
H. W. Longfellow.

MANUSCRIPT: Massachusetts Historical Society.

1. Chester Harding (1792–1866), a fashionable portrait artist of Boston.
2. Leonard Jarvis (1782–1854), U.S. Representative from Maine, 1831–1837.
3. Longfellow's solicitation here and in the following letter did not procure the commission for his friend Cooke.

255. *To Peleg Sprague*[1]

Bowdoin College   Feby. 23rd. 1834.

Hon. Peleg Sprague,
Dear Sir,

I must apologize for troubling you with a letter at a time, when you are so much engaged, as at the present moment. I certainly should not do so, were it not in behalf of a friend, and upon business, which, in a certain sense, is of a public nature.

I see by the papers, that four American artists are to be employed to execute paintings upon national subjects for four vacant pannels in the Rotunda of the Capitol. A very intimate friend of mine, Mr. George Cooke of New York, is very desirous of this opportunity to distinguish himself. He already enjoys a high reputation as a portrait and landscape painter, and I have every reason to believe, that he will become equally celebrated in historic painting.

I passed nearly a year with Mr. Cooke in Italy; and I can bear witness to his ardent and assiduous application in his profession. He passed, I think, four years in Europe; and returns home, full of zeal and enthusiasm for his art, and burning to distinguish himself by some great work. His age cannot be far from thirty-five — so that he is in his prime — a man of fine powers and long experience. His style of painting is exceedingly finished and beautiful, and his coloring very excellent.

I believe our Representative Mr. Jarvis is one of the Committee, to whom this subject is refer[r]ed. If you should have leisure to speak with him, I must beg of you to mention Mr. Cooke, as a man, who would not be likely to disappoint the expectations of the Committee.

Will you excuse me, Sir, if having thus far pleaded the cause of my friend, I take the liberty of asking a favor for myself? From reasons, which I need not here mention, I have become desirous of leaving Brunswick. My ardent desire is to obtain an appointment as Secretary of Legation in some foreign Embassy; — but this I suppose is impossible at the present moment. I have no friends in power under the present Administration; though I hope hereafter to procure such a situation. *En attendant*, a gentleman from Virginia — a friend who is much interested in my success in life — informs me, that in all probability I should be able to procure the professorship of Mod. Langs. in the University of V.

I have requested Mr. Cooke, who is acquainted with Mr. Rives,[2] Senator from Va. to write to him upon the subject, to see if there is a vacancy. If you will ask Mr. Rives, (who is one of the Govt. of the University), what the state of the institution is, and what the salaries, or perquisites of the professors are — you will do me a great favor.

I hope, Sir, you will not think I have presumed too far, in this letter. I should not have written, were not the subject of much importance to me and I will request you, in conclusion, not to put yourself to any inconvenience in these matters, but let them wait your leisure.

I am, Sir, very respectfully,

Your Obt. Ser[v]t.

Henry W. Longfellow.

MANUSCRIPT: Duxbury Rural and Historical Society. ADDRESS: Hon. Peleg Sprague/Washington. POSTMARK: BRUNSWICK ME. FEB 23 ENDORSEMENT: Professor Longfellow/Mar — 1834 — /Ansd PUBLISHED: *Massachusetts Historical Society Proceedings*, LVI (Boston, 1923), 160–161.

1. U. S. Senator from Maine, 1829–1835.
2. William Cabell Rives (1793–1868), statesman and biographer of James Madison, was at this time a U. S. Senator from Virginia. Longfellow's letters to Cooke have not survived, but Cooke's replies reveal that he made inquiries on his friend's behalf.

256. *To Romeo Elton*[1]

Bowdoin College, March 4th 1834.

Dear Sir,

You will see by the accompanying package, that although I have long delayed, I have not finally forgotten to send you the books I promised you in September last, when I had the pleasure of seeing you in Providence. This is the first opportunity I have had.

I am sorry, that these little books are not more worthy of your acceptance. I send them, however, without an apology for their want of merit, trusting to your courtesy for any excuses, that may be necessary.

Have the goodness, Sir, to present my best respects to Dr. Wayland.[2] With much regard,

> Very truly yours
> Henry W. Longfellow

Prof. Elton.

MANUSCRIPT: Brown University Library.

1. Longfellow met Romeo Elton (1790–1870), professor of Latin and Greek at Brown University, when he visited Greene in Providence after delivering his Phi Beta Kappa poem at Harvard in August.

2. Francis Wayland (1796–1865), a doctor of medicine as well as of divinity, was the president of Brown University.

257. *To an Unidentified Bookseller*

> Bowdoin College   March 18. 1834

Gentlemen,

Will you have the goodness to send me by mail a copy of your "Catalogue of Books recently purchased in London," and mark in the margin the price at which you will let me have the following books:

213. Dict. in Six Languages. 1. 4to

580. Minsheu's Guide into 11 Tongues. 1 vol. fol.

777. Sammes's Antiquities of Ancient Britain. 1 vol fol.

876. Teutonic Dictionary. 1 vol.

233. Dutch book (very curious) 3. fol.[1]

If you have any Anglo-Saxon books, please let me know it, with their prices.

> Very respectfully yours
> Henry W. Longfellow.

MANUSCRIPT: Berg Collection, New York Public Library. ADDRESS: *cut away.* POSTMARK: BRUNSWICK ME. MAR 18

1. Two of these books can be identified: John Minsheu, *The Guide into the Tongues. With their agreement and consent one with another, as also their etymologies* (London, 1617); and Aylett Sammes, *Britannia antiqua illustrata: or, The antiquities of ancient Britain . . .* (London, 1676).

258. *To Margaret Potter*

> [Bowdoin College, March, 1834][1]

> Here comes Doctor Moses,[2]
> So stop all your noses,
> For the smell of his clothes is
> Not Otter [*sic*] of Roses.

I thought it would not do to let *Old Mose* go to Portland without a letter of introduction to you, so I have given him one. Pray observe the *silver lace of time* on the seams of his coat! Did you ever see such a complete embodiment of a country practitioner? I am sorry, *on your account*, that he has left his saddle-bags behind, for I think that with those he would have been irresistibly ludicrous. To you, little Madge, whose affections are as yet disengaged, he will doubtless appear in all the brilliancy of youthful beauty. What a convenient thing it would be to have a *doctor* in the family!

Very affectionately your friend and Obt. Servt.

Henry.

MANUSCRIPT: unrecovered; text from "New Longfellow Letters," p. 781.

1. The date is conjectural.
2. This is possibly a reference to Moses Parker Cleaveland (1807–1840), son of Prof. Cleaveland, a Bowdoin graduate of 1827, and a country medical practitioner. He was unmarried at this time.

259. *To Mary Longfellow*[1]

[Brunswick, April 14, 1834]

P.S. When you send next to the post-office, will you have inquiry made, whether there are any letters for Cortés?

MANUSCRIPT: Longfellow Trust Collection. ADDRESS (*by Mary Potter Longfellow*): Miss Mary Longfellow./Care of Hon. Stephen Longfellow./Portland. POSTMARK: BRUNSWICK ME. APR 14

1. A postscript to Mary Potter Longfellow's letter to Mary Longfellow, Sunday evening [April 14, 1834].

260. *To George Washington Greene*

Bowdoin College   April 26. 1834

My dear Greene,

The books have arrived safely, and I am as delighted with them, as a child with a new drum. The present, I assure you, is most acceptable, and of great value to me. I hope I understood you aright — that they were duplicates in your library; — otherwise my conscience will not allow me to keep them.

Your letter of the 6th still unanswered! It seems utterly impossible to me, that so many days, can have slipped away since its reception! Let me see; where shall I begin — "package of books" — "*Willis*" — I will begin with him — and am sorry to say that the Review of his poems is still *in the ink-stand* — not a word of it written — and before me yawns a letter from *Mellen* reminding me of my unfortunate promise, and *urging* me to fulfill it; — and another from McLellan of Boston requesting me to write a Review of his brother's *Journal*, which is just out of the press. Both of these letters must be answered in the negative — and I fear Willis must be upon the same shelf, for the present at least, but not for ever and aye.[1]

What you say, concerning the impression which your own writing leaves upon your mind, after the excitement of composing is over, I am very *glad* you can say. Woe be to you, if it were otherwise. It is to be sure a cruel pang; — but it is one which I feel, often — often — every time I open a page of my own writing. However, I console myself with thinking — what is very true — that to be fully satisfied with what one has done, is but a sad prognostic of what one is going to do.

I am very much rejoiced at your enthusiasm on the subject of Italian Literature — the History of this beautiful province of Letters. Let me advise you — whisper it to no one; — keep the plan a secret in your own bosom — to think about when you are sad. Believe me — these plans we form, are of so etherial an essence, that the moment you uncork them, the flavor escapes.

I write this in great haste, as usual. No news from Virginia. When it comes, it will probably be unfavorable to my wishes.

Addio!

Much love to your wife from both of us. We expect to hear from you soon about the anxiously expected visit.[2] O vile pen, ink, and paper! I write this in agony.

Very truly yours
H. W. Longfellow

MANUSCRIPT: Longfellow Trust Collection. ADDRESS: To/George W. Greene Esq./Providence/R. I. POSTMARK: BRUNSWICK ME. APR 26

1. Longfellow refers to his fellow townsman Nathaniel Parker Willis, to Grenville Mellen (1799–1841), minor poet and brother of Frederic Mellen, and to Isaac McLellan, who had just published a *Journal of a Residence in Scotland, and a Tour through England and France*, compiled from the manuscripts of his brother H. B. McLellan.

2. Greene visited Longfellow in May.

261. *To Stephen Longfellow*[1]

[Bowdoin College, May 30, 1834]

My dear Father,

The box of wine came safely, and could not have come more *à propos*. Accept our best thanks therefor.

We are trying to enjoy ourselves as much as possible, though we have had but one pleasant day since Mr. Greene came.

437

I will send the Library book by the first opportunity; and shall probably come up next week — unless Mr. Greene stays till the close of it.

We are expecting George and Anne, and are very sorry that Mary is taken sick, just at this time. Hope she is better ere this.

Much love to all.

Very truly yours
Henry W. Longfellow.

MANUSCRIPT: Longfellow Trust Collection.   ADDRESS: To/Miss. Mary Longfellow./ Care of S. Longfellow Esq/Portland.   POSTMARK: BRUNSWICK ME. MAY 31 ENDORSEMENT: Ellen May 30th. 1834./Brunswick.

1. This note accompanied letters to Mary and possibly Ellen Longfellow, now lost.

262. *To Romeo Elton*

Bowdoin College   June 3rd [1834]

Dear Sir,

Please accept my best thanks for your obliging letter, and for the books you were kind enough to send me by Mr. Greene. I have not yet had time to read them, but both appear to be very interesting. The Historical Collections, Vol 1. I have seen noticed in the papers, and I regard it as a most valuable publication. *Whatcheer*, I presume, is equally good in its kind, and I promise myself much pleasure in its perusal.[1]

Present, if you please, my respects to Dr. Wayland, and believe me, with much esteem,

very truly yours
Henry W. Longfellow.

Prof. Elton.

MANUSCRIPT: Brown University Library.

1. In a letter to Longfellow dated May 19, 1834, Elton identifies the volumes referred to as *Collections of the Rhode Island Historical Society*, Vol. I (Providence, 1827), and Job Durfee's *Whatcheer, or Roger Williams in Banishment, a Poem* (Providence, 1832). Longfellow presented the Historical Society volume to the library of the University of Upsala (see Letter No. 405); the latter volume, inscribed by Elton to Longfellow, May, 1834, is in the Houghton Library of Harvard University.

263. *To George Washington Pierce*

[Bowdoin College, June 14, 1834][1]

My dear George,

On the first page is Puff. No. 2. which you must get Genl. Todd to publish *incontinent* in the Argus "because she's your wife." They tell me that Cort' really deserves this praise — and when I say *"we have been informed"* it is no invention of mine, — but really so, — we *have* been informed.[2]

When are you and Anne coming down to Brunswick? *Do* come soon — for now the season is in its *prime*, and will soon *go off*. Therefore be quick. I hardly think I shall see you in Portland before commencement.

When you call upon Mr. Todd, tell him to stop Cortés' advertisement — and that I will settle with him when I come to Portland.

Love unto all. Truly yours
Harry.[3]

Our neighbor opposite — Peter O'Slender by name,[4] amuses his leisure hours by killing *skunks*. He has just sent one into eternity, and the *odor* thereof fills the whole neighborhood. Important!

MANUSCRIPT: Longfellow Trust Collection. ADDRESS: George W. Pierce Esq/ Portland. POSTMARKS: BRUNSWICK ME. JUNE 15/PAID POSTAL ANNOTATION (*by Longfellow*): Paid. H. W. L. ENDORSEMENT: Henry and Mary/ June 15th. 1834.

1. The date is established by Mary Potter Longfellow's postscript, headed "Saturday" [June 14].

2. The allusion is not clear; it presumably has to do with Cortés' success as a Spanish teacher. The phrase "because she's your wife" suggests that Anne Longfellow Pierce took Spanish lessons from him. Thomas Todd was proprietor and publisher of the Portland *Eastern Argus*.

3. A note from Mary Potter Longfellow (who wrote "old" in front of "Harry") to Anne Pierce follows the signature and precedes the postscript.

4. That is, Peter O. Alden (162.6).

264. *To George Ticknor*

Brunswick. June 16. 1834.

Dear Sir,

I so seldom have occasion to write to you without asking a favor, that I fear you will soon begin to look upon a letter from me as a kind of premonitory musket and cross-sticks, such as the *"especie de soldado"*[1] exhibited to Gil Blas on the road to Peñaflor, — and asked an alms withal. Nor will the present letter have a tendency to do away that impression, for I am going to ask your assistance in a matter, to which my imagination, if not my judgment, has given much importance.

You have doubtless seen by the New York papers, that Cabrera, late Prof. of Spanish in the N. Y. University, has resigned his professorship and returned to his native land.[2] The vacancy is to be filled on the first of July next; and some of my friends have, with my consent, nominated me for the place. One of the Corporation writes me, that it will be necessary to present credentials of my competency etc. and the favor I am going to ask of you is to say what you can con[s]cientiously in my behalf. I requested my friend Mr. Greene to see you upon this subject, on his return to Boston, a few days since; but fearing that he may not have found you at home, I take the liberty of renewing my request by letter.

If perchance you are not acquainted with Dr Matthews,[3] Chancellor of the University, nor with any member of the corporation, any letter you may be inclined to favor me with may be addressed to the care of Dr. Eben[eze]r Storer Jr. No 622 Broadway.[4]

I do not know how this step will strike you; inasmuch as the N. Y. University has not yet raised her head very high among her sister colleges. But I have grown *very* tired of Brunswick; and N. York — businesslike and unintellectual as it is reported to be — offers a great many advantages to one of my way of thinking.

Excuse the trouble I wish to give you, and present, if you please, my respectful regards to Mrs. Ticknor.

Very truly your Obt Ser[v]t.

Henry W. Longfellow.

P.S. Mr. Cortés desires me to present his best respects.

MANUSCRIPT: Dartmouth College Library.

1. "Kind of soldier." See *Gil Blas*, Chap. II.

2. Miguel Cabrera de Nevares, who held the original appointment in Spanish at the university, resigned on April 12, 1834, to return to Spain.

3. James McFarlane Mathews (1785–1870), a founder of New York University and its first chancellor, 1831–1839.

4. Storer acted as one of Longfellow's unofficial agents in his maneuvering for the New York position. Ticknor's letter of recommendation, dated June 18, 1834, is in the Dartmouth College Library. For excerpts, see *Young Longfellow*, pp. 171–172.

265. *To George Washington Pierce*

Bowdoin College   June 30. 1834

My dear Geordie

Your letter was so full of gossip, that it was charming. How could it be otherwise, when you made the feathers fly so from our best friends? I am sorry I cannot send you in return something as high-seasoned — a cannibal repast. But alas! I have nobody here to serve up, except my wife — and I cannot think of that *yet*. To be sure — I might skin the lady, *what* wears mustachoes, or *clean* some of your political friends — my next-door neighbours to make you out a dinner. But I shall not encourage these carniverous — these anthropophagi[c] propensities. The bill of fare will be scanty.

If you have not already given up the idea of going to Bangor, you had better do so as quick as you can. I cannot possibly go with you, having promised little Mary, that I would take her to Portland. Besides, I suppose Pitt [Fessenden] will deliver the same Oration as last year — and who wants to go to Bangor to hear it again. So stay at home, and see company. We shall take the Sunday morning stage, and be in Portland about 10 or 11 o'ck.

Much obliged to you for the newspaper of last week, and the *puff*. Blow, breezes, blow! I have seen two or three others in the Boston papers; thus far everything favorable. I am engaged on No. 3 — and as the matter in hand is more original, I think the next Volume will be better than the last.[1]

Very glad, that the Old Roman enjoyed herself so much in Portland.[2] We have had a short letter from her lord and master, informing us of their safe arrival home — and nothing more.

Bad news for you; — I have not smoked yet.

Mr. Mossie has been here. Bright, but vulgar in some things. Not exactly the gentleman. Strange mixture of common sense and *un*common nonsense. Much better than the Fire King.[3]

Nothing more. Love to all. Farewell. Until the pleasure of to see you again.

Your Obt. Ser[v]t. by courtesy

H. W. Longw.

MANUSCRIPT: Longfellow Trust Collection. ADDRESS: To/George W. Pierce Esq./Portland. POSTMARK: BRUNSWICK Me. JUN 30

1. Longfellow refers to *Outre-Mer*. The *"puff"* was presumably a review of No. II in the *Eastern Argus* for June 25, 1834.

2. A facetious reference to Greene's Roman wife.

3. The persons referred to in this paragraph are unidentified.

266. *To Lewis Gaylord Clark*[1]

[Bowdoin College, July 20, 1834]

I DO not know how your subscription-list stands; but I know that the reputation of your magazine stands high. Your efforts have met with at least this success. I am happy to see you so zealous in the cause of the KNICKERBOCKER; and so long as this zeal continues, I have no doubt of your complete success. Never was magazine born with so good a name. I give you my best wishes; and whenever it is in my power, shall give you what little aid I can.

MANUSCRIPT: unrecovered; text from the *Knickerbocker, or, New-York Monthly Magazine*, LVII (February 1861), 226.

1. Clark (1810–1873) had recently become editor of the *Knickerbocker*. This fragment (the date supplied by Clark) was apparently in response to a request for contributions. Longfellow was to meet Clark in New York on the visit alluded to in Letter No. 267.

267. *To George Washington Greene*

Bowdoin College. Sunday noon. July 20. 1834

My dear Greene

Yours of the 15th has just reached me — not an hour ago. What your New York correspondent writes you concerning the income of the former Professor of Spanish, agrees with what I have heard from other sources. Still I perceive you are in a misunderstanding about it. That income did not come from the University only, — nor from teaching Spanish only — but from teaching the Spanish guitar, — an instrument which I do not play upon. The Prof. of Span[is]h has no salary whatever — only the tuition of scholars; and I am informed that the number of Spanish Scholars in the University never exceeded 30 at any one time. At present there are but 7. A letter now lies before me from Mr. Bush,[1] one of the N. Y. Professors, to Prof. Upham, in which the writer says, that although "Mr. L's reputation is with us very high, the Council will doubtless find it difficult to overlook the claims of Mr. Rabadan,[2] the present incumbent etc etc etc."

Well, the upshot of the whole matter is, that at so great a distance it is impossible to obtain *satisfactory* information. Therefore, on the 31st day of this month I shall leave Brunswick, and on the third of August I shall be in New York. Having started in this matter, I shall not abandon it without having seen with my own eyes.

The postponement of the election at N. Y. is a *contre-temps* for our arrangements here. All that I can do shall be done — n'en doutez pas [doubt it not]. Your name is already before the Executive government of the College backed by my recommendation. I have also spoken with my father upon the subject; and shall converse with other members of the Boards, as soon as I have an opportunity. But all this is of course conditional. I cannot do anything decisive until I have been in N. York. But more of this when we meet. All I can feel sure of is, that if any one takes my place here next autumn you will be the man. Credentials "setting forth your pretentions in all their amplitude," will not be needed until the first week in September next.

I am almost sorry about your making application to Dr Wayland,[3] not that I thank you the less for your good intentions, but because being almost an entire stranger to him personally, I fear he thought it strange. I hope, and trust, that you told him in so many words, that the application was not made at my request or instigation. Otherwise I shall feel unpleasantly about it.

Outre Mer No. 2. seems to succeed admirably. The critics say "he is a fine boy, and looks very much like his *pa*." In the Knickerbocker you have been anticipated; Lewis Gaylord [Clark] having taken pen in hand to salute me.[4] I am glad your paper on Petrarca is so nearly completed. You must send it soon, or Everett will give it the go-by in the next No. which would be *à regretter*.[5]

Felton and Dr. Beck[6] of Cambridge are coming to make me a visit. I expect them daily. We shall *toast* your wife, and drink your health in *Vin de Bordeaux*, of which I have lately made provision in Portland. I wish you could be with us.

I do not think that I shall stop in Providence on my way to New York. I had rather stop on my way back; for then I shall have more to tell you. You must try to be at the boat. I shall pass through either on Friday or Saturday. If I am not, I will inform you (confound the pen).

Farewell. Yours very truly
H. W. L.

MANUSCRIPT: Longfellow Trust Collection.

1. George Bush (1796–1859), professor of Hebrew and Oriental literature.

2. Carlos Rabadan had succeeded Cabrera as professor of Spanish, a position to which he was formally elected on September 25, 1834.

3. President Wayland had written a letter of recommendation for Longfellow at Greene's request.

4. *Knickerbocker*, IV (July 1834), 72–75. Clark began his review by stating, "There is not in our country, a writer who so nearly approaches the ease and grace of style, the purity of sentiment and language, which distinguish the Sketch Book and Bracebridge Hall, as the author of Outre-Mer."

5. The article was published in the *North American Review*, XL (January 1835), 1–26.

6. Charles Beck (1798–1866), professor of Latin at Harvard.

268. *To Maria Greene*[1]

[Bowdoin College]
Lunedì mattino. [July 21, 1834]

Car[issi]ma Sign[or]a Maria,

Vorrei che poteste vedere in questo momento la mia *libreria*, ossia *biblioteca*, se si può qualificar di nome di biblioteca la picciola mia collezione di libri. Ma ora non si trat[t]a dei libri: — solamente della camera che in questa stagione è bellissima. Oggi abbiamo una di quelle belle giornate che di quando in quando ci fornisce anche il cattivo clima nostro. È di buon' ora assai; ed eccomi qui scrivendo al tavolino, quasi quasi credendomi in Italia, così bella è la mattina. Un venticello spira poeticamente attraverso la finestra, il canto degli augelli, l'odor dei fiori — la freschezza dell' aria mattutina, e lo splendor del sole fanno balzar d'allegria il cuore. Certamente se ora foste quà, non mancava altro d'innamorarvi davvero di Brunswick, e particolarmente di questa camara, che forse fra pochi mesi sarà la camara di quel birbonacci||o|| marito, ch' avete sposato oltramare, e chi m'è tanto antipatico!

Ecco un assai pulito pezzo d'eloquenza poetica; adesso parliamo [in] prosa. Nella lettera che ho scritto a Greene sentirete tutto ciò che sappiamo fin' ora dell' Univers[i]tà di N. York. Questo ritardo mi dispiace assaissimo; ma che volete? Le cose si fanno con tutta la celerità che puossi aspettare da uomini grandi, che sono quasi tutti pigri, e sogliono andare a passo di lumaca.

Tante grazie per la vostra amabil[e] lettera. Il ritratto mio[2] vi piace; — bene — me ne allegro. Ma bisogna dir la verità; sempre quel ritratto mi fa pensare a un certo Pippo nel "Pittore Capriccioso" di Gozzi, il quale aveva "un visaccio largo, con certi line[a]menti, o piuttosto colpi sì fieri, che l' avrebbe quasi ritratto ognuno col carbone; bocca larga, labbra grosse, colorito piuttosto pagonazzo [pavonazzo] che vermiglio, occhi grandi e celesti, e uno sperticato nasaccio, verso le ciglia schiacciato e appuntato sopra la bocca."[3] Eccomi — servo suo!

Voi dite che avete imparato a vivere felice in qualunque parte del mondo, e che non sarebbe gran cosa per voi il dover cangiar Providenza con Brunswick. Lo credo bene. In questo di cangiar città e paesi il più duro passo è quel della soglia. Nel lasciare un luogo dove abbiamo passato molto tempo, sempre si sente un certo non so che di tristezza. Nelle parole di Lord Byron.

> In leaving even the most unpleasant people
> And places; — one keeps looking at the steeple.[4]

Addio. Ben presto ci rivedremo. Addio.

Vostro sincero amico
Enrico

Mia moglie vi manda un bacio, ed io ve ne mando due — s' è lecito.

MANUSCRIPT: Longfellow Trust Collection. ADDRESS: George W. Greene Esqr./ Providence/R. I. POSTMARK: BRUNSWICK ME. JUL 21

TRANSLATION:

Monday morning.

Dearest Signora Maria,

I wish you could see at this moment my *bookshop*, or rather *library*, if my small collection of books may be described as a library. But books are not the point just now: — only the room which at this season is very beautiful. Today we have one of those lovely days that even our bad climate occasionally provides us with. It is very early; and here I am writing at my desk, almost believing I am in Italy, so beautiful is the morning. A breeze blows poetically through the window, the song of the birds, the smell of the flowers — the coolness of the morning air, and the spendor of the sun make the heart leap with joy. Certainly if you were here now, you could not fail to fall really in love with Brunswick, and especially with this room, which perhaps a few months from now will be the room of that rascal husband whom you married overseas and whom I find so unpleasant!

There is a highly polished piece of poetic eloquence; now let us speak in prose. In the letter I have written to Greene, you will hear all we so far know of the University of N. York. This delay annoys me very much indeed; but what can one do? Things are being done with all the speed one may expect of great men, who are almost all lazy, and used to traveling at a snail's pace.

Many thanks for your kind letter. You like my portrait; — good — I am delighted. But I must tell the truth; that portrait always makes me think of one Pippo in Gozzi's "Playful Painter," who had "a broad ugly face, with such deep lines, or rather cuts that it was almost as if each of them had been drawn with charcoal; broad mouth, thick lips, complexion not so much ruddy as violet, great blue eyes, and an exaggeratedly large nose, flat toward the brow and sharply pointed over the mouth."[2] There I am — your servant!

You say you have learnt to live happily in any part of the world, and it would not be any great trouble to you to have to exchange Providence for Brunswick. I can well believe it. In leaving for new cities and countries the hardest step is the doorstep. In departing from a place where we have passed a good deal of time, one always feels an indefinable sadness. In the words of Lord Byron.

> In leaving even the most unpleasant people
> And places; — one keeps looking at the steeple.[3]

Adieu. We shall meet again very soon. Adieu.

Your sincere friend
Henry

My wife sends you a kiss, and I send you two — if that is allowed.

1. This letter presumably served as the cover sheet for Letter No. 267.

2. Possibly the Badger portrait (see frontispiece).

3. Longfellow had printed "Il Pittore Capriccioso" by Count Gasparo Gozzi (1713-1786) in his *Saggi de' Novellieri Italiani d'Ogni Secolo* (Boston, 1832). For the description of Pippo, see p. 24.

4. *Don Juan*, Canto II, stanza XIV.

269. *To George Washington Pierce*

[Bowdoin College]
Wednesday afternoon [July 23, 1834][1]

My dear George

I find I shall be able to leave Brunswick a day or two sooner, than I expected. If nothing new turns up I shall be in Portland on Tuesday next at noon. The only thing that can interfere with this arrangement, will be a visit from Mr. Felton of Cambridge, whom I have been for some days expecting, and who has not yet arrived. If you hear of his being in Portland, stop him; for a host detained against his will cannot possibly render agreeable the visit of the guest. If you can contrive to let Henry Nichols[2] know, that I am expected on Tuesday, with the intention of going Westward, it may save a clash.

My plan is to take the Bangor on Wednesday morning. I am very sorry to hear, that your eye is so completely *bunged*. I hope and trust, that it will be entirely well before the close of the week.

Señor Cortés sailed from New York for Malaga on Sunday last.

In haste yours

Henry.

MANUSCRIPT: Longfellow Trust Collection. ADDRESS: To/George W. Pierce Esqr./Portland. POSTMARK: BRUNSWICK ME. JUL 23

1. The date is approximate.
2. Presumably George Henry Nichols (1814–1890), son of Rev. Ichabod Nichols of Portland.

270. *To George Guelph Barrell*

Bowdoin College, Brunswick   August 1st 1834.

My dear Sir,

Your kind and very acceptable letter of the 26th October, reached me in due season from its date. I am very happy to find, that I am still remembered in Malaga. Your former letter never reached me; and but for the one now before me I should never have known that you had written in answer to mine from Marseilles, dated ever so many years ago.[1]

My recollections of Malaga are of the most delightful kind. Everything remains distinctly impressed upon my mind. Your house — its balcony — the pleasant sea-breeze of November — and your own personal kindness to me, are images and recollections never to be effaced.

How different the scene with me now! A professor in a college —

a married man — and living in a climate — ye Gods! — what a climate! To-day the thermometer at 98°. — tomorrow, shivering over a fire in an evening of August. How I envy you the sea-shore of the Mediterranean! My prayer is that I may visit Spain again; and I hope the prayer may be answered before many years. In the mean time I amuse the few leisure moments which now and then fall to my lot in dreaming of the past, and in writing down in such prose as flows from my pen, the thoughts that come up in my mind. A few of these sketches I here send you. I hope they may amuse a dull hour, if you have any such; — and who has not?

I intended to send this letter and the accompanying volume by my friend Don José Cortés, who sailed from New York, a few days ago for Malaga. I was disappointed in his slipping away so soon; and now avail myself of another opportunity.

The first volume of my "pilgrimages" is devoted to France; the second will treat of Spain; the third of Italy — and the fourth of Germany, and England. I shall send them all to you as occasion may offer.

In the mean time, I remain, my dear Sir, with the greatest regard,

very sincerely yours
Henry W. Longfellow.

MANUSCRIPT: Bowdoin College Library. PUBLISHED: *Bowdoin College Bulletin*, Number 327 (December 1957), p. 34.

1. A reference to Letter No. 121.

271. *To George Pope Morris*[1]

Bowdoin College
Brunswick Me. August 18. 1834.

George P. Morris Esq. —
Dear Sir,

I regretted very much, that I should be obliged to leave New York without seeing you again. I mentioned to you casually in our short interview, that I contemplated removing to your city; and upon this subject I wished to have some conversation with you. It is proposed to me to take a situation in the New York University — a professorship of Modern Languages. This professorship, if created, will be without a salary, tuition for instruction and lectures only being given. Should, therefore, the appointment be made, and should I accept, I shall be obliged to look for my support, in part at least, to sources disconnected with the University; and I wished to enquire of you whether it would be possible and desirable for me to make some arrangement, by which I could assist you in the discharge of your duties connected with the *Mirror*.

I do not put this into the form of a direct proposition, because my ideas upon the subject are rather indefinite at present; and I know not whether you desire any farther assistance, than what you have already. I should, however, be glad to hear from you upon this subject; and to be informed whether there is room for negociation of any kind.

Have the goodness to consider this letter as confidential, and to excuse the liberty I take in writing upon this subject so unceremoniously. Will you have the goodness to write me a few lines, as soon as possible?

Very respectfully yours
Henry W. Longfellow.

Geo: P. Morris Esq.

MANUSCRIPT: Clifton Waller Barrett Collection, University of Virginia. ADDRESS: To/George P. Morris Esq./(Ed. N. Y. Mirror.)/New York. POSTMARKS: BRUNSWICK ME. AUG 19/PAID POSTAL ANNOTATION (*by Longfellow*): Paid. H. W. L.

1. Morris (1802–1864) had founded the *New York Mirror* in 1823.

272. *To George Washington Pierce*

[Bowdoin College]
Wednesday morng. [August 20, 1834]

My dear George

I have just recd. this — and reply straightway upon the back thereof — no other sheet of paper being so convenient.[1]

Unfortunately my robe of office is still in Cambridge, where I left it two years ago. I intended to bring it home last week — but passing so rapidly through Boston, it escaped my mind. It is in the safe keeping of Mr. Charles Folsom; and if Appleton can find any way of getting it brought safely from Cambridge he is entirely welcome to wear it all day long if he wishes.

Have just recd. a letter from little Mary. She will be here to-night. Good bye. Love to all.

Truly yours
Henry. or Lord Harry —

MANUSCRIPT: Longfellow Trust Collection. ADDRESS: George W. Pierce Esq/ Portland POSTMARK: BRUNSWICK ME. AUG 20 POSTAL ANNOTATION (*by Longfellow*): Single ENDORSEMENT: H. W. Longfellow/Aug. 20. 1834

1. On the other side of the sheet is a note from Pierce, written on August 19, the first sentence of which reads, "Can you let John Appleton have your surplice at commencement?" Appleton (1815–1864) was a member of the Bowdoin class of 1834.

273. *To Charles Stewart Daveis*

Bowdoin College   August 26, 1834.

My dear Sir,

Mr. and Mrs. [Alexander H.] Everett will stay with us at Commencement,[1] and I write to request, that you and your lady would favor us with your company at the same time. We promise you no regal entertainment, but shall be exceedingly happy to have you with us.

Present our best regards to Mrs. D. and do me the favor of a line in answer.

Very truly yours
Henry W. Longfellow

Charles S. Dav[e]is Esq.

MANUSCRIPT: unrecovered; text from typewritten transcript, Longfellow Trust Collection. ADDRESS: Charles S Daveis, Esq., Portland POSTMARKS: BRUNSWICK ME. AUG 26/SIX CENTS PD.

1. Everett delivered the Phi Beta Kappa address at Bowdoin on September 3 (see Letter No. 281).

274. *To James McFarlane Mathews*

Bowdoin College   August 30. 1834.

Dear Sir,

Your favor of the 27th inst. has just reached me. I regret very much, that circumstances should be just as they are; but as they cannot be moulded to my wishes in every respect, I must try to adapt myself to them.

To come then at once to the point, without wearying you with a long preamble, I will say, that in reference to the Professorship of Spanish, I wish it may be considered, that my pretensions are withdrawn, and would hereby request you to withdraw them. For the Prof[essorshi]p of Modern Languages and Literature, I wish still to be considered a candidate; unless you find an objection in what follows.

I do not feel authorised under the circumstances of the case to resign the situation I now hold. Should I be appointed, therefore, to a professorship in your institution, it would not be in my power to enter upon the duties of that station immediately; certainly not before next Spring, unless some unforeseen facilities should occur. I am not aware that my immediate presence in New York would be necessary; indeed, I should imagine from the nature of the case, that it would not be so.

Should, therefore, the new professorship be founded, as anticipated,

I am desirous of obtaining the appointment, with the liberty above refer[r]ed to.

Requesting that you would present my respectful regards to your family and to Dr. Cox,[1] I am, Sir,

> Very respectfully yours
> Henry W. Longfellow.

Revd. Dr Mathews.

MANUSCRIPT: Historical Society of Pennsylvania. ADDRESS: Revd. Dr. Mathews/ Chancellor of the Univy. of/New York [*Redirected to New Haven and then again to New York in another hand*] POSTMARKS: BRUNSWICK‖ME.‖AUG. 30/ NEW YORK SEP 2/PROVIDENCE [?] OCT 1/PAID POSTAL ANNOTATION (*by Longfellow*): Paid. H. W. L.

1. Rev. Samuel Hanson Cox (1793–1881), a founder of New York University, had nominated Longfellow for the professorship of Spanish on June 3.

275. *To George Washington Greene*

> Brunswick. Me. Saturday   Sept. 6. '34.

My dear George,

The matter is brought to a stand-still at last. About a week ago I received a letter from Dr. Mathews, saying that as most of the gentlemen of the Council were out of town, nothing could be done before the first Tuesday in Septr. (last Tuesday). I wrote him in answer, that under those circumstance[s] I should not think of resigning my present situation; — that so far as regards the Span[is]h Profship first spoken of — I withdrew my pretensions unconditionally; and that in case I should be appointed to the profship. (confound the pen!) of Modern Langs. and Lit[eratur]e it would not be in my power to go to New York immediately — certainly not before Spring.

Our commencement is just over, and I have not resigned my place here; though I have reserved the right of doing so at any time during the year. Prudence dictated this step. I found that if I withdrew myself there was no possibility — no chance whatever of getting you appointed to my place. It would have been left vacant. As the matter now stands, the Executive Govt. have the power of employing one or more persons as Tutors in case of vacancy in any professor[shi]p.

Meanwhile no opportunity shall be lost of presenting your claims "in all their amplitude"; and I have little doubt of final success. Therefore go at your *Spanish* with energy — etc, etc, etc.

I write you these few lines in a restless, impatient mood, — being rather nervous from tea-drinking and cigars. I have had a very fatiguing, though pleasant Commen[cemen]t. Mr. Everett and lady left us yesterday; and now we feel the desolation of

"The banquet-hall deserted
Whose lights are fled — whose garlands dead
And all save *us* departed."[1]

I am in a sorry humour for a letter, and therefore cease grinding;
my ideas being like the *grinders* spoken of in Ecclesiastics [*sic*] — who
shall cease because they are few.[2]

Love to little Maria from *all* of us.

Very truly yours
Lord Harry

P.S. The affair in New York is decided ere this. I daily expect a letter
from Dr. Mathews.

Septr. 8. Monday.

I have left my letter open for two days in the hope of hearing from
New York; but in vain.

MANUSCRIPT: Longfellow Trust Collection. ADDRESS: George W. Greene Esq./
Providence. POSTMARK: BRUNSWICK ME. SEP 8

1. Cf. Thomas Moore, "Oft in the Stilly Night," stanza 2.
2. Eccles. 12:3.

276. *To George Guelph Barrell*

Portland. Septr. 15. '34

Geo: G. Barrell Esq.

My dear Sir,

About a month ago I wrote you a few lines from New York, and
sent you a small volume of sketches of Travels in Europe, which I hope
reached you safely. In the same package was a letter for my friend
Dr. José Cortés of Madrid. I now take the liberty of troubling you
again with letters to him; and would also request the favor of occasionally sending letters for him to your care. I know that it will put
you to some inconvenience but I hope you will excuse it on account
of my having no more direct way of sending to Madrid. I suppose,
too, that the expence of the packages sent, and which I may hereafter send will be considerable; but if you will have the goodness to
make a minute of the same, the amount shall be paid here or there
as you may direct.

Nothing new has transpired since I last wrote you. I have returned
from New York, and am now passing a College Vacation in this place,
which is rather dull.

With this, I send 1. a letter to Cortés, which I will thank you to send by mail, as soon as you receive it. 2. a package for the same, which being less important and of greater weight, please keep for some private opportunity, or until Cortés writes you.

In the freedom with which I make use of your friendship, I trust you will see nothing but an expression of the readiness I feel to render you service on all occasions.

With much regard

Very truly your friend and Obt. Ser[v]t.
Henry W. Longfellow.

Geo: G. Barrell, Esqre.

MANUSCRIPT: Clifton Waller Barrett Collection, University of Virginia.

277. *To Edward Gray Fales*[1]

Portland   Tuesday afternoon. Septr. 16. '34.

Dear Edward,

Yours of Sunday eve[nin]g reached me this morning, and I send you an answer by return of mail that there may be no delay nor misunderstanding touching the cloth. I have seen Pierce and he says, that unless I take the *blue* with him, he does not wish to take it. This, however, I cannot do; so that you will be spared the trouble of sending it. The *black* please send as you noted it down; — your *best*, — recollect.

I was sorry and disappointed not to see you again. I expected you to remain until I came back that evening; though I staid later than I intended. Excuse my want of ceremony. I did not deem it necessary.

I have just recd. a letter from your mother. The[y] reached Boston in safety, and all are well. Mary (*Black* Mary) was careless enough to leave her cloak in the Portland stage and her trunk on board the Steamer, and your mother writes that the Doctor has had more trouble on her account, than on that of all the *other* ladies put together. This is Domestic Felicity.

Write me, when you feel disposed so to do. I shall always be happy to hear from you; though you must not expect long and regular answers.

Very truly yr. friend
Henry W. Longw.

P.S. Remember me [to] Mr. Whitwell.[2]

MANUSCRIPT: Boston Public Library.   ADDRESS: To/Mr. Edward G. Fales/Calais/ (Me)   POSTMARK: PORTLAND Me. SEP 17

1. Fales (1812–1842), a member of the Bowdoin class of 1832 and the son of

Longfellow's former landlady (191.1), was in the dry goods business in Calais, Maine.

2. William Augustus Whitwell (1804–1865), a Harvard graduate, served as the first pastor of the Unitarian Church of Calais, 1833–1839.

278. *To Lewis Gaylord Clark*

Bowdoin College. October 13. 1834.

My dear Sir,

Permit me to congratulate you upon your marriage, which I see announced in the New York papers. May you live long and happily, with your fair lady,

> "And when with envy Time transported
> Shall think to rob you of your joys,
> She in her girls again be courted,
> And you go wooing in your boys." [1]

Let me congratulate you also upon your brother's joining you in the Editorship of the Knickerbocker. I think it an excellent arrangement — a union of the Lucky Dog and the Happy Man; and surely you must be happy, having wed both a wife and a brother. May all go "merry as a marriage bell." [2]

While your affairs look thus bright with the honey moon, those of your friend have passed into the yellow leaf. I hear nothing from New York, on the subject of the Professorship. Lilly Wait & co. of Boston object to my publishing a new edition of Outre Mer at present; — you do not write to acknowledge the arrival of a package I sent you a month ago, with a story for the Knicker, and another for the New Yorker, the latter from the elegant pen of *my friend* Mr. Browne. [3] Nor does Geo. P. Morris Esqe. deign to answer two letters I have written him, which I think uncivil. One of the letters was in your package and I trust that it reached him. The other being sent by mail, possibly miscarried. [4]

Thus you see I am left to my solitary reflections here in the far East, somewhat disappointed in my hopes and expectations, albeit not entirely dejected and desponding.

I hope to hear from you soon — indeed I am in daily expectation of your October package which has not yet reached me. Have the goodness to suggest to Mr. Morris the propriety of answering my letters; and tell the Harpers that I shall write them as soon as I can bring the Lilly & Wait concern to terms. [5]

What do you think of the Coplas de Manrique? Would it not be a good plan to embody ||some of it|| with Outre Mer? I think it would. With my best regards to you and ||your lady,

Very truly yours
Henry W. Longfellow.||

MANUSCRIPT: Longfellow Trust Collection. ADDRESS: ||To/Lewis|| Gaylord Clark Esq/New York.

1. See 148.10. Clark married Ella Maria Curtis, described by his brother Willis as "one of the fairest daughters of Eve" (*Clark Letters*, p. 33).
2. Lord Byron, *Childe Harold*, III, 21.
3. The second story, entitled "The Wondrous Tale of a Little Man in Gosling Green," was submitted through Clark to Horace Greeley's *New Yorker*. Written under the pseudonym Charles F. Brown, it won Longfellow a prize of $50. See *Young Longfellow*, pp. 200–201.
4. One of these letters is No. 271; the other is unrecovered.
5. The publishers of *Outre-Mer No. II* "wished to use the surrender of their copyright as a means of relieving themselves of the remaining stock" (*Young Longfellow*, p. 198).

279. *To Charles Stewart Daveis* [?] [1]

Bowdoin College, October 23rd, 34.

My dear Sir,

When I recd yr. last letter, I had just dispatched an answer to Mr. Bowen's enquiries concerning the no. of copies, which would be sold here, and making myself responsible for $50. On these conditions he is willing to undertake the publication, if Mr. Everett will consent.

I have since had a letter from Mr. Everett. He hesitates and doubts. I know not what his final resolution will be.

I thus report progress — no great progress either.[2] Profr. Newman has returned. His health is improved.

With best regards to yr. lady, in which mine joins,

Very truly yrs
Henry W. Longfellow.

MANUSCRIPT: unrecovered; text from typewritten transcript, Longfellow Trust Collection.

1. The identification is conjectural. Daveis had presumably attended the commencement (see Letter No. 273) and in his capacity as a Bowdoin overseer would have been interested in the publication of Everett's address.
2. These remarks concern the plan to publish Everett's Phi Beta Kappa address of September 3. Everett later consented, and Bowen published it by the end of the year. See 281.1.

280. *To George Washington Greene*

[Bowdoin College] October 28. '34.

My dear Greene,

It is somewhat past midnight by the clock, and before me lies "The Journey into Italy," which I have just completed.[1] The motto will give you the character of the chapter. It is from Goethe's Faust. "What I catch is at present only sketch-ways [as it were]; but I prepare myself betimes for the Italian journey." I do not give a regular and long-drawn description of all I saw between Marseilles and Rome, but only touch the salient points, and that very lightly. My next chapter, which I shall write soon, will be "Rome in Summer." And here I beg of you, that if you or your Roman lady can call to mind any quaint adage of the common people, or quaint domestic trait, either of high-born cavalier or low-born *minente*,[2] and which I peradventure have never heard of, or have forgotten — note it down for me — and send it in your next.

The No. on Spain is finished. Its papers are; 1. Spain; being a general introduction. 2. El Cajon de Sastre; — a collection of sketches in Madrid. 3. The village of El Pardillo. 4. The Ancient Spanish Ballads. 5. Leaves from my Journal; embracing my journey to Andalusia, and sketches of Cordova, Cadiz, Seville, and Granada. A thousand topics are touched upon; and I think this No. far superior to either of the preceding. The style is more spirited and vigorous, — and the subjects less familiar to most people. You see, I am pushing on with vigor; and unless the *estro* [inspiration] leaves me, I shall have Italy finished before I write you again. There is nothing like writing, when one is in the vein. The moment you stop you grow cool, and then it is all over with you.

And lo! as I write this — one lamp has shut its burning eye — and the other begins to wink. I will light my bed-lamp, and — go to bed? No, smoke a pipe.

What is the tree called in the garden of St. Onofrio — Tasso's *oak*, or Tasso's *elm* — or what?[3]

29th.

Last night I was too lazy to get your letter which happened to be in my study — and therefore instead of answering you began to discourse about myself. Yours is now before me, and shall receive a due response.

I am very glad to hear that you are in East Greenwich and have thrown off the weary yoke for a season at least. No doubt you will find your health much improved, and that the fruits of your leisure will be abundant. Need I say how much pleasure we should take in visiting you at yr. father's? But the cruel winter! Oh no, my friend, it is impossible. Our visit shall be a Summer visit — so as to give you an opportunity of drowning us in the Bay, in testimony of yr. skill as Palinurus.

We are very sorry to hear that "little Maria" has been so sick; and could not account for her long silence, till yr. letter came with the unpleasant reason. Give our love to her; and tell her not to mind it. She will be the better for it, which is after all rather poor consolation.[4]

Howe has written me to say, that he is going to take charge of the New Eng[lan]d Mag[azi]n[e].[5] He wished me to write but I have refused, not having time.

The Rev[ie]w of Outre-mer was written by Peabody.[6] I think it rather in the *cucumber* style — quite cool. No matter. Everett spoke to me highly of yr. Article.[7] He said the translations were equal to anything, that had been executed on this side of the water. This he told me when here, about a month ago.

I have at length recd. a letter from N. York, which amounts to nothing. It is from my cousin,[8] who says he has seen Dr. Mathews who informs him, that probably nothing will be done before Spring. Very shabby behavior!

A new edition of the Vocab. della Crusca is in press at Florence.[9]

Present my kind regards to yr. parents and brother and write me again very soon. There is no very good reason why two months should elapse between our letters is there?

Yrs, in full communion,
Henry W. Longw.

MANUSCRIPT: Longfellow Trust Collection.   ADDRESS: To/Geo: W. Greene Esqr./ East Greenwich/R. I.   POSTMARK: BRUNSWICK ME. OCT 29

1. Longfellow refers to his work on *Outre-Mer*.

2. An inhabitant of Trastevere on the right bank of the Tiber. Longfellow describes a *Minente* in *Outre-Mer* (*Works*, VII, 250–251).

3. Tasso's oak. Longfellow does not identify it as such in *Outre-Mer*.

4. In his letter of October 9, 1834, Greene wrote that his wife had had "a severe attack of bilious fever."

5. Samuel Gridley Howe and John Osborne Sargent (500.3) edited the magazine during January and February, 1835, having succeeded the founder, James T. Buckingham.

6. Oliver William Bourn Peabody (1799–1848) wrote a review of *Outre-Mer* for the *North American Review* (XXXIX [October 1834], 459–467), of which he was an assistant editor.

7. The article on Petrarch (267.5).

8. Dr. Eben Storer.

9. This was not, however, the edition that Longfellow owned. His copy of the

work (*Vocabolario degli Accademici della Crusca* [Verona, 1804-1806]) contains his signature and the following note: "Bought at the sale of Mr. Cogswell's books in February. 1834. — paid $18."

281. *To Alexander Hill Everett*

Bowdoin College. Nov. 2. 1834.

My dear Sir,

Your favor of the 17 Octr. was duly recd. and we feel very happy to have had it in our power to contribute in any way to the pleasure of your Eastern journey. Your short visit here afforded us much gratification; and in regard to the impression which your Discourse made upon the public mind in this region — *si qua ea gloria est* [if that is any glory] — you may be assured, that it was very vivid, and will be very lasting. A strong desire has been manifested here to have it published; but you can turn it to so good account in the many calls, that are made upon your time in the way of public addresses, that I fear you may not be willing to relinquish it. I hope, however, to have the pleasure of reading it ere long either in a pamphlet or in the Review.[1]

Please present my thanks to Mr. Peabody for his very indulgent notice of Outre Mer. It is this same book, which prevents me from sending you an Art. for the Jany. No. of the Review. I give my leisure time to the completion of the book, which if no accident prevents, will be published entire in two vols. during the Winter. I intend to send you a paper on the Hist. of the French Lang. in England for April. I have some very curious material on hand, and only want time to copy the extracts — the most irksome and laborious part of the business, -- inasmuch as the Art. will consist mainly of extracts.[2]

My wife joins me in the kindest regards to your lady.

Very sincerely your friend and Obt. Ser[v]t.
Henry W. Longfellow.

MANUSCRIPT: Longfellow Trust Collection.

1. Longfellow read it in a 55-page pamphlet: *Address to the Phi Beta Kappa Society of Bowdoin College, on the present state of polite learning in England and America, delivered at Brunswick, Me., September 3, 1834, by Alexander H. Everett* (Boston: Charles Bowen, 1834).

2. This article did not appear in the *North American Review* until October 1840 (LI, 285-308).

282. *To Edward Gray Fales*

Bowdoin College   Nov. 5. 1834.

Dear Edward,

I wish you would send me cloth for a cloak if you have any on hand such as I shall straightway describe. Color, blue — fabric stout, strong and thick — and price not more than $4. per yd. I do not wish for a dandy cloak, to flourish in the sun withal, but a good, substantial winter garment, that will keep out the wind and rain, and yet not be vulgar nor unseemly.

If you have an article of this kind, please cut me off four times the width of the cloth, and a half yd. extra: that is, if the cloth is one and a half yd. wide — send six and a half yds. and so in proportion. By the way, it must not be less than a yd and a half wide; I suppose no broad-cloths are. My reason for this is, that I wish to make a *whole-circle* cloak, in the Spanish fashion; and the cloth, when cut in two and spread on the floor should make a square, after this fashion.[1]

The cloak is cut round in this way, and has but one seam. It is as long as the cloth is wide; and has the most superlative *hang* imaginable!

The extra half yd is for the cape.

I have described this to you, as if you were an ass, and could not understand by few words. Excuse my being so minute.

If there is likely to be a quarrel about the price write me as soon as you get this, and tell me what is the best you can do.

I am in no great hurry about the cloth, so that if you expect to come this way early in the Winter, you shall have the privilege of bringing it in yr. trunk.

Yr. mother and Jane are well. Caro started for Boston day before yesterday.[2]

Very truly yrs &c

H. W. Longw.

☞ I take it for granted that my last, acknowledging the black cloth reached you.[3]

MANUSCRIPT: Clifton Waller Barrett Collection, University of Virginia.   ADDRESS: To/Mr. Edward G. Fales/Calais./Me.

1. Longfellow's sketch of a bisected circle within a square follows this sentence.
2. Longfellow refers to Edward Fales's mother (191.1) and to his two sisters, Jane Minot Fales and Caroline Danforth Fales.
3. This letter is unrecovered, but see Letter No. 277.

283. *To Stephen Longfellow*

Brunswick   December 2nd 1834.

My dear Father,

I here send you a copy of a letter which I recd. this afternoon from Cambridge,

"Confidential

Cambridge 1. Decr 1834.

Dear Sir,

Professor Ticknor has given notice that it is his intention to resign his office of Smith Professor of Modn. Langs. in Harvard University, as soon as the Corporation shall have fixed upon a successor.

The duty of nominating to that office devolves upon me, and after great deliberation and inquiry, my determination is made to nominate you for that office, under circumstances which render yr. appointment not doubtful; provided I receive from you a previous assurance of your acceptance.

To ascertain this is the object of the present letter. In case of your declining to be considered a candidate, I shall rely upon your regarding this expression of my intent as confidential.

The salary will be 1500 dollars a year. Residence in Camb[rid]ge will be required. The duties of the Profship. will be of course those which are required from the occupant of a full Profship. and such as the Corporation and Overseers may appoint.

If a relation, such as I suggest in the above outline, with this University be one acceptable, I shall be obliged by an early answer.

Should it be yr. wish, previously to entering upon the duties of the office to reside in Europe at yr. own expense a year or 18 months for the purpose of a more perfect attainment of the German, Mr Ticknor will retain his office until your return. Very respectfully &c. &c,

Josiah Quincy."

Good fortune comes at last; and I certainly shall not reject it. The last paragraph of the letter, though put in the form of a permission seems to imply a request. I think I shall accept that also.

I wish this communication had reached me three or four days sooner. We could then have discussed the matter at Thanksgiving.

Very truly yr aff[ectiona]te son
Henry W. Longw.

Ed[war]d Fales starts tomorrow in his gig. I shall write Mary by him.[1]

MANUSCRIPT: Longfellow Trust Collection. ADDRESS: To/Hon. Stephen Long-fellow/Portland POSTMARK: SASSY ANNOTATION (*on outside cover*): The fire snapped out as I did this — as letter lay on the table [*in explanation of several burn holes*].

1. This letter is unrecovered.

284. *To Josiah Quincy*

Bowdoin College   December 3rd 1834.

Dear Sir,

I received, by yesterday's mail your favor of the 1st inst. and feel highly honored, by the distinction you have been pleased to confer upon me, in selecting me as a candidate for the Smith Profship. of Modn. Langs. in Harvd University.

A connection with yr. University would be very acceptable to me for reasons so obvious, that I need not mention them. Still, before saying, that I am ready to accept the situation proposed, I am desirous of learning more in detail the duties of that situation, in order to avoid any misunderstanding hereafter. Have the goodness to favor me with farther information upon this subject. Mr. Ticknor's Profship. embraces the French and Spanish Languages only. Is a change proposed, so as to embrace other Modn. Langs? Does residence at Cambridge constitute me one of the College Faculty?

If elected to this office, I shall probably wish to avail myself of the permission granted of visiting Europe. Upon this point, however, I shall be able to decide more definitively, when I obtain farther information respecting the duties of the Profship.

With thanks for the honor you have done me, I am, Sir,

Very respectfully yr. Obt. Ser[v]t.
Henry W. Longfellow

Hon. Josiah Quincy.

MANUSCRIPT: Harvard College Papers, Second Series, VI, 296. ADDRESS: Hon. Josiah Quincy/Prest. of Harvd. University/Cambridge. POSTMARK: BRUNS-WICK ME. DEC 4 PUBLISHED: *Professor Longfellow of Harvard*, p. 10.

285. *To Stephen Longfellow*

[Bowdoin College]
Tuesday eve[nin]g. December 9. 1834

My dear Father,

Since my last letter to you I have answered President Quincy and heard from him again. My answer to his first letter was in substance this; That for obvious reasons a Profship at Cambridge would be very pleasant to me; but that before saying I was ready to accept an appointment there, I was desirous of receiving further information respecting the duties of the situation proposed &c. In answer to this letter I have just received the following.

Harvd Univy. Dec. 6. '34. Dear Sir, In reply to yours of the 3rd. It is intended the Profship. shall embrace all the Modn Langs. At present *five* are taught by the *four* instructors, exclusive of the Professor. The number of native teachers of the respective languages will depend upon the proportion of teaching the Professor may be able to assume.

The salary ($1500) is proportioned to the service contemplated. Mr. Ticknor's was $500; but he neither lived in Cambridge, nor was a member of the College faculty. Both will be required of the Professor hereafter.

As to an exact specification of duties, they are not yet marked out. A committee are on the subject. Before completing their task they would be happy to have an interview with you. If this is impracticable, the proposed plan of duties shall be sent you, as soon as prepared, if the knowledge of this be your only difficulty.

Yrs truly and respectfully

Josiah Quincy

To this letter I have written the following answer to go by the next mail.

Dear Sir, I had the pleasure of receiving by last evening's mail yr. favor of the 6th. It will give me great satisfaction to meet the committee on the Course of Study, and it will be in my power to do so, unless they are required to complete their plans before the 1st of Jany. which I presume is not the case. I had contemplated a visit to the South during the winter, and under existing circumstances shall endeavor to be in Boston before the close of the year. I shall then be able to satisfy myself fully respecting many points connected with a residence in Cambridge which I am desirous of knowing, but which it would be hardly possible for me to learn by letter. I shall then be enabled to give a final answer to yr. proposition.

I trust, Sir, this delay will not be considered unreasonable. It seems to me desirable that I should have an interview with you and the gentlemen of the committee. It would tend to facilitate any arrangement that might be entered into, by making us more fully acquainted with each other's views.

Hoping soon to have the pleasure of presenting my respects to you in person, I remain, Sir, &c. &c. &c.[1]

I leave the subject of going to Europe undiscussed until I find what the wishes and expectations of the Committee are; and you will see by this correspondence that I am not acting precipitately in any one thing. The Boards of our College will have no cause to complain, though it will hardly be possible for ||me to re||main here until next Commencement, as the ||college|| year at Cambridge commences before that time.

10th

I saw Mr. Codman at the Tavern to-day ||and was|| sorry to hear that mother has not recovered||. I shall|| write to Mary tomorrow.[2]

Affectionately yrs.

H. W. Longw.

MANUSCRIPT: Longfellow Trust Collection. ADDRESS: Hon. Stephen Longfellow/ Portland POSTMARK: BRUNSWICK Me. DEC 10

1. This is a copy, with insignificant changes, of Letter No. 287.
2. This letter is unrecovered. It is possibly the same letter promised in No. 283.

286. *To George Washington Pierce*[1]

[Bowdoin College, December 9, 1834]

My dear George,

Thank you for yr. congratulatory epistle. I am certainly a very "Lucky dog," unless this whole business fails, as I trust it will not. However it is not yet settled. But away with all inauspicious fears.

> "Hurra! for the brother of the Son!
> Hurra! for the father of the Moon!
> Throughout the whole world there is none
> Like Quashiboo — the only one
> Descended from the great baboon,
> Baboon! Baboon!"[2]

I have the Cooper Story, and will bring it up next week.

Truly yrs

H. W. Longw.

MANUSCRIPT: Longfellow Trust Collection. ADDRESS: To/Mrs H. W. Longfellow/ Portland POSTMARKS: BRUNSWICK ME. DEC 11/PAID POSTAL ANNOTATION (*by Longfellow*): Single paid. H. W. L. ENDORSEMENT: H. W. Longfellow/ Dec. 9/1834.

1. This note accompanied a letter to Mary Potter Longfellow, now lost.
2. Altered from verses appearing in a humorous sketch called "Specimens of a Timbuctoo Anthology," *New Monthly Magazine and Literary Journal,* American edition, VIII (July–December 1824), 25.

287. *To Josiah Quincy*

Bowdoin College   Dec. 10. 1834.

Dear Sir,

I had the pleasure of receiving by last even[in]g's mail yr. favor of the 6th. It will give me great satisfaction to meet the committee on the Course of Study, and it will be in my power so to do, unless they are required to complete their plans before the 1st of January, which I presume is not the case. I had contemplated a visit to the South during the winter, and under existing circumstances shall endeavor to be in Boston before the close of the year. I shall then be able to satisfy myself fully respecting many points connected with a residence in Cambridge, which I am desirous of knowing, but which it would be hardly possible for me to learn by letter. I shall then be enabled to give a final answer to yr. proposition.

I trust, Sir, that you will not consider this delay unreasonable. It seems to me desirable that I should have an interview with you, and, the gentlemen of the committee. It would tend to facilitate any arrangements that might be entered into, by making us more fully acquainted with each other's views.

Hoping soon to have the pleasure of presenting my respects to you in person, I remain, Sir,

Very respectfully yr. Obt. Ser[v]t.
Henry W. Longfellow

Hon. Josiah Quincy.

MANUSCRIPT: Harvard College Papers, Second Series, VI, 300. ADDRESS: Hon. Josiah Quincy/Prest. Harvd Univy/Cambridge POSTMARK: BRUNSWICK ME. DEC 10 PUBLISHED: *Professor Longfellow of Harvard,* p. 11.

288. *To Nathaniel Haynes*[1]

Bowdoin College   Decr. 13 1834.

Dear Sir,

I return with many thanks Sagra's History of Cuba,[2] which you were kind enough to send me for my perusal. I have looked it over with great pleasure and instruction. It is certainly a very valuable book; though I doubt whether there would be sufficient demand for it in an English dress to repay the toil of translating it.

Very respectfully yours
Henry W. Longfellow

Nathan[ie]l Haynes Esqre.

MANUSCRIPT: The Berkshire Museum, Pittsfield, Massachusetts.

1. Haynes (1799–1836), a member of the Bowdoin class of 1823, edited the *Eastern Republican* of Bangor, Maine. He had spent the previous winter in Cuba for his health.

2. Ramón de la Sagra, *Historia economico-politica y estadistica de la isla de Cuba* (Habana, 1831).

289. *To George Washington Greene*

Bowdoin College   Dec. 15. 1834.

My dear George,

Yr. letter of the 11th reached me this morng. and I am heartily glad to see, that the world wags so merrily with you. You must have enjoyed yr. visit to Boston very highly, and I am sorry I could not be with you, in yr. goblets of "racy Burgundy and bright Champagne." I am sorry, too, that this letter must be a messenger of mingled good and evil. Great things have happened since I last wrote you. A few days ago — *this is confidential* — I received a letter from Prest. Quincy of Harvd. University, informing me, that Mr. Ticknor had signified his intention to resign his Profship as soon as a successor should be appointed, and that if I would give him assurances of accepting the situation, he would nominate me, under circumstances, that would render my election not doubtful. Some farther correspondence has passed between us, and next week I am going to Cambridge to meet the gentlemen, satisfy myself upon some points, which I wish to know — and the whole business will be then brought to a close. Now tell me — am I not a very lucky fellow? Do you not wish me joy of my good fortune? Is it not most cheering to have such a place offered one — without the intrigues of rich friends, without solicitation — without making an effort to obtain it? How different from that infernal New York business.

Well — I pass a few days in Boston — and then I go to New York to publish my book,[1] for which I am to be paid part in advance. A lady has put herself under my charge for this delightful winter excursion — which lady not being my wife, will deprive me of the pleasure of visiting you in yr. nest at E. Greenwich — a pleasure which I mean to enjoy, however, on my return — wind and tide permitting. But if Narraganset takes it into its head to freeze — farewell that promised pleasure.

These are the good tidings of my letter. The bad are a corollary thereunto. My fears gain strength, that my Profship here being vacated, will not be immediately filled. The cry is still for Tutors — and as my salary will pay for two — I fear it will be devoted to that purpose in spite of all I can do. It is unpleasant for me to write this; — yet I do it in all friendship, that you may not be deceived. More when we meet.

In great haste, and very cold, though yr. warm friend,
Longw.

P.S. Recollect that this letter is strictly confidential. No one must know of this saving yr. wife, to whom I dedicate the remainder of this sheet. Hope to receive a letter from you in Boston; direct care of Isaac McLellan Jr. Esqr.

Car[issi]ma Maria,

Eccomi! Avete ragione. Fa molto tempo che non vi ho scritto nulla. Sono colpevole, ma con tutto ciò ho scappato da quella tirata d'orecchio ch' avete avuto la bontà di mandarmi. Tantissime grazie! Ho lasciato la mia moglie a Portland, tre settimane fa. Mi scrive che non stà bene, — si è raffreddata — influenza — tante cose! — in somma, incomodità della stagione. Oimè! ci vuol gran pazienza con questa moglie ammalata!

Se mai posso, vi voglio fare una visita quest' inverno; e starò con voi fino che dite "Andate — niente pigliate, e mai ritornate" — che vuol dire, due o tre giorni.

Addio. Il papa non è Rè — e questo bigliettino non è lettera. Ma non c'è rimedio. Sono occupatissimo; poi dopo domani me ne vado a Portland, e negli ultimi giorni sempre c'è da fare.

Vostro aff[ezionatissi]mo amico
Longw.

MANUSCRIPT: Longfellow Trust Collection. ADDRESS: To/Geo. W. Greene Esqr./ East Greenwich/R. I. POSTMARK: BRUNSWICK ME. DEC 16

TRANSLATION:

Dearest Maria,

Here I am! You are right. It is a long time since I last wrote to you. I am guilty, but all the same I have avoided the box on the ears you were so kind as to send me. Very many thanks! I left my wife in Portland, three weeks ago. She writes that she isn't well, — she has caught a cold — influenza — so many things! — in short, seasonal discomforts. Alas! One needs a lot of patience with this sick wife of mine!

If I'm at all able to, I want to visit you this winter; and I will stay with you until you say, "Go away — take nothing, and never come back" — that is to say, for two or three days.

Adieu. The Pope isn't King — and this little note isn't a letter. But there's no help for it. I am very busy; and the day after tomorrow I go off to Portland, and there is always a lot to do in the last few days.

Your most affectionate friend
Longw.

1. *Outre-Mer.*

290. *To Josiah Quincy*

Boston. — Jany. 1. 1834 [1]

Hon Josiah Quincy
Sir,

Your letter of to-day inclosing the Vote of the President and Fellows of Har[var]d University in relation to the Professorship of Modn. Langs. has been received, and in expressing anew my desire to meet your wishes fully in the matter before us, I beg leave to defer an official answer until my return from the South, in about three weeks hence.

In the mean time may I take the liberty of calling your attention once more to the subject of our last conversation. I feel it important that I should be regularly appointed before sailing for Europe. Otherwise I present myself as any private individual whatever. But if I go as one of your professors — I carry with me in that very circumstance my best letter of recommendation. It gives me a character — and a greater claim to attention abroad, than I can otherwise take with me. Judge Story is ready to consent to this arrangement — so is Mr. Gray — so is Mr. Ticknor.[2] If you could bring the subject once more before the corporation, I think the objections suggested by you when I saw you this morning will be found to give way before the good results, which I think may be reasonably anticipated from change in your vote where respectfully suggested.

Very respect[full]y yr. Obt. Ser[v]t.
Henry W. Longfellow

MANUSCRIPT: Harvard College Papers, Second Series, VII, 1. ADDRESS: Hon. Josiah Quincy/Cambridge POSTMARK: BOSTON MS JAN 2 ENDORSEMENT: Longfellows Letter/1. Jan. 1835 PUBLISHED: Higginson, *Longfellow*, pp. 85–86.

1. Longfellow miswrote the date. Quincy corrected the manuscript with the note: "— 5 it ought to have been."

2. Judge Joseph Story and Francis Calley Gray (1790–1856) were Fellows

of Harvard University. Longfellow's request for an immediate appointment was not granted, but President Quincy assured him that the position was his. He was formally elected Smith Professor on November 17, 1836. See *Professor Longfellow of Harvard*, pp. 13–14.

291. *To Parker Cleaveland*

Portland   Feby. 2nd 1835

My dear Sir,

I intended to write you a letter from Boston or New York — but in the hurry-skurry of travelling I found it quite impossible to write to any one, except my wife — and even in that quarter I have had a lecture for remissness.

I reached town on Saturday last — after riding all night in that sweet rain-storm. All your commissions have been faithfully executed — with the exception of the *Mann* of birds.[1] Him I did not see. I postponed that business till my return from the South; and then stopped so short a time in Boston, that I had not time. Dr. Webster is living in Cambridge.[2] I sent the package to him, but did not see him. In New York I passed an hour or two in inspecting the Hydro-Oxigen Microscope. It is nothing more nor less than a very fine Solar Mic[rosco]pe lighted by the gasses of a Compound blowpipe. The two streams of gass play upon a little ball of lime, about the size of a rifle bullet, and very powerful reflectors throw the whole volume of light through the lenses of the instrument. The screen is about twenty feet in diameter. The greatest magnifying power used was 10 millions! The wing of a common fly was enlarged into a huge fan — one hundred feet in length, and the shadow was some minutes travelling over the screen. In a drop of water — sea-serpents and dragons without number. In fine — all the usual phantasmagoria of the solar microscope.[3]

In Philadelphia I was introduced to Prof. Hare. He looks something like the Ink-merchant Mons. Le Bron.[4] The utmost I can say for his behavior is, that he is a well educated bear. I leave you to infer how much I was pleased with shaking a paw with him.

Well — I have concluded to accept the offer at Cambridge, and shall go to Europe in the Spring. I want to sail, if possible on the first of April; and in order to do this must dissolve my connection with Bowdoin as early as the first of March. Or would the Govt. prefer that I should not enter on the duties of the next term? I will do as they think best. Mr. Greene says he is willing to supply for me till the close of the College year; so that on that point there will be no embarrassment, if the Govt. wish the course of instruction to go on unchanged. P||lease|| communicate this to the other gentlemen.

I intend to be in Brunswick about [a] week before the beginning of the term — probably on Monday next. I am not perfectly satisfied with all the manoeuvres of the Cambridge corporation; but have concluded after much debate to accede to their terms. This is *sub rosa.* I will tell you more when we meet; and if you do not exclaim *"That is just like them"* — I am mistaken.[5]

Kind regards to all yr. family.

Very truly yrs.
Henry W. Longw

MANUSCRIPT: Maine Historical Society. ADDRESS: Professor Cleaveland/Brunswick. POSTMARK: PORTLAND ME FEB 3

1. Presumably James Mann, a taxidermist of Boston.
2. John White Webster (1793–1850) was professor of chemistry and mineralogy at Harvard. He later achieved notoriety and was hung for the murder of Dr. George Parkman, whose body he had dismembered in his college laboratory.
3. The Hydro-Oxygen Microscope, which Longfellow saw on display at the American Museum in New York, had only recently been brought from London, where it had been a popular and financial success.
4. A Monsieur Le Bron of Portland manufactured an "Indestructible Ink" that had been chemically tested and approved by Prof. Cleaveland. An advertisement of Le Bron's product appeared intermittently in the *Eastern Argus.*
5. Longfellow refers to the refusal of the Harvard Corporation to appoint him officially at this time.

292. *To Josiah Quincy*

Portland   February 3rd   1835.

Hon Josiah Quincy
Sir,

Placing entire confidence in the assurances of the President and Fellows of Harvard University in reference to my election to the Smith Professorship of Modern Languages and Belles Lettres in that institution, which assurances were communicated to me in yr. favor of the 1st January, together with their Vote upon the subject, — I have the honor to inform you, that I shall sail for Europe in the month of April next, and remain there till the summer of 1836.

Very respectfully
Henry W. Longfellow

MANUSCRIPT: Harvard College Papers, Second Series, VII, 10. ADDRESS: Hon Josiah Quincy/Prest. of Harvd Univy/Cambridge POSTMARK: PORTLAND ME FEB ‖3? 4?‖ [*date faint*] ENDORSEMENT: Mr Longfellow/Feb. 10. 1835 PUBLISHED: Higginson, *Longfellow,* pp. 86–87.

293. *To George Washington Greene*

Bowdoin. Feb 11 1835

My dear George,

"The great drama is completed"[1] and we are completely *dished*. As soon as I reached Portland I wrote to the Executive Govt. of our College, informing them, that I should leave in March; and on arriving here I find the state of affairs this. They tell me they have the power of filling my place by Tutors only; that a Tutor's salary is but five hundred a year; and that there is not the least prospect of a Professor's being chosen to fill the vacancy at present. Under such circumstances I would NOT advise your coming to finish my course, as one great object of such a step is defeated beforehand. The Govt. will procure some one to take my classes until next Autumn. What will then be done by the Boards of the College, it is impossible to foresee; but from all I hear and see I can draw no favorable augury for our hopes and wishes.

I write this unsavory information as early as possible, that yr. movements in regard to Boston may be unembar[r]assed. I saw Howe but once on my return. He mentioned the proposition he had made to you touching the Magazine; which I thought would be acceptable to you. He did not seem to know much respecting the Athenaeum.[2] I intended to see him again before leaving town; but the weather was so unpleasant and I was so busy with Cambridge matters, that I could not call upon him a second time.

I write you these few lines in great haste, but shall write again soon. Some of my books I shall sell. You shall have a list with prices ere long.

My kindest regards to your family — one and all. My wife, like Martha of old, is "troubled about many things."[3] This breaking up housekeeping is dire work. She sends her love to Maria, and says she shall write her soon.

Very truly yrs.

H. W. L.

P.S. Bowen paid me twenty five dollars for Petrarca. The balance waits yr. order.[4]

Have you seen anything of a stray cotton night-shirt — of coarse fabric — in yr. dominions? I left one on the road somewhere.

I suppose you imagine, that I had a solitary time in Providence, after leaving yr house? "On the contrary — quite the reverse" — I passed a very pleasant eve[nin]g with Dr. Wayland, with whom I *tea'd*. Several of the Profs were there.

MANUSCRIPT: Longfellow Trust Collection. ADDRESS: George W. Greene Esq/ East Greenwich/R. I. POSTMARK: BRUNSWICK ME. FEB 12

1. Longfellow may be paraphrasing the common Italian idiom, "La commedia è finita."

2. Samuel Gridley Howe presumably asked Greene to write for the *New-England Magazine* (see 280.5). The reference to the Boston Athenaeum is inexplicable.

3. Luke 10:41.

4. Greene was apparently in debt to Longfellow and had authorized Bowen to pay him from his fee for the article on Petrarch (267.5).

294. *To George Ticknor*

Bowdoin College   Feb 12. 1835

My dear Sir,

I have read the volumes of Entremeses you were kind enough to lend me — and read them with care. Among them all I find but two, which it will be possible to reprint — and even these two will require some expurgation, being not entirely free from indecencies. They are "El Capeador" and "La Muela." The first — which I prefer, if but one is wanted, is in the thin 4vo vol. The other in Vol 2. of the larger collection.[1]

I am now very busy in selling my furniture, and making all necessary arrangements for leaving town as soon as may be. I shall probably remain till the Second of March, which closes our first half year — and no longer. By that time the instructor who takes my place will be here. I am sorry that Greene cannot have the place. But there is no possibility of his being appointed Professor in the Autumn — and therefore I am not desirous of having him here to work for a small compensation; and have written to tell him so. I regret that matters have taken this turn; but there is no remedy.

With my best regards to your lady,

very truly yours
Henry W. Longfellow

I am making a list of books, and shall bring it with me to Boston, to add to yours, if you can find time to make one.[2]

MANUSCRIPT: Dartmouth College Library. ADDRESS: Professor Ticknor/Boston.

1. "Entremes de la Muela" is No. 12 in George Ticknor's copy of *Entremeses, Sainetes,* etc., n.d., Vol. II, now in the Boston Public Library. The thin volume containing "El Capeador" is unidentified, nor is it known to what use the sketches were to be put.

2. On April 10, 1835, the Corporation voted "That the Treasurer place at the disposal of Prof. Longfellow the sum of One thousand dollars to be expended by him in the purchase of books relating to Modern languages & literature, not now in the Library" (*Professor Longfellow of Harvard*, p. 16).

295. *To Stephen Longfellow*

[Bowdoin College]
Sunday eve[nin]g   [February 15, 1835][1]

My dear father,

I suppose that Prof Cleaveland gave you an account of the doings of the Executive Government after the receipt of my letter. They are in negociation with Mr. Goodwin — a student of Andover, who graduated here about three years ago.[2] He wants higher wages than were first offered him, and I think it probable, that he will accede to the last proposition made him; which is to give him four hundred dollars for the remainder of the College year. They do not seem to have taken a fancy to Mr. Greene and are fearful, that he would not get along very well with the students. Under such circumstances it would be useless to urge his claims. The favorite project at present is to let some graduate of the institution go abroad, as I did, and appoint him Professor on his return.

We advertised our furniture yesterday — and made some sales forthwith, though not to a very great amount. It is quite an amusing business after all; and the trouble is somewhat alleviated by the diverting remarks of our customers.

Tuesday Eve[nin]g [February 17]

I have kept my letter back in the hope of sending some news; but none offers. The sales go on pretty well as regards the cheaper articles though the more expensive remain still on hand. There are, however, some premonitory symptoms of selling the sofa and centre table, which I hope will develope themselves tomorrow.

No farther news from Mr. Goodwin. I have entered upon duties and shall continue till the Ides of March.

Very truly yrs
Henry W. Longfellow.

MANUSCRIPT: Longfellow Trust Collection.

1. The date is questionable. The letter might have been written the Sunday before or the Sunday after.

2. Daniel Raynes Goodwin (1811–1890), a member of the Bowdoin class of 1832, succeeded to Longfellow's duties, first as a tutor. He subsequently enjoyed a distinguished career as professor of modern languages at Bowdoin, as president of Trinity College, as provost of the University of Pennsylvania, and as a minister in the Episcopal Church.

296. *To George Washington Greene*

Bowdoin College. Feb. 21. 1835

Histoire Littéraire de la France. 16 vols. 4to $72.00
Tiraboschi. Storia Let. &c 20 vols in 9. 8 vo. 25.00
Andres. Storia d'ogni Let. 22 vols in 11. 12 mo 25.00
Bouterweck. Geschichte &c. 12 vols. 8vo (half-calf) 18.00
Ersch. Handbuch der Deutschen Lit. 8 vols. 8vo (German boards) $6.00
Von der Hagen. Der Nibelungen Lied, in der Ursprache, mit Einleitung und Wörterbuch. Erster Band. 8vo boards. (Vol. 2. not yet pubd. The first contains poem and glossary.) $3.25
Von der Hag[e]n. Lit. Grundriss zur Geschichte d. deutschen Poesie von der ältesten Zeit. 8vo paper. $3.00
Von d. Hag[e]n. Der Heldenbuch in d. Ursprache. 2 vols. 4to paper. $8.00
Von d. Hag[e]n. Altnordische Sagen & Lieder. (Icelandic) 8vo paper. $2.25
Von d. Hag[e]n. Nord. Heldenromane. Übersetzt &c. 5 vols. 12 mo paper. $3.50
Grimm. Lieder d. alten Edda. Erster B. (2nd not yet p.) 8vo. paper. $1.75
Berington. Lit. Hist. Middle Ages. 4to boards. $7.00
Bene[c]ke. Beyträge z.d. altdeutschen Sprache. 2 vols 8vo paper $3.00 [1]

My dear George;
I here send you a list of such books as you probably would yourself have selected from my library had you been here. The prices of many of them are high; but they are rare works; and hoping that you would take them all, I have put them to you at less than they cost me, having deducted $25.00 from the amount of the lot.

Quadrio and Crescembeni I do not wish to sell, on account of certain associations connected with them, which I cannot stop to explain here, being in great haste. [2]

Everything is in utter confusion in our poor deserted home. All day long rap! rap! ting-a-ling-ling! at the door. Hurry-skurry upstairs and down! &c &c &c which means that we are selling off. Both tables — the chairs and the carpet are already gone from my study; the bookcases stand ajar — and beneath yawn sundry boxes, ready to receive their precious freight of books.

Therefore no more for the present. I desire you will lose no time in writing me, for certain obvious reasons. Mary joins me in kindest regards to your little dear wife; and you will not fail to greet for me *ganz freundlich* [most amicably] your father and all the family.

Yours in earnest,
Henry W. Longw.[3]

MANUSCRIPT: Longfellow Trust Collection. ADDRESS: George W. Greene Esq/ East Greenwich/R. I. POSTMARK: BRUNSWICK ME. FEB 22

1. The complete titles of these works are: *Histoire littéraire de la France; ouvrage commencé par des religieux bénédictins de la Congrégation de Saint Maur, et continué par des membres de l'Institut* (Paris, 1733-1824), 16 vols.; Girolamo Tiraboschi, *Storia della Letteratura Italiana* (Firenze, 1805-1813), 11 vols.; Giovanni Andres, *Dell' Origine, dei Progressi e dello Stato Attuale d'ogni Letteratura* (Pistoja, 1821-1823), 11 vols.; Friedrich Bouterwek, *Geschichte der poesie und beredsamkeit seit dem ende des dreizehnten jahrhunderts* (Göttingen, 1801-1819), 12 vols.; Johann Samuel Ersch, *Handbuch der deutschen literatur seit der mitte des achtzehnten jahrhunderts bis auf die neueste zeit* (Amsterdam und Leipzig, 1812-1814), 8 vols.; *Der Nibelungen Lied in der Ursprache mit den Lesarten aller Handschriften* . . . herausgegeben durch Friedrich Heinrich von der Hagen zu Vorlesungen (Breslau, 1820); *Literarischer grundriss zur geschichte der deutschen poesie von der ältesten zeit bis in das sechzehnte jahrhundert*, durch Friedrich Heinrich von der Hagen und Johann Gustav Büsching (Berlin, 1812); *Der Helden Buch* in der Ursprache herausgegeben von Friedrich Heinrich von der Hagen und Anton Primisser (Berlin, 1820-1825), 2 vols.; Friedrich Heinrich von der Hagen, ed., *Altnordische Sagen und Lieder welche zum Fabelkreis des Heldenbuchs und der Nibelungen gehören* (Breslau, n.d.); Friedrich Heinrich von der Hagen, tr., *Nordische heldenromane* (Breslau, 1814-1828), 5 vols.; The Brothers Grimm, eds., *Lieder der alten Edda* (Berlin, 1815), Vol. I; Joseph Berington, *A Literary History of the Middle Ages; comprehending an account of the state of learning from the close of the reign of Augustus, to its revival in the fifteenth century* (London, 1814); George Friederich Benecke, *Beyträge zur Kenntniss der altdeutschen Sprache und Litteratur* (Göttingen, 1810-1832), 2 vols.

2. Francesco Saverio Quadrio, *Della Storia e Della Ragione D'Ogni Poesia* (Bologna, Milano, 1739-1752), 7 vols.; and Giovan Mario Crescimbeni, *Dell' Istoria della Volgar Poesia* (Venezia, 1730-1731), 5 vols. The first volume of each set contains Longfellow's note to the effect that he bought the works at the sale of Mr. Van der Kamp's library in Boston in July 1830.

3. A postscript from Mary Longfellow to Maria Greene follows this letter.

297. *To William Allen*

Brunswick   March 2nd 1835

Dear Sir,

Enclosed is a copy of my resignation of the office of Professor of Modn. Langs. and Librarian in Bowdoin College. Will you have the goodness to communicate it to the gentlemen of the Executive Government, at their next meeting, and to the Trustees and Overseers in September next.

I write these words with sorrowful feelings. For when I sum up the pains and pleasures of the last five years of my life, I find the former few and the latter many. I cannot reasonably hope for a more tranquil, nor for a happier life, than that which I have led here.

Have the goodness to express to each of the Executive Govt. the sincere regret I feel in thus dissolving the bonds of fellowship, which have so long united us. I shall always retain a grateful remembrance of the kindness I have experienced from all and each of you; and I hope that a friendly recollection of me will often mingle with your thoughts. It is indeed in sadness that I now take you each by the hand for the last time. Farewell.

Very truly and respectfully your Obt. Ser[v]t.
Henry W. Longfellow.

MANUSCRIPT: Historical Society of Pennsylvania. ADDRESS: To/Revd. Dr. Allen/ Prest. of Bowdoin College/Brunswick.

298. *To President and Trustees of Bowdoin College*

Brunswick   March 2nd 1835

To the President and Trustees of Bowdoin College.
Gentlemen,
I respectfully ask leave to hand you my resignation of the office of Professor of Modern Languages and Librarian in Bowdoin College.

I regret, that circumstances compel me to dissolve my connexion with your Institution, before the close of the College year, upon which we have now entered. But this regret is much diminished by the entire confidence I feel in the ability of the gentleman, who will perform the duties of my office, until the time of your next annual meeting. Permit me, in this connection, to express the hope, that the Professorship will not long remain vacant.

During my residence here I have endeavored to discharge faithfully the duties, which have devolved upon me. And yet at this moment — as I consider the time past — I feel how much less I *have* done, than I *might* have done. *Veniam pro laude peto.*[1]

I have the honor to be, Gentlemen,

your Obt. Ser[v]t.
Henry W. Longfellow

MANUSCRIPT: Bowdoin College Library.

1. "I seek pardon instead of praise." Ovid, *Tristia*, I, vii, 31.

299. *To Lewis Gaylord Clark*

Bowdoin College   March 3rd   1835

My dear Clark,

This is the last letter you will ever receive from me with date of Bowdoin College; as I have dissolved my connexion with that institution, and shall leave town next week. I shall sail for London on the first of April — from your city, unless I find a very good opportunity in Boston. I look forward to my foreign travel with feelings of enthusiasm. The anticipation is truly thrilling. However, upon this point I will not enlarge, because it would be "superfluous, and not only so, but likewise supererogatory, besides being principally adscititious."

I have been much too busy to write to you earlier, though courtesy and good breeding required more speed in the wielding of my pen. I have had a great many things to attend to, both in College and out. I am selling off all my household matters, and every thing about me is topsy-turvy. I trust that this is excuse enough for my delay in writing.

How go matters with you in the Maga?[1] and what are Harper & brothers doing with my book?[2] They promised to send me the sheets, but not one has come; and Greene writes me, that you have forgotten to send any to him, wherefrom he may prepare a review. I presume there is time enough, however; as I do not see the book announced in the N. York papers yet. I shall probably see you again before the book is published. In the last "N. Yorker" Dr. Caruthers has got a rap on the pate, wonderful to be read. Who has treated him so *"cavalierly"*?[3]

I shall not have time to write you the paper you desired in the vein of Youth and Old Age.[4] I am sorry; but I am too much occupied to think of writing anything but a few farewell letters. I shall not write again for the press, until I get upon the dark blue sea. Then I shall throw the reins upon the neck of fancy — and in my next book — which will be forth coming some years hence — — — Oh fie! what a boaster! I had better see first how Outre Mer turns out.

I have no literary news to tell you. In sooth, this village is too secluded; and on that account I am not sorry to leave it — though there are regrets at leaving a place, where I have passed so many quiet and happy hours. Quoth my Lord Byron

> "In leaving even the most unpleasant people
> And places — one keeps looking at the steeple."[5]

True enough — true enough. So I will take a glass of wine. Your good health! I wish you were here to drink mine, as I am all alone, *Madame* having retired for the night. My cigar is burnt to the roots — my lamps are dim — and "the bawdy hand of Time is on the —— k of one" — as Shakespear hath it.[6] Therefore, my friend, good night.[7]

MANUSCRIPT: Yale University Library. ADDRESS: Lewis G. Clark Esqr/New York. POSTMARK: BRUNSWICK ‖ME. M‖AR ‖3‖

1. A colloquialism for *Blackwood's Magazine*, applied here to Clark's *Knickerbocker Magazine*.

2. *Outre-Mer*.

3. A review of William Alexander Caruthers' *The Cavaliers of Virginia, or, The Recluse of Jamestown* (New York, 1834–1835) appeared in the *New-Yorker*, I, No. 50 (Saturday, February 28, 1835). The reviewer ridiculed the book by insisting that he could not read beyond the first few pages.

4. An essay written by Longfellow some eleven years earlier (see 56.4).

5. *Don Juan*, Canto II, stanza 14.

6. "The bawdy hand of the dial is now upon the prick of noon" (*Romeo and Juliet*, II, iv, 118).

7. The complimentary closing and signature have been cut from the manuscript.

300. *To Dr. Jean Zéphirin Nault*[1]

Brunswick, 10th March, 1835.

My dear friend —

I send you two words to say good-bye; I have not time to write more. In my last letter I spoke to you of the post as professor which has been offered me at Cambridge. I have accepted it; but before taking it up I am going to travel for two years in Europe. Charming, isn't it? I have already taken leave of my pupils in college; and the day after tomorrow I shall say my last good-bye to Brunswick. I shall probably embark on April first, at New York, for London; and after a sojourn of several weeks there I shall go to Stockholm in Sweden to study the Swedish language and literature. I shall pass next winter in Germany, probably at Berlin; and after a stay of several months in Copenhagen I shall return by way of Paris. There's a lot of work for two years! But it is magnificent. My wife and two of her intimate friends accompany me on the trip, and I hope that we shall take from it as much profit as we will pleasure. I hope also that I shall have the pleasure of meeting you in Paris, when I arrive in the world's great metropolis. What a pleasure to walk with you on the boulevards, in the Jardin des Plantes, in the Tuileries, indeed, everywhere you wish. Come, my dear friend, follow my advice and my example. Take your wife, and set out! You have thought of this trip before. There will never be a more propitious time than the present. As soon as you reach Paris, write to me in Berlin, and you will have news from me at once. What say you?

But what a going-on it is to prepare for such a trip! I have sold all my furniture, my books are packed, and I leave Brunswick at the very moment when a protracted meeting begins here. You will easily realize, with so many things to do, that I have not had time to reply to your recent letters, for which I send you a thousand thanks; also for the two packages of books, which you had the kindness to send me. Much obliged.

Many thanks on Mrs. Longfellow's part, both for you and for Mlle. ——. The little [birch?]-bark case is very pretty, and the savages' shoes [moccasins?] are magnificent, whatever you may say of them.[2]

I do wish I could be present at your wedding, my dear friend, but you see that it is impossible. Give our best respects to Madame Nault;[3] we wish you all the prosperity which you deserve — and that means much, very much.

Give my respects to Mr. Allsopp,[4] and pray accept assurance of my sincerest friendship.

> Good-bye till Paris.
> Henry W. Longfellow

MANUSCRIPT: unrecovered; text from the *Boston Evening Transcript*, Saturday, March 6, 1926.

1. The following letter was written by Longfellow in French, but with the exception of the last two paragraphs, only the English translation is now available.

2. The words in brackets were supplied by the translator. The French original is available from this point from a newspaper photograph of the letter: "disiez./ Je voudrais bien assister à vos noces, mon cher ami‖. Ma‖is vous voyez bien que cela ne se peut pas. Présentez nos meilleurs respects à *Mme Nault* no[us] vous souhaitons toute la prosperité que vous meritez c'est-a-dire beaucoup — beaucoup!/ Présentez mes respects à Monsieur Allsopp et veuillez bien recevoir l'assurance de mon amitié la plus sincere. Au revoir a Paris!/Henri W. Longfellow"

3. Nault had married, or was about to marry, Louise Caroline Durette.

4. Robert Allsopp (1802–1858), a lawyer in Quebec, was the son of George Allsop (d. 1806), a prominent English merchant of Cap-Santé. It is not known how Longfellow became acquainted with him, but the fact that Cortés writes of him in letters to Longfellow suggests that he was a visitor in Brunswick or Portland in 1832 or 1833.

301. *To Parker Cleaveland*

> Portland   March 17. 1835

My dear Sir,

Yr. favor of the 14 reached me yesterday; but I could not obtain Mr. Wood's address soon enough to answer you at an earlier moment.

1. Dr. Wood. Care of Edwards &co. No 9. Rue de Cléry.[1] Perhaps

this had better be put into French thus. "Mr. Wood — *Aux soins de M. M. Edwards & cie.* No 9" &c &c.

2. I am glad to hear from Grimm, the Dutchman. You may keep him until my return, if you have room for him on yr. shelves.[2] If you have not, please send him to S. Longw. Portland.

3. I missed my *stickee* at North Yarmouth and not before. Did you get the *card* from that place? Mitchell will take charge of said *stickee*.[3]

4. The Letters by the driver of [the] *Daily* came safe. I am much obliged to you for them. They will be of great service.

5. Berzelius' address for Letters and Boxes I will send you in my first letter from Stockholm.[4]

6. My own address I do not yet know. As soon as I reach Boston I shall find a Banker in London, who will take charge of all money, letters &c. To him everything for me will be sent, and he will forward to me. I will let you know his name and address through my father.

With kind regards to all the family

in great haste, very truly yrs.

Henry W. Longw.

MANUSCRIPT: Historical Society of Pennsylvania. ADDRESS: To/Prof. Parker Cleaveland/Brunswick POSTMARKS: PORTLAND Me. MAR 17/PAID POSTAL ANNOTATION: Single: paid

1. William Wood (1810–1899), a member of the Bowdoin class of 1829, received his medical degree in 1833 and was pursuing further medical studies in Paris at this time. He later became a prominent Portland physician and is said to have had a predilection for natural science, which explains his relationship with Cleaveland.

2. Grimm's *Die Lieder der alten Edda* (see Letter No. 296).

3. The allusion is obscure. "Stickee" is possibly a coined diminutive for "stick." Benjamin Francis Mitchell (1816–1865) of North Yarmouth was a member of the Bowdoin class of 1838.

4. Longfellow describes his visit to Jöns Berzelius, the eminent Swedish scientist, in Letter No. 319.

302. *To William Goddard*

Portland   March 18. 1835

My dear Sir,

Yr. favor of the 16 reached me yesterday. I agree with you entirely in thinking, that it will be best to take the packet of the 16th. We shall be less hurried — have a pleasanter time — and after all reach London about as soon. If you can find time to write to New York soon, we can doubtless have our choice of state-rooms.

As to the price of passage never varying, I think you must have been misinformed. When Mr. Preble of this place sailed for London with his family (our Minister to the Netherlands) they made a handsome deduction; so he informs me.[1] Another friend of mine sailed for Havre with his wife some years ago; they put their passage at one hundred each. However, I do not wish to put yr. friend to any inconvenience on this head. It might not be amiss to suggest such a thing; though I by no means wish to urge it.

We shall remain a few days longer with our friends in Portland; and start for yr. city on Tuesday next — should the weather be pleasant. Otherwise, on Wednesday or Thursday.

With kind regards to all yr. family

Very sincerely yours
Henry W. Longfellow

P.S. Will Mary Caroline have the goodness to call upon Miss. Crowninshield and inform her of the change in our arrangements and the reasons therefor?[2]

MANUSCRIPT: Clifton Waller Barrett Collection, University of Virginia. ADDRESS: To/Mr. William Goddard/Hamilton Place/Boston. POSTMARK: PORTLAND ME MAR 19/PAID POSTAL ANNOTATION (by Longfellow): single paid

1. See 162.1.

2. Mary Caroline Goddard's father had first been married to Mary Storer, Mary Potter Longfellow's aunt; she was, therefore, a kind of cousin, although not related by blood. Clara Crowninshield (234.3) had spent the winter of 1832–1833 with the Longfellows in Brunswick. For a discussion of their participation in the journey see the *Diary of Clara Crowninshield.*

303. *To George Washington Greene*

Portland   Saturday   March 21. 1835

My dear Greene,

Yr. letter relating to the books was duly received, and Bouterwek is done up in a package for you. I shall leave it in Boston in the hands of yr. friend Howe, unless you request otherwise. You will recollect that I have in hand fifteen dollars of yrs. which I received from Bowen; if convenient please send the remainder of yr. debt in a letter directed to the care of Harper & Brothers, 82 Cliff St. N. York.[1]

I expected to have been ere this in Boston but having heard that the Hannibal, which sails on the 1st April, and in which I had intended to take passage, is an inferior vessel both in her speed and accommodations, I have concluded to wait until the 16th, and take the Philadelphia for London. This will give me more time in Boston and New

York — a circumstance much to be desired, in order to obtain letters &c. &c.

I have concluded you see to go first to London. I shall remain there two or three weeks, and then make the best of my way to Stockholm, where I shall remain until October. The winter will be passed in Berlin — and the succeeding summer in Copenhagen. This is in brief the plan of my journey.

We go in a company of four; two Boston ladies Miss. Goddard and Miss. Crowninshield having joined our party. This will be very pleasant — and leave me more leisure than if Mary went alone; — for being in such a goodly number the ladies will amuse each other, without too much of my assistance. This is a very uncivil speech for me to make; but as I go for the purpose of studying, I shall want as much of the time to myself as possible. I hardly need say that we are all on tiptoe to be gone; as the advancing season admonishes us that there is no time to lose. Even a day's delay is irksome — having completed our arrangements. We hope that Wednesday next will find us in Boston, and the week afterwards in New York. I shall not feel easy until I get things safely on board ship, and the wind begins to fill our sails.

Will you believe it — Prof. Ticknor sails for Europe in June with his family for a residence of three or four years on the Continent. I am afraid they will want me to give up my projected Tour, which I will not do, on any consideration. Mr. Ticknor goes on account of his wife's health, which is failing rapidly; at least, so I hear.[2]

Boston 27. March

Thus far we run before the wind. We reached this city on Wednesday eve[nin]g last; and the first news we hear is that a new arrangement has been made in the London packets. They are to sail in future on the 1st, 10th and 20th. We go therefore on the 10th instead of the 16th. This disarranges some of our plans, and hurries us a little. Yr. good father was kind enough to invite us to pass a day or two with you on our way to N. York; but it will be totally out of our power. Present my best regards to him and all the family. The letters you promised me to Botta[3] and to Maria's father — please send to N. York care of Harper & brothers.

Farewell. In great haste

Very truly yours
Henry W. Longfellow

Addio, Maria.[4]

MANUSCRIPT: Longfellow Trust Collection. ADDRESS: To/George W. Greene
Esq/East Greenwich/R. I. POSTMARK: BOSTON MAR 28 [*faint*]

1. Longfellow first wrote "I. McLellan Jr. Esq. Boston" as his forwarding address,
deleted it, and substituted Harper & Brothers.

2. For verification, see Ticknor to Charles S. Daveis, March 19, 1835 (George
S. Hillard, ed., *Life, Letters, and Journals of George Ticknor* [Boston, 1876],
I, 401).

3. Carlo Giuseppe Guglielmo Botta (1766–1837), the Italian historian.

4. A brief postscript from Mary Longfellow to Maria Greene follows this letter.

304. *To Parker Cleaveland*

Boston   Wednesday mor[nin]g   March 31. 1835

My dear Sir,

I write you a few lines in great haste to ask a favor of you in regard
[to] a small account, which I have just found in my Note Book. It is
a charge against students for books — made in October last — and of
course *payable* (perhaps I should say PAID) in March. It stands as
follows.

Juniors.	Goodenough, — Harwood — .30 each	.60
Sophs.	Andrew — Barker — Clark —	
	Crosly — Dunning — Kimball —	
	Lamb — Lunt — Scammon —	
	Talbot — Warren — Sweat 1st — each .75	9.00
	Gray .35[1]	.35
		$9.95

It is possible that this bill was paid. But I have not marked it so in
my Note Book, nor have I any recollection of having received the
money. Will you have the goodness to see; and if the payt. has not been
made, draw for the same, and use it in my book account?[2]

I shall leave here on Saturday or Monday next, and sail from New
York to London on the 10th of April. I did not go in the ship of the
1st, because its accommodations were inferior to those of the Philadelphia, the packet of the 10th.

Kind regards to yr. family, and remembrances to the gent[leme]n
of the govt. Once more good bye.

In inconceivable haste

very truly yrs.

H. W. Longfellow

MANUSCRIPT: Bowdoin College Library. ADDRESS: To/Professor Cleaveland/

Bowdoin College/Brunswick/Me POSTMARKS: BOSTON ‖MASS‖ APRIL 2/ PAID POSTAL ANNOTATION: Paid

1. The students listed here were John Goodenow (1817–1898); Thomas Stetson Harlow (1812–1901); John Albion Andrew (1818–1867), the Civil War governor of Massachusetts; Fordyce Barker (1818–1891); William Henry Clark (1819–1898); Josiah Crosby (1816–1904); Andrew Dunning (1815–1872); Thomas Glidden Kimball (1811–1879); George W. Lamb (1818–1853); Horace Lunt (1818–1837); John Quincy Adams Scammon (1814–1898); George Foster Talbot (1819–1907); William Warren (1806–1879); Lorenzo De Medici Sweat (1818–1898); and John Gray (1811–1860).

2. These accounts payable concerned his own textbooks, which Longfellow had sold to his students.

PART FOUR

EUROPE

1835–1836

EUROPE

1 8 3 5 – 1 8 3 6

FROM THE TIME Longfellow left Portland in March, 1835, until he returned at the end of 1836 to assume his duties at Harvard, he wrote at least seventy letters and possibly as many as a hundred, of which fifty-seven have been recovered. In general, these letters differ from those he had written earlier from Europe by being more matter-of-fact and less concerned with the enthusiasms of the romantic pilgrim. It would be difficult, of course, to identify oneself with Childe Harold when escorting a pregnant wife and two young ladies. Besides, Longfellow now took his scholarship seriously and spent most of his time in professional conversation, in antiquarian bookshops, and in libraries. When he later relived the experience in the privacy of his Cambridge study, he softened some bitter memories: Sweden, which he had found cold, wet, and uncultured, became a country of long summer nights and an idealized peasantry; and Germany, where he had suffered the sharpest pangs of bereavement after Mary's death in Rotterdam, became the misty scene of the sentimental romancing in *Hyperion*.

Although a "more perfect attainment of the German" was the principal reason for his second voyage to Europe, Longfellow decided to add another feather to his cap by studying the Scandinavian languages at the same time. He therefore planned an itinerary that would take him to Stockholm for the summer of 1835, to Berlin for the following winter, and to Copenhagen for another northern summer before returning home. He clung bravely to this schedule through the first months until Mary Longfellow's pregnancy, miscarriage, and final illness forced him into delay and improvisation. His actual itinerary — reconstructed from his private journals — reveals that he spent more time in Holland and less in Denmark than he had planned, and that, as an afterthought, he enjoyed a holiday in Switzerland, which had the auspicious consequence of his meeting Fanny Appleton.

May 8–12, 1835: Portsmouth, Isle of Wight, en route London.

May 13—June 9: London.

June 10–28: En route Stockholm via Hamburg, Copenhagen, Gothenburg.

June 29—August 26: Stockholm (July 31—August 5, excursion to Upsala, Dannemora).

August 27—September 9: En route Copenhagen via Göta Canal, Gothenburg (September 2–8).

September 10–23: Copenhagen.

September 24—December 11: En route Heidelberg via Kiel, Hamburg, Amsterdam (October 1–19), Rotterdam (October 22—December 1), the Rhine.

December 12, 1835—June 24, 1836: Heidelberg (April 10–15, Frankfurt; June 11–19, tour of the baths).

June 25—August 20: Excursion to Switzerland.

August 21–26: Heidelberg.

August 27—October 6: Heidelberg to Le Havre via Baden, Strasbourg, Metz, Paris (September 4—October 5), Rouen.

October 7–11: Le Havre.

October 12: Sail for New York.

The climactic event of the tour occurred in Rotterdam on November 29, 1835, when Mary Longfellow died of an infection following a miscarriage on October 5 in Amsterdam. Longfellow gives us little information, however, either in his extant letters or in his journal, about his wife's last illness; and one must turn to the diary of Clara Crowninshield for the details of that tragic affair. Longfellow's silence cannot be explained, of course, as the result of unconcern. His genteel sensitivity made him reluctant to commit himself in writing on such delicate subjects as pregnancy and miscarriage; he may also have hesitated to admit that he was in trouble, remembering his father's expressed doubt about the European tour; and finally, it seems clear that he did not believe, until the day before her death, that Mary was in serious danger. This underestimation increased the shock of the event.

During the Heidelberg winter that followed, Longfellow's grief grew slowly into a nostalgic melancholy, which he nourished in the recesses of his mind for several years. Although he had the resilience of youth to give him strength, new acquaintances to comfort him, and the study of German to occupy him, occasional anguished sentences in his letters make clear that he now underwent the first real emotional crisis of his life. More subtly than he realized, this crisis turned him from scholarship to poetry as a means of self-expression. He had always, of course, had the instincts of the poet but few of the raw materials of inspiration. During these months he developed a maturity that after his return to America converted the synthetic melancholy of his juvenile poetry into the more meaningful emotion of *Voices of the Night*. With the publication of that volume his career as a poet really began.

Longfellow assumed the professorship at Harvard at the peak of his reputation as a scholar, with his mastery of German established and his study of Swedish, Danish, and Dutch adding a new luster to his name. If, in his innermost reflections, he thought of Mary's death as a sacrifice to his ambition, he must have regretted his insistence on the journey; but he knew also that it had had its rewards in his new knowledge and his new maturity. In Fanny Appleton, furthermore, he had met a woman who was to play a more important role in his life than he could have imagined at the time. At twenty-nine, then, where the letters in Part IV end, Longfellow stood on the threshold of fame. "I think your ambition must be satisfied," wrote his father, who had quietly guided him through his restless youth and early manhood, "and your only object now will be to fill with eminence and distinction the office in which you are placed, and to become distinguished among the literary men of the age."

305. *To Alexander Wadsworth Longfellow*

New York   April 9. 1835

My dear Alexander

I write you a few lines in great haste, merely to tell you, that I am on my way to Europe, with Mary and Clara Crowninshield. We sail for London tomorrow in the ship Philadelphia from this port. I have been appointed Professor of Modern Langs. at Harvard University, in place of Mr Ticknor; (resigned) and have a *furlough* of eighteen months, with permission to visit Europe. After passing a few weeks in London we shall go to Sweden and pass the Summer there and in Denmark. The next winter will be devoted to Berlin — and the succeeding Summer to the Rhine, Switzerland and France. My principal object in going to the North of Europe is to give some attention to the Northern Languages and Literature.

Clara will continue with us all the time and go whithersoever we go. Another lady, a Miss Goddard of Boston — will pass the Summer with us, and leave us in the autumn to travel in Italy with her brother. We anticipate a great deal of pleasure; and are going off in grand spirits.

You complain in yr. last letters that I have not written to you. You are mistaken. I have written four or five times;[1] and sent you *two* enormous packages of Magazines and such *Trash* from this city. I shall make up another package to-day, to go by the first ship to Valparaiso. This letter I send by way of Washington. *Outre Mer* in two vols will be in the package; — it is on the point of being published here by the Harpers.

Yesterday I met yr. friend *Merrick* in the street. He wrote a few lines to you and handed them to me; but unfortunately the letter got placed with some other papers and was sent on board our ship in my trunks. The ship has hauled off into the stream; so that you will not be likely to get the letter very soon, though I will send it if I get a chance. You can answer it notwithstanding. Merrick has established himself as a merchant in Hallowell.[2]

Wood has not yet returned from Paris. He means to remain there another year. Jim Greenleaf[3] has gone to Calcutta, as you probably know.

My best regards to the Commodore.

Very affectionately yr. brother
Henry[4]

MANUSCRIPT: Longfellow Trust Collection. ADDRESS: To/Mr Alexander W. Longfellow/care of Commodore Wadsworth/U. S. Navy./Valparaiso. POSTMARK: FORWARDED BY JB FERAUD PANAMA ENDORSEMENT: Henry W. Longfellow/ New York City/April 9th 1835/Received at Cambridge/May 11. 1836

1. These letters are unrecovered.

2. This could be any one of several Merricks from Hallowell, but is most likely George Merrick (1807–1862), later a merchant in New Orleans.

3. James Greenleaf (1814–1865), son of Simon Greenleaf, the jurist, and brother of Patrick Henry Greenleaf, Longfellow's classmate, married Mary Longfellow in 1839.

4. Postscripts follow by Mary Potter Longfellow and Eliza Potter, who was in New York to see the travelers leave.

306. *To Stephen Longfellow*

New York   April 9. 1835

My dear Father,

We have sent our trunks on board ship, — she has hauled off into the stream — and we are only waiting for the morning to go on board. The weather to-day is lovely and like summer. We hope to have as pleasant a day tomorrow.

We sail in the ship Philadelphia — Capt. Morgan, a very pleasant and good-natured man; who promises to take us to London in three weeks.[1] If he is longer than that, he shall call it a long passage and feel badly about it. The accommodations of the ship are very good — the state-rooms large — and the cabin airy. Here is a sketch.[2]

My book is all printed — but not yet bound up, so that I cannot send you a copy. You will have one soon. I have made out to get one for Alexander, and one or two to take with me. It is very well printed — and will look handsomely.

Three days here have passed with wonderful rapidity. It was hardly enough to do all I had to do. I have a great many letters of introduction — but not too many — and we are all in good spirits and ready to sail to-morrow. The steam-boat takes us down the bay to Staten Island where the ship is anchored, at 11 o'clock tomorrow; and we set sail without delay if the wind be fair. Otherwise the steam-boat will tow us out to sea.

Once more then farewell. My Banker in London is Timothy Wiggin Esq.[3] Direct all letters to him, and he will forward them to any point on the Continent.

My love to all. Mary and Eliza send kind regards. Good bye.

Very truly and affect[ionatel]y yours
Henry W. Longfellow

P.S. I have made up a package for Alexander, which will go by the first opportunity, and a letter, which I shall send *via* Washington.

MANUSCRIPT: Longfellow Trust Collection. ADDRESS: To/Stephen Longfellow Esq/Portland/Me POSTMARK: NEW YORK APL 10

1. Elisha Ely Morgan (c. 1805–1864), one of the most prominent and popular of the packet captains, had taken command of the *Philadelphia* in 1833. His promise to his passengers was rash, since it took his ship thirty days to cross to Portsmouth. Longfellow was seasick much of the time. See the *Diary of Clara Crowninshield*, p. 3.

2. Of the stateroom deck of the *Philadelphia*. See Plate VIII.

3. A former Manchester merchant, Timothy Wiggin (1774–1856) had established in 1825 a London merchant-banking house to compete with the noted firm of Baring Brothers.

307. *To Stephen Longfellow*

London   May 14. 1835

My dear father,

We were very sorry to find on our arrival at Portsmouth that owing to the new arrangement of packets, there would be none for New York before the 20th inst. I have therefore postponed writing till our arrival in London, or as the[y] say here, till "we came up to town."

We reached Portsmouth on Friday eve[nin]g May 8. The ship hove to about six in the evening, and a little sloop took us on board with our luggage, and carried us within a stone's throw of land, whence we were taken ashore in *wherries*, at a shilling a head! Almost the first expression I heard in England was a compound of Cockney and Yankee. One of the boatmen cried out "We towed the *w*essel in, I *expects*."

On saturday we took a sail in the harbour, and visited the Navy yard. The boatman pointed out to us all the wonders thereof, and sometimes in ludicrous phraseology. "That large ship yonder is the Belly-ruffian (Bel[l]erophon)." And what is that crazy looking thing on the left? "That is the *Mud injun* (engine) for making more water in the 'arbour!" We went on board the King's Yacht — a splendid little schooner of some 150 tons, I should think; and afterwards visited the St. Vincent, a *first rate*, of 120 guns.

Sunday afternoon [May 10] we took the steam-boat to Cowes, Isle of Wight, and the next morning visited Newport and Appuldurcombe (Ápple-dur-combé) the seat of Lord Yarborough.[1] Thence we crossed to Ryde and returned to Portsmouth in Monday eve[nin]g's boat. We came up to London in Tuesday's coach — seventy two miles — and are at Waterloo Hotel, Jermyn Street.

May 15th. We have taken lodgings to-day in Regent Street, one of the thronged and fashionable streets of the West End, and shall commence our rambles tomorrow. For two days past it has rained so incessantly, that the ladies have not been able to go out much.

May 16th. Walked up to Regent's Park to see the so-called Coliseum — a fine building, in which is exhibited a panoramic view of London as seen from the dome of St. Paul's church. I think you will find a description of this in "Leigh's picture of London."[2] This, with a drive in the afternoon into some of the by-corners of the city, in search of a Mr. Adams, watchmaker,[3] consumed the day. It is astonishing how little can be accomplished here in a day! You can do nothing before 10 o'clock in the morning, and then the distances from point to point are so great — London is on so vast and magnificent a scale, that it is impossible to kill many *lions* in the course of a day, and at night you are so thoroughly tired, that you sleep late into the next morning.

May. 17th Sunday. In the morning, took a drive in Hyde Park with Mr. Amory of Boston.[4] In the afternoon went to hear service in St. Paul's church. A thousand echoes mock the hymn and the peal of the organ; and the continuous rattling of coaches on the pavements without seems like the unbroken roar of the sea.

Passed the eve[nin]g at Mr. Bates's (Firm of Baring & brothers). Present Mr. and Mrs Sturgis of Boston — old friends of Clara — Col. Aspinwal, U. S. Consul in London — and Mr. Vail, Chargé &c.[5] Mr. Vail retains a lively recollection of George [Pierce], and the many civilities he received from him during his visit to Portland. I have not presented my letters of introduction to him, but shall do so tomorrow or next day.

I have not yet attended to that business matter for Mr. Becket not having had leisure; but will see to it soon, and you shall have notice thereof in my next.[6]

If you want to find the exact point of our residence, look on the map for Regent street — left hand side going up toward the Park — about half way between Conduit St. and New Burlington St.

We have not yet recd. letters from you. I shall go to my banker's again tomorrow morning in hope of finding some.

May 18th. Recd. a letter from Mother — with a few lines from Eliza and Margaret — all of which were very acceptable. My love to all.

Most affectionately yours
Henry W. Longfellow

Please write often, and send no half sheets. They go as double letters and postage from Liverpool to London is 75 cents for double letters.

On Friday we change our lodgings to No. 8. Princes Street near Cavendish Square.[7]

MANUSCRIPT: Longfellow Trust Collection. ADDRESS: Hon. Stephen Longfellow/ Portland. Maine./U.S. of America POSTMARKS: NEW YORK SHIP JUNE 28/ FORWARDED BY CARDWELL BROS LIVERPOOL. ANNOTATION (*in another hand*): Independence ENDORSEMENT: H W. and Mary Longfellow/May 18. 1835 Recd June 30. 1835/An[s]d. July 5. 1835

1. Charles Anderson-Pelham, Baron Yarborough (1781–1846), was "best known," according to Cockayne's *Complete Peerage*, "for his princely hospitality to members of the yacht club."

2. Samuel Leigh, *Leigh's New Picture of London* (several editions).

3. Of F. B. Adams & Sons, Watch-Manufacturers, 21 St. John's Square, Clerkonwell.

4. Presumably Charles Amory (204.2).

5. Joshua Bates (1788–1864), head of the banking firm of Baring Brothers & Company, was born in Weymouth, Massachusetts, and subsequently became one of the principal patrons of the Boston Public Library; Elizabeth Knight Hinckley, a schoolmate of Clara Crowninshield in Hingham, was the wife of William Sturgis (1806–1895), a merchant of Boston; Thomas Aspinwall (1786–1876) served as U. S. Consul in London, 1815–1853; Aaron Vail (1796–1878) was chargé d'affaires in London, 1832–1836.

6. See 308.1.

7. A postscript by Mary Potter Longfellow follows.

308. *To Stephen Longfellow*

No. 3. London   June 6. 1835

My dear father,

Since my last I have been at Wandsworth, and settled the business with Mr. Blackmore, receiving from him the sum of £23.6.8, being the amount of both legacies due to the Beckets. Wandsworth is a pretty little town, about six miles from the point of our residence in London: — near the Thames, though not upon its banks — surrounded with green trees and hedge-rows, and surmounted by several long tube-like chimneys, vomiting forth dense clouds of smoke. Unfortunately Mr. Blackmore was not at home, having come to London for the day. He called next morning and paid the money. My expenses only fifty cents — the drive being short.[1]

We are on the tiptoe of departure from London, having engaged our passages [to Hamburg] for Tuesday eve[nin]g next June 8.[2] This is the most direct and expeditious way of reaching Stockholm; for we expect to find at Lubeck, a steam-boat direct to that city, one being advertised. If we are mistaken in this, we shall either take shipping for Stockholm direct from Lubeck, or go by the way of Kiel and Copenhagen, as circumstances may [decide].

I have made arrangements with Bentley, *the* great — or *one* of the great London Publishers,[3] to publish Outre Mer. The terms are half the profits. The work will appear in the course of a few days — in two volumes; and Bentley has promised to send you two or three copies without delay. He pretends to think highly of the book, and says he has no doubt of its success.

Mr. Brooks (J. G.) of Portland has just reached London, bringing us no letters from Portland, but a package of papers from New York.[4] I see that my book is announced by a flourish of trumpets in the Knickerbocker, and the American Monthly Magazine.[5]

June 9. — when I commenced this letter I intended to make it a long one. But I am disappointed, and write these few lines amid the hurry and bustle of packing, and in the intolerable heat of an afternoon in June. We go on board the Steamer for Hambro' [Hamburg] to-night, and sail at 1 o'clock in the morning.

Love to all.

> In the greatest haste, most affect[ionatel]y yrs.
> H. W. Longw.

MANUSCRIPT: Longfellow Trust Collection. ADDRESS: To/Hon. Stephen Longfellow/Portland. Maine/U. of America POSTMARKS: BOSTON AUG 10/SHIP ANNOTATION (*by Stephen Longfellow*): Augt. 15 1835 Paid Mr Beckett for Henry $103.10.

1. See Stephen Longfellow's annotation at the end of this letter. There were a number of Beckets (Becketts) living in Portland in 1835, any one of whom may have been Stephen Longfellow's client. Mr. Blackmore, as the remarks imply, was a Wandsworth solicitor.

2. Penciled words "to Hamburg" in another hand. Longfellow corrected the date at the end of the letter.

3. Richard Bentley (1794–1871), the founder in 1837 of *Bentley's Miscellany* and later publisher of the well-known *Library of Standard Novels*. His firm was absorbed by Macmillan & Company in 1898.

4. James Brooks (1810–1873), a correspondent of the Portland *Advertiser*, later achieved distinction in both journalism and politics. See Letter No. 323.

5. *The Knickerbocker*, V (May 1835), 454–456; *The American Monthly Magazine*, V (May 1835), 247–248.

309. *To Stephen Longfellow*

Gothenburg   June 22nd 1835.

My dear Father,

Since my last I have commenced one or two letters to you, but have been obliged to leave them unfinished. Even the present must be short, as I have business, which calls me out in a few minutes. Mary's letters to her father and to Anne will inform you of our journey hither — from London thro' Hamburg, Lübeck and Copenhagen. Being too late for the steamboat which runs between this place and Stockholm — (once a fortnight! only think of it) we have been obliged to purchase a travelling carriage, and start tomorrow morning for Trollhättan. This will be our first day's journey. If you take a map you will find the place — nearly north of Gothenburg, and not far from the outlet of the Wenern Lake. It is noted for possessing the finest waterfall in Europe — and a series of *locks* on a canal — said to be surpassed by none in the world. We shall see how it is; and report to you in due time. Thence onward we propose to reach on the second day the town of Lidköping, on the third day, Hofva, a small town northeast of Maria-stad — on the fourth day Fellsingbro [Fellingsbro], near the head of the Mälar lake, not far from Arboga — the fifth Enköping on the northern shore of the lake; and the sixth Stockholm. This is our present plan. But if weather and everything proves favorable, and the ladies do not complain of fatigue we may accomplish the whole journey in four days instead of six. At all events we shall be in Stockholm before the first of July. This is rather later than I expected when I left home. But it will answer very well.

Gothenburg is a very neat, pretty city — built for the most part on a level lap of land, intersected by the little River Gotha, and surrounded on three sides by high and rocky hills, stripped of all vegetation. The streets run at right angles to each other — one or two canals intersect the city crosswise — and the pavement is one of the worst I ever trode upon. This city was originally built by the Dutch,[1] of wood for the most part — but a fire consumed the whole town, with the exception

493

of four or five houses, in the year 1804. It has since been rebuilt with stone and brick, and is certainly a very handsome town for a small one. Population about twentyfive thousand. Last year it was thirty; — five thousand died of cholera.

Yesterday being sunday I attended the English church in the morning — and afterward the Swedish — where I heard *violent* preaching, and saw a large and attentive congregation. The people are evidently a church-going people.

The weather is quite cold here — very much like October; and to day it rains, and there is a high wind — bad prognostics of our approaching journey.

Farewell. Love to all.

Very affectionately yrs
Henry W. Longw.

By the same vessel that takes this, Mary has written to Anne and to her father.

MANUSCRIPT: Longfellow Trust Collection. ADDRESS: To/Hon. S. Longfellow/ Portland/U. S. of America POSTMARKS: NEW BEDFORD MS. AUG 7/SHIP PUBLISHED: *Longfellow and Scandinavia*, pp. 149–150.

1. Longfellow is in error here. Dutch architects merely laid out the city for Gustavus Adolphus in 1619.

310. *To Karl August Nicander*

Stockholm   June 29. 1835

My dear sir,

I trust you have not forgotten Rome — the Piazza Madama — and your American friend who lived in the *casa Persiani*. If you have not, I know, that you will not be sorry to hear, that he is now in your fatherland.

In fact, I have come to Sweden to pass the summer; and reached Stockholm yesterday. I can hardly express to you my extreme regret, at finding you absent from town; and had I not a wife and two young ladies with me, I should certainly go to Nyköping to see you.

My object, in visiting Sweden, is to study its language and literature. I need your advice upon this subject; for in choosing my place of residence, I wish to study economy as well as convenience. Had I better remain here or go to Upsala? or whither shall I go?

Will you have the goodness to inform me where you intend to pass the summer, and when you shall probably return to Stockholm, and to give me any information you think may be useful in reference to lodgings &c &c here in Sweden.

I write these few lines in haste; not knowing whether they will ever reach you, and yet hoping to hear from you before many days have elapsed.

Very truly your friend and Obt. Ser[v]t.

Henry W. Longfellow

Please direct to the care of D. Erskine, American Consul, Stockholm.[1]

MANUSCRIPT: Royal Library, Stockholm. ADDRESS: À Monsieur/Monsieur Carl Augt. Nicander/Nyköping POSTMARK: STOCKHOLM $\frac{30}{6}$ 1835 PUBLISHED: "Some Unpublished Longfellow Letters," p. 178.

1. David Erskine (1787–1860), a Scottish immigrant to Sweden, was the first American consul in Stockholm.

311. *To George Washington Pierce*

[Stockholm, July 8, 1835][1]

My dear George,

This is a regular *rum* country. Everybody takes a *dram* before sitting down to dinner; and again after dinner. The *clergy* frequent confectioners shops — drink punch in public coffee rooms — play cards on Sunday — and smoke cigars in the street. All which things are *contra bonos mores* [contrary to good manners] and quite scandalous.

The Swedes are a free-and-easy race, and generally very liberal in their political notions. In everything else, they are a century behind most parts of Christendom. They are all half-asleep — want enterprise — and I suppose want *capital* also.

Living is cheap — books are cheap — newspapers cheap and abundant, and the Op[p]osition press violent. Stockholm is a pleasant, pretty city — though rather dull in Summer. The environs beautiful. Hope to hear from you soon.

Truly yr. friend

H. W. Longw

MANUSCRIPT: unrecovered; text from photostat, Longfellow Trust Collection. ADDRESS (*by Mary Potter Longfellow*): Mrs Anne L. Pierce./Care of George W. Pierce. Esqr./Portland. Maine./U.S. of America. POSTMARK: BOSTON MS SEP 22 ANNOTATION (*by Longfellow*): Mail from Boston ENDORSEMENT: Mary P. L./Stockholm July 15th/1835 PUBLISHED: "New Longfellow Letters," p. 786.

1. This is a postscript to Mary Potter Longfellow's letter to Anne Longfellow Pierce begun on July 8, 1835. The exact date of the postscript is questionable. For Mrs. Longfellow's letter, see "New Longfellow Letters," pp. 784–786.

312. *To Karl August Nicander*

Stockholm   July 10. 1835

Min Kära Vän [My dear friend],

I was very happy to receive your friendly letter of the 6th;[1] and should have sent you an immediate answer by the return of post, had I been able to get the necessary information, relative to the facilities of going to Nyköping by water. I am sorry to say, that the answer to my inquiries is not very satisfactory. I find that the steam-boat goes but once a week; and that in order to accomplish the journey and return to Stockholm, I should have to be absent a whole week or more, from my family. Much as I want to see you, therefore, I have been obliged to give up the idea of going to Nyköping. How much I regret this! The difficulty is, that the "wife and two young ladies" do not speak Swedish, and very little French — so that I could not leave them here in a strange land without a protector. Now, can you not so arrange your affairs as to come to Stockholm for a few days without great inconvenience to yourself? If you *can* — I shall be delighted; — but if you *cannot* — I must submit to the disappointment I shall feel; though a "still, small voice"[2] within says, that I shall certainly see you before I leave Sweden.

Apropos de bottes! How long do you intend to remain at Boo? I shall be here and in Upsala till the middle of September — unless something new occurs to change my plans. I am much pleased with *"Sveriges hufvudstad — den stora staden Stockholm* [Sweden's capital — the great city of Stockholm]"; and have lodgings at No 22 Drottninggatan. Will it not be possible for us to be together after your return from the Hamiltonian *villeggiatura* [country residence]?[3]

And now I will satisfy your curiosity about the *mysterious* ladies. *Whose* wife do you please to imagine I am living with, if not with *my own!* I have been married now nearly four years — but have no children *living*.[4] The two young ladies are friends of my wife, who have taken this opportunity to visit Europe. Our present plan is to pass the summer here — the winter in Germany, and the next summer in Copenhagen. The object of this my second visit to Europe is wholly literary. I am studying the Scandinavian languages and literature; as I occupy at home the Chair of Modn. Literature and Belles Lettres in one of our Universities; — which by the way, has been the case ever since I left you in Rome.

So much for me and my doings. And I know likewise what you have been doing; for I have now upon my table your "Hesperider" — "Minnen från Södern" and "Runeswärdet."[5] I congratulate you, my friend, on your great literary success; and the praises I hear of you from all mouths. I would fain add my own to these; but alas! I am not yet sufficiently master of your language to render my opinion of any value. I can only say, that I have read several of your papers with the greatest pleasure.

I trust, that if it is impossible for you to come to Stockholm at present, I shall have the consolation of hearing from you often. I hoped, that I should find you passing the Summer in Stockholm; but as this cannot be, let me know, where you are, and how you are passing your time; as much in detail as possible.

I have some friends here, who are very kind and attentive, — particularly the Antiquarian, Mr. Liljögren. I know also Mr. Arvidsson of the Royal Library — and one or two of the Upsala Professors. Old Mr. Lignel, is my instructor in Swedish.[6]

Where the deuce is *Boo*? I cannot find it on the map — nor the province of *Nerike*, either.[7] Please enlighten my darkness.

Most truly yr. friend
Henry W. Longfellow

MANUSCRIPT: Royal Library, Stockholm. ADDRESS: Till/Herr Karl Aug. Nicander/ Nyköping. POSTMARK: STOCKHOLM $\frac{10}{7}$ 1835 PUBLISHED: "Some Unpublished Longfellow Letters," pp.179–180.

1. See *Longfellow and Scandinavia*, pp. 163-165. Nicander had invited Longfellow to visit him at Nyköping.

2. I Kings 19:12.

3. See note 7.

4. This is the first suggestion in the letters that Mary Longfellow was pregnant.

5. *Hesperider* (Örebro, 1835) and *Minnen från Södern*, Första Delen (Örebro, 1831) were products of Nicander's continental tour in 1827–1829; *Runeswärdet och Den förste Riddaren* (Upsala, 1820), a poetic tragedy, was his first literary success.

6. Johan Gustaf Liljegren (1791-1837) was master of the Royal Archives; Adolf Ivar Arwidsson (1791-1858), an historian and political writer, was first assistant librarian at the Royal Library in 1835; and Karl Fredrik Lignell (1778– 1846) held the title "Linguæ Gallicæ et Anglicæ Magister" at Upsala.

7. Nerike (Närke) lies directly west of Stockholm in south central Sweden; Boo, an estate in the southeast part of the province, was owned by Nicander's patron, Baron Hugo Adolf Hamilton (1802–1871).

313. *To Stephen Longfellow*

No 1: from Stockholm. July 18. 1835.

My dear father,

I wrote you last from Gothenborg date June 21.[1] Since then we have crossed the country and reached the Capital in safety and good health. Mary has described the journey in her letters, so that I shall not go over the ground again. Instead thereof, I send you a large map of Sweden, which will enable you to follow every step of the Northern Army. Our march was through Trollhättan, Lidköping, Bodarne, Fellingsbro, Enköping, — stopping a night at each of these places; and we reached Stockholm on the afternoon of Sunday June 28. somewhat weary and travel-worn, with sun-burnt cheeks and copper noses.

I send you also a map of Stockholm, which will give you a good idea of the town and of our *whereabout*. We first stopped at the Hotel Garni, near the foot of the Drottning-gatan, the principal street in Stockholm. We then took lodgings in the same street, a little farther up; but finding the situation rather noisy and public, we have removed to the Clara Södra Kyrko Gatan. These points are near each other on the map; and thinking that these matters — trifles as they are — may not be wholly without interest for you, I have painted these places red, so that you may easily put your finger upon them.

Professor Cleaveland gave me a letter of introduction to Berzelius, the celebrated chemist. I saw him but once; and two days afterward he started for Paris, where he will pass the summer. So I shall see no more of him. Acquaintances, however, I have already in great abundance. One of these is a young poet and clergyman, by the name of *G. Mellin*;[2] another is Mr. Liljegren, a gentleman, who has charge of the Royal Archives, a scholar of note in the ancient language and literature of the land. Then there are two or three Librarians — a Professor or two from Upsala — and young artists and *authorlings* by the dozen. So that we do not want society, and time flies away very rapidly. Mr. Boyd's letters have been of great service to me, and secured me many attentions. Please tell him that I have dined with his friends Erskine, Stockoe, and Arfwedson, who all bear him in cordial remembrance.[3] Mr. Arfwedson Jr. married a Philadelphia lady, and has written a book on America, which is spoken well of by the critics.[4] I dined with him to-day, and met there Baron *Stackleback,* (or some such thing) who was for fourteen years Swedish Minister in the United States; a very agreeable man, who speaks good English, and a good deal of it, too.[5] He promises to call tomorrow, and is quite *empressé* [earnest] in his offers of friendship and attention. In fine, all to whom we brought letters, have been very kind and hospitable.

The Swedish language is soft and musical, with an accent like the lowland Scotch. It is an easy language to read, but a difficult one to speak with correctness, owing to some gram[m]atical peculiarities. Its literature swarms with translations. Cooper and Irving are well known here; and most of their works have been translated into Swedish, and are read here with delight. I have, also, a Swedish copy of Slidell's "Year in Spain." [6]

King Bernadotte [7] I have not seen. He is now out of town. His royal consort rides about in her coach, and looks, at a distance, not unlike Mrs. Hez. Winslow, being *rosy*-cheeked, and in person *instar montis* [just like a mountain].[8]

We feel quite out of the world here. Occasionally Mr. Hughes [9] sends us a few American newspapers, wherein we read of steamboat explosions and the down-fall of houses and so forth. Farther than this we hear but little from over the sea; very few letters having yet reached us in this remote corner of christendom.

In the course of a few days I think we shall go to Upsala for a week or so. This is the seat of the principal University of Sweden. They are now in vacation. There is a steam-boat on the lake, from this place thither. Speaking of steam-boats, there is one plying in the harbor of only 2 horse-power! It is a little open *yawl*, about as large as a nutshell, and holds from a dozen to twenty persons; — the merest plaything you ever saw.

The climate of Sweden seems to be very variable and subject to *sudden* changes like our own. Its greatest beauty is the long evening twilight. On mid-summers night I read with perfect ease at midnight. This, however, was but a few lines; and now, that the days have grown shorter, I cannot study without a candle later than half past nine or ten, though it is not *dark* all the night through.

My most affectionate love to mother, and to all the family. I who am so negligent a son and brother at home, bear you all in constant remembrance when absent.

How does my book make its way in the world? If there is anything peculiarly *piquant* in any criticism, I wish you would send it to me, when a good opportunity offers.

Farewell.

Most affectionately yours
Henry W. Longfellow

I shall write to Professor Cleaveland on my return from Upsala. Please say so, when you see him.

MANUSCRIPT: Longfellow Trust Collection. ADDRESS: Mail from Boston/To/Hon. Stephen Longfellow/Portland/Maine POSTMARK: BOSTON MS SEP 22 PUBLISHED: *Longfellow and Scandinavia*, pp. 150–152.

1. See Letter No. 309. The date was June 22.

2. Gustaf Henrik Mellin (1803–1876), a leader in Stockholm literary society and a popular historical novelist, became acquainted with Longfellow through Nicander. He subsequently gave Longfellow lessons in Finnish and escorted him about the city.

3. John James Boyd, the Swedish vice-consul in New York City, had provided Longfellow with letters to David Erskine and Ralf Stokoe (1786–1836), merchant

partners of Stockholm, and to Carl Abraham Arfwedson (1774–1861), wealthy merchant and intimate friend of Queen Désirée. For Longfellow's relationship with Stokoe, see Andrew Hilen, "The Longfellows and the Stokoes: A Forgotten Friendship," *Studia Neophilologica*, XXIII (1951), 17–36.

4. Carl David Arfwedson (1806–1881), exiled to America for some youthful indiscretions in print, had written of his experiences in *The United States and Canada in 1832, 1833, and 1834* (London, 1834), 2 vols. His wife was the former Elizabeth Alice Ashhurst (1814–1899) of Philadelphia.

5. Berndt Robert Gustaf Stackleberg (1784–1845) was the Swedish chargé d'affaires in Washington, 1820–1832.

6. *Ett År i Spanien. Af en ung amerikanare.* Öfversättning från engelskan i två volymer (Stockholm, 1832).

7. That is, Charles XIV, the former Marshal Bernadotte.

8. Désirée reminded Longfellow of Jane Crane Winslow, wife of Hezekiah Winslow, a lumber dealer of Portland.

9. Christopher Hughes (1786–1849), the American chargé d'affaires in Stockholm.

314. *To Thomas Wren Ward*[1]

Stockholm   July 23. 1835

T. W. Ward Esq.

Dear Sir,

I have the honor to acknowledge the receipt of your letters (Nos 1 and 2.) of the 10th April, containing copies of the Votes of the Corporation of Harvard College, authorising me to expend the sum of Two hundred pounds Sterling in the purchase of Books for the College Library.

The List of Books, which I made out at Mr. Ticknor's request, and which was to have been transmitted with the letters, did not come with them; and unfortunately a copy of the same, which I had in my possession was accidentally lost in London, in one of my rambles among the booksellers' shops.

Thinking, however, that I was not to abide strictly and entirely by the List — (indeed this being the understanding before I left America) I made a collection of some rare and curious works in London, which were shipped by Rich,[2] and which, I trust, have safely reached you. The amount expended was £41.11.6.

I intend to expend about the same amount here for Swedish books — and about as much more in Copenhagen for Danish and Icelandic — this being the department in which the Library is most deficient.

The Corporation desire another List of books to be made out with the prices. This I would willingly do, had I the necessary materials by me; but I have not.[3] I deem it, however, of the greatest importance to the Department of Modern Literature in Harvard College, that a still farther sum should be voted for German Works; particularly Philological works, and republications of the old literature of the country — a branch of learning, which at the present moment excites great attention in Germany, and upon which much is written and published.[4]

I expect to be in Berlin, about the 1st of October, and hope to hear from you again upon this subject as soon as possible.

With much respect, Yr. Obt. Ser[v]t.

Henry W. Longfellow

MANUSCRIPT: Harvard College Papers, Second Series, VII, 138. ADDRESS: To the Treasr. of Harvd. College/T. W. Ward Esq/Boston/U.S.A. POSTMARK: PLYMOUTH MS [?] SEP 29 ANNOTATION: Boston Oct 4 1835. The Treasurer/ submits this letter from Mr./Longfellow to the corporation —/TW Ward/ Treasr — PUBLISHED: *Professor Longfellow of Harvard*, pp. 17-18.

1. Ward (1786-1858), a prominent merchant and the American agent of Baring Brothers & Company, was at this time treasurer of Harvard College.

2. Obadiah Rich (114.5), whom Longfellow had met in Spain, served Harvard as an agent for rare books.

3. In *Professor Longfellow of Harvard* (p. 17, n. 8), Johnson observes, "Longfellow apparently misunderstood the third vote of the corporation, in which the Harvard officials requested that he observe the books available in other fields than modern languages and note their prices."

4. On October 17, 1835, Longfellow's request for more funds was considered at a meeting of the corporation and rejected as "not expedient" (see *Professor Longfellow of Harvard*, p. 18).

315. *To Lewis Gaylord Clark*

Stockholm, July 29 [1835]

WELL, — here I am in the far North, — a regular *rum* country, — where the clergy drink punch in the coffee-houses, and smoke in the streets, — and where most people take a dram before dinner to help their appetite, and a dram after dinner to help their digestion.

Stockholm is a very pretty city, — built upon some fifteen small islands in the Mäler lake, — a few miles from the Baltic. It has a large and magnificent palace — narrow streets without side-walks — a corn-giving pavement — and a bathing-house; where you can be *shampooed* with a coarse towel by an elderly maiden for two shillings and sixpence. I cannot vouch for the truth of this last statement, having never personally undergone the operation. I get my information from those who have.

I find that American literature is not unknown here: most of the works of IRVING and COOPER have been translated into Swedish, and are read and admired here as elsewhere. "A Year in Spain" is also translated into Swedish; and a day or two ago I saw a copy of Miss SEDGWICK's "Redwood," which is here published as one of COOPER's Novels.[1] This is probably a book-seller's speculation, thinking the book might have a better run under his name.

Ding — dong — bell! They are tolling for fire!

There — since writing these words, the oldest and finest church in Stockholm has been burnt to the ground; — *Riddarholm's Church*, in which are buried all the Kings of Sweden!

Yesterday morning the steeple was struck by lightning, and has been burning ever since, though supposed to be extinguished. It was about five o'clock P.M. when I wrote "ding — dong — bell," above. It is now midnight, and I have just returned from the conflagration. When I went out, I could see nothing but a little quiet flame curling round the ball on the top of the spire. It gained slowly: the spire crumbled and fell piece-meal, and by ten o'clock the body of the church was in flames. It was a magnificent spectacle:

> What light through the heav'ns in a sudden spire
> Shoots quivering upward? Fire! 'tis fire!
> There are wild forms, hurrying to and fro,
> Seen darkly clear on that lurid glow;
> There are shout, and signal-gun, and call
> And the dashing of water — but fruitless all!
> Man may not fetter nor ocean tame
> The might and wrath of the rushing flame.[2]

P.S. The interior of the church, being arched with brick, has been saved; including many fine paintings, and the tombs of the ancient Kings.

MANUSCRIPT: unrecovered; text from the *Knickerbocker*, VI (November 1835), 479.

1. Longfellow is correct; see James Fenimore Cooper, *Redwood. Nordamerikansk roman* (Stockholm, 1826), 2 vols.

2. The quotation is unidentified. Longfellow described the burning of Riddar-holm's Church in more detail in his journal (*Longfellow and Scandinavia*, pp. 125–128). See also the *Diary of Clara Crowninshield*, pp. 64–66.

316. *To Zilpah Longfellow* [1]

[Stockholm,   August 5, 1835]

My dearest mother,

As a little blank space is left, I will fill it with a postscript. We have just returned — that is to say, day before yesterday, — from a visit to the University of Upsala, and the Iron mines of Dannemora; — of which Mary will give you descriptions all in good time. We already begin to think of leaving Stockholm — and shall probably take the steamboat to Gothenburg in about three weeks. For my own part, I should like to go sooner if we could. I am disappointed in Sweden. The climate is too cold and unpleasant. I want a little warm sunshine. Something that I can feel, as well as see. From Gothenburg we shall go to Copenhagen, and after passing a month there, take steamboat to Stettin, and so to Berlin. We shall not return to the *North* again but pass the next summer in Germany and France.

Much love to all.

Very affectionately your Son
H. W. Longfellow

MANUSCRIPT: unrecovered; text from photostat, Longfellow Trust Collection. ADDRESS (*by Mary Potter Longfellow*): Mrs Stephen Longfellow./Care of Hon. Stephen Longfellow./Portland. Maine./U.S. of America. POSTMARKS: NEW YORK OCT 13/SHIP PUBLISHED: Higginson, *Longfellow*, pp. 97-98.

1. Postscript to Mary Potter Longfellow's letter to Zilpah Longfellow, August 5, 1835.

317. *To Johan Henric Schröder* [1]

Stockholm, ce 7. Août. 1835.
Clara Södra Kyrko gatan No 5.

Monsieur,

Ayant un[e] occasion d'examiner les "Scriptores Rerum Svec. Medii Aevi," [2] j'ai troubé une feuille, tellement déchirée, que je ne saurai m'en servir. La moitié de cette feuille manque dans tous les deux exemplaires. C'est la première page d'un des cahiers; et commence ainsi;

"I.
Ex Langfedgatal
ab Odino ad Olavum Trätälja.

Ex Codice Donationis Magnæanæ, No
415. in Bibliotheca. &c &c."

C'est curieux, que dans les deux exemplaires, la même feuille soit ainsi déchirée au beau milieu de la page.

Veuillez bien m'envoyer, par quelque bonne occasion, deux copies de cette feuille — une pour chaque exemplaire du livre.

Agréez, je vous prie, les sentimens de considération avec lesquels j'ai l'honneur d'être

Votre très humble Serviteur

H. W. Longfellow

MANUSCRIPT: Carolina Rediviva, University of Upsala. PUBLISHED: "Some Unpublished Longfellow Letters," p. 182.

TRANSLATION:

Stockholm, August 7, 1835

Sir,

Having an opportunity to examine the "Scriptores Rerum Svec. Medii Aevi," I have discovered a leaf so torn that I will not be able to use it. One half of this page is missing in each of the two copies. It is the first page of one of the books; and begins thus . . .

It is curious that in both copies the same leaf should be torn right in the middle of the page.

Would you please send me, on some convenient occasion, two copies of this leaf — one for each copy of the book.

Accept, I pray you, those feelings of respect with which I have the honor to be

Your most humble servant

H. W. Longfellow

1. Schröder (1791–1857) was librarian of Carolina Rediviva, the library of the University of Upsala.

2. Ericus Michael Fant, ed., *Scriptores Rerum Svecicarum Medii Aevi* (Upsaliæ, 1818), Vol. I.

318. *To George Washington Greene*

Stockholm   Aug. 10. 1835

My dear George,

We have now been about two months in Sweden; and shall leave it without regret in about a fortnight, to return no more forever — I trust. From which pious ejaculation you will infer, that I have not been much pleased with my "Summer in the North." It is indeed so. Stockholm is a very pretty city; — "et quand on a dit cela, on a tout dit [and when one has said that, one has said every thing]." There is no spirit — no life — no enterprise — in a word — "*no nothing.*" Literature is in an abject condition; and notwithstanding the many great names, that adorn the armorial bearings of Sweden, you cannot help seeing all around you, that "la stupidité est d'uniforme [stupidity is universal]." And then it is so cold here! It is August — but it is not summer. The rain it raineth every day; and the air is like November. I was simple enough to go out yesterday without a great-coat and umbrella; for which scandalous conduct I was drenched through by a tremendous rain; and pelted for fifteen minutes with hail-stones as large as peas. I was on the water, in an open boat. "O for a beaker full of the warm south!"[1] I shall seek one soon. I wish it were to-day.

The Swedish language is soft and musical; but it wants the energy of the German and the English. Sweden has *one great* poet — and only one. That is Tegnér — Bishop of Wexiö — still living. His noblest work is "Frithiofs Saga," an heroic poem, founded on old tradition. Franzén, — Stagnelius, — Bellman, — Atterbom, — *Nicander* — these are other Scalds of the North;[2] and then there is a multitude of small *authorlings*, just as with us. You will be curious to know something about Nicander. I am sorry to say, that I have not seen him. He has gone to pass the *summer*, (they call it so here) with a friend in the country. How delightful, to be running about in the wet grass, with an umbrella! How poetical! A few days after my arrival here, I wrote him a letter, which he answered. I have written twice since; and have received no answer; which I do not understand.[3] Besides his poems, he has published two volumes of prose; "Hesperider," — containing sketches of Italy; and "Minnen från Södern" — souvenirs of the South — a book of Travels through Denmark, Germany, Switzerland and Italy. Of this there is to be a second volume. Nicander ranks among the Swedish authors, about as high as [Grenville] Mellen does with us. There is no resemblance, however, between the styles of these two writers. Nicander is remarkably clear and simple. He is a sweet writer — not a great one. From what I hear, he has not fulfilled the promise of his youth. He is now thirty six years old. Quite venerable.

I have been to Upsala — the seat of the largest Swedish University. It is a pleasant little place; and the University library quite renowned. It contains about 80 thousand volumes. It is now vacation; and all the Professors, with one or two unimportant exceptions, are away. I did not see them. There is one other University in the South of Sweden at Lund. Nicander is a candidate for the Profship. of Belles Lettres there.

I forgot to tell you how we reached Stockholm. We came through Hamburg, Lubeck, Copenhagen, and Gothenburg. On leaving here, we take the steamboat to Gothenburg through the lakes and the great canal.[4] From Gothenburg to Copenhagen — thence to Stettin — and thence to Berlin. In Copenhagen I shall make a sojourn of some weeks.

I saw [Nathaniel Parker] Willis in London. His orbit is *high* among the stars and *garters* of the fashionable zodiac. He was very polite; — but there was no very hearty fellowship between us. It was evident that I hung heavy upon his skirts, like a country cousin. He is too artificial. And his poetry has now lost one of its greatest charms for me — its sincerity. This is strictly *sub rosa*. I do not wish to join the hue and cry against him.

I made an arrangement with Bentley to publish Outre Mer in London. I have not yet seen the London edition; but it will be elegant of course. All Bentley's books are so. I am to have half the profits, which I suppose means, what he chooses to give me — that is, nothing.[5] I have no golden dreams. This place is so far out of the world — the communication[s] between it and London are so long and difficult — that I have not yet heard a syllable about my book since I left London. Bentley was very sanguine of its success.

And now what are you doing all this time? I wish you and Maria were with us, from the bottom of my heart. A traveller's life is after all so "Remote, unfriended, melancholy, slow."[6] You must take your friends with you, to be quite happy. I hope you are "casting many a northward look"[7] to Boston or Cambridge as a home, that we may be together; and if you could come to Europe and we could eat fresh figs together in Italy once more, it would be glorious! But these perhaps are dreams.

I shall stay in Berlin till May or June next year. Thence shall go probably into Switzerland — thence to Paris. However this is uncertain. One cannot speak surely of the future.

How goeth the life of Petrarca? If I find anything which can assist you, I shall send it.[8] Of course there is nothing here in Stockholm.

Let me hear from you very soon — a long letter — without margin — and lines close together. You can hardly imagine how *hungry* I am for letters from America. I have had but two since I left home. I expect some next Spring. Please direct to the care of Baring, Brothers &c. London.

Give a great deal of love from us both to your wife. Mary will write to her before long; but cannot by the present opportunity; being very much engaged to-day.

Addio. Kind regards to yr father and family.

Very truly yr friend
Henry W. Longw.

MANUSCRIPT: Longfellow Trust Collection. ADDRESS: To/George W. Greene Esq./East Greenwich/Rhode Island/United States of America   POSTMARKS: BOSTON MS OCT 2 [*faint; reading doubtful*]/SHIP   PUBLISHED: *Longfellow and Scandinavia*, pp. 152–154.

1. John Keats, "Ode to a Nightingale," l. 15.

2. As the translator of *Nattvardsbarnen* ("Children of the Lord's Supper") and of excerpts from *Frithiofs Saga*, Longfellow did much to establish Esaias Tegnér's reputation in America. For details, see *Longfellow and Scandinavia*, chap. IV. Frans Michael Franzén (1772–1847), Carl Michael Bellman (1740–1795), and Nicander are mentioned by Longfellow in his *Poets and Poetry of Europe*, pp. 130–131, and P. D. A. Atterbom (1790–1855) and Erik Johan Stagnelius (1793–1823) are represented by selections, pp. 170–177.

3. Of the three letters, only two (Nos. 310 and 312) survive. Nicander answered the last two on August 16, 1835. See *Longfellow and Scandinavia*, pp. 165-167.

4. The Göta Canal connects the great inland Lakes Wetter and Wäner on its course from Stockholm to Gothenburg.

5. As Longfellow suspected, there were no profits.

6. Oliver Goldsmith, *The Traveller*, l. 1.

7. Cf. *Henry IV, Part 2*, II, iii, 13.

8. Greene's ambition seems to have been satisfied with his article on Petrarca (267.5), for he never completed the contemplated biography.

319. *To Parker Cleaveland*

Stockholm August. 22. 1835.

My dear sir,

I have been already two months in this city, and am on the eve of my departure for Copenhagen. Before I go, however, let me write you a few lines by a ship sailing direct to Boston.

A few days after my arrival here, I called upon Berzelius, with your letter of introduction. He has his rooms in a large stone building belonging to the Academy of Sciences. I inquired at the door if Berzelius was at home. "Yes; up one pair of stairs." So up I went, knocked at the first door I came to, and went in. I found myself in a large room, neatly furnished, but without carpets. With my hat in one hand, and your letter in the other I marched forward towards an inner door, from which at the same moment came forth a person about my own height, but much larger, with smooth, light hair, blue eyes, and a smiling, youthful face. He was carelessly dressed in a long green frock-coat. I said to him in French,

"Have I the honor to speak with Professor Berzelius?"

"That is my name."

"Then, Sir, I have the pleasure of presenting you a letter from Professor. C. of the United States of America."

"Oh! I am happy to see you" — taking the letter and reading it; and then speaking English. "I am happy to see you. Have the goodness to walk in."

And accordingly we went into an adjoining parlor, handsomely furnished with sofas etc. but no carpets. We sat down and talked a few minutes together, when he informed me that in two days he should leave town for Paris, where he should pass the summer, and return home by the way of Bonn, on the Rhine, where he is to attend the next meeting of the "*Naturforscher.*" [1] Supposing that he was busy in making preparations for his departure I made but a short call. He gave me some letters of introduction to Upsala; — and I took my leave, thanking him for his kindness; to which he replied, "That is the least

I can do for one, who comes recommended from Prof. Cleaveland."
And that is all I saw of Berzelius. He is very much liked in Stockholm;
is about fifty years of age, and next winter is to be married to a young
lady of twenty-four! [2] What do you think of that?

I have since been at Upsala, the seat of the principal Swedish University. Unfortunately it was vacation, and all the Professors and
students gone — with one or two exceptions, of no great moment.
They have but one Vacation during the year, and make the most of it.
At present Geijer, Prof. of History, is their greatest man. Afzelius is
still living but is very old, and does nothing.[3] There are a great many
farms belonging to the University, and the college salaries are paid in
corn, so many barrels a year — ranging from two to three hundred. Of
course the income of the Professors depends somewhat upon the
crops; tho' they have fees for private lessons. The most remarkable
things at Upsala are the old Cathedral, and the *Codex Argenteus*, a
M.S. of the Bible in Gothic of the VI century.[4]

From Upsala I went to the Mines of Dannemora — some twenty
miles farther North. These are Iron Mines — and very striking in
appearance. The principal shaft is a huge gulf from which you in-
stinctively draw back. It makes you giddy to look down. It is nearly
five hundred feet perpendicular in depth, and perhaps two hundred in
its longest diameter. I was let down in a bucket to the bottom, where
it was cold and damp. I found a bank of ice and snow not yet thawed,
from the last winter. I picked up a specimen of the ore for you, stepped
into the *bucket*, and reached the top again, without *kicking the
bucket*.

By the same ship, which brings you this; I send a box of books to
Cambridge. In this box go also the specimens of Iron ore from Dannemora; and a collection of fifteen beautiful specimens of Porphyry
from the mines of Elfdal[e]n, in Dalecarlia. The pieces are numbered,
with a list.

Mrs. L. joins me in kindest regards to all your family; and to all
our friends in Brunswick, particularly to the Welds and to Mrs. Fales.
Present my cordial remembrances, also to the College Govt. in general
and several; and believe me

Very truly yours etc. etc.,
Henry W. Longfellow.

I expect to be in Berlin about the first of October. If I can do anything for you or for College in Germany you have only to say the
word. A letter will reach me directed to the care of *Timothy Wiggin*,
London.

MANUSCRIPT: Berg Collection, New York Public Library. ADDRESS: To/Professor Cleaveland/Bowdoin College/Brunswick/Maine. POSTMARK: BOSTON MS OCT 23 PUBLISHED: *Longfellow and Scandinavia*, pp. 155-156.

1. An annual convention of scientists inaugurated at Bern in 1816. Longfellow himself attended the convention in 1842 (see Letters No. 720 and 721).

2. Berzelius was fifty-six when he married Johanna Elisabeth Poppius (1811–1884) in 1835.

3. Longfellow refers to Erik Gustaf Geijer (1783-1849), a poet and historian, and either to Adam Afzelius (1750-1837), the successor of Linnaeus at Upsala, or to his brother, Professor Johan Afzelius (1753-1837).

4. For more on the Upsala Cathedral and the *Codex Argenteus*, see Longfellow's journal (*Longfellow and Scandinavia*, pp. 129-130, 131-132).

320. *To Thaddeus William Harris*

[Stockholm, August, 1835] [1]

Dr. Harris,

Dear Sir,

I hope the box of books from London reached you without accident. In my estimation, they were very valuable. It cost me many days, and not idle ones to collect them, here and there, in the great metropolis; and I trust the purchase is satisfactory to you all in Cambridge. Among them were some shabby-looking Italian plays; *very valuable*; — containing specimens of many of the Italian dialects.

The books I now send are of more modern date. They comprise all the Modern Lit. of Sweden. Old books are not to be bought here. I hope to send you some from Copenhagen, in a few weeks.

I have been requested, through Mr. Ward, to make out a list of books, which I should think it expedient to purchase after the expenditure of the first Thousand Dollars voted. I have answered, that as any farther appropriation would be expended in Germany, I had not the materials necessary for such a list, but hoped, that another thousand dollars would be voted notwithstanding. I trust you will do all in your power to help forward this matter; and I will send from Germany such a collection of rare things, as is not to be found under the Western star.

In the present box, as in the last, are some books of my own, which you may deliver to Felton, or place in some quiet corner till my return. I also take the liberty of troubling you with a few packages. So good an opportunity could not be resisted. With much regard

Very truly yrs.

Henry W. Longfellow.

MANUSCRIPT: Harvard College Library. ADDRESS: To/Doctor Harris/Librarian of Harv. Univ./Cambridge POSTMARKS: BOSTON ‖MS‖ OCT 23/SHIP EN-

DORSEMENT: Recd. Oct. 23, 1835. PUBLISHED: *Professor Longfellow of Harvard*, pp. 18–19.

1. The date is conjectural.

321. *To Stephen Longfellow*

Gothenburg   September 2. 1835

My dear father,

We arrived here last evening in the steam-boat from Stockholm; having passed through the great Götha Canal and the large lakes of the interior. From Stockholm to Gothenburg is about 300 English miles; but owing to the great number of locks and the difficult navigation of the lakes we were six days on the way. Of the 300 miles only 60 are canal. There are 72 locks; and very fine ones. The canal is a noble work, built under the superintendence of Admiral von Platen.[1]

I write these few lines in great haste, not wishing to suffer an opportunity of sending to Boston to escape. We find one direct from this place.

I am now going to send our luggage on board the steamer for Copenhagen. We start at 3 o'clock this afternoon.

In the greatest haste, and with much love to all

Very truly and affect[ionatel]y yours
Henry W. Longfellow

From Stockholm Mary sent letters to her father by the ship *Talma,* a few days ago.[2]

I wrote by the *Talma* — a letter to you.[3]

3 o'clock afternoon. Well, our heels have been tripped up in fine style. The Steamer has arrived from Christiania (Norway) quite full. There are no vacant places except on deck — and as it is a night-passage to Copenhagen, this will not do for us. So here we remain a whole week. It will be stupid enough.

Thursday. Sept. 3rd.

Called upon Olof Wijk,[4] for whom I luckily had a letter of introduction. A giant in person — and a pleasant giant withal. He called this eve[nin]g with his carriage and took us out into the environs of the town, which are pleasant. Gothenburg stands on a level strip of land, into which stretches an arm of the sea, to meet the Götha Elf, a little stream running from Lake Wener. Every landscape near town has something wild about it; — some huge, round, sterile hill — or barren crag — something of untamed and untameable nature. This gives striking contrasts at every view. The town itself is well built — the houses being in general much finer than those in Stockholm.

Met to-day Capt. Condry of the Tasso.[5] The first thing he did was to whip out of his pocket, in true Yankee style, a sovereign remedy for the tooth-ache! He sails tomorrow for Boston; and takes this letter and one from Mary to her father.

We hope to find letters from you, when we reach Copenhagen. It is very long since we heard. I have received no letter, except from Mother. I write as often as an opportunity presents itself.

I have not yet fully determined where we shall pass the Winter — that is in what part of Germany. I am hesitating between Berlin and Bonn on the Rhine. We shall remain in Copenhagen about a month; and in all probability shall not return thither again.

Affectionately yours

Henry W. Longw.

MANUSCRIPT: Longfellow Trust Collection. ADDRESS: Stephen Longfellow Esq/ Portland Me/Fav[ore]d by Capt. Condry/Ship Tasso POSTMARKS: BOSTON MS OCT 19/SHIP ENDORSEMENT: H. W. Longfellow/Gothenburg Sept 3. 1835/Recd. Octr. 20. PUBLISHED: *Longfellow and Scandinavia*, pp. 156–158.

1. Baltzar Bogislaus von Platen (1766–1829), the Swedish admiral, and Thomas Telford (1757–1834), a Scottish engineer, superintended the construction of the Göta Canal. It was completed in 1832.

2. Mary Potter Longfellow interrupted at this point with a postscript: "No — — only a note and package by the Talma. I sent a letter to Father by the post the day before we left Stockholm; should write now, but we are in great haste as we leave Gothenburg in a few hours. I shall write when we reach Copenhagen. I have not yet received the letter sent from Boston directly to Sweden, and fear now, it will never reach me. With much respect and love and many kind wishes to all my friends/I remain as ever/Your affectionate/Mary —"

3. This letter is unrecovered.

4. Olof Wijk (1786–1856), a well-known merchant and politician, entertained the Longfellows on several occasions during their week in Gothenburg.

5. Capt. Dennis Condry (1794–1876) of Newburyport, Massachusetts.

322. *To Richard Bentley*

Copenhagen   September 13. 1835

Dear Sir,

I am sorry that no opportunity has yet presented itself, by which you can send me a copy of Outre Mer. The friends, whom I expected in Sweden during the summer, and who promised to take charge of any package for me from London, seem all to have turned their backs upon the North, and taken flight southward. So that I have been disappointed; and have not yet seen a copy of my book, nor heard what success or want of success it has had.

I am now on my way to Holland. Would you have the goodness to send a few copies — together with any notices which may have appeared — to the care of some book-seller in Rotterdam. They can go by the steam boat without much expense. And please write me a line by mail, care of John Hodshon & Son Amsterdam — informing me where to go for the books in Rotterdam.

Can you find time to do all this?

Very respectfully yr. Obt. Ser[v]t.
Henry W. Longfellow

Richard Bentley Esq.

MANUSCRIPT: Clifton Waller Barrett Collection, University of Virginia. ADDRESS: To/Richard Bentley Esqr./8 New Burlington St./London POSTMARKS: PORTSMOUTH SE 20 1835/F SE 21 1835

323. *To George Washington Pierce*

Copenhagen   September 20. 1835

My dear George,

Your very acceptable letter of June 30, did not reach me till day before yesterday; and yet it was the second I have received since I left home; a fact worth noting down in your journal. The puffs you sent were quite luxuriant; yet not to be compared with the *palmy exuberance* of the London press. Take the following "beautiful morceau" as a sample.

"— The scenes among which our traveller loves to linger are the gothic temple, the neglected, the deserted or the ruined castle, and the softer kind of landscape. His favorite stories are the humorous, with a touch of the satirical, or *the elegantly pensive* — MELANCHOLY, YET NOT DESPAIRING! (O Cockney!) Either the author of the Sketch Book has received a warning, or there are two Richmonds in the field."

If you do not laugh heartily at this, I shall feel hurt. Notwithstanding all this, I believe the book is doing well in London; but having received no exact intelligence from the publisher, I cannot speak with certainty. I have not even seen a London copy.

Mr. Woodside our new Chargé at this court arrived a few weeks ago. He *means* well;

> But isn't it a pity, such a pretty man as he
> Should harness plural nouns, when he talks in companie,
> With verbs *as what is* singular, and therefore dont agree,
> According to the latest rules laid down in Grammarie.

He is a brisk little man, about forty; either a bachelor, or a widower, or has run away from his wife; which of the three he has not vouchsafed to inform me. He does not seem to like Copenhagen very much; and thinks he shall soon get tired of an idle life. He is from Ohio.[1] If you were in his place I should stay here all Winter; so much am I delighted with Copenhagen. As you are *not*; we shall leave town next Thursday (24th.) for Hamburg, via Kiel.

Now let me answer your letter. Shall I go to Paris before I return? Yes, that I shall. So, you have only to transmit your money to Baring & brothers; and your list of books, and they shall be bought.

Lucky dog! to have gone into the land speculations, under the wing of a Knowing one! I hope you may be a rich man by the time I return. With this pleasant expectation before me, I shall be gratified to exhume your Uncle at Munich,[2] as my winter quarters will not be far therefrom.

You mention [James] Brooks of the Advertiser. He appeared suddenly in London one afternoon, looking very *foxy* indeed. You would have been tickled to see him parading through Bond Street, with *dandy* [Nathaniel Parker] Willis on one side, and the meek Gorham Abbot on the other.[3] He sported buckskin boots, and carried in his hat, a bandanna handkerchief and the Eastern mail. His plans of travel were of the *intense* order, like his style of writing; for he was going "from St. Petersburg to Constantinople, from the Baltic to the Balkan, from the frozen regions of the North to the burning luxuriance of the South." What the deuce has become of him with all this *sail*, I cannot conjecture and dare not surmise. At the rate he was going when I saw him last he is probably somewhere in the Carpathian mountains, by this time.

I have heard of Forrest,[4] but have not met him. When we were in Stockholm, we understood he was directing his steps thitherward. But he did not make his appearance.

As this letter, though short, is full of privacy and scandal, I trust you will not let it fall into the hands of anyone, who would make an improper use of what it contains. Read it to Pitt [Fessenden]; and tell him to take it as a letter to himself. I have no time to write, being very busy — *very*. And tell him, furthermore, that I am pleased with his favorite *"Ancient Scandinavian."*[5]

I have changed my plans for the Winter. Instead of going to Berlin, I shall go to Heidelberg on the Neckar, in the South of Germany; for many reasons, which I will explain when I get home — perhaps.[6] There I shall pass the winter. We shall probably take the steamer from Hamburgh to Amsterdam; and again from Rotterdam up the Rhine to Manheim. As my stay here is short, I have my hands full; — examining Libraries — buying books, and trying to find out what is "rotten in the State of Denmark."

Love to all.

Truly your *"elegantly pensive"* friend,

Henry W. Longw.

N.B. With this same date I write to my Father.

MANUSCRIPT: Longfellow Trust Collection. ADDRESS: To/Geo. W. Pierce Esqr/ Portland. POSTMARKS: NEW YORK DEC 5/SHIP ANNOTATION ON COVER (*by Longfellow*): Sept. 28. Two letters to my Father by this ship.[7] PUBLISHED: *Longfellow and Scandinavia*, pp. 158–160.

1. Jonathan F. Woodside (1799–1845), an Ohio lawyer and Democratic politician, had just been appointed American chargé d'affaires to Denmark. He served until 1841.

2. Presumably Benjamin Thompson, Count Rumford (1753–1814), half-brother of Pierce's father. Longfellow tried to obtain information about him on May 1, 1836, in Heidelberg. See the *Diary of Clara Crowninshield*, p. 236.

3. Rev. Gorham Dummer Abbott (1807–1874) was a member of the Bowdoin class of 1826.

4. Presumably Edwin Forrest (1806–1872), the American actor, who was in Europe at this time.

5. The allusion is vague. It may refer to Peder Pedersen (1774–1851), a former Danish consul and chargé d'affaires in Philadelphia and Washington, whom Longfellow had met on September 14.

6. One reason, and perhaps the principal one although not mentioned until later, was his wife's pregnancy. Longfellow wished for her sake to avoid overland travel; and most of the journey to Heidelberg could be made by boat. For his other reasons, see Letter No. 331.

7. Longfellow refers to Letter No. 324 and to the letter from Mary Potter Longfellow to Stephen Longfellow, September 21. See his annotation on the cover of Letter No. 324 and his postscript to his wife's letter (No. 329).

324. *To Stephen Longfellow*

Copenhagen   September 20. 1835

My dear Father,

On the 3d[1] of this month I wrote you a few lines from Gothenburg, by the ship Tasso, Captain Condry, which letter I hope you will have received before this reaches you. By the same opportunity Mary wrote to her father.

Two days ago we received the package of letters, which was to have been sent by Wm. Goddard;[2] containing letters from Mother, George Pierce and Anne, and Eliza Potter. I was sorry to have no letter from you; and still more sorry to hear that you have been so unwell. I hope and trust, that the contemplated journey was not abandoned, but that you returned from it quite renovated. But alas! this can only be for a season; unless you will give up the Law into younger hands; and I hope you will delay no longer. Do think of Cambridge, or of Brooklyn [Brookline]. You could live so quietly there — it would be so much pleasanter than Gorham. Do think of this, I beseech you.

With Copenhagen I am much delighted. It is a finely-built city, — with spacious streets and handsome houses. In parts, however, it has a desolate look; there is a marble church, left half-built — and now falling to decay — and they will get quite a crop of grass this year from the great paved square in front of the King's palace. But other quarters of the city are more lively. Then there is a Library of 400,000 volumes — a crowd of literary men, and a great deal of mental activity. I brought letters to Molbech, Thomsen, Rafn, and Finn Mágnusen.[3] A word or two of each.

Molbech is one of the Librarians of the Royal Library. He is a little, awkward man, "without form and void"[4] — with an enormous head, and lobster eyes. He is a philologist, a maker of Dictionaries, and a compiler of Anthologies &c. &c.

Thomsen has charge of the Cabinet of Northern Antiquities. A gigantic man, with coal-black hair and eyes — and a long-waisted snuff-colored coat. He is learned in antiquarian lore, and takes delight in expatiating on the age of an old rusty nail, or bit of broken glass, dug up in some out-of-the-way corner of the earth.

Rafn is an Historian and publisher of old Icelandic books, which he transcribes from the M.S.S. of which the libraries are full. A tall, thin man — with white hair, or rather bristles, standing out in all directions, like a brush; added to which his eyes are always staring wide, so that he looks like the picture of a man who sees a ghost. He is, however, a very, friendly, pleasant man, and gives me lessons in Icelandic.

Finn Mágnusen is one of the great scholars of the North; an Icelander by birth, and learned in the literature, language and antiquities of his native island. A man of medium stature, high cheek bones, and a tawny skin. He resembles the Laplanders we see in picture books.

I have given up the plan of passing the winter in Berlin. I prefer some place upon or near the Rhine, both on account of climate and expense. Heidelberg on the Neckar, a few miles from Manheim, will probably be the place. We leave here on Thursday next (24) for Hamburgh. Thence take the steamer for Amsterdam, cross to Rotterdam, and take a steamer again up the Rhine to Manheim.

September 29. Hamburg.

We left Copenhagen on the 24eve — reached Kiel the next day in the afternoon, and passed Saturday the 26th there. It is a lively little place of some 12,000 inhabitants with charming environs. It is likewise the seat of a German University, with about 300 students and a Library of 70.000 vols. I saw some of the Professors, who were very polite as Professors always are.[5]

From Kiel to Hamburg the road is most excellent. Macadamised and as level as a floor. Distance fifty English miles. Country flat and rather uninteresting. So — we are safe in Hamburg once more. The weather delightful in the morning — clear and bright — and just warm enough for travelling. We start tomorrow in the steamer for Amsterdam, and shall go up the Rhine just in the vintage time. We go through Holland, because it will be less fatiguing and less expensive — as we have much luggage.

I must not forget to tell you, that in Copenhagen I was made a member of the Northern Antiquarian Society, whose object is the cultivation of the ancient Literature of the North.[6]

Farewell. We hope to find letters from you at Amsterdam. I fear that some of mine have miscarried. I wrote you twice from London, informing you in the last, that I had recd. the money from Blackmore for the Beckets — £23.6.8. Twenty three pounds, six shillings and eight pence.[7]

Since then I have written every month — sometimes twice a month. Long passages have perhaps prevented you from receiving these letters regularly. With much love to all, very affectionately yrs.

Henry W. Longfellow.

MANUSCRIPT: Longfellow Trust Collection. ADDRESS: Hon. Stephen Longfellow/ Portland./Maine POSTMARKS: NEW YORK DEC 5/SHIP ANNOTATION ON COVER (*by Longfellow*): September 28. A double letter to you, by the same ship that brings you this. A letter to George by same. ENDORSEMENT: H. W. Longfellow to his father/Sept 20 and 29. 1835/[Received] Decr. 15 — PUBLISHED: *Longfellow and Scandinavia*, pp. 160–161.

1. The date is added in pencil.

2. William Warren Goddard (b. 1812), the brother of Mary C. Goddard, their traveling companion, was to have met the party in Copenhagen. An injury to his hand had delayed his sailing for Europe, and the death of his father shortly afterwards prevented it entirely. See the *Diary of Clara Crowninshield*, p. 115, and Letter No. 326.

3. Christian Molbech (1783–1857), First Secretary of the Royal Library; Christian Jürgensen Thomsen (1788–1865), director of the Oldnordisk Museum; Carl Christian Rafn (1795–1864), secretary of the Royal Society of Northern Antiquaries; and Finn Magnusen (1781–1847), professor of Old Norse literature and mythology at the University of Copenhagen.

4. Gen. 1:2.

5. In his journal entry for September 26 Longfellow identified these professors as Niels Nikolaus Falck (1784–1850), professor of law, and Kristian Flor (1792–1875), professor of the Danish language and literature. He also called upon the librarian of the University of Kiel.

6. Longfellow was formally elected to membership in the Nordiska Oldskriftssel-skab (Royal Society of Northern Antiquaries) on October 24, 1835. His certificate of membership is preserved in the files of the Longfellow Trust Collection. See *Longfellow and Scandinavia*, pp. 24–25.

7. See 308.1.

325. *To James Fenimore Cooper*

Copenhagen   September 23. 1835

Dear Sir,

During my residence in this city, I have become acquainted with a Mr. Riise, a "worthy Dane," who has translated many of your Romances into his mother-tongue.[1] He has expressed to me a wish to forward a copy of some of them to you; and I have taken charge of the package. It will be sent in a box of books for Harvard University, and I shall request the Librarian, Dr. Harris, to send you the package by the earliest opportunity.

I cannot forbear expressing to you the pride I have felt as an American in finding your honorable fame so wide-spread through the North — in Denmark, Norway and Sweden. You have struck a chord, which thrills rapturously in the hearts of these descendants of the ancient Sea-Kings; and Riise tells me, that in Denmark your writings are more read than those of Scott; and not only read in the city, but among the peasantry of the land. This is true, substantial fame. God grant that you may long enjoy it!

Pray excuse the liberty, which a stranger takes in thus addressing you. I should not intrude upon you, were it not for the very natural wish, which Mr. Riise has expressed, and which I have promised him to execute.

I have the honor to be

Very respectfully yours
Henry W. Longfellow.

MANUSCRIPT: Paul Fenimore Cooper, Cooperstown, New York. ADDRESS: To/J. Fenimore Cooper Esq/New York. PUBLISHED: *Correspondence of James Fenimore Cooper*, ed. J. F. Cooper (New Haven, 1922), I, 352–353.

1. Jacob Riise (1791–1872), an antiquarian book-dealer, helped Longfellow select Danish books for his personal library and for Harvard. For Longfellow's copies of his Cooper translations, see *Longfellow and Scandinavia*, p. 171.

326. *To David Erskine*

Copenhagen   Sept. 23. 1835

My dear Sir,

We leave this city tomorrow for Kiel; but before we go I must seize a moment to thank you for your kindness in forwarding a package of letters which reached you after we left Stockholm. These letters brought us very melancholy news; — nothing less than tidings of the sudden death of Mr. Wm. Goddard of Boston — *our* Miss Goddard's father. In consequence of this Miss. G. left us; and went under Mr. Appleton's[1] charge to London. We have just had a letter from her. She embarked for New York on the 20th (last Sunday) in the Ship Philadelphia, Capt. Morgan. She was so much afflicted at the news of her father's death, that she would not listen to any entreaties to stay in Europe, even until the Spring. Under these circumstances, Mr Appleton's presence was very fortunate.

In her letter she says that Mr. Wiggin had forwarded another package of letters to Stockholm; which be it said in parenthesis, was very stupid on his part, as I wrote to him not to send any after the 15th. Miss. G. is very anxious to get these letters. I suppose they must have gone to Kantzow's[2] care. Would you do us the favor to get them from him; and forward them to me, care of John Hodshon & Son Amsterdam?

By this direction you will see that we have changed our route. We shall not go to Berlin; but shall pass the winter at Heidelberg on the Neckar.

Have the goodness to transmit all accounts of postages, which are due to you from us, — to Barings & co and excuse the trouble we give you.

Mrs L. and Miss. C. join me in the kindest regards to your family and to the Stokoes.

In great haste, very truly yours
Henry W. Longfellow

MANUSCRIPT: Royal Library, Stockholm. ADDRESS: Mr. David Erskine/Stockholm ENDORSEMENT: 1835. Hy. W. Longfellow/Copenhagen 23d. Septr/Recd. 29 do./Answd. PUBLISHED: Paul Elmen, "A New Longfellow Letter," *American Literature*, XXV (January 1954), 498–499.

1. John James Appleton (1792–1864) served twice as American chargé d'affaires to Sweden, 1826–1830 and 1833–1834. Longfellow had met him in Stockholm.
2. Baron Johan Albert Kantzow (1788–1868), a partner in the merchant firm of Kantzow & Biel, had been Longfellow's banker in Stockholm.

327. *To Carl Christian Rafn*

[Copenhagen] Wednesday eve[nin]g   Sept 23. 1835

Dear Sir,

Inclosed is my answer to your letter, as Secretary of the Nordiske Oldskrift Selskab; and I take this opportunity to thank you once more for the great kindness you have shown me during my short stay in your city, and to express the hope that it may be in my power to return here again before leaving Europe.

There is no doubt that I shall pass the winter in Heidelberg. Should I determine otherwise on reaching Germany, I will take the liberty of writing you a line.

With much esteem,

very respectfully yours
Henry W. Longfellow

MANUSCRIPT: Royal Library, Copenhagen. PUBLISHED: Allen Wilson Porterfield, "Eight Unpublished Letters of Longfellow," *Scandinavian Studies and Notes*, V (1918–1919), 171.

328. *To Carl Christian Rafn*

Copenhagen   Sept. 23. 1835.

Sir,

I have had the honor of receiving this evening a letter from you as Secretary of the Royal Society of Northern Antiquaries, informing me that the managing Committee have kindly expressed a wish to nominate me as a Member, at their next meeting &c.

Have the goodness to express to the gentlemen of the Committee the high sense I entertain of the honor done me, and assure them that I embrace with eagerness the opportunity now offered me of becoming a member of their learned body.

Your Obt. Ser[v]t.
Henry Wadsworth Longfellow

Professor of Belles Lettres in Harvard University, Cambridge, United States of America

MANUSCRIPT: Royal Society of Northern Antiquaries, Copenhagen.

329. *To Stephen Longfellow*

[Copenhagen, September 21, 1835]

September 28. I have written by the same ship that brings you this. H.W.L. Also a letter to George [Pierce].[1]

MANUSCRIPT: unrecovered; text from Higginson, *Longfellow*, p. 99.

1. This is a postscript on the outside of a letter from Mary Potter Longfellow to Stephen Longfellow, September 21, 1835. Longfellow refers to Letters No. 321 and 322.

330. *To William Warren Goddard*

Rotterdam   October 23rd. 1835

My dear Sir,

I have taken the liberty to send to your care, by the Brig Hollander, Capt. Kelly — which sails from this port in a few days — two boxes of books. As a declaration of the number of volumes goes with the boxes, I presume they will not be opened at the Custom house. In case they should be opened, and the vols. counted — they will find some thirty vols. more than in the declaration. These extra vols. belong to Harvard College, and of course pay no duties; so that the custom house officers may be satisfied, that no deception was intended. Most of the books are Dutch, and will therefore pay but 4 cents pr. vol. There are however 2 large folio English books — but they were printed before 1775 — and consequently do not go by weight — but at the same rate with the Dutch books. On that account I have let them all pass as Dutch books in the Invoice.

In box No. 2. you will find 4 work-boxes, — one of which is for your sister Mary; and contains a letter for her. Three other letters — two of them from America — the other from Clara [Crowinshield] — I shall send by the way of London, and by the same post that takes this.[1] With regard to the books — will you have the goodness to put them in some snug corner of your countinghouse — where they will be safe and *dry* until my return?

We are very anxious to hear of Mary's safe arrival. She was so much afflicted by the melancholy news we received at Copenhagen, and expressed so strong a desire to return home, that I could not advise her to act otherwise than her heart prompted her. Under Mr. Appleton's charge she went safely to London; — and I doubt not has reached you in safety. Under the present afflicting circumstances, I feel, that she is infinitely happier with her mother, than she could have been with us, and that had she remained in Europe, the winter would have been inexpressibly gloomy to her. Besides, it must be a great consolation to you all, to have her with you.

Present our kindest remembrances to your mother, Mary and Lucy;[2] and excuse the trouble I give you about the books.

Very truly your friend
Henry W. Longfellow.

MANUSCRIPT: Clifton Waller Barrett Collection, University of Virginia.   ADDRESS. To/Mr. William W. Goddard/Boston./United States./America.   POSTMARKS: NEW-YORK DEC 24/SHIP/Forwarded by THOS CARDWELL, Jun. LIVERPOOL.

1. Longfellow's footnote at this point: "Since writing this, I have heard of a

direct opportunity from this place to Boston; I shall therefore send Mary's letters by the galliot Concordia, Capt. Eddes." For Capt. Eddes, see 331.9.

2. Lucy was presumably Mary Goddard's sister.

331. *To Stephen Longfellow*

Rotterdam. October. 25. 1835.

My dear Father,

On the 20. September I wrote you from Copenhagen, and at the same time wrote to George [Pierce]. Both these letters were sent a few days afterwards from Hamburg, together with Extracts from Journal, which Mary copied and sent for your amusement.[1] Have these arrived safe?

From Hamburg we took the steamboat for Amsterdam, having as I mentioned in my last, relinquished the idea of passing the winter at Berlin. My reasons were, 1. that Berlin is a very unpleasant city, compared with most of the German cities; 2. that it is the dearest of them all; and 3rd, that the objects I had in view could be equally well accomplished in some pleasanter and cheaper place. This place is Heidelberg on the Neckar, the seat of an University, and renowned for its beautiful situation.

We have now been a month in Holland. I have been buying books for the College, and studying the Dutch language; — in sound the most disagreeable I remember to have heard; — except the Russian. It is, however, a very important language to me, being of all the modern Gothic tongues, the one which bears the strongest resemblance to the mother-tongue, from which they all come. It has also a strong affinity with our own; as may be seen by the following old saying;

Dutch. Waneer de wyn is in den   *Engl*[*ish*]. Whene'er the wine is
     man.   in the man
     Dan is de wysheid in de   Then is the wisdom in
     kan.   the can.

We made our longest stay in Amsterdam, — circumstances not inclination determining us.[2] Thence passing through Haarlem, Leyden, the Hague, and Delft, to this place. At the Hague we stopped but one day; and am sorry to say did not see any of Marianne's friends, saving the gallant Major Davezac.[3] He was very gracious — even *empressé* [earnest] in his attentions. Marianne's letters which I sent over from London in May, were duly recd. by him and sent to their several addresses. Mr. Grattan[4] is in Brussels; Mr. Money[5] in Heaven, and his wife in Venice. The Major is fat as a brick; but lives in mean lodgings, in a narrow lane, leading out upon a narrow canal. He indulges the hope of being promoted to *Chargé* at Brussels, when Mr. Legaré[6] withdraws, or is withdrawn. He had a great many questions to ask, and a great deal to say about Judge Preble and family — particularly Marianne and *Longfellow.* Then we dug up Christopher Hughes Esq, and picked his bones; during which repast, the Major, while blaming Hughes's egotism, showed a particle thereof himself always *"coming back to his mutton."*[7] He spoke also of the pleasant recollections he retained of Portland — the kind attentions he received there &c. &c. In fine we gossiped an hour or more together. I was pleased with him; for you know he is quite insinuating in his manners; and has a sly way of slipping a compliment into your pocket, without your knowing it; — so that you are constrained to say "the Major *is* a pleasant man." This I must say; — he was more civil and attentive, than either Vale, in London; — Woodside, in Copenhagen, or Hughes, in Stockholm; and I am very sorry, that I could not stay longer at the Hague. I think it a *very* beautiful place; and our lodgings were in the most beautiful part of it, — at the *"Nieuwe Doelen"* — with windows looking out upon the Vijuerburg. The Park, too, is magnificent. Marianne will recollect how quiet and beautiful it is in Autumn — the foliage of the large trees bronzed — not gilded — by sun and wind; the walks all carpeted with yellow leaves, — under the trees all shade; above, all sunshine — and the little blue lake, — and the rustic bridges — and the seats beneath the trees — and the names cut on the bark. Among them all we looked in vain for hers. There were so many, that it was quite impossible to find any particular *one.*

On reaching Rotterdam we found a package of American newspapers and Magazines, sent by [Lewis Gaylord] Clark of New York, which have given us great amusement. But there were no letters from home; and that was a great disappointment to us. Yesterday, however, I had the pleasure of a letter from Wm. Wood, who is now doubtless on his way homeward; and consequently will reach Portland before this letter does. He was in Antwerp, while we were in Amsterdam; I regret extremely that we did not have the pleasure of seeing him. Please remember us to him, and thank him for his very acceptable letter.

About the time that Outre Mer was published in America — a work on the West Indies — with the same title made its appearance in Paris.[8]

There are several vessels here bound for New York and Boston; so that I may possibly write again before leaving Rotterdam. By one of them — the Brig Hollander — I shall send the College books. By the same vessel, that brings you this, Mary writes to her father. She joins me in kindest remembrances to all.

Your affectionate Son
Henry W. Longw.

By the Concordia, Capt. Eddes.[9] for Boston.

MANUSCRIPT: Longfellow Trust Collection. ADDRESS: To/Hon. Stephen Long-fellow/Portland./Maine. POSTMARKS: BOSTON MS JAN 2 [*faint; reading doubtful*]/SHIP   ENDORSEMENT: H W. Longfellow/Recd. Jany 9. 1836/ [Ansd] Feby 14.

1. The extracts have not survived, but the journal belongs to the Longfellow Trust Collection.

2. Longfellow's wife suffered a miscarriage on October 5, five days after their arrival in Amsterdam. Her resulting weakness forced the travelers to remain in the city until the 20th. See the *Diary of Clara Crowninshield*, pp. 136ff.

3. Auguste Geneviève Valentin D'Avezac (1780-1851), the American chargé d'affaires in The Hague.

4. Thomas Colley Grattan (1796-1864), popular novelist and historian, had resided briefly in The Hague in 1830, at which time Marianne Preble Long-fellow had met him. He subsequently served as British consul in Boston. Longfellow wrote a review of his *Highways and Byways* in 1824. See 60.2.

5. In his journal entry for October 22, Longfellow wrote, "Discussed Mr. Grattan — and Mr. Consul Mooney, who lies dead and buried at Venice." There is no record of a Money, or Mooney, in either the British or American consular service in the Netherlands.

6. Hugh Swinton Legaré (1797-1843) had served as chargé d'affaires in Brussels since 1832 and was about to return to the United States. A distinguished lawyer, he later became a member of Congress and Attorney General under Tyler.

7. Longfellow approximates the proverbial phrase "Revenons à ces moutons" from the anonymous fifteenth-century farce *Maistre Pierre Pathelin*.

8. Louis de Maynard de Queilhe, *Outremer* (Paris, 1835), 2 vols.

9. F. Eddes, master of the *Concordia*, was presumably a Dutchman, since *Lloyd's Register* lists his ship as a galiot, 141 tons, of Dordrecht.

332. *To Joseph Bosworth* [1]

[Rotterdam]
Thursday. afternoon. [November 26, 1835]

My dear Sir,

I am glad to say that my wife is better to-day; though on Tuesday evening, after I left you, she seemed to be dying. I think the crisis is now passed, and have strong hopes of her recovery.

I am sorry, that I cannot accept yr. kind invitation for tomorrow evening. I must not yet leave my wife's chamber.

In regard to the Swedish Alphabet, I will not forget yr. request; but I must see you again first, in order to be sure of understanding you.

Can you lend me a Dutch and English Dictionary?
In great haste

very truly yrs.
Henry W. Longfellow

I must not forget to say that we have an excellent Nurse in the Scotch-woman. Many thanks for yr. renewed kindness, and that of Mrs. B. We want nothing at present.

MANUSCRIPT: Boston Public Library. ADDRESS: Revd. Dr. Bosworth

1. Rev. Joseph L. Bosworth (1789–1876), lexicographer and chaplain of the English Church in Rotterdam, had befriended Longfellow by finding an English-speaking nurse for his wife and inviting him to furnish Scandinavian materials for his *Dictionary of the Anglo-Saxon Language* (London, 1838). For Longfellow's contributions, see *Longfellow and Scandinavia*, pp. 30–31 and 77.

333. *To Stephen Longfellow*

Rotterdam   Nov. 26. 1835

My dear Father,

If you received in due season my last, written at this place and sent by the Concordia, — you will be much surprised and justly so, at finding us still here. This detention is much against our will, and the cause of it is one which I am much grieved to mention. Mary has been quite ill; and though convalescent, is not yet well enough to travel. You will find the particulars in a letter, which I shall write to Judge Potter to-day, and send by the same conveyance with this. Some of our plans have thus been retarded, though not thwarted. We still go up the Rhine — either to Bonn or to Heidelberg, I cannot say which.

I have availed myself of this unlooked for opportunity to study the Dutch Language, though as Shylock says it was "not in the bond."[1] This is so much gained; and in consideration thereof, I should not regret the delay, were the cause other than it is.

Some of our letters have been sent forward to Heidelberg. Since we have been here we have received three, all of them for Mary. Two from Margaret, dated Oct. 11 and 28. and one from Judge Potter and Eliza, dated Oct. 16. They came in good season to cheer Mary's drooping spirits.[2] I am glad to hear that you have given up a part at least of your business in Court, and that as the cold weather advances, your health improves. All I now wish is, that you would relinquish all business, and look towards Cambridge — not Gorham — as a home.

My own health is perfectly good. I pass most of the time in reading and writing; having one or two acquaintances here who supply me with books. The days have grown very short, already; it is now but half-past two in the afternoon, and at two yards from the window I can barely see to write. True, the day is overcast. The cold weather has not yet commenced — and with the exception of one or two days, it has not been necessary to put on an overcoat. The only unpleasant thing about it, is the dampness of the atmosphere.

The most agreeable and friendly man I have met here is an English Clergyman, by the name of Bosworth. He is quite advanced in life — and is known in the Literary world by an Anglo-Saxon Grammar. He is now publishing a dictionary of the same language. My other acquaintances are those I meet at table here in the hotel.

Rotterdam is rather a pretty place. The houses are large and many of them fine; and there are public walks along the banks of the river — though at this season the trees are bare and black, and the only green thing about them is the moss on their trunks.

Nov. 28.

I am very much grieved to say, that Mary is not so well to-day. She is extremely feeble; and the physic[i]ans tell me that her situation is dangerous. It is the effect of a miscarriage, which happened some weeks ago, in spite of all our precautions. I hope she may yet revive; but my anxiety is very great; and I write this to prepare your minds for what may happen. She suffers no pain — and is perfectly calm; but does not regain her strength. The energies of her constitution seem to be exhausted. God grant, that she may recover; — but if this be not his will, may we all be resigned to whatever he may ordain.

It is a great consolation to us to have Clara here. She takes the place of a sister — if anyone can fill the place of a sister, — and does all she can to ||aid|| and soothe us.

I have not written to Judge Potter, as mentioned above; but shall write by the next packet. Our love to all.

Very truly and affectionately

Your Son

Henry W. Longfellow

MANUSCRIPT: Longfellow Trust Collection.   ADDRESS: To/Stephen Longfellow Esq/ Portland, Maine./U.S. America/["Baring Brothers & Co *London*" *deleted*]/ *Per* "United States"/["Per Batavier" *deleted*; *ship names in another hand*] POSTMARKS: ROTTERDAM 1 DEC/FPO DE-3 1835/NEW YORK SHIP JAN 12/ FORWARDED BY BARING BROTHERS & CO. London   ENDORSEMENT: H. W. Longfellow/Nov: 26. & 28. 1835/Recd. Jany 15. 1836/[Ansd.] Feby 14.

1. *Merchant of Venice*, IV, i, 261.

2. What Longfellow does not say is that he dared not read the last two letters to his wife at this time because of her extreme debility. He read them to her on November 27 and 28 after it became apparent that she would not live. See the *Diary of Clara Crowninshield*, pp. 179-182, and Letter No. 334.

334. *To Barrett Potter*

Rotterdam, Dec. 1, 1835.

My Dear Sir, —

I trust that my last letter to my father has in some measure prepared your mind for the melancholy intelligence which this will bring to you. Our beloved Mary is no more. She expired on Sunday morning, Nov. 29, without pain or suffering, either of body or mind, and with entire resignation to the will of her heavenly Father. Though her sickness was long, yet I could not bring myself to think it dangerous until near its close. Indeed, I did not abandon all hope of her recovery till within a very few hours of her dissolution, and to me the blow was so sudden, that I have hardly yet recovered energy enough to write you the particulars of this solemn and mournful event. When I think, however, upon the goodness and purity of her life, and the holy and peaceful death she died, I feel great consolation in my bereavement, and can say, "Father, thy will be done."

Knowing the delicate state of Mary's health, I came all the way from Stockholm with fear and trembling, and with the exception of one day's ride from Kiel to Hamburg we came the whole distance by water. Unfortunately our passage from Hamburg to Amsterdam in the Steamboat was rather rough, and Mary was quite unwell. On the night of our arrival the circumstance occurred to which I alluded in my last,[1] and which has had this fatal termination. . . . In Amsterdam we remained three weeks; and Mary seemed to be quite restored and was anxious to be gone. To avoid a possibility of fatigue we took three days to come to this place — a distance of only forty miles; and on our arrival here Mary was in excellent spirits and to all appearances very well. But alas! the same night she had a relapse which caused extreme debility, with a low fever, and nervous headache. This was on the 23d October. In a day or two she was better, and on the 27th worse again. After this she seemed to recover slowly, and sat up for the first time on the 11th, though only for a short while. This continued for a day or two longer, till she felt well enough to sit up for nearly an hour. And then she was seized with a violent rheumatism, and again took to her bed from which she never more arose.

During all this she was very patient, and generally cheerful, tho' at times her courage fainted and she thought that she should not recover, — wishing only that she could see her friends at home once more before she died. At such moments she loved to repeat these lines, which seemed to soothe her feelings: —

"Father! I thank thee! may no thought
E'er deem thy chastisements severe.
But may this heart, by sorrow taught,
Calm each wild wish, each idle fear." [2]

On Sunday, the 22nd, all her pain had left her, and she said she had not felt so well during her sickness. On this day, too, we received a letter from Margaret [Potter], which gave her great pleasure, and renovated her spirits very much. But still from day to day she gained no strength. In this situation she continued during the whole week — perfectly calm, cheerful and without any pain. On Friday another letter came from Margaret, and she listened to it with greatest delight. A few minutes afterwards a letter from you and Eliza was brought in, which I reserved for the next day. When I went to her on Saturday morning I found her countenance much changed, and my heart sank within me. Till this moment I had indulged the most sanguine hopes; — but now my fears overmastered them. She was evidently worse, though she felt as well as usual. The day passed without change; and towards evening, as she seemed a little restless and could not sleep, I sat down by her bedside, and read your letter and Eliza's to her. O, I shall never forget how her eyes and her whole countenance brightened, and with what a heavenly smile she looked up into my face as I read. My own hopes revived again to see that look; but alas! this was the last gleam of the dying lamp. Towards ten o'clock she felt a slight oppression in the chest, with a difficulty of breathing. I sat down by her side and tried to cheer her; and as her respiration became more difficult, she said to me, "Why should I be troubled; If I die God will take me to himself." And from this moment she was perfectly calm, excepting for a single instant, when she exclaimed, "O, my dear Father; how he will mourn for me." A short time afterwards she thanked Clara for her kindness, and clasping her arms affectionately round my neck, kissed me, and said, "Dear Henry, do not forget me!" and after this, "Tell my dear friends at home that I thought of them at the last hour." I then read to her from the Church Litany the prayers for the sick and dying; and as the nurse spoke of sending for Dr. Bosworth, the Episcopal clergyman, Mary said she should like to see him, and I accordingly sent. He came about one o'clock, but at this time Mary became apparently insensible to what was around her; and at half-past one she ceased to breathe.

Thus all the hopes I had so fondly cherished of returning home with my dear Mary in happiness and renovated health have in the providence of God ended in disappointment and sorrow unspeakable. All that I have left to me in my affliction is the memory of her goodness, her gentleness, her affection for me — unchangeable in life and in death — and the hope of meeting her again hereafter, where there shall be no more sickness, nor sorrow, nor suffering, nor death. I feel, too, that she must be infinitely, oh, infinitely happier now than when with us on earth, and I say to myself, —

> "Peace! peace! she is not dead, she does not sleep!
> She has awakened from the dream of life."[3]

With my most affectionate remembrance to Eliza and Margaret, and my warmest sympathies with you all,

very truly yours,
Henry W. Longfellow.

MANUSCRIPT: unrecovered; text from Higginson, *Longfellow*, pp. 107–111.

1. Longfellow is not accurate here; see 331.2.
2. Andrews Norton, "Trust and Submission," stanza 1.
3. Cf. Shelley, *Adonais*, stanza xxxix, lines 343–344.

335. *To William Warren Goddard*

Friday   December 4. 1835 — On board the steamer
from Rotterdam to Cologne, on the Rhine.

My dear Sir,

I write you these few lines to communicate to you and to my other friends in Boston the mournful intelligence of my dear Mary's death. She expired on Sunday morning Nov. 29. at Rotterdam, in peace and perfect resignation; in her death as in her life mindful more of others than herself, and saying, among the latest words she uttered, "Tell my dear friends at home, that I thought of them at the last hour." Her death was occasioned by extreme debility — the effect of a *miscarriage*, which took place in Amsterdam, on the 1st of October. Three weeks afterwards, on reaching Rotterdam, she had a relapse, which has terminated fatally. For the particulars of her sickness and death, I refer you to my letter to her father, and to Clara's letters.

I have had her body embalmed — inclosed in a leaden coffin, and that again in an oaken one — and the whole put into a case, and directed to yr. care. It will leave Rotterdam on Wednesday next, by the *Brig Elizabeth*, Capt. Long. Have the goodness to pay the charges; and to have the body deposited, *encased as it now is*, in the *Tomb of the Mount Auburn Cemetery*. I have heard there is such a tomb for the safe-keeping of bodies, until such a time as preparations for their final burial can be made. On my return I shall purchase a spot in Mount Auburn for a tomb. Let me hear by letter of the safe arrival of the body. By the same vessel I send two trunks containing her clothes; and some things of my own. I do not wish these to be opened until my return, unless it be necessary to open them at the Custom house, which I can hardly think will be the case, under the present circumstances. If it is thought necessary, you will find the key of the large trunk tied to one of the handles; the small trunk is not locked. Have the kindness to take charge of these, until I return to Boston. I do not wish to have them sent to Portland.

This affliction has been very sudden and unexpected to me. Till the last day — and almost till the last hour I cheered myself with vain hopes. And even now I ask myself if it can indeed be true, that she is dead. It seems to me as if we were separated but for a short season, and were soon to meet again. Indeed, I know and feel that such is the case. It gives me a melancholy pleasure to recall the goodness of her life and the calmness of her death; and to think that she is far happier now than we, who have been left behind her. So that I do not mourn as those who are without hope; but think of those words, which *she* loved to repeat in her last sickness;

> "Father! I thank thee! May no thought
> E'er deem thy chastisements severe;
> But may this heart, by sorrow taught,
> Calm each wild wish — each idle fear." [1]

With my affectionate regards to all, I remain

Very truly yr. friend
Henry W. Longfellow

MANUSCRIPT: Clifton Waller Barrett Collection, University of Virginia. ADDRESS: To/Mr. Wm. W. Goddard/(Late Wm. Goddard & Son)/Boston,/America./ Baring, Brothers &co/["London" *deleted*]   POSTMARKS: COBLENZ 5–6 $\frac{8}{12}$ /FPO DE 14 1835/NEW-YORK SHIP JAN 1‖2?‖/FRANCO   POSTAL ANNOTATION (*in another hand*): *Per* S. America   ENDORSEMENT: Henry W. Longfellow/ Cologne Decr. 4th. 1835

1. See 334.2.

336. *To George Ticknor*

Heidelberg. Dec 19. 1835

My dear Sir,

I write you a few words, to inform you of my arrival in Germany, and of the great affliction I am in. My wife is dead; and could you feel the unspeakable anguish it gives a man to write these words I am sure you would excuse me from saying anything more, than this. She expired with perfect calmness and resignation, three weeks ago this night, at Rotterdam after an illness of two months, — occasioned by a miscarriage. I had no idea before, that death could be so divested of all terror; and in my bereavement I have the consolation of feeling, that she is now beyond the reach of all sorrow and sickness, and can say to myself with some degree of composure,

"Peace! peace! She is not dead! she does not sleep!
She has awakened from the dream of life." [1]

It was in part on account of the feebleness of my wife's health, that when in Copenhagen in September last, I abandoned the idea of passing the winter in Berlin, and fixed upon this place as being more to the South and in the immediate neighborhood of the Springs of Nassau, to which I intended to go as early next summer, as circumstances would permit. We accordingly ordered our letters to be sent here, and came through Hamburg to Amsterdam by the Steam boats; and on leaving Holland, I felt a disinclination to go elsewhere, than to this place.

Have you been in Heidelberg? It is one of the most beautiful places I ever beheld. The ruins of the old castle, and the valley of the Neckar below remind me constantly of the Alhambra and the valley of the Darro. I have been lucky enough to obtain lodgings, which command the finest points of view. The prospect from my windows is magnificent. Miss Crowninshield has come thus far with me, and is in a German family. Miss Goddard has returned home on account of her father's death.

I heard of you from Schlegel in Bonn;[2] and since my arrival here Mr. Oppenheimer[3] has informed me of your being in Dresden. I should have written you sooner, but I have been here but a single week, and have been very much occupied in making arrangements, first for Miss. C. and then for myself.

I must not forget to mention that Bryant is here with his family; a very pleasant circumstance.[4] By the way, have you heard anything of my friend G. W. Greene? He is somewhere in Europe, and I am inclined to think in Germany, tho' I know not where. If you know anything of his movements I wish you would inform me of them.[5]

With my best regards to Mrs. Ticknor,

Very truly yours
Henry W. Longfellow

You have of course heard that the North American Review has passed into Palfrey's hands.[6]

Have you heard anything from Dr. Bode? Is he going to Cambridge?

MANUSCRIPT: Dartmouth College Library. ADDRESS: à Monsieur/Monsieur le Professeur Ticknor/aux soins de Messrs. Bassange & cie/à *Dresde* POST-MARKS: HEIDELBERG 21 DEC 1835/ST. POST 24 DEC N.4U.

1. See 334.3.

2. Augustus Wilhelm von Schlegel, the critic, was a professor at Bonn. Longfellow had called on him on December 7.

3. George Oppenheimer, a former Bond Street merchant and father-in-law of Francis Lieber, the publicist, had retired to his native Germany, where he died in 1837.

4. William Cullen Bryant, his wife, and two daughters, had arrived in Heidelberg a few weeks before Longfellow and Clara Crowninshield, intending to spend the winter there.

5. Greene had left America in August and was by this time established in Florence.

6. Rev. John Gorham Palfrey (1796–1881), professor of sacred literature at Harvard, served as editor of the *North American Review*, 1835–1843. See Letter No. 339.

337. *To Carl Christian Rafn*

Heidelberg. Dec. 23. 1835

Dear Sir,

Having been delayed in my journey to this place for two whole months by the illness of my wife in Holland, your friendly letter of Nov. 26. did not reach me till a few days since, when I received it from Professor Schlosser.[1] This will explain to you, why I have not sent you a more speedy reply.

The Diploma of the Royal Society of Antiquaries came safely; and I beg you to return my thanks to them for the honor they have done me, assuring them that I shall do all in my power to make the Literature of the North better known to my countrymen, on the other side of the Atlantic.

In reply to the questions you ask concerning the Indians of Massachusetts, Rhode Island and Connecticut, I can give you but vague and unsatisfactory information, it being a subject to which I have never given any particular attention.

1. Much information may still be gathered concerning the state of these Indians, though scattered through many volumes. These I have not the means of pointing out to you at the present moment; you can however easily obtain what you want on this head from a gentleman whom I shall presently name. On an island in Buzzards Bay, in the

South Eastern part of Massachusetts, still exists a small remnant of a tribe called the *Marshpee* Indians. Not many years ago, there was also a remnant of a tribe in *Stockbridge*, in the North west corner of the state. But they migrated westward to the Oneida Indians in the State of New York, and afterwards still farther west to Green Bay in the North West. Territory. They had with them an American by name *John Sargent* as their interpreter. I believe he is still living.[2]

2. 3. 4. On the subject of the Indian Languages I can say nothing. I am not acquainted with them. But I refer you to *John Pickering Esq* of Boston, as a gentleman both able and willing to give you information on all points relating to Indian History and Language.[3] He probably can tell you more about *John Sargent*.

In regard to the Indians of the South and West much information may be found in

Heckewalder's Account of the Indians, and residence among them. Tanner's Narrative of Residence among the Indians.[4]

The *Hon. Lewis Cass*, present Secretary of War, at Washington, can also give you information on this head. In the *North American Review*, about the year 1825, a paper or two from his hand may be found.[5]

Are you aware that among the Cherokees of Georgia a Newspaper is published in their Language? It is edited by the Rev. Mr. Boudinot, and called the Cherokee Phœnix.[6]

As to the list of names, which I here return as you requested, I agree with you in supposing them all Indian. But upon this point I am no authority.

Since I left you a great change has taken place in my situation. After an illness of two months my wife died in Rotterdam on the 29th November last. I have also received intelligence from home of the death of my brother-in-law, and very dear friend.[7] These circumstances will probably hasten my return; so that I fear I shall not have the pleasure of seeing you again in Copenhagen.

Have the goodness to present my respects and remembrance to your friend and fellow-laborer Finn Magnusen and believe me,

With the highest regard, yours
Henry W. Longfellow

MANUSCRIPT: Royal Library, Copenhagen. ADDRESS: à Monsieur/Monsieur le professeur C.C. Rafn/Kronprindsensgade No. 40./à Copenhague. POST-MARKS: HEIDELBERG 25 DEC 1835/T.T. HAMBURG 30. DEC. 35. SEAL: HWL PUBLISHED: Benedict Grøndal, *Breve fra og til Carl Christian Rafn, med en Biographi* (Copenhagen, 1869), pp. 177–179.

1. Friedrich Christoph Schlosser (1776-1861), professor of history at Heidelberg.

2. Longfellow's information is not quite accurate. John Sergeant (1747-1824), a Congregational minister, shared the migration of the Stockbridge Indians to Madison County, New York, where he died among them.

3. Pickering (218.2), "the leading authority of his time on the languages of the North American Indians" (*Dictionary of American Biography*, XIV, 565), was the author of *An Essay on a Uniform Orthography for the Indian Languages of North America* (Cambridge, 1820).

4. *Narrative of the Captivity and Adventures of John Tanner during Thirty Years' Residence among the Indians*. ed. Edwin James, M.D. (New York, 1830). Longfellow had read Heckewelder's book as early as 1823 (see Letter No. 31).

5. *North American Review*, XXII (January 1826), 53-119; XXIV (April 1827), 365-442; and XXVI (April 1828), 357-403.

6. Elias Boudinot (c. 1803-1839), a Cherokee Indian leader, edited the weekly *Cherokee Phoenix* from February 21, 1828, to October 1835. He was assisted by Rev. Samuel A. Worcester, a medical missionary.

7. George Pierce had died of typhus fever on November 15, 1835.

338. *To Carl Christian Rafn*

Heidelberg. Jany. 1. 1836

My dear Sir,

In my last letter I forgot to ask you one important question, and therefore trouble you with the present, by way of postscript to the last. Will you have the goodness to inform me how I shall transmit to you the 150 francs, which the Members of the Northern Society of Antiquaries pay on receiving their diplomas; and whether there are any other expenses.

With the friendly salutations of the season

Very truly yours
Henry W. Longfellow

MANUSCRIPT: Royal Society of Northern Antiquaries, Copenhagen. ADDRESS: Herre Professor Rafn/40 Kronprindsensgade/Copenhagen POSTMARK: T.T. HAMBURG 6. JAN. 36.

339. *To John Gorham Palfrey*

Heidelberg. January 4. 1836.

Dear Sir,

On reaching this city a few days since I had the pleasure of receiving your very friendly letter of October 10. I thank you for bearing me in mind, when the North American Review passed into your hands, and on my return to Cambridge, I shall cordially enter into your views and wishes, so far as my duties in the University give me leisure. Sooner than this it will not be in my power to do anything farther, than collect materials. This I have already done, having in view the North American, in whose welfare and success, I have always felt the most lively interest.

The mournful events of the last few months of my life, — the sickness and death of my wife — sorrow unspeakable — and the loneliness of my situation in a foreign land, at a moment when I need — absolutely *need* the consolations of friendship — have given me a longing desire to be once more at home. And yet the advantages I can derive from a long residence here are so great, and so strong the wish I feel to improve to their full extent the advantages now within my reach, that I think it not impossible I may remain here longer than I originally intended. This will depend much upon my pecuniary resources, which by late events here and at home, have been scattered to the four winds of heaven.[1] At present, all is uncertainty; and this is one reason why I cannot promise to send you any Articles for the Review: for if I must return in the course of a few months, I have not a single moment to employ in anything but the precise object which brought me here.

Will you do me the favor to execute the following commission for me: To request Hilliard & Gray, or any Boston booksellers to procure, and charge to me the following works.

1. The Revised Statutes of Massachusetts.
2. The 10th Report of the Boston Prison Discipline Society.
3. The American Jurist for the year 1835.

These to be sent — with a bill of expenses inclosed, to Professor Mittermaier,[2] Heidelberg; care of Perthes & Basser, *Hamburg,* or of *Heyze,* bookseller, *Bremen,* as occasion may offer. I will give you no farther trouble about the business, than to hand the list of books to some bookseller, with a request, as above.

Wishing you and all my friends in Cambridge a happy New Year,

I am very truly yours
Henry W. Longfellow.

MANUSCRIPT: Harvard College Library. ADDRESS: Rev. John G. Palfrey./Cambridge, Mass./U.S. America./Via Hâvre de Grace/et *New York.* POSTMARKS: NEW-YORK/SHIP/FEB [*date illegible*]/HEIDELBERG 4 ‖JA‖N 18‖3‖6/ALLEMAGNE [*remainder illegible*]/A.E.D. POSTAL ANNOTATION: *franco.*

1. Longfellow alludes not only to the expenses of his wife's last illness but also to the difficulty caused by the death of Mary Goddard's father, who had promised to help him with the cost of the journey. See Letter No. 341.

2. Karl Joseph Anton Mittermaier (1787–1867), professor of law at Heidelberg.

340. *To Joseph Bosworth*

Heidelberg, January 10, 1836

I have a void in my heart — a constant feeling of sorrow and bereavement, and utter loneliness, which deprives me of all mental effort.

At Bonn I had the pleasure of seeing and conversing with Schlegel. He is a very amiable and talkative old gentleman: and withal perhaps a little vain. . .

MANUSCRIPT: unrecovered; text from catalogue of Robert H. Dodd Collection, Anderson Galleries, New York, November 21, 1918.

341. *To Richard Bentley*

Heidelberg. January 10. 1836.

Dear Sir,

I have not had the pleasure of hearing from you since I left London, though I wrote to you both from Stockholm and Copenhagen.[1]

I have seen from time to time the flattering notices of Outre Mer, which have appeared in the London periodicals; and I hope that the success of the work has equalled your expectations.

With me some painful circumstances have occur[r]ed since I saw you. The long illness of my wife, which terminated in death, — and at home the sudden death of the person, upon whom I relied for my travelling expenses[2] — have thrown my financial arrangements into confusion. I mention this, hoping that it may be in your power to send me something from the profits of my book.

Have the goodness to write to me immediately; and if you can send me a copy of Outre Mer, through Perthes & Basser, Hamburg, or by private hand to this place, where I shall remain for some months, I shall be obliged to you.

Respectfully yours
Henry W. Longfellow

Richard Bentley Esq
London

MANUSCRIPT: Clifton Waller Barrett Collection, University of Virginia. ADDRESS: To/Richard Bentley Esq/8 New Burlington St./London. POSTMARKS: HEIDELBERG 10 JAN 1836/FPO JA 18 1836 ENDORSEMENT: Ansd C:O.

1. The letter from Stockholm is unrecovered; for the other, see Letter No. 322.
2. That is, William Goddard, Sr. (see 339.1 and Letter No. 343).

342. *To George Washington Greene*

Heidelberg. Jan 22. 1836.

My dear Greene,

Your letter of Jan. 1. did not reach me till yesterday. I am indeed thankful to hear from you at last; for I began to fear, that I should return home without even hearing in what part of Europe you had taken up your abode. Having heard from Mr. Ticknor a few days since, that your intention was to visit the South of Europe, I wrote immediately to Ombrosi in Florence, to learn if you were there. He has probably shown you the letter; or told you its contents; so that I shall not be the first to communicate to you the most afflicting intelligence of my dear Mary's death. Yes; she is gone to return no more; and all my bright hopes have ended in sorrow unspeakable. She died on the 29th November at Rotterdam from great debility brought on by a miscarriage, which happened in Amsterdam nearly two months before. I little thought, that death could be so stripped of all its terrors. She died as calmly and willingly as if she were but going to sleep. Thus — But I can write no more. The whole scene comes rushing back upon me — and I cannot command my feelings. O, my dear George; what have I not suffered during thes[e] last three months! I am completely crushed to the earth; and I have no friend with me, to cheer and console me. I had indulged the hope, that you were in Germany, and wrote to you at Berlin,[1] thinking it possible you might be there, and that we might pass the Winter together. But that is now impossible. The Alps are between us, and I am neither Hannibal nor Napoleon; and so far as you are concerned the climate of this place would kill you in a week. For my own part, I shall be obliged to remain here till the close of the Summer, when I shall return home, unless some unexpected occurrence enables me to remain longer in Europe. I hope, however, not to go back without seeing you, and if possible I shall make you a visit in the course of the Summer — provided you promise me one of your six rooms in the Via Mazzetta; otherwise, no.

Now let me tell you very briefly, how my time has been passed since leaving home. One month at Sea — one in London — two in Sweden — one in Denmark — two in Holland — and one here. I did not see Nicander; — he left Stockholm for the country a few days before I arrived there. On the whole I was disappointed in this Northern Tour. You will thank me for not going into particulars. It would take the whole sheet, and I have things of more importance to say. We will talk this matter over hereafter. By the way, I wrote you a letter from

Stockholm, which of course you never received, having left America before it could have arrived there.[2]

I am most sincerely grieved to hear the cause of your leaving home. Mr. Ticknor writes me, that [it] is on account of ill-health. What is the matter with you? Recollect I know nothing of this — your letter from Paris never reached me. This last of Jan 1. contains all I know of you for eight months. I hope it is nothing more serious than usual. Be careful. Above all put your heart at ease; and banish that *"corroding ambition"* which you speak of. O I wish I could be with you, speak with [you] for one half-hour. I think I could set that matter in such a point of view, that you would feel the tooth of the destroyer no more. You have a higher and nobler motive of action within you, believe me; tho' I think you are not aware of it, not having reflected much upon this subject, I imagine. Have you? Look into your own heart, and you will find the motive there. It is the love of what is intellectual and beautiful — the love of literature — the love of holding converse with the minds of the great and good — and then speaking the truth in what you write, and thereby exercising a good influence on those around you, bringing them so far as you may, to feel a sympathy with "all that is lovely and of good report."[3] Think of this my dear George, and your heart will be lighter. For my own part, I feel at this moment more than ever, that fame must be looked upon only as an accessary. If it ever has been a principal object with me — which I doubt — it is now no more so. We will speak of this, too, hereafter.

Cortés is in Italy — probably in Florence at this very moment. Do make an effort to see him by sending to the Police Office or the Spanish Minister. Of course, you have heard of the tremendous conflagration in New York?[4]

Since my arrival here I have heard very bad news from home; the death of my brother-in-law and dear friend Geo: W. Pierce. He died of a fever, about the time Mary did. I cling the more closely to the very few friends I have left, and fold you and your beloved wife, in my heart of hearts.

The North American has passed from Everett to Palfrey of Cambridge. I trust it will in future be less political. Why did you not tell me, what subject you had been writing upon? Let me suggest one, which will be very interesting: The Living poets of Italy, with a word about Mathias, who has just gone.[5]

Bryant is here with his family, passing the winter. Miss Crowninshield, our travelling companion in the North, is also here. She will return in the Spring or Summer, with the Bryants, unless she finds a good opportunity of visiting Italy. The other lady who was with us went home from Copenhagen on account of her father's death, which was very sudden.

I rejoice, that you are so quietly and happily situated in Florence. Enjoy all with a good conscience and God's blessing. What other Americans are in Flor[enc]e? I feel so much better in writing to you, that I have a great mind to indulge in another sheet. But no. Good bye. My love to Maria.

Truly your friend
H.W.L.

If you see Cortés, tell him my intention of remaining here, and that he will find a letter from me when he returns to Lucca.[6] Let me know in yr. next, whether you have seen him.

The package you brought from [Lewis Gaylord] Clark and which reached me in Rotterdam, informed me of yr. arrival in Europe.

I cannot give you the No. of my house. It is not necessary. Direct to *Heidelberg*. That will be sufficient.

Write me very soon — immediately — and as I never make any marginal notes in your letters, you need not trouble yourself to leave a margin.

MANUSCRIPT: Longfellow Trust Collection. ADDRESS: All' Illmo. Signore/Il Signor G. W. Greene/Via Mazzetta, 2090./Firenze/*Italia* POSTMARKS: HEIDELBERG 2 IAN 1836/2 FEBBRAIO 1836/CONTRO BOLLO

1. This letter and the letter to Ombrosi, mentioned previously, are unrecovered.
2. Letter No. 318.
3. Cf. Phil. 4:8.
4. The Great Fire of December 16–18, 1835, destroyed property worth some $20,000,000.
5. Thomas James Mathias (1754?–1835), satirist and scholar, had spent the last eighteen years of his life in Italy. "No Englishman, probably, since the days of Milton, had cultivated the Italian language with so much success" (*Annual Register for 1835*).
6. If Longfellow wrote this letter, it is unrecovered.

343. *To Stephen Longfellow*

Heidelberg Jan 24 1836

My dear Father,

It is now two months since I have written you, and yet I have hardly courage to begin this letter. I feel very lonely and dejected, and the recollection of the last three months of my life overwhelms me with unceasing sorrow. Every day makes me more conscious of the loss I have suffered in Mary's death, and when I think how gentle and affectionate, and good she was, every moment of her life — even to the last — and that she will be no more with me in this world — the sense of my bereavement is deep and unutterable.

You can well imagine that it required a great effort for me to discipline my thoughts to regular study. I am doing however all that I can. Fortunately Heidelberg is a very beautiful place; tho' the climate in Winter very disagreeable. The town stands between steep and high mountains on the Neckar, just where the valley, before so narrow, that you can almost throw a stone across, — spreads out trumpet-mouthed into the broad, level plain of the Rhine. The change in the face of the landscape is sudden and beautiful; — no gradual transition, with broken and irregular hills: — but the mountains go down with a grand sweep into the plain. Overlooking the town stand the ruins of a magnificent old castle — the finest I have seen in Europe, excepting the Alhambra. Indeed, the whole scene reminds me [of] Granada, and the valley of the Darro, and is hardly less beautiful.

The University of Heidelberg is celebrated as a Law School; having three very great men in this faculty; Mittermaier, Thibaut, and Zacchariae.[1] Its Literary faculty is null and void; Tho' the Library is large and good, and very rich in old manuscripts. The students are not very numerous — about four hundred, and for the most part rather a swinish multitude. They smoke in the streets, and even in the Lecture rooms. The people in general seem to be rather limited in their notions; and one of the Professors' wives said the other day — that in America, the ladies sit with their feet out of the window!

Mr. Bryant, the poet, who has been here through the winter, leaves town for America tomorrow; affairs of importance requiring his immediate return.[2] His family remains here till Spring; and perhaps will not return until I do in the Summer. It has been fortunate for Clara that they were here on our arrival. She finds their society very pleasant. Clara is in a German family, and I have lodgings in the neighborhood. She will not probably return before Mrs. Bryant does.

Professor Ticknor is in Dresden, but will be here in the Spring on his way to Italy. My friend Greene has established himself in Florence, where he means to remain for some years, in order to reestablish his health, and pursue his Italian Studies, to good advantage.

In future have the goodness to send all letters to the care of Welles &co Place St. George, Paris, directed to this place, where I intend to remain, until I leave Germany. The postage by way of London is very great. By the way — the only letter I have recd. from you is that of Oct. 18. The New Gloucester letter of July never reached me.

Alexander is by this time with you. Tell him to write to me. I should like also to have a letter from Sam at Cambridge.[3] The last letter from Portland was from Judge Potter, Nov. 15. which was answered immediately. Mary's commission about music shall be attended to.

The manner in which Wm. Goddard has slipped out of his father's engagement to me in regard to money, is what I little expected. It is very unfortunate, as my expenses of late have been very great, as you will see by my last letter to Judge Potter.[4] Fortunately living is cheap here, and I shall be able to economize.

The news of George's sickness and death was very sudden and unexpected. I warmly sympathize with you all, and in particular with Anne in this great affliction; and desire most ardently to be with you once more. At most, it will not be long: — only a few months after this letter reaches you. And thus will end a tour which has been productive of very little pleasure and much pain.

I hope the return of cold weather has restored you to at least your customary health, if it has not done much more; and I trust, that the relinquishing of your practice in Court, has been productive of good results. Pray do not go back again to the Law.

With much love to you all, and to Judge Potter and family

Very sincerely yrs. &c &c

H. W. Longfellow

MANUSCRIPT: Longfellow Trust Collection. ADDRESS: To/Stephen Longfellow Esq/Portland/Me./Fav[ore]d by Mr. Bryant. POSTMARK: NEW YORK MAR 28 ENDORSEMENT: H W Longfellow/Heidelberg Jany 24 1836/Recd April 1 —/Ansd: — April 3 —/and June 3d —

1. Anton Friedrich Justus Thibaut (1772–1840) and Karl Salomo Zachariae (1769–1843).
2. The illness of William Leggett, his editorial colleague on the *New York Evening Post*, necessitated Bryant's return.
3. Samuel Longfellow was in his freshman year at Harvard.
4. This letter is unrecovered.

344. *To George Washington Greene*

Heidelberg, February 11, 1836.

. . . Let me persuade you [to write a History of Italian Literature]. Just *this niche* seems to be left in the wall, into which you must put just this statue. The sooner you are about it the better. And here allow me to suggest a plan which I am myself pursuing in collecting and arranging materials for a Literary History of the Middle Ages (which you must remember is a secret, — not the plan, but my proposed work.) I have a blank book, which I divide into centuries. Under each century I write down the names of the authors who then flourished, when they wrote, where their works, or extracts from them, may be found, and what editions are best. This is done in as few words as possible, prose and poetry being separated. At the beginning of the blank book is a list of works cited, the full title being given, with date and form very exact. This saves the trouble of writing and re-writing as you go along. The name standing alone shows that the entire work or poem is to be found on the page noted. When only an extract is given, I say, "Extract," etc. This avoids all confusion. I have already accumulated six centuries of German literature in this way.[1] I hardly know what put this idea into my head; it is one of the most useful that ever found its way thither. The advantages of this plan are obvious. You have thus the whole field of your labor before you. In a moment you can put your finger upon anybody and anything you want. If you think the plan worth adoption, be careful to leave blank pages and spaces enough between the paragraphs for corrections and additions. I am sorry you should feel any misgivings as to your success in the literary world. Believe me, your love for literary labor is a sure guarantee of success. Go on quietly and without anxiety, enjoying the present in the blessing of a mind contented and self-possessed, and you will wake up some morning and find yourself famous, as Byron says he did.[2] All this good advice is sufficiently prosaic, and will remind you of that class of books which goes under the title, "Letters to a Younger Brother," etc., — very didactic and very dull. You must remember I only *suggest plans for your consideration.* I feel a lively interest in your success, and am anxious that you should so commence your Literary History of Italy as to waste no time nor labor. About my proposed visit to Italy I can say nothing now. How ardently I desire such a visit, you can imagine. If the thing is possible, it shall be done. God bless you!

MANUSCRIPT: unrecovered; text from *Life,* I, 226–228.

1. In Letter No. 588 Longfellow mentioned his intention of publishing a "Syllabus of the History of German Literature during the Middle Ages" in the New York *Eclectic Review.* This plan does not seem to have been carried out nor, indeed, did an *Eclectic Review* exist at that time (see 588.2). Greene, however, published a *History and Geography of the Middle Ages* in 1851.

2. In his *Memoranda,* quoted by Thomas Moore in the *Letters and Journals of Lord Byron: with Notices of his Life* (London, 1830), I, 347.

345. *To George Washington Greene*

Heidelberg. March 25 1836

My dear Greene,

If you have been disappointed in not receiving a more speedy answer to your last kind letter, attribute it in a great measure to your cousin Sam Ward,[1] who arrived here a fortnight since and has gone again, directing his face homeward. During his stay here I was a good deal with him; and accompanied him as far as Manheim on his journey towards Paris. He intends to take the Havre packet of the 8th or 16th April, being in haste to reach New York before his father's birth-day. And now you will ask, how I like your cousin. To which question I answer; — there are many things in his character which I prize highly — and some things which I dislike. Foremost among the former are his frankness and his great talent: of the latter nought shall be said at present. He has been passing the winter in Berlin and Dresden, and was intimate at Ticknor's whom he represents as living at ease — in good ardor at the Saxon court, and enjoying himself very highly. Ward tells me that he does not intend to pursue Mathematics as a profession. On his return to New York he goes into his father's counting-house — at which intelligence you will probably say *pish*! He intends, however, to devote his leisure to literary pursuits and has collected materials for writing a history of Mathematics. One thing seems quite evident to me; — and that is, that after four years roving through France and Germany with *carte blanche* as to his expenses — and a *temperament* of at least sixty-horse-power — he is wholly unfitted for going through the drudgery of a Professor's life. You of course know his early history. To use his own more energetic than elegant expression, he was in youth "completely *dunged* with flattery." His Review of Locke is certainly very fine for a boy of seventeen.[2] And so we leave him for the present.

Before answering your letter, let me say a thing or two of minor importance, lest I forget them. The volume of the *Corpus. Poet. Lat.* you need not look for any longer, for you will look in vain. The missing vol. was never published. The work is complete as it is. By strange oversight, the publishers made a mistake in numbering the volumes. So says a German Catalogue on the subject. What does the entire collection of the Italian Classics (Milano 8°) cost? There is a copy of Metastasio for sale here, which I think of buying — large octavo — sixteen vols. (Firenze 1819). What is the price in Florence, unbound?[3]

And now to your letter. Thanks for your kind remembrance of my dear Mary. You knew her well — you know how great my loss is. But alas! you do not know how it has prostrated me. I cannot recover my energies, either mental or bodily. I take no interest in anything — or at most only a momentary interest. All my favorite and cherished literary plans are either abandoned, or looked upon as a task which duty requires me work out, as a day-laborer. Other tastes and projects have begun to spring up in my mind, though as yet all is in confusion. In a word, sometimes I think I am crazed — and then I rally — and think it is only nervous debility; — sometimes I sit at home and read diligently — and then for days together I hardly open a book, but stroll about over hill and dale, and am idle and indolent: — and at all times and in all places I move about among men and things as if invisible, and of course as taking no part in what is going on around me. I do not know as I have expressed myself very intelligibly but I think you will understand me.

Greenough's criticism on your poetry is certainly correct.[4] The figure he finds fault with is not a good one. You *can* make a better; and therefore *will*. I have still more *friendly fault* to find with the piece; and simply this, — the poverty of its rhyme. *Strain* and *again* are repeated twice; — then you have *hour* and *bower,* and *hour* and *power*; — *day* and *gray, ray* and *away*; — and in eight successive lines *thee, tree,* — *thee, memory.* This constant recurrence of the same sounds — and consequent want of richness in cadence injures the piece very much. These are the defects — or rather this is *the* defect which struck me, on first reading the piece; and I think it will strike others. The ear requires greater variety. Am I not right? With this deduction the poem pleases me; and particularly the stanza beginning;

> "I think of thee — not as thou art,
> All chill and cold and silent now."[5]

To come into Italy with Ticknor as you suggest will be quite ||out|| of my power. *If at all* — I cannot come before the month of July or August. My last letters from home urge my return immediately; but I shall not go before Autumn. I must see Switzerland first — and if possible Florence, tho' I cannot promise myself that pleasure with any great hope of seeing the promise fulfilled. If I could stay another winter in Europe there would be no difficulty. But of this there is little hope. I believe I mentioned in my last, that my finances had been thrown into confusion by the death of the person who had promised me money, and the unwillingness of the son to fulfil his father's engagements. This will render any extensive plan of travel out of the question. The matter is bad enough as it is: for after a fatiguing expedition of some eighteen months I must return home with broken spirits and a debt of some thousand dollars.

I have had a letter from Ombrosi. He said he called several times upon you before he could find you. His letter is a *natural curiosity*.

I presume you have heard of Nat Willis's marriage; and his foolish affair with Capt. Marryat &c &c.[6] If you have not, you have only to say so, and I will tell you about it in two words.

The new Editor of the N. A. Review I know but slightly.[7] He is considered a man of talent; tho' not equal to the Everetts. Nevertheless he may conduct the Review equally well; since talent is not all that is wanting in such an undertaking.

Farewell. Do not follow my bad example and delay yr. answer, as I have done. Much love to your dear wife. Tell her I shall do all in my power to come to Florence.

Very truly yours
H. W. L.

MANUSCRIPT: Longfellow Trust Collection. ADDRESS: To/Geo: W. Greene Esq./ Via Mazzetta 2090/*Firenze/Italia* POSTMARKS: HEIDELBERG 26 MAR 1836/ APRILE 1836/CONTRO BOLLO

1. Samuel Ward became one of Longfellow's intimate friends and admirers. See Introduction. His blood relationship to George W. Greene was tenuous, his grandfather having married a member of the Rhode Island Greene family.

2. Ward had written a review of Lord King, *The Life of John Locke*, for the *American Quarterly Review*, XII (December 1832), 354–379.

3. The books mentioned are: *Corpus Omnium Veterum Poetarum Latinorum cum eorundem Italica versione* (Mediolani, 1731), 17 vols.; *Classici Italiani* (Milano, 1802–1818), 250 vols.; and *Opere di Pietro Metastasio* (Firenze, 1819), 16 vols.

4. Horatio Greenough (1805–1852), the sculptor, was living in Italy at this time.

5. In his letter of February 27, 1836, Greene had sent Longfellow a poem of twenty-four verses to be criticized. These are lines 13 and 14.

6. Willis had married Mary Stace, daughter of Gen. William Stace of Woolwich, on October 1, 1835. Shortly afterwards, as the result of a quarrel in print, Capt. Marryat challenged him to a duel. Willis accepted, but the intervention of the seconds prevented the duel from taking place. See Henry A. Beers, *Nathaniel Parker Willis* (Boston, 1885), pp. 197–205.

7. That is, John G. Palfrey.

346. *To Samuel Ward*

Heidelberg, April 3, 1836.

My Dear Sir,

Yours of March 26 did not reach me until last evening; which is the reason that you have not a more speedy reply. I am indeed very sorry to hear of your serious misfortune;[1] but you have left me a little in doubt *how far* I am to condole with you. What you say of "the amputation crisis" is somewhat in the Jean Paul vein; and I have not yet made up my mind whether you have lost your leg or not. I trust, however, that you have been rescued from so great a misfortune as this would be. Could I for a moment imagine otherwise, I should not allow myself to speak so lightly on the subject. But as you are doubtless fast recovering — and I hope, ere this reaches you, quite recovered — you will perhaps be amused to see into what a perplexity you threw me by a Jean-Paulism.[2]

I hope you have at least good weather to cheer you in your confinement. If you were here, you would probably die — unless your heart carries an umbrella — or has an oil-cloth hatcase for its pericardium (there's one for you, Sir, to pay you for yours of the 26th March) — for it has been raining ever since you left us, winding up this morning with a furious snow-storm. At this present moment the sunshine is breaking through the mist. More in my next.

Yesterday between ten and eleven I had a distant street view of your friend the Baron of Schwatzingen. He was passing down the Haspelgasse — all clad in green from top to toe — and looked like a large cucumber.[3] By his side crept a little man in black, without form, and void — representing a bug on the said cucumber. Whereupon I made this polymeter: "Well art thou long, and green, and fair to see — and like thy fellow cucumbers art nourished by the vine."

You will perceive that I have been reading the Flegeljahre since you left us. I am delighted with Richter's magnificent and gorgeous imagination, which makes his descriptions of nature like Claude Lorraine's sunset landscapes. What exquisite beauty and lavish prodigality of figurative language! His wit does not please me so much; for though perhaps as spontaneous as his poetic imagery and expression — it is by no means so unrivalled. Strange that a man, whose soul was so overflowing with poetry, should wear a yellow nankeen frock-coat, and get maudlin on beer! His life of Quintus Fixlein has been translated into English.[4] I doubt, however, whether his works would please the English public, in general. He is too gigantic and misty. Reading his writings is like climbing in merry company up a steep hill to see the sun rise; — half the time you are in mist and vapor — and the trees swim around you like shadowy spectres — and then arises the sweet and manifold fragrance of flowers — and the birds sing in the air — and a glorious burst of sunshine darts athwart the vapory landscape — and you are revelling, like the lark, in the freshness of morning when some merry fellow at your elbow makes a bad pun — or offers you a piece of Bologna sausage. Is it not so?

My whisper about a fall from a carriage was unfortunately prophetic.

I hope you will look upon some other things I said as possibly, and if so, fortunately prophetic. I refer to your getting married. It is a shame that a young man of your feelings should suffer them to run to waste. Excuse my frankness. Laugh, if you will, at my simplicity — but by all that is pure and lovely and of good report[5] — think of these things.

A letter from Ticknor has just been put into my hands, and has snapped short my good advice. Listen: — hear what he says of you. "Has young Ward of N. Y. been in Heidelberg, and if so how long did he stay and what did he do there? He was with us in Dresden about two months ago, and left us very anxious to hear good things of him because he is capable of doing so much!" There's a sugar-plum for you.

Half-past twelve o'clock. I see from my window a tremendous storm coming along the Manheim road. Mercy on us!

Farewell. I hope you will soon be able to write me in your own hand, to say that you are well. Excuse the nonsense of this letter, and for your sentiments of friendship and regard receive mine in return.

Truly yours, &c, &c.,

H. W. Longfellow.

MANUSCRIPT: unrecovered; text from Henry Marion Hall, "Longfellow's Letters to Samuel Ward," *Putnam's Monthly*, III (October 1907), 39.

1. On his way to Luxembourg after leaving Longfellow at Mannheim on March 20, Ward fell from his carriage and injured his right knee severely. See 372.3.

2. The influence of Jean Paul Richter on Longfellow's own style is the subject of a German dissertation: Otto Deiml, *Der Einfluss von Jean Paul auf Longfellows Prosastil* (Erlangen, 1927).

3. Baron Emmerich von Wamboldt (d. 1839) lived at Schwetzingen, once the seat of the Grand Duke of Baden. Longfellow described him in similarly colorful detail in his journal entry for March 20, 1836: "Accompanied Ward to Manheim, passing through Schwezingen, where we called upon the old *Baron Wamboldt*, an Austrian officer — living in quiet — smoking his *meerschaum*, drinking ale — and feeding high. Of the last there can be no doubt — his belly declares it — and his rubicond nose stands forth like a tavern-bush — a sign of good liquor and good company."

4. See Thomas Carlyle in *German Romance; Specimens of its Chief Authors* (Edinburgh, 1827), Vol. III.

5. Cf. Phil. 4:8.

347. *To Daniel Raynes Goodwin*

Heidelberg   April 17. 1836.

My dear Sir,

I am quite ashamed when I look at the date of your long unanswered letter. But as I can give *myself* no satisfactory reason for neglecting to write you, I will not attempt to give *you* any. I dare say you have sometimes found yourself in this same situation. You intend from day to day to write — but the favorable moment does not come. However, I should have written a little sooner, had I not been out of town. I have been passing a week in Frankfort. On my return — three days ago, I had the pleasure of receiving the books you were kind enough to send — and yesterday your letter of April 1. I find by looking at the preface of the last volume — Vol 15 — that three more volumes were to follow. "Le seizième Volume, qui est actuellement sous presse, commencera en 1722 et finira en 1730." "Enfin, toute notre Histoire sera terminée par deux autres volumes, qui rendront un compte exact du Théatre jusqu' à la clôture de Pâques 1752; on va les mettre sous presse incessamment."[1] When you see Mons. Truchy I wish you would ask him about these remaining vols. as he probably sold you the work as complete. You need not, however, give yourself any trouble about the matter. The first vols. are the ones I most wanted; and you have procured them much cheaper than I expected.[2]

I have been all the morning making plans for you; — thinking what I should do if I were in your place; and how your time may be turned to the best advantage in every respect. Of one thing I am certain. I should divide the time to be passed in Paris — and reserve three or four months till my return from Italy. I am sure you will find this advantageous. I think I should try to be in Germany as early as July — and go into Italy in December; so that I could get back to Paris again in July; thus completing the year.

Now, a little more in detail. And first, in regard to a place of residence in Germany. One of three, I think you will choose; either Berlin, Göttingen or Heidelberg. Each has its advantages and disadvantages. The University of Berlin is decidedly the foremost in Germany; — a fine Library — Professors of great fame in every branch — the head-quarters of Literature and criticism — Theatre — Opera — in fine, the united advantages of a city and a University. But in Summer it is a disagreeable place of residence. It lies in a sandy plain — there are no pleasant walks and villages around it; and as to its great literary advantages, — it requires a previous knowledge of the language to enjoy them; and just as you reached this point your time would have expired. Your expenses likewise in Berlin would be certainly double what they would be here or in Göttingen. Göttingen is a cheap place, its Library a very fine one; — and there is a good deal of Literary spirit there. The town itself is not unpleasant — but the environs are nothing — the only pleasant walk is round the walls of the town, which are planted with trees and make an agreeable promenade.

The great advantage it holds out to foreigners is the great purity [with] which all classes speak their native tongue. And this is certainly a great advantage. Heidelberg is a very beautiful place; one of the most beautiful you will see in Europe. It lies close on the bank[s] of the Neckar and all around it rise high hills. You have every variety of pleasant walks — from the gardens of the old castle — with its ruins and terraces; to the level plain of the Rhine and the deep valley of the Neckar. It is moreover a very quiet and a very cheap place. Your necessary expenses will not excede 50 cents daily; this includes two rooms, lights, breakfast, dinner and supper. By breakfast and supper I mean tea or coffee with bread. The usual price of rooms — parlor and bed-room furnished — is 20 dollars for 6 months; or by the month, $4. Dinner at a *table d'hôte*, 16 cents; — coffee in the morning with bread 6 cents. I give you these minutiae, because it is necessary for every one to know them. But Heidelberg has also its disadvantages. The language spoken here is not pure. The pronunciation is bad, and the words are curtailed in every way: for instance — *"kaps kapt"* is Heidelbergish for *"Ich hab' es gehabt* [I've had it]" — *"eine Flasche* [a bottle]" becomes *"ein Flasch,"* — *"guten Morgen* [good morning]" is *"gute Morge* (pr. *morge* in French) &c. &c. &c. This is bad: but as you know what the good pronunciation is, you can avoid the bad. If you choose to take an instructer you can find some one from the North; and in a word can keep clear of these provincial peculiarities. Taking everything into consideration, then, I should advise you to come to this place in July; — stay here till the close of November; — then go to Munick, — and through the Tyrol into Italy. In Italy make Rome your head-quarters BY ALL MEANS; and return to Paris through Switzerland the following Summer.

Here you have as good a plan as I can make. From Heidelberg in the vintage time you can make an excursion down the Rhine — you will see the Tyrol, and you will see Switzerland — and this is doing a great deal, without interfering with your plans of study. I shall see you either here or in Paris in the course of the Summer; and we can talk the matter over again. I shall probably remain here until July or August, and then go into Switzerland, and to Paris on my way home. I will write you more definitely as to time and place at a later period, so that we may not miss seeing each other.

I am sorry to hear of the fire in Brunswick, and that Dr. Adams should have preferred jumping out of the window to going quietly down stairs or up through the skuttle. I hope the burning of the Ath[enaea]n Library will unite the two societies into one — so that out of seeming evil some good may spring.[3]

On looking over what I have written, I find I have laid much stress upon pleasant scenery &c in choosing a place of residence. In this I think I am right. A visit to Europe is for us, who have to toil for our daily bread — the great vacation of Life. We can bury ourselves in books when at home. Here we must do something likewise for the imagination — for our poetic education. Hence I envy you the Italian Tour.

Let me hear from you soon. Tell me what Americans are in Paris, and what they are doing. I hear something of a Mr. Thorn who is making a fool of himself by giving parties to the English Nobility and *cutting* his own countrymen. I am told he invites the former to his suppers and soirées — the latter to his *church* — for he has also a church establishment. Is this true or fabulous?[4]

Very truly your friend
Henry W. Longfellow.

MANUSCRIPT: Bowdoin College Library. ADDRESS: À Monsieur/Monsieur le Professeur Goodwin/aux soins de Messrs Welles & cie/à Paris. POSTMARK: HEIDELBERG 20 APR ‖1836‖ [*other postmarks illigible*] POSTAL ANNOTATION: franco

1. " 'The sixteenth Volume, which is now in press, will begin with 1722 and end with 1730.' 'Finally, our entire History will end with two other volumes, which will give an exact account of the Theater up to its Easter closing in 1752; they are being prepared for publication without delay.' "

2. *Histoire du Theatre François depuis son Origine jusqu'à présent, Avec la Vie des Plus Célèbres Poets Dramatiques, un Catalogue exact de leurs Piéces. & des notes Historiques & Critiques* (Paris, 1745-1749), 15 vols. The concluding volumes seem never to have been printed. M. Truchy was presumably a Paris bookseller.

3. In the early morning of February 17, 1836, a fire swept through Maine Hall, destroying classrooms and dormitories and the Athenaean Society library of over 3000 volumes. The library of the Peucinian Society was saved. In the excitement, Samuel Adams (1806-1877), the tutor in modern languages and college librarian, jumped out of his window in the northeast corner of the building and broke his leg. Adams, who was filling in for Goodwin while the latter was abroad preparing himself to succeed Longfellow, received his M.D. from Bowdoin in 1836. He was later associated for many years with Illinois College, Jacksonville.

4. Herman Thorn (c. 1784-1859), formerly a purser in the U. S. Navy, had been a shipmate of James Fenimore Cooper aboard the *Wasp 18* (James Franklin Beard, *The Letters and Journals of James Fenimore Cooper* [Cambridge, Mass., 1960], II, 16). By his marriage to Jane Mary Jauncey, daughter of an English financier on Wall Street, he entered a family of great wealth. He, his wife, and their bevy of attractive children were living in Paris in great style at this time, entertaining extravagantly and cultivating the European nobility. Some indication of the attitude that Longfellow deplores may be had from Moses Beach, *Wealth and Biography of the Wealthy Citizens of the City of New York* (New York, 1855, 12th edition), p. 72: "Made foreign excursions and acquired the grace and dignity of the ancient dukes. Has now the bearing of Majesty, and treads the earth as if he would aspire to the gods."

348. *To Stephen Longfellow*

[Heidelberg.] May 8. 1836.

My dear Father,

Here is a sketch of Heidelberg,[1] which will give you some faint idea of the beautiful landscape in which it lies. I have made a + to show you the part of the town in which I live. The house stands close beneath the Castle; and from the garden behind, a winding pathway leads up to the terrace, which you see supported by arches, and which forms a part of the extensive and beautiful gardens of the Castle. This terrace looks westward. The view from it is magnificent. Right under you is the town, running a mile along the bank of the river, with one long street from gate to gate. Beyond, the valley of the Neckar opens, like the mouth of a trumpet, into the level plain of the Rhine. You see the spires of Manheim in the distance; and farther westward the blue summits of the Donnersberg and the mountains of Alsatia. The Castle is now a complete ruin and uninhabited. It has been thrice struck by lightning, and has endured ten sieges. One of its huge corner towers has been rent from top to bottom, and half has toppled down the hill. Another has been sprung by a mine. Mutilated statues in armor look down from their niches in the walls; ivy and wild-flowers grow about them; and great trees wave on the roofless towers. Excepting the Alhambra of Granada, I have seen nothing to compare with this ruin. And this is the public promenade of Heidelberg. In the evening there is music in the gardens; you meet your friends and acquaintances there; there are shady walks and fountains; and the nightingales sing all night long. But amid all this enchantment a sense of loneliness hangs over me constantly. The scene of Mary's death — and the consciousness of what I lost in loosing her — are ever present to my mind; and I recall the last words written with a pencil in her Journal; — on her death-bed — which I litt[l]e thought then would be such; — "O, if we ever reach Heidelberg, I shall be too happy!" But I will not make you sad with my sadness; nor dwell longer on those mournful events, which so suddenly changed our tour of pleasure into a funeral procession.

I am very happy to hear of the safe arrival of the Brig Elizabeth.[2] I had some apprehensions, as the Autumn and Winter have been so stormy. The Hollander is lost. I had two large boxes of very curious Dutch books on board of her, and in one of the boxes were some presents which Mary sent to her sisters. There was also a case of books for College. Fortunately all were insured; but nevertheless I regret the loss very much. The books were very rare — many of them — and I know that nothing could have been more valuable than those little parcels, which Mary put up with her own hand for her sisters. I wish Sam would mention to Dr. Harris, that the books were insured. I may have forgotten to mention it in my letter to him, written when the books were sent.[3] I wish also that Dr. Harris (the Librarian) would write, informing me what cases of books have been received and whether any farther appropriations of money have been made for the purchase of German and French books. They do business in a strange way at Cambridge. I have not had a word from any of them on this subject.

All the letters you mention in your last have been received — those of October and November, — of February — and the last, April 3rd. making three in all. The date of my last I have forgotten; — and I fear that from the long interval which has elapsed since then, you will imagine me on my way home, and be disappointed at finding me still here, and to learn, that I cannot possibly return before the close of the Summer. I have still a great deal to do; and I mean to pass a month or so in Switzerland. My health is very good: you need feel no apprehensions on that point. I wish yours were as good, and hope it may be. Only do not build a house in Gorham. You may depend upon it you can live just as well in the neighborhood of Boston — and save yourself the vexation of building. You can at least go and see, and I feel pretty sure the matter will be placed in a new light.

I feel under very great obligations to Judge Potter for his kindness and promptitude in assisting me unasked, in a matter which might have been embarrassing. It was my earnest desire from the beginning not to be a burden either to you or him; and hence made the arrangements with Mr. Goddard, which his booby of a son sees fit not to recognize, and thus throws me into the very position I wished to avoid. This was not because I thought, that you and the Judge would feel any reluctance to making the same arrangements yourselves; but because I wanted you to see my feelings upon this subject — and to know that I laid no claims to assistance from the circumstances of kindred and relationship. It was a business affair altogether; and as such I wished to manage it. This does not however prevent me from being under much obligation to you ||and the Judge for fulfilling|| Mr. Goddard's engagements: and on ||this point I feel once more|| [4] at ease.

I am glad that Alex has got safe home from the South Sea bubble [5] — and often wish he were here to keep me company in my rambles about the castle and the hills. We speak of him often among the ruins. They would please him much. For Mary I am making a small collection of German Music; which will be remarkable for quality more than quantity. Ask Anne what I shall get for her.

Clara's kind regards to the girls. I shall write again soon.

When you write to Cambridge ask Sam to say to Mr. Felton, that I wish to make the same arrangements there for boarding and lodging, as I intended when I last saw him. He will understand my meaning. I consider Mother's letter as a part of yours, and answer both in this. My affectionate ||remembrances to all.||

Very truly &c &c

||Henry W. Longfellow||

MANUSCRIPT: Longfellow Trust Collection. ADDRESS: To/Stephen Longfellow Esq./Portland/Maine/États Unis d'Amérique./par le Hâvre/et New York. POSTMARKS: HEIDELBERG 9 MAR 1836/NEW-YORK SHIP JUNE 10 POSTAL ANNOTATION: franco ENDORSEMENT: H. W. Longfellow/Heidelberg. May 8. 1836/Recd. June

1. This sketch is the printed letterhead of the sheet and includes the title "Heidelberg." See Plate VIII.

2. The *Elizabeth*, under Capt. William Long, had carried the body of Mary Potter Longfellow to Boston. See Letter No. 335.

3. This letter is unrecovered, but see Letter No. 330.

4. The manuscript has been mutilated by the cutting away of the signature. The restored words, in another hand, were apparently supplied at the time of the mutilation.

5. That is, from his cruise with the Pacific Fleet under his uncle, Commodore Wadsworth. See 240.2.

349. *To George Ticknor*

Heidelberg   May 9. 1836

My dear Sir,

How shamefully I have neglected to answer your last friendly letter! When I compare its date with the present, I am at a loss what to say for myself. This delay admits of no excuse. I will not even attempt to palliate it; but take refuge under the hope, that you will not consider it a matter of much importance.

Ward was here about a week. I saw a good deal of him. He had much to say of you and Mrs. Ticknor, and I was sincerely glad to learn from an eye-witness how very pleasantly and comfortably you were living in Dresden; for I had a lurking apprehension, that Mrs. Ticknor might find an unpleasant contrast between a Boston fire-place and a Saxon stove. Then he had long stories to tell me — wherein he figured as the hero; and he gave me a cigar, which, he said, came from you, and which I smoked with gratitude. I liked his open and generous character, and that ardor of temperament which so fully develops his talent — in itself not small. What I did not like in him, I leave unsung. You can easily imagine it. His defects are as obvious as his good qualities. We parted very good friends. I had a letter from him a few weeks ago. He has met with a very serious accident; and still lies quite ill at Luxembourg. In jumping out of his carriage at a friend's door, he fell upon his knee on the pavement, and it was long doubtful whether he would not lose one of those handsome legs which have figured so advantageously at the various courts of Europe. It is probable he will be lame for life. This I hear from others, not from him. His account of the matter is this. "I fell headlong from the carriage, and thus nearly fulfilled your hypothesis, that it was possible for me to fall from my chaise and thereby lose my life. A knee, whose amputative crisis has this day passed, saved my life and manuscripts." This is a little in the Jean-Paul vein. The accident, however, is a very serious one, and I am very sorry to hear of it, notwithstanding the frivolous way.

Curious! I had just written this word, when in came the postman with a letter from Ward, dated Luxembourg May 5. He says; "I am almost entirely recovered, although as yet unable to travel. I am assured, that on the 8th or 9th inst. I shall be allowed to set out upon my journey, and my present intention is to embark on the 24th for New York." So, the affair is not so serious, after all — and our sympathies have been in some degree superfluous.

I have lately received some bad news from America. The Brig Hollander, bound from Rotterdam to Boston — after beating about the ocean all winter long, went down in sight of her port, and was lost "with man and mouse." On board of her were three cases of rare and curious Dutch books; the harvest of a months toil among the antiquarian book-stalls of Amsterdam. Fortunately they were insured; — a poor consolation, at best, for me, though doubtless not despised by the Treasurer. The books were really too good to be sunk; — they were food for worms — not fishes. And so goes the entire collection of Dutch Literature.

I regret very much that you are not coming to Heidelberg, and that I cannot go to Dresden. I do not however abandon the hope of seeing you during the Summer. I shall probably go to Munick, and, if possible, into the Tyrol, and thence through Switzerland into France. Miss. Crowninshield is desirous of making this tour, and if we can find suitable travelling companions, we shall no doubt do it.[1] This will probably be in July. If you can say with any degree of certainty, when you shall be in those regions — if at all — I will do all in my power to join you, if it be only a few days or even hours.

Dr. Julius[2] has arrived here. I have not yet seen him, ||but|| am going out to look for him. I am curious to hear what he has to say about America. The most important news I have heard lately from that quarter, came in a letter from a German *woman*, who writes to her friends here, that no lady in America has more than one pocket-handkerchief, and most of them none. I suppose she means those ladies, who sit with their feet out of the window, — as mentioned in my last letter, if I mistake not.[3]

You see that I found the Doctor, and that he has been with me. He dresses in black and wears gaiters and a low-crowned hat, as of yore. No shadow of change.

My kindest regards to Mrs. Ticknor.

Very truly yours &c

Henry W. Longfellow

MANUSCRIPT: Dartmouth College Library. ADDRESS: To/George Ticknor Esq./ Care of H. Bassange & co/Dresden POSTMARKS: HEIDELBERG 11 MAI 1836/ ST. POST 14 MAI N.4U.

1. No suitable traveling companions were found, and Miss Crowninshield remained unhappily in Heidelberg while Longfellow made the tour alone.

2. Nicolaus Heinrich Julius (1783–1862), a medical doctor and authority on prison reform, had recently returned from a two-year sojourn in the United States, where apparently Longfellow had met him.

3. Longfellow mentions this phenomenon in Letter No. 343 to his father. He may have repeated it in a letter to Ticknor, now lost. The following note from Dr. Julius to Ticknor is inserted at this point: "My dear friend!/ The day before yesterday I got here from Strasburg, and found your dear Letter of the 24th of April. On comparing the dates and what I still have to do, to go to Belgium and Holland, before I can call at Hamburgh, you will find that it is impossible, unfortunately impossible, to meet you this year somewhere in Germany. I pray to God that I may be able to do it next year. As I have found no address of your's, I shall continue to write to you to Dresden. If you choose to write to me *soon*, do it to Brussels (care of Professor Quetelet) where I shall be before the end of this month. In June your letters will find me at Hamburgh (Dr Julius, Hamburgh). I am very happy to hear that the power of the genius of art has got hold of Mrs. Ticknor, and the countries she will visit this year and the next, will continue to cultivate this taste which may form the finest ornament of her future life. Anna [Ticknor's eldest daughter], I hope, will trie to emulate her amicable mother. God bless you all in your undertakings and may you reap from what you have to see, all the enjoyments you are meriting so well. Pray, remember me to all our Boston friends, and principally to the Guild and Norton families. Farewell./Your true friend Julius." Lambert Adolphe Jacques Quetelet (1796–1874), mathematician, astronomer, and physicist, was secretary of the Belgian Academy of Sciences. Mrs. Ticknor's sisters, Eliza and Catherine Eliot, had married, respectively, Benjamin Guild and Andrews Norton.

350. *To George Washington Greene*

Heidelberg. June 5. 1836.

My dear George,

I thank you for your last kind letter, and for the information about the Italian Classics. Unfortunately — most unfortunately, by the treachery of a gentleman in Boston my finances have been thrown into utter confusion;[1] and consequently an outlay of two hundred dollars, in addition to my necessary travelling expenses, would be extremely inconvenient for me at the present moment. I must therefore delay the purchase of these books for the present.

I foresee by the way in which I have commenced this letter, that it will not be worth the trouble of reading. I think one feels from the "dear Sir" — from the very first word he writes, — whether he is going to write a *letter*, properly so called, or only a thing with a date at one end of it, and a "yours and so forth," at the other. The soul betrays itself, as well in the movement of a pen, as in a glance of the eye. I have not felt really like writing a letter for a very long time; and this is the reason why I have not answered your last sooner. However, I have a proposition to make to you, which must be made now. I am on the eve of my departure for Munick. I wish I could say for Florence. But alas! that lies not within the circle of possibilities. I cannot do it; tho' my very soul languishes "for a beaker full of the warm South."[2] From Munick I intend to go to Milan; then cross the Simplon into Switzerland and return to Heidelberg; — and after a few days tarry here start for home by way of Paris. Now, will you and Maria meet us in Milan, and travel in Switzerland with us? I say *us,* because Miss. Crowninshield goes with me.[3] At all events come to Milan, that we may pass a day or two together. As soon as you get this letter, therefore, write me. *Munick, poste restante.* I shall be there probably as soon as your letter.

Your Cousin Sam Ward has met with a very serious accident. On his way to Paris, he fell from his carriage, and injured his knee so badly, that he was confined a month in Luxemburg; from which place he wrote me. He resumed his journey too soon, and I hear with sincere regret, that he is ill again in Paris, and may loose his leg. Horrible. I shall write him immediately and so must you — care of Messrs. Hottinguer & cie Rue Bergère No 11. Paris. He will be glad to hear from you, for he holds you in high esteem. So does Felton. See what he says in his last letter to me. "Greene has uncommon talent. His article in the N. A. Review on Machiavelli is admirable.[4] I hope he will go on, and take the opportunity his residence affords him to let us know all about the literary doings of Italy." I am glad — sincerely glad to hear this from Felton; and I let you hear it also, because it is of great importance for a man to know how he stands with his friends. At least I think so; and it has often given me pain to think, that some of my friends set no very high value upon me. Through good report and through evil report the voice of a friend has a wonder-working power; and from the very hour we hear it "the fever leaves us."[5]

You ask for German catalogues with prices. Infatuated young man!

Did you not know that Germany is full of Antiquarian booksellers from whom you can obtain everything you want at about half the price marked in the *Trade* catalogues! These marked prices are always very high; and unless you have drawn the capital prize in a lottery, you must not think of ordering many books from regular booksellers. Deal with Antiquaries through some friend. Let me recommend the following works, which may be had here at the prices marked.

Herders Werke.	45 vols. small 8° — 22 florins	= $9.
Lessings do	30 vols do — 12 do	= 4.80
Schillers do	12 vols. do (beautiful edit.) 16 fl.	= 6.40. Fine paper.
Göthes do	55 vols. 16 mo — — 14. fl.	= 5.60

Unfortunately the price of this last work has been lately doubled; but may possibly come down again. Upon about the same terms you can have all the old German writers — [Friedrich Gottlieb] Klopstock — [Christian Fürchtegott] Gellert — &c — &c. They have been published uniform at Carlsruhe — some two hundred volumes; — sold separately, each work by itself. The new works are all dear. Every miserable little authorling sets a price upon his writings, which would astonish you. So much for literary statistics.

From Munick I will let you know where I shall probably be in Milan: that is, if I hear from you there, and it is in your power to come so far to meet me. Do not fail to write.

Since I last wrote you I have met with a serious loss. Two large boxes of books — mostly Dutch — ponderous folios with brass clasps and curious engravings — in fine a treasure in their way — all gone down into the great deep — food for fishes. The vessel sank in sight of Boston harbour, and went to the bottom "with man and mouse."

And thus my epistle takes an end. My warmest regards to Maria. You must come to Milan. The Lago di Como is beautiful — and the Alps sublime. You have seen them only once. To me it is all new. Farewell.

Truly yours

H. W. L.

MANUSCRIPT: Longfellow Trust Collection. ADDRESS: George W. Greene/Borgo di Pinti No. 6718./Firenze./Italia. POSTMARKS: HEIDELBERG 6 IUN 1836/ CONTRO BOLLO

1. The gentleman referred to was William Warren Goddard (see Letter No. 348). For the Italian classics, see 345.3.

2. See 318.1.
3. See 349.1.
4. *North American Review*, XLI (July 1835), 70–94.
5. Longfellow is possibly recalling the story of Jesus and Simon's mother-in-law, who lay sick with a fever: "And he came and took her by the hand, and lifted her up; and immediately the fever left her" (Mark 1:31).

351. *To Carl Christian Rafn*

Heidelberg   June 7. 1836

My dear Sir,

I here send you an order upon the house of Chapeaurouge & cie in Hamburg for the sum of 150 francs or 80 Marks; the amount of my contribution on becoming a member of the Society of Northern Antiquarians. Will you have the goodness to notify me of its arrival and acceptance.

Your very friendly letter of the 12th [of] February was duly received. I need not assure you that it would give me great pleasure to visit you again before my return to America; but it will not be in my power. I shall be obliged to go home before the close of the season; and shall probably sail from Hâvre in August or September.

I have something to communicate to you, which I think will not be without interest. Dr. *Julius* of Berlin has just returned from a journey in the United States, where he has been examining our Penetentiaries and prisons. During his journey he became very much interested in the History and fate of the North American Indians; and made a very interesting and valuable collection of books and papers relating to them. He informs me that he shall publish a book upon this subject, as soon as he has leisure to arrange his materials.[1] To him — a very friendly and obliging person — I refer you for any information you may wish. He will doubtless be very happy to be serviceable to you.

Present, if you please, my respectful remembrance to your friend Magnussen, and to Mr. Bölling, in whose affliction I can truly sympathize.[2] Please tell him (Mr. Bölling) that I shall send him a small package with a letter in the course of a few days.

With sentiments of high regard and bidding you an affectionate farewell,

I am, dear Sir, your Obt. Ser[v]t.

Henry W. Longfellow

MANUSCRIPT: Royal Society of Northern Antiquaries, Copenhagen. ADDRESS: To/ Professor Chs. C. Rafn/Copenhagen. POSTMARKS: HEIDELBERG 8 IUN 1836/ T.T. HAMBURG 12. JUN

1. Julius did not complete a book on the Indians, but his *Nordamerikas sittliche*

Zustände, Nach eignen Anschauungen in d. Jahren 1834–36 was published in Leipzig in 1839.

2. Jørgen Andresen Bølling (1792–1862), First Secretary of the Royal Library in Copenhagen, had given Longfellow lessons in Danish during the previous September. His wife had died on January 24, 1836. See Letter No. 355.

352. To Otto Heinrich Thilenius [1]

[Ems, June 14, 1836] [2]

My dear Sir

The ladies have looked into their bandboxes and consulted their glasses, and after passing in review before each other, we have come to the conclusion, that we look so much like *"Wilden aus Canada* [savages from Canada]" that we fear our presence would only disturb your festivities to-day.

Allow us therefore to follow our first impulse, which led us to refuse your kind civilities, only from a sense of what we owe to the *bienséances* [proprieties] of society.

Respectfully yours

H. W. Longfellow

MANUSCRIPT: Goddard-Roslyn Collection, Roslyn, New York. PUBLISHED: *Diary of Clara Crowninshield*, p. 275, n. 11.

1. Thilenius (1800–1867), a physician of Ems, had invited Longfellow, Clara Crowninshield, Mrs. Bryant, and her daughter Fanny — then on a tour of the German baths — to his sister's birthday celebration. Longfellow wrote this letter of refusal, but after considerable hesitation they all went, and the letter was never delivered. For details, see the *Diary of Clara Crowninshield*, pp. 273–276.

2. Longfellow mistakenly wrote "June 13" on the backflap of the letter.

353. To Samuel Ward [1]

Heidelberg, June 22, 1836

My dear Sir:

I think you must be crazy. The phantoms of your brain are beautiful, but they are not holy, and in the silence of the night they visit ladies' chambers. There is a wild beauty in your episode of the Creole girl, but I must tell you as I have told you before: these matters belong to the great volume of unwritten sensations which ought to remain unwritten. Let me speak candidly. Your imagination needs baptism in cool pure water. You have suffered it to lie too long in the seething Kock-brunnen of modern French literature. It must come out now and be shampooed with a coarse towel, and believe me you will feel both lighter and better for the operation. The bed of flowers is in truth an exquisite image, and I doubt not was original in your own mind, as you say it is. You little imagined when you wrote it that another had written it before you — but you shall have proof of this on the next page and you will see that this other has a great advantage over you in having exhibited his figures through a thin, transparent veil instead of bringing them before us in a state of absolute nudity. Wilhelm Müller, a German poet, is the author of the following which he entitled: *Die Brautnacht.*[2]

So there, you have my criticism and a poem in return for yours. Moreover, you have herein, by inference, an answer to your proposition, *"si vous aimiez mieux un autre style épistolaire, dites le moi."*

Et, voilà que je vous l'ai dit, sans vouloir le dire. La prochaine fois vous m'écrierez plus tranquillement, n'est-ce pas?[3]

I hope this letter will reach you before you leave Paris, otherwise you will go on your way wondering at my silence. I should have written you sooner, but have been sometime absent on a Tour down the Rhine and through the Baths of Ems, Langen-Schwalbach, Wiesbaden, &c.[4] On my return two days ago I found your letter waiting for me. I regret to hear you have had a relapse. Take better care of yourself, I pray you, or one of those legs, which have figured so extensively at the various courts of Europe, may figure no more anywhere.

I shall soon have the pleasure of seeing you again, for I intend to be in Paris about the close of August, and shall sail for New York either in September, or at the latest in October. I shall leave Heidelberg in a few days for Munich — the Tyrol and Switzerland. Why can't you return and make this journey with me? Will you? I have written to George Greene, to meet me in Milan.[5]

Excuse my laconic epistle in answer to your long one. I am busy, and have several letters to write before I can leave town. A pleasant voyage to you.

Very truly your friend,
Henry W. Longfellow.

P.S. By the way, who do you think has made his appearance here from New York? — No less a personage than young Zimmern, "son of the Brothers Zimmern & Co." — as he himself once said.[6] He says he did not like New York and the people in New York did not like him. So here he is once more.

MANUSCRIPT: unrecovered; text from *Uncle Sam Ward and His Circle,* pp. 111–112, and Henry Marion Hall, "Longfellow's Letters to Samuel Ward," *Putnam's Monthly,* III (October 1907), 39–40.

1. This letter, the manuscript of which is unrecovered, is a composite of two printed texts, neither of which is complete. The date is questionable. Hall, in the *Putnam's Monthly* text, states that Longfellow wrote it on June 23, 1836. Maude Howe Eliott, in *Uncle Sam Ward and His Circle,* supplies the earlier date.

2. Elliott interpolates in brackets at this point: "Here follow seven verses in German." The poem, of seven four-line stanzas, may be found in James Taft Hatfield, ed., *Wilhelm Müller Gedichte* (Berlin, 1906), pp. 264–265. Ward's poem is unfortunately unrecovered.

3. " 'if you should prefer a different epistolary style, tell me.'/And now I have told you, without meaning to do so. The next time you will write me more calmly, won't you?"

4. For details of this tour, see the *Diary of Clara Crowninshield*, pp. 264–286.

5. See Letter No. 350.

6. The "Gebrüder Zimmern" were prominent bankers and cloth-merchants of Heidelberg. One of them, August Zimmern, had entertained both Longfellow and Ward, and the young Zimmern here referred to was possibly his son.

354. *To Robert Storer* [1]

Heidelberg   June 23. 1836

My dear Sir,

I have taken the liberty to send to your care two small casks of Rhenish wine; marked as follows,

> P.L.F. #1. One cask Johannisberger.
> " " "   2. One cask Scharlachberger.

Each cask contains a German Ohm — Nassau measure. How many English gallons, I cannot ascertain exactly. They cost both together $ — 116. which I mention, because I have heard that the duties on the Rhine wines was a certain pr. cent on their cost. They will be forwarded to you by Quack Balck &co Rotterdam; and I shall be much obliged to you if you will have them placed in some cool place until my return. Excuse the liberty I take in troubling you in this way, being assured that I shall always be most ready and happy to serve you, whenever an occasion offers.

I have still to thank you for your kindness on a late painful occasion, of which I can yet hardly think with composure — much less speak. Excuse me if I say no more, therefore; and be assured of my grateful remembrance of your kindness.[2]

In September or October I hope to have the pleasure of seeing you again in Boston. Until then farewell. With particular regards to your brothers and sisters

Very truly yours
Henry W. Longfellow

MANUSCRIPT: unrecovered; text from photostat, Longfellow Trust Collection.

1. On June 17 Longfellow purchased the two casks of wine referred to in this letter from Jacob Bertram, a wine merchant of Wiesbaden (*Diary of Clara Crownin-*

shield, p. 283). Bertram's bill, preserved among the Longfellow papers, identifies the person to whom the wine was shipped as Robert Storer of Boston, Mary Potter Longfellow's half-uncle.

2. Storer had presumably helped with the arrangements for receiving Mary Potter Longfellow's body in Boston. See Letter No. 335.

355. *To Jørgen Bølling*

Heidelberg June 24. 1836

My dear Sir,

I have delayed for a long time to fulfil my promise of writing to you. Circumstances of a very painful nature, which you have probably heard from Prof. Rafn — I allude to the sickness and death of my wife — have thrown such a gloom over me, that I have not had heart to write to anyone. Besides which, the books I promised you, have but lately reached me.

You too — My dear Sir, — have suffered affliction; and I can truly sympathize with you in your loss, as the same bereavement has been mine.[1] How little did we think, when we walked together about [the] environs of your native city — that each of us was so soon to lose his best earthly friend. Such, however, has been the will of Providence. We have left to us the pleasant recollection of the goodness of the departed — the trust that they are happier, than if they had remained with us — and the cheering hope of meeting them again, where there will be no more sorrow nor parting.

The two volumes of Outre Mer I shall put into the bookseller's hands to-day, to be sent by the best opportunity. I hope they may afford you some amusement. At all events, they will be a slight token of my friendly remembrance.

I shall leave Heidelberg tomorrow for a Tour to Munick and the Tyrol. On my return I hope to find a letter from you, informing me of your health and well-being. Present my best regards to Professor Rafn, and to our friend Riise, in whose rooms we passed so many pleasant hours together.

Very truly yours
Henry W. Longfellow

MANUSCRIPT: Royal Library, Copenhagen. ADDRESS: To/Mr. Bölling/Assistant Librarian in the/Royal Library at/Copenhagen. POSTMARK: HEIDELBERG 24 IUN 1836. PUBLISHED: Allen Wilson Porterfield, "Eight Unpublished Letters of Longfellow," *Scandinavian Studies and Notes,* V (1918–1919), 172.

1. See 351.2.

356. *To George Ticknor*

Munich   Wednesday   June 29 — 1836

My dear Sir,

I write you these few lines to say, that I am in Munich, and shall probably be in Salzburg on Friday night. If so, I promise myself the pleasure of passing Saturday and Sunday with you at Ischl.[1] It is, however, possible, that I may not get away from this city before Monday.

For fear I should not see you, I will mention, that the best hotel here is *Der goldene Hirsch*. I am in *Der goldene Hahn*, which I beg you to avoid. It is an *abschenliches Nest*.[2]

Not doubting, that you will be in Ischl by July 1. — as was your plan, when you last wrote me — I shall be sadly disappointed if anything has delayed you in Vienna, so as to prevent our meeting. I should like at all events to see Ischl, being so near it as Salzburg, and should probably go there, even did I not expect to meet you. I must say, however, that the views I have seen of the place do not strike my fancy. It looks like Ems — one of your regular, fashionable watering places — with lodging houses like hospitals.

With kindest regards to Mrs. Ticknor. —

very sincerely yours
Henry W. Longfellow.

MANUSCRIPT: University of Washington Library.   ADDRESS: à Monsieur/Monsieur Geo: Ticknor/poste restante./à Ischl.   POSTMARK: MÜNCHEN [*remainder illegible*]

1. Longfellow spent Monday, July 4, in Ischl, but as the Ticknors had not yet arrived, he did not remain.

2. Longfellow recommends "The Golden Stag" because "The Golden Cock" is an "abominable nest."

357. *To Stephen Longfellow*

Geneva   July 29. 1836.

My dear Father,

I mentioned in my last letter, whose date I have as usual forgotten, that I should take an opportunity of visiting Switzerland before my return home. I have accordingly left Clara with Mrs. Bryant in Heidelberg, and am now at Geneva; having already completed — or nearly so — the Tour I proposed. As I keep a day-book, and note down all my movements and all that strikes me as novel or curious, I shall not here give you any description of my journey. On my return you shall have the whole series, from the moment we reached London down to the present moment, hardly a day omitted. Suffice for the present to say that thus far my journey has not had much effect in cheering, or even soothing me. On the contrary I have frequently thought, as I pursued my way alone, that it was the worst thing I could have done, thus to have undertaken a solitary expedition among these mountains. I am satisfied, however, that in the end I shall not regret it; and having now visited all the most important parts of Europe, I shall return home without a desire to recross the Atlantic.

I start tomorrow on my return to Heidelberg, in company with Mr. T. Motley and wife of Boston.[1] It was quite delightful to me to meet them here. In truth, it has revived me more than anything else, and seems to bring me somewhat nearer home, as we have necessarily some recollections and sympathies in common.

At Heidelberg I shall stop but a few days — merely long enough to pack up my books, and despatch them to Boston; and shall then go to Paris with Clara and Mrs. Bryant. I think I told you, that Mr. Bryant left his family at Heidelberg, and that they will return with me. In Paris I shall not stay long; and you may expect to see me in September or October.

One thing troubles me very much. It is this arrangement about money. Whether I shall ever forgive Mr. Goddard for his misconduct requires some consideration. He could not have done anything to offend me more. I am afraid I have put you and Judge Potter to a good deal of inconvenience; and as this is what I wished and intended from the beginning to avoid, it causes me no little uneasiness.

The towns in Switzerland have disappointed me. Even Geneva is much less beautiful than I imagined. The country, however, has equalled, if not surpassed my expectations. I have just returned from the Valley of Chamouni and Mont Blanc. Coleridge's poem beginning "Hast thou a charm to stay the morning star"[2] — will convey to you a better idea of the sublimity of the scene, than any description. Of all places I have ever visited, this is the most sublime; and yet not desolate; for the valley is rich and fruitful, and vegetation climbs up to the very snows and ice-bergs of the mountains.

Of the Lake of Geneva, I think too much has been said. The eastern extremity of this Lake is the most beautiful. Ther‖e is‖ the scene of Rousseau's Nouvelle Héloise; Bryon describes it in the Third canto of Childe Harold; and there, too, is the castle of Chillon, the most beautiful prison I was ever in. The dungeons, to which description has added so many horrors, are high, vaulted chambers; and have light and air from narrow windows looking upon the lake.

Lausanne pleases me most of any city in Switzerland. It is not upon the lake, but over-looks it; and the houses rise up on terraces, and public walks and gardens look towards the Alps. The house in which Gibbon lived is shown. I visited the garden, and walked along the avenue of trees, which he mentions — when he walked out at night, after writing "the last word of the last page" of his history. You will find the description in his Memoirs.[3]

I have also been at Ferney — Voltaire's residence — about three miles north of Geneva. His parlor and bed-room, with the ancient furniture, are still exhibited. The visit gave me no great pleasure. I have no regard nor respect for the memory of this evil spirit — whose countenance was "half eagle, half monkey" — and whose mind partook of the character of his countenance.

Farewell. I hope, on reaching Heidelberg, to find letters from you; and to hear good accounts of your health. Give my affectionate regards to the Judge [Barrett Potter] and his family, and in fine to all at home.

Very truly yours
H. W. Longfellow

MANUSCRIPT: Longfellow Trust Collection. ADDRESS: To/Stephen Longfellow Esqr./Portland/Maine./par le Hâvre et New York. États Unis d'Amerique POSTMARKS: GENEVE 30 JUILLET 1836/SUISSE PAR FERNEY/NEW-YORK SHIP SEP 19 ["19" *inverted*]/A.E.D./PP POSTAL ANNOTATION: franco

1. Thomas Motley (1781–1864), a well-to-do Boston merchant, was the father of John Lothrop Motley. His wife was Anna Lothrop Motley.
2. "Hymn Before the Sunrise in the Vale of Chamouni," l. 1.
3. Cf. *The Autobiography of Edward Gibbon*, ed. J. B. Bury (World's Classics Edition, London, New York, and Toronto, 1907), p. 205.

358. *To Stephen Longfellow*

Paris September 8. 1836

My dear Father

I wrote you last from Geneva: from which place I returned to Heidelberg, where I remained only long enough to make the necessary arrangements for our return, and we are already thus far on our way back. We shall sail from Havre on the 8th of October, in the Silvie de Grace.[1] This is the first good vessel; and is one of the best in the line. I hope therefore to be with you as early as the middle of November; quick passages being made in October.

After leaving Geneva with Mr and Mrs Motley, we joined Mr. Appleton's family at Interlaken,[2] and remained together for a fortnight. And suddenly one day as we sat at dinner in Schaffhausen, the door opened and — enter Mr. Ticknor! He is fat and hearty, and looks as robust as an oak. Mrs T. is well; but rather dejected. This for Mr. Daveis.[3]

On reaching Heidelberg I found Goodwin there and a letter from you, and also one from the Judge [Barrett Potter]. I shall be at home so soon, that it will not be necessary to answer either. Mrs. W. C. Bryant is with us, and her two daughters; so that I have charge of three ladies and a child: for which I am very glad. It is much pleasanter than being alone, though it has some inconveniences. It diverts my thoughts, however, from myself in some degree; and so far has a good effect. We shall probably all return together. It was very fortunate for Clara, that Mrs. Bryant happened to be in Heidelberg.

With much love to you all, and in great impatience to see you once more

Very truly yours
Henry W. Longfellow

MANUSCRIPT: Longfellow Trust Collection. ADDRESS: To/Stephen Longfellow Esq/Portland/Maine/États Unis d'Amerique, par le Hâvre et New York. POSTMARKS: NEW-YORK OCT 21/FORWARDED BY YR. OB. SERVT. WELLES & CO. PARIS/FORWARDED BY GRACIE & SARGENT NEW YORK POSTAL ANNOTATION: *Per* Normandie

1. Because of the weather, the sailing date had to be postponed, and the *Sylvie de Grace* did not sail until October 12 (see the *Diary of Clara Crowninshield*, p. 298 and n. 24).

2. Nathan Appleton (1779–1861) had gone to Europe with his daughters Frances and Mary, his son Tom, and their cousins Isaac Appleton Jewett and William Appleton. The latter died in Switzerland of tuberculosis. Longfellow discreetly foregoes mentioning that the charms of Fanny Appleton (whom he married in 1843) caused his unscheduled delay in Interlaken.

3. Charles S. Daveis was one of Ticknor's oldest friends.

359. *To George Washington Greene*

Paris   September 12 1836

My dear Greene

I suppose you imagine me dead of cholera at Milan, in trying to penetrate from the Tyrol into Italy. Such a destiny has not been mine, you perceive. Your letter reached me at Munich; and I got as far as Innsbruck on my way to Milan, and the Lakes; nothing intimidated by the rumours of cholera and sudden death. I had even engaged my passage for Italy: when some informality in my passport put a stop to my march southward, and sent me forthwith into Switzerland, where I remained six weeks, and where I saw Mr. Ticknor, who is on his way to Italy, and for ought I know may now be with you in Florence. I am thus far on my way home, without having seen you; and Heaven only knows when and where we shall meet again: I hope it may be soon, and at home.

On returning to Heidelberg I expected to find a letter from you, as you owe me one or two; unless you call your last a letter. But all in vain. We commune together sufficiently *à la Chartreuse*; and the word *silence* seems to be written over our doors: and over *yours* in larger letters than over *mine*. How am I to make my letters reach you in future? Felton will tell me.

My journey through the Tyrol and parts of Switzerland was very lonely, having no companions but those, whom I picked up one day, and was glad to drop the next. And then those grand and solitary regions made a most melancholy impression upon my sick soul; and at times when I stood all alone on the tops of the great mountains, and saw around me only barren cliffs, and icebergs, whose breath was like the breath of the grave, — cold and appalling, — I thought I should have gone mad forever. Such a journey, under such circumstances, proves to me, that travelling is not always a cure for sadness. So far from dissipating my thoughts it concentrated them; so that in this experiment of moral alchymy — this search after the philosopher's stone — this turning of lead into gold — the crucible was near being burst asunder.

And now, my dear George, farewell; and to your good and lovely wife, farewell. Never let one thought, word or deed of yours be such as to throw a shadow upon her gentle spirit, as you value your own peace of mind hereafter. These things give sharpness to the shafts of death; and these are the words of one "who has himself been hurt by the archer."[1]

I intend to sail from Havre on the 8th of October in the ship Silvie de Grace;[2] and if you receive this in season for an answer to reach me before the 3rd of Oct. — do not fail to write, care of Welles & co, Place St. George. After my return no letters must be directed to him as I shall leave no account open with him; but you will write to me as to yr. other friends in America.

Good bye, my dear Greene

Affectionately your friend
H. W. L.

MANUSCRIPT: Longfellow Trust Collection. ADDRESS: To/Mr George W. Greene/ at Greenough's in the Borgo di Pinto/Florence/Italy. POSTMARKS: 13 SEPT 1836 [*remainder illegible*]/13 SETTEMBRE 1836 [*faint*]/PONT BEAUVOISIN

1. Cf. Cowper, *The Task*, III, 112–113.
2. See 358.1.

360. *To Joseph Bosworth*

Paris, Sept. 12, 1836

Did I inform you of the disaster which befel my Dutch books? Three large cases, my whole collection of Dutch Literature have been sunk to the bottom of the sea; old chronicles and all — not a leaf saved. This is a great loss; as I cannot easily replace the books. Thus most of my recollection of Holland must be of a mournful kind.

MANUSCRIPT: unrecovered; text from typewritten transcript, Longfellow Trust Collection.

361. *To Stephen Longfellow*

Cambridge   Dec. 7. 1836

My dear Father,

I have just received yours of the 5th and here send you a list of my drafts upon Wiggin since January last.

Feb. 2. 1836	£25
April 5.	25
— 25	25
August. 26.	35
September 6.	40
— 12.	40
October 3.	80

What the extra £10 are charged for I know not: unless it be Mr. Wiggin's charge for brokerage &c &c. When we get the items of the account, we shall see. I have not yet found it convenient to settle with Wm Goddard.[1] My time is very much taken up with furnishing my rooms, and in making and receiving calls. This is the reason why I have not written before. I have not yet entered upon my College duties; nor shall I this term. What these duties will be seems quite uncertain though I think I shall have nothing to do but lecture. I have already begun my preparations for a course of German Literature, which I hope to deliver next Summer.

On Thanksgiving day I dined with Judge Prescott in Boston. You know him; a very cordial old gentleman. His son is one of our Examining Committee in the Mod. Langs. and a man of letters.[2]

Profs. Hedge and Popkin I have had a glimpse of.[3] I fancy it must make them feel rather old, to see the son of one of their pupils here as Professor; placed before them as a kind of living mile-stone or finger-post, pointing both ways on the road of life.

All the world here has the influenza; so that I am not surprised to hear that you have all had it.

Sam[ue]l and Alex are well.[4]

Very truly yours
H. W. Longfellow

Please make due acknowledgements to the Judge for his great kindness in assisting me with my accounts. I feel under much obligation to him.[5]

The reason of my drawing so much in Paris was that I got an abundant supply of clothing there.

MANUSCRIPT: Longfellow Trust Collection. ADDRESS: To/Hon. Stephen Longfellow/Portland./Maine POSTMARK: CAMBRIDGE MS DEC 7 ENDORSEMENT: Henry to his Father/Decr. 22. 1836

1. Longfellow's statement of account with the estate of William Goddard, dated December 12, 1836, is in the Clifton Waller Barrett Collection of the University of Virginia. It reveals that Miss Goddard's expenses amounted to $684.27. The statement contains no charge for Longfellow's services as chaperon.

2. Judge William Prescott (1762-1844) was the father of the historian William Hickling Prescott.

3. Levi Hedge (1766-1844) and John Snelling Popkin (1771-1852) had both retired from Harvard — the former as professor of natural theology, moral philosophy, and political economy; the latter as Eliot Professor of Greek.

4. Samuel Longfellow, as noted above (343.3), had recently entered Harvard; Alexander was studying engineering and surveying in Cambridge.

5. In a letter dated September 26, 1836, Judge Potter asked Longfellow not to make an issue of the Goddard debt: "Do not my Dear Sir, let it cause you a moments pain, and permit me to hope on your arrival in Boston, that you will not take the least notice of the affair, not even to allude to it. And if they mention the subject I would say it was not of the least inconvenience as your father and Mr. P had assured you that it was perfectly in their power to afford you any accom[m]odation you wished." There is no record of William Goddard's having met his father's obligation, other than to recompense Longfellow for Mary Goddard's actual traveling expenses.

362. *To Eliza Ann Potter*

Cambridge, Sunday evening [1836].

My Dear Eliza, —

By tomorrow's steamboat I shall send you two trunks, containing the clothes which once belonged to your sister. What I have suffered in getting them ready to send to you, I cannot describe. It is not necessary, that I should. Cheerful as I may have seemed to you at times, there are other times, when it seems to me that my heart would break. The world considers grief unmanly, and is suspicious of that sorrow, which is expressed by words and outward signs. Hence we strive to be gay and put a cheerful courage on, when our souls are very sad. But there are hours, when the world is shut out, and we can no longer hear the voices, that cheer and encourage us. To me such hours come daily. I was so happy with my dear Mary, that it is very hard to be alone. The sympathies of friendship are doubtless something — but after all how little, how unsatisfying they are to one who has been so loved as I have been! This is a selfish sorrow, I know: but neither reason nor reflection can still it. Affliction makes us childish. A grieved and wounded heart is hard to be persuaded. We do not wish to have our sorrow lessened. There are wounds, which are never entirely healed. A thousand associations call up the past, with all its gloom and shadow. Often a mere look or sound — a voice — the odor of a flower — the merest trifle is enough to awaken within me deep and unutterable emotions. Hardly a day passes, that some face, or familiar object, or some passage in the book I am reading does not call up the image of my beloved wife so vividly, that I pause and burst into tears, — and sometimes cannot rally again for hours.

And yet, my dear Eliza, in a few days, and we shall all be gone, and others sorrowing and rejoicing as we now do, will have taken our places: and we shall say, how childish it was for us to mourn for things so transitory. There may be some consolation in this; but we are nevertheless children. Our feelings overcome us.

Farewell. Give my kind regards to all, and believe me most truly and affectionately,

> your friend,
> Henry W. Longfellow.

MANUSCRIPT: unrecovered; text from Higginson, *Longfellow*, pp. 113–115.

SHORT TITLES OF WORKS CITED
INDEX OF RECIPIENTS

SHORT TITLES OF WORKS CITED

Clark Letters

Leslie W. Dunlap, ed., *The Letters of Willis Gaylord Clark and Lewis Gaylord Clark* (New York, New York Public Library, 1940).

Diary of Clara Crowninshield

Andrew Hilen, ed., *The Diary of Clara Crowninshield: A European Tour with Longfellow, 1835–1836* (Seattle, University of Washington Press, 1956).

Higginson, *Longfellow*

Thomas Wentworth Higginson, *Henry Wadsworth Longfellow* (Boston and New York, Houghton Mifflin Co., 1902).

Life

Samuel Longfellow, ed., *Life of Henry Wadsworth Longfellow with Extracts from His Journals and Correspondence* (Boston and New York, Houghton Mifflin Co., 1891), Standard Library Edition, 3 vols.

Longfellow and Scandinavia

Andrew Hilen, *Longfellow and Scandinavia: A Study of the Poet's Relationship with the Northern Languages and Literature* (New Haven, Yale University Press, 1947).

Longfellow and Spain

Iris Lilian Whitman, *Longfellow and Spain* (New York, Instituto de las Españas en los Estados Unidos, 1927).

"New Longfellow Letters"

Mary Thacher Higginson, "New Longfellow Letters," *Harper's Monthly Magazine*, CVI (April 1903), 779–786.

Poets and Poetry of Europe

Henry Wadsworth Longfellow, ed., *The Poets and Poetry of Europe. With Introductions and Biographical Notices* (Philadelphia, Porter and Coates, 1871).

Professor Longfellow of Harvard

Carl L. Johnson, *Professor Longfellow of Harvard* (Eugene, University of Oregon Press, 1944).

"Some Unpublished Longfellow Letters"	Amandus Johnson, "Some Unpublished Longfellow Letters," *German-American Annals*, V, N.S. (May and June 1907), 172–192.
Uncle Sam Ward and His Circle	Maud Howe Elliott, *Uncle Sam Ward and His Circle* (New York, MacMillan Co., 1938).
Works	Samuel Longfellow, ed., *The Works of Henry Wadsworth Longfellow with Biographical and Critical Notes* (Boston and New York, Houghton Mifflin Co., 1886), Standard Library Edition, 11 vols.
Young Longfellow	Lawrance Thompson, *Young Longfellow* (New York, MacMillan Co., 1938).

INDEX OF RECIPIENTS

(References are to letter numbers)

INDEX OF RECIPIENTS